## READINGS

# Real students
# Real challenges
# Real success

## THIRD EDITION

# Real
# Writing

### with Readings

Paragraphs and Essays for
College, Work,
and Everyday Life

## SUSAN ANKER

BEDFORD / ST. MARTIN'S

*Real Writing with Readings,*
Third Edition
ISBN 0–312–40521–9

*Real Writing,* Third Edition
ISBN 0–312–40522–7

Instructor's Annotated Edition
ISBN 0–312–41006–9

Practical Suggestions
for Teaching *Real Writing*
ISBN 0–312–41005–0

Additional Resources
to Accompany *Real Writing*
ISBN 0–312–41007–7

# Real Writing

*Paragraphs and Essays for College,*
*Work, and Everyday Life*

## THIRD EDITION

Susan Anker

**R**eal Writing has helped thousands of students become better writers by addressing the major writing challenges they face in college, at work, and in their everyday lives. With its practical, realistic coverage of paragraphs and essays and its motivational real-world emphasis, *Real Writing* proves to students that they can master writing— and helps them do it.

Based on extensive class-testing and guidance from ten expert advisory board members from two- and four-year schools across the country, the third edition has been revised to provide even more writing, reading, and editing help. Also, a new full-color design and other features make it easier to use than ever.

> " The title captures the greatest strength of the text — 'real writing.' Students will relate to real students commenting on their apprehensions about writing. Real people, not just teachers, talk about the importance of writing. "
>
> — *Debbie Stallings, Hinds Community College*

# Real Writing...

## Motivates students with a real-world emphasis:

**Real-world content throughout provides a practical focus.**
All of the assignment topics, exercises, and models in *Real Writing* are drawn from real-world situations that will resonate with students.

**Profiles of Success show that success is within reach.**
These interviews with—and real-world writing from—former students show students that writing skills are critical to their success in college and beyond.

## Prepares students for success with the best coverage of basic skills:

**Comprehensive coverage of writing and editing helps students build these crucial skills.** *Real Writing* covers every stage of the writing process—and all the rhetorical modes of development—with plenty of model paragraphs and essays. The editing chapters offer clear explanations and abundant examples and practices to help students understand key grammar concepts.

**Thorough treatment of critical thinking and reading prepares students for college-level work.** Critical Thinking boxes help students think through writing and editing tasks before beginning them. The version of the book with readings contains detailed advice for critical reading.

**CRITICAL THINKING: SUPPORTING YOUR POINT**

**FOCUS**
Read your topic sentence or thesis statement.

**ASK YOURSELF**
- What do my readers need to know?
- What facts, details, or observations will help me show, explain, or prove my main point to readers?

**WRITE**
- Use a prewriting technique to generate possible support.
- Add supporting details.

## Focuses on key writing and editing issues so students are not overwhelmed:

**Writing coverage emphasizes the "four basics."**
Every chapter covering the modes now opens with a list of the four basic features of the type of writing covered in the chapter. This list is followed by a paragraph that is annotated to show these features.

**Grammar coverage emphasizes the "four most serious errors."** *Real Writing* concentrates first—with fuller coverage and plenty of practice—on four errors identified by instructors as the most serious: fragments, run-ons, subject-verb agreement problems, and verb form problems.

**The Four Most Serious Errors**

This book puts special emphasis on the four grammar errors that people most often notice. These four errors may make your meaning harder to understand, but even if they don't, they give a bad impression of you.

**The Four Most Serious Errors**

1. Fragments
2. Run-ons
3. Problems with subject-verb agreement
4. Problems with verb form and tense

If you can edit your writing to correct the four most serious errors, it will be clearer, and your grades will improve. By focusing on these errors, this book will help you make a big difference in your writing.

This chapter will review the basic elements of the sentence to help set up the detailed coverage of the four most serious errors in the next four chapters.

# Now it does more to help students become better writers...

## 1

### The Basics
*What You Need to Get Started*

Course Basics 103
Writing Basics 110

This chapter reviews basic information you will need to get off to a good start in your writing class. Please take the time to read it through carefully: It provides you with a solid foundation for the course.

#### Course Basics

The students who are pictured in this chapter recently completed the course you are now taking. For this section, we asked them to tell you "things they wish they'd known." Below are their best tips for succeeding in the course.

##### 1. Have a Positive Attitude

A few of you may think that you don't belong in this class because you always got good grades in writing when you were in high school. Of course, this isn't high school. If you were given a test that determined you should be here, accept this and think of this course as an opportunity. Get everything you can from the class: You need to write in every other course you will take and in any job you will want.

Also remember that you get from this course only what you give. For example, your instructor doesn't decide what grade to give you: He or she evaluates and translates into a grade the work that you do—or don't do. If you fail the course, don't think, "My teacher flunked me" or "My teacher gave me an F."

A few of you may think that you don't belong in this class because you always got good grades in writing when you were in high school. Of course, this isn't high school. If you were given a test that determined you should be here, accept this and think of this course as an opportunity. Get everything you can from the class: You need to write in every other course you will take and in any job you will want.

**MARK BALDERAS:** "If you really want to learn to write, and you follow the clear and simple steps in this 'Course Basics' and in the book, you will get a good grade."

103

■ **A new Chapter 1 prepares students for college writing.** Suffused with the voices (and photos) of developmental writing students who have recently passed the course using *Real Writing*, this chapter offers practical advice for becoming a successful student and a successful writer.

■ **A focus on the "four basics" promotes successful writing.** This helpful distillation begins each chapter on the methods of development.

### Understand What Narration Is

Narration is writing that tells the story of an event or an experience.

**FOUR BASICS OF GOOD NARRATION**

1. It reveals something of importance to you (your main point).
2. It includes all of the major events of the story (primary support).
3. It brings the story to life with details about the major events (secondary support).
4. It presents the events in a clear order, usually according to when they happened.

The following paragraph illustrates the four basics of narration.

(1) Last night my husband saved my life. We were sitting out on the porch with a couple of friends, enjoying the cool breeze of the evening. (2) While eating a piece of melon that was dessert, I laughed at something my friend said, and suddenly the fruit stuck in my windpipe, entirely blocking any air. (3) I tried to swallow hard and dislodge it, b... di... ...en I tried taking...

■ **Writing chapters teach problem solving and teamwork.** A special section at the start of these chapters helps students understand how to use problem-solving and teamwork skills to address life challenges. Then, writing assignments pose real-world problems for students to solve.

■ **Streamlined writing coverage simplifies learning and instruction.** Coverage of paragraphs and essays has been combined wherever this is useful. However, the book provides abundant models of, and separate assignments for, paragraphs and essays.

> ❝ If you really want to learn to write, and you follow the clear and simple steps in the book, you will. ❞
> — *Mark Balderas, Student and* Real Writing *user*

# better editors of their writing . . .

■ **More exercises in the book and online provide additional practice.** Additional exercises cover the four most serious errors, pronouns, and ESL concerns. Also, Exercise Central, the largest online bank of editing exercises, offers an expanded set of exercises for *Real Writing*.

■ **Visual guides help students find and correct grammar problems.** These guides, preceding many of the practices in the editing chapters, show students—at a glance—how to identify and correct sentence problems on their own.

> 66 The explanations are clear, straightforward, and precisely stated. They can be easily applied to student work — and understood by students when working at home without a teacher to explain. . . . 99
>
> — *William Shute,*
> *San Antonio College*

---

**FINDING AND FIXING RUN-ONS:**
Correcting a Run-On with a Comma and a
Coordinating Conjunction

↓

**FIND**

Foods <u>differ</u> from place to place <u>your favorite treat</u> <u>might disgust</u> someone from another culture.

1.  To determine whether there are two independent clauses in a sentence, **underline** the subjects and **double-underline** the verbs. *There are two independent clauses.*
2.  **Ask:** If there are two independent clauses in the sentence, are they separated by either a period or a semicolon? *No. It is a run-on.*

↓

**FIX**

            *and*
Foods differ from place to place, your favorite treat might disgust someone from another culture.

3.  **Correct the run-on** by adding a comma and a coordinating conjunction between the two independent clauses.

---

■ **A handy Quick Reference Card helps students with editing (and much more) as they write their papers.** Students can prop this card next to their computers for quick advice on editing, writing and revising, word processing, and Internet searches.

# and better readers
# of words and visuals...

**A strengthened emphasis on finding the main idea and support in readings improves comprehension.** This advice is part of a chapter on critical reading that precedes the 20 readings in the longer version of *Real Writing*.

**New marginal questions by readings encourage closer reading.** These questions get students to think critically as they read.

## 39
## The Basics of Critical Reading

In Chapters 40–48, you will find twenty essays that demonstrate the types of writing you have studied in this book: narration, illustration, description, process analysis, classification, definition, comparison and contrast, cause and effect, and argument. However, these readings provide more than just good models of writing. They also tell fascinating stories, argue passionately about controversial issues, and present a wide range of perspectives.

Some of the essays may even help you work more efficiently, with strategies for successful job interviews and tips on using exercise to improve mental functioning. These essays can also provide you with ideas for your own writing, both in and out of school. Most important, they offer you a chance to practice your reading skills — skills that will help you to become a better writer.

Reading good models will improve your writing by showing you how other writers have handled certain elements — for example, main points and supporting information, organization of ideas, and introductions and conclusions. The following basics will help you understand and respond to the reading you will do in this course and others. They will also help you get information you need in other areas of your life.

**FOUR BASICS OF READING**

1. Preview the essay, article, or chapter.
2. Find the main idea.
3. Find the support for the main idea.
4. Review and respond to what you have read.

A piece of advice before getting into the basics: Be an active reader. An active reader takes part in the experience of reading and doesn't passively sit and look at the words. Before beginning to read, prepare to actively engage in reading. Find a place where you can be comfortable and where you won't constantly be distracted or interrupted. You need to be mentally alert and

631

...the traffic had been bad. When my partner came ...ace told me his day hadn't gone any better than mine, How was your day?"

PREDICT: Pause here. Try to predict what the author's main point will be:

" knowing that one more straw might break his back. A ...nted to take me to lunch. I said I was busy. Four lies in ...none of which I felt the least bit guilty about.

. We exaggerate, we minimize, we avoid confrontation, ...elings, we conveniently forget, we keep secrets, we jus- ...guy institutions.

whole week without telling a lie, and it was paralyzing. 5

**New color visuals, with assignments, get students thinking and writing about images.**

**ASSIGNMENT 9   WRITING ABOUT IMAGES**

In either a paragraph or an essay, describe a process (humorous or otherwise) for breaking a bad habit. Make sure to include details about the steps.

**ASSIGNMENT 2   WRITING ABOUT IMAGES**

Look carefully at this photograph. In a paragraph or essay, either tell the story of what might have happened to bring the couple to this point or tell a story about an argument you had with someone you loved.

...h makes me stop smoking, one makes me eat less,
...akes me put my clothes in the hamper instead
...leaving them on the floor, one makes me
put the toilet seat back down..."

> **❝** *Real Writing* is crisp and contemporary. The graphics, layout, use of color, and photographs make it lively.... **❞**
> — *Carol Abbott Kontos, University of Maine at Augusta*

# and it's even easier to use.

■ **A clean new full-color design helps students navigate the book more easily.** The design makes key information easier to find and connects related elements.

■ **A new tutorial in the Introduction for Students shows students how to log on to and use Exercise Central.**

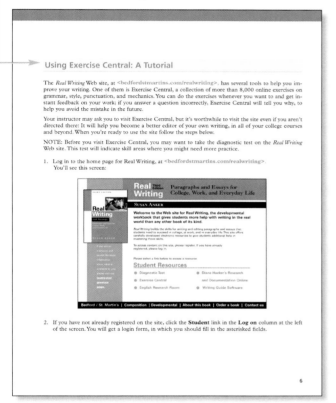

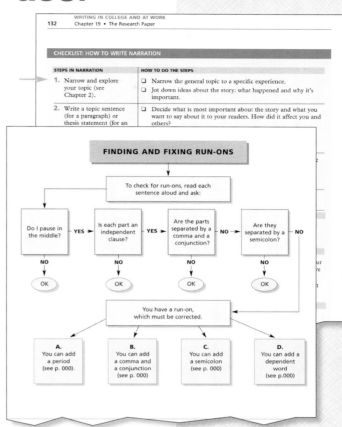

■ **New cross-references provide closer integration between the book and its electronic resources.** New marginal notes in the student edition direct students toward specific topics in Exercise Central and the Writing Guide Software. Also, Exercise Central and the software have been enhanced to integrate seamlessly with one another, allowing students to move easily from skill diagnostics to tutorials to practice.

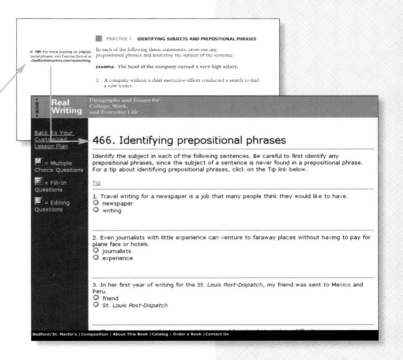

# Part of a series that puts writing in a practical context

## The Anker Series

Beginning with the publication of the first edition of *Real Writing* in 1998, the Anker Series was the first to put writing in a real-world context and to cement the connection between what students learn in their college composition course and how they live their lives. The second book in the series—*Real Essays*, launched in 2003—offers this same unique approach for courses that emphasize essays. The series helps students succeed because of its thorough, practical writing instruction and the message that writing well is both an essential and achievable skill. Featuring photos, quotes, profiles, and advice, Susan Anker's texts are infused with the voices and concerns of developmental writing instructors and their students.

## An Author with a Unique Perspective

SUSAN ANKER (B.A., M.Ed., Boston University) brings a unique perspective to the teaching of the developmental writing course. She taught English and developmental writing for several years before entering college publishing, where she worked for 18 years: as a sales representative and English/ESL editor at Macmillan Publishing Company; as developmental English/ESL editor, executive editor, and editor in chief at St. Martin's Press; and as editor in chief for humanities at Houghton Mifflin

Company. In each of these positions, she worked with developmental writing instructors, maintaining her early interest in the area. Anker and her husband are the principals of Anker Publishing Company, which publishes professional development materials for higher education instructors and administrators. Her many years of experience talking and working with hundreds of developmental writing instructors across the country, and developing textbooks that meet the needs of these instructors and their students, have culminated in *Real Writing* and *Real Essays*.

# A wide array of new media and print resources

## Electronic Ancillaries

**Give Students More Practice and More Help with Writing**

**bedfordstmartins.com/realwriting**

**Book Companion Site.** The companion Web site for *Real Writing* provides additional resources for students and instructors as well as links to Exercise Central and other resources.

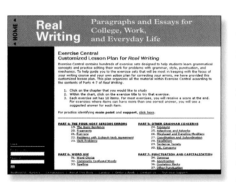

**Exercise Central** With more than 8,000 items, **Exercise Central** is the largest online collection of grammar exercises available. A new diagnostic helps students identify areas where they need more help, and multiple exercise sets on every topic, at a variety of levels, ensure that they get as much practice as they need.

**Writing Guide Software.** This software leads students step by step through the process of writing various types of paragraphs and essays. Also included are diagnostic tests, grammar tutorials, and a customizable error log that links to Exercise Central. To order this software with each student copy of *Real Writing with Readings*, use ISBN 0–312–41231–2. To order it with *Real Writing*, use ISBN 0–312–41229–0.

## Print Ancillaries

**Take Instructors' Busy Lives into Account**

**Instructor's Annotated Edition.** Gives practical page-by-page advice on teaching *Real Writing*, with marginal teaching tips and much more. Also contains answers to all exercises. ISBN 0–312–41006–9.

**Practical Suggestions for Teaching *Real Writing*,** Merrill Glustrom, Front Range Community College, and Eddye Gallagher, Tarrant County College. Contains advice on teaching with *Real Writing*, including expanded advice on student collaboration and tips on assessing work in electronic classrooms. ISBN 0–312–41005–0.

**Additional Resources to Accompany *Real Writing*,** Susan Anker. Supplements the instructional materials in the text with a variety of transparency masters and other reproducibles for classroom use. ISBN 0–312–41007–7.

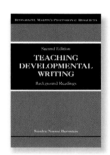

**Teaching Developmental Writing: Background Readings,** Second Edition, A Bedford/St. Martin's Professional Resource, Susan Naomi Bernstein, University of Houston, Downtown. Offers more than 30 professional essays on topics of interest to basic writing instructors. ISBN 0–312–41189–8.

### More Help for Students

**Quick Reference Card.**
A handy card offering tips on writing, revising, editing, word-processing, and Internet research. Students can prop it up next to their computers for easy reference while they're writing. To order this card with each student copy of *Real Writing with Readings*, use ISBN 0–312–41249–5. To order it with each copy of *Real Writing*, use ISBN 0–312–41250–9.

**Notebook Dividers to Accompany *Real Writing*,** Lois Hassan, Henry Ford Community College. Helps students get organized by providing dividers for three-ring binders with preprinted tabs and useful tips on managing various aspects of the course. To order these dividers with each student copy of *Real Writing with Readings*, use ISBN 0–312–41511–7. To order them with each copy of *Real Writing*, use ISBN 0–312–41514–1.

# More reviewer praise...

## Clear, Thorough Explanations

"Susan Anker has ... tremendous talent in writing clear, complete explanations that communicate extremely well to the developmental student."

—*Daniel L. Moody,*
*Southwestern College*

## Clean, Helpful Design

"The book is well laid out so that even the weakest English student can follow the information and learn."

—*Dee Pruitt,*
*Florence-Darlington Technical College*

## Strong Focus on Students' Needs

"Susan Anker does a splendid job with 'talking' to students on their level. The new Chapter 1 [on course basics and writing basics] will serve as a foundation not only to their writing class but to all their other classes as well. It also serves to motivate, encourage, and challenge students."

—*Sandra Torrez,*
*Texas A&M University, Kingsville*

## Appealing Profiles of Success

"The Profile of Success feature is very effective. I have been telling students about the practical benefits of the skill of writing for almost thirty years. I have even had an editor and other professional friends visit classes to underscore this point, but I have never seen so simple, obvious, and effective a lesson in that regard. And including a sample of student writing as a model is brilliant!"

—*David Rollinson,*
*College of Marin*

## Engaging Readings

"The readings ... always spark interest and subsequent class discussion. The readings are so varied that they interest all the students."

—*Paul Vantine,*
*Cameron University*

## A Proven Success

"It works beautifully for my students."

—*Julie Hanwell,*
*Tri-County Community College*

"This is the textbook I have been waiting for and the one I wish I had written!"

—*Kathleen S. Britton,*
*Florence-Darlington Technical College*

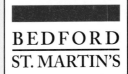

# Professional Resources for Instructors

We offer something for every writing instructor — from the first-time teaching assistant to the program director — including practical guides on teaching, ancillary volumes of pedagogical readings, landmark works of reference, and collections of important scholarship.

## BIBLIOGRAPHIES

**Linda Adler-Kassner,**
*Eastern Michigan University*

**Gregory R. Glau,**
*Arizona State University*

2002 Paper 125 pages ISBN 0–312–39475–6
www.bedfordstmartins.com/basicbib

*The Bedford Bibliography for Teachers of Basic Writing* is a new resource, compiled by members of the Conference on Basic Writing under the general editorship of Linda Adler-Kassner and Gregory R. Glau. The text provides an annotated list of books, articles, and periodicals selected specifically for their value to teachers of basic writing.

**Nedra Reynolds,**
*University of Rhode Island*

**Patricia Bizzell,**
*College of the Holy Cross*

**Bruce Herzberg,**
*Bentley College*

2004 Paper 150 pages (approx.)
ISBN 0–312–40501–4

An essential, highly praised resource for writing teachers for over 15 years, *The Bedford Bibliography* provides an annotated list of books, articles, and periodicals devoted to composition and rhetoric — updated to include the most recent research — together with a historical overview of these fields.

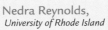

**Norman A. Stahl,**
*Northern Illinois University*

**Hunter Boylan,**
*Appalachian State University*

2003 Paper 350 pages ISBN 0–312–24774–5

Offers 37 professional essays by writers such as Martha E. Casazza, Michele L. Simpson, and David C. Caverly, on topics that will engage teachers of basic reading, including strategic learning, the reading/writing connection, and teaching new-to-English learners.

## BACKGROUND READINGS

**Timothy Barnett,**
*Northeastern Illinois University*

2001 Paper 470 pages ISBN 0–312–39161–7

Offers a range of perspectives, from Aristotle to the present day, on argument and on teaching argument. The 28 readings — many of them classic works in the field — present essential insights and practical information for instructors using any of Bedford/ St. Martin's argument texts and readers.

**Glenn Blalock,**
*Stephen F. Austin State University*

2002 Paper 528 pages ISBN 0–312–39049–4

Contains 43 articles on the teaching of writing, a critical thinking section, an appendix of articles on writing with a computer, and a bibliography for further reading.

**T. R. Johnson,**
*Boston University*

**Shirley Morahan,**
*Northeast Missouri State University*

2002 580 pages ISBN 0–312–39711–9

Professional readings on composition and rhetoric written by leaders in the field such as Peter Elbow, Nancy Sommers, and David Bartholomae are accompanied by chapter introductions, headnotes, and activities for classroom use.

**Susan Naomi Bernstein,**
*University of Houston, Downtown*

2004 Paper 378 pages ISBN 0–312–41189–8

Offers more than 30 professional essays on topics of interest to basic writing instructors, along with useful editorial apparatus that points out practical classroom applications.

**Cheryl Glenn,**
*Pennsylvania State University*

**Robert J. Connors,**
late of *University of New Hampshire*

**Melissa Goldthwaite,**
*St. Joseph's University*

2003 Paper 560 pages (approx.) ISBN 0–312–40417–1

This guide to teaching writing and to major theoretical issues includes a brief anthology of scholarly essays and new coverage of computer-mediated instruction, Web-based research, and other uses of new technologies.

New

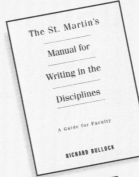

**Richard Bullock,**
*Wright State University*

Paper 76 pages ISBN 0–312–09573–2

This practical guide provides tips for instructors interested in teaching writing in courses across the curriculum.

**Edward M. White,**
*University of Arizona*

1999 Paper 171 pages ISBN 0–312–19732–2

Practical advice on creating assignments, tests, and diagnostics, along with a guide for meaningful assessment.

**Nedra Reynolds,**
*University of Rhode Island*

2000 Paper 74 pages ISBN 0–312–19809–4

Provides the practical information instructors and writing program administrators need to use the portfolio method successfully in a writing course. An ideal companion to *Portfolio Keeping: A Guide for Students.*

**Leigh Ryan,**
*University of Maryland*

2002 Paper 86 pages ISBN 0–312–39051–3

Contains suggestions and strategies to give tutors the skill and confidence to help students in the writing center.

**Christina Murphy,**
*Marshall University*

**Steve Sherwood,**
*Texas Christian University*

2003 Paper 116 pages ISBN 0–312–18850–1

A brief guide with an anthology of essays, updated to include more on writing centers and tutoring with technology

New

**Gesa E. Kirsch, Faye Spencer Maor, Lance Massey, Lee Nickoson-Massey, and Mary P. Sheridan-Rabideau**

2003 Paper 636 pages ISBN 0–312–40764–5

Collects the most influential and frequently cited articles published in feminist composition over the last 25 years. A valuable reference, the volume surveys the history of feminist pedagogy, theory, and research, as well as the politics of the profession.

New

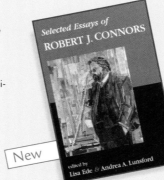

**Lisa Ede,**
*Oregon State University*

**Andrea A. Lunsford,**
*Stanford University*

2003 Paper 500 pages ISBN 0–312–40279–1

One of the most influential scholars in the field of rhetoric and composition, Robert J. Connors argued vigorously for the importance of grounding contemporary theories and practice in a richly historicized understanding of the past. This chronological collection provides a representative sample of Connors's most significant work throughout his 20-year career.

New

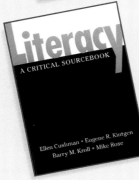

**Ellen Cushman, Eugene R. Kintgen, Barry M. Kroll, and Mike Rose**

2001 Paper 804 pages ISBN 0–312–25042–8

This new collection of both landmark and current essays provides a comprehensive overview of literacy studies today. An indispensable reference tool, the book is ideally suited for use in a wide range of upper-division and graduate classes.

**Lisa Ede,**
*Oregon State University*

1999 Paper 496 pages ISBN 0–312–20264–4

Includes all the Braddock essays, recently written afterwords as each author reflects on his or her essay, and an introduction that revisits the essays and the field to explore where it has been — and where it is going.

# Also in the Anker Series

# Real **Essays**

*Writing Projects for College,
Work, and Everyday Life*

Susan Anker

**R**eal Essays builds and strengthens the writing and editing skills that students need to succeed in college, at work, and in everyday life. *Real Essays*

- teaches writing, reading, and editing as practical and essential processes

- includes clear models and step-by-step guidance for writing nine types of essays

- covers all grammar topics — with an emphasis on fragments, run-ons, subject-verb agreement, and problems with verb forms

- fosters critical reading skills that help students comprehend, analyze, and respond to readings

*Real Essays with Readings*
2003 Paperbound 816 pages
ISBN 0–312–39915–4

*Real Essays*
2003 Paper 720 pages
ISBN 0–312–39914–6

Instructor's Annotated Edition
ISBN 0–312– 39916–2

Writing Guide Software
ISBN 0–312–41184–7

bedfordstmartins.com/realessays

> " This text challenges students to reach beyond what they have been told they can achieve. I like that very much. "
> — *Anne Gervasi, DeVry University*

# Real Writing
## with Readings

*Paragraphs and Essays for College,*
*Work, and Everyday Life*

# Real Writing

## with Readings

*Paragraphs and Essays for College, Work, and Everyday Life*

Susan Anker

---

Bedford / St. Martin's                    *Boston* ◆ *New York*

**For Bedford / St. Martin's**

*Developmental Editor:* Beth Castrodale
*Associate Editor:* Karin Halbert
*Production Editor:* Deborah Baker
*Senior Production Supervisor:* Joe Ford
*Marketing Manager:* Brian Wheel
*Editorial Assistant:* Caryn O'Connell
*Copyeditor:* Alison Greene
*Text Design:* Claire Seng-Niemoeller
*Cover Design:* Billy Boardman
*Photo Researchers:* Martha Friedman and Alice Lundoff
*Cover Art:* "Four Students Using a Computer." © NAVASWAN/Getty Images
*Composition:* Monotype Composition Company, Inc.
*Printing and Binding:* R. R. Donnelley & Sons Company

*President:* Joan E. Feinberg
*Editorial Director:* Denise B. Wydra
*Editor in Chief:* Karen S. Henry
*Director of Marketing:* Karen Melton Soeltz
*Director of Editing, Design, and Production:* Marcia Cohen
*Managing Editor:* Elizabeth M. Schaaf

Library of Congress Control Number: 2003107466

8   7   6   5   4   3

f   e   d   c   b   a

*For information, write:* Bedford/St. Martin's, 75 Arlington Street, Boston, MA 02116
(617-399-4000)

ISBN: 0–312–40522–7 (*Real Writing*)
　　　0–312–40521–9 (*Real Writing with Readings*)
　　　0–312–41006–9 (*Instructor's Annotated Edition*)

**Acknowledgments**

Isaac Asimov. "What Is Intelligence, Anyway?" Published by permission of the Estate of Isaac Asimov, c/o Ralph M. Vicinanza Ltd.

Russell Baker. "The Plot against People." From the *New York Times*, June 18, 1968. Copyright © 1968 by the New York Times Company. Reprinted by permission.

Nell Bernstein. "The Drug War's Littlest Victims." From *Salon.com*, October 30, 2002. Copyright © 2002 Salon.com. Reprinted by permission of Salon.com. <www.Salon.com>.

Bill Bryson. "Snoopers at Work." From *I'm a Stranger Here Myself* by Bill Bryson. Copyright © 1999 by Bill Bryson. Used by permission of Broadway Books, a division of Random House, Inc.

*Consumer Reports.* "Laptop Computers." Copyright © 2003 Consumers Union of U.S., Inc. Yonkers, NY 10703-1057, a non-profit organization. Reprinted with permission from the March 2003 issue of *Consumer Reports* for educational purposes only. No commercial use or photocopying permitted. To learn more about Consumers Union, log onto <www.ConsumerReports.org>.

Chitra Banerjee Divakaruni. "Common Scents." From *Salon.com*, June 26, 1997. Copyright © 1997. Reprinted with the permission of Salon.com. <www.salon.com>.

Tim Duncan. "To Avoid a Failed System, Vote 'No.'" From the *Boston Globe*, October 28, 2002. Copyright © 2002 by Globe Newspaper Company (MA). Reproduced with permission of Globe Newspaper Company (MA) in the format Textbook via Copyright Clearance Center.

Daryn Eller. "Move Your Body, Free Your Mind" and "A Workout for Your Brain." From *Health Magazine*, May 2002. Copyright © 2002. Reprinted by permission of the author.

Stephanie Ericsson. "The Ways We Lie." © 1992 by Stephanie Ericsson. Originally published by the *Utne Reader*. Reprinted by the permission of Dunham Literary as agents for the author.

Gabrielle Glaser. "Scents." From *Health Magazine*, July/August 2001. Copyright © 2001. Reprinted by permission of Writers' Representatives, Inc. on behalf of the author.

Jim and Ed Gogek. "Seeing Criminal Addicts through Middle-Class Eyes." From the *San Diego Union Tribune*, August 10, 2000. Copyright © 2000. Reprinted by permission of the authors.

Google search screens reprinted by permission of Google.

Marcia Hill Gossard. "Taking Control." From *Newsweek*, July 15, 2002. Copyright © 2002 Newsweek, Inc. All rights reserved. Reprinted by permission.

Dianne Hales. "Why Are We So Angry?" From *Parade* magazine, September 2, 2001. Copyright © 2001. Reprinted by permission of *Parade* and the author.

Adora Houghton. "My Indian." Originally published in *Multitude: Cross-Cultural Readings for Writers* (McGraw-Hill, Inc.), 1993. Copyright © 1993 by Adora Houghton. Reprinted by permission of the author.

Robyn Griggs Lawrence. "Wabi-Sabi: The Art of Imperfection." From *Natural Home*, May/June 2001. Published by Interweave Press, Loveland, Colorado. Reprinted with permission from *Natural Home* and Robyn Griggs Lawrence, author.

Andrea Lee. "Mother." Edited excerpt from *Sarah Phillips* by Andrea Lee. Copyright © 1984 by Andrea Lee. Used by permission of Random House, Inc.

*Acknowledgments and copyrights are continued at the back of the book, which constitutes an extension of the copyright page. It is a violation of the law to reproduce these selections by any means whatsoever without the written permission of the copyright holder.*

# Preface

More than ever, students aren't only students: They are also workers, parents, people with diverse responsibilities for whom "student" is just one of many demanding roles. If what they learn is not directly related to the rest of what they do, it is easily lost among other pressing concerns. When their textbooks fail to make the connection, it is not surprising that writing remains for students something that is done only in college, or even only in the writing class.

The success of *Real Writing,* along with the many endorsements of this approach that I have received from students and instructors, has confirmed the absolute necessity of making this connection between writing and students' lives. It remains the primary goal of this new edition of *Real Writing.* In each chapter, students can see people like themselves—students, workers, and parents—who have struggled with writing, who have wondered why it is important, and who are learning that good writing is not a mysterious, divinely inspired gift but a skill that can be learned by any person who is willing to pay attention and practice. Students also see that competence in any activity, whether it be playing a sport, cooking a meal, replacing a flat tire, or learning a dance, requires close attention to the necessary steps in the process and repeated practice, practice, practice. Throughout *Real Writing,* photos, quotes, profiles, and advice from real students help to emphasize both the hard work involved in becoming a competent writer and the absolute necessity of learning this skill. This new edition, as you will see, does even more to inspire students and help them master writing skills.

## Features

Many of the features of the second edition of *Real Writing* have been carried over to the third edition, with significant revisions based on suggestions from a large number of instructors. Several new features have also been added as a result of my observations of students using the second edition in class, discussions with both faculty and students who use the text, and other extensive comments from users and reviewers (these new features are described in the shaded section on pp. xii–xiv).

### Provides Clear, Detailed Writing Guidance

*Real Writing* teaches writing strategies as practical, essential processes. It first takes students step-by-step—with plenty of examples and models—through every stage of the writing process. It then shows them how to write effective paragraphs and essays using all the major modes of development, in academic, professional, and personal settings. A special section on essay exams, timed writing, and the research essay provides concrete strategies for succeeding in these writing situations. Throughout, the instruction is infused with appealing real-world examples and writing assignments.

## Motivates Students As No Other Text Does

That's quite a claim, but that's what users — professors and students alike — tell us. They point to the following features:

### The Real-World Context

Throughout, *Real Writing* shows students how they will actually use writing and editing skills in other college courses, in their work, and in their everyday lives. *Real Writing* teaches writing forms and strategies as practical, essential processes. All the assignment topics, exercises, and models in the book are drawn from real-world situations that are relevant to students.

### The Profiles of Success

All Part Two chapters (covering the methods of development) include interviews with, and photos of, former students who have overcome significant challenges to succeed in the real world. These profiles show students that success is within reach, but more important, they demonstrate very explicitly how writing is used in the workplace. For example, in the Profile of Success in Chapter 8 (Narration), a nurse describes how writing good narration is important in her job. Her comments are followed by an actual narrative that she wrote on the job.

### The "Can Do" Attitude

Students who have used and reviewed *Real Writing* have responded enthusiastically to the "can do" tone and to the examples and activities that are relevant to their lives. For the first time, many students have told us, they are motivated to read and use a textbook. One of the many features they single out is the "You Know This" boxes that begin many of the chapters. With concrete, specific examples, these boxes link the content of the chapter to activities that students are already familiar with.

## Makes Grammar Less Overwhelming

*Real Writing* gives special emphasis to the four most serious errors. In a survey conducted for the first edition, instructors throughout the country identified four errors as the most serious: **fragments**, **run-ons**, **subject-verb agreement problems**, and **verb form problems**. These four errors are each covered in a separate chapter in Part Four, which opens the "Editing" section of the book. By concentrating on a limited number of major sentence problems as they begin to edit their papers, students feel they have a shot at mastering these problems and are more likely to remember strategies for avoiding them. Other important grammar concepts and problems are covered thoroughly in Part Five, "Other Grammar Concerns," after students have gained confidence by focusing on the most troublesome errors.

*Real Writing* gives students **practice**, **practice**, and **more practice** with grammar and editing. We have tried to make sure that each exercise is on a high-interest topic and have carefully chosen language that is neither too simple nor too difficult for students. In addition, every chapter in Parts Four through Seven ends with a practice that asks students to edit one or more paragraphs for the sentence problems covered in that chapter, which helps them learn to edit their own paragraphs and essays.

## Is Easy for Students to Use

The consistent, three-part format of most chapters (either Understand/ Practice/Write, or Understand/Practice/Edit) helps students successfully navigate the information. **(See pp. xii–xiii for a description of how paragraph and essay coverage has been revised with an eye to ease of use.)** Most chapters end with a chapter review that can be used as a review quiz. In addition, nearly every chapter in the Editing section ends with a flowchart designed to help students, especially visual learners, find and correct errors.

An Introduction for Students helps students find information they need and introduces the important features of the book.

## Helps Students Think Critically

Many students come to college needing to learn how to learn. "Critical Thinking" boxes throughout the book get students to *focus* on the matter at hand, *ask* themselves some key questions, and *write* or *edit* based on their answers. This process of reflection benefits not only students' writing and editing but also every aspect of their lives.

## Provides a Reader that Connects Reading and Writing

The "Readings" section at the end of the longer edition of *Real Writing* is a collection of twenty-one high-interest selections in the areas of college, work, and everyday life, all of which have been reviewed and approved by students. The selections are organized according to rhetorical mode, which parallels the arrangement of the writing chapters, making it easier for students to see the connection to their own writing and for instructors to link the readings to the writing instruction. An introduction to reading (Chapter 39) explains and models strategies for active, critical reading, and the unique apparatus includes not only headnotes, comprehension and critical thinking questions, and writing prompts, but also guiding questions that give students a focus as they read.

## New to This Edition

### Even Stronger, More Focused Writing Coverage

The third edition of *Real Writing* helps students focus on writing basics so they aren't overwhelmed. It also offers more writing support than ever before. New writing features include:

• **A new Chapter 1 that prepares students for college writing.** In the "Course Basics" section of this chapter, students who had recently completed their first college writing course offer candid, practical advice on how to succeed in the course and in college. This chapter also offers "Writing Basics," introducing students to two essential features of all good writing: main idea and support.

• **An increased emphasis on main idea and support throughout the book.** As in previous editions, these crucial concepts are detailed in separate chapters of Part One, which covers the writing process. Then, each chapter of Part Two, which covers writing various types of paragraphs and essays, includes new sections on main idea and support that point out considerations that are specific to particular modes of development. These sections offer plenty of explanations, examples, and practices. Similarly, the introductory chapter to the readings now includes full sections on finding main idea and support. And the reading selections themselves have added apparatus that specifically asks students to restate the main idea and identify major support.

• **A focus on the "four basics" of each type of writing.** Each chapter on the methods of development now begins with a list of four important features of the type of writing covered in the chapter. This list, which highlights the essential elements needed to understand and use a rhetorical strategy, is followed by a new model paragraph that is annotated to show these basic features.

• **Exciting new writing assignments.** Each of the writing chapters in Part Two now offers—in addition to the "Writing for College, Work, and Everyday Life" assignments—a new assignment, "Writing about Images." This option presents a provocative color photograph or cartoon with a writing prompt. Additionally, a new section on problem solving and teamwork at the start of Part Two reinforces the fact that writing and collaboration are often the means of addressing real-world problems. Special assignments ask students to use these skills to solve a problem from college, work, or everyday life.

• **A more sensible treatment of paragraphs and essays.** Recognizing that the processes for generating ideas, drafting, and revising are in many ways similar for paragraphs and essays—and to avoid needlessly repetitive coverage—the third edition combines the discussions of the processes wherever this is useful.

However, paragraphs and essays are treated separately wherever the needs and conventions for them differ—such as in drafting, where students writing essays need help with introductory and concluding paragraphs and use of transitions between paragraphs. Additionally, the core assignment chapters in Part Two contain separate writing assignments for paragraphs and essays, with plenty of models for both.

The new organization has two advantages: (1) students see the relationship between paragraphs and essays so they aren't intimidated by essays, and (2) students don't have to flip back and forth between paragraph coverage and an essay chapter that appears in isolation much later in the book.

For those instructors who prefer essay coverage to be separate from that of paragraphs, we have added **Appendix A, "The Basics of Writing an Essay."** This appendix has the same material as books with separate essay coverage in the middle of the book; however, because the material here is at the end of the book, it's much easier to find and refer to.

- **A "Computer Basics" appendix that helps students use technology to become better writers.** This section shows students how to start a paper, save and manage files, revise and edit, format and print work, and search the Web effectively and efficiently.

### Even More Editing Help and Practice

- **Additional exercises in the book and online provide more practice.** The third edition offers more exercises covering the four most serious errors, pronouns, and ESL concerns. Additionally, one-third of the exercises have been replaced or revised in response to user suggestions. Also, the online resource Exercise Central (described below under "Ancillaries") has been expanded with new practice items for *Real Writing*. A new tutorial in the Introduction for Students shows students how to log on to and use this important resource.
- **Visual guides to help students correct grammar problems.** These guides, preceding many of the practices in the Editing chapters, show students at a glance how to find and fix sentence problems on their own.

### Easier to Use

- **A clean, new full-color design helps students navigate the book more easily.** *Real Writing* has been redesigned to make key information easier to find and to connect related elements.

(continued)

*New to This Edition (continued)*

• **New cross-references provide closer integration between the book and its electronic resources.** New marginal notes in the student edition direct students toward specific topics in Exercise Central and the Writing Guide Software (described below under "Ancillaries"). In addition, Exercise Central and the Writing Guide Software have been enhanced to integrate seamlessly with one another, allowing students to move easily from skill diagnostics to tutorials to practice.

*More Resources to Improve Students' Reading Skills*

• **An expanded introduction to the readings in the longer edition offers more advice on critical reading.** As noted earlier, this introduction reinforces the new emphasis on main idea and support in the writing instruction and includes several new practice items.
• **New questions in the margins of readings engage students as they read.** These questions get students to think critically and to consider important features of the writing as they read.

## Ancillaries

The ancillary program that accompanies *Real Writing* is as realistic about instructors' busy lives as the text is about students' lives. Because instructors and students are relying more and more on computers for writing, research, and instruction, the electronic ancillaries that accompany the third edition of *Real Writing* are designed to enhance the text instruction and give you and your students plenty of options. The print ancillaries for instructors provide practical, useful advice as well as additional resources. The print ancillaries for students offer quick-reference information for those working on computers and help with managing the course.

### Electronic Resources

•   **Book Companion Site.** The companion Web site for *Real Writing,* at **<bedfordstmartins.com/realwriting>**, provides additional resources for students and instructors, including links to Exercise Central practices written expressly for *Real Writing* and to resources for research and documentation.
•   **Exercise Central.** With more than 8,000 items (4,000 more than for the second edition of *Real Writing*), this is the largest online collection of grammar exercises available. Exercise Central is thorough, easy to use, and convenient for both students and instructors. A new diagnostic helps students identify areas where they need more help, and multiple exercise sets on every topic, at a variety of levels, ensure that they get as much practice

as they need. Customized feedback for all answers assures that skills practice becomes a learning experience, and a reporting feature allows both students and instructors to monitor and assess student progress.

• **Writing Guide Software.** This software, available for $5.00 when packaged with the text, leads students step by step through the process of writing each of the types of paragraphs and essays covered in the text. Also included are diagnostic tests, grammar tutorials, and a customizable error log that links to Exercise Central.

## Print Ancillaries for Instructors

• **Instructor's Annotated Edition.** This resource gives practical page-by-page advice on teaching *Real Writing*, with marginal tips including teaching advice, discussion prompts, collaborative activities, strategies for teaching ESL students, and more. It also contains answers to all exercises and suggestions for using the other ancillaries.

• **Practical Suggestions for Teaching REAL WRITING,** Merrill Glustrom, Front Range Community College, and Eddye S. Gallagher, Tarrant County College. This useful volume contains information and advice on working with basic writers, bringing the real world into the classroom, building critical thinking skills, teaching ESL students and speakers of non-standard dialects, and assessing student progress. It now offers updated and expanded advice on using technology in the classroom, peer review, conferencing, and much more.

• **Additional Resources to Accompany REAL WRITING,** Susan Anker, and Eddye S. Gallagher, Tarrant County College. This resource supplements the instructional materials in the text with a variety of transparency masters and other reproducibles for classroom use.

• *Teaching Developmental Writing: Background Readings,* Second Edition, A Bedford/St. Martin's Professional Resource, Susan Naomi Bernstein, University of Houston, Downtown. This helpful volume offers more than 30 professional essays on topics of interest to basic writing instructors, along with editorial apparatus pointing out practical applications for the classroom.

## Print Ancillaries for Students

• *Real Writing* **Quick Reference Card.** This handy, three-panel card offers concise tips on the four basics of good writing, on editing the four most serious grammar errors, and on word processing and Web research. Students can prop it up next to their computers for easy reference while they're writing. This card is packaged free with the text when you use the following ISBNs: *Real Writing with Readings:* 0–312–41249–5; *Real Writing:* 0–312–41250–9.

• **Notebook Dividers to Accompany *Real Writing*,** Lois Hassan, Henry Ford Community College. These dividers for three-ring binders—with preprinted tabs and useful tips on managing various aspects of the course—help students get organized. These dividers are packaged free with the text when you use the following ISBNs: *Real Writing with Readings:* 0–312–41511–7; *Real Writing:* 0–312–41514–1.

# Acknowledgments

While my name is the only one that appears on the cover of this book, this revision of *Real Writing* was anything but a solo enterprise: The supporting cast was both immense and instrumental in conceiving and implementing new ideas, in refining existing ones, and in making the book happen. To those whose names follow, I am deeply grateful.

## Editorial Advisory Board

The ten members of our Editorial Advisory Board (listed below) have graciously offered thoughtful and insightful suggestions that are reflected on each page of *Real Writing*. The stacks of their reviews in my office are a monumental testament to the amount of reading and writing each board member has done on this revision. I can only hope that I've done justice to the sage ideas they sent my way. This is their book as much as mine, and I am beholden to each of them.

> Sandra Barnhill, South Plains Community College (TX)
> Kathleen Beauchene, Community College of Rhode Island
> Karen Eisenhauer, Brevard Community College (FL)
> Steven A. Garcia, Riverside Community College (CA)
> Merrill Glustrom, Front Range Community College (CO)
> Earl Hawley, College of DuPage (IL)
> Timothy L. Roach, St. Louis Community College, Forest Park (MO)
> Tamara Shue, Georgia Perimeter College
> William Shute, San Antonio College (TX)
> Sandra A. Torrez, Texas A&M University, Kingsville

Merrill Glustrom also revised the eminently thorough and useful *Practical Suggestions for Teaching REAL WRITING*. Merrill came to be a part of the *Real Writing* team through a suggestion from Tom Kling, a brilliant senior sales representative at Bedford/St. Martin's.

I want to single out those advisers who have been with me through two revisions because our lives have become intertwined: Karen Eisenhauer, Steve Garcia, Tim Roach, Tamara Shue, and Bill Shute. I have consulted with Steve and Tamara from the start of the first edition of *Real Writing*, and I started consulting with Bill Shute while the first edition was just a twinkle in our eyes.

I also want to thank Eddye Gallagher, who helped form the initial plans for *Real Writing* and who was instrumental in shaping the second edition. Eddye is coordinating a wide-ranging program at Tarrant County College, and though she was not actively involved in this third edition, her work remains an important part of *Practical Suggestions*. And she remains a friend.

## Student Advisory Board

Although we always have students review certain parts of *Real Writing*, this time we wanted more direct student involvement. Specifically, we wanted to work with some conscientious students who had just taken the course using the book. We found just such students through recommendations from trusted editorial advisers and reviewers. They are:

- Mark Balderas, San Antonio College
- Michelle Bassett, Quinsigamond Community College
- Michelle Bostick, Brevard Community College
- Nicole Day, Brevard Community College
- Katilya Labidou, Brevard Community College

Beyond their behind-the-scenes suggestions about things that worked or didn't work in *Real Writing*, we wanted these students to speak—student-to-student—to those who are just beginning the course. The result is the new Chapter 1, which includes candid, practical advice from the students about how to succeed in the course. That advice applies to other college courses as well as the writing course. I'm so pleased with the chapter; it's a useful, real store of sound tips that only real students could supply.

I'm honored to have been able to work with these student advisers, who gave us lots of time, thought, and careful suggestions. Thanks so much to each of you, and I hope to keep in touch as you continue through college and beyond.

## Other Student Contributors

Aside from the student advisers, many current and former students have contributed to this book. The nine former students featured in the "Profiles of Success" have been an inspiration, and I have been honored to talk with them. I thank them all for their hard work, their writing, and their well-deserved successes. The "Profiles of Success" are:

- Rosalind Baker (Human Services Director)
- Celia Hyde (Police Chief)
- Len Lacy (Manufacturing Manager)
- Kelly Layland (Nurse)
- Rocío Murillo (Teacher)
- Yuan Ping (Financial Manager)
- Sandro Polo (Architect)
- Walter Scanlon (Consultant)
- Alan Whitehead (Builder)

Other current and former students contributed model paragraphs and essays to the book, or provided quotes and other helpful suggestions: Carol

Benson, Karen Branch, Jesse Calsado, Jeanette Castro, Amy Cork, Robert Crider, Lidia Figueroa, Danny Fitzgerald, Lorenzo Gilbert, Dale Hill, Carol Parola, Rupa Patel, Suzanne Robinson, Jason Sifford, Cathy Vittoria, and Dana Williams.

## Reviewers

In addition to the Editorial Advisory Board, a large group of reviewers helped to develop and fine-tune the third edition of *Real Writing* and its ancillaries. I would like to thank Althea Allard, Community College of Rhode Island; Marla Allegre, Allan Hancock College; Andre Belyi, Brevard Community College; Denise Bostic, Nicholls State University; Mike Chu, College of DuPage; Joseph Colavito, Northwestern State University; Dawn Copeland, Motlow State Community College; Judy D. Covington, Trident Technical College; Linda Elaine, College of DuPage; Julie Hanwell, Tri-County Community College; Robin Havenick, Linn-Benton Community College; Deanna S. Highe, Central Piedmont Community College; Yvonne Robinson Jones, Southwest Tennessee Community College; Edwina Jordan, Illinois Central College; Kevin Kelly, Andover College; Melissa Knous, Angelina College; Carol A. Kontos, University of Maine at Augusta; Catherine Lally, Brevard Community College; Reginald F. Lockett, San Jose City College; Susan Lockwood, Chattahoochee Valley Community College; Catherine A. Lutz, Texas A&M University, Kingsville; Eric Meyer, St. Louis Community College-Meramec; Heather L. Morgan, Bakersfield College; Diane Payne, University of Arkansas-Monticello; Betty Peterson, Somerset Community College; Diane L. Polcha, Tulsa Community College; Melissa Price, Piedmont Technical College; Dee Pruitt, Florence-Darlington Technical College; Sharon Race, South Plains College; Renee Santos, Piedmont Technical College; Shaheen Sayeed, Moraine Valley Community College; Richard A. Schmitt, Nunez Community College; Kimberly Shuckra, Harrisburg Area Community College; William E. Smith, Western Washington University; Lerah A. Spikes, Georgia Perimeter College; Debbie Stallings, Hinds Community College; Geraldine Stiles, Andover College; James E. Twining, Community College of Rhode Island; Gregory J. Underwood, Pearl River Community College; Paul Vantine, Cameron University; Linda VanVickle, St. Louis Community College-Meramec; Kenneth R. Vorndran, Pima Community College; Barbara Schwarz Wachal, St. Louis Community College-Forest Park; and Susan Waugh, St. Louis Community College-Meramec.

The following instructors contributed to previous editions and have given us valuable insights and suggestions: Norman Asmar, Miami-Dade Community College; William Boggs, Slippery Rock University; Kathleen Briton, Florence-Darlington Technical College; Sandra Chumchal, Blinn College; Norma Cruz-Gonzales, San Antonio College; Sarah Harris, Southern Mississippi Planning and Development District; Claudia House, Nashville State Technical Institute; Michael Hricik, Westmoreland County Community College; Gloria Isles, Greenville Technical College; Patricia Malinowski, Finger Lakes Community College; Dan Moody, Southwestern College; Mercy Moore, Broward Community College; Patricia Pallis, Naugatuck Valley Community-Technical College; Verlene Pierre, Southeastern Louisiana University; Linda Rollins, Motlow State Community College; David Rollinson, College of Marin; Ingrid Schreck, Chaffey College; and Linda Whisnant, Guilford Technical Community College.

## Contributors

Carolyn Lengel continues to have my highest respect for her ability to create carefully conceived grammar practices on interesting topics. Carolyn not only contributed many exercises to the book and to Exercise Central, but she also crafted interesting, insightful headnotes for the new readings, while updating those that appeared in the second edition.

One of our very able editorial advisers, Kathleen Beauchene, developed a brilliant new series of activities and questions to accompany the readings. We really wanted to beef up the reading activities because so many students need help with active, critical reading and with identifying—in engaging ways—the main idea and support in an essay. Kathleen met and exceeded our hopes, providing new marginal questions that ask students about the readings as they read and new writing activities that develop both comprehension and critical, close reading skills.

Martha Friedman helped find thought-provoking visuals for the new image-based writing assignments, and Alice Lundoff diligently searched for part-opener photographs.

Merrill Glustrom, Editorial Advisory Board member and a steady supplier of pragmatic advice and ideas, revised *Practical Suggestions,* the wonderfully useful instructor's manual that provides practical advice on teaching the basic writing class and, specifically, teaching it using *Real Writing.*

Susan Naomi Bernstein, University of Houston, Downtown, wrote and revised the *Background Readings* with thoughtful editorial guidance from Karin Halbert of Bedford/St. Martin's.

## Bedford/St. Martin's

Bedford/St. Martin's is not your run-of-the-mill publisher, and I say this having spent many years at other publishing companies. It has earned its reputation as the premier publisher of English texts by devoting inordinate time, brainpower, money, and plain old blood, sweat, and tears to each of its books. Each project is a messy, collaborative, draining, and finally inspiring effort. They demand an incredible amount; they give even more than they demand.

Karin Halbert, associate editor, solved all kinds of problems and played a key role in finding new sources of readings, amassing and annotating a vast array of possibilities. Karin also helped develop and edit most of the ancillaries with the third edition, including Exercise Central and the companion Web site. Karin has a fine editorial eye and incredible stamina. She juggled multiple projects, ably, under tight deadlines. Caryn O'Connell, editorial assistant, also played a big part in this revision, helping to coordinate the extensive review program, working closely with student advisers and commentators, and assisting with research and many other tasks. She did all of this not only with great competence but with infectious good cheer.

The new media team at Bedford/St. Martin's was instrumental in developing the innovative electronic resources for *Real Writing*. Nick Carbone, director of new media, and Harriet Wald, associate editor of new media, helped ensure that the Writing Guide Software integrated smoothly with Exercise Central, while providing much more help along the way. David Mogolov, associate editor of new media, helped with the tutorial for Exercise Central that appears in the Introduction for Students and offered many suggestions for improving this resource. Capably, patiently, and with endless good humor, new media coordinator Coleen O'Hanley produced the indispensable companion Web site.

Alison Greene copyedited the final manuscript, catching and querying infelicities and errors and offering sure remedies for them all.

Deborah Baker, production editor, managed, once again, to organize late, long, and out-of-sequence manuscript so that it ran smoothly through the many steps of the production process. Also, she oversaw a complicated and extended redesign process with incredible patience and insight. I also want to thank Elizabeth Schaaf, managing editor, for reviewing the manuscript and pointing out any repetitiousness of subjects and needlessly negative examples or practices. Marcia Cohen, vice president and director of editing, design, and production, has admirably survived yet another challenging production and manufacturing process.

Text designer Claire Seng-Niemoeller has demonstrated her ability to work with complex design elements (and people who request endless revisions, making an already-strong design more dynamic and user-friendly). Art director Donna Dennison and design associate Billy Boardman created lively new book covers, and both shared invaluable insights about the interior design. Promotion manager Tom Macy and project manager Pelle Cass helped create engaging promotional materials for the book under tight deadlines.

I am lucky enough to live in the same area as my publisher: Boston. I'm even luckier to have known many of the people at Bedford/St. Martin's for many years. They are old and trusted friends. And with each book and each new edition, I work with these old friends and new, brilliant, sensitive people who somehow seem to work round-the-clock with good cheer and clear, fertile minds. I'll thank some of those people here, though over the years many others have contributed to the success of *Real Writing*.

Karen Melton Soeltz, director of marketing, Brian Wheel, marketing manager, and Jimmy Fleming, marketing specialist, have helped ensure that the revision of *Real Writing* is soundly and consistently connected to the marketplace. Honest and intelligent feedback from the sales force and from the regional sales managers has helped ensure that *Real Writing* reflects what's going on in all areas of the country.

The editorial team that produced this edition of *Real Writing* is extensive, and each person named here had deep involvement: Joan Feinberg, president and longtime friend, still manages somehow to find time to imprint books with her keen and legendary editorial wisdom; Denise Wydra, editorial director and the editor for the first edition of *Real Writing*, not only lends expert word help but also is the one among us who has a natural talent for seeing how words can be expressed visually; Karen Henry, editor in chief, absorbs ideas, understands our intentions, and helps us to shape them into features that meet the needs of students and instructors.

Although no longer a full-time presence at Bedford/St. Martin's, Chuck Christensen is still a force, and I thank him for first involving me in *Real Writing*.

Finally, thanks to Beth Castrodale, my multitalented editor and co-author. Beth learned and sharpened her editorial skills under the tutelage of the very best: other Bedford players including Jane Betz, Karen Henry, and—of course—Joan Feinberg and Chuck Christensen. She now is one of the very best and helps others learn the art of being a Bedford/St. Martin's editor. She is also a writer, a quilter, a student of languages, and a person who makes you feel that there's no one she'd rather be talking with than you, any time of day or night. She contributed so many new ideas and revised so many awkwardly rendered ones that her work really deserves more than a paragraph at the end of a preface. Maybe I'll think of something more apt, but I might need her help.

Always last, but never least, I thank my husband, Jim Anker, for his professional wisdom and personal strength.

—Susan Anker

# Contents

# Introduction for Students

## *How to Use This Book*

## Why Use *Real Writing*?

The easy answer is that your instructor assigned it for this course. But a better answer is that *Real Writing* will benefit you personally. Probably you're juggling lots of time-consuming commitments (such as college, a job, and family responsibilities). You need to choose tools that will help you spend your time in the most useful ways.

As the title suggests, *Real Writing: Paragraphs and Essays for College, Work, and Everyday Life* isn't just an academic text. Its purpose is to improve your writing so that you can succeed not only in this course but in other courses, on the job, and in your everyday life. Writing is a skill that you'll use throughout college, but it is also a skill that you will need for most jobs. In fact, employers usually cite good communication skills as the number-one ability they look for in job candidates. Mastering basic writing skills may turn out to be your most significant college achievement.

How will *Real Writing* help? It focuses on the practical: It zeroes in on the most important writing and editing skills you need to succeed. It gives you simple explanations, reality-based assignments, concrete steps for completing tasks, and tips for moving ahead if you get stuck. *Real Writing* isn't removed from your life; it starts where you are and helps you get to where you want to go.

Make sure to read Chapter 1 carefully. In it, students who have completed the writing course you are taking offer practical advice on how to succeed in the course. The chapter also gives you a quick head start on the basics of the writing process.

## How to Find Information in *Real Writing*

There are many ways to find information in this book. You can use different tools to find what you are looking for, depending on the help you need.

## To Find a Chapter or Section

**BRIEF CONTENTS AND DETAILED CONTENTS**    A brief table of contents is printed on the inside of the front cover. Here you can scan all the chapter titles and see at a glance where the various writing and editing topics are. You'll also notice that the topics of the book begin with Writing Paragraphs and Essays (Parts One, Two, and Three), move to Editing (Parts Four through Seven), and finish with Readings (Part Eight), if you are using *Real Writing with Readings.* If you're looking for a whole chapter or a general section of the book, the brief contents is a good place to turn.

A longer, more detailed table of contents is at the beginning of the book (pp. xxiii–xxxi). When you are trying to find something specific in a chapter, the detailed contents may be more useful than the brief contents. For example, you might recall that there's coverage of drafting paragraphs early in Part One but not remember where it is. The detailed contents will show you that "Practice Writing a Draft Paragraph" and "Write Your Own Draft Paragraph" are sections in Chapter 6 and give their exact page numbers.

**INDEX**    At the end of *Real Writing* is a complete index that lists the topics covered in the book, in alphabetical order, and indicates what page each topic is on. Using the index will almost always get you to the right place. For example, to find information on how to write a topic sentence, you would look up *topic sentence.* There you would find the page number not only for the section that deals with topic sentences in general but for other sections that cover topic sentences in specific types of writing. The index includes many of the terms you might use to look up a particular concept or topic, so you won't have to look in several places.

## To Find Help with Writing or Grammar Problems

**CHART OF CORRECTION SYMBOLS**    In the back of the book is a chart of the symbols that many instructors use to indicate writing or grammar problems in student work. If your instructor uses these symbols, this chart will help you understand what they mean.

**LIST OF USEFUL CHARTS AND QUICK REFERENCES**    On the inside of the back cover is a list of charts and quick reference tools (such as writing checklists, a list of irregular verbs, and so on) that you will find helpful as you write and edit.

## To Find the Page You Need

**HEADINGS AT THE TOPS OF PAGES**    Next to the page number at the top of each page is a heading that will tell you exactly where you are in the book. The first line of the heading is the part title—the name of the part of the book you're in. On each left-hand page under the part title are the chapter number and title. On each right-hand page under the part title is the name of the major section you're in. The following sample, for instance, shows that you are in the part "How to Write Paragraphs and Essays," in Chapter 1, "The Basics." Within that chapter, you are in the major section "Writing Basics."

# How to Use *Real Writing* When You Write

*Real Writing* is filled with charts, checklists, and other aids to help you complete your writing assignments successfully and become a better writer. Here are descriptions of a few of these aids with samples from the book.

**MARGINAL NOTES**    Throughout the book you will see two kinds of notes in the margins. Tips provide hints on how to do a particular writing task, remind you of information you may have forgotten, refer you to other pages where you can review material, and offer other kinds of advice. Idea journal and learning journal notes suggest topics for you to write about in your journal.

**MODELS**    Each chapter includes examples that provide good models for writing. For example, there are many models of the various stages of the writing process showing you examples of topic sentences, thesis statements, and support. Also, model paragraphs illustrate the "four basics" of writing various types of paragraphs and essays.

> ■ **TIP** Showing involves providing visual details or other supporting observations. Explaining involves offering specific examples, or illustrating aspects of the main point. Proving involves providing specific evidence, sometimes from outside sources.
>
> ■ **IDEA JOURNAL** Write about a time that you were overcharged for something. How did you handle it?

## ■■ **FOUR BASICS OF GOOD NARRATION**
1.  It reveals something of importance to you (your main point).
2.  It includes all of the major events of the story (primary support).
3.  It brings the story to life with details about the major events (secondary support).
4.  It presents the events in a clear order, usually according to when they happened.

In the following paragraph, each number corresponds to one of the Basics of Good Narration.

1 Last night my husband saved my life. We were sitting out on the porch with a couple of friends, enjoying the cool breeze of the evening. 2 While eating a piece of melon for dessert, I laughed at something my friend said, and suddenly the fruit stuck in my windpipe, entirely blocking any air. 3 I tried to swallow hard and dislodge it, but it didn't move. 3 When I tried taking a deep breath, I couldn't get one. 2 Fortunately, my husband, seated across the table from me, saw that something was wrong and asked me if I needed help. 2 Close to panic, I nodded yes.

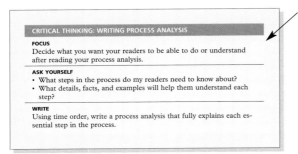

**CRITICAL THINKING GUIDES**   Many chapters include short guides that help you focus on specifics as you begin a task. These guides help you to complete assignments and give you useful practice in thinking before acting—a skill you'll use both in and out of college.

**CHECKLISTS FOR WRITING**   Each chapter on writing paragraphs and essays has checklists that will help you complete the assignment. These checklists contain specific steps for writing either a paragraph or an essay.

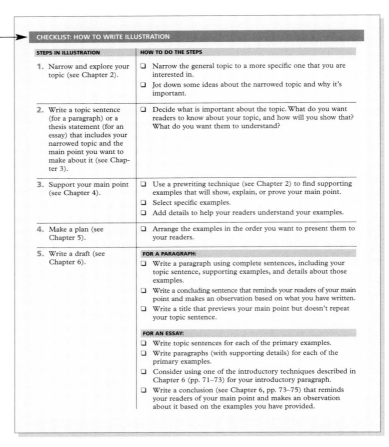

**GUIDED EXAMPLES THAT SHOW HOW TO FIND AND FIX ERRORS**  Many of the chapters on grammar, word use, and punctuation include charts that take you through the steps of finding and correcting specific types of sentence errors. Each chart includes a sentence with an error that is corrected according to the steps. The example is followed immediately by practices with the same type of error, making it easy for you to refer to the example as you complete the exercises. You can also use these examples to check your work.

**CHAPTER REVIEWS AND QUICK REVIEW CHARTS**
Each chapter ends with a review that tests your understanding of key concepts. Additionally, most of the chapters on editing end with quick review charts, which present all the types of errors covered in the guided examples (described on the preceding page) and help you decide what type of error you have and how to fix it. You can use the charts to troubleshoot for problems in your writing.

## Helpful Appendices

*Real Writing* has four appendices that will aid you in college, work, and everyday life. The first appendix covers the basics of essay writing. You may read this as an assignment, or you can use this as a refresher on essay writing in this course or later in college. The remaining three appendices contain useful information, tips, and strategies for three important activities: giving oral presentations, writing a résumé and cover letter, and using the computer to write and search for information.

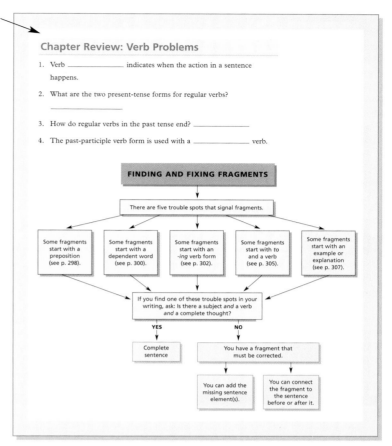

# How to Use Exercise Central: A Tutorial

The *Real Writing* Web site at **<bedfordstmartins.com/realwriting>** has several tools to help you improve your writing. One of them is Exercise Central, a collection of more than 8,000 online exercises in grammar, style, punctuation, and mechanics. You can do the exercises whenever you want to and get instant feedback on your work; if you answer a question incorrectly, Exercise Central will tell you why, to help you avoid the mistake in the future.

Your instructor may ask you to visit Exercise Central, but it's worthwhile to visit the site even if you aren't directed there: It will help you become a better editor of your own writing. When you're ready to use the site, follow the steps below.

**NOTE:** Before you visit Exercise Central, you may want to take the diagnostic test on the *Real Writing* Web site. This test will indicate skill areas where you might need more practice.

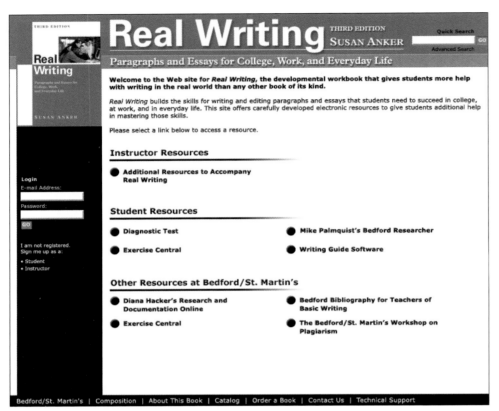

1. Log in to the home page for *Real Writing* at **<bedfordstmartins .com/realwriting>**. You'll see the screen shown at left:

2. If you have not already registered on the site, click on the **Student** link in the **Log on** column at the left of the screen. You will see the form shown at right:

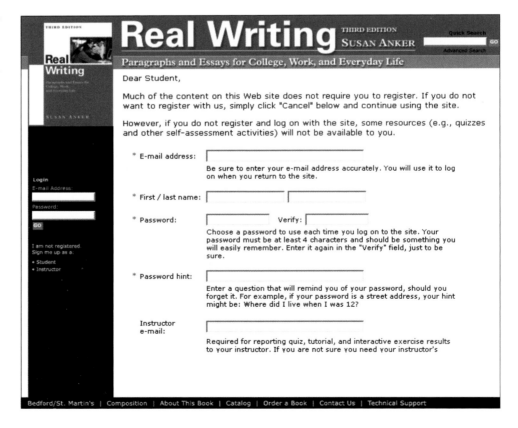

3. Make sure to fill in the asterisked fields with your information. (Your instructor's e-mail address is optional, although you will have to enter it if your instructor wants to monitor your work.) When you have completed the form, click on **Submit** at the bottom of the screen. You will be asked to validate the information; when you've finished, click on **Continue**.

4. You will be returned to the home page, where you should click on the **Exercise Central** link.

You will get a chart (the Customized Lesson Plan) that organizes exercises by subject, according to parts and chapters in *Real Writing.* Choose a subject/chapter from this chart and click on it. For instance, if you choose Chapter 20 (Fragments), the screen shown at right will appear.

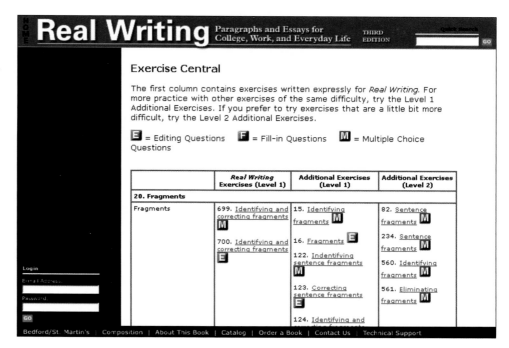

5. Make your choice from the exercise chart. Note that the first column contains exercises written especially for *Real Writing.* For more practice, try the exercises in the other columns.

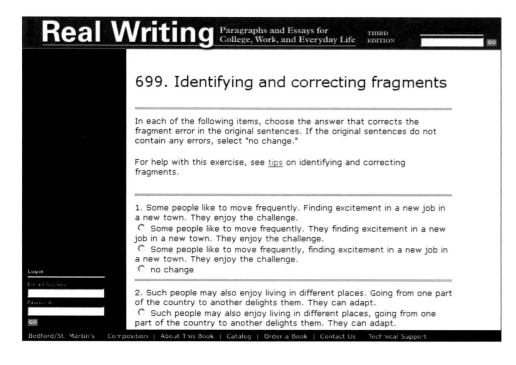

Let's try the multiple-choice exercise for "Identifying and Correcting Fragments" from the first column.

6. Read the instructions first. In this case, choose your answer by clicking on the circle to the left of it.

7. When you're done with the exercise, click on **Submit** at the bottom of the screen.

8. Exercise Central will calculate your score and give you feedback on any incorrect answers.

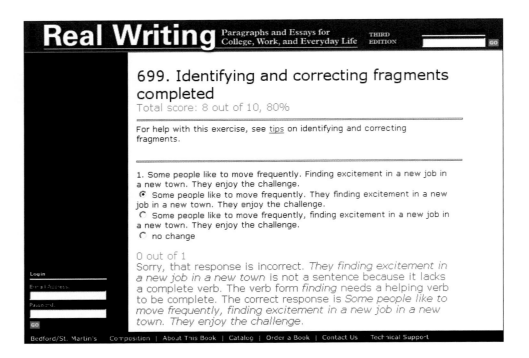

Note the "total score" under the exercise title. Because the answer for number 1 is incorrect, Exercise Central explains the reason why.

9. When you're done with your Exercise Central session, be sure to log out.

## Part One

# How to Write Paragraphs and Essays

# 1
# The Basics
## *What You Need to Know to Get Started*

This chapter reviews basic information you will need to get off to a good start in your writing class. Please take the time to read it through carefully: It provides you with a solid foundation for the course.

## Course Basics

The students pictured in this chapter recently completed the course you are now taking. For this section, we asked them to tell you "things they wish they'd known." Throughout this chapter you'll find their best tips for succeeding in the course.

**MARK BALDERAS:** "If you really want to learn to write, and you follow the clear and simple steps in this Course Basics and in the book, you will get a good grade."

### Have a Positive Attitude

A few of you may think that you don't belong in this class because you always got good grades in writing when you were in high school. Of course, this isn't high school. If you were given a test that determined you should be here, accept this and think of this course as an opportunity. Get everything you can from the class: You will need to write in every other course you will take and in any job you will want.

**NICOLE DAY:** "It is very important to have a positive attitude when starting the class and going through it. This way you can open your mind to a variety of lifetime learning experiences. Having a positive attitude lets your teacher know that you are willing to try."

**NICOLE DAY:** "Doing the assignments is crucial to your grade in the class and to your future. By doing the assignments, you might learn something that you never knew before."

**KATILYA LABIDOU:** "I'm not one who grasps things easily. I had to go to my instructor's office every chance I had, both before class and also on days when I didn't have to be at school. I finally understand my writing better as well as my speech."

Also remember that you get from this course only what you give. For example, your instructor doesn't decide what grade to give you: He or she evaluates and grades the work that *you* do—or don't do.

### Do the Assignments

Take the course and the course work seriously. Do not make the mistake that a couple of our student advisers did of thinking that you can do nothing and still manage to pass. Although no one will make life difficult or uncomfortable for you if you choose not to do the work, you risk failing the course. More important, you will not learn to be a better writer, and that will affect your future plans.

### Make Sure You Understand, and Get Help if You Don't

If you don't understand a concept during class, the quickest way to clear up your confusion is to raise your hand and ask the instructor to go over it again or to give another example. If you don't understand, probably others don't either, so don't feel foolish asking for clarification.

If you get confused while you are doing an assignment, ask your instructor for help either after class, during office hours, or via e-mail. In addition to your instructor, you have other possible sources of help, such as the library, computer lab, writing center, and tutors. Your tuition pays for these resources, so find out how they can help you and use them. Whatever you do, don't remain confused.

## Manage Your Time

Passing this course requires—at the very least—that you attend class and that you complete the homework and writing assignments. To do so, you need to manage your time effectively. Here is some advice about time management that our student advisers wanted to pass on to you.

### Get to Class (on Time) and Stay until the End

Make a commitment to go to every class. Things do come up in life that may conflict with your class, but if you are going to miss a session, be late, or leave early, let your instructor know in advance, if possible, and ask what you should do on your own.

**MICHELLE BASSETT:** "You'd be surprised at how much you miss when you're absent for just one class. As for getting there on time, two things: Many instructors give out important information right at the start of class. Also, many consider coming in late an absence."

## Make a Schedule for Writing Assignments

It's tempting to put off doing the assignment until the last minute, but there are several stages to the process of writing a good paper, and the process as a whole takes some time. Working back from the due date of your assignment, make up a written schedule that leaves enough time for the various steps. Then stick to it. Here is a sample schedule that one student developed.

**ASSIGNMENT:** *Write an essay describing an important event in your life.*

**DUE DATE:** *10/8/03*

| TASKS FOR COMPLETING ASSIGNMENT | FINISH BY |
|---|---|
| *Decide on a topic.* | *9/28/03* |
| *Complete a draft (with a main point you care about and enough information to support that point).* | *10/3/03* |
| *Reread the draft, looking for ways to improve it. Then revise it.* | *10/5/03* |
| *Proofread the draft, correcting any errors in grammar, spelling, and punctuation.* | *10/7/03* |

**MICHELLE BASSETT:** "Make sure you begin writing assignments long before they're due. Then you have time to revise and edit before handing in something that you know isn't as good as it could be."

Write down the instructor's directions and the due date.

This step is unnecessary if the topic (for example, "Describe your first day of college") has been assigned.

■ **RESOURCES** A blank schedule appears in *Additional Resources.* You can reproduce it for students to help get them started with making schedules.

## Be a Part of the Class

As we all know, it's possible to go to every class and still not be part of it. Decide that you will be an active part of the class; you are more likely to do well. Our student advisers offer these suggestions, as a start.

### Make a Friend

In most classes, students sit in about the same place in each session. Take advantage of this, and get to know at least one other person in the class. Exchange names, phone numbers, and e-mail addresses with students who sit near you. That way, if for some reason you can't make it to a class, you'll know someone who can fill you in on what you missed. Also, if you find you aren't exactly clear on what an assignment is, you can double-check with another student. You might also want to study with other students.

■ **TEACHING TIP** Devote a few minutes of class time to allowing students to get to know their neighbors and to exchange contact information if they wish.

### Get to Know Your Instructor

Your instructor wants you to succeed in the class as much as you want to. It helps him or her to know you a little bit: who you are, what you do, what you need help with. Make an appointment to visit your instructor during his or her office hours. When you go, ask questions about material you are not sure you understood in class or problems you have with writing. You and your instructor will get the most out of these sessions if you bring examples of your writing or specific assignments you're having trouble with.

**NICOLE DAY:** "Knowing your instructor is important because then they know who you are and what you need help with. When you're having trouble with something, you feel more comfortable going to your instructor when you know her."

**MICHELLE BOSTICK:** "Going to see your instructor in her office allows you to identify areas where your writing is weak, and you can get help that might embarrass you if you had to ask in class. It helps you become a more confident student. It also shows the instructor that you are concerned about your writing and will take initiative."

Using e-mail is not quite as good as talking face-to-face, which allows for more personal interaction. You may need to use e-mail if, for some reason, you can't see your instructor during office hours.

If you do e-mail your instructor, remember this: Whenever you communicate, you create an impression of yourself. Even though e-mail is less formal than, for example, a writing assignment, what you say and how you say it are still important. Reread your e-mail messages before sending them to make sure that they are clear and they don't have spelling or grammar errors.

### Sit Near the Front

**NICOLE DAY:** "Sitting in front is very beneficial to your learning. You can see everything, and it lets your teacher know that you want to learn and not just hide in the back."

■ **RESOURCES** *Practical Suggestions* includes more advice on fostering class participation.

Don't hide in the back of the class and hope that no one will notice that you're there. Instead, when you go to the first class, sit in one of the first few rows. It really is easier to learn when you're closer to the instructor (and other students who are brave enough to choose seats near the front).

### Speak Up

For many students, speaking in class is difficult: You're not sure you have the right answer, or you think your question might be stupid. But speaking up in class is important. School is exactly the right place for getting over the fear of talking in a group, and the ability to speak to people in a group will help you at work and in your everyday life. Speaking up also allows you to get answers to questions and respond to class discussion right away. If you wait until later, you may forget your questions or the points you wanted to make.

Once you get used to speaking in class, you'll find that it's not hard, and you will get more out of the course. Challenge yourself, early on, to participate orally in the class: Volunteer to answer a question or to ask a question. Here are some tips that might help you:

• Don't be afraid to make a mistake. No one in the class, including your instructor, will make fun of you. As teachers are fond of saying, "There's no such thing as a dumb question."

- When you speak, look at your instructor (or whomever you're speaking to).

- Speak loudly enough for people to hear; otherwise, you'll have to repeat yourself.

## Identify Your Goals and Needs

What do you, personally, want from this course? Once you have a good idea of what you want, you will be more able to focus on what you need and to get specific help from your instructor.

First, what are some of your real-world goals, both small and large, right now and in the future? Some short-term goals, for example, might be persuading your boss to give you a raise, getting a loan from the bank, or getting a promotion. Longer-term goals might include deciding what kind of job or career you hope to have or what degree you want to finish. Do some thinking about your real-life goals and list at least five short-term and longer-term ones, the more concrete and specific the better (for example, "be happy" is too general and abstract).

Once you have some real-world goals in mind, try to link those goals to the writing skills you want to learn or improve in this course. For example, if one of your real-world goals is to convince your boss that you deserve a raise, you might want help with making a good argument for that.

Use the worksheet on page 8 to fill in these goals. Your instructor may or may not want a copy of this worksheet, but, in any case, *you* need it.

> **MARK BALDERAS:** "Be sure to set your *own* goals. They will help you succeed."

## Hang in There

Don't give up on yourself if things get hard. You can get help, and you can become a better writer and pass this course. If you drop out, you'll either have to take the same course next term or have the same writing problems that you had coming in. This course is the time and place to improve your writing, and better writing skills will give you more control over your life and how you communicate with others.

Believe in your ability to pass this course and stay focused; don't panic and run away. If you want some inspiration, check out the former students highlighted in the Profiles of Success at the beginning of Chapters 8–16. All of these people are successful, yet all of them had to overcome some major obstacles, often their own fear of writing.

> **KATILYA LABIDOU:** "Acknowledging your faults is the first step. I was really surprised when I first got a failing grade. Wanting to be better than average is what got me through. Sometimes I wasn't sure I could do it, but I stuck with it, and spent time learning about writing and grammar."

**NAME:** _____

**COURSE:** _____  **DATE:** _____

**REAL-WORLD GOALS**

_____

_____

_____

_____

_____

_____

_____

**COURSE GOALS**

Think about your writing and comments you have received about it in the past. What do you think your major problems with writing are? What should you work on improving? Jot down a few ideas and then, based on your answers to these questions, list three specific skills you want to improve during this course. Keep your real-world goals in mind as you decide on your course goals because what you learn in this class should be related to what you want to do with what you have learned.

_____

_____

_____

_____

_____

_____

_____

_____

# Writing Basics

This section will give you basic information on writing that you need to get off to a good start in this course. Chapters 2–7 cover all of the important stages of writing in more detail, with complete explanations and practice exercises.

## The Writing Process

A complete piece of writing does not happen all at once. Writers go through several steps, each bringing them closer to a finished piece of writing. All of these steps taken together are called the **writing process**.

    The writing process is not so different from other processes you use every day, for example, while parking a car or tying a shoelace: They seem complicated at first, but once you become familiar with the steps, you hardly notice that you are doing them.

    The chart that follows shows the five basic stages of the writing process and steps within those stages. Note that a chapter number appears after many of the steps. This number indicates where that step is covered in detail in this book. Your instructor may or may not assign these chapters to you. In either case, take a look at them because, in addition to providing complete explanations, Chapters 2–7 show how a student does each of the steps. Seeing how others go through the writing process will help you work through these steps in your own writing.

■ **DISCUSSION** Tell students about your own writing process. Let them know that sometimes you struggle and sometimes you don't. Tell them which parts are most difficult for you. Also let them know that different people emphasize different parts of the writing process: There isn't just one way to write.

---

## THE WRITING PROCESS

↓

### GENERATE IDEAS

**CONSIDER:** What is my purpose in writing? Given this purpose, what interests me? Who will read this? What do they need to know?

- Narrow and explore your topic (Chapter 2).
- Make your point (Chapter 3).
- Support your point (Chapter 4).

↓

### PLAN

**CONSIDER:** How can I organize my ideas effectively for my readers?

- Arrange your ideas and make an outline (Chapter 5).

↓

---

↓

> ### DRAFT
>
> **CONSIDER:** How can I show my readers what I mean?
>
> - Write a draft, including an introduction that will interest your readers, a strong conclusion, and a title (Chapter 6).

↓

> ### REVISE
>
> **CONSIDER:** How can I make my draft clearer or more convincing to my readers?
>
> - Look for ideas that do not fit (Chapter 7).
> - Look for ideas that could use more detailed support (Chapter 7).
> - Connect ideas with transitional words and sentences so that they flow smoothly (Chapter 7).

↓

> ### EDIT
>
> **CONSIDER:** What errors could confuse my readers and weaken my point?
>
> - Find and correct errors in grammar (Parts Four through Seven). Focus first on finding sentence fragments (Chapter 20), run-on sentences (Chapter 21), places where subjects and verbs don't match (Chapter 22), and other problems with verbs (Chapter 23).
> - Look for errors in word use (Chapters 31–32), spelling (Chapter 33), and punctuation and capitalization (Chapters 34–38).

## Four Basic Elements of Good Writing

Four elements are key to good writing and should be kept in mind throughout the writing process.

■■
■■ **FOUR BASICS OF GOOD WRITING**

1. It considers the needs and knowledge of the audience.
2. It fulfills the writer's purpose.
3. It includes a clear, definite main point.
4. It provides support that explains or proves the main point.

### 1. Audience

■ **TIP** All of the chapters in Part Two include a list of "four basics" to help you focus on important aspects of various types of writing.

The person or people who will read what you write. Whenever you write, always have at least one real person in mind as your reader. Think about what that person already knows and what he or she will need to know to understand your main point. In most cases, assume that your readers know only what you write on the page about your topic and main point. Sometimes writers — particularly when they are writing about a very familiar topic — make the mistake of assuming that their readers already know everything that they do. As a writer, however, it's up to you to recreate the situation so that your readers get the full picture.

What you say and how you say it may be very different for two different audiences. Consider the two examples below, which refer to the same situation but are written for different audiences. Notice the tone and content of each note.

**SITUATION:** Marta woke up one morning feeling very sick. When she went into the bathroom, she saw in the mirror that her face was swollen and red. Then she was hit with a violent attack of nausea. She could tell that she had a fever. Marta immediately called her doctor who said she could come right in. Marta's mother was coming to stay with the children in a few minutes, so Marta asked a neighbor to keep an eye on her children until her mother got there. Marta then left a note for her mother telling her why she had already left. When she got to the doctor's office, the nurse asked her to write a brief description of her symptoms for the doctor.

**MARTA'S NOTE TO HER MOTHER**

*Mom,*
*I wasn't feeling very well this morning, so I'm going to stop by the doctor's office before work to have her check me out. Don't worry, I'm okay, but before this develops into a flu or something, I thought I'd get some medication or a shot just in case. You know that I can't afford to miss any more work. See you later.*

**MARTA'S NOTE FOR HER DOCTOR**

*When I woke up this morning, I could tell I had a fever because I was sweating, and my head was throbbing. When I looked in the mirror, I saw that my face was very swollen, especially around my eyes, which were almost swollen shut. My lips were also very swollen and dry. The skin on my forehead, nose, and cheeks was bright red and itchy. Within a few minutes, I had to vomit and had several such episodes before calling your office.*

## 2. Purpose

The reason you are writing. In college, your purpose for writing is usually to show something, to explain something, or to create a convincing argument. Your purpose can depend on your audience, as shown by the examples in the previous section (the notes from Marta): Marta's purpose in the first note was to briefly explain her situation to her mother and to provide reassurance; her purpose in the second was to give her doctor a detailed description of her symptoms so that she could get effective treatment. Before you begin to write, ask yourself — and answer — exactly what your purpose is.

Both before you begin to write and at every step along the way, you need to think about both purpose and audience very carefully; the following chart can help.

■ **TEACHING TIP** Reinforce the ideas of audience and purpose by having students write two letters concerning a contemporary issue, for example, gun control. One letter could be to the National Rifle Association and the other to a crime prevention group.

## *Considering Your Audience and Purpose*

| STEP | HOW TO DO IT | STUDENT EXAMPLES |
|------|-------------|------------------|
| Prepare to meet the needs of your audience. | • Ask yourself: Who will be reading this?<br>• Figure out what you need to explain to these readers so that they will understand the topic/situation and your point of view. (Make a list, if this helps.) | See the notes from Marta above. |
| Prepare to fulfill your purpose. | • Ask yourself: What does the assignment/writing situation require?<br>• Ask yourself: What point do I want to make? (See the next section for more details.) | See the notes from Marta above. |

### 3.  Main Point

The point you want to make to your readers. You need to have a clear, central point in mind as you write your paper, and everything in the paper should support that point. In paragraphs the main point is known as the *topic sentence,* and in essays it is known as the *thesis statement.*

Your main point should be some aspect of a general topic that you care about—something that you are motivated to show, explain, or prove to your readers. If you start your paper with a weak main point, chances are that your support of that point will also be weak.

Consider the example of a student who was assigned the general topic of "an important daily routine." First she narrowed the general topic to a specific one that she was interested in: commuting by car. Then, she wrote a sentence that includes her main point:

Narrowed topic                                              Main point

Because commuting by car has increased my stress level, insurance rates, and gas consumption, I have decided to give it up and take the train instead.

Note that she picked an aspect of the topic that she cares about: namely, that commuting by car has such significant personal drawbacks that she has decided to give it up in favor of taking the train. In the body of the paper (the supporting paragraphs between the introduction and the conclusion), she would provide more details on the drawbacks of car commuting and explain how she arrived at her decision to take the train.

It is also important that you be able to identify the main point in others' writing; doing so is a key part of active reading, as we discuss in Chapter 39 of this book.

The following chart presents steps for making and reinforcing your main point.

## Making Your Main Point

| STEP | HOW TO DO IT | STUDENT EXAMPLES |
|---|---|---|
| • Choose a topic that you can get interested in (see Chapter 2). | • Ask yourself some questions about the general topic (which may be assigned to you) to help you narrow it to something that you are personally interested in. | *Assigned General Topic:* "drug abuse"<br>• Does drug abuse have any effect on my life?<br>• Do I know someone who has a drug problem?<br>• If so, how did that person become involved with drugs?<br>• Does alcohol count as a drug? |
| | • Based on your answers to the previous questions, explore ideas that interest you (see Chapter 2). Jot them down. | • My father was an alcoholic. He was a great guy sometimes, but then he'd start drinking and become really mean. He'd pick fights with my mother and hit her. My brother and sisters and I would try to defend her without getting hit ourselves. |
| | • Ask yourself: Is there a good narrowed topic—one that I'm personally interested in—in any of the ideas? | • How alcoholism affects the family of an alcoholic |
| • Write a topic sentence (for a paragraph) or a thesis statement (for an essay; see Chapter 3). | • Write a complete sentence that includes your narrowed topic and the main point you want your readers to understand about that topic. | • My father's alcoholism affected my family.<br>*Narrowed Topic:* My father's alcoholism<br>*Main Point:* affected my family. |
| • Rewrite the topic sentence or thesis statement to make it more forceful, confident, and specific (see Chapter 3). | • No one writes a perfect topic sentence or thesis statement the first time. Before you start writing the rest of your essay or paragraph, rewrite this sentence at least once to make it more specific. You should revisit it several times before you finish your paper.<br>• Read the sentence aloud. Does it sound forceful and confident? If not, try out some variations using different words. | • My father's alcoholism not only changed him but also deeply affected each person in the family.<br>*Narrowed Topic:* My father's alcoholism<br>*Main Point:* not only changed him but also deeply affected each person in the family. |

(continued)

## Making Your Main Point (cont'd.)

| STEP | HOW TO DO IT | STUDENT EXAMPLES |
|---|---|---|
| | • If you need to add more specifics, look back on the notes you jotted down earlier for some ideas. Or generate some additional ideas (see Chapter 2).<br>• Get input from your instructor or peers (see Chapter 7, pp. 81–82). | |
| • Reinforce the main point in your conclusion (see Chapter 6). | • Take a final opportunity to underscore your main point to help ensure that your readers will understand and agree with your main point. Remind them of that main point and make an observation based on the points you have raised in your paper. | • My father loved his family, but his drug of choice— alcohol—nearly destroyed us. |

### 4. Support

The information and ideas you use to show, explain, or prove your main point. Support points make up the largest part (the body) of your paragraph or essay.

There are two basic kinds of support:

- **Major (or primary) support:** the sentences that present the information and ideas that directly support your main point.
- **Supporting details (secondary support):** the sentences that give readers more detail about your major support points.

Support allows you to control your readers' experience. The more detailed and exact the support, the more you help readers understand your experience, idea, or position. Always think about how you can make your support more specific or concrete (something that readers can easily visualize or feel, because of details you provide), and choose your details carefully so that readers see or feel something as you do. When you read someone else's writing, make an effort to identify that writer's support for his or her main point. The chart on page 15 provides some tips for developing effective support.

Here is an example of a paragraph that has a topic sentence, major support points, and a concluding sentence. The major support is underlined.

■ **DISCUSSION** After students have read the two versions of the same paragraph on pages 14 and 15, discuss with them the fact that the second paragraph provides more specific and vivid details than the original. How does this affect their experience as readers?

Topic sentence ——————

Having an ice cream cone on a hot summer day is my favorite eating experience. As I wait in the heat to place my order, I start thinking about how cool and refreshing my favorite flavor will be. When I take that first lick, it's even better than I imagined. I dig out a big chunk of chocolate and hold it on my tongue just where the first lick melted. Soon, the top edge of the sugar

## Supporting Your Point

| STEP | HOW TO DO IT | STUDENT EXAMPLES |
|---|---|---|
| • Generate support for your topic sentence (for a paragraph) or thesis statement (for an essay; see Chapter 4). | • Reread your topic sentence or thesis statement and write as many ideas as you can think of to support it.<br>• Review your ideas, keeping your main point, audience, and purpose in mind.<br>• Select the ones that you think will best convince readers of your main point. (Get instructor or peer feedback if you can; see Chapter 7, pp. 81–82.)<br>• For each major support point, add specific, concrete details that will help your reader see your topic as you do. | See the examples below. |

cone gets a little soggy. The cone is my favorite part because I eat it just the way I did when I was a little kid. Eating that ice cream cone brings me back to the wonderful, carefree summer days of childhood, and I am happy. — Concluding sentence

You might think the example isn't bad, and it's not, but it doesn't have many descriptive details. Compare it with the following paragraph, with the major support still underlined and the supporting details added in italics.

Having an ice cream cone on a hot summer day is my favorite eating — Topic sentence
experience. As I wait in the heat to place my order, I start thinking about how cool and refreshing my favorite flavor will be. *Mine is mocha chocolate chunk, and all I can think about as I stand there is the coffee and chocolate flavors.* When I take that first lick, it's even better than I imagined. *The ice cream is cold, so cold it gives me a headache, for just a minute. The creamy mocha flavor, sweet with just a hint of bitter coffee, explodes against my taste buds, and I hold the first bite there until it melts on my tongue.* I dig out a big chunk of chocolate and hold it on my tongue just where the first bite melted. *In contrast to the creamy ice cream, the chunk is hard. I don't let it melt; instead I bite right into it, so I get the full effect of the chocolate.* Soon, the top edge of the sugar cone gets a little soggy. *That's because the ice cream has melted into it, and now the cone is part crunchy and part puffy with absorbed ice cream. I nibble at the edges, turning the cone round and round and mixing it with licks of ice cream.* The cone is my favorite part because I eat it just the way I did when I was a little kid. *When the cone is down to about two inches, I raise it above my mouth, point my head up, bite off the point, and drain the remaining ice cream. Finally, I pop the part of the cone that's left into my mouth and lick my lips to catch any stray ice cream.* Eating that ice cream cone brings me back to the wonderful, carefree summer days of childhood, and I am happy. — Concluding sentence

## Paragraph and Essay Structure

In this course (and in the rest of college), you will write paragraphs and/or essays. Each of these has a basic structure that you should know.

### Paragraph Structure

A **paragraph** has three necessary parts—the topic sentence, the body, and the concluding sentence.

| | |
|---|---|
| 1. The **topic sentence** | states the **main point**. The topic sentence is often the first sentence of the paragraph. |
| 2. The **body** | supports (shows, explains, or proves) the main point. It is usually made up of about three to five **support sentences**, which contain facts and details supporting the main point. |
| 3. The **concluding sentence** | reminds readers of the main point and often makes an observation. |

Read the paragraph that follows with the paragraph parts labeled.

Topic sentence

Body support

Concluding sentence

Gambling is a growing addiction in this country. As more casinos open, more people have the opportunity to try gambling. For most people, a casino is simply a fun place to visit, filled with people, lights, noise, food, and a feeling of excitement as patrons try to beat the odds and win. Most people set a limit on how much money they are willing to lose, and when they reach that amount, they stop. Addicts, however, can't stop. They always want to play just one more game to get back what they lost. If they do recoup their losses, they feel lucky and don't want to end their winning streak. Win or lose, they keep playing, and the vast majority lose, returning repeatedly to the cash machine to replenish their funds, or getting cash advances on their credit cards. People have been known to spend their entire savings because they are caught up in the frenzy of trying to win. Because casinos and gambling games like keno are now more widespread, more addicts are surfacing, and the casinos encourage the addiction: It means more money for them. The gamblers' support group, Gamblers Anonymous, based on the principles of Alcoholics Anonymous, has seen vastly increased membership in the last few years as more potential addicts are introduced to gambling, fall into its clutches, and struggle to get free. Clearly, gambling needs to be taken as seriously as any other addiction.

### Essay Structure

An **essay** has multiple paragraphs and, like a paragraph, three necessary parts: an introduction that includes a thesis statement, a body, and a conclusion.

1. The **introduction** may be a single paragraph or multiple paragraphs, but it must contain the main point in a single, strong statement known as the *thesis*. One popular way to structure an essay is to write a three-point thesis that previews three aspects of the topic that will be detailed in each of the three body paragraphs of the essay.

> **EXAMPLE:** Responsible driving involves (1) paying attention to your own driving, (2) being aware of other cars, and (3) always putting safety first.

A five-paragraph essay could be developed from this thesis. It would have (in addition to an introductory paragraph and a concluding paragraph) one body paragraph on paying attention to your own driving, a second body paragraph on being aware of other cars, and a third body paragraph on putting safety first.

2. The **body** supports (shows, explains, or proves) the main point. As already noted, it usually has at least three **support paragraphs**, each of which contains facts and details that support the main point. Each of the support paragraphs begins with a **topic sentence**, a major support point for the thesis statement.

3. The **conclusion** reminds readers of the main point. It may summarize the support and make an observation based on that support.

The following diagram shows how the parts of an essay correspond to the parts of a paragraph.

■ **RESOURCES** *Additional Resources* contains reproducible forms that students can use to plan their paragraphs and essays. The forms detail the steps of the writing process and provide spaces for the main point, support, and so on.

**RELATIONSHIP BETWEEN PARAGRAPHS AND ESSAYS**

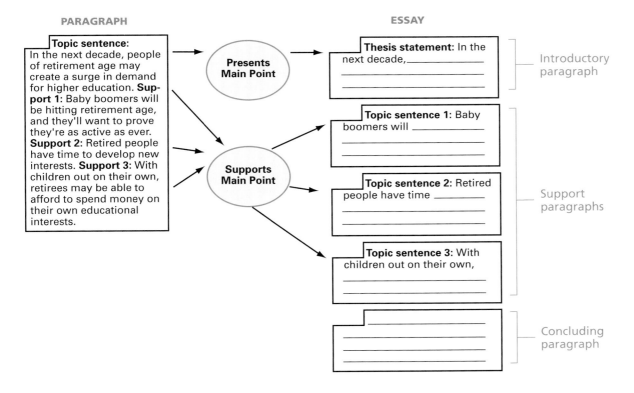

## A Final Note: Avoiding Plagiarism

■ **TIP** For more information on avoiding plagiarism, and citing and documenting outside sources, see Chapter 18.

■ **RESOURCES** Visit the Bedford/St. Martin's Workshop on Plagiarism at <www .bedfordstmartins.com/ plagiarism/> for online re- sources on avoiding plagiarism. These resources include a "quick reference" flyer that helps students manage writing and research so they don't - accidentally plagiarize. Also included is an instructor flyer that describes books, Web sites, software, and faculty service workshops that Bedford/ St. Martin's has developed to help faculty make sure their students understand how to avoid plagiarism.

In all the writing you do, it is important to avoid plagiarism—passing off information you gather from another source as your own. Writers who pla- giarize, either on purpose or by accident, risk failing a course, being expelled from school, or losing their jobs and damaging their reputations. Be aware that your instructors are savvy about plagiarism and know how to look for it; so if you plagiarize, you have a good chance of getting caught.

To avoid plagiarism, take careful notes on every source (books, inter- views, television shows, Web sites, and so on) you might use in your writing. When recording information from sources, try to take notes in your own words, unless you plan to use direct quotations. In that case, make sure to record the quotation word for word and include quotation marks around it, both in your notes and in your paper.

When you use material from other sources—whether you directly quote or paraphrase—you must name these sources in your paper. Therefore, as you take notes from sources, record the author's name, the title of the work, the date and place of publication, the publisher and its location, page num- bers of the referenced material, and volume numbers (if relevant). With Web sites, be sure to also record the URL (the "address" where the Web site is located), the date you accessed the site, the date of publication or latest up- date, and the name of the sponsoring organization.

## Chapter Review: The Basics

1.  What are the five "course basics" that can help you succeed in this course and others?

    *Have a positive attitude.*

    *Manage your time.*

    *Be a part of the class.*

    *Identify your goals and needs.*

    *Hang in there.*

2.  What are the five steps of the writing process?

    *Generate ideas*

    *Plan*

    *Draft*

    *Revise*

    *Edit*

3.  Your *audience* consists of the person or people who will read what you write, and your *purpose* is the reason you are writing.

4.  A topic sentence or thesis statement states your _main point_.

5.  The body of a paragraph or essay _supports_ the main point.

## What Will You Use?

How might the "course basics" described in this chapter also help you with work and everyday life? What particular basics would you like to improve on in college, work, and everyday life?

# 2

# Finding, Narrowing, and Exploring Your Topic

## Choosing Something to Write About

## You Know This

You already know what a topic is:

- What was the topic of a movie you saw recently?
- What topic is in the headlines this week?
- What was the topic of a conversation you had recently?

## Understand What a Topic Is

A **topic** is who or what you are writing about. A good topic is one that interests you, that you can say something about, and that is specific. Any topic you choose should be able to pass the Three-Question Test for Good Topics:

**THREE-QUESTION TEST FOR GOOD TOPICS**

| | |
|---|---|
| **Does it interest me?** | If you don't care about a topic, you will find it hard to write about it. You will get bored and so will your audience. Try to find a topic that you care about. If you are assigned a topic, try to find some part of it that interests you. |
| **Can I say something about it?** | If no ideas come to mind, even after you've thought about this question for a few minutes, you might want to choose another topic. |
| **Is it specific?** | Whether you are writing a paragraph or an essay, if your topic is too general (for example, "world peace"), it will be difficult to focus in enough to say anything meaningful about it. As you choose a topic, keep in mind that you will need to make some meaningful point about it in either a paragraph or a short essay. |

When your instructor assigns a general topic, it may at first seem uninteresting, unfamiliar, or very general. It is up to you to find a good, specific topic based on the general one. There are two steps involved: narrowing the topic and exploring the topic.

## Practice Narrowing a Topic

To **narrow** a general topic, focus on the smaller parts of it until you find one that is interesting and specific.

There are many ways to narrow a topic. For example, you can try dividing a general category into smaller subcategories. Or you can think of specific examples from your life or from current events.

### Divide it into smaller categories

### Think of specific examples

ASSIGNED
GENERAL TOPIC  **Crime**
Stolen identities (how does it happen?)
When I had my wallet stolen by two kids
   (how? what happened?)
The telemarketing scam that my grandmother lost
   money in (how did it work?)

ASSIGNED
GENERAL TOPIC  **Web sites**
Shopping online (for what, and where?)
Music (what kind? what can I get?)
My favorite sites (why do I like them?)

### Think of something related to the topic that happened in the last two weeks (or past month or year)

ASSIGNED
GENERAL TOPIC  **Environmental problems**
Water in the reservoir found to have high *E. coli* levels
Hot weather causing the state to run out of power

ASSIGNED
GENERAL TOPIC  **Heroism**
The guy who pulled a perfect stranger from a
   burning car
The people who stopped the robbery in the North End

A topic for an essay can be a little broader than one for a paragraph, because essays are longer than paragraphs and allow you to develop more ideas. But be careful: Most of the extra length in an essay should come from developing ideas in more depth (giving more examples and details, explaining what you mean), not from covering a broader topic.

Read these examples of how a general topic was narrowed to a more specific topic for an essay, and an even more specific topic for a paragraph.

■ **TEACHING TIP** Give students examples of questions they might be asked that are too "big" to answer in a paragraph or essay. Have them figure out how to narrow the question or assignment.

| ASSIGNED GENERAL TOPIC | NARROWED ESSAY TOPIC | NARROWED PARAGRAPH TOPIC |
|---|---|---|
| Drug abuse | How alcoholism affects family life | How alcoholism affects a family's budget |
| Public service opportunities | Volunteering at a homeless shelter | My first impression of the homeless shelter |
| A personal goal | Getting healthy | Eating the right foods |
| A great vacation | A family camping trip | What I learned on our family camping trip |

When you have found a promising topic for a paragraph or essay, be sure to test it by using the Three-Question Test for Good Topics. You may need to narrow and test several times before you find a topic that will work for the assignment.

■ **RESOURCES** For separate coverage of essays, see Appendix A, The Basics of Writing an Essay.

■ **PRACTICE 1    NARROWING A GENERAL TOPIC FOR AN ESSAY**

Read each of the five general topics. In the space provided, write a narrower topic that would be good for an essay. Make sure that what you write passes the Three-Question Test for Good Topics.

1. A living hero _____ *Answers will vary.* _____

2. A controversy on this campus _____

3. A future goal _____

4. An essential survival skill _____

5. Problems of working students _____

■ **PRACTICE 2    NARROWING A GENERAL TOPIC FOR A PARAGRAPH**

Read each of the five general topics. In the space provided, write a narrower topic that would be good for a paragraph. Make sure that what you write passes the Three-Question Test for Good Topics.

1. A living hero _____ *Answers will vary.* _____

2. A controversy on this campus _____

3. A future goal _____

4. An essential survival skill _____

5. Problems of working students _____

■ **PRACTICE 3   CHOOSE A NARROWED TOPIC**

The next section of this chapter gives you a chance to try out several ways to come up with ideas about a topic. But first you need a narrowed topic. Your instructor will either assign one or ask you to choose your own and write it in the space provided here. Don't forget to put it to the Three-Question Test for Good Topics.

My narrowed topic: _Answers will vary._____

## Practice Exploring Your Topic

You will want to explore your narrowed topic to get ideas you can use in a paragraph or essay. Use **idea-generating** (also called **prewriting**) techniques to investigate what you already know about the narrowed topic, and to find out what you want to write about.

Use prewriting techniques to come up with ideas at any time during your writing: to find a topic, to get ideas for what you want to say about it, and to support your ideas. Ask yourself: What interests me about this topic? What do I know? What do I want to say? Then use one or more of the idea-generating techniques to find the answers.

This section presents six different idea-generating techniques. No one uses all of them; writers choose the ones that work best for them. To find out which ones work best for you, though, you'll need to try them all out.

**SIX PREWRITING TECHNIQUES**

1. Freewriting
2. Listing/brainstorming
3. Questioning
4. Discussing
5. Clustering/mapping
6. Keeping a journal

When using idea-generating techniques, don't judge your ideas. Later you can decide whether or not you will use them. At this point, your goal is to come up with as many ideas as possible, so don't say, "Oh, that's stupid" or "That won't work." Just get your brain working by writing down all the possibilities.

A student, Carol Parola, was assigned the general topic "A survival skill," which she narrowed to "The importance of listening." The following pages show how she used the first five idea-generating techniques to explore

■ **COMPUTER** Emphasize to students how useful computers are for prewriting. Using computers, students can easily move ideas around as they prewrite. Later, when students review their prewriting, they can highlight (with bold or underlining) ideas that seem especially relevant. Also, they can cut and paste text from their prewriting into working drafts. (For more on using computers in writing, see Appendix D.)

her topic. The sixth technique, using a journal, is a little different from the others in that it involves making entries over a period of days or weeks; therefore, this technique will be discussed after the first five.

## Freewriting

**Freewriting** is like having a conversation with yourself, on paper. To freewrite, just start writing everything you can think of about your topic. Write nonstop for five minutes. Don't go back and cross anything out, and don't worry about using correct grammar or spelling; just write.

■ **TIP** If you are writing on a computer, try a kind of free-writing called "invisible writing." Turn the monitor off, or adjust the screen so that you cannot see what you are typing. Then write quickly for five minutes without stopping. After five minutes, read what you have written. You may be surprised by the ideas that you can generate this way.

### FREEWRITING EXAMPLE

*People don't really listen very well, like I know I don't always. Sometimes I'm just kinda listening to what someone's saying cause I'm really thinking about something else. I'm not paying attention really and then later I can't remember what the person said. That's OK if it's not important but what if it is. Like sometimes I've forgotten an appointment or took the wrong train or did the wrong assignment because I was distracted. At work this week I had to take an order back because I wasn't really listening to the customer. My boyfriend doesn't listen to what I'm really saying and sometimes when I call him on it he kinda repeats what I'm saying but I know he didn't get the message. Or he pretends like he's listening but he's really thinking about a football game or his car. Once I wasn't listening when one of my friends was talking about something really important to her and I really hurt her feelings. I felt bad because I try to be a good friend but when you're not listening you can't really be good at anything.*

### PRACTICE 4    FREEWRITING

On a separate sheet of paper, or on the computer, freewrite on the narrowed topic you chose in Practice 3. To get started, ask yourself these questions: What interests me about this topic? What do I know about it? What do I want to say?

*Answers will vary.*

## Listing/Brainstorming

List all of the ideas about your topic that you can think of. Write as many as you can in five minutes without stopping.

### LISTING EXAMPLE

*Understand what others are saying*

*Understand directions on a test*

*Understand a job you're supposed to do*

*I've fouled up a lot when I haven't listened, like when I didn't follow the assignment*

*My boyfriend doesn't listen to me and it hurts my feelings*

*Got way lost getting to the church*

*Most people are too busy thinking of what they're going to say to listen carefully*

*Lots of misunderstandings, causes lots of problems at work like when we lose business or have to take something back*

### PRACTICE 5 LISTING/BRAINSTORMING

On a separate sheet of paper, or on the computer, list as many ideas as you can about the following topic: "Problems at this school." Or use a topic of your own. To get started, ask yourself these questions: What interests me about this topic? What do I know about it? What do I want to say?

*Answers will vary.*

## Questioning: Asking a Reporter's Questions

Ask questions to start getting ideas. The following questions, which reporters use, give you different angles on your narrowed topic: Who? What? Where? When? Why? How? You can use these prompts to make up questions of your own that are more tailored to your topic, as Carol does.

■ **TEAMWORK** Break the class up into pairs and have them ask and answer the reporter's questions about their topics.

**QUESTIONING EXAMPLE**

**What is good listening?**
*It's when people really pay attention to what someone is saying. They're not distracted.*

**Who's a good listener?**
*My grandmother's a great listener. She hears what I'm saying and always has, so she knows what's important and can give me great advice.*

**Why do I think listening's important enough to write about?**
*Because it helps you not to make mistakes, it helps you understand things, and it helps you relate to people.*

**What happens when people don't listen?**
*They can forget when a test's scheduled and not study, or not turn a paper in on time and get their mark lowered. They can even fail a class. They can mess up at work and even lose a job. Or they can cause an accident. They can hurt other people's feelings and end up alone.*

**How do people become good listeners?**
*They learn how to focus on one thing at a time, and they can figure out what's important in a whole bunch of words and sentences. Kinda like they're trying to get the main idea.*

 ### PRACTICE 6 QUESTIONING

Use questioning (either the reporter's questions of *who, what, where, when, why,* and *how* or some that you tailor yourself) to explore the following topic: "An obnoxious person." *Answers will vary.*

## Discussing

■ **TIP** If you find that talking about your ideas with someone is a good way to get going, you might want to ask another student to be your regular partner and discuss ideas before beginning any paragraph or essay assignment.

Many people find it helpful to discuss ideas with another person before they write. As they talk, they get more ideas, and they get immediate feedback from the other person.

Team up with another person. If you both have writing assignments, first explore one person's topic, then the other's. The person whose topic is being explored is the interviewee; the other person is the interviewer. The interviewer should ask questions about anything that seems confusing or unclear and should let the interviewee know what sounds interesting. The interviewee should give thoughtful answers and keep an open mind. It is a good idea to take notes when you are the interviewee.

**DISCUSSING EXAMPLE**

Carol: I think I'm going to write about how important listening is.

Terry: What are you going to say?

C: I don't know, but I know that it's important to listen.

T: Why?

C: Because otherwise you can make all kinds of mistakes.

T: Like what?

C: Well, you might get directions wrong or answer the wrong question at an interview, or not get a loan because you didn't fill out the application right. Anytime you don't listen you risk making a mistake. Or you can hurt people.

T: I don't know what you mean.

C: If I were telling you how depressed I was or something and then found out you weren't listening, I'd think you didn't care about me and weren't my friend. My feelings would really be hurt, and I might not want to be friends anymore. Sometimes I wonder if even stuff like wars could be avoided if people just really listened and focused on what the other person was saying and tried to understand that other person's point of view. I mean really get inside the person's head.

T: Do you think you're a good listener?

C: No, not really. I'm always in a hurry and thinking about a million different things and not concentrating on any one thing. But I want to change that. Listening's important.

PRACTICE 7    **DISCUSSING**

Use discussion with a partner to come up with ideas about the narrowed topic you chose in Practice 3 (p. 23) or about another narrowed topic. The interviewer can try asking these questions: What interests you about the narrowed topic? What do you know about it? What do you want to say?

## Clustering/Mapping

Clustering, also called mapping, is like listing except that you arrange your ideas in a more visual way. Start by writing your narrowed topic in the center. Then write the questions Why? What interests me? What do I know? and What do I want to say? around the narrowed topic. Circle these questions and draw lines to connect them to the narrowed topic. Next, write three things in response to each of these questions. Circle these ideas and connect them to the questions. Keep branching out from the ideas you have added until you feel that you have fully explored your topic. Below is an example of Carol's clustering.

**CLUSTERING EXAMPLE**

**PRACTICE 8**

On a separate piece of paper, use clustering to explore the narrowed topic you chose at the end of Practice 3 (p. 23) or another narrowed topic.

*Answers will vary.*

■ **RESOURCES** It is helpful to provide students with a form they can use for clustering. A form is provided in *Additional Resources.*

## Keeping a Journal

Another good way to get ideas is to write in a journal. Setting aside a few minutes on a regular schedule to write in the journal will give you a great source of ideas when you need them. Another benefit is that you will get used to writing regularly, so writing will not seem like such a chore.

■ **RESOURCES** For tips on helping students keep journals, see *Practical Suggestions*.

To get the most from your journal writing, you should commit yourself to keeping a journal all term and writing in it for at least ten minutes (or write ten lines) at least three times a week. What you write doesn't need to be long or formal. Your journal is for you.

You can use a journal in many ways:

- To record and explore your personal thoughts and feelings
- To comment on things that happen, either to you, or in politics, in your neighborhood, at work, in college, and so on
- To explore ideas to see what you know and think about them
- To explore situations you don't understand (as you write, you may figure them out)

List three other ways you might use a journal (there are no wrong answers).

1. _____

2. _____

3. _____

■ **TEACHING TIP** Some students may feel uncomfortable with journal writing. Emphasize that journal entries will not be graded, are confidential, and don't have to be written in polished prose.

Jack was assigned to write in his journal, and at first he didn't like the idea: It seemed too much like a girl keeping a diary. But as he got used to writing in one, he found that it not only gave him ideas he could use in writing assignments but also helped him understand his own behaviors.

**JOURNAL ENTRY**

*12/13/03--I've been doing some kinda weird things, like worse than usual road rage (yelling at other drivers, hitting the steering wheel, tailgating) and getting really mad at my girlfriend. At first I thought other people were just doing stupid things, like my girlfriend bugging me about Christmas presents and stuff, but it's happening so often I'm starting to wonder if it's me. But I don't know why I'd be mad except everyone's all whipped up about this dumb Christmas thing. I hate this season. Everyone's got this fake cheery stuff going and buying like crazy and pretending the world is like a fairy tale. It's not and I hate Christmas, always have. Might want to think about when I started hating it and what happened to start it.*

■ **TEACHING TIP** Here are some suggestions for weekly journal assignments for students: a different positive thing that happens each day and why it is positive; item in the newspaper or on the news (not only the facts, but observations as well); a personal goal and what steps are necessary to achieve it; and two personal interests and why. *Practical Suggestions* includes additional ideas about student journals.

This book contains two kinds of journal assignments.

**IDEA JOURNAL:** a place to record and explore your personal ideas. (Jack's journal entry, above, is from an idea journal.) Many chapters in this book have idea journal assignments on the first page or somewhere in the margins. These ask you to think about and comment on your personal experience with a topic or idea. They can be very useful in helping you finish the assignments—and besides, they are interesting possibilities for future writing.

**LEARNING JOURNAL:** a written record of what you have learned. A learning journal helps you see where you have improved—and where you still have questions. Many chapters include assignments for such a learning journal.

■ **PRACTICE 9   WRITING IN A JOURNAL**

For the next week, write in a journal for ten minutes (or write at least ten lines) each day at the same time of day. Put the date and time at the start of each entry. For each of the entries, write on the topic "Something I noticed about myself today."

At the end of the week, reread the entries and write a sentence or two about an observation you can make based on what you noticed about yourself all week. Don't worry; these entries will not be graded.

# Write Your Own Topic and Ideas

If you have worked through this chapter, you should have both your narrowed topic (recorded in Practice 3) and ideas from your prewriting. Now is the time to make sure your topic and ideas about it are clear. If you don't have a narrowed topic, choose one now, using the Critical Thinking box below. Then referring again to the steps in the box, make sure you are satisfied with your topic and ideas.

---

**CRITICAL THINKING: WORKING WITH YOUR TOPIC**

**FOCUS**
Read the general topic you have chosen or been assigned.

**ASK YOURSELF**
- How can I divide this topic?
- Which of these parts would be a good narrowed topic?
- Does this topic pass the Three-Question Test for Good Topics?
- What do I already know about this topic?
- What do I want to write about?

**WRITE**
Narrow to find a good topic and then use prewriting techniques to explore your ideas about the topic. Before going on to the next chapter, complete the following checklist. If you did the earlier practice exercises, you may already have a narrowed topic and ideas from prewriting. Choose the best of those ideas now.

---

■ **TEACHING TIP** It is important for students to use the Critical Thinking guides and checklists rather than skipping over them. You might want to read each question in the Critical Thinking guide aloud to students and give them a minute or so between questions to jot down their responses. After they have finished an assignment, have them complete the checklist. You may want students to turn in these responses along with their drafts.

---

**CHECKLIST: EVALUATING YOUR NARROWED TOPIC**

- ❑  This topic interests me.
- ❑  My narrowed topic is specific.
- ❑  I can write about it in a paragraph or an essay (whichever you have been assigned).
- ❑  I have generated some things to say about this topic.

Now that you know what you're going to write about, you're ready to move on to the next chapter, which shows you how to express what's important to you about your narrowed topic.

## Chapter Review: Narrowing and Exploring a Topic

1. The three questions for good topics are

   *Does it interest me?*

   *Can I say something about it?*

   *Is it specific?*

■ **LEARNING JOURNAL** What prewriting technique or techniques work best for you, and why?

2. Name five prewriting techniques

   *freewriting*

   *listing/brainstorming*

   *questioning*

   *discussing*

   *clustering/mapping*

3. What are two kinds of journals?

   *idea journal*

   *learning journal*

## What Will You Use?

How might you use idea-generating techniques to investigate possible career choices? Explore possible academic goals or plans? Find possible solutions to problems?

# 3

# Writing Your Topic Sentence or Thesis Statement

*Making Your Point*

## Understand What a Topic Sentence and a Thesis Statement Are

Every good piece of writing has a **main idea**—what the writer wants to get across to the readers about the topic, or the writer's position on that topic. If you have narrowed and explored your topic, as discussed in Chapter 2, you may already have a sense of your main idea. Clearly and definitely conveying your main idea to your readers is fundamental to the success of any piece of writing. If your readers don't know from the start what your main idea is, they will not read the rest of what you have written with any clear thought in mind.

A **topic sentence** (for a paragraph) and a **thesis statement** (for an essay) express the writer's main idea and include both the topic and the main point the writer wants to make about that topic. To see the relationship between the thesis statement of an essay and the topic sentences of paragraphs that support this thesis statement, see the diagram on page 34.

In many paragraphs, the main idea is expressed in either the first or last sentence. In essays, the thesis statement is usually one sentence (often first or last) in an introductory paragraph that contains several other sentences related to the main idea. (In Chapter 6, you will learn more about writing introductions for essays.)

One way to write a topic sentence for a paragraph or a thesis statement for an essay is to use this basic formula as a start:

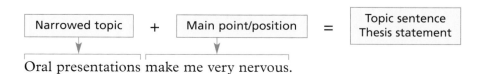

Oral presentations make me very nervous.

### You Know This

You already have experience in making your point:

- You explain the point of a movie to someone who hasn't seen it.
- When a friend asks you, "What's your point?" you explain it.
- When you persuade someone to do something you want, you make your point about why they should.

■ **IDEA JOURNAL** What are your strongest communication skills? What other skills or talents do you have?

■ **TIP** For more information on what a complete sentence is, see Chapter 19, The Basic Sentence: An Overview.

■ **PRACTICE 1    FIND THE TOPIC SENTENCE AND MAIN POINT**

Read the paragraph that follows and underline the topic sentence. In the spaces below the paragraph, identify the narrowed topic and the main point.

A recent survey reported that employers consider communication skills more critical to success than technical skills. Employees can learn technical skills on the job and practice them every day. But they need to bring well-developed communication skills to the job. They need to be able to make themselves understood to colleagues, both in speech and in writing. They need to be able to work cooperatively as part of a team. Employers can't take time to teach communication skills, but without them an employee will have a hard time.

**NARROWED TOPIC:**    *communication skills*

**MAIN POINT:**    *Employers consider communication skills more critical to success than technical skills.*

■ **PRACTICE 2    IDENTIFYING TOPICS AND MAIN POINTS**

In each of the following sentences, underline the topic and double-underline the main point about the topic.

**EXAMPLE:**  Aging airplanes have increased the likelihood of plane crashes.

1. The level of nicotine in cigarettes is kept high by the tobacco industry.

2. The oldest child in the family is often the most independent and ambitious child.

3. Gadgets created for left-handed people are sometimes poorly designed.

4. The city's new mayor enjoys practical jokes.

5. Dinnertime telephone sales calls should be illegal.

6. The magazine *Consumer Reports* can help you decide which brands or models are the best value.

7. Of all the fast-food burgers, <u>Burger King's Whopper</u> <u>is the best buy</u>.

8. At 5:00 every afternoon, <u>Route 128</u> <u>becomes a parking lot</u>.

9. <u>Some song lyrics</u> <u>have serious messages about important social issues</u>.

10. <u>The beach on a hot midsummer day</u> <u>is a great place for people-watching</u>.

Your first try at your topic sentence or thesis statement will probably need some tweaking to make it better. Before you write sentences to support your topic sentence, or paragraphs to support your thesis statement, you may want to change some words to make sure that the topic sentence or thesis statement is clear, specific, and forceful. As you get further along in your writing, you may go back several times to revise the topic sentence or thesis statement, based on what you learn as you develop your ideas. Look at how one student revised the example sentence above to make it more detailed:

Planning a vacation carefully can be time-consuming.

When developing a topic sentence or thesis statement, make sure it has the following five features.

### BASICS OF A GOOD TOPIC SENTENCE OR THESIS STATEMENT

- It fits the size of the assignment.
- It states a single main point or position about the narrowed topic.
- It is specific.
- It is something you can show, explain, or prove.
- It is a forceful statement written with confidence.

Although a topic sentence or thesis statement states a single main point or position, this main point or position may include more than one idea; however, the ideas should be closely related. For example:

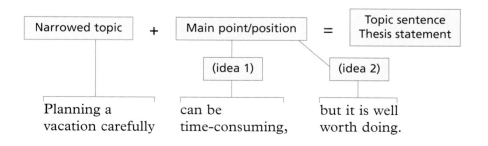

■ **ESL** Some cultures (particularly Asian ones) avoid making direct points in writing. You may need to explain that in English the rhetorical convention is that the writer make a clear, direct point. Ask students if writing conventions in their countries approach the main point differently.

■ **TIP** If you are writing on a computer, it is easy to try out different versions of your topic sentence or thesis statement. Make the same point in as many ways as you can. Try sounding silly, or angry, or puzzled. Then choose the version you like best. For more on using a computer, see Appendix D.

# Practice Developing a Good Topic Sentence or Thesis Statement

The explanations and practices in this section, organized according to the "basics" described previously, will help you write stronger topic sentences and thesis statements.

## It Fits the Size of the Assignment

■ **TIP** Expressing your main idea so that it fits the size of your assignment will get easier with practice. This section will provide some practice to get you off to a good start.

As you develop a statement (the topic sentence or the thesis statement) about your topic and main point, think carefully about the length of the assignment. Sometimes a statement could be used as a basis for either a paragraph or an essay.

Consider the following example, where the difference between the paragraph and the essay is in the depth of detail provided:

_____ Topic _____ Main point _____

In the next decade, people of retirement age may create a surge in the demand for higher education.

If the writer had been assigned a paragraph, she might write sentences that included the following support points:

**Support 1** Baby boomers will be hitting retirement age, and they'll want to prove they're as active as ever.

**RELATIONSHIP BETWEEN PARAGRAPHS AND ESSAYS**

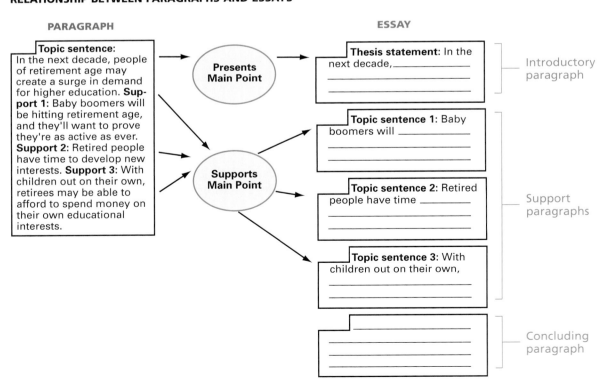

**Support 2** Retired people have more time to develop new interests.

**Support 3** With children out on their own, retirees may be able to afford to spend money on their own educational interests.

If the writer had been assigned an essay, she might develop the same support. In an essay, however, instead of writing single sentences to support her main idea, she would develop each support point into a paragraph. The support sentences she wrote in a paragraph might be topic sentences for support paragraphs. (For more on providing support, see Chapter 4.)

Other times, however, a topic sentence for a paragraph is much narrower than a thesis statement for an essay, simply because a paragraph is shorter and allows less development of ideas.

Consider how one general topic could be narrowed into an essay topic, and into an even more specific paragraph topic.

| ASSIGNED GENERAL TOPIC | NARROWED ESSAY TOPIC | NARROWED PARAGRAPH TOPIC |
|---|---|---|
| Drug abuse ⟶ | How alcoholism affects family life ⟶ | How alcoholism affects a family's budget |

**POSSIBLE THESIS STATEMENT (for the essay):** Alcoholism can destroy family life.

(The essay might go on to give several ways in which alcoholism negatively affects the family.)

**POSSIBLE TOPIC SENTENCE (for the paragraph):** Alcoholism quickly destroys a family's budget.

(The paragraph focuses on one way alcoholism affects family life—its budget—and might go on to give examples of how the budget gets destroyed.)


■ **PRACTICE 3   WRITING SENTENCES TO FIT THE SCOPE OF THE ASSIGNMENT**

For each of the three items in this practice, read how the topic has been narrowed for an essay or a paragraph. Using the following example as a guide, write a thesis statement for the narrowed essay topic and a topic sentence for the narrowed paragraph topic.

**EXAMPLE:**

Topic          Narrowed for an essay          Narrowed for a paragraph

Sports     Competition in school sports     User fees for school sports

**POSSIBLE THESIS STATEMENT (for an essay):** *Competition in school sports has reached dangerous levels.*

**POSSIBLE TOPIC SENTENCE (for a paragraph):** *This year's user fees for participation in school sports are too high.*

|  | Topic | Narrowed for an essay | Narrowed for a paragraph |
|---|---|---|---|
| 1. | Public service opportunities | Volunteering at a homeless shelter | My first impression of the homeless shelter |

**POSSIBLE THESIS STATEMENT (for an essay):** _Answers will vary._

_____

**POSSIBLE TOPIC SENTENCE (for a paragraph):** _____

_____

|  | Topic | Narrowed for an essay | Narrowed for a paragraph |
|---|---|---|---|
| 2. | A personal goal | Getting healthy | Eating the right foods |

**POSSIBLE THESIS STATEMENT (for an essay):** _____

_____

**POSSIBLE TOPIC SENTENCE (for a paragraph):** _____

_____

|  | Topic | Narrowed for an essay | Narrowed for a paragraph |
|---|---|---|---|
| 3. | A great vacation | A family camping trip | A lesson I learned on our family camping trip |

**POSSIBLE THESIS STATEMENT (for an essay):** _____

_____

**POSSIBLE TOPIC SENTENCE (for a paragraph):** _____

_____

■ **COMPUTER** When students write on the computer, have them use bold type for their topic sentence or thesis statement. This helps you see what they consider their main point and helps them stay focused as they provide support. For more information on using computers in writing, see Appendix D.

Some main ideas are too broad for either a short essay or a paragraph. A main idea that is too broad is impossible to show, explain, or prove within the space of a paragraph or short essay.

**TOO BROAD**    Art is important.

[How could a writer possibly support such a broad concept in a paragraph or essay?]

**NARROWER**    Art instruction for young children has surprising benefits.

A main idea that is too narrow leaves the writer with little to write about. There is little to show, explain, or prove.

**TOO NARROW**    One of my legs is longer than the other.

[Okay, so now what?]

**BROADER**    Although one of my legs is two inches longer than the other, technology allows me to function perfectly.

■ **PRACTICE 4:   WRITING TOPIC SENTENCES THAT ARE NEITHER TOO BROAD NOR TOO NARROW**

In the following five practice items, three of the topic sentences are either too broad or too narrow, and two of them are OK. In the space to the left of the item write either "B" for too broad, "N" for too narrow, or "OK" for just right. Rewrite the three weak sentences to make them broader or narrower as needed.

**EXAMPLE:** _B_  World War II affected many people.

_World War II gave women their first real chance to work._ _____

1.  _N_  I have a sister.

_Answers will vary._ _____

_____

2.  _OK_  This year, schools in my town face budget cuts, teacher shortages, and demands for major renovations.

_____

_____

3.  _B_  College is challenging.

_____

_____

4.  _B_  I would like to be successful in life.

_____

_____

5.  _OK_  Having a positive attitude improves people's ability to function, improves their interactions with others, and reduces stress.

_____

_____

## It Contains a Single Main Point

Your topic sentence or thesis statement should focus on only one main point. Two main points can split the focus of the writing and confuse readers.

### Main Idea with Two Main Points

High schools <u>should sell healthy food instead of junk food</u>, and they <u>should start later in the morning</u>.

The two main points are underlined. Although both are good main points, together they split both the writer's and the readers' focus. The writer would need to give reasons to support each point, and they are very different ideas.

### Main Idea with a Single Main Point

High schools <u>should sell healthy food instead of junk food</u>.

OR

High schools <u>should start later in the morning</u>.

The main point may contain more than one idea, but these ideas should be closely related and serve an overall main point you want to make. For example, some writers use a three-point topic sentence (for a paragraph) or thesis statement (for an essay) that includes the main point and previews three support points that will be explored in the body paragraphs.

### Three-Point Thesis

High schools should sell healthy food instead of junk food because (1) it is better for students, (2) it is often less expensive, and (3) it can boost levels of energy and attention.

---

▮   PRACTICE 5   **WRITING SENTENCES WITH A SINGLE MAIN POINT**

In each of the following sentences, underline the <u>main point</u>(s). Identify the sentences that have more than a single main point by marking an X in the space provided to the left of that item. Put a check (✓) next to sentences that have a single main point.

> **EXAMPLE:** ___X___ Shopping at second-hand stores is <u>a fun way to save money</u>, and <u>you can meet all kinds of interesting people as you shop</u>.

___✓___ 1.  <u>My younger sister, the baby of the family, was the most adventurous of us</u>.

___X___ 2.  <u>Political campaigns are often nasty</u>, and <u>the voting ballots are difficult to understand</u>.

___X___ 3.  <u>My brother, Bobby, is incredibly creative</u> and <u>attractive to women of all ages</u>.

___X___ 4.  <u>Pets can actually bring families together</u>, and <u>they require lots of care</u>.

✓ 5. Unless people conserve voluntarily, we will deplete our supply of water.

## It Is Specific

A good statement of a main point (topic sentence or thesis statement) gives readers specific information and concepts that allow them to understand the writer's main idea right from the start. A statement that lacks such information is considered vague.

**VAGUE** Students are often overwhelmed.

**SPECIFIC** Working college students have to learn how to successfully juggle many responsibilities.

What words in the first sentence are vague?

How does the second sentence explain more clearly the writer's main idea?

One way to make sure that your topic sentence or thesis statement is specific is to make it a preview of what you are planning to say in the rest of the paragraph or essay.

**PREVIEW:** Working college students have to learn how to juggle many responsibilities: doing a good job at work, getting to class regularly and on time, being alert in class, and doing the homework assignments.

**PREVIEW:** I have a set routine every Saturday morning that includes sleeping late, going to the gym, and shopping for food.

### PRACTICE 6 WRITING SENTENCES THAT ARE SPECIFIC

In the space below each item, revise the sentence to make it more specific. There is no one correct answer. As you read the sentences, think about what would make them more understandable to you if you were about to read a paragraph or essay on the topic.

**EXAMPLE:** Marriage can be a wonderful thing.

*Marriage to the right person can add love, companionship, and support to life.*

1. My job is horrible.

*Answers will vary.*

2. Working with others is very rewarding.

_______________

3. I am a good worker.

_____

4. This place could use a lot of improvement.

_____

5. Getting my driver's license was challenging.

_____

## It Is an Idea That You Can Show, Explain, or Prove

If a main idea is so obvious that it doesn't need support, or if it states a fact that most people would agree with, then it probably won't make a good topic sentence or thesis statement.

| | |
|---|---|
| **OBVIOUS** | Models are very thin. |
| | The Honda Accord is a popular car model. |
| | Many people like to take vacations in the summer. |
| **FACT** | The automobile industry lobby is very strong. |
| | Violent crime was up 10 percent this summer. |
| | More than 60 percent of Americans aged twenty and older are overweight. |

It would be hard for any writer to base a paragraph or an essay on these statements: There is really nothing to say about them as they are currently worded. They could be good main ideas, however, if they were revised.

| | |
|---|---|
| **REVISED** | To be thin, models maintain very strange eating habits. |
| | OR |
| | Too often, young women believe that they should be as thin as the models they see everywhere in the media. |
| | Fuel economy for SUVs will be slow to improve because the automobile industry lobby is too powerful. |
| | OR |
| | The government is afraid of clamping down on the automobile industry. |

> **PRACTICE 7    WRITING SENTENCES THAT YOU CAN SHOW, EXPLAIN, OR PROVE**

Revise the following sentences so that they contain an idea that you could show, explain, or prove.

**EXAMPLE:** Leasing a car is popular.

*Leasing a car has many advantages over buying one.*

1. I wear my hair long.

   *Answers will vary.*

2. My monthly rent is $750.

3. Health insurance rates rise every year.

4. Many people in this country work for minimum wage.

5. Technology is becoming increasingly important.

## It Is Forceful, Confident, and Definite

A good topic sentence or thesis statement is forceful, confident, and definite. Instead of announcing your topic, go ahead and make your point about it—as specifically as you can. Getting right to your point is more direct and forceful than working your way up to it. Also, keep in mind that expressions like "I think" and "I believe" can signal a lack of confidence in your point, so try to avoid them.

| | |
|---|---|
| **WEAK** | In this paragraph I will talk about why people go to college. |
| **FORCEFUL** | People have many complex reasons for going to college. |
| **WEAK** | In my opinion, everyone should exercise. |
| **FORCEFUL** | Everyone should exercise to reduce stress, maintain a healthy weight, and feel better overall. |
| **WEAK** | I think student fees are much too high. |
| **FORCEFUL** | Student fees need to be explained and justified. |

■ **PRACTICE 8    WRITING FORCEFUL, CONFIDENT, DEFINITE SENTENCES**

Rewrite each of the following sentences to make them more forceful, confident, and definite. Also, try to make up details to make sentences more specific.

**EXAMPLE:** Jason's Supermarket is the best.

*Jason's Supermarket is clean, well-organized, and filled with top-quality products.*

1. I will prove that drug testing in the workplace is an invasion of privacy.

   *Answers will vary. Possible answer: Drug testing in the workplace is an invasion of*

   *privacy and should be banned immediately.*

2. This school should consider banning cell phones from classrooms.

   *Possible answer: Because ringing cell phones are disruptive to class, this school*

   *should ban their classroom use.*

3. I strongly think that I deserve a raise.

   *Possible answer: I deserve a raise based on my strong performance over the past*

   *year.*

4. Nancy should be the head of the Students' Association.

   *Possible answer: Because she is hard-working, dedicated, and concerned about*

   *campus issues, Nancy should be the head of the Students' Association.*

5. I think my neighborhood is really nice.

   *Possible answer:  My neighborhood is safe, close to several stores, and beautifully*

   *landscaped.*

## Write Your Own Topic Sentence or Thesis Statement

If you have worked through this chapter, you should have a good sense of how to write a topic sentence or thesis statement that includes the five features of a good one (see p. 33).

To develop a good topic sentence or thesis statement, consider the process that one student, Jeanette Castro, used. First, she narrowed her general topic.

**General topic:** *an activity that you are very involved in*
**Narrowed topic (for a paragraph):** *training to run a marathon*
**Narrowed topic (for an essay):** *running a marathon*

Then she did some prewriting (see Chapter 2) to get some ideas about her narrowed topic.

**For a paragraph:**  *training to run a marathon*
*Start six months before*
*Get good shoes*
*Work up to distance*
*Use a schedule (can find one on the Web)*

**For an essay:** *running a marathon*

*Training (schedule, shoes, routine, the final practice run)*

*The day before a marathon (what to eat and drink, whether to practice, how much sleep to get)*

*The morning of the marathon (how much time to leave before the race, what to eat and drink, how to dress, how to get psyched)*

*During the run (how often to drink, what to watch out for--physical symptoms, how to pace yourself, how to stay motivated and focused on your goal)*

Next she decided on the point she wanted to make about her topic—in other words, her position on it:

**For a paragraph:** *training for a marathon is essential*

**For an essay:** *running a marathon requires lots of planning and thought*

Then she was ready to write the statement of her main point.

**Topic sentence (for a paragraph):** *Training is important if you want to run a marathon.*

**Thesis statement (for an essay):** *Running a marathon is a process, not just something that happens on one day.*

Finally, Jeanette revised this statement to make it more forceful:

**Topic sentence:** *Training for success in a marathon involves several important steps.*

**Thesis statement:** *Successfully running a marathon demands careful planning from start to finish.*

You may want to tinker with the wording of your topic sentence or thesis statement later on as you write and revise your paragraph or essay, but following a sequence like Jeanette's should start you off with a good basic statement of your main point.

## Writing Assignment

Write a topic sentence or thesis statement using the narrowed topic and ideas you developed in Chapter 2, your response to the idea journal prompt on page 31, or one of the following topics (which you will have to narrow).

| | | |
|---|---|---|
| Volunteering | Good neighbors | Exciting experiences |
| A controversial issue | Interviewing for jobs | Juggling many |
| Dressing for success | Downtown | responsibilities |
| This school | Holiday traditions | Friendship |
| Siblings | | |

■ **TEACHING TIP** Even if you aren't reading a student's entire first draft, it always helps to check the topic sentence or thesis statement, because you can clear up numerous potential problems before you have to give a grade.

Before writing, read this Critical Thinking box:

---

**CRITICAL THINKING: WRITING A TOPIC SENTENCE OR THESIS STATEMENT**

**FOCUS**
- Read your narrowed topic.
- Decide what is important to you, personally, about the topic.

**ASK YOURSELF**
- What do I want to show, explain, or prove about the topic?
- How can I state what I want to show, explain, or prove forcefully and confidently?
- Will the main point I'm considering fit the assignment?
- Can I get behind the main point I'm considering and support it for my readers?

**WRITE**
- Write a forceful, confident topic sentence (for a paragraph) or thesis statement (for an essay) that includes your topic and your main point about that topic.
- Rewrite it to improve it.

---

After writing your topic sentence or thesis statement, complete the checklist that follows.

---

**CHECKLIST: EVALUATING YOUR MAIN POINT**

❑  It is a complete sentence.

❑  It fits the assignment.

❑  It includes my topic and the main point I want to make about it.

❑  It states a single main point.

❑  It is specific.

❑  It is something I can show, explain, or prove.

❑  It is forceful and confident.

---

Coming up with a good working topic sentence or thesis statement is the foundation of the writing you will do. Now that you know what you want to say, you're ready to learn more about how to show, explain, or prove it to others. That is covered in the next chapter: Supporting Your Point.

## Chapter Review: Writing a Topic Sentence or Thesis Statement

1. The **main idea** of a piece of writing is *what the writer wants to get across to the readers about the topic.*

2.  A **topic sentence** and a **thesis statement** include *both the topic and*

    *the main point the writer wants to make about that topic.*

3.  The basics of a good topic sentence or thesis statement are

    *It fits the size of the assignment.*

    *It states a single main point or position about the narrowed topic.*

    *It is specific.*

    *It is something you can show, explain, or prove.*

    *It is a forceful statement written with confidence.*

■ **LEARNING JOURNAL** How would you help someone who said, "I have some ideas about my topic, but how do I write a good topic sentence or thesis statement?"

## What Will You Use?

Recall an assignment you have in another class or at work. How can you use what you have learned in this chapter to do the assignment? How can making a clear point help you in everyday life? In college? In your job?

# 4

# Supporting Your Point

*Finding Details, Examples, and Facts*

**You Know This**

You have lots of experience in supporting your point:

- You explain why you think a movie was boring.
- You explain to a child why locking the door is important.
- You give reasons to persuade someone of your opinion.

## Understand What Support Is

**Support** is the collection of examples, facts, or evidence that show, explain, or prove your main point. **Primary support** consists of the major ideas that back up your main point, and **secondary support** explains (or provides details to back up) your primary support.

Without support, you *state* the main point, but you don't *make* the main point. Consider these unsupported statements:

> The amount shown on my bill is incorrect.
>
> I deserve a raise.
>
> I am innocent of the crime.

The statements may be true, but without good support, they are not convincing. If you sometimes get papers back with the comment "You need to support/develop your ideas," the suggestions in this chapter will help you.

Writers sometimes confuse repetition with support. The same point repeated several times is not support. It is just repetition.

■ **IDEA JOURNAL** Write about a time that you were overcharged for something. How did you handle it?

| **REPETITION, NOT SUPPORT** | The amount shown on my bill is incorrect. You overcharged me. It didn't cost that much. The total is wrong. |
| --- | --- |
| **SUPPORT** | The amount shown on my bill is incorrect. I ordered the bacon-cheeseburger plate, which is $6.99 on the menu. On the bill, the order is correct, but the amount is $16.99. |

As you develop support for your main point, make sure that it has these three features.

**BASICS OF GOOD SUPPORT**

- **It relates to your main point**. The purpose of support is to show, explain, or prove your main point, so the support you use must be directly related to that main point.

- **It considers your readers**. Create support that will show your readers what you mean.

- **It is detailed and specific**. Give readers enough detail, particularly through examples, so that they can see what you mean.

In addition to being necessary for good writing, support has two benefits to you personally:

- It helps you meet length requirements for your assignments, not by "padding" your writing, but by providing details and examples that add substance and help you get your point across to your readers.

- It gives you control. Although you may be writing in response to an assignment, you can choose what examples, facts, and observations to include. As a result, you have control over how you fulfill an assignment and how readers perceive your topic.

Read the following two paragraphs, both written by Jeanette Castro, whose topic sentence you saw at the end of Chapter 3. In the first paragraph, she provides some support for her main point but does not give many details about it. In the second paragraph, she has added details (secondary support) to help her reader see the main point the way she does. The supporting details are in **bold**; in both paragraphs, the topic sentence is <u>underlined</u>.

**PARAGRAPH WITH PRIMARY SUPPORT**

<u>Training for success in a marathon demands several important steps.</u> Runners should first get a schedule developed by a professional running organization. They should commit to carefully following the schedule. On the night before and the morning of the big day, runners should take special steps to make sure they are prepared for the race.

**PARAGRAPH WITH SECONDARY SUPPORT ADDED**

<u>Training for success in a marathon demands several important steps.</u> Runners should first get a schedule developed by a professional running organization. **These schedules are available in bookstores or on the Web. A good one is available at <www.runnersworld.com>. All of the training schedules suggest starting training three to six months before the marathon.** Runners should commit to carefully following the schedule. **If they cannot stick to it exactly, they need to come as close as they possibly can. The schedules include a mixture of long and short runs at specified intervals. Carefully following the training schedule builds up endurance a little at a time so that by the time of the race, runners are less likely to hurt themselves. The training continues right up until the start of the**

■ **TIP** Showing involves providing visual details or other supporting observations. Explaining involves offering specific examples, or illustrating aspects of the main point. Proving involves providing specific evidence, sometimes from outside sources.

■ **TIP** Often, your topic sentence or thesis statement will suggest the kind of support you should use. For example, the topic sentence/thesis statement "Cell phone use during driving should be banned" suggests that the writer will offer reasons as major support.

■ **TIP** To see how the author of this paragraph provided support for a full essay on this topic, see Chapter 6, pages 76–77.

**marathon**. On the night before and the morning of the big day, runners should take special steps to make sure they are prepared for the race. **The night before the race, they should eat carbohydrates, drink plenty of water, and get a good night's sleep. On the day of the marathon, runners should eat a good breakfast, dress for the weather, and consider doing a light warm-up before the race's start. Before and during the race, they should drink plenty of water**. Running a marathon without completing the essential steps will not bring success; instead it may bring pain and injury.

Again, primary support shows, explains, or proves the main point. In turn, secondary support provides details, examples, or proof for the primary support. In the previous paragraphs, the writer relied largely on explanation; for example, she explained what schedules are and why they are important.

Note that support points must be factual; an opinion alone will not convince readers. If you use an opinion, you should immediately support it with a fact.

## Practice Supporting a Main Point

### Generate Support

■ **TIP** For more information on developing a topic sentence or thesis statement, see Chapter 3.

To generate support for the main point of a paragraph or essay, try one or more of these three strategies:

**THREE QUICK STRATEGIES FOR GENERATING SUPPORT**

1. **Circle an important word or phrase** in your topic sentence (for a paragraph) or thesis statement (for an essay) and write about it for a minute or two. Reread your main point to make sure you're on the right track. Keep writing about the word or phrase.

2. **Reread your topic sentence or thesis statement and write down the first thought you have**. Then write down your next thought. Keep going.

■ **TIP** For a review of prewriting techniques, see Chapter 2.

■ **TEACHING TIP** Emphasize to students that prewriting can help them at every stage of the writing process, whenever they need to develop ideas further or provide more detail.

3. **Use a prewriting technique** (freewriting, listing, questioning, discussing, clustering) while thinking about your main point and your audience. Write for three to five minutes without stopping.

 **PRACTICE 1    GENERATING SUPPORTING IDEAS**

Choose one of the following statements of a main point, or one of your own, and use one of the three strategies just mentioned to generate possible support. Because you will need a good supply of ideas from which to choose support for your main point, try to find at least a dozen possible supporting ideas. Do this practice on a separate piece of paper, or on a computer, and keep your notes because you will use them in later practices in this chapter.
*Answers will vary.*

1. This year's new TV programs are worse than ever.

2. Today there is no such thing as a "typical" college student.

3. Learning happens not only in school but throughout a person's life.

4. Practical intelligence can't be measured by grades.

5. I deserve a raise.

■ **IDEA JOURNAL** Write about any of the sentences you don't choose for Practice 1.

## Select the Best Primary Support

After you have generated possible support, you need to review your ideas and select the best ones to use as primary support. Remember, this is where you get to take control of your topic, because by choosing the support you give your readers, you are shaping the way they will see your topic and main point. These are *your* ideas, and you need to sell them to your readers.

The following steps can help:

1. Carefully read the ideas you have generated.
2. Keep in mind that you'll want to select three to five points that you think will best get your main idea across to readers. If you are writing a paragraph, these three to five points will become the primary support for your topic sentence. If you are writing an essay, these points will become topic sentences of paragraphs to support your essay's main point (thesis).
3. Identify the points that you think will be clearest and most convincing to your readers and will provide the best examples, facts, and observations to support your main point. (See the "Basics of Good Support" on p. 47.)
4. Cross out ideas that are not closely related to your main point.
5. If you find that you have crossed out most of your ideas and do not have enough left to support your main point, use a prewriting technique to find more.

■ **TIP** To see the relationship between topic sentences and support in paragraphs, and thesis statements and support in essays, see the diagram on page 34 of Chapter 3.

■ **TEACHING TIP** Remind students that just because they find a point interesting doesn't necessarily mean they should include it in their writing. It must support their main point.

As you review your ideas, you may also come up with new ones that would be good support. If you come up with a new idea, jot it down.

■ **PRACTICE 2** **SELECTING THE BEST PRIMARY SUPPORT**

For each of the following two topic sentences, put a check mark (✓) next to the three points you would choose to support it. Be ready to explain your choices.

**NOTE:** In the example, the writer has selected the best support and crossed out unrelated ideas. However, she left some ideas unmarked, thinking they might work as secondary support.

**EXAMPLE:**

**TOPIC SENTENCE OR THESIS STATEMENT:** Defrosting the freezer is definitely my most hated household task.

**POSSIBLE PRIMARY SUPPORT**

✓ Takes forever

~~I forget about half the stuff in there, one day my daughter found some hamburger that'd been in there for five years~~

✓ Creates a real mess

Running back and forth to the kitchen to refill pans with boiling water

✓ Tiring

Freezing fingers

Not supposed to use a hammer or anything pointed to help

Always wait until nothing else will fit in

~~Are there self-defrosting freezers like in my refrigerator?~~

1. **TOPIC SENTENCE OR THESIS STATEMENT:** Most Americans are not good listeners.

   **POSSIBLE PRIMARY SUPPORT:** *Answers may vary. Possible answers shown.*

   People talk more than they listen

   ✓ Competitive streak—everyone wants to say the most

   ✓ Even when quiet, thinking about what to say next, not listening

   ✓ Good listening is hard work

   Preparing a good "comeback"

   Good listening is active, not passive

   If you can't talk most of the time, talk faster

   Talk louder

2. **TOPIC SENTENCE OR THESIS STATEMENT:** Instead of being afraid of those who are different, people should learn to appreciate and learn from those differences.

   **POSSIBLE PRIMARY SUPPORT:**

   They're interesting

   ✓ Different ideas and perspectives

   Friendly

   Shouldn't teach your children to be afraid or hateful

   Gifted in other ways even if physically challenged

   ✓ Builds sensitivity

   ✓ Helps you to learn how to see and do things differently

   Shouldn't make fun of others

■ **TEACHING TIP** Tell students to ask themselves the kinds of questions their readers will ask: Such as? In what way? For example? If their support points answer those questions, readers should understand their main point.

■ PRACTICE 3    **SELECTING THE BEST SUPPORT**

Refer to your response to Practice 1 (p. 48). Of the dozen or more possible primary support points that you generated, choose three to five that you think will best show, explain, or prove your main point to your readers. Write your three to five points in the space provided here.

*Answers will vary.*

_____

_____

_____

_____

_____

## Add Secondary Support

Once you have selected your best primary support points, you need to flesh them out for your readers. Do this by adding **secondary support**, specific examples, facts, and observations to back up your primary support points.

■ PRACTICE 4    **ADDING SECONDARY SUPPORT**

Using your answers to Practice 2, choose three primary support points and write them in the spaces indicated. Then read each of them carefully and write down at least three supporting details (secondary support) for each one. For examples of secondary support, see the example paragraph on page 47.

*Answers will vary.*

   **PRIMARY SUPPORT POINT 1:**

_____

    **SUPPORTING DETAILS:** _____

_____

   **PRIMARY SUPPORT POINT 2:**

_____

    **SUPPORTING DETAILS:** _____

_____

   **PRIMARY SUPPORT POINT 3:**

_____

    **SUPPORTING DETAILS:** _____

_____

# Write Your Own Support

Before developing your own support for a main point, look at how one student, Jesse Calsado, developed support for his topic sentence.

> **TOPIC SENTENCE:** *Cheating comes in many forms, not just students cheating on tests.*

First he did some prewriting and selected the best primary support points, while eliminating ones that he didn't think he would use:

> *Being paid under the table/not reporting income*
>
> ✓ *Not telling cashiers when they've undercharged you, or getting too much money back*
>
> ✓ *Doctors and dentists who tell patients they need stuff that's not really necessary because the insurance company will pay*
>
> *Not reporting stuff you find*
>
> *Trying to sneak in free*
>
> *Even perfect Martha Stewart*
>
> *Cheating on a partner*
>
> *Cheating at games*
>
> ✓ *Cheating on company time by using computers to e-mail friends or surf the Web*
>
> *Scam artists*
>
> ✓ *Then there are the big cheaters: CEOs*

■ **COMPUTER** Have students first type in possible support and then cut and paste to group it. They can easily move the points around to try new groupings. For more on using computers in writing, see Appendix D.

Then Jesse added supporting details for his possible primary support points. Before thinking of new supporting details, he reread his list of prewriting ideas to see if any of them would work. As he added detail, he wrote down other things that he thought of, too.

> **PRIMARY SUPPORT POINT:** *Not telling a cashier you've been undercharged, or getting too much money back*
>
> > **SUPPORTING DETAIL:** *A report in last week's paper: During a one-month period, reporters noted each instance of a customer being undercharged or getting too much change, and not once did the customer report it.*
>
> **PRIMARY SUPPORT POINT:** *Professionals recommend treatments that may not be necessary, just because the insurance company will reimburse the patient.*
>
> > **SUPPORTING DETAIL:** *My dentist recommended that I get crowns for two teeth, for $1,400, and said my insurance would cover it. After I told him I didn't have insurance, he said that fillings would probably be fine.*

**PRIMARY SUPPORT POINT:** *Cheating on company time*

    **SUPPORTING DETAIL:** *Using computers to write e-mails to friends and spending lots of time surfing the Web. Not as easy for supervisors to see as personal phone calls.*

**PRIMARY SUPPORT POINT:** *Speaking of cheating, CEOs who mislead investors, spend company money on personal stuff, and cheat employees*

    **SUPPORTING DETAIL:** *Enron's creative accounting hid debt and inflated profits, and bosses sold stock off but wouldn't let employees. WorldCom also used accounting to hide losses. Executives at Adelphia Communications used shareholder money to purchase the Buffalo Sabres, and for other stuff. Employees left with no jobs or savings plans or pensions. Even Martha Stewart has been accused of getting "inside information" that allowed her to sell stock before it dropped in value.*

## Writing Assignment

Develop primary support points and supporting details using either your topic sentence or thesis statement from Chapter 3, your response to the idea journal prompt on page 49, or one of the following topic sentences/thesis statements.

Same-sex marriages hurt the institution of marriage. ***Or*** It's time to legalize same-sex marriages.

Companies expect too much of their employees.

All families have some unique family traditions.

People who don't speak "proper" English are discriminated against.

Many movies have important messages for viewers.

First read this Critical Thinking box:

| **CRITICAL THINKING: SUPPORTING YOUR POINT** |
| --- |

**FOCUS**
Read your topic sentence or thesis statement.

**ASK YOURSELF**
- What do my readers need to know?
- What facts, details, or observations will help me show, explain, or prove my main point to readers?

**WRITE**
- Use a prewriting technique to generate possible support.
- Select the best primary support from your prewriting.
- Add supporting details.

■ **TEACHING TIP** Because support is essential and often difficult for students, walk them through the Critical Thinking guide, using a very simple topic sentence or thesis statement about something familiar—the classroom, the college, the town (for example, "Parking on this campus is inadequate.").

After developing your support, complete the following checklist:

| CHECKLIST: EVALUATING YOUR SUPPORT |
| --- |
| ❑  It is related to my main point. |
| ❑  It uses examples, facts, and observations that will make sense to my readers. |
| ❑  It includes enough specific details to show my readers exactly what I mean. |

Once you've pulled together your primary support points and secondary supporting details, you're ready for the next step: arranging them into a plan for a draft of a paragraph or essay. For information on making a plan, go on to the next chapter.

## Chapter Review: Supporting Your Point

**■ LEARNING JOURNAL** In your own words, explain what good support points are and why they are important.

1.  Support points are examples, facts, or evidence that <u>_show_</u>, <u>_explain_</u>, or <u>_prove_</u> your main point.

2.  Three basics of good support points are:

    _It relates to your main point._

    _It considers your readers._

    _It is detailed and specific._

3.  To generate support, try these three strategies:

    _Circle an important word or phrase in your topic sentence or thesis statement and write about it._

    _Reread your topic sentence or thesis statement and write down the first thought you have, then your second, and so on._

    _Use a prewriting technique._

4.  When you have selected your primary support points, what should you then add?

    _secondary support (or supporting details)_

5.  In addition to being necessary for good writing, support has two bene-

    fits to you personally. What are they?

    *It helps you meet length requirements for assignments.*

    *It gives you control.*

## What Will You Use?

How could knowing how to support your main point help you in college or
at work?

# 5

# Making a Plan

*Arranging Your Ideas*

■ **IDEA JOURNAL** Write about a plan you came up with recently. How well did it work?

■ **TIP** For more information on supporting a main point, see Chapter 4.

## Understand What a Logical Order Is

In writing, **order** means the sequence in which you present your ideas: what comes first, what comes next, and so on. If you don't put your points in a logical order, they will not be easy for your readers to follow. There are three typical ways of ordering—arranging—your ideas: time order (also called chronological order), space order, and order of importance.

Read the paragraph examples that follow. In each paragraph, the primary support points are underlined, and the secondary support is in *italics*.

### Use Time Order to Write about Events

Use **time order** (chronological order) to arrange points according to when they happened. Time order works best when you are writing about events. You can go from

- First to last/last to first
- Most recent to least recent/least recent to most recent

**EXAMPLE USING TIME ORDER**

Because I'm not a morning person, I have to follow the same routine every morning or I'll just go back to bed. <u>First I allow myself three "snooze" cycles on the alarm.</u> *That gives me an extra fifteen minutes to sleep.* <u>Then I count to three and haul myself out of bed.</u> *I have to do this quickly, or I may just sink back onto the welcoming mattress.* <u>Next I head to the shower.</u> *I run the water for a minute so it will be warm when I step in. While waiting for it to warm up, I wash my face with cold water. It's a shock, but it jolts me awake.* <u>After showering and dressing, I'm ready for the two cups of coffee</u> *that are necessary to get me moving out of the house.*

What kind of time order does the author use? *first to last*

## Use Space Order to Describe Objects, Places, or People

Use **space order** to arrange ideas so that your readers picture your topic the way you see it. Space order usually works best when you are writing about a physical object or place, or a person's appearance. You can move from

- Top to bottom/bottom to top
- Near to far/far to near
- Left to right/right to left
- Back to front/front to back

### EXAMPLE USING SPACE ORDER

Donna looked very professional for her interview. <u>Her long, dark, curly hair was held back with a gold clip.</u> *No stray wisps escaped. Normally wild and unruly, her hair was smooth, shiny, and neat.* <u>She wore a white silk blouse</u> with *just the top button open at her throat. Donna had made sure to leave time to iron it so it wouldn't be wrinkled. The blouse was neatly tucked in to her* <u>black A-line skirt,</u> *which came just to the top of her knee.* She wore <u>black stockings</u> that she had *checked for runs* and <u>black low-heeled shoes.</u> Altogether, her appearance marked her as serious and professional, and she was sure to make a good first impression.

What type of space order does the example use? *top to bottom*

■ **IDEA JOURNAL** What would you wear to look professional?

## Use Order of Importance to Emphasize a Particular Point

Use **order of importance** to arrange points according to their importance, interest, or surprise value. Usually, save the most important for last.

### EXAMPLE USING ORDER OF IMPORTANCE

People who keep guns in their houses risk endangering both themselves and others. <u>Many accidental injuries occur when a weapon is improperly stored or handled.</u> *For example, someone cleaning a closet where a loaded gun is stored may handle the gun in a way that causes it to go off and injure him or her.* <u>There have also been many reports of "crimes of passion" with guns.</u> *A couple with a violent history has a fight, and in a fit of rage one gets the gun and shoots the other, wounding or killing the other*

■ **IDEA JOURNAL** What do you think about keeping guns in your house? Does it guard against robberies? Is there risk involved?

*person.* Most common and most tragic are incidents in which children find loaded guns and play with them, accidentally killing themselves or their playmates.

What is the writer's most important point? *that children sometimes find loaded guns and accidentally kill themselves or their playmates*

## Practice Arranging Ideas in a Logical Order

### Choose an Order

After you have generated support for your main point (as discussed in Chapter 4), you need to decide how to arrange your ideas so that they will be most understandable to your readers. While you might not always strictly follow one of the orders of time, space, or importance, they will help you to begin organizing your ideas.

**PRACTICE 1   CHOOSING AN ORDER**

Read each of the three topic sentences and the support points that follow them, and decide what order you would use to arrange the support in a paragraph. Indicate which point would come first, second, and so on by writing the number in the blank at the left. Then indicate the type of order you used (time, space, or importance).

> **EXAMPLE: Many grocery stores share the same basic layout so that shoppers will have a sense of where to find what they want.**

_6_ bakery on the far left

_2_ deli section back right corner

_3_ meat and seafood next to each other running across the back

_4_ freezer section a little to the left of center in wide aisle

_1_ produce section (fruits and vegetables) to right at front of store

_5_ refrigerated foods to left of freezer

Type of order: *space*

1. It was one of those days when everything went wrong.

    _4_ My boss was waiting for me.

    _2_ I had no hot water for a shower.

    _6_ I got sick at lunch and had to go home.

_3_ I missed the regular bus to work.

_1_ My alarm didn't go off.

_5_ I forgot to save work on my computer and lost it.

Type of order:  _time: first to last_

2. For his fiftieth birthday, Elton John threw himself a huge party and dressed like a king from the eighteenth century.

   _4_ a powdered white wig of long curls

   _2_ tight white satin pants that came only to the knee

   _5_ a headdress made of feathers and long plumes

   _3_ a blue satin jacket with a high neck and diamonds sewn into it

   _1_ blue satin high-heeled shoes studded with diamonds

   Type of order:  _space: bottom to top_

3. Properly extinguishing a campfire is every camper's duty.

   _3_ You can even get a fine.

   _1_ It cuts down on the smell of smoke, which can bother other campers.

   _2_ If you don't extinguish well, you can get a citation.

   _4_ Partially doused fires can ignite and burn wild.

   Type of order:  _importance_

> ■ **TIP** Try using the cut-and-paste function on your computer to experiment with different ways to order support for your main point. Doing so will give you a good sense of how your final paragraph or final essay will look. For more on using computers in writing, see Appendix D.

## Make a Written Plan

When you have decided how to order your primary support points, it's time to make a more detailed plan for your paragraph or essay. A good, visual way to plan a draft is to arrange your ideas in an outline. An **outline** lists the topic sentence (for a paragraph) or thesis statement (for an essay), the primary support points for the topic sentence or thesis statement, and secondary supporting details for each of the support points. It provides a map of your ideas that you can follow as you write. Below are sample outlines for a paragraph and for an essay.

### Outlining Paragraphs

**SAMPLE OUTLINE FOR A PARAGRAPH**

Topic sentence
  Primary support point 1
    Supporting detail for point 1

Primary support point 2
    Supporting detail for point 2
Primary support point 3
    Supporting detail for point 3
Concluding sentence

### Outlining Essays

If you are writing an essay, the primary support points for your thesis statement will become topic sentences for paragraphs that will make up the body of the essay. These paragraphs will consist of details that support the topic sentences. To remind yourself of the differences between paragraph and essay structure, see the diagram on page 34.

The outline below is for a typical five-paragraph essay, in which three body paragraphs support a thesis statement, which is included in an introductory paragraph; the fifth paragraph is the conclusion. However, essays may include more or fewer than five paragraphs, depending on the scope of the topic.

**SAMPLE OUTLINE FOR A FIVE-PARAGRAPH ESSAY**

This example uses "standard" outline form, in which letters and numbers distinguish between primary support and secondary supporting details. Some instructors may require this format. If you are making an outline just for yourself, you don't have to use the standard system—but you do need a plan to place the points you want to make in order. In an informal outline, you might want to simply indent the secondary supporting details under each primary support.

**Thesis statement** (part of introductory paragraph 1)
    **A. Topic sentence for support point 1** (paragraph 2)
        1. **Supporting detail 1 for support point 1**
        2. **Supporting detail  2 for support point 1** (and so on)
    **B. Topic sentence for support point 2** (paragraph 3)
        1. **Supporting detail 1 for support point 2**
        2. **Supporting detail 2 for support point 2** (and so on)
    **C. Topic sentence for support point 3** (paragraph 4)
        1. **Supporting detail 1 for support point 3**
        2. **Supporting detail 2 for support point 3** (and so on)
**Concluding paragraph** (paragraph 5)

■ **TIP** For an example of a five-paragraph essay, see Chapter 6, pages 76–77.

■ **TIP** For an example of a five-paragraph essay, see Chapter 6, pages 76–77.

**PRACTICE 2   MAKING AN OUTLINE**

The paragraph in this practice appeared earlier in this chapter to illustrate time order of organization. Read it and make an outline for it in the space provided.

Because I'm not a morning person, I have to follow the same routine every morning or I'll just go back to bed. First I allow myself three "snooze" cycles on the alarm. That gives me an extra fifteen minutes to sleep. Then I count to three and haul myself out of bed. I have to do this quickly, or I may just sink back onto the welcoming mattress. Next I head to the shower. I run the water for a minute so it will be warm when I step in. While waiting for it to warm up, I wash my face with cold water. It's a shock, but it jolts me awake. After showering and dressing, I'm ready for the two cups of coffee that are necessary to get me moving out of the house.

**TOPIC SENTENCE:** *Because I'm not a morning person, I have to follow the same routine every morning or I'll just go back to bed.*

    **A. PRIMARY SUPPORT 1:** *First I allow myself three "snooze" cycles on the alarm.*

        **1. SUPPORTING DETAILS:** *That gives me an extra fifteen minutes to sleep.*

    **B. PRIMARY SUPPORT 2:** *Then I count to three and haul myself out of bed.*

        **1. SUPPORTING DETAILS:** *I have to do this quickly, or I may just sink back onto the welcoming mattress.*

    **C. PRIMARY SUPPORT 3:** *Next I head to the shower.*

        **1. SUPPORTING DETAILS:** *I run the water for a minute so it will be warm when I step in.*

        **2. SUPPORTING DETAILS:** *While waiting for it to warm up, I wash my face with cold water. It's a shock, but it jolts me awake.*

    **D. PRIMARY SUPPORT POINT 4:** *After showering and dressing, I'm ready for the two cups of coffee*

        **1. SUPPORTING DETAILS:** *that are necessary to get me moving out of the house.*

■ **COMPUTER** Have students outline on a computer so that they can easily rearrange their ideas. Remind them to save their work. For more information on using computers in writing, see Appendix D.

## Make Your Own Plan

Before making your own plan, consider the process that another student used. In Chapter 2, you saw Carol Parola's prewriting on the subject of the importance of listening. After reviewing her prewriting, she saw that she'd mentioned the importance of listening in several different contexts. She

■ **RESOURCES** A reproducible blank outline for essays is in *Additional Resources.*

grouped her support according to the importance of listening in school, at work, and in her everyday life. When she considered various ways in which to order her points (time, space, importance), she decided to present her ideas in the order of their importance to her, with the personal context last.

Here is Carol's outline for a paragraph or an essay on the importance of listening.

**Topic sentence/thesis statement:** *Taking the time to listen carefully can help you avoid a whole range of problems.*

> **Primary support point 1:** *In school: Listening can help you prevent stupid mistakes that cause low grades.*
>
> > **Supporting detail:** *doing wrong assignment, getting due date wrong, getting test date wrong*
>
> **Primary support point 2:** *At work: Listening can help you avoid mistakes that can get you in trouble.*
>
> > **Supporting detail:** *shipping the wrong order, causing an accident with machinery*
>
> **Primary support point 3:** *Personal level: Listening can help you avoid misunderstandings.*
>
> > **Supporting detail:** *once hurt a good friend by not listening to something that was important to her; can avoid lots of misunderstandings with family; not miss important appointments*

**Conclusion:** *don't know yet; maybe review the importance of listening in so many areas*

## Writing Assignment

Make a plan for a paragraph or an essay using the support you generated in Chapter 4, your responses to the idea journal prompts, or one of the following topic sentences/thesis statements.

The teacher I remember best is _____.

Whenever I think of _____, I feel happy/lonely/angry/confused.

Work to live, don't live to work.

If I could make one change in my life, it would be _____

_____.

Most people are very poor listeners.

First read the Critical Thinking box that follows.

## CRITICAL THINKING: MAKING A PLAN

**FOCUS**

Reread your topic sentence (for a paragraph) or thesis statement (for an essay). Also, reread your prewriting or other ideas you have jotted down about your topic.

**ASK YOURSELF**

- What would be the best way to organize my support points? Time order? Space order? Order of importance?
- What point should come first? What next? What after that?
- Will this organization help me get my point across to my readers?

**WRITE**

Write a plan (an outline) that shows how you want to arrange your points.

After writing your plan, complete the following checklist.

## CHECKLIST: EVALUATING YOUR PLAN

- ❑  It follows a logical order of organization.
- ❑  It includes all of my ideas, arranged in the order I want to present them.

Now that you have a plan, you're ready to write a complete draft of your paragraph or essay, so move on to the next chapter.

# Chapter Review: Making a Plan

1. In writing, what does order mean? *the sequence in which you present your* *ideas.*

2. Three ways to order ideas are _____ *time* _____, _____ *space* _____, and _____ *importance* _____.

3. Making _____ *an outline* _____ is a useful way to plan your draft.

## What Will You Use?

Explain how you might use a written plan in writing you do for a college course, at work, or in your everyday life.

■ **LEARNING JOURNAL** In your own words, explain why making a written plan for your writing is helpful.

# 6

# Drafting

*Putting Your Ideas Together*

**You Know This**

You often "give something a try," knowing that you might not get it just right the first time:

- You rehearse in your head something you want to say to someone.
- You rehearse for a big event or play.
- You put out clothes you might want to wear to an important event.

■ **IDEA JOURNAL** Write about a time when you had a trial run before doing something.

■ **TEACHING TIP** Students can refer to these characteristics of a good draft in evaluating one another's papers in peer review.

■ **COMPUTER** Have students draft on the computer, saving the draft on disk and printing it out. Explain how using the computer can make changing a draft much easier.

## Understand What a Draft Is

A **draft** is the first whole version of all your ideas put together in a piece of writing. Do the best job you can in drafting, but remember that you will have more chances to make changes. Think of your first draft as a dress rehearsal for your final paper.

**BASICS OF A GOOD DRAFT**

- It has a statement of the main point.
- It has primary support points and secondary supporting details, examples, or facts that are arranged in a logical order.
- It includes an introductory sentence (for a paragraph) or an introductory paragraph (for an essay) that draws in readers.
- It has a conclusion that reminds readers of the main point and makes an observation.
- It follows standard paragraph and/or essay form and uses complete sentences.

## Practice Writing a Draft Paragraph

### Write a Draft Using Complete Sentences

When you are ready to write a draft, you have already done most of the hardest work—next you just have to put your ideas in paragraph form. Work with your outline in front of you. Be sure to include your topic sentence (usually as your introductory sentence), and express each point in a complete sentence. As you write, you may want to add support points or details or change the order. It's okay to make changes from your outline as you write — an outline is only a plan.

Read the following paragraph, annotated to show the various parts of the paragraph.

### Narcolepsy: A Misunderstood Malady — Title

Narcolepsy, a disorder that causes people to fall asleep suddenly and — Topic sentence uncontrollably, is often misunderstood. Narcoleptics may be in the middle of a meal or a conversation or almost any other activity, and they just nod off, usually only for a minute or so. Because most of us associate falling asleep with boredom or a lack of interest, people are often very offended when someone falls asleep in the middle of something. We don't look kindly on someone whose face falls into his or her plate during a dinner conversation, for example. Students with narcolepsy are often criticized, or even ridiculed, for falling asleep in the middle of a class. On the job, narcolepsy can be even more of a problem. No one looks favorably on an employee who falls asleep in the middle of an important meeting or is found sleeping on the job. However, narcoleptics have no control over this disorder; when they suddenly fall asleep, it is not from boredom, rudeness, or lack of a good night's sleep.

— Support

Although paragraphs typically begin with topic sentences, they may also begin with a quote, an example, or a surprising fact or idea. The topic sentence is then presented later in the paragraph. For examples of various introductory techniques, see pages 71–72.

■ **TIP** For more on topic sentences, see Chapter 3. For a discussion of the parts of a complete sentence, see Chapter 19.

## Write a Concluding Sentence

A **concluding sentence** refers back to the main point in the topic sentence and makes an observation based on what you have written in the paragraph. The concluding sentence does not just repeat the topic sentence.

In the paragraph above, the main point, expressed in the topic sentence, is "Narcolepsy, a disorder that causes people to fall asleep suddenly and uncontrollably, is often misunderstood."

A good concluding sentence would be "Narcolepsy is a legitimate physical disorder, and narcoleptics do not deserve the harsh reactions they often receive."

This sentence **refers back to the main point** by repeating the word "narcolepsy" and by restating that it is a real disorder. It **makes an observation based on what is written** by stating, ". . . narcoleptics do not deserve the harsh reactions they often receive."

For more on conclusions, see pages 73–74. Although these pages cover conclusions for essays, they provide some basic tips that can help you add a satisfying ending to any piece of writing.

■ **TEACHING TIP** Tell students that the concluding sentence gives them an opportunity to express a personal opinion based on the support they have provided, but they should not use it to introduce new, unrelated ideas.

■ **TIP** In some cases, a paragraph is better off without a concluding sentence. If you want to omit a concluding sentence, be sure your instructor does not require one.

### PRACTICE 1   CHOOSING A CONCLUDING SENTENCE

Each of the following paragraphs has three possible concluding sentences. Circle the letter of the one you prefer, and be prepared to say why you chose it.

1. Have you ever noticed that people often obey minor rules while they ignore major ones? For example, most people cringe at the thought of ripping off the "Do not remove under penalty of law" tag from a new pillow. This rule is meant for the seller so that the buyer knows what the pillow is made of. The owner of the pillow is allowed to remove the tag, but people hesitate to do so. Another minor rule that people obey is the waiting-line procedure in a bank. Ropes often mark off where a line should form, and a sign says "enter here." Customers then zigzag through the rope lines. Even when there is no one in line, many people follow the rope trail rather than walking right up to a teller. The same people who tremble at the thought of removing a tag or ignoring the rope lines may think nothing of exceeding the speed limit, even at the risk of a possible accident.

   a. This doesn't make sense to me.

   b. What is it about those minor rules that makes people follow them?

   c.) Apparently "under penalty of law" is a greater deterrent than "endangering your life."

2. Student fees should not be increased without explanation. These fees are a mystery to most students. Are the fees for campus improvements? Do they support student activities and, if so, which ones? What exactly do we get for these mysterious fees? We are taught in classes to think critically, to look for answers, and to challenge accepted wisdom. We are encouraged to be responsible citizens. As responsible citizens and consumers, we should not blindly accept increases until we know what they are for.

   a.) We should let the administration know that we have learned our lessons well.

   b. Student fees should be abolished.

   c. Only fees that go directly to education should be approved.

■ **TEACHING TIP** Warn students about two common problems in endings of paragraphs: (1) stopping abruptly so it seems that the paragraph is unfinished or that the writer ran out of time; (2) changing focus so readers are left wondering what the point is.

■ **PRACTICE 2  WRITING CONCLUDING SENTENCES**

Read the following paragraphs and write a concluding sentence for each one.

1. One of the most valuable ways that parents can help children is to read to them. Reading together is a good way for parents and children to relax, and it is sometimes the only "quality" time they spend together during a busy day. Reading develops children's vocabulary. They understand more words and are likely to learn new words more easily. Also, hearing the words aloud helps children's pronunciation and makes them more confident with oral language. Additionally, reading at home increases children's chances of success in school because reading is required in every course in every grade.

Possible Concluding Sentence: *Answers will vary but should include the idea that reading helps children in many ways and/or that it is an important activity for parents and children to share.*

2. There are certain memory devices, called *mnemonics,* that almost everyone uses. One of them is the alphabet song. If you want to remember what letter comes after *j,* you will probably sing the alphabet song in your head. Another is the "Thirty days hath September" rhyme that people use when they want to know how many days are in a certain month. Another mnemonic device is the rhyme "In 1492, Columbus sailed the ocean blue."

Possible Concluding Sentence: <u>*Answers will vary but should refer to the*</u>

<u>*memory devices and how commonly they are used.*</u>

## Title Your Paragraph

The title is the first thing readers see, so it should give them a good idea of what your paragraph is about. Decide on a title by rereading your draft, especially your topic sentence. A paragraph title should be fairly short and should focus on the main point, but it should not repeat your topic sentence.

Look at the title of the paragraph on page 65. It includes the topic (narcolepsy) and the main point (that this condition is misunderstood). It lets readers know what the paragraph is about, but does not repeat the topic sentence.

For more on titles, see page 75. Although these pages cover titles for essays, they provide some basic tips that can help you add an interesting title to any piece of writing.

### PRACTICE 3    WRITING TITLES

Write possible titles for the paragraphs in Practice 2.

1. <u>*Answers will vary.*</u>

2. _____

■ **DISCUSSION** Ask students to name favorite TV shows, movies, or songs, and write them on the board. Then, invite students to discuss what makes these titles interesting or dull, topic-appropriate or irrelevant. Can they think of better alternatives?

## Write Your Own Draft Paragraph

Before you draft your own paragraph, read Jeanette Castro's annotated draft below. (You saw her developing her main point in Chapter 3 and supporting it in Chapter 4.)

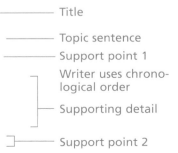

**Training for a Marathon** ———————————— Title

    Training for success in a marathon demands several important steps. ———— Topic sentence
First, runners should get a schedule that was developed by a profes- ———— Support point 1
sional running organization. These schedules are available in bookstores
or on the Web. A good one is available at runnersworld.com. All of the —— Writer uses chronological order
training schedules suggest starting training three to six months before the —— Supporting detail
marathon. Runners should commit to carefully following the schedule. —— Support point 2

Supporting detail

Support point 3

Supporting detail

Concluding sentence: refers back to main point and makes an observation

If they cannot stick to it exactly, they need to come as close as they possibly can. The schedules include a mixture of long and short runs at specified intervals. Carefully following the training schedule builds up endurance a little at a time so that by the time of the race, runners are less likely to hurt themselves. The training continues right up until the start of the marathon. Closer to the time of the marathon, runners should make sure they are prepared for the big day. The night before the race, they should eat carbohydrates, drink plenty of water, and get a good night's sleep. On the day of the marathon, runners should eat a good breakfast, dress for the weather, and consider doing a light warm-up before the race's start. Before and during the race, they should drink plenty of water. Running a marathon without completing the essential steps will not bring success; instead it may bring pain and injury.

## Writing Assignment: Paragraph

Write a draft paragraph, using what you have developed in previous chapters, your response to the idea journal prompt on page 64, or one of the following topic sentences. If you use one of the topic sentences below, you may want to revise it to fit what you want to say.

Being a good _____ requires _____.

I can find any number of ways to waste my time.

People tell me I'm _____, and I guess I have to agree.

So many decisions are involved in going to college.

The most important thing to me in life is _____.

First read this Critical Thinking box.

■ **COMPUTER** Suggest to students that they highlight (using boldface or underlining) the support points in their drafts. This keeps them on track and also helps peer editors focus on the support points. For more information on using computers in writing, see Appendix D.

---

| **CRITICAL THINKING: DRAFTING YOUR PARAGRAPH** |

**FOCUS**
Review your outline, including your topic sentence and support.

**ASK YOURSELF**
- Does my topic sentence say what I want it to, or do I need to revise it?
- Do my primary support points all relate to my topic sentence?
- Do I provide supporting details that show, explain, or prove my primary support?
- How should I turn my primary support points and supporting details into sentences?
- How can I end the paragraph?
- What's a good title?

**WRITE**
Write your draft paragraph, including a title.

■ **COMPUTER** If students have saved their prewriting on their computer, they might want to revisit it if they feel they need further support. They can cut and paste ideas from their prewriting into their draft, then flesh them out. For more information on using computers in writing, see Appendix D.

After writing your draft, complete the following checklist.

---

**CHECKLIST: EVALUATING YOUR DRAFT PARAGRAPH**

❑ There is a clear, confident topic sentence that states my main point.

❑ Each primary support point is backed up with supporting details, examples, or facts.

❑ The primary support and secondary support points are arranged in a logical order.

❑ The concluding sentence reminds readers of my main point and makes an observation.

❑ The title reinforces the main point.

❑ All of the sentences are complete, consisting of a subject and verb, and expressing a complete thought. (For more information, see Chapter 20.)

❑ The draft is properly formatted:

  • My name, my instructor's name, the course, and the date appear in the upper left corner.

  • The first sentence of the paragraph is indented, and the text is double-spaced (for easier revision).

  • I have followed any other formatting guidelines provided by my instructor.

---

# Practice Writing a Draft Essay

The draft of an essay needs to have the "Basics of a Good Draft," listed on page 64. It should also have the following characteristics:

■ **RESOURCES** For separate coverage of essays, see Appendix A, The Basics of Writing an Essay.

• Its primary support points are topic sentences that each support the main point (thesis statement).

• Each topic sentence is part of a paragraph, and the other sentences in that paragraph support the topic sentence.

## Write Topic Sentences and Draft the Body of the Essay

In an essay, each of your primary support points helps you show, explain, or prove your main point to your readers. Using your outline, or plan, you need to write complete sentences for your primary support points. These will serve as the topic sentences for the body paragraphs of your essay.

■ **TIP** For more on supporting a thesis (the main point of an essay), see Chapter 4, and for more on outlining, see Chapter 5. For a discussion of the parts of a complete sentence, see Chapter 19.

PRACTICE 4    **WRITING TOPIC SENTENCES**

Each thesis statement that follows has support points that could be topic sentences for the body paragraphs of an essay. For each support point, write a topic sentence.

**EXAMPLE:**

**THESIS STATEMENT:** My daughter is showing definite signs of becoming a teenager.

**SUPPORT POINT:** talking on the phone with friends

> **TOPIC SENTENCE:** *She talks on the phone for as long as she possibly can.*

**SUPPORT POINT:** a new style of clothes

> **TOPIC SENTENCE:** *She used to like really cute clothing, but now she has a new style.*

**SUPPORT POINT:** doesn't want me to know what's going on

> **TOPIC SENTENCE:** *While she used to tell me everything, she is now very secretive and private.*

**SUPPORT POINT:** developing an "attitude"

> **TOPIC SENTENCE:** *The surest and most annoying sign that she's becoming a teenager is that she's developed a definite "attitude."*

1. **THESIS STATEMENT:** Rhonda acts as if she is trying to fail this course.

   **SUPPORT POINT:** misses most classes

   > **TOPIC SENTENCE:** _*Answers will vary.*_____

   **SUPPORT POINT:** is always late whenever she does come

   > **TOPIC SENTENCE:** _____

   **SUPPORT POINT:** never has her book or does any homework

   > **TOPIC SENTENCE:** _____

2. **THESIS STATEMENT:** The Latin American influence is evident in many areas of U.S. culture.

   **SUPPORT POINT:** Spanish language used in lots of places

   > **TOPIC SENTENCE:** _____

   **SUPPORT POINT:** lots of different kinds of foods

   > **TOPIC SENTENCE:** _____

   **SUPPORT POINT:** new kinds of music and popular musicians

   > **TOPIC SENTENCE:** _____

Drafting topic sentences for your essay is a good way to start drafting the body of the essay (the paragraphs that support each of these topic sentences). As you write support for your topic sentences, refer back to your outline, in which you listed supporting details. (For an example, see Carol Parola's outline on page 62 of Chapter 5.) Turn these supporting details into complete sentences, and add additional support if necessary. (Prewriting techniques can help here; see Chapter 2.) Don't let yourself get stalled if you're having trouble with one word or sentence. Just keep writing. If you are writing by hand, use every other line to leave space for changes. Remember, a draft is a first try; you will have time later to improve it.

## Write an Introduction

The introduction to your essay captures your readers' interest and presents the main point. Think of your introductory paragraph as a marketing challenge. Ask yourself: How can I sell my essay to readers? You need to market your main point.

The thesis statement is usually either the first or the last sentence in an introductory paragraph.

### BASICS OF A GOOD INTRODUCTION

- It should catch readers' attention.
- It should present the thesis statement of the essay.
- It should give readers a clear idea of what the essay will cover.

■ **IDEA JOURNAL** Write about the ways that advertising attracts people's attention.

■ **ESL** Remind nonnative speakers that it is a convention of English to present the main point in the first paragraph, stated explicitly.

Here are some common kinds of introductions that spark readers' interest. In each one, the introductory technique is in **boldface**. These are not the only ways to start essays, but they should give you some useful models.

### Open with a Quote

A good short quote definitely gets people interested. It must lead naturally into your main point, however, and not be there just for effect. If you start with a quote, make sure that you tell the reader who the speaker is.

1. **"It's premature to push for federal legislation to ban cell phone use while driving."** That's according to Robert Shelton, executive director of the National Highway Safety Administration, in congressional testimony this spring. To that, we respond, "Oh, bullfeathers, Robert!"

—Tom Magliozzi and Ray Magliozzi, "Protecting Its
People: Let Our Government Do Its Job"

### Give an Example or Tell a Story

People like stories, so opening an essay with a brief story or example often draws them in.

2. **This is a true story: I was sitting at my desk, facing the challenge of how to begin a piece about the power of exercise to**

**enhance creative thinking.** Naturally, I wanted this beginning to engage you, but nothing all that engaging was coming to mind. Zilch, in fact. So I did what I often do: I went to the pool and swam for an hour. Now here I am, back at my desk typing away, my writer's block well behind me.

—Daryn Eller, "Move Your Body, Free Your Mind"

### Start with a Surprising Fact or Idea

Surprises capture people's interest. The more unexpected and surprising something is, the more likely people are to take notice of it.

■ **TEACHING TIP** In the inverted-pyramid strategy, the introductory paragraph starts with a general statement and narrows to a thesis statement.

3. Now here is something to bear in mind should you ever find yourself using a changing room in a department store or retail establishment. **It is perfectly legal—indeed, it is evidently routine—for the store to spy on you while you are trying on their clothes.**

—Bill Bryson, "Snoopers at Work"

### Offer a Strong Opinion or Position

The stronger the opinion, the more likely it is that people will pay attention. Don't write wimpy introductions! Make your point and shout it!

4. My parents and I emigrated here from Cuba. Though we are proud of our heritage and our first language, **we have always understood that success in this country is inextricably tied to the command of English.** The faster that command is achieved, the better.

—Lincoln J. Tamayo, "A 'Yes' Vote Will Benefit Kids"

### Ask a Question

A question needs an answer, so if you start your introduction with a question, your readers will need to read on to get the answer.

5. **What is intelligence, anyway?** When I was in the Army, I received a kind of aptitude test that all soldiers took and, against a normal of 100, scored 160. No one at the base had ever seen a figure like that, and for two hours they made a big fuss over me. (It didn't mean anything. The next day I was still a buck private with KP as my highest duty.)

—Isaac Asimov, "What Is Intelligence, Anyway?"

■   PRACTICE 5   **MARKETING YOUR MAIN POINT**

■ **TIP** If you get stuck while writing your introductory statement, try one or more of the prewriting techniques described in Chapter 2, pages 23–29.

As you know from advertisements, a good writer can make just about anything sound interesting. For each of the following topics, write an introductory statement using the technique indicated. Some of these topics are purposely dull to show you that you can make a punchy statement about almost any subject if you put your mind to it.

**EXAMPLE:**

**TOPIC:** Welfare to single teenage mothers

**TECHNIQUE:** Question

*What would happen if the government stopped making welfare payments to single teenage mothers tomorrow?*

1. **TOPIC:** Smoking cigarettes

   **TECHNIQUE:** Strong opinion

   *Answers will vary.*

2. **TOPIC:** Food in the cafeteria

   **TECHNIQUE:** Example or story

   _____

3. **TOPIC:** Credit cards

   **TECHNIQUE:** Surprising fact or idea

   _____

4. **TOPIC:** Role of the elderly in society

   **TECHNIQUE:** Question

   _____

5. **TOPIC:** Stress

   **TECHNIQUE:** Quote (You can make up a good one.)

   _____

■ **TEACHING TIP** Remind students that since the introduction should catch readers' attention, they should consider who their readers are and what they would find interesting.

## PRACTICE 6    IDENTIFYING STRONG INTRODUCTIONS

In a newspaper, a magazine, an advertising flier—anything written—find a strong introduction. Bring it to class and be prepared to explain why you chose it as an example of a strong introduction.

## Write a Conclusion

Conclusions too often just fade out because writers feel they're near the end and think the task is over—but it isn't *quite* over. Remember, people usually remember best what they see, hear, or read last. Use your conclusion to drive your main point home one final time. Make sure your conclusion has the same energy as the rest of the essay, if not more.

**BASICS OF A GOOD ESSAY CONCLUSION**

• It should refer back to the main point.

- It should sum up what has been covered in the essay.
- It should make a further observation or point.

In general, a good conclusion creates a sense of completion: It brings readers back to where they started, but it also shows them how far they have come.

One of the best ways to end an essay is to refer directly to something in the introduction. If you asked a question, re-ask it and answer it. If you started a story, finish it. If you used a quote, use another one — maybe a quote by the same person or maybe one by another person on the same topic. Look again at two of the introductions you read earlier, and note how the writers conclude their essays. Pay special attention to the text in bold.

### 1. INTRODUCTION

**This is a true story: I was sitting at my desk, facing the challenge of how to begin a piece about the power of exercise to enhance creative thinking.** Naturally, I wanted this beginning to engage you, but nothing all that engaging was coming to mind. Zilch, in fact. So I did what I often do: I went to the pool and swam for an hour. Now here I am, back at my desk typing away, my writer's block well behind me.

—Daryn Eller, "Move Your Body, Free Your Mind"

### CONCLUSION

You may have to experiment a little to find out what works for you. For me, a moderate workout is best — that is, one long enough to help me get an "empty mind," but not so hard that it tires me out. **Once I get to that quiet state, so many ideas start percolating in my head that when I get home I often go straight to my desk to capitalize on the momentum. Need proof that it works? I finished this article, didn't I?**

—Daryn Eller, "Move Your Body, Free Your Mind"

### 2. INTRODUCTION

My parents and I emigrated here from Cuba. Though we are proud of our heritage and our first language, **we have always understood that success in this country is inextricably tied to the command of English.** The faster that command is achieved, the better.

—Lincoln J. Tamayo, "A 'Yes' Vote Will Benefit Kids"

### CONCLUSION

Question #2 is not anti-immigrant or racist. **As an immigrant, I know firsthand that there is nothing more pro-immigrant than to provide a child with the very foundation of success here — a command of English as quickly as possible.**

Politicians have had years to make reforms in our bilingual education laws, but they have repeatedly failed to do so. It is time for voters to do the right things by voting "yes" on Question #2.

—Lincoln J. Tamayo, "A 'Yes' Vote Will Benefit Kids"

### PRACTICE 7 ANALYZING CONCLUSIONS

How is the conclusion to the essay "Move Your Body, Free Your Mind" linked to the introduction (example 1 on p. 74)? How does it refer back to the introduction? Make some notes about these questions and be prepared to discuss your answers in class.

*Answers will vary, but students might point out that the writer concludes the*

*"story" begun in the introduction by showing how exercise helps free her mind.*

_____

_____

### PRACTICE 8 FINDING GOOD INTRODUCTIONS AND CONCLUSIONS

In a newspaper or magazine or anything written, find a piece of writing that has a strong introduction and conclusion. (You may want to use what you found for Practice 6.) Answer the questions that follow.

1. What method of introduction is used? *Answers will vary.* _____

2. What does the conclusion do? Restate the main idea? Sum up the support? Make a further observation? _____

   _____

3. How are the introduction and the conclusion linked? _____

   _____

■ **TEAMWORK** Scramble the examples students bring in, and have the students work in small groups to match introductions and conclusions.

## Title Your Essay

Even if your title is the *last* part of the essay you write, it is the *first* thing readers read. Use your title to get your readers' attention and to tell them, in a brief way, what your paper is about. Use vivid, strong, specific words.

**BASICS OF A GOOD ESSAY TITLE**

- It makes people want to read the essay.
- It does not merely repeat the thesis statement.
- It may hint at the main point but does not state it outright.

One way to find a good title is to consider the type of essay you are writing. If you are writing an argument (as you will in Chapter 16), state your position in your title. If you are telling your readers how to do something (as you will in Chapter 11), try using the term *steps* or *how to* in the title. This way, your readers will know immediately not only what you are writing about but how you will discuss it.

■ **TIP** Center your title at the top of the page before the first paragraph. Do not put quotation marks around it or underline it.

■ **PRACTICE 9** **TITLING AN ESSAY**

Reread the paired paragraphs on page 74, and write alternate titles for the essays that they belong to.

Introduction/conclusion 1: _Answers will vary._

Introduction/conclusion 2: _____

# Write Your Own Draft Essay

Before you draft your own essay, read Jeanette Castro's annotated draft below. (You saw her developing her main point in Chapter 3 and supporting it in Chapter 4.)

Title indicates main point ———————— **A Plan to Cross the Finish Line**

Introductory paragraph: Writer opens with a quote.

Writer uses chronological order; each primary support point is a topic sentence presenting a step in a process.

Thesis statement ——————

Topic sentence ——————
Support point 1

Supporting details ——————

Topic sentence ——————
Support point 2

Supporting details ——————

"I want to run a marathon by the time I'm forty," I announced to my family last year. Little did I know what that would mean for a slightly lumpy, out-of-shape thirty-nine-year-old. I soon found out and now have some important information to pass on to any of you who are interested in running a marathon. Successfully running a marathon requires careful planning from start to finish.

The whole process begins three to four months before the race. The first step is to get a good training schedule from a reliable source. I used the Web to find one at www.runnersworld.com, which has a variety of useful information in addition to schedules. The schedule is detailed and easy to understand, though quite rigorous. Around the time you get the schedule, buy a good pair of shoes. The *Runner's World* Web site has lots of advice about these, too. Go to a real runner's shoe store rather than a discount store where clerks don't know anything about shoes. Without good shoes, you will mangle your feet and run the risk of greater injury, so even if they're expensive, they are worth every penny.

Next comes the actual training. Understanding the schedule is easy; following it isn't. Training takes a good deal of time, which I didn't have, and you probably don't either. Try to stick closely to the schedule, though. Finding a training partner can keep you on track: You can help each other make the time and go out in the bad weather, deal with aching muscles, and face other unpleasantness along the way. If possible, try to run part of the actual course. Vary short and long runs as recommended to develop muscles and endurance and to avoid injury. A final practice run before the race will set you up physically and mentally. You might do this practice run two or three days before the marathon, leaving yourself some resting time before the race.

Finally, the night before the marathon arrives. Eat a nutritious, carbohydrate-rich meal and get a good night's sleep. Avoid coffee, alcohol, or sleep remedies. When you get up on the morning of the race, eat a good breakfast. Then, make sure to dress appropriately for the weather. If it's a cool day, you might want to bring layers that you can strip off. Allow plenty of time to get to the start of the race. In the minutes before the start cue, breathe deeply, relax, and psyche yourself up. During the run, pace yourself and drink plenty of fluids at rest stops. If this is your first marathon, you probably aren't in it to win, so don't push yourself to the point of injury. After the race, drink more water if you need it, and cover up to avoid hypothermia. You will need a lot of rest and recovery time in the hours and days that follow.

> Topic sentence
> Support point 3

> Supporting details

Anyone who is in reasonably good shape can run a marathon by carefully following several important steps. All that is required are patience, persistence, and determination. I should know, because, guess what? I ran a marathon before I turned forty, and you can run one, too.

> Concluding paragraph: First sentence relates back to thesis statement.
> Refers back to opening quote

## Writing Assignment: Essay

Write a draft essay using what you have developed in previous chapters, your response to the idea journal prompt on page 64, or one of the following thesis statements. If you choose one of the thesis statements below, you may want to modify it some to fit what you want to say.

Taking care of a sick (child/parent/spouse/friend) can test even the most patient person.

Being a good _____ requires _____ .

Doing _____ gave me a great deal of pride in myself.

A good long-term relationship involves flexibility and compromise.

Some of the differences between men and women create misunderstandings.

Before writing your draft, read the Critical Thinking box that follows.

### CRITICAL THINKING: DRAFTING YOUR ESSAY

**FOCUS**
Review your outline, including your thesis statement and support.

**ASK YOURSELF**
- Does my thesis statement say what I want it to, or do I need to revise it?
- Do my primary support points relate to my thesis statement?
- Do I provide supporting details that show, explain, or prove my primary support?

(continued)

- How should I turn my primary support points into topic sentences for their own paragraphs?
- Is there an introductory technique that might work especially well for my paper's topic and focus?
- What should I say in my concluding paragraph? How can I remind my readers of my main point without just repeating the thesis statement?
- Can I use my introductory technique in my conclusion?
- What observation do I want to make to my readers in my conclusion?
- In my title, how can I get readers' attention and highlight my main point?

**WRITE**

Write a draft essay, including a title.

After you have finished writing your draft, complete the following checklist.

---

**CHECKLIST: EVALUATING YOUR DRAFT ESSAY**

- ❑ There is a clear, confident thesis statement that states my main point.
- ❑ The primary support points are now topic sentences that support the main point.
- ❑ Each topic sentence is part of a paragraph, and the other sentences in the paragraph support the topic sentence.
- ❑ The primary support and supporting details are arranged in a logical order.
- ❑ I have tried to draw readers' interest in my introduction.
- ❑ The conclusion reinforces my main point and makes an additional observation.
- ❑ The title reinforces the main point.
- ❑ All of the sentences are complete, consisting of a subject and verb, and expressing a complete thought. (For more information, see Chapter 20.)
- ❑ The draft is properly formatted:
  - My name, my instructor's name, the course, and the date appear in the upper left corner.
  - The first sentence of each paragraph is indented, and the text is double-spaced (for easier revision).
  - The pages are numbered.
  - I have followed any other formatting guidelines provided by my instructor.

Don't think about your draft anymore—for the moment. Give yourself some time away from it—at least a few hours, preferably a day. Taking a break will allow you to return to your writing later with a fresher eye and more energy for revision, resulting in a better piece of writing—and a better grade. After your break, you'll be ready to take the next step: revising your draft.

## Chapter Review: Drafting

1. A draft is _the first whole version of all your ideas put together in a piece of writing_ .

2. Five basic features of a good draft are _It has a statement of the main point. It has primary support points and secondary supporting details, examples, or facts that are arranged in a logical order. It includes an introductory sentence or paragraph that draws in readers. It has a conclusion that reminds readers of the main point and makes an observation. It follows standard paragraph and/or essay form and uses complete sentences._

■ **LEARNING JOURNAL** In your own words, explain how you write a draft.

**FOR AN ESSAY:**

3. Five ways to start an essay are

   _Open with a quote._

   _Give an example or tell a story._

   _Start with a surprising fact or idea._

   _Offer a strong opinion or position._

   _Ask a question._

4. Three features of a good conclusion are

   _It refers back to the main point._

   _It sums up what has been covered in the essay._

   _It makes a further observation or point._

5. Three basic features of a good essay title are

   _It makes people want to read the essay._

   _It does not merely repeat the thesis statement._

   _It may hint at the main point but does not state it outright._

## What Will You Use?

How can understanding the process of drafting help you in classes other than this one? In your everyday life or at work?

# 7

# Revising
*Improving Your Paragraph or Essay*

## You Know This

You often make changes to improve things:

- You dress for an important occasion then decide to try other clothes you think will be more suitable.

- You go to a store to buy a specific model of something (such as a CD player or a computer) and then, based on the information the salesperson gives you, you rethink your decision.

- You arrange furniture one way and then rearrange it a couple of times until it's right.

## Understand What Revision Is

Revising and editing are two different ways to improve a paper.

**Revising** is changing the ideas in your writing to make it clearer, stronger, and more convincing. In other words, it involves looking at the "big picture" and making sure it's the picture you want your readers to "see." When revising, you might add, cut, or change whole sentences or groups of sentences.

**Editing** is finding and correcting problems with grammar, style, word choice and usage, and punctuation. While editing, you usually add, cut, or change words and phrases. Editing and proofreading concern the "little picture": your writing at the word level rather than at the idea level. (Note that the Editing section of this book begins on p. 285.)

Most writers find it difficult to revise and edit well if they try to do both at once. It is more efficient to solve bigger, idea-level problems first (by revising) and then to correct smaller, word-level ones (by editing).

### REVISION STRATEGIES

- Search for ideas that do not fit.
- Search for ideas that are not as specific or complete as they could be.
- Search for ways to connect ideas so that they flow smoothly from one to the next.
- Search for ways to improve your overall paper.

Revision is critical to good writing. No one gets everything right in one draft, so do not skip the revising stage. Commit yourself to making at least four changes in any draft. Revising isn't optional: It is a critical part of any kind of writing you do, whether it is for college, for work, or for every-day life.

**FIVE REVISION TIPS**

1. Give yourself a break from your draft (a few hours or a day).
2. Read your draft aloud and listen to your words.
3. Imagine yourself as your reader.
4. Get feedback from a friend, classmate, or colleague (see the next section).
5. Get help from a tutor at your college writing center or lab.

## Understand What Giving and Getting Feedback Are

One of the best ways to get help with revising your writing is to exchange drafts with one or more students. Other people can look at your work with a fresh perspective, and they often see things that you might not — parts that are good and parts that need to be strengthened or clarified.

To get useful feedback, exchange papers with a partner. Each partner should read the other's paper and jot down a few comments. If you are working in a small group, you may want to read each paper aloud. Group members can make notes while each member is reading. Then offer comments to one another that will help improve the paper. The first time someone comments on what you have written, you may feel a little awkward or embarrassed, but you'll get over it.

**BASICS OF USEFUL FEEDBACK**

- It is given in a positive way.
- It is specific.
- It offers suggestions.
- It is given in writing (although people may also provide feedback orally).

Often it is useful for the writer to give the person or people providing feedback a few questions to focus on as they read or listen.

**QUESTIONS FOR REVIEWERS OF A DRAFT**

1. What is the main point?
2. Can I do anything to make the introduction more interesting?
3. Do I have enough support for my main point? Where could I use more support?
4. Where could I use more details?
5. Are there places where you have to stop and reread something to understand it? If so, where?

■ **TIP** Among the useful Internet resources for writers revising a draft, three good online writing labs can be found at the University of Missouri, **<web.missouri.edu/~writery>**; Purdue University, **<owl .english.purdue.edu>**; and Capital Community College, **<webster.commnet.edu/ grammar/index.htm>**.

■ **TEAMWORK** Try modeling peer review. Bring in a short paragraph or essay, and have students answer the Questions for Reviewers of a Draft in small groups, with one person acting as a recorder. You can join each group for a few minutes to make sure each group understands the process. Then discuss the answers as a class.

■ **RESOURCES** *Practical Suggestions* contains a discussion of peer feedback.

6. What about the conclusion? Does it just fade out? How could I make my point more forcefully?

7. Where could the paper be better? What would you do if it were your paper?

8. If you were getting a grade on this paper, would you turn it in as is?

9. What other comments or suggestions do you have?

## Practice Revising for Unity, Detail, and Coherence

To revise your writing, you will need to reread it carefully with an objective and critical eye. You may need to read what you have written several times before deciding what changes would improve it. Remember to consider your audience and your purpose and focus on three areas: unity, detail, and coherence.

### Revise for Unity

■ **TIP** Problems with unity can also result when your writing lacks a main point, or if the main point isn't clearly or specifically stated. For more information on stating your main point, see Chapter 3.

**Unity** in writing means that all the points you make are related to your main point; they are *unified* in support of your main point. As you draft a paragraph or an essay, you may detour from your main point without even being aware of it, as the writer of the following paragraph did with the underlined sentences. The diagram after the paragraph shows what happens when readers read the paragraph.

First, double-underline the main point in the paragraph that follows. This will help you see where the writer got off-track.

■ **TEACHING TIP** Read the paragraph aloud to the class, and ask students to stop you as soon as they hear it detouring from the main point.

Car mechanics don't always have the answers to car problems. Today while I was driving, my car started weaving and wobbling, and the steering seemed loose. I pulled into a gas station and asked the mechanic to take a look at it. He seemed to know what he was doing as he walked around the car, looking at various parts, nodding his head, and saying, "Uh huh." The mechanic told me his cousin has a Tracker just like mine and loves it. I really like mine, too. It's like a sports car. The mechanic finished his inspection of the car and told me there was absolutely nothing wrong. I got back in and continued driving. After about half a mile, one tire spun right off the car and rolled off the road, leaving my car lying on its side. I learned later that two of the lug nuts attaching the tire to the wheel had come loose and that the mechanic should have checked them first. Next time I won't be so quick to accept a mechanic's answer.

■ **IDEA JOURNAL** Have you ever had a bad experience with an "expert" who turned out not to be so expert? If you could relive the experience, what would you do differently?

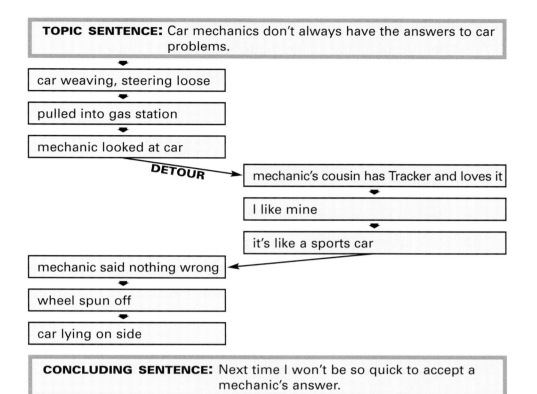

**TOPIC SENTENCE:** Car mechanics don't always have the answers to car problems.

car weaving, steering loose

pulled into gas station

mechanic looked at car

DETOUR → mechanic's cousin has Tracker and loves it

I like mine

it's like a sports car

mechanic said nothing wrong

wheel spun off

car lying on side

**CONCLUDING SENTENCE:** Next time I won't be so quick to accept a mechanic's answer.

Detours in your writing lead readers away from your main point and weaken it because the readers' focus is shifted. As you revise, check to make sure that your paragraph or essay has unity.

### ■ PRACTICE 1    REVISING FOR UNITY

Each of the following paragraphs contains a sentence that detours from the main point. First double-underline the <u>main point</u>, then underline the <u>detour</u> in each paragraph.

**EXAMPLE:**

"Education is one of the few things people are willing to pay for and not get." When we buy something expensive, we make sure we take it home and use it. For example, we wouldn't think of spending a couple of hundred dollars on a new coat and shoes only to hide them away in a closet never to be worn. And we certainly wouldn't pay for those items and then decide to leave them at the store. I once left a bag with three new shirts in it at the cash register, and I never got it back. People pay a lot for education, but sometimes look for ways to leave the "purchase" behind. They

■ **COMPUTER** If you can send material to students' computers, type in a short paragraph or essay and have students add a sentence to the paragraph (or to each paragraph in the essay) that doesn't support the main point. Then have students move to another computer and find the unrelated sentence or sentences that other students have input. They should put the detouring sentences in italics. Have them return to the original computer and see if the correct sentences are italicized.

■ **IDEA JOURNAL** Write about the statement "Education is one of the few things people are willing to pay for and not get." Do you agree? How does this statement apply to you?

cheat themselves by not attending class, not paying attention, not studying, or not doing assignments. At the end of the term, they have a grade but didn't get what they paid for: education and knowledge. They have wasted money, just as if they had bought an expensive sound system and had never taken it out of the box.

■ **IDEA JOURNAL** Today, what are your must-do, want-to-do, and hope-to-do activities? Keep track of these for a week.

1. One way to manage time is to keep a written calendar or schedule. It should have an hour-by-hour breakdown of the day and evening, with space for you to write next to the time. As appointments or responsibilities come up, write them in on the right day and time. Before the end of the day, consult your calendar to see what's in store for the next day. Using a calendar saves you trouble, because once you write down the appointment or activity, you don't have to think about it anymore. Calendars come in all sizes, colors, and shapes. Once you are in the habit of using a calendar, you will see that it frees your mind because you are not always trying to think about what you're supposed to do, where you're supposed to be, or what you might have forgotten.

■ **TIP** For more advice on managing your time, see Chapter 1, pages 4–5.

2. As you use a calendar to manage your time, think about how long certain activities will take. A common mistake is to underestimate the time needed to do something, even something simple. For example, when you are planning the time needed to get cash from the cash machine, remember that there may be a line of people. Last week in the line I met a woman I went to high school with. When you are estimating time for a more complex activity, such as reading a chapter in a textbook, block out more time than you think you will need. If you finish in less time than you have allotted, so much the better. Allow for interruptions. It is better to allow too much time than too little.

3. Effective time management means allowing time for various "life" activities. For example, it is important to budget time for chores, like paying bills, buying food, picking up a child, or going to the doctor. It seems as if my dentist is always a half hour behind schedule. A daily schedule should also account for communication with other people, such as family members, friends, service people, and others. It is impor-

tant to allow time for relaxation. Do not schedule an activity for every minute; give yourself some "down" time. Finally, leave time for unexpected events that are a huge part of life, like last-minute phone calls, a car that won't start, or a bus that is late.

## Revise for Detail and Support

When you revise a paper, look carefully at the support points and supporting details you have developed, and imagine yourself as your reader: Do you have enough information to understand the main point? Are you convinced of the main point?

In the margin of your draft (or between the lines), note ideas that seem weak or unclear. (As we noted in Chapter 6, you should double-space your drafts to allow room for revisions.) As you revise, add at least three additional support points or supporting details to your draft.

■ **TIP** One advantage of writing on a computer is that revision is made easier. You can even try out different versions and then decide later which one you like best. In Microsoft Word you can save different versions using the Save As feature under the File menu. For more information on using computers in writing, see Appendix D.

**PRACTICE 2   REVISING FOR DETAIL AND SUPPORT**

Read the following paragraph, double-underline the main point, and add at least three additional support points or supporting details to it (you will have to make them up). Write them in the spaces provided under the paragraph, and indicate where they should go in the paragraph by writing in a caret (∧) and the number.

**EXAMPLE:**

My two-year-old son, Angelo, is not always the angel that his name suggests. When I came home from work, I saw that he was very upset.1 The babysitter told me that he had been behaving badly all day.2 Just before I came home, she told him he could not play outside until he behaved better, but he only acted worse. But by the time my husband came home, Angelo was his old self.3

1. *He was crying hysterically and screaming.*

2. *For example, he threw his breakfast and lunch on the floor and had a tantrum*
   *when the babysitter told him it was time for his nap.*

3. *He was playing with his favorite truck and laughing.*

A simple hamburger can be built into a feast. Start by slathering the bun with your favorite condiment. Then stack on your favorite toppings.

The top of the bun then holds the sandwich together. Bite into it; it's delicious!

1. *Answers will vary but may specify ingredients or sensory details.* _____

2. _____

3. _____

## Revise for Coherence

Even if you have expressed all of your points and arranged them in a logical order, your writing may still seem choppy, and your ideas may be hard to follow. If so, you need to improve the coherence of your paper.

**Coherence** in writing means that all of your points and details connect to form a whole. In other words, even when the points and details are assembled in an order that makes sense, they still need "glue" to connect them.

Coherence in writing helps readers see how one point leads to another — a piece of writing that lacks coherence can sound like a string of unrelated statements. Individual ideas should be so well arranged and connected that they leave readers with a clear overall impression. A good way to make sure that your writing is coherent is to use transitions.

**Transitions** are words, phrases, and sentences that connect your ideas so that your writing moves smoothly from one point to the next. Use transitions when moving from one main support point to another. Also use them wherever you want to improve the flow of your writing. The next page shows some common transitional words and phrases. These are not the only transitions, however.

Here are two paragraphs, one that does not use transitions and one that does. Read them and notice how much easier the second paragraph is to follow. Both paragraphs make the same points, but the transitions (underlined) in the second paragraph help "hold it together."

**NO TRANSITIONS**

It is not difficult to get organized — it takes discipline to stay organized. All you need to do is follow a few simple ideas. You must decide what your priorities are and do these tasks first. You should ask yourself every day: What is the most important goal I have to accomplish? Make the time to do it. To be organized, you need a personal system for keeping track of things. Making lists, keeping records, and using a schedule help you remember what tasks you need to do. It's a good idea not to let belongings and obligations stack up. Get rid of possessions you don't need, put items away every time you use them, and don't take on more responsibilities than you can handle. It isn't a mystery; it's just good sense.

**TRANSITIONS ADDED**

It is not difficult to get organized — <u>even though</u> it takes discipline to stay organized. All you need to do is follow a few simple ideas. You must

## *Common Transitional Words and Phrases*

**SPACE**

| | | | |
|---|---|---|---|
| above | below | near | to the right |
| across | beside | next to | to the side |
| at the bottom | beyond | opposite | under |
| at the top | farther/further | over | where |
| behind | inside | to the left | |

**TIME**

| | | | |
|---|---|---|---|
| after | eventually | meanwhile | soon |
| as | finally | next | then |
| at last | first | now | when |
| before | last | second | while |
| during | later | since | |

**IMPORTANCE**

| | | | |
|---|---|---|---|
| above all | in fact | more important | most |
| best | in particular | most important | worst |
| especially | | | |

**EXAMPLE**

| | | | |
|---|---|---|---|
| for example | for instance | for one thing | one reason |

**AND**

| | | | |
|---|---|---|---|
| additionally | and | as well as | in addition |
| also | another | furthermore | moreover |

**BUT**

| | | | |
|---|---|---|---|
| although | in contrast | nevertheless | still |
| but | instead | on the other hand | yet |
| however | | | |

**SO**

| | | | |
|---|---|---|---|
| as a result | finally | so | therefore |
| because | | | |

decide what your priorities are and do these tasks first. For example, you should ask yourself every day: What is the most important task I have to accomplish? Then make the time to do it. To be organized, you also need a personal system for keeping track of things. Making lists, keeping records, and using a schedule help you remember what tasks you need to do. <u>Finally</u>, it's a good idea not to let belongings and obligations stack up. Get rid of possessions you don't need, put items away every time you use them, and don't take on more responsibilities than you can handle. Organization isn't a mystery; it's just good sense.

■ **PRACTICE 3  ADDING TRANSITIONS**

■ **TIP** More help with editing (and writing) is offered in the Writing Guide Software included with this book. For online editing exercises, visit Exercise Central at <bedfordstmartins.com/ realwriting>.

Read the following paragraphs. In each blank, add a transition that would smoothly connect the ideas. In each case, there is more than one right answer.

**EXAMPLE:**

Life Gem, a Chicago company, has announced that it can turn cremated human ashes into high-quality diamonds. _After_ cremation, the ashes are heated to convert their carbon to graphite. _Then_, a lab wraps the graphite around a tiny diamond piece and again heats it and pressurizes it. _After_ about a week of crystallizing, the result is a diamond. _Because of_ the time and labor involved, this process costs about $20,000. _Although_ the idea is very creative, many people will think it is also very weird.
*Answers will vary.*

1. Selena Quintanilla's story is both inspiring and tragic. _When_ she was very young, Selena sang in English in her father's band. _As_ a teenager, she started singing Tejano music in Spanish. Tejano literally means "Texan," but it has come to represent a culture of Mexican Americans. Selena's new Tejano music became very popular and successful, and she was ready to release an album in English. _However_, she was murdered right before the album's release. _After_ it was released, her album sold 175,000 copies in a single day, becoming one of the best-selling albums in history. Selena's death and stardom occurred almost simultaneously, when she was only twenty-four.

2. Smoking should be banned at all restaurants. The smell of cigarette smoke is downright unpleasant. _Also_, it makes my eyes water and sting, which is not a very pleasant experience while I am try-

ing to eat. _In addition_ , it ruins the taste of the food I've just paid for. _Most important_ , inhaling secondhand smoke is nearly as unhealthy as smoking yourself. Smokers may claim that having separate smoking and nonsmoking sections is enough, but it isn't. Smoke from the smoking section wafts steadily over to the nonsmoking one, damaging both my evening out and my good health.

One other way to give your writing coherence is to repeat a **key word**, a word that is directly related to your main point. For example, look back at the paragraph on p. 86, the example with transitions added. The main point of the paragraph is that it's not difficult to get organized. Note that the writer repeats the word "organized" several times throughout the paragraph. Repetition of a key word is a good way to keep your readers focused on your main point, but make sure that you don't overdo the repetition.

## Revise Your Own Paragraph

In Chapter 4, you saw Jesse Calsado developing support for his main point. Before you revise your own paragraph, read Jesse Calsado's paragraphs below. The first is his draft with his notes for revision. The second shows the revisions he made to his draft to make sure that it has unity, that it provides enough support and detail for his topic sentence, and that it is coherent.

### Cheating: It's Not Just a Classroom Concern

Cheating is not just a classroom concern: It affects nearly every aspect of life. Probably the most widespread and costly kind of cheating occurs in the workplace. Employees use computers to write e-mails to friends on company time. Speaking of corporate cheating, let us not forget CEOs who spend company money on personal stuff and cheat employees out of pensions and benefits when the company goes bankrupt. People usually do not speak up when being undercharged or getting too much money back. Cashiers really should be paying better attention; that's a real problem I've noticed lately. An article in last week's paper had information about that. Another example of cheating outside the classroom occurs when health care providers recommend treatments that may not be necessary, just because the insurance company will reimburse the patient. I have had that experience with my dentist. When people hear the word *cheating*, they often think of students and tests, but there are lots of ways of cheating and lots of people doing it.

*Is "affect" the right word? Work on this topic sentence.*

*Add some kind of transition.*

*Add some kind of transition? This seems jumpy.*

*Add a transition.*

*Does this sentence really belong?*

*Be more specific about article.*

*Give more detail about experience.*

*This last sentence sounds weird.*

*Something seems wrong with the support. Rearrange points? Save worst or most common for last?*

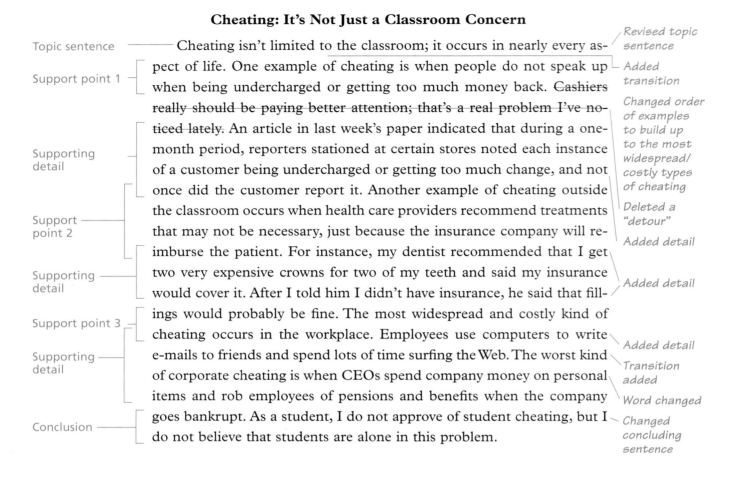

**Cheating: It's Not Just a Classroom Concern**

Topic sentence ——— Cheating isn't limited to the classroom; it occurs in nearly every aspect of life. One example of cheating is when people do not speak up when being undercharged or getting too much money back. ~~Cashiers really should be paying better attention; that's a real problem I've noticed lately.~~ An article in last week's paper indicated that during a one-month period, reporters stationed at certain stores noted each instance of a customer being undercharged or getting too much change, and not once did the customer report it. Another example of cheating outside the classroom occurs when health care providers recommend treatments that may not be necessary, just because the insurance company will reimburse the patient. For instance, my dentist recommended that I get two very expensive crowns for two of my teeth and said my insurance would cover it. After I told him I didn't have insurance, he said that fillings would probably be fine. The most widespread and costly kind of cheating occurs in the workplace. Employees use computers to write e-mails to friends and spend lots of time surfing the Web. The worst kind of corporate cheating is when CEOs spend company money on personal items and rob employees of pensions and benefits when the company goes bankrupt. As a student, I do not approve of student cheating, but I do not believe that students are alone in this problem.

Labels on left: Topic sentence, Support point 1, Supporting detail, Support point 2, Supporting detail, Support point 3, Supporting detail, Conclusion

Annotations on right: *Revised topic sentence*, *Added transition*, *Changed order of examples to build up to the most widespread/costly types of cheating*, *Deleted a "detour"*, *Added detail*, *Added detail*, *Added detail*, *Transition added*, *Word changed*, *Changed concluding sentence*

## Writing Assignment: Paragraph

Revise the draft paragraph you wrote in Chapter 6.

Before revising the paragraph, read the Critical Thinking box that follows and make notes on your draft as you work through the steps.

| CRITICAL THINKING: REVISING YOUR DRAFT PARAGRAPH |
| --- |

**FOCUS**

• After a break, reread your draft with concentration and a fresh perspective.

• If your paragraph has been reviewed by an instructor or your peers, look over those comments now.

**ASK YOURSELF**

• Did I make my main point clearly and confidently?

• Does everything in my paragraph relate to my main point?

• Do I have enough primary support and supporting details to back up my main point?

• Is it clear how one idea in my paragraph connects to another?

• Would transitions help?

• Would repeating a key word help?

- Is my support organized in a logical, effective way (for example, by time, space, or order of importance)?
- How can I address any concerns or suggestions from my instructor or peers?

**WRITE**

Revise your draft paragraph, making at least four changes.

After revising your draft, complete the following checklist.

---

**CHECKLIST: EVALUATING YOUR REVISED PARAGRAPH**

- ❏  My topic sentence is confident and definite, and my main point is clear.
- ❏  My ideas are detailed and specific.
- ❏  My ideas flow smoothly from one to the next.
- ❏  This paragraph fulfills the original assignment.
- ❏  I am ready to turn in this paragraph for a grade.
- ❏  This is the best I can do.

After you have finished revising your paragraph, you are ready to edit it. See the Important Note about this on page 94.

## Revise Your Own Essay

In Chapter 4, you saw Jesse Calsado developing support for his main point. Before you revise your own essay, read Jesse Calsado's essays below. The first is his draft with his notes for revision. The second shows the revisions he made to his draft to ensure that it has unity, that it provides enough support and detail for his topic sentence, and that it is coherent.

### Cheating: It's Not Just a Classroom Concern

Cheating is not just a classroom concern: It affects nearly every aspect of life. By making that claim, I am not defending student cheating. I am saying, however, that our society has problems with all kinds of cheating, and we should recognize, admit to, and deal with those, too.

*Is "affects" the right word? Work on this thesis statement.*

Probably the most widespread and costly kind of cheating occurs in the workplace. Employees use computers to write e-mails to friends on company time. Speaking of corporate cheating, let us not forget CEOs who spend company money on personal stuff and cheat employees out

*Add some kind of transition? This seems jumpy.*

*This one does, too. Do I know enough to be more specific? If not, maybe cut.*

*Add a transition.*

*Does this sentence really belong?*

*Be more specific about article.*

*Give more detail about experience.*

*Something seems wrong with the order of my support. Rearrange points? Save worst or most common for last?*

*This last sentence sounds weird.*

of pensions and benefits when the company goes bankrupt. Enron and WorldCom used creative accounting, and even Martha Stewart isn't perfect. Long-time employees were left with no jobs or savings plans or pensions.

People usually do not speak up when being undercharged or getting too much money back. Cashiers really should be paying better attention; that's a real problem I've noticed lately. An article in last week's paper indicated that during a one-month period, reporters stationed at certain stores noted each instance of a customer being undercharged or getting too much change, and not once did the customer report it.

Another example of cheating outside the classroom occurs when health care providers recommend treatments that may not be necessary, just because the insurance company will reimburse the patient. I have had that experience with my dentist. He recommended that I get two very expensive crowns for two of my teeth and said my insurance would cover it.

When people hear the word cheating, they often think of students and tests, but there are lots of ways of cheating and lots of people doing it. Student cheating is not right. Neither is cheating by anybody else.

### Cheating: It's Not Just a Classroom Concern

Introduction: Thesis statement is first sentence

Cheating is not just a classroom concern: It is all around us. By making that claim, I am not defending student cheating. I am saying, however, that our society has problems with all kinds of cheating, and we should recognize, admit to, and deal with those, too. Cheating isn't just for students.

*Changed thesis statement*

*Added transition sentence*

Topic sentence: support point 1

One common example of cheating happens when people are undercharged or get too much money back. They never report it. ~~Cashiers really should be paying better attention; that's a real problem I've noticed lately.~~ An article in last week's paper indicated that during a one-month period, reporters stationed at certain stores noted each instance of a customer being undercharged or getting too much change, and not once did the customer report it. When customers were overcharged or did not get enough change, they were very quick to speak up. However, they were quite comfortable cheating when the error was to their benefit.

*Changed order of support points to build up to most widespread/costly form of cheating*

*Added transition*

*Deleted a "detour"*

Supporting detail

Topic sentence: support point 2

Supporting detail

Another example of cheating outside the classroom occurs when health care providers recommend treatments that may not be necessary, just because the insurance company will reimburse the patient. I have had that experience with my dentist. He recommended that I get two

very expensive crowns for two of my teeth and said my insurance would *Added detail*
cover it. After I told him I didn't have insurance, he said that fillings
would probably be fine. I had another experience like that, too. When my *Transitional sentence added*
father was in the hospital with what turned out to be the flu, doctors or-
dered the most expensive and complicated tests available. They said they
wanted to rule out serious problems, but I'm not convinced that they
thought he really needed the tests. The more tests, the more money for
the hospital.

**Topic sentence: support point 3**

The most widespread and costly kind of cheating occurs in the
workplace. Employees use computers to write e-mails to friends on *Added detail*
company time and to amuse themselves by surfing the Web. The worst *Transition added*
kind of corporate cheating happens when CEOs spend company money
on personal items and cheat employees out of pensions and benefits *Word change*
when the company goes bankrupt. For example, executives at Adelphia *Added information about CEOs spending money on personal items and dropped WorldCom and Martha Stewart; not enough information*

**Supporting detail**

Communications used shareholder money to purchase the Buffalo
Sabres, and to buy personal items. Also, Enron used creative accounting
to hide debt and inflate profits, misleading investors. Then, when the
company got in trouble, top executives sold off stock but wouldn't let
employees do the same. This kind of cheating robs long-time employees
of jobs, savings plan monies, and pensions, and it robs the public of trust
in corporations.

**Conclusion**

When people hear the word cheating, they often zero in on students
and tests, but cheating really is all around us. Student cheating is not
right and should not be practiced or tolerated. But we are surrounded
by even more damaging cheating practices, and we should be aware of *Added to conclusion*
that as well. Cheating, whoever is doing it, is harmful to our society.

## Writing Assignment: Essay

Revise the draft essay you wrote in Chapter 6.

Before revising your essay, read the Critical Thinking box that follows
and make notes on your draft as you work through the steps.

### CRITICAL THINKING: REVISING YOUR DRAFT ESSAY

**FOCUS**
- After a break, reread your draft with concentration and a fresh
  perspective.
- If your essay has been reviewed by an instructor or your peers, look
  over those comments now.

**ASK YOURSELF**
- Did I say what I wanted to say?

(continued)

- Have I tried to catch readers' attention in my introduction?
- Does the introduction include my thesis statement?
- Do all of the topic sentences support my thesis statement?
- Does everything in each paragraph relate to the topic sentence for that paragraph?
- Do I have enough support for each topic sentence? Can I add any details, examples, or facts?
- Does one idea move smoothly into the next?
- Would transitions help?
- Would repeating key words help?
- Is my support organized in a logical, effective way (for example, by time, space, or order of importance)?
- Does my conclusion remind my readers of my main point? Have I made an observation based on what I've written that ends the essay on a strong note?
- How can I address any concerns or suggestions from my instructor or peers?

**WRITE**

Revise your draft essay, making at least four changes.

■ **TEACHING TIP** Ask students to write you an informal letter and attach it to their paper. In the letter, they should comment on the assignment: whether it was easy or hard, interesting or not. They should also indicate what they might change about their own writing process if they were to do the assignment again.

### CHECKLIST: EVALUATING YOUR REVISED ESSAY

- ❑ My thesis statement is confident and definite, and my main point is clear.
- ❑ My ideas are detailed and specific.
- ❑ My ideas flow smoothly from one to the next.
- ❑ This essay fulfills the original assignment.
- ❑ I am ready to turn in this essay for a grade.
- ❑ This is the best I can do.

**IMPORTANT NOTE:** Editing—making changes in grammar, word use, punctuation, and capitalization—follows revising and is the final stage in the writing process. After you have revised your writing to make the ideas clear and strong, you need to edit it to be sure there are no errors or distractions that could prevent readers from understanding your message. When you are ready to edit your writing, turn to Part Four, the beginning of the editing chapters.

## Chapter Review: Revising

1. Revising is _changing the ideas in your writing to make it clearer, stronger, and more convincing._

2. Why is revision important? (See p. 80.) *No one gets everything right in one*
   *draft. Revision is critical to good writing.*

3. Four basic features of useful feedback are

   *It is given in a positive way.*

   *It is specific.*

   *It offers suggestions.*

   *It is given in writing.*

4. As you revise, make sure that your paragraph or essay has these three
   things: *unity* , *detail/support* , and *coherence* .

5. *Unity* means that all the points you make are related to your
   main point.

6. Coherence means *that all of your points and details connect to form a whole.*

7. An important way to ensure coherence in your writing is to *use*
   *transitions.*

8. Transitions are *words, phrases, and sentences that connect your ideas so*
   *that your writing moves smoothly from one point to the next.*

■ **LEARNING JOURNAL:** How would you explain the terms *unity, support,* and *coherence* to someone who had never heard of them?

## What Will You Use?

How can what you have learned about revising in this chapter help you in other areas of your life? How can you use what you know about revising in your other courses?

# Part Two

# Writing Different Kinds of Paragraphs and Essays

# 8

# Narration

## *Writing That Tells Stories*

## Understand What Narration Is

**Narration** is writing that tells the story of an event or an experience.

### ■■ FOUR BASICS OF GOOD NARRATION

1. It reveals something of importance to you (your main point).
2. It includes all of the major events of the story (primary support).
3. It brings the story to life with details about the major events (secondary support).
4. It presents the events in a clear order, usually according to when they happened.

In the following paragraph, each number corresponds to one of the Basics of Good Narration.

**You Know This**

You often use narration:

- You tell a friend what you did or where you went over the weekend.
- You explain the plot of a movie you saw to people who haven't seen it.
- You say, "You won't believe what happened the other day." Then you tell the story.

1 Last night my husband saved my life. We were sitting out on the porch with a couple of friends, enjoying the cool breeze of the evening. 2 While eating a piece of melon for dessert, I laughed at something my friend said, and suddenly the fruit stuck in my windpipe, entirely blocking any air. 3 I tried to swallow hard and dislodge it, but it didn't move. 3 When I tried taking a deep breath, I couldn't get one. 2 Fortunately, my husband, seated across the table from me, saw that something was wrong and asked me if I needed help. 2 Close to panic, I nodded yes. 3 My eyes were filled with tears, and I could hear the blood pounding in my ears. 3 I thought, briefly, *I could die*. 2 My husband ran in behind me, pulled me up, and placed his arms around me. My heart was really

*Events in chronological order*

**■ IDEA JOURNAL** Write about something that happened to you this week.

beating hard by this time, and I was panicky. **2** He jerked his fists firmly into my body, under my rib cage. **2** The melon flew out of my mouth. **2** I breathed in precious air and hugged my husband for a long time, half laughing, half crying. For a while, at least, I'll try to remember that I owe him my life and not get irritated when he forgets to do something.

You can use narration in many practical situations. Consider the following examples:

COLLEGE                  In a reading or English course, you are asked to tell, in your own words, the basic story of a piece of literature.

WORK                     Something goes wrong at work, and you are asked to explain to your boss — in writing — what happened.

EVERYDAY LIFE            In a letter of complaint about service you received, you need to tell what happened that upset you.

## PROFILE OF SUCCESS: Narration in the Real World

**Kelly Layland**
Registered Nurse

The following profile gives more insight into a work application of narration. In particular, it provides some information about a nurse, including the kinds of writing she does at work and, specifically, how she uses narration on the job. Following the profile is an example of narration Kelly has done at work.

**BACKGROUND:** In high school, I wasn't a good student. I had a lot of other things to do, like having fun. I'm a very social person; I loved my friends, and we had a great time. But when I decided I wanted to go to college, I had to pay the price. I had to take lots of noncredit courses to get my skills up to college level because I'd fooled around during high school. The noncredit English course I took was very beneficial to me. After I passed it, I took English 101 and felt prepared for it.

**COLLEGE(S)/DEGREES:** A.S., Monroe Community College; L.P.N., Isabella Graham Hart School of Nursing; R.N., Monroe Community College

**EMPLOYER:** Rochester General Hospital

**WRITING AT WORK:** I don't write long pieces at work, but I write every day, mostly patient notes, summaries, and reports. The accuracy of my writing affects patient treatment.

**HOW KELLY USES NARRATION:** Every day I write brief narratives that recount all that went on with the patient during the day: things that went wrong and things about his or her treatment that need to be changed.

**COMPUTER SKILLS:** Word processing and computer searches

**TEAMWORK ON THE JOB:** Health care is increasingly team-based. Team members have different responsibilities, all of which need to be coordinated, so clear communication — both oral and written — is essential. I work directly with a team that includes a secretary and a licensed practical nurse. Each of us performs a different but related service for the patient.

**A TYPICAL PROBLEM AT WORK:** Occasionally, something important (but not life threatening) will happen just as I'm about to go off shift, and I can't stay to deal with it. I have to carefully write down, in detail, what happened so that the next nurse will know what is going on and will take care of it.

**KELLY LAYLAND'S NARRATION**

The following paragraph is an example of the daily reports that Kelly Layland writes on each patient. The name of the patient has been changed.

■ **RESOURCES** For a discussion of how to use the profiles in Part Two, see *Practical Suggestions.*

Margaret Hoffman's condition, though still in need of close monitoring, is steadily improving. She started the day with a chest X-ray, which was clear. This is the biggest improvement in her condition. Throughout the day, the patient was on oxygen, but her cough is now productive, indicating a positive change in her level of congestion. By late this afternoon, she was no longer experiencing shortness of breath and wheezing. However, also by late afternoon, she had developed a raised red rash all over her upper back, which she reported was itchy and uncomfortable. I administered Benadryl to her, and she is now resting quietly. I will continue to monitor her condition.

1. Double-underline the **main point** of the narration.
2. Underline the **major events**.
3. What order of organization does Kelly use? *time order*

## Main Point in Narration

The explanations, examples, and practices in the next two sections will help you develop a good main point and support for your narration. As noted earlier, in narration the **main point** is what is important about the story—to you (and to your readers). To help you discover the main point for your own narration, complete the following sentence:

**What's important to me about the experience is . . .**

Doing so can help you avoid the "So what?" response from readers. Notice the difference between the following two opening sentences in a narration:

**IMPORTANCE NOT CLEAR**    My child plays soccer. [So what?]

**IMPORTANCE CLEAR**    Soccer takes up all of my child's free time.

Although writers usually reveal the main point either at the beginning or at the end of their narration, here we suggest that you start off with your main point and remind readers of that main point at the end of your paragraph or essay.

You can express your main point in a topic sentence (paragraph) or thesis statement (essay) that contains both your narrowed topic and your main point.

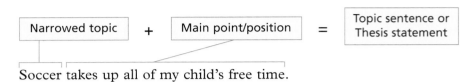

Soccer takes up all of my child's free time.

### PRACTICE 1    DECIDING ON A MAIN POINT

For each of the following topics, write what main point you might make in a narration. There is no one correct answer; you are practicing how to decide on a main point about a topic. Before writing your answer, you may need to make some notes about the topic.

**EXAMPLE:**

**TOPIC:** A fight I had with my sister

**MAIN POINT:** *learned it's better to stay cool*

1. **TOPIC:** A commute to work or school

   **MAIN POINT:** *Answers will vary.*

2. **TOPIC:** An embarrassing experience

   **MAIN POINT:** _____

3. **TOPIC:** A funny incident that you witnessed

   **MAIN POINT:** _____

4. **TOPIC:** A typical evening at home

   **MAIN POINT:** _____

5. **TOPIC:** A funny or frightening dream

   **MAIN POINT:** _____

## Support in Narration

■ **TIP** In an essay, the major events may form the topic sentences of paragraphs. The details supporting the major events then make up the body of these paragraphs.

In a narration, the **support** consists of the major events you include (primary support) and the details (secondary support) you give the reader about those events. Your support should demonstrate your main point—what's important to you about the story. Think of major events as the key steps or stages in the story and the details as examples or illustrations that elaborate on the major events, bringing them to life or indicating why they are important. For an example of how major events and details are used in narration, see the paragraph on pages 99–100.

The way you describe events creates a story with a certain point of view. For example, two people who witness or participate in the same series of events may give very different accounts of it because they either focused on different events or perceived those events differently. The stories Charlene and Daryl tell in the following two paragraphs reflect different points of view. Read these two accounts of the same experience.

### CHARLENE'S STORY

This morning I could have killed my husband. While I was running around yelling at the kids, trying to get them fed and off to school, he sat there reading the newspaper. When I finally sat down, he just kept on reading that newspaper, even though I needed to talk with him. After several attempts to get through to him, I finally barked out, "Daryl! I have a few things I need to say!" He looked up, smiled, got another cup of coffee, and said, "What?" But as I began talking, he resumed reading the paper. Does he live in another world?

■ **TIP** In writing a narration, you may use direct quotations (as this writer did) or indirect quotations. For more information on how to incorporate and punctuate quotations, see Chapter 18, pages 270–72.

### DARYL'S STORY

This morning my family enjoyed some "quality time" together. The children were all in the kitchen eating and talking with each other. After they left for school, my wife and I were able to sit and share some quiet time at the table. We chatted about various things while drinking coffee and looking at the newspaper. It really started the day out right.

As you can see, the events are the same, but the stories aren't; they are told from two different points of view. Be careful to describe events in a way that will tell the story you want to tell.

■ **ESL** Ask students if they have seen certain events differently than other people because of language or cultural differences.

### Choosing Major Events

When you tell a story to a friend in person or on the phone, you have the luxury of including events that aren't essential to the story or of going back and filling in events that you've forgotten. When you are writing a narration, however, you need to make choices about which events to include, selecting only those that most clearly demonstrate your main point. If you find later that you've left out an important event, you can add it when you are revising.

■ **TEACHING TIP** Ask students to write a narrative joke they've heard—then examine the structure of one or two of these jokes.

### ■ PRACTICE 2   CHOOSING MAJOR EVENTS

This practice uses three items from Practice 1, where you wrote main points for topics. Using your main points from that practice, for each numbered item write three events that would help you make your main point. Remember, there is no one correct answer: What you want to do is think logically about three essential events that will demonstrate your main point to readers.

**EXAMPLE:**

**TOPIC:** A fight I had with my sister

**MAIN POINT:** *learned it's better to stay cool*

**EVENTS:** *We disagreed about who was going to have the family party.*

*She made me so mad I started yelling at her, and I got nasty.*

*I hung up on her, and now we're not talking.*

1. **TOPIC:** A commute to work or school

   **MAIN POINT:** *Answers will vary.*

   **EVENTS:** *Answers will vary.*

2. **TOPIC:** An embarrassing experience

   **MAIN POINT:** _____

   **EVENTS:** _____

3. **TOPIC:** A typical evening at home

   **MAIN POINT:** _____

   **EVENTS:** _____

## Giving Details about the Events

When you write a narration, look for examples and details that will make each event more realistic and specific. Remember that you want your readers to share your point of view and see the same message in the story that you do. One way to give readers more information is to add at least one or two details that explain each event.

■ **PRACTICE 3   GIVING DETAILS ABOUT THE EVENTS**

Choose two of the items in Practice 1 and write a topic sentence or thesis statement for each. Then write the major events in the spaces provided. (These are the same events you wrote for Practice 2.) Give a detail about each event.

**EXAMPLE:**

**TOPIC SENTENCE:** *After a horrible fight with my sister, I learned the value of*

*staying cool.*

**EVENT:** *We disagreed about who was going to have the family party.*

   **DETAIL:** *Even though we both work, she said she was too busy and that I*

*would have to do it.*

**EVENT:** *She made me so mad I started yelling at her, and I got nasty.*

**DETAIL:** *I brought up times in the past when she'd tried to pawn responsibilities off on me and told her I was sick of being the one who did everything.*

**EVENT:** *I hung up on her, and now we're not talking.*

**DETAIL:** *I feel bad, and I know I'll have to call her sooner or later because she is my sister. I do love her even though she's a pain sometimes.*

1. **TOPIC SENTENCE:** *Answers will vary.*

   **EVENT:** *Answers will vary.*

   **DETAIL:** *Answers will vary.*

   **EVENT:** _____

   **DETAIL:** _____

   **EVENT:** _____

   **DETAIL:** _____

2. **TOPIC SENTENCE:** _____

   **EVENT:** _____

   **DETAIL:** _____

   **EVENT:** _____

   **DETAIL:** _____

   **EVENT:** _____

   **DETAIL:** _____

**NOTE:** Another "basic" of good narration (see p. 99) is that events are presented in a clear order, usually according to when they happened (time order, or chronological order). For more details on using time order, see Chapter 5, pages 56–57.

## Read and Analyze Narration

Reading examples of narration and analyzing their structure will help you understand what good narration looks like before you write your own. The first example is paragraph-length, and the second is essay-length. Your instructor may ask you to read and answer the questions for one or both of these.

■ **READING SELECTIONS**
For further examples of and activities for narration, see Chapter 40.

## Narration: Paragraph

At age fourteen, a gawky and shy James Earl Jones was transformed. Transplanted from rural Mississippi, he felt out of place at Dickson High School in Brethren, Michigan. His stutter was so pronounced that he never spoke out in class. Understandably, he often felt alone. Jones found refuge in writing poetry. One day in class, he wrote a poem and submitted it to his English teacher. The teacher, surprised at how good it was, wondered whether Jones had copied it and challenged Jones, "The best way for you to prove that you wrote this poem yourself is for you to recite it by heart to the class." Jones then walked to the front of the room, thinking it would be better to be laughed at for stuttering than to be disgraced. He was scared, but he opened his mouth and began to speak. To the astonishment of everyone in the class, the words flowed smoothly. The stutter disappeared. He had stumbled upon what speech therapists would one day discover: that the written page can be a stutterer's salvation. He went on to become a high school public-speaking champion and won a scholarship to the University of Michigan. Today, fifty years later, the voice of James Earl Jones is among the most familiar in the world.

—Wallace Terry, "When His Sound Was Silenced"

1. The **topic sentence** of a narration paragraph usually includes the topic and the **main point** the writer wants to make about it.

My first day at my new job was nearly a disaster.

Double-underline the **topic sentence** of the previous paragraph.

2. What is important about the story?  *A fourteen-year-old boy with a stutter became a man with one of the most recognizable voices in the world.*

3. The **support** in a narration paragraph is a series of events and details about these events. The events tell readers what happened. Underline the **major events** in the paragraph.

4. Narration usually uses **time order** to organize the events and time **transitions** to guide readers from one step to the next.

**COMMON TIME TRANSITIONS**

| | | | |
|---|---|---|---|
| after | eventually | meanwhile | soon |
| as | finally | next | then |
| at last | first | now | today |
| before | last | second | when |
| during | later | since | while |

Circle the (transitions) the writer used in the sample paragraph.

5. Does the paragraph have the Four Basics of Good Narration (see p. 99)? Why or why not?

   *Yes. Specific answers will vary, but students should be able to give examples of the*

   *Four Basics.*

## Narration: Essay

Dale Hill, a student at Kaskaskia College in Illinois, wrote the following essay, which received an honorable mention in the 2002 Paul Simon Student Essay Contest sponsored by the Illinois Community College Trustees Association.

■ **TEACHING TIP** You might check to see if there is any contest in your community, county, or state similar to the one Hill entered; you could then work with students who are interested in entering.

### How Community College Has Changed My Life

*Dale Hill*

Grandpa was a sharecropper. With only a second-grade education, he planted his seeds and raised his family of seven sons and three daughters. My father, third eldest of the sons, broke new ground when he became the first person ever in the family to graduate from high school. Although Dad was very bright, it never occurred to him to go on to college. He and Grandpa shared the attitude that college was only for rich people and that you cannot change a sow's ear into a silk purse. Dad was expected to work to help support his younger brothers and sisters, and that is what he did. And that is what I did, too, for a long while. (Now, however, my attitude has changed, and I have learned that there are other ways to seed future growth. The change did not happen overnight.

(While) I was growing up in the same small farming town and attending Dad's same high school, people still thought that college was only for the rich. College was my dream deferred. Like my father before me, I was expected to work after graduation to help support the family, and like my father before me, that is what I did. What followed was twenty wasted and fruitless years of unfulfilling factory and retail jobs. Only last year, faced with the prospect of starting over again with a son of my own to set an example for, did I return to my dream.

The prospect of attending college, leaving old attitudes and beliefs behind, was daunting. The world I knew was greatly different from the academic world, and I was unsure that I would fit in. I was twenty years older than traditional students and was not confident that I could compete. Going to a university full-time would require a commitment of time and money that would cause hardship for my family. My wife suggested that I enroll at my local community college first, which I did.

I discovered that community college acts as the perfect stepping stone between the mundane life that I wished to leave behind and the new one I wished to begin. The proximity, affordability, and flexibility offered by my local community college lessen the sacrifices my family is called upon to make. Community college allows me to test the waters of an academic environment without fear of plunging in over my head. It encourages me to challenge myself and build my confidence even as it expands my horizons. My community college nourishes me and helps me to grow.

I have discovered that my father's and grandfather's attitudes about college were right. College education *is* for the rich: the rich in mind and spirit, the rich in wonder and curiosity. How has community college changed my life? It has shown me how rich I am. I am planting a new seed for my family now, a crop that will bear fruit for generations to come.

1. The thesis statement of a narration essay usually includes the **topic** and the **main point** the writer wants to make about it.

My first date with Pat was full of surprises.

Double-underline the **thesis statement** of the previous essay.

2.  The **support** in a narration essay is the series of events (and details about these events) that tell readers the story. These major events should also be topic sentences for paragraphs in the body of the essay. Underline the **topic sentences** in each paragraph.

3.  Writers of narration usually use **time order** to organize their events and time transitions to guide readers from one step to the next. Writers may also use **transitional sentences** to move from one paragraph to another. (For a list of common time transitions, see p. 107.)
     Circle the (transitions) the writer used in the sample essay.

4.  Double-underline the **sentence in the last paragraph** that summarizes Dale's main point for the reader.

5.  Does the essay have the Four Basics of Good Narration (see p. 99)? Why or why not?

    *Yes. Specific answers will vary, but students should be able to give examples of*

    *the Four Basics.*

## Write Your Own Narration

In this section you will write your own narration paragraph or essay based on your (or your instructor's) choice among three assignments on pages 112–13.
    To complete your narration, follow this sequence:

■ **TIP** Look back at your idea-journal entry (p. 99) for ideas.

1.  Review the Four Basics of Good Narration (p. 99).
2.  Choose your assignment (see pp. 112–13).
3.  Read the Critical Thinking box on page 113.
4.  If you are asked to complete Assignment 3, read Using Problem Solving and Teamwork in Writing, below.
5.  Write your narration using the Checklist: How to Write Narration on pages 114–15.

### Using Problem Solving and Teamwork in Writing

Writing in the Real World/Solving a Problem (Writing Assignment 3 in Chapters 8–16) offers you the opportunity to solve real-world problems by working alone or as a part of a team. Your instructor will probably decide whether you will do these assignments independently or in groups.
    Problem solving and teamwork are important in today's workplace as well as in your college courses and in everyday life, so this is great real-world practice. The former students whose stories are highlighted in the Profiles of Success in Chapters 8–16 all emphasize the importance of teamwork and give examples of how they use teamwork in their jobs.

(continued)

This section will explain both what skills are and how to use them effectively.

### Problem Solving

Problem solving is the process of identifying a problem and figuring out a reasonable solution.

Problems range from minor inconveniences like finding a rip in the last clean shirt you have when you're running late to more serious problems such as being laid off from your job. While such problems disrupt our lives, they also give us opportunities to tackle difficult situations with confidence.

Too often people are paralyzed by problems because they don't have strategies for attacking them. However, backing away from a problem rarely helps solve it. When you know how to approach a challenging situation, you are better able to take charge of your life.

Problem solving consists of five basic steps, which can be used effectively by both individuals and groups of people.

### The Problem-Solving Process

**Understand the problem.** You should be able to say or write it in a brief statement or question.

**EXAMPLE:**

Your ten-year-old car needs a new transmission, which will cost at least $750. Do you keep the car or buy a new one?

**Identify people or information that can help you solve the problem (resources).**

**EXAMPLES:**

- Your mechanic
- Friends who have had similar car problems
- Car advice from print or Web sources

**List the possible solutions.**

**EXAMPLES:**

- Pay for the transmission repair.
- Buy a new car.

---

**Evaluate the possible solutions.**

1. Identify the steps each solution would require.

2. List possible obstacles for each solution (like money or time constraints).

3. List the advantages and disadvantages of the solutions.

**EXAMPLES** (considering only advantages and disadvantages):

- Pay for the transmission repair.

  **Advantage:** This would be cheaper than buying a new car.

  **Disadvantage:** The car may not last much longer, even with the new transmission.

- Buy a new car.

  **Advantage:** You'll have a reliable car.

  **Disadvantage:** This option is much more expensive.

---

**Choose the most reasonable solution,** one that is realistic—the simpler the better. Be able to give reasons for your choice.

**Solution:** Pay for the transmission repair.

**Reasons:** You do not have money for a new car, and you don't want to assume more debt. Opinions from two mechanics indicate that your car should run for three to five more years with the new transmission. At that point, you'll be in a better position to buy a new car.

---

## Teamwork

Teamwork is working with others to achieve a common goal. Working with others to solve a problem has many benefits: more possible solutions, more people to share the work, more ideas and perspectives. But effective teamwork involves more than simply meeting with people: You need to understand and apply good teamwork skills. For example, sports teams don't win merely because the individual players are talented; they win because the individual players pool their individual talents into a co-ordinated whole. Each player on the team works hard, but each player also supports and cooperates with other players. Players may also discuss strategies together to help ensure the team's success. The same is true of teamwork in other arenas as well.

Following are some basics to keep in mind when you are part of a team.

(continued)

**BASICS OF EFFECTIVE TEAMWORK**

- The team establishes ground rules that ensure each person on the team can contribute.
- Members listen to each other and respect different points of view.
- Although one person may function as team leader, all individuals play an equal role and are equally appreciated.
- Members recognize that they must depend on one another.
- All members contribute and feel responsible for their own work because it affects the outcomes of the team's efforts.

■ **TEACHING TIP** Suggest to students that they make journal entries on some of the topics that they don't write about for this assignment.

■ **TIP** If you use the Writing Guide Software with this book, you'll find step-by-step guidance for writing narration paragraphs and essays.

■ **ASSIGNMENT 1**  **WRITING ABOUT COLLEGE, WORK, AND EVERYDAY LIFE**

Write a narration on one of the following topics.

**COLLEGE**

| PARAGRAPH | ESSAY |
|---|---|
| • A run-in you had with someone in authority<br>• A project, assignment, or activity that was fun | • How a teacher made a difference<br>• Your most challenging college experience |

**WORK**

| PARAGRAPH | ESSAY |
|---|---|
| • A funny work story<br>• A conflict at work<br>• A work achievement you are proud of | • A work day that you'd rather forget<br>• A work achievement you are proud of<br>• Your first day at your first (or most recent) job |

**EVERYDAY LIFE**

| PARAGRAPH | ESSAY |
|---|---|
| • A childhood memory<br>• A mistake you made that helped you learn a lesson | • A day when everything went right (or wrong)<br>• Your biography<br>• An experience that triggered a strong emotion in you: happiness, sadness, relief, fear, regret, nervousness |

■ **ASSIGNMENT 2**  **WRITING ABOUT IMAGES**

Look carefully at the photograph at the top of page 113. In a paragraph or essay, either tell the story of what might have happened to bring the couple to this point or tell a story about a time when you felt the same way as one of the people in this photograph.

■ ASSIGNMENT 3  **WRITING IN THE REAL WORLD/SOLVING A PROBLEM**

**PROBLEM:**  You are the supervisor of a small office. You come back from your lunch break to hear arguing coming from the conference room. One employee (whose voice you recognize) is yelling threats at another, and you are worried that the argument will become violent. However, just as you enter the room, the argument stops. The employee who had been threatening the other has stopped, and neither will admit there is a problem, even after you have asked pointed questions. What do you do?

**ASSIGNMENT:** Write a narration (paragraph or essay) of the incident for your boss, adding details and examples of your own to make the situation clear. Then, using the problem-solving steps on page 110, recommend a course of action to your boss at the end of the narration. You can do the problem solving in a small group or on your own.

■ **TEAMWORK** For more detailed guidance on group work, see *Practical Suggestions.*

Before writing in response to any of the previous assignments, read the Critical Thinking box that follows.

## CRITICAL THINKING: WRITING NARRATION

**FOCUS**
Think about your story and what you want your readers to know about it.

**ASK YOURSELF**
• What is important about this story?
• What major events do I need to tell about?
• What details will bring the story to life for my readers?

■ **TEACHING TIP** After students have chosen their topics, read these questions aloud and model the process.

**WRITE**
Using time order, write a narration that vividly recreates the story for your readers.

Use the checklist that follows to help you write your narration. Check off the steps as you complete them. If you need help completing a step, read the information in the right-hand column.

## CHECKLIST: HOW TO WRITE NARRATION

| STEPS IN NARRATION | HOW TO DO THE STEPS |
|---|---|
| **1.** Narrow and explore your topic (see Chapter 2). | ❑ Narrow the general topic to a specific experience.<br>❑ Jot down ideas about the story: what happened and why it's important. |
| **2.** Write a topic sentence (for a paragraph) or thesis statement (for an essay) that includes your main point about the story (see Chapter 3). | ❑ Decide what is most important about the story and what you want to say about it to your readers. How did it affect you and others? |
| **3.** Support your main point (see Chapter 4). | ❑ Use a prewriting technique (see Chapter 2) to recall what the major events were.<br>❑ Choose the most important events.<br>❑ Write specific, concrete details to describe each event. |
| **4.** Make a plan (see Chapter 5). | ❑ Arrange the major events in time order. |
| **5.** Write a draft (see Chapter 6). | **FOR A PARAGRAPH:**<br>❑ Write a paragraph using complete sentences, including your topic sentence, your major events, and details about those major events.<br>❑ Write a concluding sentence that reminds your readers of your main point and makes an observation based on what you have written.<br>❑ Write a title that previews your main point but doesn't repeat your topic sentence.<br><br>**FOR AN ESSAY:**<br>❑ Write topic sentences for each of the major events.<br>❑ Write paragraphs (with supporting details) for each of the major events.<br>❑ Consider using one of the introductory techniques described in Chapter 6 (pp. 71–73) for your introductory paragraph.<br>❑ Write a conclusion (see Chapter 6, pp. 73–75) that reminds your readers of your main point and makes an observation based on what you have written.<br>❑ Write a title that previews the main point but does not repeat your thesis statement. |

| STEPS IN NARRATION | HOW TO DO THE STEPS |
|---|---|
| **6.** Revise your draft, making at least four changes (see Chapter 7). | ❑ Get feedback from others if possible (see Chapter 7, pp. 81–82). <br> ❑ *Review for unity:* Ensure that major events help show, explain, or prove your main point and that there are no detours. <br> ❑ *Review for support:* Ensure that all major events are included, each supported with concrete, specific details. Add any details that occur to you that would help your readers understand the event. <br> ❑ *Review for coherence:* Add time transitions to move readers smoothly from one idea to the next. Consider repeating a key word. <br> ❑ Read your topic sentence (for a paragraph) or thesis statement (for an essay), as well as your conclusion, to make sure that they are as clear, confident, and definite as you can make them. |
| **7.** Edit your revised draft (see Parts Four through Seven). | ❑ Find and correct problems with grammar, spelling, word use, and punctuation. <br> ❑ Print out a clean copy. |
| **8.** Ask yourself: | ❑ Does my paper include the Four Basics of Good Narration? <br> ❑ Is this the best I can do? <br> ❑ Is the paper ready to be graded? |

# Chapter Review: Narration

1. Narration is writing that  *tells the story of an event or experience*  .

2. List the Four Basics of Good Narration.

   *It reveals something of importance to you.*

   *It includes all of the major events of the story.*

   *It brings the story to life with details about the major events.*

   *It presents the events in a clear order, usually according to when they happen.*

3. The topic sentence in a narration paragraph or the thesis statement in a narration essay usually includes what two things?

   *your narrowed topic*

   *your main point*

4. What type of organization do writers of narration usually use?

   *time order*

■ **RESOURCES** All chapters in Part Two have writing checklists, which have been reproduced in *Additional Resources.* Photocopy and distribute them if you want students to hand in the checklists with their assignments.

■ **RESOURCES** A blank diagram of a narration (big enough to write in) is in *Additional Resources.* You may want to copy it and give it to students to plan their writing.

5.  List five common transitions for this type of organization.

*Answers will vary.*

_____

_____

_____

_____

_____

■ **IDEA JOURNAL** Reread your idea-journal entry from page 99. Write another entry on the same topic, using what you have learned about narration.

## What Will You Use?

Give some examples of how you will use narration in your own life, either in your other courses or on the job.

# 9

# Illustration

## Writing That Gives Examples

## Understand What Illustration Is

**Illustration** is writing that uses examples to show, explain, or prove a point. Giving examples is the basis of all good writing and speaking: You make a statement, and then you give an example that shows (illustrates) what you mean.

### ■■ FOUR BASICS OF GOOD ILLUSTRATION

1. It makes a point.
2. It gives specific examples that show, explain, or prove the point.
3. It gives details to support these examples.
4. It uses enough examples to get the writer's point across.

In the following paragraph, each number corresponds to one of the Four Basics of Good Illustration. Notice that the writer also uses narration (see Chapter 8).

**1** Working full time while going to college requires good time management skills, and planning ahead is essential. **2** Because mornings are hectic around my house, I try to collect what I need for work and school the night before. **3** For example, before bedtime I make sure to put the books and papers I'll need the next day into my backpack. **2** At work, I always try to stay in control of my time. **3** I limit socializing and breaks, because if I don't leave by 5:05 P.M. I'll have a hard time finding a parking space, and I'll also miss the beginning of class. **2** The biggest time management challenge is finding time to do homework. **3** When I'm home, everyone in my family wants a piece of me, and it's really easy to

### You Know This

You use examples to illustrate your point in daily communication:

- You answer the question "Like what?"
- You tell a friend that she's been acting weird, and she asks, "How?" You remind her of something she did.

■ **IDEA JOURNAL** Give some examples of things that annoy you.

Enough examples to make the writer's point

**117**

respond to their requests and put off my work. Therefore, I try to set aside a specific time slot to do my school work, and to stay focused on it until it's done. Before I started school, I thought my life was pretty busy already. Now that I'm combining work, school, and family, time management is a must.

It is hard to explain anything without using examples, so you use illustration in almost every communication situation. Consider the following examples:

| | |
|---|---|
| COLLEGE | An exam question asks you to explain and give examples of a concept. |
| WORK | Your boss asks you to tell her what office furniture or equipment needs to be replaced and why. |
| EVERYDAY LIFE | You complain to your landlord that the building superintendent is not doing his job. The landlord asks for examples. |

## PROFILE OF SUCCESS: Illustration in the Real World

**Alan Whitehead**
Home Development
Company Vice President

The following profile gives more insight into a work application of illustration. In particular, it provides some information about a home development company vice president, including the kinds of writing he does at work and, specifically, how he uses illustration on the job. Following the profile is an example of illustration Alan has done at work.

**BACKGROUND:** I grew up in Maryville, Tennessee, and after graduating from high school worked in a foundry for six years. After my wife and I had our first child, I decided that I would like to be a better provider for them, so I enrolled in a local community college, where I developed computer-aided design skills. Upon graduation, I was offered a job using those skills at Richmond American Homes. Since then, I have risen steadily in the company.

**COLLEGE(S)/DEGREES:** A.A.S. in computer-aided design and drafting, Pellissippi State Technical College

**EMPLOYER:** Richmond American Homes

**WRITING AT WORK:** Memos listing and describing changes or additions to blueprints, detailed letters to architects about products in order to bid for design services, letters to developers or city-government officials requesting architectural approval, e-mail to employees and subcontractors

**HOW ALAN USES ILLUSTRATION:** In nearly every type of writing I do, I have to give examples to explain what is being done or needs to be done.

**COMPUTER SKILLS:** Word processing and computer-aided design programs

**TEAMWORK ON THE JOB:** In order to build homes, teamwork and communication within the architecture department are essential. A team within the department consists of a general manager, a project manager, an architect, and various draftspeople, all of whom work together on building homes to detailed specifications.

**A TYPICAL PROBLEM AT WORK:** Increasingly, municipalities are imposing their own architectural requirements for subdivisions, based on the town's vision of what it wants new houses to look like. The municipality will present the developer of a subdivision with definite architectural styles it will allow, and the developer must then come up with a plan that balances the municipality's requirements with those of buyers. This plan is then negotiated with the town.

**ALAN WHITEHEAD'S ILLUSTRATION**

Alan wrote the following memo to keep his coworkers in the company informed about a project he was working on.

To:    President, Richmond American Homes

        Vice President of Construction

        Vice President of Purchasing

Fr:    Alan Whitehead

Re:    Replacement plans, the "Aspen" (model 2180)

To improve ease of access, the following changes are being made to the Aspen plans, as I pointed out during our walk-through of the frame last Tuesday. Enlarge the master bedroom door to a pair of 2668 double-doors. The space to enlarge the door will be taken from the master closet. The kitchen island will shift 12 inches toward the family room, and the eating bar will become optional. The curved stairs have been increased in width to 4 feet, 6 inches (please note the radius change in the attached drawings). The revised drawings are now available for the subcontractors who will be affected by these changes. Please see the attached drawings to clarify the changes I have indicated above.

■ **RESOURCES** For a discussion of how to use the profiles in Part Two, see *Practical Suggestions.*

1. Double-underline the **main point** of the paragraph.
2. Number the **major examples** Alan provides.
3. Underline the **specific details**.

## Main Point in Illustration

The explanations, examples, and practices in the next two sections will help you develop a good main point and support for your illustration. In illustration, the **main point** is the message you want your readers to receive and understand, and it is often based on a set of examples you have in mind at the outset.

When you are assigned a general topic to illustrate, first narrow the topic (see Chapter 2). Then, to discover your main point, consider what is important about the topic to you and your readers. It can help to complete the following sentence:

**What I want readers to know about this topic is . . .**

■ **TEACHING TIP** It might help to tell students that with illustration, examples often come to mind before the main point does. For example, it's not uncommon in work situations for someone to notice several examples of a problem, and then to write an e-mail or memo summing up the problem and listing examples. That writing typically contains a subject line expressing the main point.

When you know what your main point is, you can then express it in a topic sentence (paragraph) or thesis statement (essay) that contains both your narrowed topic and your main point.

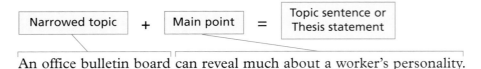

An office bulletin board can reveal much about a worker's personality.

### PRACTICE 1  MAKING A MAIN POINT

Each of the items in this practice is a narrowed topic. Think about each of them, and in the space provided, write a main point about each topic.

**EXAMPLE:** Early morning walks (or runs) *give me energy and a positive outlook*

1. A few moments alone *Answers will vary.*

2. A course I'm taking _____

3. The busiest time at work _____

4. Being a parent of a newborn baby _____

5. Working with other people _____

## Support in Illustration

In illustration, the **support** consists of examples and details that explain your main point to readers.

### Examples

The best way to generate good examples (if you don't already have some in mind) is to use one or more prewriting techniques, like those discussed in Chapter 2. First, write down all of the examples you can think of. Then, review your examples and choose the ones that will best communicate your point to your readers. As much as possible, choose examples that are different from one another and that illustrate your point in different ways.

■ **TEACHING TIP** Tell students that the number of examples they will need for each assignment will vary. For some topics, one extended example is enough; other topics call for more examples presented in less detail.

### PRACTICE 2  SUPPORTING YOUR MAIN POINT WITH SPECIFIC EXAMPLES

Read the following main points and jot down three examples you might use to support each one.

**EXAMPLE:** My boss is very frugal.

*makes us reuse envelopes*

*has a lock on the phone*

*gives us only a certain amount of paper each week*

1. My (friend, sister, brother, husband, wife — choose one) has some very admirable traits.

   *Answers will vary.*

2. My boss is fair (unfair). [Choose one or the other.]

3. This weekend is particularly busy.

4. This school is user-friendly (user-unfriendly). [Choose one.]

5. Computers make some tasks very easy.

## Details

Your illustration paragraph or essay will only be as good as the examples you provide, and your examples will only be as good as the details you use. Details make your examples stronger and/or more easily understandable for the reader. Once you have chosen examples, you need to look for details that describe or give more information about your examples.

■ **PRACTICE 3   GIVING DETAILS ABOUT THE EXAMPLES**

Choose two of the items from Practice 2, where you wrote specific examples to support main points. In the spaces provided, first copy the main point you are using and your examples from Practice 2. Then write a detail that further shows, explains, or proves what you mean.

**EXAMPLE:**  My boss is very cheap.

**EXAMPLE:** _makes us reuse envelopes_

   **DETAIL:** _have to tape them shut_

**EXAMPLE:** _has a lock on the phone_

   **DETAIL:** _have to find him and get him to unlock the phone for business calls_

**EXAMPLE:** _gives us only a certain amount of paper each week_

   **DETAIL:** _have to cut up into pieces to make sure we don't run out_

1. **MAIN POINT:** _Answers will vary._

   **EXAMPLE:** _Answers will vary._

      **DETAIL:** _Answers will vary._

   **EXAMPLE:** _____

      **DETAIL:** _____

   **EXAMPLE:** _____

      **DETAIL:** _____

2. **MAIN POINT:** _____

   **EXAMPLE:** _____

      **DETAIL:** _____

   **EXAMPLE:** _____

      **DETAIL:** _____

   **EXAMPLE:** _____

      **DETAIL:** _____

# Read and Analyze Illustration

■ **READING SELECTIONS**
For further examples of and activities for illustration, see Chapter 41.

Reading examples of illustration and analyzing their structure will help you understand what good illustration looks like before you write your own. The first example is paragraph-length, and the second is essay-length. Your instructor may ask you to read and answer the questions for one or both of these.

## Illustration: Paragraph

Although they don't consider it stealing, many people regularly take things from their companies. The most common items to disappear are pens and pencils that employees almost unconsciously stuff into their purses, knapsacks, or briefcases. Over time, they may accumulate quite a stash of them. Another big item is all kinds of paper: pads of lined paper, handy little notepads that can be used for shopping lists and phone messages, and file folders to organize home records. Yet another "innocent" theft is the long-distance personal phone call. Those calls cost the company in two ways: They use company time for personal business, and the company has to pay for the calls. Even though companies may have special discounted telephone rates, no call is free. Finally, one of the more significant ways people steal is by taking home samples of the products the company makes: food, clothing, supplies, and so on. Employees seem to think they are entitled to these products and even give them to friends. By doing so, they hurt the company by robbing it of a product it depends on for revenue. These examples may not seem like stealing, but the results are the same: extra costs to the company, which may result in lower pay raises.

1. The **topic sentence** of an illustration paragraph usually includes the **topic** and the **main point** the writer wants to make about it.

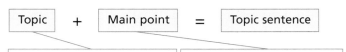

| Topic | + | Main point | = | Topic sentence |

The bus drivers in my city have no sense of courtesy.

Double-underline the **topic sentence** of the previous paragraph.

2. The **support** in an illustration paragraph consists of the examples writers provide to demonstrate their main point to their readers. Underline the **examples** that support the main point.

3. In illustration, **transitions** signal readers that they are moving from one example to another. Transitions help writers make such moves smoothly.

**COMMON ILLUSTRATION TRANSITIONS**

| | |
|---|---|
| also | for instance |
| another | for one thing |
| finally | in addition |
| for example | |

Circle the (transitions) in the example paragraph.

4. Does the paragraph have the Four Basics of Good Illustration (p. 117)? Why or why not? *Yes. Specific answers will vary, but students should be able to give examples of the Four Basics.*

## Illustration: Essay

### Scents

*Gabrielle Glaser*

People have been using fragrance to cure what ails them for thousands of years. Yet until recently, scientists have viewed aromatherapy as hocus-pocus. Now researchers are finding that some scents really can give you a psychological lift.

Some scents seem to have the ability to boost one's confidence. In a recent study, the pungent aroma of peppermint helped college athletes perform better with less effort, or at least it made them *feel* like superstars. In fact, according to measurements such as heart rate and blood pressure, the athletes got just as much benefit from the scent of jasmine and a stinky chemical called dimethyl sulfite. But in sports, believing you have a mental edge can translate into the real thing—and that's all that matters, right?

(Other scents have the effect of calming one down). When you're anxious, sniff something that you associate with a more relaxed time in your life, suggests Will A. Wiener, Ph.D., a psychologist and director of the Institute for Performance Enhancement in Manhattan. This strategy has helped one of Wiener's clients, a professional basketball player who gets petrified at the free-throw line. Just before he shoots a basket, the player buries his nose in a handkerchief scented with a loved one's favorite cologne. The smell allows him to block out the jeering crowd and concentrate.

Still other scents appear to improve one's focus. Researchers in Miami found that adults who sniffed lavender before and after tackling simple math problems worked faster, felt more relaxed, and made fewer mistakes. The fragrant herb can also improve your nights: In a small study, a British doctor found that lavender helped elderly insomniacs fall asleep sooner—and slumber longer—than sedatives did.

Researchers continue to study the effects of other herbs on people's moods. Because herbs are natural substances, they are less expensive to produce, and do not require Federal Department of Agriculture (FDA) approval. The old saying, "Take time to stop and smell the roses" may, after all, be good advice for us all.

—From *Health* magazine, July/August, 2001

1.  The **thesis statement** of an illustration essay usually includes the **topic** and the **main point** the writer wants to make about it.

This year, the city council has passed four unpopular regulations.

2.  Double-underline the **thesis statement** of the previous essay.

3.  The **support** in an illustration essay consists of specific examples that back up the main point. Each major example of the main point should be the topic sentence of a paragraph in the body of the essay. Underline the **topic sentences/major examples** in the essay.

4.  In illustration, transitions signal readers that they are moving from one example to another. Transitions help writers make such moves smoothly. Transitional sentences are often used to move from one paragraph to another. (For a list of common illustration transitions, see p. 124.)

    Circle the **transitional sentences** in the example essay.

5.  Double-underline **sentence in the concluding paragraph** that relates back to the introduction and the main impression.

6.  Does the essay have the Four Basics of Good Illustration (p. 117)? Why or why not?

    *Yes. Specific answers will vary, but students should be able to give examples of*

    *the Four Basics.*

# Write Your Own Illustration

■ **TIP** Look back at your idea-journal entry (p. 117) for ideas.

In this section, you will write your own illustration paragraph or essay based on your (or your instructor's) choice among three assignments.

To complete your illustration, follow this sequence:

1. Review the Four Basics of Good Illustration (p. 117).
2. Choose your assignment.
3. Read the Critical Thinking box on page 127.
4. If you are asked to complete Assignment 3, read Using Problem Solving and Teamwork in Writing (Chapter 8, pp. 109–11).
5. Write your illustration using the Checklist: How to Write Illustration (pp. 128–29).

### ASSIGNMENT 1  WRITING ABOUT COLLEGE, WORK, AND EVERYDAY LIFE

■ **TIP** If you use the Writing Guide Software with this book, you'll find step-by-step guidance for writing illustration paragraphs and essays.

Write an illustration on one of the following topics.

**COLLEGE**

| PARAGRAPH | ESSAY |
| --- | --- |
| • Your goals for taking this course | • Obstacles to coming to college |
| • Things to consider before registering for a course | • Today's students |

**WORK**

| PARAGRAPH | ESSAY |
| --- | --- |
| • Skills you have | • Jobs you've had |
| • Information to include on a résumé | • Odd things about your job or the place you work |

**EVERYDAY LIFE**

| PARAGRAPH | ESSAY |
| --- | --- |
| • Stresses in your life | • Stresses in your life |
| • Pet peeves, annoying things | • Pet peeves, annoying things |

■ **TEACHING TIP** Suggest to students that they make journal entries on some of the topics that they don't write about for this assignment.

### ASSIGNMENT 2  WRITING ABOUT IMAGES

Write a paragraph or essay about what the drawing at the top of page 127 illustrates. Think not just about the individual gestures, but also about what the illustration as a whole says about the meaning of gestures. Alternatively, you might want to consider why graphic illustrations, not words, are used in this case. Try to think of other things that you might illustrate with pictures instead of words. What particular features would you include in such pictures?

# The Olympic don'ts of gestures

Olympic volunteers who will be working with international visitors are being trained to be careful what they say or what they gesture. Here's what gestures mean in other countries:

**OK sign**
**France:** you're a zero; **Japan:** please give me coins; **Brazil:** an obscene gesture; **Mediterranean countries:** an obscene gesture

**Thumbs-up**
**Australia:** up yours; **Germany:** the number one; **Japan:** the number five; **Saudi Arabia:** I'm winning; **Ghana:** an insult; **Malaysia:** the thumb is used to point rather than the finger

**Thumbs-down**
**Most countries:** something is wrong or bad

**Thumb and forefinger**
**Most countries:** money; **France:** something is perfect; **Mediterranean:** a vulgar gesture

**Open palm**
**Greece:** an insult dating to ancient times; **West Africa:** You have five fathers, an insult akin to calling someone a bastard

Source: Atlanta Committee for the Olympic Games

By Sam Ward, USA TODAY

This guide to the cultural meaning of gestures was published for volunteers working with international visitors during the 1996 Olympic games.

---

■ **ASSIGNMENT 3    WRITING IN THE REAL WORLD/SOLVING A PROBLEM**

**PROBLEM:** Your college is increasing its tuition by $500 next year, and you can't afford to continue in your program. Going to college has been hard, but you've done pretty well so far, and you'd like to get a degree. Rather than dropping out or hoping that tuition costs will go down in the future, what options do you have?

**ASSIGNMENT:** In a small group or on your own, use the problem-solving steps on p. 110 to come up with options you might pursue to continue in college. Write a paragraph or essay that uses illustration to give examples of those options.

■ **TEAMWORK** For more detailed guidance on group work, see *Practical Suggestions.*

Before writing, read the Critical Thinking box that follows.

## CRITICAL THINKING: WRITING ILLUSTRATION

**FOCUS**
Think about the point you want to make about your topic.

■ **TEACHING TIP** Walk students through the Critical Thinking guide, explaining the importance of asking and answering the questions.

**ASK YOURSELF**
• How much will my readers already know about this topic?
• What are some examples I've experienced myself?
• What kinds of examples will my readers relate to?
• What specific details will help my readers see or understand what I mean?

**WRITE**
Using specific, detailed examples, write your illustration.

Use the checklist that follows to help you write your illustration. Check off the steps as you complete them. If you need help completing a step, read the information in the right-hand column.

## CHECKLIST: HOW TO WRITE ILLUSTRATION

| STEPS IN ILLUSTRATION | HOW TO DO THE STEPS |
|---|---|
| **1.** Narrow and explore your topic (see Chapter 2). | ❑ Narrow the general topic to a more specific one that you are interested in.<br>❑ Jot down some ideas about the narrowed topic and why it's important. |
| **2.** Write a topic sentence (for a paragraph) or a thesis statement (for an essay) that includes your narrowed topic and the main point you want to make about it (see Chapter 3). | ❑ Decide what is important about the topic. What do you want readers to know about your topic, and how will you show that? What do you want them to understand? |
| **3.** Support your main point (see Chapter 4). | ❑ Use a prewriting technique (see Chapter 2) to find supporting examples that will show, explain, or prove your main point.<br>❑ Select specific examples.<br>❑ Add details to help your readers understand your examples. |
| **4.** Make a plan (see Chapter 5). | ❑ Arrange the examples in the order you want to present them to your readers. |
| **5.** Write a draft (see Chapter 6). | **FOR A PARAGRAPH:**<br>❑ Write a paragraph using complete sentences, including your topic sentence, supporting examples, and details about those examples.<br>❑ Write a concluding sentence that reminds your readers of your main point and makes an observation based on what you have written.<br>❑ Write a title that previews your main point but doesn't repeat your topic sentence.<br><br>**FOR AN ESSAY:**<br>❑ Write topic sentences for each of the primary examples.<br>❑ Write paragraphs (with supporting details) for each of the primary examples.<br>❑ Consider using one of the introductory techniques described in Chapter 6 (pp. 71–73) for your introductory paragraph.<br>❑ Write a conclusion (see Chapter 6, pp. 73–75) that reminds your readers of your main point and makes an observation about it based on the examples you have provided. |

| STEPS IN NARRATION | HOW TO DO THE STEPS |
|---|---|
| | ❏ Write a title that previews the main point but does not repeat your thesis statement. |
| **6.** Revise your draft, making at least four changes (see Chapter 7). | ❏ Get feedback from others if possible (see Chapter 7, pp. 81–82). <br> ❏ *Review for unity:* Ensure that major examples help show, explain, or prove your main point and that there are no detours. <br> ❏ *Review for support:* Ensure that all major examples are supported with concrete, specific details. Add any other details that occur to you as you read your draft. <br> ❏ *Review for coherence:* Add transitions to move readers smoothly from one idea to the next. Consider repeating a key word. <br> ❏ Read your topic sentence (for a paragraph) or your thesis statement (for an essay), as well as your conclusion, to make sure that they are as clear, confident, and definite as you can make them. |
| **7.** Edit your revised draft (see Parts Four through Seven). | ❏ Find and correct problems with grammar, spelling, word use, and punctuation. <br> ❏ Print out a clean copy. |
| **8.** Ask yourself: | ❏ Does my paper include the Four Basics of Good Illustration (see p. 117)? <br> ❏ Is this the best I can do? <br> ❏ Is the paper ready to be graded? |

# Chapter Review: Illustration

1. Illustration is writing that  *uses examples to show, explain, or prove a point.*

2. What are the Four Basics of Good Illustration?

   *It makes a point.*

   *It gives specific examples that show, explain, or prove the point.*

   *It gives details to support these examples.*

   *It uses enough examples to get the writer's point across.*

## What Will You Use?

List some advice from this chapter that you will use in the future, either in other courses or in your job.

■ **RESOURCES** All chapters in Part Two have writing checklists, which are also reproduced in *Additional Resources.* You can photocopy and distribute them if you want students to hand in the checklists with their assignments.

■ **RESOURCES** A blank diagram of an illustration (big enough to write in) is in *Additional Resources.* You may want to copy it and give it to students to plan their writing.

■ **IDEA JOURNAL** Reread your idea-journal entry from p. 117. Write another entry on the same topic, using what you have learned about illustration.

# 10

# Description

*Writing That Creates Pictures in Words*

## You Know This

You use description every day:

- You describe what someone looks like.
- You describe an item you want to buy.
- You describe a place you visited to a friend.

■ **IDEA JOURNAL** Describe what you are wearing.

Examples and details bring the subject to life.

## Understand What Description Is

**Description** is writing that creates a clear and vivid impression of the topic. Description translates your experience of a person, place, or thing into words, often by appealing to the physical senses: sight, hearing, smell, taste, and touch.

### ■■ FOUR BASICS OF GOOD DESCRIPTION

1. It creates a main impression—an overall effect, feeling, or image—about the topic.
2. It uses specific examples to support the main impression.
3. It supports those examples with details that appeal to the five senses: sight, hearing, smell, taste, and touch.
4. It brings a person, place, or physical object to life for the reader.

In the following paragraph, each number corresponds to one of the Four Basics of Good Description.

1 A tour of Robinson Hall, a historic home in an early stage of renovation, feels like entering a scene out of a horror movie. 2 Just inside the arched entrance is a small foyer with a stairwell set in the corner. 3 The paint is peeling, some of the floorboards are missing, and there is trash on the floor. 3 With many of the windows broken, the cold, damp air from outside comes right in. To the left is a door that leads to the front room, or living room. 2 From here, one can see through a wide doorway into the dining room and then into the kitchen, which is rec-

130

ognizable only by the **3** old farm sink, knocked onto the floor. **2** To the left of the kitchen are two small rooms, one of which will become a bathroom. **2** The entire floor on the first level looks as if it is about to fall out of the house. But the restorer, John Carroll, is enthusiastic about the prospects for the renovation. While he admits the restoration will take a long time, he has already made some headway with the shell, which was filled with knee-deep debris when he first saw it. He hopes that Robinson Hall will be transformed within a year from a scary spectacle to an elegant historic building.

—Sophie Fleck

Being able to describe something or someone accurately and in detail is important in many situations. Consider the following examples:

| | |
|---|---|
| COLLEGE | On a nursing test, you describe the symptoms you observed in a patient. |
| WORK | You write a memo to your boss describing how the office could be arranged for increased efficiency. |
| EVERYDAY LIFE | You have to describe something you lost to the lost-and-found clerk at a department store. |

## PROFILE OF SUCCESS: Description in the Real World

The following profile gives more insight into a work application of description. In particular, it provides some information about the chief of police in a small town, including the kinds of writing she does at work and, specifically, how she uses description on the job. Following the profile is an example of description Celia has done at work.

**BACKGROUND:** When I graduated from high school, I wasn't particularly interested in academics. I took some courses at a community college, then got the travel bug and dropped out. After traveling, being a tennis bum, and trying several different colleges, I returned home. The police chief in town was a friend of the family's and encouraged me to think about law enforcement. I entered that field and have been there since.

**COLLEGE(S)/DEGREES:** Greenfield Community College, Mt. Wachusett Community College, Fort Lauderdale Community College

**EMPLOYER:** Town of Bolton, Massachusetts

**WRITING AT WORK:** As chief of police, I do many kinds of writing: policies and procedures for the officers to follow; responses to attorneys' requests for information; letters, reports, and budgets; interviews with witnesses; statements from victims and perpetrators; accident reports. In all of the writing I do, detail, clarity, and precision are essential. I have to choose my words carefully to avoid any confusion or misunderstanding.

Celia Hyde
Chief of Police

■ **RESOURCES** For a discussion of how to use the profiles in Part Two, see *Practical Suggestions*.

**HOW CELIA USES DESCRIPTION:** When I am called to a crime scene, I have to write a report that describes precisely and in detail what the scene looks like.

**COMPUTER SKILLS:** Word processing, spreadsheets, police department software, photo imaging

**TEAMWORK ON THE JOB:** Police officers always work as a team. Each officer has a partner and they support each other in every action. We also work with other town boards, such as the Board of Selectmen and the schools, to coordinate safety issues and public education. I also consult with the town counsel for advice on legal issues.

**A TYPICAL PROBLEM AT WORK:** When officers disagree either with each other or with a policy, they come to me for clarification. I have to resolve internal disputes, often after consulting town counsel. My explanations must be detailed and given in writing.

**CELIA HYDE'S DESCRIPTION**

The following report is one example of the descriptive reports Celia Hyde writes every day. The name of the homeowner has been changed.

> **Report, Breaking and Entering scene**
>
> **Response to burglar alarm, November 15, 2003, 17:00 hours**
>
> The house at 123 Main Street is situated off the road with a long, narrow driveway and no visible neighbors. The dense fir trees along the drive block natural light, though it was almost dusk and getting dark. There was snow on the driveway from a recent passing snow squall. I observed one set of fresh tire marks entering the driveway and a set of footprints exiting it.
>
> The homeowner, Mr. Smith, had been awakened by the sounds of smashing glass and the squeaking of the door as it opened. He felt a cold draft from the stairway and heard a soft shuffle of feet crossing the dining room. Smith descended the stairs to investigate and was met at the bottom by the intruder, who shoved him against the wall and ran out the front door.
>
> While awaiting backup, I obtained a description of the perpetrator from Mr. Smith. The subject was a white male, approximately 25–30 years of age and 5'9"–5'11" in height. He had jet-black hair of medium length, and it was worn slicked back from his forehead. He wore a salt-and-pepper, closely shaved beard and had a birthmark on his chin the size of a dime. The subject was wearing a black nylon jacket with some logo on it in large white letters, a blue plaid shirt, and blue denim jeans.

1. What is your **main impression** of the scene and of the intruder? *a dark,*
   *isolated crime scene/an ordinary-looking man*

2. Underline the **details** that support the main impression.

3. What senses do the details appeal to? *sight, hearing, touch*

4. How is the description organized? *time order*

## Main Point in Description

The explanations, examples, and practices in the next two sections will help you develop a good main point and support for your description. In description, the **main point** is the main impression—the overall effect, feeling, or image—you want to create for your readers. Every good description has a main impression—and the details in the description help to create it.

If you do not have a main impression about a topic you wish to describe, it usually helps to list ideas and details about it, thinking about the senses it appeals to (smell, hearing, sight, taste, and/or touch). You may also want to do some freewriting. To help you discover the main point for your description, complete the following sentence:

**What's most vivid and important to me about this topic is . . .**

■ **COMPUTER** Have students select a classmate or a well-known place on campus and, using the computer, have them write descriptive terms about the person or place (without naming their subject). Students should then move to another computer, read the other student's description, and try to guess who or what the subject is. If students can't guess, the original writer should add more description.

> ### PRACTICE 1   FINDING A MAIN IMPRESSION

For the following general topics, jot down four impressions that appeal to you, and circle the one you would use as a main impression. Base your choice on what is most interesting, vivid, and important to you.

**EXAMPLE:**
**TOPIC:** A vandalized car
    **IMPRESSIONS:** *wrecked, smashed, damaged*

1. **TOPIC:** A movie-theater lobby
    **IMPRESSIONS:** *Answers will vary.*

2. **TOPIC:** A fireworks display
    **IMPRESSIONS:** _____

3. **TOPIC:** A pizza place
    **IMPRESSIONS:** _____

4. **TOPIC:** An old person
    **IMPRESSIONS:** _____

5. **TOPIC:** The room you're in

   **IMPRESSIONS:** _____

When you know what your main impression is, you can then express it in a topic sentence (paragraph) or thesis statement (essay) that contains both your narrowed topic and your main impression.

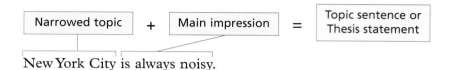

New York City is always noisy.

To be effective, your topic sentence or thesis statement should be specific. You can make it specific by adding details and using descriptive words that appeal to the senses. Here is a more specific version of the sentence in the preceding example.

   **MORE SPECIFIC:** Even in the middle of the night, New York City is alive with the noises of people at work and at play.

### PRACTICE 2   WRITING A STATEMENT OF YOUR MAIN IMPRESSION

Choose three of the items from Practice 1 to use in this practice. In the spaces below, write the topic and the main impression you chose. Then write a statement of your main impression. Finally, revise the sentence to make the main impression sharper and more specific.

   **EXAMPLE:**

   **TOPIC/MAIN IMPRESSION:** *A vandalized car/battered* _____

   **STATEMENT:** *The vandalized car on the side of the highway was battered.*

   **MORE SPECIFIC:** *The shell of a car on the side of the road was dented all over,*

   *apparently from a bat or club, and surrounded by broken glass.*

1. **TOPIC/MAIN IMPRESSION:** *Answers will vary.* _____

   **STATEMENT:** _____

   **MORE SPECIFIC:** _____

2. **TOPIC/MAIN IMPRESSION:** _____

   **STATEMENT:** _____

   **MORE SPECIFIC:** _____

3. **TOPIC/MAIN IMPRESSION:** _____

   **STATEMENT:** _____

   **MORE SPECIFIC:** _____

## Support in Description

In description **support** consists of specific details that appeal to one or more of the five senses: sight, hearing, smell, taste, and touch. Your description should show your readers what you mean, not just tell them. Sensory details can bring your description to life. Here are some qualities to consider as you develop sensory details to support a main impression.

■ **TEAMWORK** Put students in small groups, and give each group an object to describe using the questions in the text.

| SIGHT | SOUND | SMELL |
|---|---|---|
| Colors? | Loud/soft? | Sweet/sour? |
| Shapes? | Piercing/soothing? | Sharp/mild? |
| Sizes? | Continuous/off and on? | Good? (Like what?) |
| Patterns? | Pleasant/unpleasant? (How?) | Bad? (Rotten?) |
| Shiny/dull? | | New? (New what? Leather? Plastic?) |
| Does it look like anything else? | Does it sound like anything else? | Old? |
| | | Does it smell like anything else? |

| TASTE | TOUCH |
|---|---|
| Good? (What does "good" taste like?) | Hard/soft? |
| Bad? (What does "bad" taste like?) | Liquid/solid? |
| Bitter/sugary? Metallic? | Rough/smooth? |
| | Hot/cold? |
| Burning? Spicy? | Dry/oily? |
| Does it taste like anything else? | Textures? |
| | Does it feel like anything else? |

### PRACTICE 3   FINDING DETAILS TO SUPPORT A MAIN IMPRESSION

Read the statements below and write four sensory details you might use to support the main impression.

**EXAMPLE:**

Even at night, New York City echoes with noise.

a. *police and fire sirens* _____

b. *people on the street* _____

c. *sounds of music from clubs* _____

d. *car horns* _____

1. My favorite meal smells as good as it tastes.

   a. *Possible answers: sweetness of sweet potatoes*

   b. *sage in stuffing*

   c. *buttery roasting turkey*

   d. *cinnamon apple pie*

2. The new office building has a very contemporary look.

   a. *Possible answers: lots of glass*

   b. *concrete*

   c. *steel*

   d. *tall*

3. A classroom during an exam echoes with the "sounds of silence."

   a. *Possible answers: people coughing*

   b. *rustle of papers*

   c. *radiator hissing*

   d. *sounds of pens scratching paper*

4. The Elvis impersonator looked like Elvis's twin.

   a. *Possible answers: sequined jumpsuit*

   b. *ornate gold sunglasses*

   c. *dyed black hair and sideburns*

   d. *quivering upper lip*

5. The person sitting next to me has a terrible cold.

   a. *Possible answers: sneezing*

   b. *coughing*

   c. *face flushed with fever*

   d. *blowing nose*

## Read and Analyze Description

■ **READING SELECTIONS**
For further examples of and activities for description, see Chapter 42.

Reading examples of description and analyzing their structure will help you understand what good description looks like before you write your own. The first example is paragraph-length, and the second is essay-length. Your instructor may ask you to read and answer the questions for one or both of these.

## Description: Paragraph

### The Peach Tree
*Cathy Vittoria*

When I reminisce about my childhood, the fondest memories I have revolve around food. Our family often went on picnics to the beach. There at the water's edge, my father would struggle to light the charcoal in the gusty wind. My mother's anise-flavored bread was the perfect match for ham on Easter morning and the days that followed. On my birthday we always had gnocchi, fluffy pillows of pasta that melted in my mouth, tossed with a heavenly tomato sauce. In August we had peaches, not just any peaches, but the peaches from our own peach tree. I loved our peach tree; it produced the sweetest, most succulent peaches I've ever eaten. When I think about my past, that peach tree plays an integral part in my childhood memories.

—From Cathy Vittoria, "The Peach Tree," Diablo Valley
Community College Web site, (Brian McKinney, instructor)

1. The **topic sentence** of a description paragraph usually includes the topic and the **main impression** the writer wants to make about it.

Topic    +    Main impression    =    Topic sentence

My van has all the comforts of a studio apartment.

Double-underline the **topic sentence** of the previous paragraph.

2. The **support** in a description consists of the details that create the main impression. These details often appeal to the senses of sight, hearing, smell, taste, and touch. Underline the **details** in the sample paragraph that create the main impression.

3. Description often uses **time order** or **space order**. Some common time transitions are listed below. (For space transitions, see Chapter 7, p. 87.)

**COMMON TIME TRANSITIONS**

| | | | |
|---|---|---|---|
| after | eventually | meanwhile | soon |
| as | finally | next | then |
| at last | first | now | today |
| before | last | second | when |
| during | later | since | while |

Circle the (**time transitions**) in the sample paragraph.

4. Does the paragraph have the Four Basics of Good Description (p. 130)? Why or why not?

*Yes. Specific answers will vary, but students should be able to give examples of the*

*Four Basics.*

## Description: Essay

### The Peach Tree

*Cathy Vittoria*

Although it may seem an odd childhood memory, a peach tree was an important part of my childhood. The peach tree was special to my sisters and me. It was, in fact, the only tree in our small yard. We grew through the seasons with it. Every February the first (bits of pink) showed through the (tightly closed flower buds). By March it was (covered in pink,) like overgrown cotton candy. (In April) (little flecks of green) accented the (pink blossoms) and slowly pushed out the pink until a (fresh, vibrant green) blanketed the crown of the tree. During this transition, the lawn became a (carpet of pink). Then slowly the fruit came, growing from (little nubs like pumpkin seeds) to the (size of walnuts). In June, the tree dropped its excesses, and (green fruit, hard as golf balls), would bomb us as we played in the yard. After that, it was just a matter of waiting. Being children, we put the time to good use. We climbed and swung on the tree's branches. We played house and frontier fort in the tree. We were pirates, Tarzan, Jane, and George of the Jungle.

By mid-August the fragrance perfumed the air. The fruit, the (size of softballs), bent the branches. Not heeding our parents' advice, we would sneak a peach, unable to resist. We were usually greeted by a (tasteless, crunchy disappointment). One day, Mom and Dad would summon us to tell us it was time. We picked baskets full of peaches, more than we could eat. We stood on the lawn eating while leaning forward to keep the juice from dripping onto our clothing. The (juice still ran down our faces and arms onto everything). We were (sticky but satisfied). Mom would make the best peach pies, but my father's favorite dessert was peaches and red wine. We would have peaches on pancakes, peaches on ice cream, peaches on cereal, and peaches on peaches. After that, the canning began. Mom would peel, slice, and carefully cut away any of the bad parts of the peach before canning. The jars would be lined up on the kitchen counter under the open window, waiting to cool before being stored in the basement. Knowing that there would be peaches for us during the other eleven months of the year was always great comfort.

The peach tree declined in health as we grew up. Peach leaf curl was a chronic problem. Winter storms caused some damage; limbs cracked and broke off. Eventually, the old tree was producing only a few runt-sized fruit. One winter my parents cut down the tree. It left a scar on the lawn and a barren space in the yard. I hadn't thought much about that old tree for some time, even though it was the peach tree that planted the seed, so to speak, of my passion for gardening. The first fruit trees I planted in my own back yard were peaches. When I told my sisters that I was writing about the peach tree, they both smiled a familiar smile. For a moment, they were transported to another place and time. And I knew that it wasn't simply nostalgia; it was real. In the years that have followed, I have never found a peach as large, juicy, and luscious as the ones from our tree.

—Diablo Valley Community College Web site
(Brian McKinney, instructor)

1. The **thesis statement** in a description essay usually includes the **topic** and the **main impression** the writer wants to make about it.

The condition of my apartment was an assault on the eyes.

Double-underline the **thesis statement** of the previous essay.

2. Each main support point should be a topic sentence for a paragraph in the body of the essay. Underline each **topic sentence**.

3. The **support** in a description essay consists of the details that create the main impression. These details often appeal to the senses of sight,

hearing, smell, taste, and/or touch. Circle the (**details**) in the sample essay that help to create the main impression.

4. Description often uses **time order** or **space order**. (For space transitions, see Chapter 7, p. 87. For time transitions, see p. 137.)

Underline the **time transitions** and any **transitional sentences** in the sample essay.

5. Double-underline the **sentence in the concluding paragraph** that relates back to the introduction and the main impression.

6. Does the essay have the Four Basics of Good Description (p. 130)? Why or why not?

*Yes. Specific answers will vary, but students should be able to give examples of the*

*Four Basics.*

## Write Your Own Description

■ **TIP** Look back at your idea journal entry (p. 130) for ideas.

In this section, you will write your own description paragraph or essay based on your (or your instructor's) choice among three assignments.

To complete your description, follow this sequence:

1. Review the Four Basics of Good Description (p. 130).
2. Choose your assignment.
3. Read the Critical Thinking box on page 142.
4. If you are asked to complete Assignment 3, read Using Problem Solving and Teamwork in Writing (Chapter 8, pp. 109–11).
5. Write your description using the Checklist: How to Write Description (pp. 142–44).

### ASSIGNMENT 1   WRITING ABOUT COLLEGE, WORK, AND EVERYDAY LIFE

■ **TIP** If you use the Writing Guide Software with this book, you'll find step-by-step guidance for writing description paragraphs and essays.

Write a description on one of the topics.

**COLLEGE**

| PARAGRAPH | ESSAY |
| --- | --- |
| • A classroom just before the start of class | • The library |
| • Sounds in the cafeteria | • The cafeteria |
| • The entrance to the student center | • The scene outside the student center |

**WORK**

| PARAGRAPH | ESSAY |
|---|---|
| • The physical sensations you experience as you work<br>• A coworker or a boss<br>• Your own work space | • The sounds and smells of your workplace<br>• Your favorite (or least favorite) coworker<br>• The products your workplace produces |

■ **ESL** Have students describe a famous place or popular meal in their native countries.

**EVERYDAY LIFE**

| PARAGRAPH | ESSAY |
|---|---|
| • A favorite photograph<br>• A season<br>• Your favorite piece of clothing | • A busy department store<br>• Music you like or a concert you attended<br>• A favorite photograph |

■ **TEACHING TIP** Suggest to students that they make journal entries on some of the topics that they don't write about for this assignment.

■ **ASSIGNMENT 2  WRITING ABOUT IMAGES**

This picture is from a book that shows families' possessions in various places in the world. In either a paragraph or an essay, describe the photograph, including what certain possessions tell you about the particular family and their world.

■ **ASSIGNMENT 3   WRITING IN THE REAL WORLD/SOLVING A PROBLEM**

**PROBLEM:** You are the chief of police in a small town, with a small police force. For the most part, everyone gets along well, but occasionally there's a conflict that you must resolve. For instance, one of the junior officers on the force has recently come back from vacation with a neatly trimmed beard, and most people compliment him on it. However, one of the more senior officers comments that a beard is not appropriate for a police officer. The tension grows between the two officers, and people start taking sides. The current rules-and-regulations manual hasn't been revised for quite some time, and because the force is small and usually congenial, the dress code in the manual is brief, vague, and doesn't mention facial hair. You know that you now need to write a more specific code.

■ **TEAMWORK** For more detailed guidance on group work,
see *Practical Suggestions.*

**ASSIGNMENT:** In a small group or on your own, come up with specific rules that the dress code should include. (You may want to work on a dress code for high school students rather than for police officers.) Then write a paragraph or essay that describes the dress code very specifically. Make sure to use vivid and specific examples.

Before writing, read the Critical Thinking box that follows.

## CRITICAL THINKING: WRITING DESCRIPTION

### FOCUS

■ **TEACHING TIP** Walk students through the Critical
Thinking guide, explaining the
importance of asking and
answering the questions.

Think about what you want to describe and the overall impression you want to give your readers.

### ASK YOURSELF

- What is the main impression I want to create about this topic?
- What details will help my readers see my topic as I do? Which senses should I appeal to?
- How should I arrange these images?

### WRITE

■ **RESOURCES** All chapters in
Part Two have writing checklists, which are reproduced in
*Additional Resources.* You can
photocopy and distribute them
if you want students to hand in
the checklists with their assignments.

Using time or space order, write a description that brings your topic to life for your readers.

Use the checklist that follows to help you write your description. Check off the steps as you complete them. If you need help completing a step, read the information in the right-hand column.

## CHECKLIST: HOW TO WRITE DESCRIPTION

| STEPS IN DESCRIPTION | HOW TO DO THE STEPS |
| --- | --- |
| **1.** Narrow and explore your topic (see Chapter 2). | ❑ Jot down ideas about the topic, thinking of the various senses it appeals to, and your own experiences. |
| **2.** Write a topic sentence (for a paragraph) or thesis statement (for an essay) | ❑ Review the ideas you jotted down about your topic, then close your eyes and try to visualize or experience your topic. What |

| STEPS IN DESCRIPTION | HOW TO DO THE STEPS |
|---|---|
| that includes your narrowed topic and the main impression you want to give readers about that topic (see Chapter 3). | major impression comes to your mind as you think about it? What do you want your readers to experience? |
| **3.** Support your main impression with sensory details (see Chapter 4). | ❏ Use a prewriting technique (see Chapter 2) to discover concrete, sensory details (sight, hearing, smell, taste, and touch) that will make your readers experience your topic as you did.<br>❏ Drop details that don't directly support your main impression.<br>❏ Add additional specific and vivid details to make your topic come alive for your readers. |
| **4.** Make a plan (see Chapter 5). | ❏ Arrange your details in a logical order (usually according to time or space order). |
| **5.** Write a draft (see Chapter 6). | **FOR A PARAGRAPH:**<br>❏ Write a paragraph using complete sentences, including your topic sentence, which should include the main impression you want to make. Then, provide examples and details that bring your subject to life.<br>❏ Write a concluding sentence that reminds readers of your main impression and makes an observation based on what you have written.<br>❏ Write a title that previews your main point but does not repeat your topic sentence.<br><br>**FOR AN ESSAY:**<br>❏ Write topic sentences for each of the major examples that support your main impression.<br>❏ Write paragraphs (with supporting details) for each of the major examples.<br>❏ Consider using one of the introductory techniques described in Chapter 6 (pp. 71–73) for your introductory paragraph.<br>❏ Write a conclusion (see Chapter 6, pp. 73–75) that reminds your readers of your main impression and makes an observation based on what you have written.<br>❏ Write a title that previews the main impression but does not repeat your thesis statement. |
| **6.** Revise your draft, making at least four changes (see Chapter 7). | ❏ Get feedback from others if possible (see Chapter 7, pp. 81–82).<br>❏ *Review for unity:* Ensure that all examples contribute to the main impression. |

(continued)

| STEPS IN DESCRIPTION | HOW TO DO THE STEPS |
|---|---|
| | ❑ *Review for support:* Ensure that your examples and details recreate the topic for your readers. Close your eyes after reading the draft: Do you see anything you should add? |
| | ❑ *Review for coherence:* Add transitions (especially time or space transitions) to take readers from one example to the next. Consider repeating a key word. |
| | ❑ Read your topic sentence (for a paragraph) or thesis statement (for an essay), as well as your conclusion, to make sure that they are as forceful and specific as you can make them. |
| **7.** Edit your revised draft (see Parts Four through Seven). | ❑ Find and correct problems with grammar, spelling, word use, and punctuation. <br> ❑ Print out a clean final copy. |
| **8.** Ask yourself: | ❑ Does my paper include the Four Basics of Good Description (see p. 130)? <br> ❑ Is this the best I can do? <br> ❑ Is the paper ready to be graded? |

# Chapter Review: Description

■ **RESOURCES** A blank diagram of a description (big enough to write in) is in *Additional Resources.* You may want to copy it and give it to students to plan their writing.

1. Description is writing that *creates a clear and vivid impression of the topic.*

2. What are the Four Basics of Good Description?

   *It creates a main impression about the topic.*

   *It uses specific examples to support the main impression.*

   *It supports those examples with details that appeal to the five senses.*

   *It brings a person, place, or physical object to life for the reader.*

3. The topic sentence in a description paragraph or the thesis statement in a description essay includes what two elements? *a narrowed topic and main impression about that topic*

4. Description often uses what kinds of organizational order? *time order or space order*

■ **IDEA JOURNAL** Reread your idea-journal entry from p. 130. Write another entry on the same topic, using what you have learned about good description.

## What Will You Use?

List some ways that you might use description in your college courses, your job, and your everyday life.

# 11

# Process Analysis

*Writing That Explains How Things Happen*

## Understand What Process Analysis Is

**Process analysis** either explains how to do something (so your readers can do it) or explains how something works (so your readers can understand it). Both types of process analysis present the steps involved in the process.

### ■■ FOUR BASICS OF GOOD PROCESS ANALYSIS
### ■■

1. It tells readers what process you want them to know about and makes a point about it.
2. It presents the essential steps in the process, so readers can either do the process themselves or understand how something works.
3. It explains the steps in detail.
4. It presents the steps in a logical order (usually time order).

In the following paragraph, each number corresponds to one of the Four Basics of Good Process Analysis.

> **1** Making microwave popcorn is a snap. **2** First read the box to find out how many minutes the popcorn should cook in the microwave oven. **2** Next place the popcorn bag in the microwave oven, **3** making sure that the correct side is facing up, as written in big letters on the bag. **2** Then close the door **3** firmly and **2** push the "cook" button, if your microwave oven has this feature. **2** Press the number buttons to indicate the amount of time that you want the popcorn to pop. **2** Next push the "start" button. Stay close by and **3** listen for when the popping slows

**You Know This**

You often use process analysis:

- You teach a friend or a family member how to do something.
- You read a manual to figure out how to fix something.

■ **IDEA JOURNAL** Write about something you recently learned how to do—and how you do it.

Time order used.

down to two or three seconds between pops. **2** When that happens, even if the time isn't yet up, push the "stop" button. **2** Take the bag out and **3** open it just a little bit at first to let the burst of hot steam escape. **2** Then rip the rest of the top off, **2** pour the popcorn into a big bowl, and top it with whatever you like: **3** salt, butter, cheese, chili powder — use your imagination. The whole process takes well under five minutes, and you're then ready to enjoy that great popcorn.

You use process analysis in many situations. Consider the following examples:

COLLEGE      In a science course, you explain how photosynthesis works.

WORK      You write instructions to explain how to operate something (the copier, the fax machine).

EVERYDAY LIFE      You write out a recipe for an aunt.

## PROFILE OF SUCCESS: Process Analysis in the Real World

**Rocío Murillo**
Teacher

■ **RESOURCES** For a discussion of how to use the profiles in Part Two, see *Practical Suggestions*.

The following profile gives more insight into a work application of process analysis. In particular, it provides some information about a teacher, including the kinds of writing she does at work and, specifically, how she uses process analysis on the job. Following the profile is an example of process analysis Rocío has done at work.

**BACKGROUND:** Both of my parents had only elementary school educations because they had to work. I grew up speaking only Spanish because my father was adamant that we not forget our native language. When I started school and learned English, I did well, and my teachers encouraged me. But when I got to high school, I changed schools, and it was an uphill battle. My counselor insisted that I did not have what it takes to go to college. He would counsel me to prepare for my reality by taking home economics classes. Fortunately, I didn't listen to him, but I wasn't confident about my abilities.

After high school, I went to El Camino College and found out about the Puente Project. In this specialized program I was blessed with a caring Latino counselor, a gifted English teacher, and an inspiring mentor. I blossomed in this program and realized that I was good enough to be accepted as a University of California, Irvine student.

At the age of twenty-two, I left home and moved to Irvine. That first quarter at UC Irvine was incredibly difficult. I was working three jobs, and I received a letter of probation that stated that if I did not better my grades by the next quarter I would be kicked out. I remember sitting on the outside steps of a building one lonely afternoon and crying. But I was determined to go on. I got a job at the Science Library at the university, and did better the next quarter.

The subsequent years have not always been easy. I was diagnosed with serious and chronic diabetes, which at first made me very angry. Now, I am determined to live a full life, and I am an advocate for diabetic education. I have worked hard, and now have a master's degree, a job I love, and a wonderful husband; also, I am expecting twins. I am a survivor.

**COLLEGE(S)/DEGREES:** A.A., El Camino College; B.A., University of California, Irvine; M.Ed., Pepperdine University

**EMPLOYER:** Lennox (California) School District

**WRITING AT WORK:** Regular lesson plans and the dreaded lesson plans for substitute teachers; materials for students on almost every topic (because for some reason there is no book that has these materials); letters to parents, administrators, and businesses; memos to other teachers; grant proposals; e-mails, conference notes, and, most important, thank-you notes.

**HOW ROCÍO USES PROCESS ANALYSIS:** Every time I give students directions for an assignment or activity, I use process analysis—explaining, step-by-step, how to do something. Understanding the steps of the process before they do it helps students learn. Among other things, I teach writing to my students. Some students and teachers would rather spend their day in the bathroom than write. So I think of how to connect writing to my students' everyday lives. Finding ways of helping students to see why writing is important is a huge part of my job.

**COMPUTER SKILLS:** PowerPoint, several word-processing programs, Hyperstudio, Excel, PowerSchool

**TEAMWORK ON THE JOB:** Teamwork is most definitely one of the most important parts of my job. I am currently in a classroom with forty students and two other teachers. The other teachers and I work as a team to teach those students. Also, all of the grade-level teachers meet once a week to collaborate, support, and laugh with one another. Our cohesive team is the glue that holds our grade level together. I am proud to be a member of this particular group.

**A TYPICAL PROBLEM AT WORK:** Many of our students carry around so much emotional baggage that sometimes learning is just too much for that child for that day. Students have problems such as parents who abuse alcohol or drugs or their children, abandonment, poverty, hunger, gangs, and so on. The other teachers in the room and I have to share information with one another and find creative ways to combat the problem that a particular child may be facing.

**ROCÍO MURILLO'S PROCESS ANALYSIS**

Rocío wrote the following paragraph for her students. After she and her students read this process analysis together in class, and after her students made a commitment to try to follow it, the students' reading improved, a result she had expected. Two other important results also came from this process: The students' writing improved, and their self-esteem soared.

We are not all born good readers, but there are steps that you can take to become good readers.[1] First, you have to read, period. <u>Read anything you can get your grubby little hands on, such as magazines,</u>

(continued)

newspapers, and books of all kinds, including comic books.² Second, read every single day. To be good at anything (sports, music, academics), you have to practice daily. The same is true of reading.³ Third, reflect on what you are reading or have read. This means you need to talk to someone about what you are reading, just as you talk to a friend about a movie that you have seen. The more you are able to share what you are reading, the more you will comprehend. These three steps are the three golden rules of reading, and practicing them will definitely make you a better reader and probably a better writer, too.

1. What **process** is being analyzed? *reading*

2. What is the **main point**? *There are steps you can take to become a good reader.*

3. Is this a paragraph that tells how to do something or a paragraph that explains how something works?
   *It tells how to do something.*

4. Number the **major steps**.

5. Underline the **specific details**.

6. What order of **organization** does the writer use? *time order*

7. Does it include the Four Basics of Good Process Analysis (p. 145)? *Yes.*
   *Specific answers will vary, but students should be able to give examples of the Four Basics.*

## Main Point in Process Analysis

The explanation, examples, and practices in the next two sections will help you develop a good main point and support for your process analysis.

As noted earlier, in a process analysis you explain to your readers how to do something or how something works by presenting the steps in the process. Most readers will want to know why they need to understand the process you are writing about. Your **main point** should tell them what about the process you want them to know. Your topic sentence (paragraph) or thesis statement (essay) should not simply state the process: It should make a point about it.

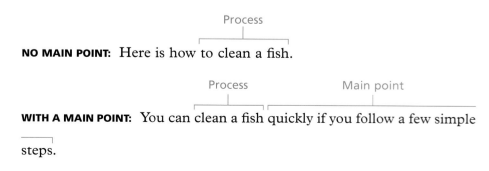

Process

**NO MAIN POINT:**  Here is how to clean a fish.

Process                     Main point

**WITH A MAIN POINT:**  You can clean a fish quickly if you follow a few simple

steps.

To help you discover the main point for your process analysis, complete the following sentence:

**What I want readers to know about this process is that . . .**

When you know what your main point is, you can then express it in a topic sentence (paragraph) or thesis statement (essay) that contains both your narrowed topic (the process) and your main point.

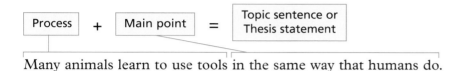

Many animals learn to use tools in the same way that humans do.

## Support in Process Analysis

To perform or understand a process, your readers must know all of its essential steps; those steps are the **support** for your main point in a process analysis.

Because you are describing a process that you are familiar with, you may not think about each individual step. For example, as you tie your shoes, you probably aren't aware of the steps involved; you just do them. But when you explain a process in writing, you need to think carefully about what the individual steps are so that you do not leave out any essential ones.

Your readers may also need to know details, facts, or examples that will help them understand each step. As you describe the process, think about what you would need to know about each step in order to understand it or perform it. For example, you'll want to warn your readers if a step will be difficult or time-consuming.

PRACTICE 1   **FINDING THE MAIN POINT AND SUPPLYING MISSING STEPS**

In each of the following process analysis paragraphs, an essential step is missing. In real life, the writer would naturally do that essential step, but he or she left it out of the paragraph.

Either by yourself, with a partner, or in a small group, first identify the main point, then underline it. Next supply the missing step in each paragraph. Indicate with a caret sign (∧) where it should appear in the paragraph.
*Placement of carets may vary.*

1. Getting myself ready for work in the morning is a mad dash. First I shut off the alarm clock and drag myself out of bed. I turn on the shower and splash cold water on my face while waiting for the shower to get hot. Then I jump into the shower for a quick shampoo and lather up with soap. After rinsing myself off and shutting off the water, I grab the

towel and dry myself off. Blow-drying my hair takes just two minutes. Then I go down to the kitchen for coffee that my roommate has already made. I gulp down one cup at the table and then walk around with a second one, gathering up what I need to take with me to work. After running a comb through my hair, I'm out the door. I run down to the bus stop, and I'm off to another fast-paced day. From beginning to end, the whole process takes only twenty minutes.

**WHAT'S MISSING?** *getting dressed* _____

2. Anyone can make a cake from a packaged cake mix; it's easy. First get the package and read the directions. Then assemble the ingredients you will need to add. These usually include water, eggs, and sometimes oil. If the instructions say so, grease and flour the cake pan or pans you will use to bake the cake. Next mix the ingredients together in a bowl and stir or beat as directed. Then transfer the batter into the right-sized cake pans. Put the pans into the oven and set the timer for the baking time indicated. It's hard to go wrong.

**WHAT'S MISSING?** *turning on the oven* _____

### PRACTICE 2   FINDING AND CHOOSING THE ESSENTIAL STEPS

For each of the following topics, write the essential steps in the order you would perform them.

1. Making (your favorite food) is simple.

   *Answers will vary.* _____

   _____

2. I think I could teach anyone how to _____ .

   _____

3. Operating a _____ is _____ .

   _____

   _____

### PRACTICE 3   ADDING DETAILS TO ESSENTIAL STEPS

Choose one of the topics from Practice 2. In the spaces that follow, first copy down that topic and the steps you wrote for it in Practice 2. Then add a detail to each of the steps. If the process has more than four steps, you might want to use a separate sheet of paper.

**TOPIC:** *Answers will vary.* _____

**STEP 1:** _____

     **DETAIL:** _____

**STEP 2:** _____

     **DETAIL:** _____

**STEP 3:** _____

     **DETAIL:** _____

**STEP 4:** _____

     **DETAIL:** _____

When you are describing a process, most often you will arrange the steps according to time: what should be done first, second, third, and so on. When you are writing a process analysis paragraph or essay, review the steps you have chosen to make sure that they are arranged in a logical time sequence.

## PRACTICE 4    ARRANGING STEPS IN TIME ORDER

The steps following each topic sentence are out of order. Number the steps according to time sequence, using *1* for the earliest and so on. There may be more than one correct order.

1. To choose the course(s) you will take next semester, just follow a few simple steps.

   _1_ Get the current course catalog and schedule.

   _4_ Decide which of the courses you want to take match your schedule.

   _2_ Decide what courses you need most.

   _3_ Find out when the courses you want are scheduled.

   _5_ Make a list of the courses you have chosen.

2. Most computers start up in similar ways.

   _2_ Wait for the screen and icons to appear.

   _3_ Move the cursor to the application you want and click on it.

   _1_ Find the "start" button and push it.

   _4_ When the application opens, click on the specific operation or file you want.

> ■ **TIP** If you have written a narration paragraph already, you will notice that narration and process analysis are alike in that they both usually present events or steps in time order—the order in which they occur. The difference is that narration reports what happened, whereas process analysis describes how to do something or how something works.

3. Everyone should know how to use a checkbook register to keep track of the money in a checking account.

___4___ Write the new balance in the next space.

___1___ Record the number of the check, the date, and the payee.

___2___ Write the amount of the check in the "amount" column.

___5___ Check against the bank statement to make sure there are no mistakes.

___3___ Subtract the amount of the check from the balance in the account.

# Read and Analyze Process Analysis

■ **READING SELECTIONS** For further examples of and activities for other process analysis paragraphs and essays, see Chapter 43.

Reading examples of process analysis and analyzing their structure will help you understand what good process analysis looks like before you write your own. The first example is paragraph-length, and the second is essay-length. Your instructor may ask you to read and answer the questions for one or both of these.

## Process Analysis: Paragraph

### A Workout for Your Brain

*Daryn Eller*

Brain gym movements, created in the 1970s by educator Paul E. Dennison, Ph.D., are short, easy exercises that are designed to enhance neural connections and reduce stress. Most of the brain gym movements are designed to help shuttle information between the left and right sides of your brain. When you don't have time to squeeze in a longer workout, try this simple brain gym movement: Stand with your arms at your sides. At the same time, bend your right knee and left elbow at a 90-degree angle and move them toward each other (don't crouch to make them meet; it's not necessary that they touch). Return to the starting position, then repeat with your left knee and right elbow. Continue at a moderate pace for about one minute. You can find this move and others at **<www.braingym.org>**. Using the brain gym regularly will keep your brain in good shape and help you deal with daily stress more efficiently.

> —Daryn Eller, sidebar from "Move Your Body, Free Your Mind," *Health* magazine, May 2002

1. The **topic sentence** of a process analysis paragraph usually includes the **process** being analyzed and the **main point** the writer wants to make about it. In process analysis, the topic is the process.

Applying for a driver's license is time-consuming and exhausting.

Double-underline the **topic sentence** in the example paragraph.

2. Is this a paragraph that tells how to do something or a paragraph that explains how something works?

    *It tells how to do something.*

3. The **support** in a process analysis paragraph is a series of steps. The steps tell readers how to do the process or how the process takes place. Number the **steps** in the sample paragraph.

4. Underline the **details** the writer includes for each step.

5. Writers of process analysis usually use **time order**: The first step in the process is described first, and so on. They also use **time transitions** to guide readers from one step to the next.

    **COMMON TIME TRANSITIONS**

    | | | | |
    |---|---|---|---|
    | after | eventually | meanwhile | soon |
    | as | finally | next | then |
    | at last | first | now | when |
    | before | last | second | while |
    | during | later | since | |

    Circle the (transitions) the writer used in the sample paragraph.

6. Does the paragraph have the Four Basics of Good Process Analysis (p. 145)? Why or why not?

    *Yes. Specific answers will vary, but students should be able to give examples of the*

    *Four Basics.*

## Process Analysis: Essay

### How to Apply for Financial Aid

*Karen Branch*

Why do so many students who qualify for financial aid fail to receive it? Many students simply don't know how to apply for it. The process of applying for financial aid is time-consuming, but not difficult — and it's a process you should learn. If you think there's any chance you will be attending college in the fall, start the process by April 1.

*1* The first step is to call the college admissions department and ask to speak to the financial-aid department. Ask if you can make an appointment to talk with a financial-aid officer. Also ask for information on all available financial aid. The person will ask for your name and address, and will mail you information or direct you to where you can find it online. Through the regular mail, it should arrive in a few days, so if you haven't received the package in a week, call again.

*2* When you receive the package, take a quick look at everything to see what's there. The package should include information from the college and information from the U.S. Department of Education. For example, you should receive a pamphlet on direct loans, a Free Application for Federal Student Aid, and a copy of Student Guide: Financial Aid from the U.S. Department of Education. If you are missing any of these items, call the college again and request them.

*3* Next review the forms and booklets for deadlines. Financial-aid officers say the biggest reason students don't get loans or aid is that they miss deadlines. Don't lose out on real money because you've missed a deadline. Start a file labeled "Financial Aid," and staple a sheet of paper with deadlines to the inside front. Also mark important dates on your personal calendar.

*4* After this previewing, you then need to discover what aid you are eligible for. Read the information you have received very carefully, and determine what you should apply for. If you are confused, call the financial aid office again; it is the job of people there to help you, so don't hesitate to call.

*5* Once you know what aid you will apply for, gather together all the forms you will need to complete. Fill in the application completely. Most people make mistakes on forms, so it is smart to make a couple of copies of the application forms and fill out the information on the copies first. Then proofread the information carefully, and when you're sure it's right, transfer it to the real application. If you have any questions, call the financial-aid office again. You might want to have someone there review your draft application.

6⟨When⟩ you have completed the actual application, make sure that you attach any additional information requested. For example, you will probably have to attach a financial statement or your high school transcripts. Reread the pamphlet and the application to make sure your package is complete. When everything is ready, make a copy for your file and mail the application materials. If you are using an online site, read the directions for how the materials should be returned (in electronic form or in hard copy).

7⟨Then⟩ you wait for a while. The financial-aid office can tell you when you should expect a response. If you haven't heard anything within that time, call financial aid to see if you should follow up in any way. With any luck, you should be notified that you have received some money. This news will make the whole procedure worth it. <u>Don't miss out on easy money just because you didn't understand the process!</u>

1.  The **thesis statement** of a process analysis essay usually includes the **process** being analyzed and the **main point** the writer wants to make about it.

Completing an income-tax form is very taxing.

Double-underline the **<u>thesis statement</u>** in the example essay.

2.  The **support** in a process analysis essay is a series of steps in the process. Each major step in the process should be a topic sentence for one of the paragraphs in the body of the essay. Number the **steps** in each **topic sentence** in the essay.

3.  Each step in a process analysis is explained with details that help the reader understand how to do that step or how it works. Underline the **details** the writer of the sample essay gives for the first step.

4.  Writers of process analysis usually use **time order**: The first step in the process is described first, and so on. They also use **time transitions** to guide readers from one step to the next and transitional sentences to move from one paragraph to the next. (For a list of common time transitions, see p. 153.)

Circle the (transitions) the writer uses in the sample essay.

5. Double-underline the **sentence in the concluding paragraph** that ties the concluding paragraph to the introductory paragraph.

6. Does the essay have the Four Basics of Good Process Analysis (p. 145)? Why or why not?

   *Yes. Specific answers will vary, but students should be able to give examples of the*

   *Four Basics.*

# Write Your Own Process Analysis

In this section, you will write your own process analysis paragraph or essay based on your (or your instructor's) choice among three assignments.

To complete your process analysis, follow this sequence:

■ **TIP** Look back at your idea-journal entry (p. 145) for ideas.

1. Review the Four Basics of Good Process Analysis (p. 145).
2. Choose your assignment.
3. Read the Critical Thinking box on page 158.
4. If you are asked to complete Assignment 3, read Using Problem Solving and Teamwork in Writing (Chapter 8, pp. 109–11).
5. Write your process analysis using the Checklist: How to Write Process Analysis (pp. 158–59).

■ **TIP** If you use the Writing Guide Software with this book, you'll find step-by-step guidance for writing process analysis paragraphs and essays.

■ **ASSIGNMENT 1**  **WRITING ABOUT COLLEGE, WORK, AND EVERYDAY LIFE**

Write a process analysis on one of the following topics.

**COLLEGE**

| PARAGRAPH | ESSAY |
|---|---|
| How to<br>• Register for a course<br>• Use a spell-checker<br>• Get a parking permit | How to<br>• Find a book in the library<br>• Apply for admission to the college<br>• Study for an exam |

**WORK**

| PARAGRAPH | ESSAY |
|---|---|
| How to<br>• Use a piece of equipment or office machine<br>• Perform a specific task at work | How to<br>• Prepare for a job interview<br>• Make a product that your company produces |

■ **ESL** Suggest that students write about a process that they used in their native country or culture but don't use where they live now.

EVERYDAY LIFE

| PARAGRAPH | ESSAY |
|---|---|
| How to | How to |
| • Operate a household appliance | • Discipline a child |
| • Do something that you are good at | • Do something that you are good at |
| • Politely get rid of a telephone sales call | • Plan a surprise party |

■ **TEACHING TIP** Suggest to students that they make journal entries on some of the topics that they don't write about for this assignment.

■ **ASSIGNMENT 2   WRITING ABOUT IMAGES**

In either a paragraph or an essay, describe a process (humorous or otherwise) for breaking a bad habit. Make sure to include details about the steps.

**"One patch makes me stop smoking, one makes me eat less, one makes me put my clothes in the hamper instead of leaving them on the floor, one makes me put the toilet seat back down..."**

■ **ASSIGNMENT 3   WRITING IN THE REAL WORLD/SOLVING A PROBLEM**

**PROBLEM:** It is late at night on the day before a major paper is due for your English course. The paper is worth 30 percent of your grade for the course, and your instructor has emphasized that no late papers will be accepted. You've worked hard on this assignment and have carefully saved all of your ideas and your first draft on your personal computer. Unfortunately, your computer breaks down. Despite repeated tries, it won't start, and the paper is due the next day at 11:00 A.M.

■ **COMPUTER** Have students write about how to do something on a computer (open programs, highlight, delete, underline, and so on). Read some of the finished papers aloud to compare the steps.

■ **TEAMWORK** For more detailed guidance on group work, see *Practical Suggestions.*

**ASSIGNMENT:** In a small group or on your own, work out a process to solve this problem and to avoid it in the future. You might want to refer to the problem-solving steps on page 110. Then, in a paragraph or essay, describe the process.

Before writing, read the Critical Thinking box that follows.

## CRITICAL THINKING: WRITING PROCESS ANALYSIS

■ **TEACHING TIP** Walk students through the Critical Thinking guide, explaining the importance of asking and answering the questions.

**FOCUS**

Decide what you want your readers to be able to do or understand after reading your process analysis.

**ASK YOURSELF**

- What steps in the process do my readers need to know about?
- What details, facts, and examples will help them understand each step?

**WRITE**

Using time order, write a process analysis that fully explains each essential step in the process.

■ **RESOURCES** All chapters in Part Two have writing checklists, which are reproduced in *Additional Resources.* You can photocopy and distribute them if you want students to hand in the checklists with their assignments.

Use the checklist that follows to help you write your process analysis. Check off the steps as you complete them. If you need help completing a step, read the information in the right-hand column.

## CHECKLIST: HOW TO WRITE PROCESS ANALYSIS

| STEPS IN PROCESS | HOW TO DO THE STEPS |
|---|---|
| **1.** Narrow and explore your topic (see Chapter 2). | ❑ Narrow the general topic to a specific process that you are familiar with. |
| **2.** Write a topic sentence (for a paragraph) or a thesis statement (for an essay) that includes the process you are describing and the point you want to make about it (see Chapter 3). | ❑ Decide what you want your readers to understand about the process. |
| **3.** Support your main point by choosing the essential steps in the process (see Chapter 4). | ❑ Use a prewriting technique to list all the steps you can think of. <br> ❑ Choose steps that are necessary for the reader to perform or understand the process. <br> ❑ Add specific details to help the reader do or understand the process correctly. |
| **4.** Make a plan (see Chapter 5). | ❑ Arrange the steps in time order. |

| STEPS IN PROCESS | HOW TO DO THE STEPS |
|---|---|
| **5.** Write a draft (see Chapter 6). | **FOR A PARAGRAPH:**<br>❑ Write a paragraph using complete sentences, including your topic sentence and the steps in the process.<br>❑ Write a concluding sentence that reminds your reader of your point about the process and makes an observation about it.<br>❑ Write a title that previews your main point about the process but doesn't repeat it.<br><br>**FOR AN ESSAY:**<br>❑ Write topic sentences for each of the major steps in the process.<br>❑ Write paragraphs for each of those steps, giving specific details about each of the steps.<br>❑ Consider using one of the introductory techniques described in Chapter 6 (pp. 71–73) for your introductory paragraph.<br>❑ Write a conclusion (see Chapter 6, pp. 73–75) that reminds your readers of your main point about the process and makes an observation about it.<br>❑ Write a title that previews the process but doesn't repeat the thesis statement. |
| **6.** Revise your draft, making at least four changes (see Chapter 7). | ❑ Get feedback from others if possible (see Chapter 7, pp. 81–82).<br>❑ *Review for unity:* Ensure that the steps are all part of the process.<br>❑ *Review for support:* Ensure that all of the essential steps are included, with enough specific detail about each that readers should be able to readily perform or understand the process.<br>❑ *Review for coherence:* Make sure that the steps are arranged chronologically and that time transitions help the reader understand the sequence of steps in the process. Consider repeating a key word.<br>❑ Read your introduction and conclusion to make sure they are related, specific, and firm. |
| **7.** Edit your revised draft (see Parts Four through Seven). | ❑ Find and correct problems with grammar, spelling, word use, and punctuation.<br>❑ Print out a clean copy. |
| **8.** Ask yourself: | ❑ Does my paper include the Four Basics of Good Process Analysis (see p. 145)?<br>❑ Is this the best I can do?<br>❑ Is the paper ready to be graded? |

## Chapter Review: Process Analysis

■ **RESOURCES** A blank diagram of a process analysis (big enough to write in) is in *Additional Resources.* You may want to copy it and give it to students to plan their writing.

1. Process analysis is writing that *either explains how to do something or explains how something works.*

2. What are the Four Basics of Good Process Analysis?

   *It tells readers what process you want them to know about and makes a point about it.*

   *It presents the essential steps in the process, so readers can either do the process themselves or understand how something works.*

   *It explains the steps in detail.*

   *It presents the steps in a logical order (usually time order).*

3. The topic sentence (paragraph) or the thesis statement (essay) in a process analysis usually includes what two things? *the process being analyzed and the main point about the process*

■ **IDEA JOURNAL** Reread your journal entry on how to do something you recently learned (p. 145). Make another entry on the same process, using what you have learned about process analysis. Assume you are teaching someone else this process.

## What Will You Use?

List some situations in your college courses, work, or everyday life where you will use process analysis.

# 12

# Classification

*Writing That Sorts Things into Groups*

## Understand What Classification Is

**Classification** is writing that organizes, or sorts, people or items into categories.

### ■■ FOUR BASICS OF GOOD CLASSIFICATION

1. It makes sense of a group of people or items by organizing them into categories.
2. It uses a single organizing principle.
3. It applies useful categories.
4. It gives examples of what fits into each category.

In the following paragraph, each number corresponds to one of the Four Basics of Good Classification.

> 1 Since I've been working as a cashier at Wal-Mart, I've discovered there are several kinds of 2 customers who drive me crazy. 3 First are the openly rude ones. 4 They frown and make loud, sarcastic remarks about how long the line is and how long they've been waiting. 4 They throw their money on the counter and never say hello or acknowledge me as anything but human scum. I'm embarrassed for myself, but I'm also embarrassed for them. 3 Second are the silent but obviously impatient customers. 4 Although they don't say anything, you've been aware of them since the time they got in line. 4 They make faces, roll their eyes, and look at their watches every ten seconds. What do they expect? This is Wal-Mart; there are always lines. 3 The third kind is really my

**You Know This**

You have had experience classifying various items:

- You see how movies in a video store are arranged.
- You group items into boxes when you move.
- You sort laundry by color before washing it.

■ **IDEA JOURNAL** Write about the different kinds of students in this class or the different kinds of friends you have.

**161**

least favorite: suspicious customers who watch my every move as if my goal in life is to overcharge them. 4 They turn the monitor so they can see every price, but that's not enough. 4 After looking at the price there, they lean over the counter toward me and look at what price comes up on the register. 4 Then their heads snap back to look at the monitor. They clearly don't trust me and are just waiting for me to make a mistake, at which point they will jump all over me. This kind of customer make me nervous and a lot more likely to mess up. If you are one of these three kinds of customers, remember me next time you're at Wal-Mart; I'm the one just trying to do my job, and you're driving me crazy!

—Joyce Kenneally

Sometimes when you are writing a classification (or reading one), it helps to think of classification in diagram form. Here is a diagram of the previous paragraph:

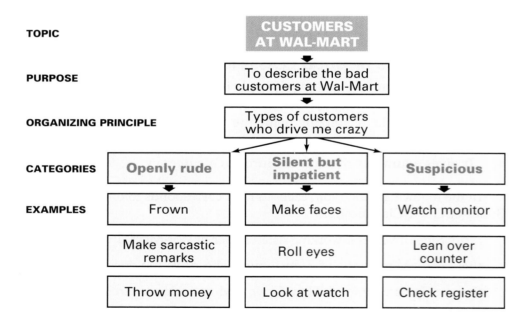

You use classification any time you want to organize people or items. Consider the following examples:

COLLEGE    In a criminal justice course, you are asked to discuss the most common types of chronic offenders.

WORK    For a sales presentation, your boss asks you to classify the kinds of products your company produces.

EVERYDAY LIFE    You classify your typical monthly expenses to make a budget.

## PROFILE OF SUCCESS: Classification in the Real World

The following profile gives more insight into a work application of classification. In particular, it provides some information about a director of human services, including the kinds of writing she does at work and, specifically, how she uses classification on the job. Following the profile is an example of classification Rosalind has done at work.

**BACKGROUND:** At eighteen, I was a complete mess. I was a homeless single mother living in a shelter for abused women and children. I realized that things weren't going to get any better unless I helped myself, so I enrolled in a community college, where I met some teachers who encouraged me. Going to school was hard because of my situation and location, but my teachers kept encouraging me. Once I'd taken a few courses, I got the hang of it and started to do better. I knew it was the only good way out for me.

**COLLEGE(S)/DEGREES:** A.A., Massachusetts Bay Community College; B.S. in history from Suffolk University, with a minor in public policy

**EMPLOYER:** City of Marlborough, Massachusetts

**WRITING AT WORK:** Reports, proposals, summaries, letters, requests for proposals, memos

**HOW ROSALIND USES CLASSIFICATION:** Many of the grants and proposals I write classify people, projects, or funding into different categories. Breaking things down into categories helps other people understand the whole project and who it benefits.

**COMPUTER SKILLS:** PowerPoint, word processing, and spreadsheet programs

**TEAMWORK ON THE JOB:** The Human Services Department is a government agency, so part of my job is to coordinate programs with other agencies in the city. Often a program is sponsored by two or more cooperating organizations, and people in all of them have to band together to implement a program.

**A TYPICAL PROBLEM AT WORK:** Because Human Services is a municipal agency, there are often other government bureaucracies to work with. Sometimes it seems to take forever to get through all the red tape in order to create necessary programs that will help real people.

Rosalind Baker
Director of Human Services

■ **RESOURCES:** For a discussion of how to use the profiles in Part Two, see *Practical Suggestions.*

### ROSALIND BAKER'S CLASSIFICATION

This paragraph was part of a grant proposal that Rosalind Baker completed at her job. The grant application requires the applicant to describe how the funds will be spent, who will receive the money, and what the outcome will be. In the paragraph that follows, Rosalind classifies the population that will be served by the grant program.

The funding from this grant would subsidize training programs and child-care arrangments for three types of currently unemployed residents of this city, making it possible for them to become self-supporting. One group consists of those who were laid off when Johnson Rubber closed its factory here. Many workers who had been employed at Johnson Rubber for decades have been unable to find other work and need

(continued)

to learn new skills. Another group consists of recent immigrants to this country who are eager to work but need instruction in English-language skills in order to find jobs. The third major group targeted for funds from the grant are single mothers, many of whom are presently on welfare because they cannot afford child care. Our agency has already identified and interviewed many people from each of these three groups, and they are very eager to do whatever they can to find suitable jobs in our area.

1. Double-underline the **topic sentence**.
2. What is the **main point**? *that the grant would help unemployed residents become self-supporting*
3. How many **categories** are there? *three* _____ What are they? *unemployed factory workers, recent immigrants, single mothers*
4. Underline the **examples of people or items** in each category.

## Main Point in Classification

The explanations, examples, and practices in the next two sections will help you develop a good main point and support for your classification. The **main point** in classification depends on the system, or **organizing principle**, you use to sort information about your topic for your readers. First think about your purpose: What do you want to help your readers do or understand? That will help you decide on the best way to organize (or sort) your topic.

To help you discover the organizing principle for your classification, complete the following sentences:

**My purpose for classifying my topic is . . .**

**It would make most sense to my readers if I sorted this topic by . . .**

The organizing principle is the single guideline you use to sort the group of people or items, not the categories into which you group the information.

Imagine the following situation in your college bookstore. The purpose of sorting textbooks is to help students find them. The best way to organize the books is by subject area or course number. But not in this bookstore . . .

You walk into the bookstore looking for an algebra text and expect to find it in the math textbook area, classified according to its subject area. Instead, the books on the shelves aren't classified in any way you can make sense of.

When you ask the sales clerk how to find the book, he says, "What color is it? The right half of the store has them arranged by color: blue over there, green in the middle, and so on. The left half of the store has them arranged by author."

You may never find your book. The first problem is that books are not shelved according to a single organizing principle. Instead there are two: by color and by author. The other problem is that the categories of organization (color and author) are not useful for the purpose of helping you to find the text you want. Even if you know the color of the book, you still won't know whether you will find it in the color section; it might be in the author section. The following diagram shows how you would expect textbooks to be classified.

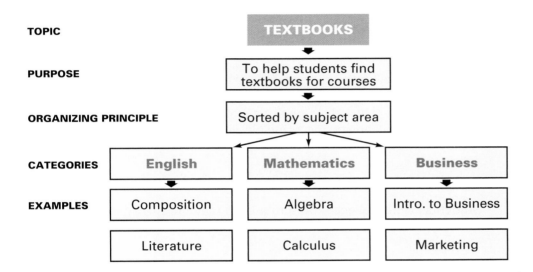

| TOPIC | **TEXTBOOKS** |
| PURPOSE | To help students find textbooks for courses |
| ORGANIZING PRINCIPLE | Sorted by subject area |
| CATEGORIES | **English** / **Mathematics** / **Business** |
| EXAMPLES | Composition / Algebra / Intro. to Business |
| | Literature / Calculus / Marketing |

## PRACTICE 1   USING A SINGLE ORGANIZING PRINCIPLE

For each topic that follows, one of the categories does not fit the same organizing principle as the rest. Circle the letter of the category that does not fit, and write the organizing principle the rest follow in the space provided. *Answers may vary.*

**EXAMPLE:**

**TOPIC:** Shoes

**CATEGORIES:**

a. Running     c. Golf
b. Leather     d. Bowling

**ORGANIZING PRINCIPLE:** *by type of activity*

1. **TOPIC:** Relatives

   **CATEGORIES:**

   a. Aunts     c. Sisters
   b. Uncles     d. Nieces

   **ORGANIZING PRINCIPLE:** *female relatives*

■ **COMPUTER** Have students type in a topic and write one example of a category. Then have them move to the next computer and write another category that would fit that topic. They should keep moving and adding categories until each topic has five categories. Then have students return to their original computers and see if the categories all follow one organizing principle. Have students read the categories aloud, and let the class decide whether they fit.

2. **TOPIC:** Jobs

   **CATEGORIES:**

   a.  Weekly         c.  Monthly

   b.  Hourly         (d.) Summer

   **ORGANIZING PRINCIPLE:** *pay period*

3. **TOPIC:** Animals

   **CATEGORIES:**

   a.  Dogs          c.  Rabbits

   b.  Cats          (d.) Whales

   **ORGANIZING PRINCIPLE:** *pets; four legs*

In classification, writers may go right to the categories themselves instead of stating their organizing principle in a topic sentence or thesis statement. Read the examples that follow: one that states the organizing principle, one that states both the organizing principle and the categories, and one that states only the categories.

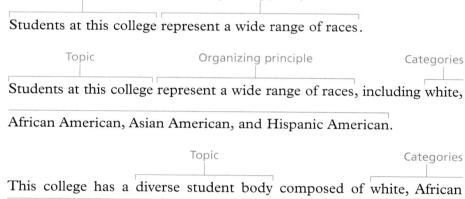

Topic | Organizing principle

Students at this college represent a wide range of races.

Topic | Organizing principle | Categories

Students at this college represent a wide range of races, including white, African American, Asian American, and Hispanic American.

Topic | Categories

This college has a diverse student body composed of white, African American, Asian American, Hispanic American, and Portuguese American students.

## Support in Classification

In classification, **support** consists of the categories you sort information into and the examples of things that fit into each category. First you need to choose useful categories; then you need to find the best examples for these categories.

### Choose Useful Categories

The categories you choose for your classification will tell your readers how you are organizing your topic. First, though, you need to find useful categories.

Suppose, for example, that you work in an office and need to sort the stack of papers on your desk. Before making random piles, you decide on some useful categories: papers that can be thrown away; memos you need to take action on; articles you need to read; information that can be passed on to others; paperwork that you've seen and that needs to be filed; and so on. Deciding on such categories is the first step in classification.

### PRACTICE 2   CHOOSING USEFUL CATEGORIES

In the items that follow, you are given a topic and a reason for sorting. For each item, list three useful categories. (There are more than three correct categories for each item.)

■ **TEACHING TIP** Walk students through this step. Use a simple topic (stores in town or a local mall, clothing students are wearing, courses offered at the college) and demonstrate how you would classify it. Or break the class into small groups and give each group a topic. Then call on students from each group to tell what they did.

**EXAMPLE:**

**TOPIC:** Pieces of paper in my wallet

**REASON FOR SORTING:** To get rid of what I don't need

**CATEGORIES:**

a. *Things I need to keep in my wallet*

b. *Things I can throw away*

c. *Things I need to keep, but not in my wallet*

1. **TOPIC:** Animals in a pet shop

   **REASON FOR SORTING:** To decide what kind of pet to get

   **CATEGORIES:** *Answers will vary. Possible answers:*

   a. *Dogs*

   b. *Birds*

   c. *Fish*

2. **TOPIC:** College courses

   **REASON FOR SORTING:** To decide what I'll register for

   **CATEGORIES:** *Answers will vary. Possible answers:*

   a. *English*

   b. *Accounting*

   c. *Math*

3. **TOPIC:** Stuff in my notebook

   **REASON FOR SORTING:** To organize my schoolwork

   **CATEGORIES:** *Answers will vary. Possible answers:*

   a. *Homework*

   b. *Notes*

   c. *Doodles*

4. **TOPIC:** Wedding guests

   **REASON FOR SORTING:** To arrange seating at tables

   **CATEGORIES:** *Answers will vary. Possible answers:*

   a. *Family members*

   b. *Neighbors*

   c. *Friends*

5. **TOPIC:** Clothing

   **REASON FOR SORTING:** To get rid of some clothes

   **CATEGORIES:** *Answers will vary. Possible answers:*

   a. *Out of style*

   b. *Don't fit*

   c. *Good*

### Give Examples of People or Items That Fit in the Categories

Your readers need specific examples of things that fit into each category. After you find useful categories, look for examples. You will also need to add facts and details about your examples to make them clear for your readers. To find examples and details, you might want to use some of the prewriting strategies discussed in Chapter 2.

**PRACTICE 3   GIVING EXAMPLES**

In the spaces provided for each topic, give at least two examples of people or items that fit into each category. Then add a fact or detail about one example.

**EXAMPLE:**

**TOPIC:** Pieces of paper in my wallet

**REASON FOR SORTING (PURPOSE):** To get rid of what I don't need

a. **CATEGORY:** Things I need to keep in my wallet

   **EXAMPLES:** *money, license, phone numbers*

   **FACT OR DETAIL:** *I always keep at least ten dollars in my wallet.*

b. **CATEGORY:** Things I can throw away

   **EXAMPLES:** *ticket stubs, old receipts, old grocery lists*

   **FACT OR DETAIL:** *Sometimes I find ticket stubs from movies I can't even remember.*

c. **CATEGORY:** Things I need to keep, but not in my wallet

   **EXAMPLES:** *bank receipts, addresses on slips of paper*

   **FACT OR DETAIL:** *I'll add the addresses to my address book and throw the slips away.*

1.  **TOPIC:** Animals in a pet shop

    **REASON FOR SORTING:** To decide what kind of pet to get

    a.  **CATEGORY:** Dogs

        **EXAMPLES:** *Answers will vary.* _____

        **FACT OR DETAIL:** _____

    b.  **CATEGORY:** Birds

        **EXAMPLES:** _____

        **FACT OR DETAIL:** _____

    c.  **CATEGORY:** Fish

        **EXAMPLES:** _____

        **FACT OR DETAIL:** _____


2.  **TOPIC:** College courses

    **REASON FOR SORTING:** To decide what I'll register for

    a.  **CATEGORY:** English

        **EXAMPLES:** _____

        **FACT OR DETAIL:** _____

    b.  **CATEGORY:** Accounting

        **EXAMPLES:** _____

        **FACT OR DETAIL:** _____

    c.  **CATEGORY:** Math

        **EXAMPLES:** _____

        **FACT OR DETAIL:** _____


3.  **TOPIC:** Stuff in my notebook

    **REASON FOR SORTING:** To organize my schoolwork

    a.  **CATEGORY:** Homework

        **EXAMPLES:** _____

        **FACT OR DETAIL:** _____

    b.  **CATEGORY:** Notes

        **EXAMPLES:** _____

        **FACT OR DETAIL:** _____

    c.  **CATEGORY:** Doodles

        **EXAMPLES:** _____

        **FACT OR DETAIL:** _____

# Read and Analyze Classification

■ **READING SELECTIONS**
For further examples of and activities for classification, see Chapter 44.

Reading examples of classification and analyzing their structure will help you understand what good classification looks like before you write your own. The first example is paragraph-length, and the second is essay-length. Your instructor may ask you to read and answer the questions for one or both of these.

## Classification: Paragraph

Test questions generally fall into two categories, depending on how they are answered: objective and subjective. (The first kind,) [objective questions], have definite right and wrong answers. Multiple-choice, matching, and fill-in-the-blank questions are objective. Although objective questions can be tricky because of their wording, most students prefer such questions, particularly multiple choice and matching. The answers are already there, and the student just has to choose the right ones. The questions in (the second category) are tougher. [Subjective test items], such as short-answer and essay questions, have no single correct answer. There is a range of possible responses. Students have to know the information in order to answer each question, and they have to present it in their own words. For most people, the more concrete, objective questions are less intimidating than the subjective ones. You can make a lucky guess on an objective question, but a subjective question doesn't offer much hope for a student relying on dumb luck.

1. The **topic sentence** of a classification paragraph usually includes the **topic** being classified and how it is being classified—the **organizing principle**. Sometimes the categories themselves are named. Remember: In classification, the organizing principle is usually (but not always) the main point.

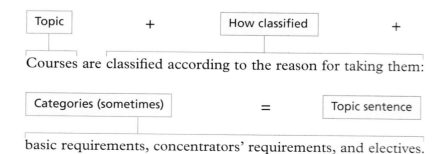

Courses are classified according to the reason for taking them:

basic requirements, concentrators' requirements, and electives.

Double-underline the **topic sentence** in the example paragraph.

2. The **support** in a classification paragraph consists of the categories used and the examples of items in each category. In the sample paragraph, what examples does the writer give of each category? Put brackets around the [categories] and underline the **examples**.

3. Writers of classification paragraphs can use time, space, or importance order. They use **transitions** to guide the reader from one category to another.

**COMMON CLASSIFICATION TRANSITIONS**

| | | |
|---|---|---|
| another | the first type | the third group |
| the final | the second group | the third kind |
| the first group | the second kind | the third type |
| the first kind | the second type | |

Circle the (transitions) used in the sample paragraph.

4. Does the paragraph have the Four Basics of Good Classification (see p. 161)? Why or why not?

*Yes. Specific answers will vary, but students should be able to give examples of the*

*Four Basics.*

## Classification: Essay

### Blood Type and Personality

*Danny Fitzgerald*

In Japan, the question "What's your blood type?" is as common as "What's your sign?" in the United States. Some Japanese researchers claim that people's personalities can be classified by their blood types. You may be skeptical about this method of classification, but don't judge its validity before you read the descriptions the researchers have put together. Do you see yourself?

If you have blood type O, you are a leader. When you see something you want, you strive to achieve your goal. You are passionate, loyal, and self-confident, and you are often a trendsetter. Your enthusiasm for projects and goals spreads to others who happily follow your lead. When you want something, you may be ruthless about getting it or blind to how your actions affect others.

■ **TEAMWORK** If most students know their blood type, form groups according to blood type and have students determine if they have the traits discussed in the essay. They could then write a classification essay on their own blood type's characteristics.

(Another) blood type, A, is a social, "people" person. You like people and work well with them. You are sensitive, patient, compassionate, and affectionate. You are a good peacekeeper because you want everyone to be happy. In a team situation, you resolve conflicts and keep things on a smooth course. Sometimes type A's are stubborn and find it difficult to relax. They may also find it uncomfortable to do things alone.

People with type B blood are usually individualists who like to do things on their own. You may be creative and adaptable, and you usually say exactly what you mean. Although you can adapt to situations, you may not choose to do so because of your strong independent streak. You may prefer working on your own to being part of a team.

(The final) blood type is type AB. If you have AB blood, you are a natural entertainer. You draw people to you because of your charm and easygoing nature. AB's are usually calm and controlled, tactful and fair. On the downside, though, they may take too long to make decisions. And they may procrastinate, putting off tasks until the last minute.

Classifying people's personalities by blood type seems very unusual until you examine what researchers have found. Most people find the descriptions fairly accurate. When you think about it, classification by blood type isn't any more far-fetched than classification by horoscope sign. What will they think of next? Classification by hair color?

1.  The **thesis statement** of a classification essay usually includes the **topic** being classified and how it is being classified—the **organizing principle**. Sometimes the categories themselves are named.

The kinds of music that I like best are rap, reggae, and jazz.

Double-underline the **thesis statement** in the example essay.

2.  In a classification essay, the **categories** are usually presented in the topic sentences. Underline the **topic sentence** for each paragraph.

3. The **support** in a classification essay consists of the categories used and the examples of items in each category. In the sample essay, what **examples** does the writer give of each category?

   *type O: leader, trendsetter; type A: peacekeeper; type B: individualist; type AB:*

   *entertainer*

4. Writers of classification essays can use time, space, or importance order. They use **transitions** and **transitional sentences** to guide the reader from one category to another. (For a list of common classification transitions, see p 171.)

   Circle the (transitions) used in the sample essay.

5. Does the essay have the Four Basics of Good Classification (see p. 161)? Why or why not?

   *Yes. Specific answers will vary, but students should be able to give examples of the*

   *Four Basics.*

## Write Your Own Classification

■ **TIP** Look back at your idea-journal entry (p. 161) for ideas.

In this section, you will write your own classification paragraph or essay based on your (or your instructor's) choice among three assignments.

To complete your classification, follow this sequence:

1. Review the Four Basics of Good Classification (p. 161).
2. Choose your assignment.
3. Read the Critical Thinking box on page 175.
4. If you are asked to complete Assignment 3, read Using Problem Solving and Teamwork in Writing (Chapter 8, pp. 109–11).
5. Write your classification using the Checklist: How to Write Classification (pp. 175–76).

### ASSIGNMENT 1  WRITING ABOUT COLLEGE, WORK, AND EVERYDAY LIFE

■ **TIP** If you use the Writing Guide Software with this book, you'll find step-by-step guidance for writing classification paragraphs and essays.

Write a classification on one of the following topics.

**COLLEGE**

| PARAGRAPH | ESSAY |
| --- | --- |
| Types of | Types of |
| • Teachers | • Courses offered |
| • Students in your class | • Degree/certificate programs |
| • Assignments | • Resources in a college library |

■ **TEACHING TIP** Suggest to
students that they make journal entries on some of the topics that they don't write about
for this assignment.

■ **ESL** Suggest to students
that they write about something unique to their native
cultures: foods, holidays, stores,
vacation spots, housing, and so
on.

**WORK**

| PARAGRAPH | ESSAY |
|---|---|
| Types of | Types of |
| • Bosses | • Positions at your company |
| • Work you like | • Work benefits |
| • Skills needed to do your last job | • Workers/employees |

**EVERYDAY LIFE**

| PARAGRAPH | ESSAY |
|---|---|
| Types of | Types of |
| • Monthly expenses | • Drivers |
| • Fast food restaurants | • Friends |
| • Cars | • Responsibilities you have |

■ **ASSIGNMENT 2**   **WRITING ABOUT IMAGES**

Write either a paragraph or an essay about what is being classified in the
series of photos and what the categories are.

 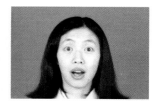

■ **ASSIGNMENT 3**   **WRITING IN THE REAL WORLD/SOLVING A PROBLEM**

**PROBLEM:** Every month you find yourself short on money, and you realize
that as a first step you need to manage your finances better. You decide to
make a monthly budget that categorizes the kinds of expenses you have.

   **ASSIGNMENT:** Working with a group or on your own, break your monthly
expenses into categories, thinking of everything that you spend money on.
Then review the expenses carefully to see which ones might be reduced.
Next write a classification paragraph or essay that classifies your monthly
expenses, with examples, and end with suggestions about how you might reduce your monthly spending. You may want to refer to the problem-solving
steps on p. 110.

■ **TEAMWORK** For more detailed guidance on group work,
see *Practical Suggestions*.

Before writing, read the Critical Thinking box that follows.

■ **TEACHING TIP** Walk students through the Critical Thinking guide, explaining the importance of asking and answering the questions.

## CRITICAL THINKING: WRITING CLASSIFICATION

**FOCUS**

Think about what you want to classify and the categories you could use.

**ASK YOURSELF**

- What is my purpose? What do I want to help my readers understand?
- How should I sort my topic according to my purpose and my readers' needs? What is my organizing principle?
- What categories will help my readers understand my topic?
- What people or items will fit into each category?

**WRITE**

Write a classification that demonstrates your main point by sorting items into useful categories and giving detailed examples.

■ **RESOURCES** All chapters in Part Two have writing checklists, which are reproduced in *Additional Resources*. You can photocopy and distribute them if you want students to hand in the checklists with their assignments.

Use the checklist that follows to help you write your classification. Check off the steps as you complete them. If you need help completing a step, read the information in the right-hand column.

## CHECKLIST: HOW TO WRITE CLASSIFICATION

| STEPS IN CLASSIFICATION | HOW TO DO THE STEPS |
| --- | --- |
| **1.** Narrow and explore your topic (see Chapter 2). | ❏ Narrow the topic to one that you are familiar with and can break into groups.<br>❏ Jot down a few ideas about the possible categories and things that might fit into the categories. |
| **2.** Write a topic sentence (for a paragraph) or a thesis statement (for an essay) (see Chapter 3). | ❏ The main point of a classification usually (but not always) includes the organizing principle.<br>❏ Use one of the following structures for your topic sentence or thesis statement:<br>topic + organizing principle<br>topic + organizing principle + categories<br>topic + categories |
| **3.** Support your main point by choosing useful categories and giving detailed examples of items that fit into those categories (see Chapter 4). | ❏ Use a prewriting technique (see Chapter 2) to find possible categories and detailed examples of items.<br>❏ Review your categories to make sure they all follow the same organizing principle.<br>❏ Find examples of people or items that fit into each category and add details about them so your readers understand the items as you do. |

(continued)

| STEPS IN CLASSIFICATION | HOW TO DO THE STEPS |
|---|---|
| **4.** Make a plan (see Chapter 5). | ❏ Arrange the categories in the order you think will best explain the topic to your readers. |
| **5.** Write a draft (see Chapter 6). | **FOR A PARAGRAPH:** |
|  | ❏ Write a paragraph using complete sentences, including your topic sentence, the categories you are using, and examples of those categories. |
|  | ❏ Write a concluding sentence that reminds your readers of your main point and makes an observation based on what you have written. |
|  | ❏ Write a title that previews your main point but doesn't repeat your topic sentence. |
|  | **FOR AN ESSAY:** |
|  | ❏ Write topic sentences for each of the categories. |
|  | ❏ Write paragraphs that explain each category in detail. |
|  | ❏ Consider using one of the introductory techniques described in Chapter 6 (pp. 71–73) for your introductory paragraph. |
|  | ❏ Write a conclusion (see Chapter 6, pp. 73–75) that reminds your readers of your main point and makes an observation based on what you have written. |
|  | ❏ Write a title that previews your main point but doesn't repeat your thesis statement. |
| **6.** Revise your draft, making at least four changes (see Chapter 7). | ❏ Get feedback from others if possible (see Chapter 7, pp. 81–82). |
|  | ❏ *Review for unity:* Ensure that the categories all follow a single organizing principle. |
|  | ❏ *Review for support:* Ensure that you provide enough specific detail about each category. |
|  | ❏ *Review for coherence:* Make sure that the categories are arranged logically and that transitions help the reader understand when you are moving from one category to another. Consider repeating a key word. |
|  | ❏ Read your introduction and conclusion to make sure they are related, specific, and firm. |
| **7.** Edit your revised draft (see Parts Four through Seven). | ❏ Find and correct problems with grammar, spelling, word use, or punctuation. |
|  | ❏ Print out a clean copy. |
| **8.** Ask yourself: | ❏ Does my paper include the Four Basics of Good Classification (p. 161)? |
|  | ❏ Is this the best I can do? |
|  | ❏ Is the paper ready to be graded? |

# Chapter Review: Classification

1. Classification is writing that *organizes/sorts people or items into categories.*

2. The organizing principle is *how you sort the group of people or items.*

3. The topic sentence in a classification paragraph or the thesis statement in a classification essay can include what elements? *The topic being classified and how the topic is being classified.*

4. What are the Four Basics of Good Classification?

   *It makes sense of a group of people or items by organizing them into categories.*

   *It uses useful categories.*

   *It uses a single organizing principle.*

   *It gives examples of what fits into each category.*

## What Will You Use?

List some situations in college, work, or in everyday life where you will use classification.

■ **IDEA JOURNAL** Reread your idea-journal entry (p. 161) on the kinds of students in this class or the kinds of friends you have. Make another entry on the same topic, using what you have learned about classification.

■ **RESOURCES** A blank diagram of a classification (big enough to write in) is in *Additional Resources.* You may want to copy it and give it to students to plan their writing.

# 13

# Definition

*Writing That Tells What Something Means*

## You Know This

You often ask, or are asked, for the meaning of something:

- When a friend tells you a relationship is "serious," you ask what he means by "serious."
- Another student calls a class you are considering "terrible," and you ask what she means.
- A child hears you use the term "hilarious" and asks what you mean.

■ **IDEA JOURNAL** Write about what success means.

■ **TEACHING TIP** This chapter is a good place to emphasize the benefits of vocabulary building and keeping a list of new words. Reinforce this practice by giving students a new word at the end of each class and challenging them to use the word during the next class.

## Understand What Definition Is

**Definition** is writing that explains what something means. Definition helps you convey what you mean and avoid being misunderstood. It also helps you understand what other people mean.

### ■■ FOUR BASICS OF GOOD DEFINITION

1. It tells readers what is being defined.
2. It presents a clear and precise basic definition.
3. It uses examples to show what the writer means.
4. It gives details about the examples that readers will understand.

Some words—like *glass, book,* or *tree*—have definite, concrete meanings, and you can depend on a dictionary definition for their meanings. The meanings of other words—like *beautiful, good,* or *fun*—depend more on a person's point of view. These words need to be carefully explained, or they could be misunderstood.

For example, if a friend says, "Don't take that class. It's terrible," you won't know exactly what she means by "terrible." Until you do, you won't know whether you would think the course is terrible or not.

You ask your friend what she means by "terrible," and she says, "It's offered only one night a week from four to seven, and you have to use computers. Plus, the class isn't on campus; it's downtown."

In fact, the time at which the course is offered fits your schedule perfectly, and you'd prefer to write with a computer. Since you work downtown, the class is also in a much more convenient location for you. By asking your friend to define "terrible," you discovered that the class is not terrible for you at all: It's ideal.

In the following paragraph, each number corresponds to one of the Four Basics of Good Definition.

A **1** stereotype **2** is a conventional idea or image that is much oversimplified — and often wrong, particularly when it is applied to people or groups of people. Stereotypes can prevent us from seeing people as they really are because they blind us with preconceived notions about what a certain type of person is like. **3** For example, I had a stereotyped notion of Native Americans until I read "My Indian" by Adora Houghton. **4** I thought all Indians wore feathers and beads, had long black hair, and avoided all contact with non-Native Americans because they resented their land being taken away. **4** After reading that essay, I understood that my stereotype of Native Americans was completely wrong. **3** Not only was it wrong, but it set up an us-them concept in my mind that made me feel that I, as a non-Native American, would never have anything in common with Native Americans. **3** My stereotype would not have allowed me to see any Native American as an individual: I would have seen him or her as part of a group that I thought was all alike, and all different from me. **3** After reading that essay, I realized that I have stereotypes not just about people of other races and religions but also about people who have different kinds of jobs or who live in different parts of the country. **4** I assumed all English teachers were interested only in grammar and would judge me by how correct I am. **4** I assumed that people who had Southern accents resented Northerners, and I assumed that people from New York were rude. Now I know that while some members of those groups do in fact have those characteristics, other individuals don't, and I do all of those groups and myself a disservice by holding on to those stereotypes. From now on, I won't assume that any individual fits my stereotype; I'll try to see that person as I'd like them to see me: as myself, not a stereotyped image.

■ **READING SELECTIONS** The essay ("My Indian") referred to in this example appears on p. 615.

You can use definition in many practical situations. Consider the following examples:

**COLLEGE**       On a math exam, you are asked to define *exponential notation.*

WORK  On an application that says, "Choose one word that describes you," you must define yourself in a word and give examples that support this definition. (This is also a very common interview question.)

EVERYDAY LIFE  In a relationship, you define for your partner what you mean by *commitment* or *communication*.

## PROFILE OF SUCCESS:  Definition in the Real World

**Walter Scanlon**
Program and Workplace
Consultant

■ **RESOURCES** For a discussion of how to use the profiles in Part Two, see *Practical Suggestions.*

■ **READING SELECTIONS** Students might also be interested in Walter Scanlon's "It's Time I Shed My Ex-Convict Status," which appears on page 565 of the Readings section.

The following profile gives more insight into a work application of definition. In particular, it provides some information about a business consultant, including the kinds of writing he does at work and, specifically, how he uses definition on the job. Following the profile is an example of definition he has done at work.

**BACKGROUND:** I grew up in a working-class neighborhood in New York City, in a family with a long history of alcohol problems. Both parents drank heavily. From my earliest days in grammar school, I assumed the role of class clown, somehow managing to just get by academically. By the time I reached high school I felt very much alone but discovered alcohol and other drugs to keep me company. It was not long before I dropped out of school. My drug use progressed, and for the next ten years I was in and out of hospitals and prisons. When I wasn't in an institution, I lived on the streets—in abandoned buildings and deserted cars. My home became anywhere I could crash, and more often than not that would be Penn Station or Port Authority Bus Terminal in New York City.

At one point after being released from yet another prison, I knew I had to do something different if I was to survive. I recalled one of my earlier hospital stays when I attended a twelve-step program. Instead of looking for a drink or a drug this time out of jail, I looked for such a meeting and found it: That set me on the right track and was the beginning of a new life for me.

I had earned a GED, and a friend suggested I try taking a course at college. Because I hadn't paid much attention in high school, I took a basic reading course to improve my reading skills. Then I took one college-level course, never intending to earn a degree but just to say I went to college. I didn't do all that well in the first course, but I wanted to keep trying. In the meantime, I had gotten a job working with alcoholics and drug addicts, and I liked that very much. Somehow I kept taking courses and, before I knew it, ended up with a bachelor's degree. I then went on for a master's and, finally, a Ph.D. Now I run my own successful consulting business in which I work with companies' employee assistance programs, private individual clients, and families with a wide range of complex problems. I have also written two books and countless articles on related subjects.

**COLLEGE(S)/DEGREES:** B.A., Pace University; M.B.A., New York Institute of Technology; Ph.D., Columbus University

**EMPLOYER:** Self

**WRITING AT WORK:** I do all kinds of writing in my job: letters, proposals, presentations, articles, books, training programs, e-mails, memos, and more. I take my writing very seriously because I know that's how people will judge me. Often I have only a few minutes to present myself, so I work hard to make my point early on, and very clearly. I believe that if you write clearly, you think clearly. In most situations there are many factors that I can't control, but I can always control my writing and the message it gives people.

People absolutely judge you by the way you write and speak. I sometimes get e-mails that have all kinds of grammar mistakes in them, and believe me, I notice them and form opinions about the sender. (For an example of an e-mail that Walter received and his reaction to it, see Chapter 22, p. 330.)

**HOW WALTER USES DEFINITION:** As I work with clients, I often have to define a term so that they can understand it before I explain its relevance to the situation or context within which we're working.

**COMPUTER SKILLS:** Word processing, PowerPoint, and others

**TEAMWORK ON THE JOB:** Everything I do involves teamwork, whether that involves me working with family members, with a human resources department, or with staff of an employee assistance program. People's problems are complex and can be solved only by a team effort in which each individual is prepared and ready to work.

**A TYPICAL PROBLEM AT WORK:** My profession is helping people solve problems. I've found that many problems can be addressed by effective communication. For example, often a client I'm working with doesn't recognize that he or she has a particular behavioral problem. I then work with the person or department to identify the problem and develop strategies for dealing with it.

**WALTER SCANLON'S DEFINITION**

In the following paragraph, Walter defines *employee assistance program* for a client.

### Employee Assistance Program

The "employee assistance program" (EAP) is a confidential, early-intervention workplace counseling service designed to help employees who are experiencing personal problems. It is a social service within a work environment that can be found in most major corporations, associations, and government organizations. EAP services are always free to the employee. While such a service is benevolent in nature, its founding objective is far more profit-driven: Employees who are free of stress and emotional problems are far more productive than those who are not. An employee whose productivity is on a decline because of a progressive drinking problem, for example, might seek help through the EAP. He/she would be assessed by a counselor and then referred to an appropriate community resource for additional services, if necessary. The *employee* is helped through the EAP while the *employer* is rewarded with improved productivity.

(continued)

1. The **topic sentence** of a definition paragraph typically identifies the term being defined and provides a brief, basic definition.

■ **TIP** For other possible patterns for a topic sentence, see pages 183–84.

| Term | + | *Means/is* | + | Basic definition | = | Topic sentence |

Basically, credit is a lender's faith that a borrower will repay a loan.

Double-underline the **topic sentence**.

2. Fill in the blanks with the term defined in the paragraph and the definition.

Term: *employee assistance program*

Definition: *a confidential, early-intervention workplace counseling service designed to help employees who are experiencing personal problems*

3. The **support** in a definition paragraph consists of the examples that demonstrate your definition and the details that explain those examples. Underline the **examples** in the paragraph.

4. Does the paragraph have the Four Basics of Good Definition (see p. 178)? Why or why not?

*Yes. Specific answers will vary, but students should be able to give examples of the Four Basics.*

## Main Point in Definition

The explanations, examples, and practices in the next two sections will help you develop a good main point and support for your definition. Typically, the **main point** in definition will include the term or concept you want to define as well as a basic definition of that term or concept.

Therefore, when you are writing a definition paper, you will first develop a basic definition. Then you have to find a good way to present it to your readers in a topic sentence (paragraph) or thesis statement (essay).

### Choose a Basic Definition

You need to understand a term before you can define it for others. Start by reading the dictionary definition of your term and writing down any ideas you have about its meaning. Then explain the term briefly in your *own words*. Do not just copy the definition from the dictionary.

To help you discover the main point for your definition, complete the following sentence:

**I want readers to understand that this term means . . .**

**PRACTICE 1    CHOOSING A BASIC DEFINITION**

Look up the meaning(s) of the following five terms in the dictionary. Then write a basic definition in your own words. It does not need to be a complete sentence.

*Answers will vary. Possible answers shown.*

1.  Stress (noun): *a mentally or emotionally upsetting condition*

2.  Vacation (noun): *time devoted to pleasure and relaxation*

3.  Confidence: *trust or faith in a person or thing*

4.  Conservation: *preservation from loss, damage, or neglect*

5.  Marriage: *a ceremonial and legal union of two people*

## Write a Topic Sentence or Thesis Statement

There are several patterns for writing a good topic sentence or thesis statement for a definition paragraph or essay. You do not have to follow one of these patterns, but they provide reliable formulas if you want to use them. This pattern is the simplest:

| Term | + | *means/is* | + | Basic definition | = | Topic sentence or Thesis statement |

This pattern presents the term, the word *means* or *is,* and the basic definition. In some cases, the basic definition might be a synonym (a word with the same meaning that your readers are more likely to know), as in the definition of *insomnia* below.

**EXAMPLE:**

| TERM | *MEANS/IS* | BASIC DEFINITION |
| --- | --- | --- |
| Assertiveness | is | standing up for your rights. |
| Insomnia | means | sleeplessness. |

Another pattern uses "class" and "detail" to help define a term:

| Term | + | Class | + | Detail | = | Topic sentence or Thesis statement |

The "class" is a larger group that the term belongs to; the "detail" is a unique characteristic that sets the thing being defined apart from other items in the class. This pattern can provide readers with a precise, basic definition of the term as long as you are clear about what the class is and can give a brief but revealing detail.

**EXAMPLE:**

| TERM | CLASS | DETAIL |
|------|-------|--------|
| Insomnia | is a sleep disorder | that prevents people from sleeping. |
| A jet ski | is a jet-propelled craft | that races across water. |

A third pattern can be effective when you are defining a word differently from what your readers may expect:

Term  +  *is not*  +  Expected definition  =  Topic sentence or Thesis statement

For example, many people think that depression is just a bad mood. The first definition that follows alerts readers that the term *depression* will be defined differently, as more than just a bad mood.

| TERM | *IS NOT* | EXPECTED DEFINITION |
|------|----------|---------------------|
| Depression | is not | just a bad mood. |
| Wealth | is not | the amount of money someone has. |

Because the topic sentence or thesis statement in this third pattern does not give the definition of the term, make sure you provide a basic definition somewhere else. You may want to state the definition clearly at the end of your paragraph or essay.

■ **TIP** Once you have a basic statement of your definition, try revising it to make it stronger, clearer, or more interesting.

■ **PRACTICE 2    WRITING A STATEMENT OF YOUR DEFINITION**

For each of the following terms, write a definition statement using the pattern indicated in brackets. First look up the meaning of each term in the dictionary. If you completed Practice 1, you can use the basic definitions you wrote there for items 1–5 instead of looking them up in the dictionary.

**EXAMPLE:**

Cirrhosis [term + class + detail]:

*Cirrhosis is a liver disease often caused by alcohol abuse.*

*Answers will vary. Possible answers shown.*

1.  Stress [term + class + detail]: *Stress is an emotionally upsetting condition that can have physical effects.*

2.  Vacation [term + *means/is* + basic definition]: *Vacation means taking time off to relax.*

3.  Confidence [term + class + detail]: *Confidence is a feeling of trust or faith.*

4. Conservation [term + *means/is* + basic definition]: <u>*Conservation means*</u>
   <u>*preserving something from damage, loss, or neglect.*</u>

5. Marriage [term + *is not* + expected definition]: <u>*Marriage is not a lifelong*</u>
   <u>*love affair.*</u>

## Support in Definition

When you have developed a clear, basic definition, you then need to provide **support**—the information to explain your definition. This information can be examples or facts or stories—whatever will help your readers understand what you mean.

**PRACTICE 3   SELECTING EXAMPLES AND DETAILS TO EXPLAIN THE DEFINITION**

List three examples or pieces of information that you could use to explain each of the following definitions.

**EXAMPLE:**

**Insomnia means sleeplessness.**

a. <u>*hard to fall asleep*</u>

b. <u>*wake up in the middle of the night*</u>

c. <u>*wake up without feeling rested in the morning*</u>
*Answers will vary. Possible answers shown.*

1. Confidence is feeling that you can conquer any obstacle.

   a. <u>*You focus on chances of success.*</u>

   b. <u>*You know you have the needed skills.*</u>

   c. <u>*You let others know you are optimistic.*</u>

2. A true vacation is not just time off from work.

   a. <u>*need to relax*</u>

   b. <u>*need to have something fun and unusual to do*</u>

   c. <u>*need enough time to unwind*</u>

3. A family is a group you always belong to, no matter what.

   a. <u>*You can always count on family.*</u>

   b. <u>*Distance, divorce, even death won't change it.*</u>

   c. <u>*Sometimes you might want to escape, but you can't.*</u>

■ **COMPUTER** In computer classrooms, have students type one example into their computers and then move to the next computer, add an example for the topic there, and continue until there are three examples for each definition.

■ **DISCUSSION** Ask students, "How has the definition of *family* changed in the last decade?"

# Read and Analyze Definition

■ **READING SELECTIONS**
For further examples of and
activities for definition, see
Chapter 45.

Reading examples of definition and analyzing their structure will help you understand what good definition looks like before you write your own. The first example is paragraph-length, and the second is essay-length. Your instructor may ask you to read and answer the questions for one or both of these.

## Definition: Paragraph

*Assertiveness* means standing up for your rights — politely but firmly. My friend Teresa is assertive. For example, once when we were in a restaurant and her hamburger was well done instead of rare, Teresa signaled the waiter and nicely asked if she could return the excellent but well-done burger for one that was a bit rarer. I braced myself for an argument, but the waiter just replaced the burger. Another time as we stood in line for movie tickets, a guy cut in front of Teresa. She tapped him on the shoulder, smiled, and said, "I see there was a gap that looked as if it were the end of the line, but it's really back there." When the guy stared at her and said, "I'll just stay here. You don't mind, right?" she answered, "Well, yes, I do mind." She then made sure the people in back of us were listening and said, "And you're not being fair to all these other people, either." The guy left. Assertiveness helps you get what you want and deserve without creating a scene.

■ **TIP** For other possible patterns for a topic sentence, see
pages 183–84.

1. The **topic sentence** of a definition paragraph typically identifies the term being defined and provides a brief, basic definition.

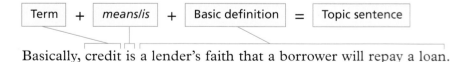

Basically, credit is a lender's faith that a borrower will repay a loan.

Double-underline the **topic sentence** in the example paragraph.

2. The **support** in a definition paragraph consists of the examples that demonstrate your definition and the details that explain those examples. Underline the **examples** in the paragraph.

3. Writers of definition may use a variety of **transitions** to indicate different relationships: *for example, for instance, for one thing,* and so forth.

(For a complete list of transitions, see Chapter 7, p. 87.) Circle the (**transitions**) used in the sample paragraph.

4.  Does the paragraph have the Four Basics of Good Definition (see p. 178)? Why or why not?

    *Yes. Specific answers will vary, but students should be able to give examples of the*

    *Four Basics.*

## Definition: Essay

### A Hero for Today

*Suzanne Robinson*

What is a hero today? Heroes of the past were larger than life. Ancient heroes such as Hercules were gods with superhuman powers. Heroic political figures, like Franklin Roosevelt, Mahatma Gandhi, and Martin Luther King Jr., operated on the world stage, hoping to improve life for all. The achievements of military heroes, like George Patton, or famous researchers, like Jonas Salk, are part of the history books. Today, some sports figures appear to be bigger than life, like Michael Jordan, but they don't seem as noble as heroes of the past. Today's heroes are likely to be more local, and their achievements may not be widely known. But today's heroes are still individuals who are selflessly devoted to making the world a better place through their heroic actions, even if they do not become a part of history.

(For example,) a few years ago, my community lost some of its heroes: Six firefighters were killed while trying to put out a fire in an abandoned warehouse that threatened to collapse on surrounding buildings. Despite the great risk, the firefighters battled the flames to save others. They didn't own the building or know anyone in the surrounding buildings, but their interest was in serving the greater good. They were selflessly devoted to the community. They were today's heroes.

A hero doesn't need to be in a dangerous profession, (however.) At my company last year, one of the supervisors realized that many women were missing work because they had no dependable child care. She could have just fired those of us who had too many absences, or she could have tolerated the absences as long as we weren't getting paid for the time we missed. Instead, Myra took action: She talked to us, did some research, and presented management with a proposal to have an on-site day-care center. When her proposal stalled, she nagged the managers until they considered it. Now that we have a place where our children are cared for during the day, absenteeism is down and morale is up. Myra devoted herself to our well-being, and her achievement is, to us, monumental. She is our hero.

Today's heroes may not gain world recognition for their actions. They may change a small part of the world just a little at a time. But today's heroes are no less devoted to work that makes the world a better place. We can find our heroes closer to home today.

1. The **thesis statement** of a definition essay typically identifies the term being defined and provides a brief, basic definition.

■ **TIP** For other possible patterns for a topic sentence, see pages 183–84.

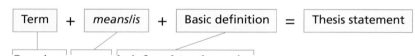

Succinct means brief and to the point.

Double-underline the **thesis statement** in the example essay.

2. The **support** in a definition essay consists of examples and details that explain what the writer means by the term. The major examples should be the topic sentences for paragraphs in the body of the essay. The rest of each paragraph gives details about a particular example. Underline the **topic sentences** in the sample essay.

3. Writers of definition may use a variety of **transitions** to indicate different relationships: *for example, for instance, for one thing,* and so forth. (For a complete list of transitions, see Chapter 7, p. 87.) Circle the transitions used in the sample essay.

4. Double-underline the **sentence in the concluding paragraph** that relates back to the introduction and the thesis statement.

5. Does the essay have the Four Basics of Good Definition (see p. 178)? Why or why not?

*Yes. Specific answers will vary, but students should be able to give examples of the*

*Four Basics.*

# Write Your Own Definition

In this section you will write your own definition paragraph or essay based on your (or your instructor's) choice among three assignments.

To complete your definition, follow this sequence:

1. Review the Four Basics of Good Definition (p. 178).
2. Choose your assignment.
3. Read the Critical Thinking box on page 191.
4. If you are asked to complete Assignment 3, read Using Problem Solving and Teamwork in Writing (Chapter 8, pp. 109–11).
5. Write your definition using the Checklist: How to Write Definition (pp. 191–192).

■ **TIP** Look back at your idea-journal entry (p. 178) for ideas.

### ASSIGNMENT 1  WRITING ABOUT COLLEGE, WORK, AND EVERYDAY LIFE

Write a definition on one of the following terms (in italics) or topics.

**COLLEGE**

| PARAGRAPH | ESSAY |
|---|---|
| • A computer term | • *Cheating* |
| • *Course prerequisite* | • *Nontraditional student* |
| • *Plagiarism* | • *Learning* |

**WORK**

| PARAGRAPH | ESSAY |
|---|---|
| • A good job | • A positive work environment |
| • *Self-starter* | • What is a good manager? |
| • A term used in your work | • *Downsizing* |

**EVERYDAY LIFE**

| PARAGRAPH | ESSAY |
|---|---|
| • *Self-esteem* | • *Discrimination* |
| • *Addiction* | • A good relationship |
| • *Common sense* | • *Heroism* |

■ **TIP** If you use the Writing Guide Software with this book, you'll find step-by-step guidance for writing definition paragraphs and essays.

■ **ESL** Suggest that students define a common term in their language that has no direct counterpart in English.

■ **TEACHING TIP** Suggest to students that they make journal entries on some of the topics that they don't write about for this assignment.

### ASSIGNMENT 2  WRITING ABOUT IMAGES

Write a paragraph or essay about how the ad on the next page defines "real Indian." If you are writing an essay, you might also want to consider whether this ad makes you rethink your previous ideas about what it means to be Native American.

■ **READING SELECTIONS** For an essay on a similar subject, see "My Indian," p. 615.

Carly Kipp, Blackfeet. Biology major, tutor, mom, pursuing a doctorate in veterinary medicine, specializing in large-animal surgery.

■ **ASSIGNMENT 3**   **WRITING IN THE REAL WORLD/SOLVING A PROBLEM**

**PROBLEM:**  You see a news report that cites a recent survey of business managers who were asked what skills or traits are most important to employers. The top five skills and traits cited were (1) motivation, (2) interpersonal skills, (3) initiative, (4) communication skills, and (5) maturity.

You have a job interview next week, and you want to be able to present yourself well. Before you can do that, though, you need to have a better understanding of the five skills and traits noted above and what examples you might be able to give to demonstrate that you have them.

**ASSIGNMENT:**  Working in a group or on your own, come up with definitions of three of the five terms and think of some examples of how the skills

■ **TEAMWORK**  For more detailed guidance on group work, see *Practical Suggestions.*

or traits could be used at work. Then, write a paragraph or essay that defines the three terms and provides examples of how you have demonstrated these skills or traits, either in a current job or in other situations.

Before writing, read the Critical Thinking box that follows.

## CRITICAL THINKING: WRITING DEFINITION

### FOCUS

Think about what you want to define for your readers and what it means to you.

### ASK YOURSELF

- What is my purpose? To give someone a formal definition? To explain what I mean when I use a certain word?
- Are my readers likely to be at all familiar with what I'm defining?
- What basic definition should I use in my topic sentence (paragraph) or thesis statement (essay)?

### WRITE

Write a working definition and give examples that show readers what the term, as you're defining it, means.

■ **TEACHING TIP** Walk students through the Critical Thinking guide, explaining the importance of asking and answering the questions.

■ **RESOURCES** All chapters in Part Two have writing checklists, which are reproduced in *Additional Resources.* You can photocopy and distribute them if you want students to hand in the checklists with their assignments.

Use the checklist that follows to help you write your definition. Check off the steps as you complete them. If you need help completing a step, read the information in the right-hand column.

## CHECKLIST: HOW TO WRITE DEFINITION

| STEPS IN DEFINITION | HOW TO DO THE STEPS |
|---|---|
| **1.** Narrow and explore your general topic — the term you will define (see Chapter 2). | ❏ Use a dictionary to find the meaning(s) of the term you plan to define. <br> ❏ Jot down a few ideas about the term's meaning. Consider both the dictionary meaning(s) and other meanings, especially the meaning you want to write about. |
| **2.** Write a topic sentence (paragraph) or thesis statement (essay) that includes the term you are defining and a basic definition (see Chapter 3). | ❏ Consider your purpose for defining this term: What do you want your readers to know about it? |
| **3.** Support your definition (see Chapter 4). | ❏ Use a prewriting technique (see Chapter 2) to find examples and details that show your readers what you mean. <br> ❏ Choose specific examples and details that demonstrate what you mean. |

(continued)

| STEPS IN DEFINITION | HOW TO DO THE STEPS |
|---|---|
| **4.** Make a plan (see Chapter 5). | ❑ Arrange the examples according to how you think your readers will best understand them. |
| **5.** Write a draft (see Chapter 6). | **FOR A PARAGRAPH:**<br>❑ Write a draft paragraph using complete sentences, including your topic sentence, supporting examples, and details about those examples.<br>❑ Write a concluding sentence that reminds readers of the term and its meaning and makes an observation based on what you have written.<br>❑ Write a title that previews your main point but doesn't repeat it.<br><br>**FOR AN ESSAY:**<br>❑ Write topic sentences for each of the examples you have.<br>❑ Write paragraphs (with details about the examples) for each of the examples.<br>❑ Consider using one of the introductory techniques described in Chapter 6 (pp. 71–73).<br>❑ Write a conclusion (see Chapter 6, pp. 73–75) that reminds readers of the term and its meaning and makes an observation about it based on the examples you've given.<br>❑ Write a title that previews the main point but does not repeat your thesis statement. |
| **6.** Revise your draft, making at least four changes (see Chapter 7). | ❑ Get feedback from others if possible (see Chapter 7, pp. 81–82).<br>❑ *Review for unity:* Cut any examples that don't help readers understand your definition of the term.<br>❑ *Review for support:* Add other examples or details that will help explain the term.<br>❑ *Review for coherence:* Make sure the sequence of examples is logical, and add transitions to take readers smoothly from one example to the next. Consider repeating a key word.<br>❑ Read your topic sentence (paragraph) or thesis statement (essay), as well as your conclusion, to make sure that they are as clear, confident, and definite as you can make them. |
| **7.** Edit your revised draft (see Parts Four through Seven). | ❑ Find and correct any problems with grammar, spelling, word use, and punctuation.<br>❑ Produce a clean copy. |
| **8.** Ask yourself: | ❑ Does my paper include the Four Basics of Good Definition (see p. 178)?<br>❑ Is this the best I can do?<br>❑ Is the paper ready to be graded? |

## Chapter Review: Definition

1. Definition is writing that *explains what something means.*

2. What are the Four Basics of Good Definition?

   *It tells readers what term is being defined.*

   *It presents a clear and precise basic definition.*

   *It uses examples to show what the writer means.*

   *It gives details about the examples that readers will understand.*

3. The **topic sentence** (paragraph) or **thesis statement** (essay) for a definition usually includes what two elements? *the term being defined and a brief, basic definition*

■ **RESOURCES** A blank diagram of a definition (big enough to write in) is in *Additional Resources.* You may want to copy it and give it to students to plan their writing.

## What Will You Use?

List some situations in your life where you will use definition. Include examples from college, work, and your everyday life.

■ **IDEA JOURNAL** Reread your idea journal entry from page 178. Write another entry on the same topic, using what you have learned about definition.

# 14

# Comparison and Contrast
*Writing That Shows Similarities and Differences*

**You Know This**

You frequently compare and contrast different items or places:

- You compare different pairs of jeans before deciding which pair to buy.
- You drive through your old neighborhood and notice that it looks the same as or different from before.
- You compare two restaurants you know for a friend so the two of you can decide which one to go to.

■ **IDEA JOURNAL** Write about some of the differences between men and women.

## Understand What Comparison and Contrast Are

**Comparison** is writing that shows the similarities among subjects—people, ideas, situations, or items; **contrast** shows the differences. In conversation, people often use the word *compare* to mean either compare or contrast, but as you work through this chapter, the terms will be separated.

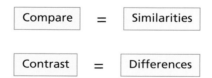

■■
■■ **FOUR BASICS OF GOOD COMPARISON AND CONTRAST**

1. It uses subjects (typically two) that have enough in common to be compared/contrasted in a useful way.
2. It serves a purpose—either to help readers make a decision or to help them understand the subjects.
3. It presents several important, parallel points of comparison/ contrast.
4. It arranges points in a logical organization.

In the following paragraph each number corresponds to one of the Four Basics of Good Comparison and Contrast.

Points arranged logically

The **1** two candidates for governor (Jackson and Centauro) have **2** dramatically different positions on key issues. **3** While Jackson supports loosening environmental restrictions, Centauro wants to establish even stricter standards and make sure they are enforced. For example,

194

Jackson has suggested that the state consider relaxing its vehicle emissions policies, in part because many larger, older vehicles will not meet standards that come into force next year. Government vehicles fall into this category. In contrast, Centauro has called for the state to sell its large, inefficient vehicles and replace them with smaller vehicles that will surpass standards and also reduce the state's consumption of gasoline. **3** The candidates' positions on raising taxes also differ. Jackson wants to roll back taxes, while Centauro wants to raise them, especially the sales tax on items such as cigarettes, alcohol, and gas. Jackson claims that returning money to the taxpayers will stimulate the sluggish economy; Centauro asserts that rolling back taxes will devastate education and other worthy programs. **3** For me personally, their most important difference is their position on the death penalty: Jackson favors it, and Centauro opposes it. Jackson and Centauro offer voters a very clear choice on these and other issues. Now it is up to the voters to educate themselves about those issues and the candidates' positions on them.

Many situations require you to understand similarities and differences. Consider the following examples.

| COLLEGE | In a pharmacy course, you compare and contrast the side effects of two drugs prescribed for the same illness. |
| WORK | You are asked to contrast this year's sales with last year's. |
| EVERYDAY LIFE | At the supermarket, you contrast brands of the same food to decide which to buy. |

## PROFILE OF SUCCESS: Comparison and Contrast in the Real World

The following profile gives more insight into a work application of comparison and contrast. In particular, it provides some information about a financial manager, including the kinds of writing she does at work and, specifically, how she uses comparison and contrast on the job. Following the profile is an example of comparison and contrast she has done at work.

**BACKGROUND:** I grew up in Shang-hai, China, during the regime of Mao Tse-Tung. When it came time for college, I was sent instead to a government farm to work, as part of Mao's program named "Sending Down Youth." I remained at the farm for eight and a half years, during which time I was vice president of manufacturing for a 600-person company. After China opened up so that the Chinese people could travel outside of China, I followed some family members to the United States. I took English-as-a-second-language courses for two semesters because my English was very

(continued)

Yuan Ping
**Accounting Manager**

■ **RESOURCES** For a discussion of how to use the profiles in Part Two, see *Practical Suggestions.*

limited. I then attended St. Cloud State University, where I did very well. However, twenty years later, I enrolled in a basic English writing course to improve my writing and grammar skills. I feel that I need better writing skills before I can advance further in my career.

**COLLEGE(S)/DEGREES:** Queens College; B.S., St. Cloud State University

**EMPLOYER:** University of Massachusetts Medical School

**WRITING AT WORK:** As a manager, I do more writing than I did as a staff accountant. I write employee reviews, explain new policies and procedures for the department, write planning and scheduling memos, and document candidate interviews. Mainly my department prepares reports that analyze financial information for various other operations. The reports explain the numbers and must be both clear and to the point. I have to think a lot about the audience—the people who will receive the report and what I can say to help them understand it.

**HOW PING USES COMPARISON AND CONTRAST:** The financial reports compare what a department has actually spent to what it was budgeted to spend. These reports let every department know how they are doing.

**COMPUTER SKILLS:** Microsoft Office, spreadsheets, word processing, Excel, and more

**TEAMWORK ON THE JOB:** To produce a report, several different people work together as a team. Each person has a different task depending on that person's abilities and position.

**A TYPICAL PROBLEM AT WORK:** Communication is the biggest problem. I can't just confront people who, for example, won't share information that we need. So we have to figure out how to work with those people so that they will willingly provide us with data.

**YUAN PING'S COMPARISON AND CONTRAST**

Every month Ping's department has to prepare financial statements that compare budgets with the actual amount spent. Below is a condensed version of one such report.

### Analysis of Operation
### One Month Ended October 31, 2002

The following Executive Summary details the financial performance of Company X for the period ending October 31, 2002. The financial highlights provided present the month and year-to-date actual activity as compared to budget.

### Results from Operations

■ **TIP** In financial reports, numbers in parentheses are negative numbers (or losses). In the tables presented below, the month and year-to-date numbers are the same because October is the first month of the company's fiscal year.

For the month of October, Company X incurred a deficiency of revenues over expenses totaling ($1,218) as compared to a budgeted deficiency of ($1,044). The tables below show the results of numerous areas of operation, with each area analyzed in terms of budgeted amounts compared to the actual amounts, and with the variance (the difference between the actual and budgeted amounts) calculated. Some of the operations resulted in better-than-budgeted revenues, but overall, the first month of this fiscal year shows a slight deficit.

**Revenue**
*Net Patient Revenue (month ended 10/31/02 and year to date)*

|  | Actual | Budget | Variance |
|---|---|---|---|
| Gross Patient Revenue | $32,880 | $35,636 | ($2,756) |
| Contractual Allowances | ($21,216) | ($22,978) | $1,762 |
| Net Patient Revenue | $11,664 | $12,658 | ($ 994) |

*Other Revenue (month ended 10/31/02 and year to date)*

| Actual | Budget | Variance |
|---|---|---|
| $ 3,232 | $ 3,409 | ($ 177) |

**Expenses**
*Salaries, Wages, and Contract Labor (month ended 10/31/02 and year to date)*

| Actual | Budget | Variance |
|---|---|---|
| $ 9,784 | $10,288 | $ 504 |

1. What are the subjects being compared or contrasted? *actual costs compared with budget*

2. What is the **purpose** of the report? *to show how a company stands*

3. What is the **main point**? *There was a slight deficit.*

4. What are the **points of comparison** that Ping presents in the illustrative tables? *net patient revenue, other revenue, expenses*

5. Does the writing include the Four Basics of Good Comparison and Contrast (p. 194)? Why or why not? *Yes. Specific answers will vary, but students should be able to give examples of the Four Basics.*

## Main Point in Comparison and Contrast

The explanations, examples, and practices in the next two sections will help you develop a good main point and support for your comparison/contrast. The first thing you need to do is to make sure that the subjects you have chosen (there will typically be two) have enough in common to make a comparison or contrast worthwhile. You may have heard people say, "That's comparing apples and oranges." This expression means that the things being compared or contrasted aren't alike enough to result in a meaningful comparison. For example, comparing or contrasting a light in your room to a running shoe wouldn't help explain either of the items; they're so different that showing either similarities or differences makes no sense.

Once you have selected your subjects, you need to be clear about what you want to achieve in your writing. Do you want to help your readers choose between the two (or more) subjects? For example, you might compare or contrast two cars, hoping to show your readers that one is better than the other. Or do you want to give your readers a clearer understanding of two subjects, without implying that one is better? For example, you might objectively compare or contrast two routes to get somewhere so that readers understand the options.

To help you discover the **main point** for your comparison/contrast, complete the following sentence:

**My purpose for comparing or contrasting these topics is to . . .**

Then you can write your **topic sentence** (for a paragraph) or **thesis statement** (for an essay). In comparison/contrast, the topic sentence or thesis statement usually identifies the subjects and tells the main point the writer wants to make about them.

| Subjects | + | Main point | = | Topic sentence or Thesis statement |

Leasing a car and buying one are very different propositions.

## Support in Comparison and Contrast

When you have your topic sentence (for a paragraph) or thesis statement (for an essay), you need to select points of comparison or contrast that demonstrate your main point to your readers; these points make up your **support**.

To do this, many people make a list with two columns, one for each subject, with parallel, or matched, points of comparison or contrast lined up underneath.

■ **COMPUTER** Have students freewrite on the computer for a minute, responding to one word that you supply. Then have them move to another person's computer and review that person's freewriting, looking for words that could be compared/contrasted. They should underline those words on the screen.

**TOPIC SENTENCE/THESIS STATEMENT:** The two credit cards I'm considering offer very different financial terms.

| BIG CARD | MEGA CARD |
|---|---|
| no annual fee | $35 annual fee |
| $1 fee per cash advance | $1.50 fee per cash advance |
| 30 days before interest charges begin | 25 days before interest charges begin |
| 15.5% finance charge | 17.9% finance charge |

Choose points that will be convincing and understandable to your readers, and explain them with facts, details, or examples.

■ **PRACTICE 1** **FINDING POINTS OF CONTRAST**

Each of the following items lists some points of contrast. Fill in the blanks with more.

**EXAMPLE:**
**CONTRAST:  Hair lengths**

*Long hair*

takes a long time to dry

can be worn a lot of ways

*doesn't need to be cut often*

gets tangled, needs brushing

*Short hair*

dries quickly

*only one way to wear it*

needs to be cut every five weeks

*low maintenance*

1.  **CONTRAST:**  Snack foods

    *Potato chips*

    high fat

    *Answers will vary but should*

    *focus on differences.*

    *Pretzels*

    low fat

    twists or sticks

2.  **CONTRAST:**  Ethnic foods

    *Mexican*

    beans as a starch

    *Chinese*

    common condiment: soy sauce

3.  **CONTRAST:**  Buildings

    *The most modern one in town*

    lots of glass

    *An older building*

    only a few stories tall

4.  **CONTRAST:**  Dancing and other forms of exercise

    *Dancing*

    purpose: social, for fun

    *Other forms of exercise*

    done at a gym

---

■  **PRACTICE 2    FINDING POINTS OF COMPARISON**

Each of the following items lists some points of comparison. Fill in the
blanks with more.

1.  **COMPARE:**  Sports

    *Basketball*

    team sport

    *Answers will vary but*

    *should focus on similarities.*

    *Soccer*

    team sport

2.  **COMPARE:**  Ethnic foods

    *Mexican*                                  *Chinese*

    relatively inexpensive                     _____

    can be mild or spicy                       _____

    _____                _____

3.  **COMPARE:**  Dancing and other forms of exercise

    *Dancing*                                  *Other forms of exercise*

    done to music                              done to music

    _____                _____

    _____                _____

    _____                _____

■ **TEACHING TIP** Point out that in a whole-to-whole essay, there usually needs to be a strong transition when the essay moves from subject 1 to subject 2.

In comparison/contrast, there are two different ways to organize your support: point-by-point or whole-to-whole. A **point-by-point** organization presents one point about the subjects (typically two) with examples for each subject and then moves to the next point with examples and so on. A **whole-to-whole** organization presents all the points about the first subject and then all the points about the second subject. You have to decide which organization will best serve your purpose. Choose one of the two organizations and stick with it; otherwise you will confuse your readers.

■ **TIP** For a review of outlining, see Chapter 5, pp. 59-60.

| POINT-BY-POINT | WHOLE-TO-WHOLE |
|---|---|
| Topic sentence or Thesis statement | Topic sentence or Thesis statement |
| Point 1 | Subject 1 |
|    Subject 1 |    Point 1 |
|    Subject 2 |    Point 2 |
| Point 2 |    Point 3 |
|    Subject 1 | Subject 2 |
|    Subject 2 |    Point 1 |
| Point 3 |    Point 2 |
|    Subject 1 |    Point 3 |
|    Subject 2 | Concluding sentence or paragraph |
| Concluding sentence or paragraph | |

■ **PRACTICE 3**   **ORGANIZING A COMPARISON/CONTRAST**

The first outline that follows is for a comparison paper using a whole-to-whole organization. Reorganize the ideas and create a new outline (#2) using a point-by-point organization. The first blank has been filled in for you.

The third outline is for a contrast paper using a point-by-point organization. Reorganize the ideas and create a new outline (#4) using a whole-to-whole organization. The first blank has been filled in for you.

**1. COMPARISON PAPER USING WHOLE-TO-WHOLE ORGANIZATION**

**MAIN POINT:** My daughter is a lot like I was at her age.

a. Me
- Not interested in school
- Good at sports
- Hard on myself

b. My daughter
- Does well in school but doesn't study much or do more than the minimum
- Plays in a different sport each season
- When she thinks she has made a mistake, she beats up on herself

**2. COMPARISON PAPER USING POINT-BY-POINT ORGANIZATION**

**MAIN POINT:** My daughter is a lot like I was at her age.

a. Interest in school
- Me: _Not interested in school_
- My daughter: _____

b. _____
- Me: _____
- My daughter: _____

c. _____
- Me: _____
- My daughter: _____

**3. CONTRAST PAPER USING POINT-BY-POINT ORGANIZATION**

**MAIN POINT:** My new computer is a great improvement over my old one.

a. Weight and portability
- New computer: _small and light_
- Old computer: _heavy, not portable_

b. _Speed_
- New computer: _fast_
- Old computer: _slow_

c. _Cost_
- New computer: _inexpensive_
- Old computer: _expensive_

**4. CONTRAST PAPER USING WHOLE-TO-WHOLE ORGANIZATION**

**MAIN POINT:** My new computer is a great improvement over my old one.

a. New computer
- _small and light_
- _____
- _____

b. Old computer
- _____
- _____
- _____

# Read and Analyze Comparison and Contrast

■ **READING SELECTIONS** For further examples of and activities for comparison and contrast, see Chapter 46.

Reading examples of comparison and contrast and analyzing their structure will help you understand good comparison/contrast writing before you write your own. The first example is paragraph-length, and the second is essay-length. Your instructor may ask you to read and answer the questions for one or both of these.

## Comparison and Contrast: Paragraph

When they get lost while driving, women and men have very different ways to find the right route. As soon as a woman thinks she might be lost, she will pull into a store or gas station and ask for directions. As she continues on, if she's still not sure of the directions, she will stop again and ask someone else for help. Until they know they are on the right track, women will continue to ask for directions. In contrast, men would rather turn around and go home than stop and ask for directions. First, a man doesn't readily admit he is lost. When it is clear that he is, he will pull over and consult a map. If he still finds himself lost, he will again pull out that map. Either the map will finally put the man on the right route, or—as a last resort—he will reluctantly stop at a store or gas station and let his wife go in and ask for directions. Many battles of the sexes have raged over what to do when lost while driving.

1.  The **topic sentence** of a comparison/contrast paragraph usually iden-tifies the subjects and tells the main point the writer wants to make about them. It should also indicate whether the subjects are being compared or contrasted, through words such as *alike, similar, same, compare, both, different, dissimilar, unlike,* or *opposite.* In comparison/con-trast, the topic is typically made up of two subjects.

My two sons are complete opposites in personality.

Double-underline the **topic sentence** in the example paragraph.

2.  Is the **purpose** of the paragraph to help readers make a decision or to help them understand the subjects better? *to help them understand*

3. The **support** in a comparison/contrast paragraph is a series of important, parallel points of similarity or difference between the two (or more) subjects. Underline **each point of contrast** in the sample paragraph. Give each parallel, or matched, point the same number.

4. Which organization (point-by-point or whole-to-whole) does the writer of the sample paragraph use? _whole-to-whole_

5. **Transitions** are used to move readers smoothly from one part of a comparison/contrast paragraph to the next.

| COMMON COMPARISON TRANSITIONS | COMMON CONTRAST TRANSITIONS |
| --- | --- |
| one similarity | one difference |
| another similarity | another difference |
| similarly | in contrast |
| like | now/then |
| both | unlike |
| | while |

Circle the (transitions) in the paragraph.

6. Does the paragraph include the Four Basics of Good Comparison and Contrast (p. 194)? Why or why not?

_Yes. Specific answers will vary, but students should be able to give examples of the_

_Four Basics._

## Comparison and Contrast: Essay

### Settling for Burt and Marjorie's Car

*Robert Crider*

How many people actually own and drive the car of their dreams? Seventy-five percent? Fifty percent? Twenty-five percent? Whatever the number, I'm not one of them. I have yet to own the car of my dreams. I've owned many cars, and (now) I own a 1986 Chevy Cavalier. None of them have I seen in my fantasies. I want a brand-spanking-new Ford Thunderbird Supercoupe, different in every way imaginable from the Cavalier.

The car I must put up with for now does not stack up well against the car of my dreams. The Cavalier is little, beige, and looks as though an old couple with names like Burt and Marjorie should be puttering around a retirement community in it, taking their friends out for breakfast at McDonald's, or traveling from their double-wide trailer to their bridge club games or the bingo hall. The car's body styling is the standard, nondescript box shape that typifies cars of the 1980s.

The interior is just as plain as the outside of the car. The only options the car had when I purchased it brand-new (because it was cheap) were power steering, power brakes, and air conditioning. Car manufacturers are so cheap they consider an in-dash cigarette lighter an option. I put in the car radio, speakers, and even the antenna myself. I wouldn't dare to install an expensive stereo system; the Cavalier is rated by insurance companies as one of the easiest cars to break into. I have had to break into it a half-dozen times myself, and if I can do it, anybody can.

On top of all this, there's the matter of the Cavalier's engine. I have to admit it's more powerful than a squirrel on a treadmill. It's more like two, possibly three, squirrels on a treadmill. Every time I try to pass another car, I wish for a downhill grade to help the engine along. On the other hand, I wouldn't want to face the prospect of having to go *up* the hill that precedes the downhill. The engine would probably die of sheer fright if I took it even near a mountain.

So, as I chug along every day to school, I envision myself a year or two from now driving along or, rather, racing along in a sleek, luxurious, eye-catching Ford Thunderbird Supercoupe. Even the name evokes visions of gracious curves, a stylish interior, room for five full-size passengers, and power to spare. The Supercoupe has little in common with the Cavalier.

Unlike the dull beige of the Cavalier, the color would be silver-gray with a touch of silver metallic in the finish. It would look at home out on the open highway with me at the wheel and a long-legged beauty beside me, her hair billowing in the rush of air from the sunroof. The car's body, not at all boxy, has entrancingly fluid lines without a harsh corner anywhere. It cannot be mistaken for any other car on the road, certainly not a Cavalier.

In contrast to the Cavalier's stripped-down approach to options, the T-bird would be equipped with every option imaginable. There would be power windows, power door locks, power side-view mirrors, a power trunk lock, power seats, and, of course, power lumbar support. Can't forget the JBL custom-designed, in-dash CD player, power booster amplifier, equalizer, and eight speakers with computer-controlled surround sound. Should I worry about car thieves? Heavens, no! The T-bird contains the latest in security systems. If an unauthorized person attempts to drive off with my baby, the car will turn itself off, lock the doors, windows, and seatbelts, and automatically dial 911. The officers would merely trigger the homing device hidden in the car's body and track it on their scanners.

Now we come to the reason why the car is called the Supercoupe. Under its front hood lies a supercharged eight-cylinder engine. The eight cylinders give it adequate power for my daily drive to work and running errands. There are always those times, though, when circumstances make me wish for some gut-wrenching, tire-burning acceleration. For that, the engine is equipped with a supercharger. A simple flick of the switch turns on a forced-air blower that pressurizes the air intake of the engine and practically doubles the horsepower. There are quite a number of cars on the road today that boast of being turbocharged, but they have no chance of overtaking a supercharged car. In this car, unlike in the Cavalier, I would fear no car or mountainous incline.

In summary, I'm driving a Cavalier and dreaming of caviar. I want a wild set of wheels but have to settle for just wheels. Maturity has taught me patience but hasn't tamed the kid in me who dreams of a car that can perform. Someday, no more Burt and Marjorie for me.

1. The **thesis statement** of a comparison/contrast essay usually identifies the subjects and tells the main point the writer wants to make about them. It should also indicate whether the subjects are being compared, contrasted, or both, through words such as *alike, similar, same, compare, both, different, dissimilar, unlike,* or *opposite.*

| Subjects | + | Main point | = | Thesis statement |
|---|---|---|---|---|

My "at work" look and my "at home" look are worlds apart.

Double-underline the **thesis statement** in the example essay.

2. Is the **purpose** of the essay to help readers make a decision or to help them understand the subjects better? *to help them understand*

3. The **support** in a comparison/contrast essay is a series of important, parallel points of similarity and/or difference between the two (or more) subjects. Underline **each point of comparison or contrast** in the sample essay.

4. Which organization (point-by-point or whole-to-whole) does the writer use? *whole-to-whole*

5. **Transitions** and **transitional sentences** are used to move readers smoothly from one part of a comparison/contrast essay to the next. (For a list of common compare and contrast transitions, see p. 203.)

   Circle the (**transitions**) and (**transitional sentences**) the writer uses to move from past to present.

6. Double-underline the **sentence in the concluding paragraph** that relates back to the introduction and main point.

7. Does the essay have the Four Basics of Good Comparison and Contrast (p. 194)? Why or why not?

   *Yes. Specific answers will vary, but students should be able to give examples of the*

   *Four Basics.*

## Write Your Own Comparison and Contrast

■ **TIP** Look back at your idea-journal entry (p. 194) for ideas.

In this section you will write your own comparison/contrast paragraph or essay based on your (or your instructor's) choice among three assignments. To complete your comparison/contrast, follow this sequence:

1. Review the Four Basics of Good Comparison and Contrast (p. 194).
2. Choose your assignment.
3. Read the Critical Thinking box on page 209.
4. If you are asked to complete Assignment 3, read Using Problem Solving and Teamwork in Writing (Chapter 8, pp. 109–11).
5. Write your comparison/contrast using the Checklist: How to Write Comparison/Contrast (pp. 209–10).

**ASSIGNMENT 1    WRITING ABOUT COLLEGE, WORK, AND EVERYDAY LIFE**

Write a comparison/contrast on one of the following topics.

**COLLEGE**

| PARAGRAPH | ESSAY |
| --- | --- |
| • Two teachers | • High school and college |
| • Memorizing versus learning | • Two courses |
| • Two kinds of tests | • Your attitude about writing now versus your attitude in high school |

**WORK**

| PARAGRAPH | ESSAY |
| --- | --- |
| • Two offices | • Two kinds of customers |
| • A good job experience or environment/a bad job experience or environment | • The job you have versus the job you'd like to have |
| • Model employee behavior versus bad employee behavior | • A job versus a career |

**EVERYDAY LIFE**

| PARAGRAPH | ESSAY |
| --- | --- |
| • How you dress now/how you dressed five years ago | • Two types of music |
| • Healthy foods/unhealthy foods | • Television shows now/five years ago |
| • Two friends or family members | • Your life now/How you would like your life to be in five years |

 **ASSIGNMENT 2    WRITING ABOUT IMAGES**

Write a paragraph or essay comparing or contrasting the photographs of man-child pairs on the next page. Include what assumptions you can make about the two different pairs from details in the photographs.

**ASSIGNMENT 3    WRITING IN THE REAL WORLD/SOLVING A PROBLEM**

**PROBLEM:** You've decided to buy a laptop computer, but it's expensive and you want to make sure you get the best computer for your money. There is a dizzying array of choices, and you want to be informed before going into a store because you know the salesperson may try to push one of the more expensive models.

---

**TIP** If you use the Writing Guide Software with this book, you'll find step-by-step guidance for writing comparison/contrast paragraphs and essays.

**ESL** Give students the option of comparing/contrasting some aspect of their native cultures with that aspect of the United States.

**TEACHING TIP** Suggest to students that they make journal entries on some of the topics that they don't write about for this assignment.

■ **TEAMWORK** For more detailed guidance on group work, see *Practical Suggestions*.

**ASSIGNMENT:** Working in a group or on your own, use the problem-solving steps on page 110 to decide what you should know before making your purchase and where you might get information. You can consult the rating chart that follows. Identify three points that are contrasted in the chart (or that you identify on your own), and make notes about why each point is important to you. Then choose the model you would buy, based on these points. Finally, write a contrast paragraph or essay that explains your decision and contrasts your choice versus another model. Make sure to support your choice based on the three points you considered.

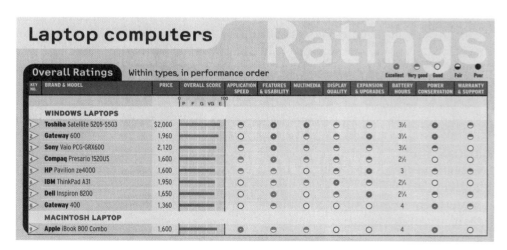

## Laptop computers

**Overall Ratings**   Within types, in performance order

Excellent • Very good • Good ○ Fair ◐ Poor ●

| KEY NO. | BRAND & MODEL | PRICE | OVERALL SCORE | APPLICATION SPEED | FEATURES & USABILITY | MULTIMEDIA | DISPLAY QUALITY | EXPANSION & UPGRADES | BATTERY HOURS | POWER CONSERVATION | WARRANTY & SUPPORT |
|---|---|---|---|---|---|---|---|---|---|---|---|
| | **WINDOWS LAPTOPS** | | | | | | | | | | |
| 1 | **Toshiba** Satellite 5205-S503 | $2,000 | | ◐ | ◑ | ● | ◐ | ◐ | 3½ | ◑ | ◐ |
| 2 | **Gateway** 600 | 1,960 | | ○ | ◑ | ◐ | ◐ | ◑ | 3¼ | ◑ | ◐ |
| 3 | **Sony** Vaio PCG-GRX600 | 2,120 | | ◐ | ◑ | ◐ | ◐ | ◐ | 3¼ | ◑ | ○ |
| 4 | **Compaq** Presario 1520US | 1,600 | | ◐ | ◑ | ◐ | ◐ | ◐ | 2½ | ○ | ○ |
| 5 | **HP** Pavilion ze4000 | 1,600 | | ◐ | ◑ | ○ | ◐ | ◑ | 3 | ◐ | ◐ |
| 6 | **IBM** ThinkPad A31 | 1,950 | | ○ | ◑ | ◐ | ◑ | ◐ | 2¼ | ○ | ○ |
| 7 | **Dell** Inspiron 8200 | 1,650 | | ○ | ◑ | ○ | ◐ | ◑ | 2¼ | ◐ | ◐ |
| 8 | **Gateway** 400 | 1,360 | | ○ | ◐ | ○ | ○ | ○ | 4 | ◑ | ◐ |
| | **MACINTOSH LAPTOP** | | | | | | | | | | |
| 9 | **Apple** iBook 800 Combo | 1,600 | | ◑ | ◐ | ◐ | ○ | ○ | 4 | ◑ | ○ |

## CRITICAL THINKING: WRITING COMPARISON AND CONTRAST

**FOCUS**

Think about what you want to compare or contrast and for what purpose.

**ASK YOURSELF**

- Are my subjects similar enough to reasonably compare or contrast?
- What do I want my readers to be able to do? Make a decision? Understand how my two subjects are alike or different? Is there some other point I want to make?
- What are some parallel points of comparison?

**WRITE**

Write a comparison/contrast that gets your point about the two subjects across to your readers.

**■ TEACHING TIP** Walk students through the Critical Thinking guide, explaining the importance of asking and answering the questions.

**■ RESOURCES** All chapters in Part Two have writing checklists, which are reproduced in *Additional Resources*. You can photocopy and distribute them if you want students to hand in the checklists with their assignments.

Use the checklist that follows to help you write your comparison/contrast. Check off the steps as you complete them. If you need help completing a step, read the information in the right-hand column.

## CHECKLIST: HOW TO WRITE COMPARISON AND CONTRAST

| STEPS IN COMPARISON/CONTRAST | HOW TO DO THE STEPS |
| --- | --- |
| **1.** Narrow and explore your topic (see Chapter 2). | ❑ Narrow your general topic to two subjects that have enough in common to be compared or contrasted.<br>❑ Jot down some ideas about the two subjects.<br>❑ Decide whether you will compare or contrast your subjects. |
| **2.** Write a topic sentence (for a paragraph) or a thesis statement (for an essay) that includes the two subjects and your main point about them (see Chapter 3). | ❑ Decide why you are comparing or contrasting these two subjects, and make sure your purpose comes across in your topic sentence or thesis statement. |
| **3.** Support your main point (see Chapter 4). | ❑ Use a prewriting technique (see Chapter 2) to find similarities or differences. Many people find that making a two-column list (one column for each subject) is the easiest way to come up with parallel similarities or differences.<br>❑ Add examples and details that will help your readers see the similarity or difference in each point of comparison or contrast. |
| **4.** Make a plan (see Chapter 5). | ❑ Decide whether to use point-by-point or whole-to-whole organization.<br>❑ Outline or diagram the paragraph or essay by arranging the points of comparison or contrast in the order you want to present them. |

(continued)

| STEPS IN COMPARISON/CONTRAST | HOW TO DO THE STEPS |
|---|---|
| **5.** Write a draft (see Chapter 6). | **FOR A PARAGRAPH:**<br>❏ Write a paragraph using complete sentences, including your topic sentence, the points of comparison or contrast, and details about those points.<br>❏ Write a concluding sentence that reminds your readers of your main point and makes an observation based on what you have written.<br>❏ Write a title that previews the main point but doesn't repeat your topic sentence.<br><br>**FOR AN ESSAY:**<br>❏ Write topic sentences for each of the points of comparison or contrast.<br>❏ Write paragraphs with supporting details for each of the points of comparison or contrast.<br>❏ Consider using one of the introductory techniques described in Chapter 6 (pp. 71–73).<br>❏ Write a conclusion (see Chapter 6, pp. 73–75) that reminds your readers of your main point and makes an observation based on what you have written.<br>❏ Write a title that previews the main point but doesn't repeat your topic sentence. |
| **6.** Revise your draft, making at least four changes (see Chapter 7). | ❏ Get feedback from others if possible (see Chapter 7, pp. 81–82).<br>❏ *Review for unity:* Cut any points of comparison that aren't parallel or don't demonstrate your main point.<br>❏ *Review for support:* Add details that help show readers the similarities or differences.<br>❏ *Review for coherence:* Make sure the organization is consistent throughout (point-to-point or whole-to-whole). Check to make sure the sequence of points is logical, and add transitions to take readers smoothly from one point or subject to the next. Consider repeating a key word.<br>❏ Read your topic sentence (paragraph) or thesis statement (essay), as well as your conclusion, to make sure that they are as clear, confident, and definite as you can make them. |
| **7.** Edit your revised draft (see Parts Four through Seven). | ❏ Find and correct problems with grammar, spelling, word use, and punctuation.<br>❏ Print out a clean final copy. |
| **8.** Ask yourself: | ❏ Does my paper include the Four Basics of Good Comparison and Contrast (see p. 194)?<br>❏ Is this the best I can do?<br>❏ Is the paper ready to be graded? |

# Chapter Review: Comparison and Contrast

1. Comparison is writing that shows *similarities*; contrast shows *differences*.

2. What are the four basics of good comparison and contrast?

   *It uses subjects that have enough in common to be compared/contrasted in a useful way.*

   *It serves a purpose — either to help readers make a decision or to help them understand the subjects.*

   *It presents several important, parallel points of comparison/contrast.*

   *It arranges points in a logical organization.*

3. The topic sentence (paragraph) or thesis statement (essay) in comparison/contrast should include what two basic parts? *the subjects being compared or contrasted and the main point of the comparison*

4. What are the two ways to organize comparison/contrast? *point-by-point or whole-to-whole*

## What Will You Use?

List some situations in your everyday life where you will use comparison/contrast. What are some college or work situations that call for this type of writing?

■ **RESOURCES** A blank diagram of a comparison/contrast (big enough to write in) is in *Additional Resources.* You may want to copy it and give it to students to plan their writing.

■ **IDEA JOURNAL** Reread your idea journal entry (p. 194) on the differences between men and women. Make another entry on the same topic, using what you have learned about comparison/contrast.

# 15

# Cause and Effect

*Writing That Explains Reasons or Results*

## You Know This

You consider causes and effects every day:

- You explain to a boss or a companion what caused you to be late.
- You consider the possible effects of calling in sick.
- After eating you feel ill and try to figure out the cause.

■ **IDEA JOURNAL** Write about a time that you did something that caused someone to be happy or unhappy.

## Understand What Cause and Effect Are

A **cause** is what made an event happen. An **effect** is what happens as a result of the event.

### ■■ FOUR BASICS OF GOOD CAUSE AND EFFECT

1. It makes clear, early on, whether you are writing about causes, effects, or both.
2. It discusses real causes, not just something that happened before another event.
3. It discusses real effects, not just something that happened after another event.
4. It gives clear and detailed examples of causes and effects.

In the following paragraph, each number corresponds to one of the Four Basics of Good Cause and Effect.

1 The next time you get a cold, don't blame the weather; blame your hands. While many people think that cold weather causes colds, the weather is not the real cause. 2 Colds are caused by viruses that are transmitted primarily from the hands to the eyes or nose. When you 2 come in contact with someone who has a cold, or just with something they have touched, 3 you often pick up germs from that person on your hands. 4 For example, when a cashier with a cold gives you change, the coins may well carry the cold germ. When you later 2 rub your eyes or nose, you 3 pass the germ on to yourself. Elementary schools and day-

care centers are cold breeding grounds **2** because children are in close contact with each other, in confined spaces; they touch the same desks, computer keyboards, and lunch tables, and each other. **3** Those same children can then infect their family members at home. Colds are more common in the winter only **2** because during the cold weather, windows are closed and less fresh air circulates. There are only two known ways to cut down on getting colds: Hibernate so you never come into contact with anyone or anything, or wash your hands with warm water and soap, often. The choice seems pretty clear.

When you are writing about causes, be careful that you don't say something caused an event or a situation just because it happened before the event or situation. For example, if you compliment a gas-company phone rep on his polite handling of a billing question, and then you don't get the next month's bill, you shouldn't assume that your nice words were the cause.

Use the same caution when writing about effects: Just because one event happens after another event doesn't mean that the second event is an effect of the first. For example, if you eat pizza and the next day you come down with the flu, you shouldn't assume that the flu was an effect of eating the pizza.

■ **TEACHING TIP** Explain to students the differences between *effect* (noun) and *affect* (verb).

Jim Rice of Quinsigamond Community College helps his students visualize the cause/effect relationship by suggesting that they think of three linked rings:

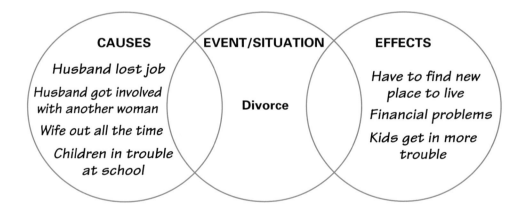

You will find causes and effects in many practical situations. Consider the following examples:

| | |
|---|---|
| COLLEGE | In a nutrition course, you are asked to identify the consequences (effects) of poor nutrition. |
| WORK | A car comes into your auto shop with a flat tire, and you are asked to determine the cause of the flat. |
| EVERYDAY LIFE | You explain to your child why a certain behavior is not acceptable by warning him or her about the negative effects of that behavior. |

## PROFILE OF SUCCESS: Cause and Effect in the Real World

**Len Lacy**
Manufacturing Manager

■ **RESOURCES** For a discussion of how to use the profiles in Part Two, see *Practical Suggestions.*

The following profile gives more insight into a work application of cause and effect. In particular, it provides some information about a manufacturing manager, including the kinds of writing he does at work and, specifically, how he uses cause and effect on the job. Following the profile is an example of cause/effect writing he has done at work.

**BACKGROUND:** I grew up in a housing project in Galveston, Texas. My mother and father were divorced when I was six, and I had a succession of three stepfathers. Fortunately, my mother was one of fifteen children, so I drew support from aunts, uncles, and cousins who lived in the area.

My mother demanded that I use good language. When I graduated from Ball High School, I received a full scholarship to Rice University, which I attended for two years. I then transferred to Southern University, where a friend's father helped me get a partial scholarship. During college, I worked in a cooperative work-study program, which gave me some real-world experience.

**COLLEGE(S)/DEGREES:** Rice University; B.S., Southern University. I am presently enrolled in an M.B.A. program at Quincy College. By the time this book is published, I'll have my degree.

**EMPLOYER:** Quincy Compressor Inc.

**WRITING AT WORK:** I write a monthly report to my supervisor that documents activity in my department regarding personnel, productivity, labor, and other matters. I also write weekly memos to the seven supervisors I manage. These written documents are essential; they ensure people understand and remember what I am asking.

**HOW LEN USES CAUSE AND EFFECT:** In memos and reports, I often have to explain why a certain manufacturing procedure worked well or didn't. I explain what caused better- or worse-than-expected performance or what effects certain actions had on the manufacturing operation.

**COMPUTER SKILLS:** Excel, all Microsoft Office components, tracking software, word processing. I also teach a computer course at a local community college.

**TEAMWORK ON THE JOB:** I directly manage seven supervisors, who in turn manage 250 workers. One of my responsibilities as a department manager is to ensure that my department's work complements the work of people in other departments, keeping to schedules and productivity goals. I emphasize the importance of excellent personal performance, but it must be aligned with company needs. A basic element of teamwork is respect. I demand consistent respect, and I return it. We don't all have to like each other, but we do need to respect each other and pull together to get the job done well.

**A TYPICAL PROBLEM AT WORK:** Problems are a fact of life in any job. Communication problems are common, as are problems with machines or operations that hold up a production schedule that we need to meet. We have to figure out how to deal with the problem.

### LEN LACY'S CAUSE AND EFFECT WRITING

The following is an excerpt from an internal report that Len wrote about the in-progress work of a particular manufacturing group. The xxx's represent identifying information that we could not publish.

The xxx group reduced cycle time for the xxx process. The basic assembly process was videotaped on March 13 to measure times for calculating the standard work cycle time. The original standard work time (videotaped on February 6, 2001) was calculated to be 26.5 minutes. The standard work cycle time on March 13 was calculated to be 19.5 minutes. In the course of four weeks, it took seven fewer minutes to build the same basic. Two things are responsible for this reduced cycle time. First, the assembly personnel learned how to build the QTS-5 basic. They modified the process and organized their materials to reduce the assembly time required for each basic. Second, a custom assembly fixture was built and installed for the QTS-5 basic. During the original standard work calculation, the crude assembly fixture that was used required considerable manual manipulation. The new fixture reduced the amount of time it took to manipulate the basic.

1. Does the paragraph discuss causes or effects? _causes_ _____

2. Double-underline the **topic sentence**.

3. Underline the **causes** Len presents.

## Main Point in Cause and Effect

The explanations, examples, and practices in the next two sections will help you develop a good main point and support for your cause/effect writing. To help you discover the **main point** for your cause/effect writing, complete the following sentence:

**The direct cause(s)/effect(s) of my subject are . . .**

*Direct* means that you are not confusing an accident of timing for causes or effects; you are sure that the causes/effects directly caused the situation or event or directly resulted from it. Also, keep in mind that there may be many causes and effects, but some are more significant than others. Make sure that you choose the most important causes or effects to write about.

For example, a student working on an essay about the effects of parents reading to children listed the following in an early outline:

Helps them learn to read

Improves their vocabulary

Builds a closer bond between parent and child

Leaves children less wound up before bedtime than playing does

Although all of these are direct effects, the writer decided to drop the last one because, as a benefit of reading, it is less significant than the others. Here is her thesis statement:

By reading to their children, parents build their kids' reading and vocabulary skills and create a closer parent-child bond.

The thesis statement (or topic sentence, in the case of a paragraph) for a cause/effect essay usually identifies the topic (the basic issue, situation, or event) and makes a point about it, often giving the reader a preview of causes and effects. In the previous example, effects are previewed.

### PRACTICE 1   CHOOSING DIRECT AND IMPORTANT CAUSES AND EFFECTS

For each of the situations that follow, create a ring diagram. Write three possible causes in the left ring and three possible effects in the right one. There is no one correct set of answers, but your choices should be logical, and you should be prepared to explain how your answers were direct causes and effects. *Answers will vary.*

**EXAMPLE:**

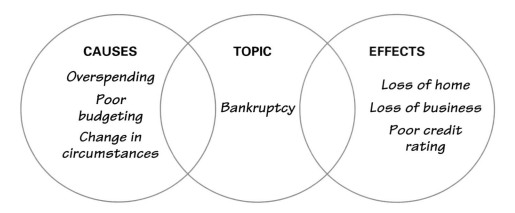

1. **TOPIC:** A fire in someone's home

2. **TOPIC:** An A in this course

3. **TOPIC:** A car accident

When you have determined the most important causes or effects, you should be ready to state your main point about the causes and/or effects of your topic in a **topic** sentence (paragraph) or thesis statement (essay). Your statement should also indicate whether you will write about causes, effects, or both. To clearly state your main point, you will often want to use a word such as *cause, because, reason, result,* or *effect.*

I had problems in school because I couldn't read the blackboard and was too shy to ask questions.

**PRACTICE 2   STATING YOUR MAIN POINT**

For each of the topics in Practice 1, review your causes and effects, and write a sentence that states a main point. First look at the following example and at the list of causes for the topic (bankruptcy) in the example in Practice 1.

**EXAMPLE:**

**TOPIC:** Bankruptcy

**MAIN POINT:** *Although many different kinds of people declare bankruptcy each year, the causes for bankruptcy are often the same.*

1. **TOPIC:** A fire in someone's home

   **MAIN POINT:** *Answers will vary.*

2. **TOPIC:** An A in this course

   **MAIN POINT:** _____

3. **TOPIC:** A car accident

   **MAIN POINT:** _____

## Support in Cause and Effect

In cause/effect writing, **support** consists of the causes or effects of the event or situation you are examining, as well as details and examples about the causes or effects.

Your reader may not immediately understand how one event or situation caused another or what particular effects resulted from a certain event or situation. You need to give specific examples and details to explain the relationship.

 **PRACTICE 3   GIVING EXAMPLES AND DETAILS**

Look at your answers to Practices 1 and 2. Choose two causes or two effects for each of the three items, and give an example or detail that explains each cause or effect.

**EXAMPLE:**

**TOPIC:** Bankruptcy

**CAUSE 1:** *Overspending*

   **EXAMPLE/DETAIL:** *bought a leather jacket I liked and charged it*

**CAUSE 2:** *Poor budgeting*

   **EXAMPLE/DETAIL:** *never keeping track of monthly expenses versus monthly income*

1. **TOPIC:**  A fire in someone's home

   **CAUSE/EFFECT 1:** *Answers will vary.* _____

       **EXAMPLE/DETAIL:** _____

   **CAUSE/EFFECT 2:** _____

       **EXAMPLE/DETAIL:** _____

2. **TOPIC:**  An A in this course

   **CAUSE/EFFECT 1:** _____

       **EXAMPLE/DETAIL:** _____

   **CAUSE/EFFECT 2:** _____

       **EXAMPLE/DETAIL:** _____

3. **TOPIC:**  A car accident

   **CAUSE/EFFECT 1:** _____

       **EXAMPLE/DETAIL:** _____

   **CAUSE/EFFECT 2:** _____

       **EXAMPLE/DETAIL:** _____

# Read and Analyze Cause and Effect

■ **READING SELECTIONS** For further examples of and activities for cause and effect, see Chapter 47.

Reading examples of cause and effect and analyzing their structure will help you understand good cause/effect writing before you do your own. The first example is paragraph-length, and the second is essay-length. Your instructor may ask you to read and answer the questions for one or both of these.

## Cause and Effect: Paragraph

Much to her surprise, lottery winner Sylvia Lee found that sudden wealth was a mixed blessing—the results were both good and bad. (After) her win was announced, she was constantly hounded by people who wanted to sell her something. She got an unlisted telephone number, but the more aggressive salespeople just camped out on her doorstep. (Another) negative result was that people started treating her differently. "I was shocked," said Lee. "Everyone from the checkout clerk at the grocery store where I've shopped for years to my next-door neighbor acted as though I had changed. I'm still the same; I've just got money now."

Lee admits, though, that most of the changes have been positive. "It really is a relief not worrying about money all the time. I actually went on my first shopping spree ever, and it was great." Lee expects that other new and unexpected results of her sudden wealth are yet to come, but she's not discouraged: So far, at least, the plusses far outweigh the minuses.

1. The **topic sentence** of a cause/effect paragraph usually includes the topic and the main point the writer wants to make about it. Typically, writers also indicate whether they will write about causes, effects, or both, often by using a word such as *cause, because, reason, result,* or *effect.*

   Prolonged exposure to the sun can cause skin cancer.

   Double-underline the **topic sentence** in the sample paragraph.

2. Does the paragraph present causes, effects, or both? *effects*

3. The **support** in a cause/effect paragraph consists of the causes or effects of the situation or event. Underline **each cause or effect** in the sample paragraph.

4. Writers often use **transitions** to move readers smoothly from one cause or effect to the next.

   **COMMON CAUSE/EFFECT TRANSITIONS**

   | | |
   |---|---|
   | also | because |
   | another | one cause, reason, effect, result |
   | as a result | a second, third, etc. |

   Circle the **transitions** in the sample paragraph.

5. Double underline the **sentence at the end that reminds the reader of the main point**.

6. Does the paragraph have the Four Basics of Good Cause and Effect (p. 212)? Why or why not?

   *Yes. Specific answers will vary, but students should be able to give examples of the*

   *Four Basics.*

## Cause and Effect: Essay

### Learning from Loss

*Carol Benson*

Two years ago, a good friend died from AIDS. Since that time, Kevin's death has had many effects on me. Although most of those effects have been painful, in the end I've grown from the experience.

The first effect I experienced was rage. How could this have happened, and why? The world seemed full of unfairness and cruelty. I spent hours crying, slamming my fist against walls and tables, cursing a world where criminals lived while Kevin died. I couldn't sleep or eat much. I lived on my rage alone.

After the feelings of rage came those of sorrow and loss. I missed my friend. I kept picking up the phone to call him, only to realize while dialing that he was dead. Something would happen at work that I knew he'd appreciate, and I'd think, "Wait till Kevin hears this." During this time I sighed a lot and felt tired. For the first time I understood what people meant by the phrase "Part of me died."

Months later, I turned a corner and stopped sitting around feeling like a victim. I had to do something. I called the local AIDS hotline and asked about volunteer opportunities. Now I visit four AIDS patients often and spend time with them. Sometimes we talk, or watch TV, or have dinner. Sometimes we just sit together, and they doze off. I also got involved in organizing an AIDS walk to raise money for research. The walk raised $5,000. About 700 people showed up, and together we marched through the streets, feeling part of a powerful group joined by the deaths of friends and family.

I still think of Kevin often, but not with rage or even so much with sorrow. In some ways I feel connected to him through my work with AIDS patients. I know that I can't control everything in life, but I can take control of my own life. The effects of Kevin's death have helped me to look beyond myself and to work for a better world.

1. The **thesis statement** of a cause/effect essay usually identifies the topic (the basic situation or event) and makes a point about it, often giving the reader a preview of what caused it or what resulted from it. In the thesis statement, writers also indicate whether they will write about causes, effects, or both, often by using a word such as *cause, because, reason, result,* or *effect.*

Getting away for a while can have definite positive effects on your mind and body.

Double-underline the **thesis statement**.

2. Does the essay present causes, effects, or both? *effects*

3. The **support** in a cause/effect essay usually consists of the major causes or effects of the situation or event that is the topic. Writers also give readers examples of or details about the causes and/or effects. The major causes or effects form the topic sentences for the paragraphs in the body of the essay. Underline the **topic sentences** in the sample essay.

4. Writers use **transitions** to move readers smoothly from one cause or effect to the next. (For a list of common cause and effect transitions, see p. 219).

   They also use **transitional sentences** to move from one paragraph to the next. Circle the **transitions** and the **transitional sentences** in the sample essay.

5. Double-underline the **sentence in the concluding paragraph that relates back to the introduction and main point**.

6. Does the essay have the Four Basics of Good Cause and Effect (p. 212)? Why or why not?

   *Yes. Specific answers will vary, but students should be able to give examples of the*

   *Four Basics.*

## Write Your Own Cause and Effect

In this section you will write your own cause/effect paragraph or essay based on your (or your instructor's) choice among three assignments.

To complete your cause/effect writing, follow this sequence:

■ **TIP** Look back at your idea-journal entry (p. 212) for ideas.

1. Review the Four Basics of Good Cause and Effect (p. 212).

2. Choose your assignment.

3. Read the Critical Thinking box on page 223.

4. If you are asked to complete Assignment 3, read Using Problem Solving and Teamwork in Writing (Chapter 8, pp. 109–11).

5. Write your cause/effect paper using the Checklist: How to Write Cause and Effect (pp. 224–25).

■ **ASSIGNMENT 1   WRITING ABOUT COLLEGE, WORK, AND EVERYDAY LIFE**

■ **TIP** If you use the Writing Guide Software with this book, you'll find step-by-step guidance for writing cause/effect paragraphs and essays.

Write a cause/effect paper on one of the following topics.

**COLLEGE**

| PARAGRAPH | ESSAY |
|---|---|
| • Causes or effects of not studying for an exam | • Effects of getting a college degree |
| • Causes of getting a failing grade in a course | • Causes/effects of plagiarism |
| • Effects of being a good student | • Causes of your interest in a particular course or major |

**WORK**

■ **ESL** Suggest that students write about the cause or effect of a cultural misunderstanding.

| PARAGRAPH | ESSAY |
|---|---|
| • Causes of frequent absences | • Causes of job satisfaction/ dissatisfaction |
| • Effects of a task you perform | • Causes/effects of stress at work |
| • Causes of stress at work | • Causes/effects of low employee morale |

**EVERYDAY LIFE**

| PARAGRAPH | ESSAY |
|---|---|
| • Causes/effects of not getting enough sleep | • Causes or effects of a major change in your life |
| • Causes/effects of stress | • Effects of a good decision you made |
| • Causes/effects of a difficult decision | • Effects of having children |

■ **TEACHING TIP** Suggest to students that they make journal entries on some of the topics that they don't write about for this assignment.

■ ASSIGNMENT 2   **WRITING ABOUT IMAGES**

Write a paragraph or an essay about the causes and effects that are the main point of the cartoon below.

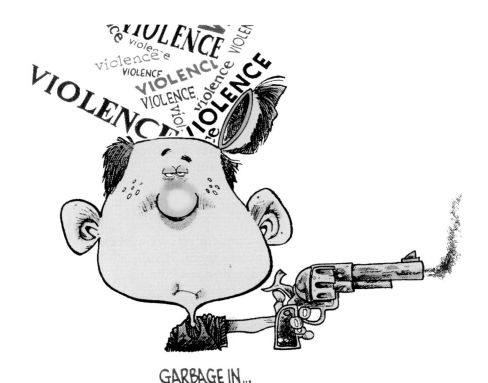

GARBAGE IN...

■ ASSIGNMENT 3   **WRITING IN THE REAL WORLD/SOLVING A PROBLEM**

**PROBLEM:** You've learned of a cheating ring at school that uses cell phones to relay test answers to students taking the test. A few students in your math class, who are also friends of yours, think this is a great idea and are planning to participate in the ring during a test you will be taking next week. You have decided not to participate, partly because you fear getting caught, but also because you think cheating is wrong. Now you want to convince your friends not to take part in the ring, because you think your teacher will catch on, and you don't want them to get caught and possibly kicked out of school. How do you make your case?

**ASSIGNMENT:** Working in a group or on your own, list the various effects of cheating—both immediate and long-term—that you could use to convince your friends. Then write a cause/effect paragraph or essay that identifies possible effects of cheating and gives examples of each.

Before writing, read the Critical Thinking box that follows.

■ **TEAMWORK**  For more detailed guidance on group work, see *Practical Suggestions.*

■ **TEACHING TIP** Walk students through the Critical
Thinking guide, explaining the
importance of asking and answering the questions.

## CRITICAL THINKING: WRITING CAUSE AND EFFECT

**FOCUS**

Think about your topic and whether you want to describe causes,
effects, or both.

**ASK YOURSELF**

- What important causes and/or effects do I need to present?
- Am I sure that the causes are real causes (not just something that
  happened before) or real effects (not just something that happened
  afterward)?
- What examples would show my readers how something is a cause
  or an effect?

**WRITE**

Write a cause/effect paragraph or essay that presents direct causes
and/or effects and gives detailed examples.

Use the checklist that follows to help you write your cause/effect paper.
Check off the steps as you complete them. If you need help completing a
step, read the information in the right-hand column.

## CHECKLIST: HOW TO WRITE CAUSE AND EFFECT

| STEPS IN CAUSE AND EFFECT | HOW TO DO THE STEPS |
|---|---|
| **1.** Narrow and explore your topic (the situation or event for which you will present causes and/or effects) (see Chapter 2). | ❑ Narrow the general topic to one that you can determine logical (and important) causes and effects.<br>❑ Jot down ideas about the narrowed topic. |
| **2.** Write a topic sentence (for a paragraph) or a thesis statement (for an essay) that presents your topic and main point (see Chapter 3). | ❑ Consider previewing the causes, effects, or both.<br>❑ Consider your purpose for writing: Do you want to explain why something happened, what happened as a result of it, or both? |
| **3.** Support your main point (see Chapter 4). | ❑ Use a prewriting technique (see Chapter 2) to find causes and/or effects.<br>❑ Choose only events or situations that are direct causes or direct effects.<br>❑ Choose the most significant causes and/or effects to use in your paragraph or essay.<br>❑ Explain the causes/effects with examples and details that your reader will understand. |

| STEPS IN CAUSE AND EFFECT | HOW TO DO THE STEPS |
|---|---|
| **4.** Make a plan (see Chapter 5). | ❏ Arrange the causes/effects in a logical order. |
| **5.** Write a draft (see Chapter 6). | **FOR A PARAGRAPH:**<br>❏ Write a paragraph using complete sentences, including your topic sentence, your cause(s) or effect(s), and detailed examples.<br>❏ Write a concluding sentence that reminds your readers of your main point and makes an observation based on what you have written.<br>❏ Write a title that previews the main point but doesn't repeat your topic sentence.<br>**FOR AN ESSAY:**<br>❏ Write topic sentences for each of the causes or effects.<br>❏ Write paragraphs with supporting details for each of the causes or effects.<br>❏ Consider using one of the introductory techniques described in Chapter 6 (pp. 71-73).<br>❏ Write a conclusion (see Chapter 6, pp. 73-75) that reminds your readers of your main point and makes an observation based on what you have written.<br>❏ Write a title that previews the main point but does not repeat your thesis statement. |
| **6.** Revise your draft, making at least four changes (see Chapter 7). | ❏ Get feedback from others if possible (see Chapter 7, pp. 81-82).<br>❏ *Review for unity:* Cut anything that doesn't directly explain what caused or resulted from the situation or event.<br>❏ *Review for support:* Add examples and details that help readers understand the nature of the cause or the effect.<br>❏ *Review for coherence:* Make sure the sequence of causes or effects is logical, and add transitions to take readers smoothly from one point or subject to the next. Consider repeating a key word.<br>❏ Read your topic sentence (paragraph) or thesis statement (essay), as well as your conclusion, to make sure that they are as clear, confident, and definite as you can make them. |
| **7.** Edit your revised draft (see Parts Four through Seven). | ❏ Find and correct problems with grammar, spelling, word use, and punctuation.<br>❏ Print out a clean copy. |
| **8.** Ask yourself: | ❏ Does my paper include the Four Basics of Good Cause and Effect (p. 212)?<br>❏ Is this the best I can do?<br>❏ Is the paper ready to be graded? |

■ **RESOURCES** All chapters in Part Two have writing check-lists, which are reproduced in *Additional Resources.* You can photocopy and distribute them if you want students to hand in the checklists with their assignments.

■ **RESOURCES** A blank diagram of cause and effect (big enough to write in) is in *Additional Resources.* You may want to copy it and give it to students to plan their writing.

# Chapter Review: Cause and Effect

1. A cause is  *what made an event happen*  .

2. An effect is  *what happens as a result of the event*  .

3. What are the Four Basics of Good Cause and Effect?

   *It makes clear, early on, whether you are writing about causes, effects, or both.*

   *It discusses real causes, not just something that happened before another event.*

   *It discusses real effects, not just something that happened after another event.*

   *It gives clear and detailed examples of causes and/or effects.*

4. The topic sentence (paragraph) and thesis statement (essay) in cause/effect writing usually include the  *topic*  , the  *main point*  , and an indication of  *whether you will write about causes, effects, or both*  .

■ **IDEA JOURNAL** Reread your idea-journal entry (p. 212) on a time you caused someone to be happy or unhappy. Make another entry on this topic, using what you have learned about cause and effect.

## What Will You Use?

List some situations in your everyday life where you will analyze causes and/or effects. What college or work situations require this kind of writing?

# 16

# Argument
*Writing That Persuades*

## Understand What Argument Is

**Argument** is writing that takes a position on an issue and offers reasons and supporting evidence to persuade someone else to accept, or at least consider, the position. Argument is also used to convince someone to take an action.

Argument helps you persuade people to see things your way, or at least to understand your position. Most of us have experienced the feeling of being a helpless victim—just standing by while something that we don't want to happen happens. Although knowing how to argue won't eliminate all such situations, it will help you to stand up for what you want. You may not always win, but you will sometimes, and you'll at least be able to put up a good fight.

### ▪▪ FOUR BASICS OF GOOD ARGUMENT

1. It takes a strong and definite position on an issue or advises a particular action.
2. It gives good reasons and supporting evidence to defend the position or recommended action.
3. It considers opposing views.
4. It has enthusiasm and energy from start to finish.

In the following paragraph, each number corresponds to one of the Basics of Good Argument.

> **1** Charging user fees for school athletics is both unfair and harmful to children. **3** While I understand that states have cut back on school aid, user fees are not justified. **2** Property taxes have already gone way up to support the schools, and over 75 percent of the town budget goes

## You Know This

You often try to persuade others or make your opinion known:

- You convince your mate that it's better to save some money than to buy a new television.
- The college announces a tuition increase, and you want to protest.
- You persuade someone to lend you money or let you borrow a car.

▪ **IDEA JOURNAL** Persuade a friend who has a dead-end job to take a course at your college.

▪ **TEACHING TIP** Explain to students that argument is not like bickering or fighting. It is a reasonable defense of a position.

Argument is enthusiastic and energetic.

to the schools. **2** And now, on top of taxes that skyrocket each year, families are being asked to pay extra for their children to participate in sports. For families with several children, each of whom participates in several sports, the cost is beyond their reach. So what are they supposed to do? How do they decide which child gets to play which sport? **3** People who don't have children in the schools may feel that it's only right for actual users to support the costs, but they overlook the important benefits of sports to children and our society. **2** In these times when obesity among children is rising to dangerous levels, sports play an important role in children's physical fitness. **2** Participation in sports also teaches children the importance of teamwork, responsibility, and discipline. If parents are unable to pay high user fees, the losers are both the children and our society at large, because our children are our future.

Knowing how to put together a good argument is one of the most useful skills you can develop. Consider the following examples:

| | |
|---|---|
| **COLLEGE** | You might argue for or against makeup exams for students who don't do well the first time. |
| **WORK** | You need to leave work an hour early one day a week for twelve weeks to take a course. You must persuade your boss to allow you to do so. |
| **EVERYDAY LIFE** | You try to negotiate a better price on an item you want to buy. |

## PROFILE OF SUCCESS: Argument in the Real World

Sandro Polo
Graduate Student in
Architecture

The following profile gives more insight into a work application of argument. In particular, it provides some information about a graduate student in architecture, including the kinds of writing he did at design firms before his graduate studies and, specifically, how he used argument on the job. Following the profile is an example of argument that Sandro did at work.

**BACKGROUND:** I was born in Peru and moved to California with my family when I was sixteen. I spent one and a half years in an ESL program; it took me about five years to learn English. I wasn't a good student, and later I was diagnosed with dyslexia, a condition that made reading very difficult for me. I enrolled at Solano Community College but was kicked out twice for a low grade-point average. To continue there, I had to go before the president of the college and make a case for my reinstatement. I told the president, "I know I can do it," and two years later, I graduated with honors. I went on to the University of California, Davis, where I received a B.S. in design. After working in several interior design/architectural firms,

I decided that I wanted my architecture degree, so I'm pursuing an M.S. at the University of Southern California.

**COLLEGE(S)/DEGREES:**  A.A., Solano Community College; B.S., University of California, Davis. Pursuing M.S. at the University of Southern California.

**WRITING AT WORK:**  Much of my writing was via e-mail, to clients, engineers, contractors, and city officials. Everything about a project had to be carefully and accurately documented so that the project would be successfully designed and built. All writing had to be saved both for future reference and to resolve any disputes.

**HOW SANDRO USES ARGUMENT:**  Often some aspect of a building project turned out to be more expensive than was originally budgeted. In such instances, I had to present a case for spending more money than was originally allocated.

**COMPUTER SKILLS:**  Word processing, computer-assisted design (CAD), Internet searches

**TEAMWORK ON THE JOB:**  Architecture relies very heavily on teamwork, with many different individuals (for example, engineers, designers, contractors, construction workers) working together in a coordinated effort to construct a building.

**A TYPICAL PROBLEM AT WORK:**  Problems related to money or insufficient budgets were common. Also, when engineers or contractors didn't do things right, I had to explain the situation in writing as the first step to resolving the conflict.

■ **RESOURCES** For a discussion of how to use the profiles in Part Two, see *Practical Suggestions.*

**SANDRO POLO'S ARGUMENT**

Often, certain items in a building project run over projected cost. When that happened on his job, Sandro needed to inform the client and, if he thought the extra costs were justified, make a case to the client that it was worth spending more than anticipated.

The ventilating system that was specified in the plans has come in at $XXXXX, significantly more than we had estimated. That is largely because since the plans were first put together, the company that designed and manufactures the ventilating system has developed a new system which is more expensive. The extra cost of the new system is, however, well worth your extra investment.

1  In the long term, your costs will be lower with the new system because it is more efficient, requiring less power. Over the years, this will save you money.

2  Because the system is new, it is more adaptable to future systems that you may need. This will avoid the costs of retrofitting an incompatible system in the future.

3  Most important, this new system is of a much higher quality. It has a far superior filtration system, which results in a healthier environment for the occupants and will avoid problems such as a "sick building," with its many accompanying costs.

*(continued)*

I would strongly advise you to go with the newer, higher-quality system despite the higher initial costs. It will save you money over the years.

1. What is the **issue** (or topic) in question? *the higher-than-projected cost of a ventilating system*

2. What is the author's **position**? *that the cost is well worth it and will save the client money in the long run*

3. Number the three **reasons** that Sandro gives and underline the **evidence** that supports each reason.

## Main Point in Argument

The explanations, examples, and practices in the next two sections will help you develop a good main point and support for your argument. Once you have an issue (or topic) in mind, you need to find a position on this issue that you are interested in writing about. Your **main point** will state this position; it may also preview the reasons you will give to support your position.

### Put the Issue into Question Form

To discover your position, try turning the issue into a question. This helps you understand what the issue is and gives you a way to frame your argument: as an answer to the question. Try starting the question with the word *should*.

For example, if you are interested in writing about a cigarette tax that your state government is considering, you might ask, "Should the sales tax on cigarettes be raised?" You might then consider the pros (reasons for) and cons (reasons against) of answering either yes or no, making notes about both sides of the argument. Next you would choose the stance you feel most enthusiastic about and write a strong statement of your position. For example:

> The sales tax on cigarettes should be raised to give the state badly needed revenue and to help discourage smoking.

■ **TIP** For more advice on building enthusiasm, see page 231. For more information on writing a statement of your position, see page 231.

■ **TIP** If your students are comfortable using the Web, have them type some key words about their topic into a search engine (e.g., <www .google.com>)—for instance *animal testing* and *pros and cons*. Seeing the points others have raised about an issue can help them consider the various sides. However, they should take care to consult only reliable sources. For more information, see Chapter 18.

■ **PRACTICE 1    TURNING THE ISSUE INTO A QUESTION**

For each of the following issues (topics), write a question. *Answers will vary. Possible answers shown.*

**EXAMPLE:**

**ISSUE:** Prisoners' rights

**QUESTION:** *Should prisoners have the rights they do?*

1. **ISSUE:** Lab testing on animals

**QUESTION:** *Should lab testing be conducted on animals?*

2. **ISSUE:** Violence in entertainment

   **QUESTION:** *Should the television industry use a ratings system for violent programs?*

3. **ISSUE:** Flat-rate income tax

   **QUESTION:** *Should the United States adopt a flat-rate income tax?*

4. **ISSUE:** Pornography on the Internet

   **QUESTION:** *Should pornography be banned from the Internet?*

5. **ISSUE:** Affirmative action in hiring practices

   **QUESTION:** *Should affirmative action in hiring practices be abandoned?*

## Build Enthusiasm and Energy

A good argument has enthusiasm and energy; when you read it you know that the writer is committed to his or her position. Get yourself energized or you aren't likely to persuade or convince anyone. You should feel like a lawyer about to go to court to present a case.

When you are free to choose an issue to write about, you will probably choose something you personally care about. But even when you are assigned an issue, you still need to defend it powerfully by finding some aspect of it that you care about.

Take a few minutes to think about the issue, talk about it with a partner, or jot down ideas about it. Here are techniques to get you started.

**TIPS FOR BUILDING ENTHUSIASM AND ENERGY**

- Imagine yourself arguing your position with someone you always disagree with (who, naturally, holds the opposite position).
- Imagine that your whole grade rests on persuading your professor of your position.
- Imagine how this issue could affect you or your family personally.
- Imagine that you are representing a large group of people who care about the issue very much and whose lives will be forever changed by it. It's up to you to win their case.

## Write a Statement of Your Position

Your topic sentence (paragraph) or thesis statement (essay) should answer your original question in a strong statement of your position.

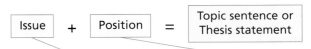

Day-care facilities should be provided at a low cost to employees.

Most good topic sentences for argument paragraphs or thesis statements for argument essays use words like these:

| | |
|---|---|
| could (not) | ought (not) |
| must (not) | requires |
| must have | should (not) |
| needs | would |

■ **TIP** For more on revising, see Chapter 7.

When you have a statement of your position, try revising it to make it sound stronger, clearer, or more interesting. Here are progressively stronger revisions:

1. Day-care facilities should be provided by companies at a low cost to employees.

2. Companies should provide day-care facilities at a low cost to employees.

3. Employees are entitled to low-cost, company-sponsored day care.

## PRACTICE 2    WRITING A STATEMENT OF YOUR POSITION

Write a statement of your position for each item in Practice 1 by answering the questions you wrote there. *Answers will vary. Possible answers shown.*

**EXAMPLE:**

**ISSUE:** Prisoners' rights

**QUESTION:** *Should prisoners have the rights they do?*

**ANSWER/POSITION STATEMENT:** *Prisoners should not have more rights and privileges than law-abiding citizens.*

1. **ISSUE:** Lab testing on animals

   **ANSWER/POSITION STATEMENT:** *Animals should continue to be used for lab testing.*

2. **ISSUE:** Violence in entertainment

   **ANSWER/POSITION STATEMENT:** *The television industry should use a ratings system for violent programs.*

3. **ISSUE:** Flat-rate income tax

   **ANSWER/POSITION STATEMENT:** *The United States should not adopt a flat-rate income tax.*

4. **ISSUE:** Pornography on the Internet

   **ANSWER/POSITION STATEMENT:** *Banning pornography from the Internet would*

   *violate the right to free speech.*

5. **ISSUE:** Affirmative action in hiring practices

   **ANSWER/POSITION STATEMENT:** *Affirmative action in hiring should be maintained.*

## Support in Argument

A strong position must be **supported** with convincing reasons and evidence. Remember that you want to persuade readers that your position is the right one. Use strong reasons and supporting evidence that will be convincing to your audience, consider opposing views, and end on a strong note.

### Present Convincing Reasons and Evidence

The strength of your argument depends on the quality of the reasons and supporting evidence that you present. **Reasons** are the points that support your position, points that must be backed by evidence. **Evidence** consists of the *facts, examples,* and *expert opinions* that support your reasons.

■ **TEACHING TIP** Go over the concept of evidence carefully. Students' arguments are often weak because of poor evidence or lack of evidence.

- **FACTS:** Things that are real; their existence can be proved. Statistics — real numbers from actual studies — can be persuasive factual evidence to back up your position.

- **EXAMPLES:** Specific information or experiences that support your position.

- **EXPERT OPINION:** The opinion of someone who is considered an expert in the field. The person must be known for his or her expertise in your topic. For example, the opinion of the head of the FBI about the benefits of a low-fat diet isn't strong evidence. The FBI director isn't an expert in the field of nutrition.

In each of the following examples, a reason and appropriate evidence provide support for a position.

**POSITION:** It pays to stay in college.

**REASON:** College graduates earn more than people without degrees.

**EVIDENCE/FACT:** Community-college graduates earn 58 percent more than high-school graduates and 320 percent more than high-school dropouts.

**POSITION:** Genetically modified foods should be banned until they have been thoroughly tested for safety.

**REASON:** Currently, nobody is certain about the effects of such foods on humans and animals.

**EVIDENCE/EXAMPLE:** The government and the biotech industry have not produced convincing evidence that such foods are as safe or nutritional as foods that have not been genetically modified.

**POSITION:** The drug Ritalin is overprescribed for attention-deficit/hyperactivity disorder (ADHD) in children.

**REASON:** It is too often considered a "wonder drug."

**EVIDENCE/EXPERT OPINION:** Dr. Peter Jensen, a pediatric specialist, warns, "I fear that ADHD is suffering from the 'disease of the month' syndrome, and Ritalin is its 'cure.'"

As you choose reasons and evidence to support your position, consider what your audience is likely to think about your view of the issue. Are they likely to agree with you, to be uncommitted, or to be hostile? Think about what kinds of reasons and evidence would be most convincing to a typical member of your audience.

When writing an argument, it's tempting to cite as evidence something that "everyone" knows or believes or does. But be careful of "everyone" evidence; everyone usually doesn't know or believe it. It is better to stick with facts (including statistics), specific examples, and expert opinions.

■ **TIP** To find good reasons and strong evidence, you may want to consult outside sources, either at the library or on the Internet. For more on using outside sources, see Chapter 18.

■ **COMPUTER** If you are working in a lab setting, have each student list the evidence for his or her topic on the computer. Then have each student move to another student's computer and write down opposition to the evidence that is listed. Students should then return to their own computers and try to answer the objections.

■ **PRACTICE 3** **FINDING EVIDENCE**

For each of the following positions, give the type of evidence indicated (you may have to make up the evidence).

**EXAMPLE:**

**POSITION:** Pesticides should not be sprayed from planes.

**REASON:** They can cause more damage than they prevent.

**EVIDENCE/FACT:** *Scientific studies prove that both plant life and people are harmed.*

1. **POSITION:** The parking situation on this campus is impossible.

   **REASON:** There are too few spaces for the number of students.

   **EVIDENCE/EXAMPLE:** *Answers will vary.*

2. **POSITION:** People should not go overboard when dieting.

   **REASON:** Losing weight quickly is unhealthy.

   **EVIDENCE/FACT:** _____

3. **POSITION:** Smoking is harmful to smokers and nonsmokers alike.

   **REASON:** Even secondhand smoke can cause lung damage.

   **EVIDENCE/EXPERT OPINION:** _____

4. **POSITION:** Wealthy people receive special privileges in our society.

   **REASON:** As the saying goes, "Money talks."

   **EVIDENCE/EXAMPLE:** _____

5. **POSITION:** Adolescents and alcohol are a dangerous mix.

   **REASON:** Alcohol can be fatal to adolescents.

   **EVIDENCE/FACT:** _____

## Review Your Reasons and Evidence, and Consider Your Opposition

Your reasons and evidence may be convincing to you, but will they persuade your readers? Review the support for your argument by using these strategies.

### TESTING YOUR REASONS AND EVIDENCE

- Reread your reasons and evidence from your opponent's perspective, looking for ways to knock them down. Anticipate your opponent's objections, and include evidence to answer them.
- Ask someone else to cross-examine your reasons, trying to knock them down.
- Stay away from generalities. Statements about what everyone else does or what always happens are easy to disprove.
- Make sure that you have considered every important angle of the issue. Take the time to present good support for your position; your argument depends on the quality of your reasons and evidence.
- Reread your reasons and evidence to make sure that they support your position. They must be relevant to your argument.

■ **DISCUSSION** Model the opponent's perspective in class. Put a topic and some evidence on the board. Ask for ideas about how the opposition would try to knock down the evidence.

■ **PRACTICE 4** **REVIEWING THE EVIDENCE**

For each of the following positions, one piece of evidence is weak: It does not support the position. Circle the letter of the weak evidence, and in the space provided state why it is weak.

**EXAMPLE:**

**POSITION:** Advertisements should not use skinny models.

**REASON:** Skinny should not be promoted as ideal.

a. Three friends of mine became anorexic trying to get skinny.

(b.) Everyone knows that most people are not that thin.

c. A survey of young girls shows that they think they should be as thin as models.

d. People can endanger their health trying to fit the skinny "ideal."

Not strong evidence because _"everyone knows" is not strong evidence; every-_

_one obviously doesn't know that._

1. **POSITION:** People who own guns should not be allowed to keep them at home.

   **REASON:** It is dangerous to keep a gun in the house.
   a. Guns can go off by accident.
   b. Keeping guns at home has been found to increase the risk of home suicides and adolescent suicides.
   c. Just last week a story in the newspaper told about a man who, in a fit of rage, took his gun out of the drawer and shot his wife.
   ⓓ. Guns can be purchased easily.

   Not strong evidence because _it is irrelevant; it doesn't support the position_.

2. **POSITION:** Schoolchildren in the United States should go to school all year.

   **REASON:** Year-round schooling promotes better learning.
   ⓐ. All of my friends would like to end the long summer break.
   b. A survey of teachers across the country showed that children's learning improved when they had multiple shorter vacations rather than entire summers off.
   c. Many children are bored and restless after three weeks of vacation and would be better off returning to school.
   d. Test scores improved when a school system in Colorado went to year-round school sessions.

   Not strong evidence because _wanting it doesn't mean it should happen; also this is a personal preference, not evidence._

3. **POSITION:** The "three strikes and you're out" law that forces judges to send people to jail after three convictions should be revised.

   **REASON:** Basing decisions about sentencing on numbers alone is neither reasonable nor fair.
   a. A week ago, a man who stole a slice of pizza was sentenced to eight to ten years in prison because it was his third conviction.
   b. The law makes prison overcrowding even worse.
   ⓒ. Judges always give the longest sentence possible anyway.
   d. The law too often results in people getting major prison sentences for minor crimes.

   Not strong evidence because _it is a generality; not all judges do this._

### End on a Strong Note

Arguments are almost always organized by order of importance. (For more information, see Chapter 5, pp. 57–58.) It is often effective to save your most persuasive reasons and evidence for the end, building up force and leaving a strong impression. In other words, consider saving the best for last.

Your conclusion is your last opportunity to convince readers of your position. Make it memorable and dramatic. Remind your readers of the issue, your position, and the rightness of your position.

Before writing your conclusion, build up your enthusiasm again. Then reread what you have written. As soon as you finish reading, write the most forceful ending you can think of. Aim for power; you can tone it down later.

## Read and Analyze Argument

Reading examples of argument and analyzing their structure will help you understand what good argument writing looks like before you do your own. The first example is paragraph-length, and the second is essay-length. Your instructor may ask you to read and answer the questions for one or both of these.

■ **READING SELECTIONS**
For further examples of and activities for argument, see Chapter 48.

### Argument: Paragraph

Prisoners should not have more rights and privileges than law-abiding citizens. [1] In the first place, they are guaranteed certain facilities that not everyone else has. For example, a prisoner in Massachusetts recently sued a prison because he didn't have a toilet in his cell and had to use one down the hall. My grandmother, who lives in a nursing home, also has to go down the hall to use the bathroom, and we pay for her to be there. [2] Prisoners have the right to three square meals a day. I eat macaroni and cheese from a box several times a week because it's cheap. Is that a square meal? [3] Worst of all, my taxes pay for prisoners to get college degrees. Last year my state proudly reported that one hundred prisoners had received college degrees. I can't even afford that for myself; why should I help someone who's being "punished"? I realize that education is supposed to help rehabilitate prisoners, but why should someone who has broken the law get more help than I do? I wish the state took as good care of me as it does of its prisoners.

1. The **topic sentence** in an argument paragraph should include the issue (topic) and the writer's position on that issue.

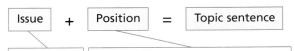

Cell phones should be banned from theaters.

Double-underline the **topic sentence** in the example paragraph.

2. The **support** in an argument paragraph consists of the reasons and evidence that back up the position. Number the three reasons that the writer gives to support his position, and **underline** the evidence that supports those reasons.

3. Writers of argument paragraphs usually use **order of importance**; they start with the least important idea and end with the most important one. They use **transitions** to move from one piece of evidence to the next and to add emphasis.

| TRANSITIONS FROM ONE POINT TO ANOTHER | | TRANSITIONS TO ADD EMPHASIS | |
|---|---|---|---|
| also | for example | above all | more important |
| another fact to consider | in addition | best of all | most important |
| another reason | in the first place | especially | remember |
| another thing | the last point to consider | in fact | worst of all |
| consider that | | in particular | |

What transition does the writer use to indicate his final, most important piece of evidence in the sample paragraph? _worst of all_

4. Double-underline the **concluding statement**.

5. Does the paragraph have the Four Basics of Good Argument (p. 227)? Why or why not?

_Yes. Specific answers will vary, but students should be able to give examples of the_

_Four Basics._

## Argument: Essay

### Life or Death: Who Decides?

*Jason C. Sifford*

Too many hospital beds are taken up by basically dead bodies. Many families who have the money to do so keep patients alive who would otherwise never wake up again. While these "dead" patients take up room in the hospitals, there are many who could be saved with immediate care but who cannot be admitted for lack of space. A different but equally problematic situation is the family who cannot make unbiased medical decisions about their spouse or family members when money is involved, be it medical bills or the anticipation of a large sum from the insurance company. In each case, families' feelings stand in the way of good medical care. Therefore, doctors should have the sole authority to recommend that a patient sustain treatment or be cut off from it.

[1] Doctors go through strenuous training for at least eight years to learn how the body works and, for that matter, how the body does not work. After the conventional four years of college comes medical school. After medical school comes the internship, which can last up to three years. Obviously, becoming a doctor is no trivial task. These doctors become, after all their studies, the most elite and intelligent people on earth, at least in the areas of health and patient care.

[2] However, too often it is the family, with its close ties to the patient and lack of training in life-or-death situations, that makes the most important medical decisions for the patient. Many families care deeply about their loved ones and would do anything to keep them alive for as long as possible. "Alive" is the key word here. Many families, with unsupported hopes that some supernatural force or miracle will happen, keep their loved ones on life support long after the brain has expired. On the other hand, some people have family members who go into the hospital and ask that needed treatment be denied. And some family members will not sign the needed waivers so that treatment may begin because they have taken out huge insurance policies on the patient and wish to collect on them. Doctors can review the facts objectively and determine if a patient will recover or not. Therefore, they should have the last word on the matter.

[3] The most tragic outcome of keeping the "dead" alive is that many people cannot enter the hospital because of a lack of beds. A recent poll by the *American Medical Journal* estimated that 15 percent of all hospital beds are taken up by clinically dead patients. These numbers are staggering, considering that another 30 percent of the general population cannot receive treatment because of hospital overcrowding. In Freemont, Georgia, Jessica Freeman, twelve years old, died in her home from an infection after being treated in the emergency room for a ruptured appendix and then released because no beds were available.

With tragedies such as Jessica's happening every day, it is evident that something is wrong with our medical system. Giving doctors authority either to dismiss patients who are not treatable or to stop treatments for those who will never recover can only help save more lives.

1. The **thesis statement** of an argument essay usually includes the issue (topic) and the writer's position on that issue. Writers may also use a thesis statement to preview the reasons they will offer to support their position.

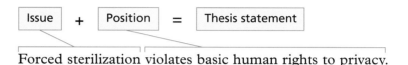

Forced sterilization violates basic human rights to privacy.

Double-underline the **thesis statement** in the example essay.

2. The **support** in an argument essay consists of reasons and evidence — facts, examples, and expert opinions. The support helps persuade readers that the position is a good one. Each major reason should be the topic sentence of a paragraph. Number the **topic sentences** in the sample essay and underline the **evidence** that backs up each reason.

3. Writers of argument essays usually use **order of importance**, starting with the least important and ending with the most important and persuasive piece of evidence. They use transitions and transitional sentences to move from one reason or piece of evidence to the next and to add emphasis. (For lists of argument transitions, see p. 238.)

   What **transition** does the writer use to indicate his final, most important piece of evidence in the sample essay? *the most tragic outcome*

4. Double-underline the **sentence in the concluding paragraph that relates back to the introduction and main point**.

5. Does the essay have the Four Basics of Good Argument (p. 227)? Why or why not?
   *Yes. Specific answers will vary, but students should be able to give examples of the Four Basics.*

## Write Your Own Argument

■ **TIP** Look back at your idea-journal entry (p. 227) for ideas.

In this section, you will write your own argument paragraph or essay based on your (or your instructor's) choice among four assignments.

To complete your argument, follow this sequence:

1. Review the Four Basics of Good Argument (p. 227).

2. Choose your assignment.

3. Read the Critical Thinking box on page 243.

4. If you are asked to complete Assignment 3, read Using Problem Solving and Teamwork in Writing (Chapter 8, pp. 109–11).

5. Write your argument using the Checklist: How to Write Argument (pp. 244–45).

## ASSIGNMENT 1   WRITING ABOUT COLLEGE, WORK, AND EVERYDAY LIFE

Write an argument paragraph or essay on one of the following topics.

■ **TIP** If you use the Writing Guide Software with this book, you'll find step-by-step guidance for writing argument paragraphs and essays.

### COLLEGE

| PARAGRAPH | ESSAY |
|---|---|
| • Take a position on a controversial issue on your campus.<br>• Argue that textbooks cost too much.<br>• Persuade your teacher to raise your grade. | • Take a position on the law that requires students to stay in school until they are sixteen.<br>• Argue that student evaluations should/should not determine teachers' pay raises.<br>• Argue for or against affirmative action in college admissions. |

### WORK

| PARAGRAPH | ESSAY |
|---|---|
| • Take a position on a controversial issue in your workplace.<br>• Persuade your boss to give you a raise.<br>• Argue for a change at work. | • Persuade someone to buy your company's product or service.<br>• Argue that "my email is private."<br>• Argue that a company policy isn't fair. |

■ **ESL** Some cultures (many Asian ones, for example) are not as direct as U.S. culture is. Emphasize to students that their positions must be clear, direct, and supported by evidence.

### EVERYDAY LIFE

| PARAGRAPH | ESSAY |
|---|---|
| • Take a position on a controversial current issue in your community.<br>• Argue for or against smoking restrictions.<br>• Argue that something should be banned. | • Argue for or against assisted suicide.<br>• Take a position on any issue you feel strongly about.<br>• Argue for or against the legalization of marijuana. |

■ **TEACHING TIP** Suggest to students that they make journal entries on some of the topics that they don't write about for this assignment.

## ASSIGNMENT 2   WRITING ABOUT IMAGES

What issue might you be willing to demonstrate publicly for or against, and why? Present your position in a paragraph or essay.

■ **ASSIGNMENT 3**    **WRITING IN THE REAL WORLD/SOLVING A PROBLEM**

**PROBLEM:** Your friend/child/relative has just turned sixteen and is planning to drop out of high school. He's always done poorly, and if he drops out he can increase his hours at the restaurant where he works. You think this is a terrible idea for many reasons.

**ASSIGNMENT:** In a group or on your own, come up with various reasons in support of your decision. Consider, too, your friend's/child's/relative's possible objections to your argument, and account for those. Then write an argument paragraph or essay to persuade him to complete high school. Give at least three solid reasons and support your reasons with good evidence or examples.

■ **TEAMWORK** For more de-tailed guidance on group work, see *Practical Suggestions.*

■ **ASSIGNMENT 4    WRITING ARGUMENT FOR A WRITING TEST**

Many states and colleges require students to take a writing test. Often the test calls for an argument paragraph or essay on an assigned topic, and students must argue for or against something, as directed. Many people believe that a good writer should be able to argue either side of an issue regardless of his or her personal feelings. Choose one of the following topics, come up with reasons and evidence to support both sides of the issue, and write a paragraph or an essay defending each side. If your instructor gives you a time limit, make sure to budget your time carefully: Allow enough time to decide on your position for each side, write a topic sentence (paragraph) or thesis statement (essay), and develop strong reasons and evidence to support your position.

■ **TIP** For more on timed writing, see Chapter 17.

1.  People convicted of drunk driving should lose their license forever.

2.  Recently a popular and well-respected high school teacher in Illinois was dismissed from his position because people found out that when he was a high-school student he had been charged with possession of marijuana (two joints). The law in the state says that no one convicted of any drug crime may serve as a teacher in a public school, so the principal had no choice but to dismiss the teacher despite his superb record of fifteen years of teaching. Argue for and against the law.

3.  A conviction for first-degree murder should carry a mandatory death penalty.

4.  The government should make it more difficult for couples to divorce.

5.  College students should be penalized for poor attendance.

Before writing, read the Critical Thinking box that follows.

■ **DISCUSSION** Organize debates on some of these topics. Poll the class on the issues, divide students into groups to develop arguments, and suggest using the library to gather evidence. Devote a class period to the debates and a discussion of the effectiveness of the arguments.

**CRITICAL THINKING: WRITING ARGUMENT**

**FOCUS**

Think about your position on the issue, perhaps putting your issue into question form. Consider how you can persuade your readers.

**ASK YOURSELF**
• Why is this issue important to me?
• What are my readers likely to know about the issue?
• What are the opposing views to my position, and how can I answer them?
• What reasons and evidence will support my position?

**WRITE**

Using order of importance, write an argument that strongly defends your position.

■ **TEACHING TIP** Walk students through the Critical Thinking guide, explaining the importance of asking and answering the questions.

Use the checklist that follows to help you write your argument. Check off the steps as you complete them. If you need help completing a step, read the information in the right-hand column.

## CHECKLIST: HOW TO WRITE ARGUMENT

| STEPS IN ARGUMENT | HOW TO DO THE STEPS |
|---|---|
| **1.** Narrow and explore your topic (see Chapter 2). | ❑ Narrow the general topic to an issue that you care about.<br>❑ Jot down ideas about the issue. |
| **2.** Write a topic sentence (for a paragraph) or a thesis statement (for an essay) that includes your topic and your position on it (see Chapter 3). | ❑ Turn the issue into a question (see p. 230) and answer the question to discover your position.<br>❑ Build energy by thinking about how you are personally affected by this issue.<br>❑ Write your topic sentence or thesis statement, including your position.<br>❑ Rewrite the topic sentence or thesis statement to make it more definite and confident. |
| **3.** Support your position (see Chapter 4). | ❑ Use a prewriting technique (see Chapter 2) to come up with reasons and evidence.<br>❑ Consider what makes strong, persuasive evidence (facts, examples, expert opinions).<br>❑ Consider what your readers' position on the issue might be and what types of reasons and evidence will most likely convince them.<br>❑ Drop reasons or evidence that are unrelated to your position and evidence that will not be convincing to your readers.<br>❑ Consider opposing views and anticipate objections. |
| **4.** Make a plan (see Chapter 5). | ❑ Arrange the reasons in order of importance, saving the most important for last. |
| **5.** Write a draft (see Chapter 6). | **FOR A PARAGRAPH:**<br>❑ Write a paragraph using complete sentences, including your topic sentence, your reasons for your position, and supporting evidence.<br>❑ Write a concluding sentence that reminds your readers of your position and makes a strong last attempt to convince them of that position, based on what you've written.<br>❑ Write a title that previews the main point but doesn't repeat your topic sentence.<br><br>**FOR AN ESSAY:**<br>❑ Write topic sentences for each of the reasons that support your position.<br>❑ Write paragraphs with supporting evidence for each of the reasons.<br>❑ Consider using one of the introductory techniques described in Chapter 6 (pp. 71–73). |

| STEPS IN ARGUMENT | HOW TO DO THE STEPS |
|---|---|
| | ❏ Write a conclusion (see Chapter 6, pp. 73–75) that reminds your readers of your position and makes a strong last attempt to convince them of that position, based on the reasons you have presented.<br>❏ Write a title that previews the main point but does not repeat your thesis statement. |
| **6.** Revise your draft, making at least four changes (see Chapter 7). | ❏ Get feedback from others if possible (see Chapter 7, pp. 81–82).<br>❏ *Review for unity:* Cut any reasons that don't directly support your position.<br>❏ *Review for support:* Add reasons and evidence that help readers understand your position. Get rid of weak reasons or evidence. Read your argument as if you hold the opposing view, and try to anticipate any criticisms.<br>❏ *Review for coherence:* Check to make sure the essay is organized by order of importance, with the most convincing reason presented last. Add transitions to take readers smoothly from one point or subject to the next. Consider repeating a key word.<br>❏ Read your topic sentence (paragraph) or thesis statement (essay), as well as your conclusion, to make sure that they are as clear, confident, and definite as you can make them. |
| **7.** Edit your revised draft (see Parts Four through Seven). | ❏ Find and correct problems with grammar, spelling, word use, and punctuation.<br>❏ Print out a clean copy. |
| **8.** Ask yourself: | ❏ Does my paper include the Four Basics of Good Argument (p. 227)?<br>❏ Is this the best I can do?<br>❏ Is the paper ready to be graded? |

# Chapter Review: Argument

1. Argument is writing *that takes a position on an issue and offers reasons and evidence to support it* .

2. What are the Four Basics of Good Argument?

   *It takes a strong and definite position on an issue or advises a particular action.*

   *It gives good reasons and supporting evidence to defend the position or recommended action.*

■ **RESOURCES** All chapters in Part Two have writing checklists, which are reproduced in *Additional Resources*. You can photocopy and distribute them if you want students to hand in the checklists with their assignments.

■ **RESOURCES** A blank diagram of an argument (big enough to write in) is in *Additional Resources*. You may want to copy it and give it to students to plan their writing.

*It considers opposing views.*

*It has enthusiasm and energy from start to finish.*

3.  Why are enthusiasm and energy important in argument? *An energetic/ passionate argument is persuasive.*

4.  The topic sentence (paragraph) or thesis statement (essay) in an argu- ment should include what two elements? *an issue and the writer's position on that issue*

5.  In an argument, reasons are *the points that support a position* .

6.  What three types of information make good evidence? *facts, examples, expert opinions*

7.  Why do you need to be aware of opposing views? *to anticipate attacks that may damage the strength of your argument*

■ **IDEA JOURNAL** Reread your idea-journal entry (p. 227) on why your friend should take a college course. Make another entry on this topic, using what you have learned about argu- ment.

## What Will You Use?

List some situations in your life where you could use argument to help you.

# Part Three
# Special College Writing Projects

# 17

# Tests, Timed Writing, and Summaries

*Writing That Shows What You've Learned*

## Studying for Tests

Everyone gets nervous about taking tests. The trick is to turn that nervousness into positive energy by learning test-taking strategies. This chapter will give you some all-purpose study strategies for different kinds of tests as well as some specific advice about essay exams and other timed writing assignments.

If you don't study for an exam, panic and poor performance are the likely results. Here are five reliable tips to help you study for any exam.

### 1. Ask about the Test

The more you know about the test, the better off you'll be. Start with the person who knows the most: your instructor. It's reasonable to ask about the test, so don't be afraid. Just know what questions to ask.

**You Know This**

You've taken lots of tests under pressure:

- You try out for a sports team or school play.
- You get your driver's license.
- You participate in a race.

| ASK | NOT |
|---|---|
| • What part of the course or text will the test cover? (A chapter? A unit?) | • What's on the test? |
| • Will the format be multiple choice? Short answer? Essay? A combination? | • You're not going to give us an essay question, are you? |
| • Will I be allowed to use notes? A textbook? Reference books? | • We can just look up the answers, right? |
| • What percentage of my course grade will this count for? | • Is this test important? |

■ **DISCUSSION** Ask students to consider why the "not" questions aren't good. If they get stuck, ask them to think what effect the questions might have on an instructor.

| **ASK** | **NOT** |
|---|---|
| • Can you recommend what to review? (the text, notes, lab reports, and so on) | • Do I need to read the book? Is the stuff you said in class important? |
| • Will I have the whole period to complete the exam? | • How long is it? Is there a makeup test? |

Also, ask if you will need any special materials (calculator, dictionary, and so on). Write down your instructor's answers to your questions. Don't rely on your memory; you will be busy enough remembering the material for the exam without having to recall what the instructor said.

## 2. Study with Others

Although everyone is busy, forming a study group is well worth the effort. Probably the most important thing you can do is exchange notes on what is likely to be on the test and how to approach it. When you study by yourself, you have only your own perception of what's important. Having others' ideas improves your ability to "scope out" the test.

Study-group members can also help each other learn and review the content of the course. Do some preparation before meeting as a group so that you make the most of your group-study time. Here are some ways to prepare and study as a group or with a partner.

- Each person could take responsibility for a particular section of the material, preparing a list of five to ten questions that might be asked about that section. The questions and possible responses could then be discussed in the group.
- Each person could copy his or her notes—including study questions—on a particular chapter, section, or topic and distribute them to group members.
- Each person could come with a list of "ten questions I'm sure will be on the test."
- Each person could come with a list of "things I don't understand."

## 3. Predict What Will Be on the Exam

Whether you are studying with other people or by yourself, it's a good idea to make a list of what you think will be covered on the exam. Look over your notes, assignments, and any previous tests or quizzes. What has the instructor stressed the most? Try writing questions for that material, and then try answering your own questions.

If you are confused about some concepts, ask your instructor about them, or ask another person in the class—someone who knows the material. If you are studying in a group, try writing a mock exam and showing it to your instructor to see if you are on the right track. Don't go into an exam knowing that you don't understand a major concept.

## 4. Use Study Aids

Reread your notes, looking especially for anything you've underlined, starred, or highlighted. You might also want to consider using one or more of the following study aids.

- If you are being tested on material from your textbook, review any chapter reviews, summaries, or "key concepts" sections.
- Review any handouts your instructor may have given you.
- Consider other available ways to review material—audiotapes, videos, computer exercises, study guides, and so on.

■ **TEACHING TIP** Walk students through a chapter of this book, pointing out the study aids in the chapter: the major headings, Critical Thinking guides, chapter reviews, and so on.

## 5. Study Actively

You are more likely to understand and remember material if you have reviewed it actively. If you're reviewing material in a book, take notes. This helps you remember information because you put it in your own words, you write the information, and you see it on the page of your notebook or in the margin of the book.

Say aloud concepts that you want to remember. Many people learn well by hearing something in addition to seeing it.

If you are studying from notes, modify your notes in some way. For example, if you've written an outline, transform it into a map, such as the clustering example in Chapter 2 (p. 27). *Do* something.

## Taking Tests

Some students who fail or get low grades on exams simply don't know or understand the material. But many others fail because they don't know how to take an exam. Here are five strategies you should use for every exam.

## 1. Be Prepared

If you've found out everything you could about the exam and studied for it using the five tips discussed previously, you've already done the most important preparation. But don't get to the exam and discover that you've left something essential at home. Do you need paper? A pen? Books? A notebook? A calculator? Make sure you have what you need.

## 2. Manage Your Nerves

Get plenty of rest the night before, and allow extra time to get to class. Arrive early enough to settle in. Sit up straight, take a deep breath, and remind yourself that you know the material. You're prepared; you're ready; you will pass. When your instructor starts to talk, look up and listen.

## 3. Understand the Directions

First, listen to the directions your instructor gives. It's tempting to start flipping through the exam as soon as you get it rather than listening to what your instructor has to say. Resist the temptation. Your instructor may be giving you key advice or information that's not written elsewhere, and you may miss it if you're not paying attention.

Second, when you begin the test (after surveying it), carefully read the written directions for each part. Sometimes students answer all of the questions in a section and then find out later that the directions said to answer only one or two. If you don't understand any part of the directions, be sure to ask your instructor for clarification.

## 4. Survey the Whole Exam before Starting

Surveying is a crucial step that will help you budget your time. Often the toughest questions (and the ones worth the most points) are at the end. You don't want to answer all the two-point questions and leave the thirty-point ones unanswered. Ask yourself:

- *How many parts does the test have?* Be sure to look on both sides of the page.
- *How many points is each part worth?* This information will help you decide how much time to spend on each part.
- *Which questions can I answer quickly and easily?* Start with these. It will get you going on the test, give you points, and build your confidence.

## 5. Develop a Plan

■ **TEACHING TIP** Tell students that surveying and developing a plan don't take much time away from the test taking; students shouldn't use more than three to five minutes for planning.

First, **budget your time**. After surveying the whole test, write down how much time you will allow for each part. Make sure to leave enough time for the parts with the highest point values. Also leave enough time for any essay questions. They usually take longer than you think they will.

As you plan your time, keep in mind how much time you really have for the exam: A "two-hour" exam may really be only one hour and fifty minutes long if it takes ten minutes for your instructor to distribute and explain the test. And remember to subtract a few minutes at the beginning for settling in and a few at the end for checking your work.

Second, **decide on an order**. Decide where you should start and what you should do second, third, and so on. Start with the parts you can answer quickly and easily.

Third, **make a schedule and stick to it.** You can calculate what time you want to start each section: Part 1 at 9:40, Part 2 at 9:55, and so on.

As you take the exam, monitor your time. If you find you're really stuck on a question and you're going way over your time budget, move on to another question or part. If you've thought about the question and can't come up with an answer, just move on. If you have time at the end of the exam period, you can always go back to it.

# Responding to Essay Questions or Timed Writing Assignments

An **essay question** is a test item that asks you to write several paragraphs explaining and illustrating your answer. A **timed writing** is an assignment that requires writing one or more paragraphs in response to a question or prompt within a set period of time and in the classroom.

Here are five steps you can take to answer essay questions and timed writing assignments.

## 1. Read the Question Carefully

Be sure to read an essay question carefully so you know exactly what to write. Look for three kinds of key words in an essay question:

- words that tell you *what subject* to write on
- words that tell you *how to write about it*
- words that tell you *how many parts* your answer should have

Circle words like these in the essay question. (For a more complete list of key words, see page 254.)

Discuss the three major stages in the consumer buying process.

Describe someone who has played an important role in your life.

### PRACTICE 1   IDENTIFYING AND DECODING KEY WORDS

Read the following essay questions, and circle the key words. In the space below each item, explain what the question asks you to do.

**EXAMPLE:** Discuss the meaning of addiction.
*Define the term addiction and give examples of it.*

1. Discuss the effects of alcohol.
*List and explain the effects of alcohol.*

■ **TEACHING TIP** Have students bring in exams with essay questions from other classes. Look for other words that are used on these exams, and discuss what they mean.

## Common Key Words in Essay Exam Questions

| KEY WORD | WHAT IT MEANS |
|---|---|
| **Analyze** | Break into parts (classify) and discuss |
| **Define** | State the meaning and give examples |
| **Describe** the **stages** of | List and explain steps in a process |
| **Discuss** the **causes** of | List and explain the causes |
| **Discuss** the **concept** of | Define and give examples |
| **Discuss** the **differences between** | Contrast and give examples |
| **Discuss** the **effects/results** of | List and explain the effects |
| **Discuss** the **meaning** of | Define and give examples |
| **Discuss** the **similarities between** | Compare and give examples |
| **Discuss** the **stages/steps** of | Explain a process |
| **Explain** the **term** | Define and give examples |
| **Follow/Trace** the **development** of | Give the history; narrate the story |
| **Follow/Trace** the **process** of | Explain the sequence of steps or stages in the process |
| **Identify** | Define and give examples |
| **Should** | Argue for or against |
| **Summarize** | Give a brief overview of narrative |

2. What are the main differences between the Senate and the House of Representatives?

    *Contrast the Senate and the House and give examples.*

3. Discuss the four main stages of collective bargaining.

    *Write a process analysis with four steps for the collective-bargaining process.*

4. Identify and discuss three major learning styles.

    *Define and give examples of three learning styles.*

5. Give examples of technological changes that affect the way businesses operate.

*Identify and describe several examples that illustrate how businesses have*

*changed.*

6. (Trace the development) of (animation) in the (movie) industry.
   *Give the history of animated films.*

## 2. Write a Thesis Statement

Write a thesis statement that is simple and clear; it should say exactly what you will cover in your answer. (In some cases, you may get partial credit for correct information contained in the thesis statement, even if you did not get the chance to write about it in your essay.)

■ **TIP** For more on writing a thesis statement, see Chapter 3.

The best way to stay on track in an essay exam is to write a thesis statement that contains the key words in the essay question and restates its main idea.

**ESSAY QUESTION:** Explore one important consequence of women entering the workforce in large numbers in the 1940s.

**POSSIBLE THESIS STATEMENT:** One important consequence of women entering the workforce in large numbers in the 1940s was the recognition that women could do "men's work."

■ **TIP** For more on developing thesis statements, see Chapter 3.

■ **PRACTICE 2   WRITING THESIS STATEMENTS**

Write thesis statements in response to the following sample essay-exam questions. Even if you do not know much about the topic, you should be able to write a thesis statement that follows the guidelines in this section.

1. Describe someone who was important to you in high school.
   *Answers will vary.*

2. Identify three ways to relieve stress; give examples.

3. Should smoking be banned from all public places?

4. Discuss the differences between your eating habits now and your eating habits five years ago.

5. Choose two people who made a difference in twentieth-century America, and explore their contributions.

## 3. Make an Outline

■ **TIP** For more on making an outline, see Chapter 5.

Before you answer an essay question, jot down some notes on how you want to answer it. Write down any important names, dates, or facts that pop into your head. Make a short outline so that you have a basic map for your answer. These notes will help you stick to your main points and remember essential details as you write.

## 4. Write Your Answer

Your answer to an essay question should always be in essay form, with an introductory paragraph, several support paragraphs, and a concluding paragraph. Don't forget to use separate paragraphs for separate support points.

Here is an essay written by Lorenzo Gilbert at Broward Community College in Florida for the final exam in his basic writing course. He wrote in response to this question: "Describe someone who has played an important role in your life."

Introduction with thesis statement

Support point 1

In today's society with all of the violence and drugs in the black community, it really helps to see a black man rise above other people's expectations.

When my uncle Dr. Gerald Johnson was a little boy, he used to take care of sick or wounded animals. When he got a little older, he worked for an animal doctor in an animal clinic. He cleaned cages, walked dogs, bathed dogs, and assisted the doctor any way he could. Although he earned only seventy-five cents an hour, the knowledge he received from working under a doctor would make him rich later.

Support point 2

Johnson graduated from Miami Central and received a band scholarship to attend Tuskegee University in Alabama. Tuskegee was an all-black school, so he felt very much at home. After marching in the band for four years and taking a lot of preveterinarian courses, it was time for him to move on. Although Tuskegee had a veterinary school, Johnson decided to go to the University of Florida since it was closer to home. Unfortunately, going to UF made him feel out of place. The university was predominantly white, and the veterinary school had only two blacks including Johnson. After the second year the only black other than Johnson dropped out because of the pressure. Since Johnson was black, none of the white students would work with him, study with him, or help him.

Support point 3

Even though he did not receive the extra help the others got, he still graduated, making him the first black to graduate from the University of Florida's veterinary school.

Support point 4

Now he owns three animal clinics and employs two assistant doctors, four receptionists, seven technicians, and one groomer.

Conclusion that summarizes the main point and makes further observations

If you really want something and work hard for it, you can have it. Johnson really wanted to be a veterinarian and he got it. That is why he plays an important role in my life. He helped me see that anything is possible.

## 5. Read and Revise Your Answer

After you have finished an essay exam, read your answer and ask yourself the following questions.

- Do I include a thesis statement that clearly states the topic and my main point about it?

- Does my essay answer the question? (Look back at the question and your notes on what it asks you to do. Have you done it?)

- Is my answer in essay form? Are there separate paragraphs for each point?

- Is my answer free of major grammar and spelling errors?

You can revise your essay by neatly crossing out mistakes, adding extra words or sentences in the margin or on extra lines, and using the paragraph symbol (¶) to show where you want a new paragraph to start.

### ASSIGNMENT    ANSWERING AN ESSAY QUESTION

Choose one of the following topics and write an essay on it, using the five steps to answer essay questions and timed writing assignments discussed in this chapter. If you are doing this independently, give yourself a forty-five-minute time limit.

1. Write an essay agreeing or disagreeing with one of the following statements.

> People should live together before they get married.
>
> Marriage is an outdated custom.
>
> People should be required to retire at age sixty-five.
>
> Most students cheat on exams.
>
> Admissions policies at colleges should be made stricter.
>
> English should be the only official language in the United States.
>
> All public schools should have metal detectors.
>
> Tobacco should be banned entirely.
>
> People would be better off if they never watched television.
>
> Violence on television and in movies results in increased violence in society.
>
> People in this state do not care about the environment.
>
> All people should have religious training.
>
> Schoolchildren have too many vacations.

2. Discuss a major problem on this campus.

3. Define *heroism*.

4. Discuss the types of crime in this area.

5. Narrate an event that impressed you in high school.

6. Summarize the events that led to your taking this course.

# Writing Summaries

A **summary** is a condensed version of a longer piece of writing. A summary presents the main idea and key support points, stripping down the information to its essential elements. A summary is always stated in your own words.

In college, you are often asked to summarize something you have read about or done in a course: a chapter in a book, an experiment, an event in history. To summarize something well, you have to understand it thoroughly so that you can explain its important parts in your own words. For that reason, teachers often ask summary questions on exams. In the workplace, you often have to summarize events, situations, or information for your boss, who needs to know what's going on but doesn't have the time to hear every small detail.

**BASICS OF A GOOD SUMMARY**

- It has a topic sentence (for a paragraph-length summary) or a thesis statement (for an essay-length summary) that identifies what you are summarizing.
- It states the main point of the longer text being summarized.
- It includes the key support points.
- It includes any concluding observations or recommendations.
- It is written in your own words.

The following example is a summary of the student essay on pages 153–55, "How to Apply for Financial Aid." First read that essay, and then read the summary.

Main point

The essay "How to Apply for Financial Aid," by Karen Branch, describes how to apply for aid. The author says that many students who are eligible for financial aid don't get it because they don't know how to apply for it. The author then presents the steps a student should follow, starting with calling the college admissions department and talking to the financial-aid officer, who can provide information, directions, and an application form. It is then up to the student to read the information, determine what aid he or she qualifies for, and accurately complete the various forms. It is important to send the forms in on time and to follow up with the financial-aid office. The author urges students not to overlook this source of funding.

**PRACTICE 3   ANALYZING A SUMMARY**

1. Double-underline the **topic sentence** of the summary.

2. What is the **main point** of the longer essay? Underline it and write "main point" in the margin.

3. What is the **final observation**? Underline it.

■ **ASSIGNMENT    WRITING A SUMMARY**

Choose any essay that you have written for this course, and write a summary of it. When you turn it in to your instructor, be sure to attach the longer piece of writing you are summarizing.

Your instructor may prefer that you summarize a paragraph you have written, a book you have read, an article he or she will give you to read, or one of the topics in the list that follows. In any case, use the Critical Thinking guide that follows the summary assignments to help you write a concise summary in your own words.

■ **ADDITIONAL SUMMARY ASSIGNMENTS**

1. Read the front page of today's newspaper and summarize one of the featured news items.

2. Summarize the cover story from a recent issue of a magazine.

3. Watch one of the television newsmagazines (such as *60 Minutes*) and summarize one of the stories. To do this assignment, take notes while you are watching and listening.

4. Summarize a movie you have seen recently.

5. Summarize the strategies for taking an exam that are presented in this chapter.

6. Summarize the information on a chart or graph from a newspaper or magazine (such as *USA Today* or *Consumer Reports*).

**CRITICAL THINKING: WRITING A SUMMARY**

**FOCUS**
Read the longer work carefully, focusing on the most important information in it.

**ASK YOURSELF**
• To sum up the main point in one sentence, what would I say?
• What other key information shows, explains, or proves the main point?
• What observations or conclusions does the author make?

**WRITE**
Write a summary, using your own words, that includes the main points of the longer piece.

■ **TEAMWORK** Bring in a short article from a newspaper, or use an essay from the end of this book (if you are using the version of *Real Writing* with readings). Divide students into small groups and have them work through the Critical Thinking guide to answer the questions about the article or essay. Compare answers and ideas. Have them write a summary.

# Chapter Review: Tests, Timed Writing, and Summaries

1. What are five strategies you can use to help you study effectively for any exam?

   *Ask about the test.*

   *Study with others.*

   *Predict what will be on the exam.*

   *Use study aids.*

   *Study actively.*

2. Why is surveying an exam before starting important?

   *You find out how many parts there are, how many points each part is worth,*

   *and which questions you can answer quickly and easily.*

3. What three steps are involved in developing a plan for taking a test once you have surveyed it?

   *budgeting your time*

   *deciding on an order*

   *making a schedule and sticking to it*

4. What is the best way to start your written response to an essay exam?

   *Write a simple and clear thesis statement that says exactly what you will cover*

   *in your essay.*

5. A summary is a  *condensed version of a longer piece of writing.*

6. What are five basics of a good summary?

   *It has a topic sentence (for a paragraph-length summary) or a thesis statement*

   *(for an essay-length summary) that identifies what you are summarizing.*

   *It states the main point of the longer text being summarized.*

   *It includes the key support points.*

   *It includes any concluding observations or recommendations.*

   *It is written in your own words.*

# 18

# The Research Essay
*Using Outside Sources in Your Writing*

This chapter will guide you through the process of writing a research essay. Throughout the chapter we show how one student, Rupa Patel, worked through key steps in the process. Rupa's completed research essay appears on pages 279–83.

**STEPS TO WRITING A GOOD RESEARCH ESSAY**

1. Make a schedule.
2. Choose a topic.
3. Find and evaluate sources.
4. Avoid plagiarism by taking careful notes.
5. Write a thesis statement.
6. Make an outline.
7. Write your essay.
8. Cite and document your sources correctly.
9. Revise and edit your essay.

**You Know This**

You have done research and reported on it:

- You find information in *Consumer Reports* about a product you want to buy and tell your spouse or friend what you've found.
- You go online to find information about something you want to do or buy.
- You ask a coworker about how to do a certain job, and you take notes.

# Make a Schedule

After you receive your assignment, create a schedule that divides your research assignment into small, manageable tasks. Keep the schedule handy because you will need to refer to it often.

You can use the following schedule as a model for making your own.

**SAMPLE RESEARCH ESSAY SCHEDULE**

Assignment: (Write out what your instructor has assigned.) _____

_____

Number of outside sources required: _____

Length (if specified): _____

Draft due date: _____

Final due date: _____

Your general topic: _____

Your narrowed topic and guiding research question: _____

_____

| STEP | DO BY |
|------|-------|
| Choose a topic. | _____ |
| Find and evaluate sources; decide which ones to use. | _____ |
| Take notes, keeping publication information for each source. | _____ |
| Write a working thesis statement by answering your guiding research question. | _____ |
| Review all notes; choose the best support for your working thesis. | _____ |
| Organize notes; make an outline. | _____ |
| Write a draft, including a title. | _____ |
| Review the draft; get feedback; add more support if needed. | _____ |
| Revise the draft. | _____ |

Prepare a list of works cited using correct      _____
documentation form.

Edit the revised draft.      _____

Submit the final copy.      _____

## Choose a Topic

Your instructor may assign a topic or want you to think of your own topic for a research paper assignment. If you are free to choose your own topic, find a subject that you are personally interested in or curious about.

Ask yourself some questions like the following, which were adapted from suggestions made by Cathryn Amdahl, Harrisburg Area Community College.

1.  What is going on in my own life that I want to know more about?
2.  What do I daydream about? What frightens me? What do I see as a threat to me or my family? What inspires or encourages me?
3.  What am I interested in doing in the future, either personally or professionally, that I could investigate?
4.  What famous person or people interest me?

Here are some current topics that you might want to research.

Abortion laws

Affirmative action

Antiterrorism measures

Assisted suicide

Behavior disorders

Environmental issues: pollution, global warming, auto emissions

Gay/lesbian marriage

Health issues

Medical issues

Music/musical groups

Obesity in the United States

Online dating services

Privacy and the Internet

Road rage

School issues: home schooling, charter schools, school choice, school funding

Stem-cell research

Stolen identities

Travel: good deals, cruises, places

Violence in the media

Volunteer opportunities

When you have an idea for a general topic, write answers to these questions.

1.  Why is this topic important to me or of interest to me? How does it affect me? What do I hope to gain by exploring it?
2.  What do I know about the topic? What do I want to find out?

■ **TEACHING TIP** Have students write an "I-search" paper —a proposal in which they report on what they are interested in learning and explain why they are interested in it. In the I-search papers, have students tell you what they know about their topics already and the specific questions they want answers to.

■ **TIP** For more on guiding research questions, see page 264.

■ **TEACHING TIP** Suggest that students work with a topic they used earlier in the course for a paragraph or essay assignment.

Although a research essay may be a bit longer than some of the other essays you have written, the topic still needs to be narrow enough to write about in the assigned length. For more on narrowing your topic, see Chapter 2.

At this point, you need to learn more about your topic before writing a thesis statement. As you begin your research, come up with a **guiding research question** about your narrowed topic that you will address in your paper. This question—often a variation of "What do I want to find out?"—will help to guide and focus your research.

---

**RUPA PATEL'S GUIDING RESEARCH QUESTION:** Rupa chose the topic of student plagiarism for her research paper. She formed the following research question to guide her research: **Why do students plagiarize?**

---

# Find and Evaluate Sources

## Consult a Research Librarian

Unless you are already familiar with finding materials in the library, you will save yourself time and possible frustration by talking with the reference librarian. Before your appointment, jot down some questions you want to ask, such as those listed here.

### QUESTIONS FOR THE LIBRARIAN

- How do I use an online catalog or a card catalog? What information will the library's catalog give me?
- What other reference tools would you recommend as a good starting place for research on my topic?
- Once I identify a source that might be useful, how do I find it?
- Can I get onto the Internet from a computer here? If so, how?
- Can you recommend a search engine to use? Can you also recommend some useful key words?
- I'm doing a research paper on _____. Can you suggest some good sources for information and articles?

## Use the Online Catalog or Card Catalog

Most libraries now list their holdings on a computer rather than in a card catalog, but both systems give the same information: titles, authors, subjects, publication data, and call numbers. Catalogs are searchable by author, title, subject, or key word. They typically contain help features, but you can also consult a librarian if you need assistance.

If you are just beginning your research, you will probably search by subject heading or key word because you may not know specific authors or titles. Here is one of the catalog entries found by searching with the key word *plagiarism*, the subject of Rupa Patel's essay.

```
Record 9 of 10

Author/Editors:    Buranen, Lise, and Alice M. Roy, eds.
Title:             Perspectives  on  Plagiarism  and  Intellectual
                   Property in a Postmodern World
Publisher:         Albany: State  University  of  New  York  Press,
                   1999
Subject:           Plagiarism.
                   Intellectual property.
Location:          Central Branch
Call Number:       PN167.P47 1999
Status:            Available
```

Think of your research question when entering key words into the catalog and other search engines. Consider, for example, Rupa's research question: *Why do students plagiarize?* Good starting key words for this question would be *plagiarism causes*.

## Use Other Reference Materials

The reference department of the library contains many reference materials, including indexes, that can point you toward useful sources for your topics. If your topic is a current one, periodicals (magazines, journals, and newspapers) may be more useful than books. Some of the more popular periodical indexes are

- *Readers' Guide to Periodical Literature*
- *NewsBank*
- *InfoTrac*
- *ProQuest*

These indexes may be available online or in print form, so you will want to check with the librarian to determine how and where they can be accessed.

## Use the Internet

The Internet provides access to all kinds of information. If you are new to using the Internet and the World Wide Web to search for information, you will want to ask the librarian or a classmate for some help in addition to reading this section.

■ **TEACHING TIP** Schedule a tour of the library, during which you can show students the reference room, the computer terminals that provide access to the online catalog and Internet, the periodical room, and the stacks.

■ **TIP** For tutorials on searching and evaluating various sources, and for help with other research tasks, visit <**www.bedfordresearcher.com/tutorials.cfm**>.

In fact, it's a good idea to get onto the Internet through your school library's Web site. You can access the library catalog and other databases electronically, and the site may also contain links to other helpful Web sites.

The easiest way to search for information on the Internet is to use a search engine. Search engines allow you to search for information by typing in your topic or by using key words about your topic. Here are some popular search engines.

| | |
|---|---|
| AltaVista **www.altavista.com** | HotBot **www.hotbot.com** |
| Ask Jeeves **www.ask.com** | Infoseek **www.infoseek.com** |
| Excite **www.excite.com** | Lycos **www.lycos.com** |
| Google **www.google.com** | Yahoo! **www.yahoo.com** |

To review possible sources, choose a search engine and type in your research question. For example, using Google, Rupa typed in "Why do students plagiarize?" and her search netted over seventeen thousand Web sites. She didn't know quite where to start, so she went to a few sites to see what they were and what information they contained. She noted that several sites were sponsored by colleges and universities and discussed what plagiarism is, how to avoid it, and the fact that many students aren't familiar with the various sorts of plagiarism.

At this point she made a note to herself that perhaps her thesis might focus on the different kinds of plagiarism. As you review sources, be ready to modify your research question based on the information you find.

**NOTE:** Consider using an "advanced search" feature for more targeted searching. For example, using such a feature in Google, Rupa could search for the **exact phrase** "Why do students plagiarize?" This phrase turns up fifty-plus results—a much smaller list than that found with a regular search. Also, the results are more focused. For more information on doing an Internet search, see Appendix D.

**RUPA PATEL'S MODIFIED RESEARCH QUESTION:** Rupa modified her research question to: **What are the different kinds of plagiarism?**

## Interview People

Interviews can be excellent sources of information. Before interviewing anyone, plan the questions you want to ask. While you will probably add to those questions as you interview the person, it is best to start with a few questions (five to ten) that you have written in advance. Make sure to record the person's name and identify how the person qualifies as a good source of information.

As you conduct the interview, listen carefully and take good notes. If you plan to use any direct quotations (a person's exact words), make sure that you put the person's actual words in quotation marks. (For more information about using direct quotations, see page 270 of this chapter.)

## Evaluate Your Sources

As you collect sources—both print materials and online information—you need to consider whether they are reliable. For example, suppose you are researching new methods of weight loss and find an ad for a weight-loss product at the back of a tabloid newspaper. The ad makes claims that seem too good to be true, such as "Lose pounds and inches while you sleep." You are right to be skeptical of this source because it is probably not reliable. Use sources that have known credibility.

When you are gathering information from Web sites, being mindful of their reliability is even more important. Anyone anywhere can put up a Web site and place whatever information he or she wants on it, whether it's true, unbiased, or not. It is up to you as the researcher to determine whether the source is reliable.

One way to evaluate a Web source is to consider the uniform resource locator (URL) extension. (*URL* is another name for a site's Internet address.) The extension is the part of the URL that follows the dot.

### *Guide to URL Extensions*

| EXTENSION | TYPE OF SITE | HOW RELIABLE? |
|-----------|-------------|---------------|
| .com | A commercial or business organization | Varies. Consider whether you have heard of the organization, and be sure to read its home page carefully. |
| .edu | An educational institution | Reliable, but may include many varied course materials. |
| .gov | A government agency | Reliable. |
| .net | A commercial or business organization, or a personal site | Varies. This extension indicates just the provider, not anything about the source. Go to the source's home page to find out what you can about the author or the sponsor. |

The following questions can also help you evaluate the reliability of sources—both print and electronic.

**TEN QUESTIONS FOR EVALUATING A SOURCE (PRINT OR ELECTRONIC)**

1. Is the source up-to-date?
2. Is the source one that you know is reliable (such as a well-known magazine or a reputable Web site)?

■ **TEACHING TIP** Have students apply these questions to an article that you bring to class. Discuss their responses, and decide as a class whether or not the source is reliable.

3. Has the author published other material on this subject?

4. Does the author offer other sources to support his or her ideas?

5. Does the author present various sides of an issue instead of ignoring opposing points?

6. Does the author have a balanced, objective tone? (In other words, he or she does not make other points of view seem wrong or dangerous.)

7. Does the author provide adequate support for his or her thesis?

8. If the source is a Web site, is the site's sponsoring organization well known and generally well respected?

9. Will using this source strengthen the point you want to make?

10. Can the information in the source be verified by checking other sources?

**NOTE:** This list of questions was adapted from Ingrid Schreck, *Working with Sources,* Boston: Bedford/St. Martin's, 2000.

The following Web page discussing types of plagiarism has been annotated to show some features you might look for when evaluating an Internet source.

*.edu* extension indicates a generally reliable source

Objective presentation of information, with source citations

Date of last update

Reliable source: University of Michigan

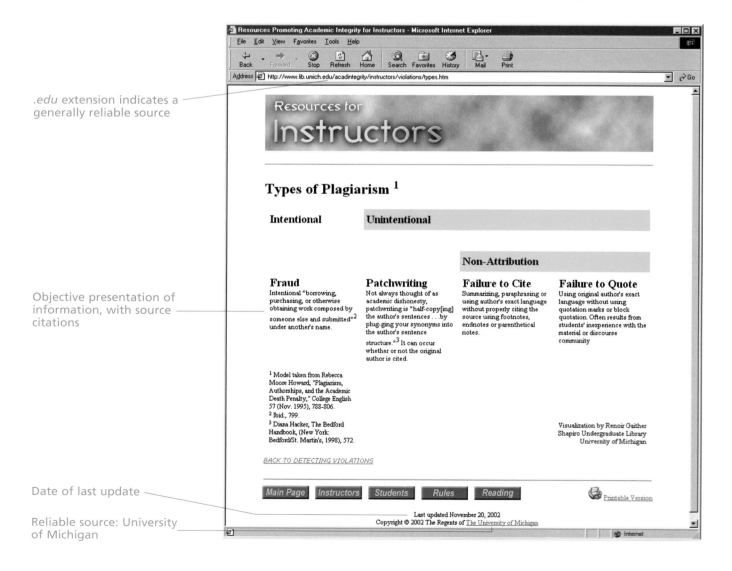

A final caution: Avoid sites that are aimed at selling products as opposed to providing balanced information, for such sites are generally biased. Be aware, though, that such sites may look "official," and the companies or industry organizations sponsoring them may try to disguise promotional material as unbiased information.

This is another good reason for checking a site's sponsorship. If you are uncertain about a site's reliability for any of the reasons outlined in this section, check with your college librarian or your instructor.

# Avoid Plagiarism by Taking Careful Notes

As you read potential sources, take lots of notes. Write down any information that might help you answer your guiding research question. If you find later that you don't want to use some of the information you have gathered, you can disregard it. But for now, you want to build a good supply of potential support (and be sure to record the source of each note).

As a responsible researcher, you must give credit to your sources. In other words, you have to acknowledge the source of any fact, supporting detail, or quotation you use in your essay. If you do not, you are committing plagiarism: passing off information you gather from another source as your own.

Using a research essay from the Web or an essay that someone else wrote—even if that person gives you permission to use it—is one very obvious sort of plagiarism. Cutting and pasting information from Web sources without properly citing the source is also plagiarism. Even using a paper that you wrote for another course is widely regarded as plagiarism, called "self-plagiarism."

Sometimes plagiarism results from taking incomplete or sloppy notes. If you forget to write down a source, to indicate in your notes whether the words are a direct quote or not, or to identify an idea as your own or that of another person, you may commit plagiarism unintentionally.

Whenever you use facts, details, and examples from outside sources in your own writing, you must cite the source (give credit to someone else's work or idea) within your paper—immediately following the material you have borrowed.

■ **TEACHING TIP** Consider visiting the Bedford/St. Martin's Workshop on Plagiarism at <www.bedfordstmartins.com/plagiarism>. This site contains various resources for helping your students to avoid plagiarism, including a flyer that you can hand out in class.

■ **TEACHING TIP** Certain software programs can help students avoid plagiarism while working with Web sources. For example, the program Net Snippets automatically captures the URL and access date for sources that students gather from the Web. The program also allows students to store comments about the sources.

## Keep a Running Bibliography

A **bibliography** is a complete list, alphabetized by author, of the outside sources you consult. A **Works Cited** list is a complete list, alphabetized by author, of the outside sources that you actually cite within your essay. Most instructors require a list of works cited at the end of research essays. Keeping a running bibliography will ensure that you have the information you need to prepare a Works Cited list. You can keep this information on note-cards or on your computer. Following is a list of information you will need to record for each bibliography entry.

| BOOKS | MAGAZINES |
|---|---|
| Author name(s) | Author name(s) |
| Complete title and subtitle | Title of article and page numbers |
| Year of publication | Title of magazine or journal |
| Publisher and location of publisher | Year, month, day of publication (2003, December 22) |

You will likely integrate source material by direct quotation, paraphrase, and summary. As you take notes, record which method you are using so you don't plagiarize accidentally.

## Direct Quotation

A **direct quotation** is using a person's exact words. Use these guidelines when you use direct quotations:

- Record the exact words of the source.
- Record the name of the writer or speaker so that you can use it later to introduce the quotation in your paper.
- Enclose the speaker's words in quotation marks.
- For written sources, include the page number on which the quote appeared in the original source in parentheses after the end quotation mark but before the period. If the person quoted is not the author of the book or the article in which you found the quote, give the author's last name in parentheses along with the page number. If there are two or three authors, give all names.

   **DIRECT QUOTATION:**  A *Christian Science Monitor* article titled "Your Work, or the Web's?" quotes Don McCabe, founder of the Center for Academic Integrity and a researcher at Rutgers University in New Jersey, as saying, " 'Unless somebody starts to teach high-school students and even middle-school students proper use of the Internet and citing resources, the problems at the college level will increase dramatically' " (Cowen 17).

The author of the article, Trisha Cowen, is different from the speaker quoted, McCabe, so Cowen's name must appear with the page reference.

## Paraphrase

When you **paraphrase**, you put someone's idea into your own words and restate it. Be careful if you choose to paraphrase. It is easy to think you are using your own words while you are actually using only some of your own and some of the author's. To paraphrase responsibly, use these guidelines:

- Don't look at the source as you write the paraphrase.
- Check your paraphrase against the original source to make sure you have not used too many of the author's words or copied the author's sentence structure.
- Cite your source in parentheses after the paraphrase. When you paraphrase, you must cite your source as you do with quotations.

■ **RESOURCES** *Additional Resources* contains exercises on integrating and citing sources within a research essay.

Read the examples that follow to see acceptable and unacceptable paraphrases.

**QUOTATION FROM ORIGINAL SOURCE**

Later in the same *Christian Science Monitor* article, Cowen writes, "The Internet provides a rich source of information, but students often don't realize that it is a flawed resource, riddled with bias, weak writing, and poor documentation" (17).

**UNACCEPTABLE PARAPHRASE (TOO CLOSE TO ORIGINAL)**

In the same article, Cowen writes that the Internet is a good information source, but users often don't understand that it's an imperfect source, characterized by one-sided information, bad writing, and bad source citation (17).

**ACCEPTABLE PARAPHRASE**

Cowen adds that the Internet can be an unreliable resource because of the poor quality of the writing and documentation in many Internet sources; also, the information is often one-sided (17).

## Summary

A **summary** presents only the main points of a source in your own words.

If you read a short article or essay that supports your thesis but has no one person's words or ideas you want to include in your paper, you may want to summarize the material. If you decide to summarize and cite the source, you will need to do the following:

- Introduce the outside source. For example, "In her article 'Avoiding Plagiarism,' Mary Jones says . . .."
- Include the page numbers of the entire section you summarized in parentheses. Include the last name(s) of the author(s) of the source either in the phrase that introduces the summary or in parentheses before the page number.

For more on writing a summary, see Chapter 17.

**SUMMARY OF AN ARTICLE**

The article "The Great Term-Paper Buying Caper" (Kleiner, Lord, and Faber 63) points out the widespread practice of buying papers from the

Web: Term-paper sites are now a big business and get thousands of hits per year. The fact remains, however, that quality is not guaranteed, and the paper a student purchases may be no better than the paper he or she would write.

## Write a Thesis Statement

■ **TIP** For more information on writing thesis statements, see Chapter 3.

After you have taken notes on the sources you gathered, you should be ready to write a thesis statement, which states the main idea of your research essay. You can start by turning your guiding research question into a statement that answers the question. Note how Rupa Patel uses her research question to write a thesis statement.

> **RUPA PATEL'S GUIDING RESEARCH QUESTION:** What are the different kinds of plagiarism?
>
> **RUPA'S THESIS STATEMENT:** To understand the reasons for plagiarism, one must understand the several kinds of plagiarists—haphazard plagiarists, paper-for-hire plagiarists, and self-plagiarists.

## Make an Outline

■ **TIP** For more information on outlining, see Chapter 5. For a discussion of major support and supporting details, see Chapter 4.

To make an outline, first write down your thesis statement. Then, review your notes to decide what your major support points will be. Write these under your thesis statement and order them with a letter or number, leaving plenty of space between each support point if you are working on paper. Under the major support points (which will become the topic sentences for the support paragraphs), write supporting details.

Many students find it helpful to use complete sentences in their outlines so that when they write a draft it will be easy to remember what they wanted to say. They then add supporting sentences as they write their drafts and can change the sentences as they write and revise.

If you've taken notes on a computer, it's easy to cut and paste information from your notes to your outline.

> **RUPA PATEL'S OUTLINE**
>
> I.  Thesis statement: To understand the reasons for plagiarism, one must understand the several kinds of plagiarists—haphazard plagiarists, paper-for-hire plagiarists, and self-plagiarists.
> II. Haphazard plagiarists
>     A.  Some do not properly cite their sources, because they did not take proper notes.

      B. Others cut and paste material from a Web site without citing the source.

      C. Still others use unreliable Internet sources or, worse, purchase entire papers from Web sites.

      D. These plagiarists should be aware that software and Web sites help professors detect plagiarism.

III. Paper-for-hire plagiarists

      A. They feel no shame because they believe that what they're doing isn't plagiarism or that it's fair practice.

      B. A San Diego State University student turned in her uncle's essays but thought this was okay because she had his permission.

      C. A Chico State University student sent his rough-draft essays to his mother for "proofreading."

      D. "Brains" at Carondelet High School write the papers for payment, and it's considered a standard and legitimate business practice.

IV. Self-plagiarists

      A. Most students don't even know what this is.

      B. Students can't believe that they would get in trouble for using their own writing.

V. Plagiarists beware

      A. Teachers are now armed with software and Web sites for detecting plagiarism.

      B. Don't be tempted.

      C. Students pay for their education: Why not take the time to learn?

## Write Your Essay

Using your outline, write a draft of your research essay in complete sentences. (For more information on writing a draft essay, see Chapter 6.)

Your **introduction** should include your thesis statement and a preview of the support that you will provide in the body of your essay. The **body** of your essay will present your major support points. Each major support point will be part of a paragraph that demonstrates or proves the point, using the source material you have collected. The **conclusion** of your essay will remind readers of your main point and make a further observation based on the information you have presented.

For the complete research paper that Rupa Patel wrote based on her previous outline, see pages 279–83.

## Cite and Document Your Sources Correctly

There are two places where you need to document, or give credit to, your sources. When you refer to a source within the body of your paper, you will use a **parenthetical reference**. At the end of your paper, you will have a **Works Cited** section, which lists all of your sources, in alphabetical order, with complete bibliographic information.

Use the following sections to guide you in including the correct information in the correct format. Almost no one can remember the specifics of how to cite an outside source; the key is to refer to this section when you are preparing your final draft.

There are several different systems of documentation. Most English professors use the Modern Language Association (MLA) system, so that is the format presented here. When you are writing a research paper in another course, your professor may want you to use another system.

## Parenthetical References

### FOR A DIRECT QUOTATION

If you refer to the author (or authors) in the phrase that introduces a quotation, just write the page number in parentheses at the end of the quotation.

> In a *Christian Science Monitor* article titled "Your Work, or the Web's?" Trisha Cowen writes, "The Internet provides a rich source of information, but students often don't realize that it is a flawed resource, riddled with bias, weak writing, and poor documentation" (17).

If you do not refer to the author(s) in an introductory phrase, write the author's name followed by the page number at the end of the quotation.

> "The Internet provides a rich source of information, but students often don't realize that it is a flawed resource, riddled with bias, weak writing, and poor documentation" (Cowen 17).

**NOTE:** The same guidelines apply to source material that is not a direct quote:

> Janelle Taylor describes several different strategies that help students avoid plagiarism (53).

> Several different strategies can help students avoid plagiarism (Taylor 53).

### FOR AN INDIRECT QUOTATION

When an author quotes another person and you want to use that quotation, use the name of the quoted person in the introductory phrase. Then, in parentheses at the end of the sentence, write the abbreviation "qtd. in," followed by the name of the author and the page number.

> According to Lorene Frame, "There are now hundreds of Web sites that teachers can use to detect plagiarism" (qtd. in Becker 40).

### FOR AN ELECTRONIC SOURCE (FROM A WEB SITE)

Cite electronic sources in the same way you do print sources, when possible. If the source does not use page numbers (and many do not), you do not need a page reference.

If the author of the information you are citing is not known, use the title of the source.

### FOR A PERSONAL INTERVIEW

Use the name of the person interviewed in the sentence and then in parentheses following the sentence write *personal interview.*

For an anonymous personal interview, describe the speaker in the sentence and in parentheses at the end of the sentence write *personal interview, anonymous.*

> A Chico State University student confessed to his friends that he sends his rough-draft essays to his mother for "proofreading" (personal interview, anonymous).

## Works Cited

Following are model Works Cited entries for major types of sources. At the end of your paper, you will need to include such entries for each source you cite in the body of the paper.

■ **TIP** If you have additional questions about MLA style—especially on how to cite electronic sources—visit the MLA Web site at **<www.mla.org>**.

## Books

**1. BOOK WITH ONE AUTHOR**

Full title

Anker, Susan. Real Writing: Paragraphs and Essays for College, Work, and
    Everyday Life. 3rd ed. Boston: Bedford/St. Martin's, 2004.

All lines after first line of entry are indented.

Author, last name first    Edition number    Place of publication    Publisher    Publication date

**2. BOOK WITH TWO OR THREE AUTHORS**

Collier, Peter, and David Horowitz. The Roosevelts: An American Saga. New York: Simon
    & Schuster, 1994.

Quigley, Sharon, Gloria Florez, and Thomas McCann. You Can Clean Almost Anything.
    New York: Sutton, 1999.

**3. BOOK WITH FOUR OR MORE AUTHORS (*ET AL.* MEANS "AND OTHERS")**

Roark, James L., et al. The American Promise: A History of the United States. 2nd
    compact ed. Boston: Bedford/St. Martin's, 2003.

**4. BOOK WITH AN EDITOR**

Tate, Parson, ed. Most Romantic Vacation Spots. Cheyenne: Chandler, 2000.

**5. WORK IN AN ANTHOLOGY**

Allison, Dorothy. "River of Names." The Story and Its Writer: An Introduction to Short
    Fiction. Ed. Ann Charters. 6th ed. Boston: Bedford/St. Martin's, 2003.

**6. ENCYCLOPEDIA ARTICLE**

"Kosovo." Encyclopaedia Britannica. 16th ed. 1999.

## Periodicals

**7. MAGAZINE ARTICLE**

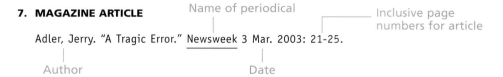

Adler, Jerry. "A Tragic Error." Newsweek 3 Mar. 2003: 21-25.

**8. NEWSPAPER ARTICLE**

Johnson, Michelle. "Making Sense of Web Searches." Boston Globe 31 Mar. 2003: B7.

**9. EDITORIAL IN A MAGAZINE OR NEWSPAPER**

Jackson, Derrick Z. "America's One-Sided Prayers." Editorial. Boston Globe 9 Apr. 2003:
   A19.

## Electronic Sources

Electronic sources include Web sites; reference databases (online or on CD-ROM); works from subscription services such as LexisNexis, Electric Library, or PsycLIT; and electronic communications such as e-mail. Because many electronic sources change often, always note the date you accessed the source as well as the date on which the source was posted or updated. To make sure your records are correct, you may want to bookmark, download, or print out hard copies of the pages you have used.

**10. AN ENTIRE WEB SITE**

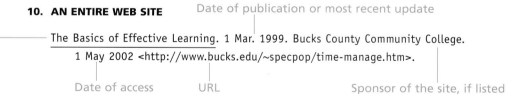

The Basics of Effective Learning. 1 Mar. 1999. Bucks County Community College.
   1 May 2002 <http://www.bucks.edu/~specpop/time-manage.htm>.

**11. A PART OF A LARGER WEB SITE**

Kelly, Meg. "Managing Your Time and Study Environment." The Basics of Effective
   Learning. 1 Mar. 1999. Bucks County Community College. 1 May 2002
   <http://www.bucks.edu/~specpop/time-manage.htm>.

**12. ARTICLE IN AN ONLINE PERIODICAL**

Weine, Stevan M. "Survivor Families and Their Strengths: Learning from Bosnians after
   Genocide." Other Voices: The (e)Journal of Cultural Criticism. 2.1 (2000). Other
   Voices. 1 May 2002 <http://www.othervoices.org/2.1/weine/bosnia.html>.

**13. WORK FROM A SUBSCRIPTION SERVICE**

Rothstein, Kevin. "MIT Student Discipline Panel Sees Rise in Dishonesty." Boston
    Herald 27 Mar. 2003. NewsBank. Boston Public Lib. 15 Apr. 2003
    <http://www.newsbank.com>.

**14. E-MAIL OR ONLINE POSTING**

Eisenhauer, Karen. "Learning Styles." E-mail to Susan Anker. 24 Apr. 2003.

Collins, Terence. "Effective Grammar Activities." Online posting. 14 Dec. 2001. CBW
    Listserv. 3 May 2002 <cbw-1@tc.umn.edu>.


## Other Sources

**15. PERSONAL INTERVIEW**

Mustard, Sam. Personal interview. 22 June 2003.

**16. FILM OR VIDEO**

None Too Soon. Dir. Carolyn Dumore, Sophie Fleck, and Mary Lovington. Universal,
    2002.

**17. TELEVISION OR RADIO PROGRAM**

"12:00 to 1:00." 24. Fox. KTTV, Hollywood. 3 May 2003.


# Revise and Edit Your Essay

After a break, reread your draft with a fresh perspective. Then ask yourself
these questions:

- Does my essay have the necessary parts (an introductory paragraph
  that states the thesis, body paragraphs that support the thesis, and a
  conclusion that reminds readers of the main point and makes an
  observation)?
- Do I use information and ideas from reliable sources?
- Do all of the major support points in my essay relate directly to the
  main point?
- Do all of the supporting details in each body paragraph relate to the
  paragraph's topic sentence?
- Do I have enough support?
- Do the paragraphs and sentences flow smoothly? Do I provide transitions to help the reader move from point to point? Do I provide identifying phrases to integrate source material effectively?

Next, revise your draft making any improvements you can. Refer to Chapter 7 if you need more help.

After you have carefully revised your research essay, take time to edit and proofread it thoroughly. (Refer to Parts Four through Seven of this book if you need more help with any problems with grammar, spelling, punctuation, or word use.) Also, be sure that your parenthetical citations and Works Cited list follow the documentation system recommended by your instructor.

**NOTE:** You may find it most effective to prepare your list of Works Cited after you have revised your paper but before you edit it. That way, you reduce the chance that the list will omit sources that you have added during revision, or show ones that you have cut.

## Sample Student Research Essay

On the following pages is a student research paper, annotated to show typical features of such papers (including references to various source materials), as well as elements of effective writing (such as the thesis statement and topic sentences). The paper also illustrates typical formatting conventions (such as margins and title placement). Your instructor may specify different or additional formatting conventions in class or in the syllabus. If you are uncertain about your instructor's formatting preferences, be sure to check.

Patel 1

Rupa Patel

Professor McKinney

English 100

May 1, 2002

Student Plagiarists: Categories and Cautions

Merriam-Webster's dictionary defines the word plagiarize as ". . . to pass off (the ideas or words of another) as one's own." Every student knows that plagiarism is dishonest and wrong, yet a growing number of students engage in it. Why do students plagiarize? To understand the reasons for plagiarism, one must understand the several kinds of plagiarists--haphazard plagiarists, paper-for-hire plagiarists, and self-plagiarists.

**Haphazard plagiarists** are the ones most people think of when they think of students who plagiarize. Some haphazard plagiarists are guilty simply of not properly citing their sources, mainly because they didn't take proper notes as they were doing their research: Their research is haphazard. They can't remember exactly what was a direct quote or where the information came from, so they cite incorrectly, or not at all. These haphazard plagiarists are sloppy, but they may not have intentionally plagiarized from the start. Other haphazard plagiarists cut and paste material from a Web site without citing the source. They weave together the words of others into a whole that they pass off as their own, not always understanding that this is wrong. Interviewed for a Christian Science Monitor article, Don McCabe, founder of the Center for Academic Integrity and a researcher at Rutgers University, reported that one in ten college students admit to cutting and pasting off the Internet (Cowen 17).

The author of the same article noted that many students use Internet sources even though they may contain weak writing, may be one-sided, or may poorly document the information (Cowen 17). Worse, students may purchase entire papers online from Web sites such as http://www.schoolsucks.com. Although purchasing whole papers is more unethical than haphazard plagiarism, it also involves the use of unreliable sources. It may also set students up for a disappointment. An article from U.S. News & World Report titled "The Great Term-Paper Buying Caper" states, "Paying top dollar for a paper is no guarantee that it's going to get an A" (Kleiner, Lord, and Faber 63). Students who buy papers online are willing to risk their academic credibility by turning

Annotations (right margin):

½" margin between top of page and header

Writer's last name and page number on every page

Title centered

Introductory technique: quotation

Thesis statement

Topic sentence, 1st major point

In-text citation

Topic sentence, supports 1st major point

Transitional sentence

In-text citation, direct quotation

Patel 2

in a paper that may include incorrect information or may be turned in by another student who also purchased the same paper.

**Topic sentence, supports 1st major point**

Students who plagiarize from the Internet should be forewarned: New Web sites, such as http://www.plagiarism.org, help professors detect plagiarism. Using the plagiarism.org Web site, professors can search the Internet for passages that match portions of student essays. This program has limitations. It is unable to detect plagiarized paragraphs that have been slightly rewritten. However, more sophisticated plagiarism detection software is available every day for professors, and many of these programs are highly accurate.

**Topic sentence, 2nd major point**

A second category of plagiarist consists of the **paper-for-hire plagiarists**, who also pass off other people's work as their own, but in an entirely different way, which--according to the individuals I interviewed--causes them to feel no guilt or shame. A first-year student at San Diego State University admitted to her friends that she was turning in her uncle's essays for every assignment (personal interview, anonymous). She felt that she was not doing harm to anyone because her uncle specifically wrote the essays for her. All she had to do was retype the essays with her name on the top of the paper. According to this student, she is not plagiarizing because her uncle has given his permission for her to use his essays. She has almost completed her first year at the school without even one teacher suspecting academic dishonesty. Although her friends and family members are appalled at her and her uncle's lack of scruples, no one has alerted the school or her teachers.

**Topic sentence, supports 2nd major point**

A Chico State University student confessed to his friends that he sends his rough-draft essays to his mother for "proofreading" (personal interview, anonymous). His mother actually rewrites the essays, leaving the basic idea intact. Her son, completely happy with the rewrites, feels that he is not plagiarizing because his mother has always done this for him. The mother does not feel that her son is plagiarizing because she approves of his using the "proofread" essays.

**Topic sentence, supports 2nd major point**

Paper-for-hire plagiarists also justify their plagiarism by thinking of it as standard business practice. Throughout Carondelet High School in Concord, California, students can be found who are willing to write other students' essays--for a price (personal interviews, anonymous). The "brains," as they are labeled at the school, do not feel that those who turn in the essays are plagiarizing. Essays are tailor-made for the students who pay the "brains." Therefore, according to the "brains," submitting those essays is not a form of plagiarism. The "brains" feel that payment for their services of writing the papers can be easily compared to the paychecks received by the president's speechwriters. In exchange for the payment, the speechwriter creates the perfect speech for the president, who in turn reads it to the country as his own words. A "brain" remarked, "If the president is not a plagiarist, then neither are the students who pay for my work!" (personal interview, anonymous).

Paper-for-hire plagiarists do not feel guilt because they actually believe that they are not doing anything wrong. They feel that they are simply using the available resources to create a paper that is academically suitable for the topic. These plagiarists also know and trust the person who is writing the paper and are therefore able to feel confident in the essay that is presented to a teacher. However, permission from the original author does not mean consent in the classroom. In his Web-based resource "What Is Plagiarism?" Michael Spears says that "using another student's work and claiming it as your own, even with permission, is academically unethical and is treated as plagiarism."

The last group of plagiarists consists of **self-plagiarists**. However absurd it may sound to a student, turning in a paper he or she wrote for another class without getting permission from the current teacher is called self-plagiarism (and the current teacher is not likely to give that permission). In a definition of self-plagiarism that appears on his "What Is Plagiarism?" Web resource, Michael Spears argues that students should "do something original and put forth some effort." Many other instructors would agree.

For their part, however, self-plagiarists often don't know that they are doing anything wrong. How many times has a generic essay assignment been tossed onto your list of homework assignments and you think, "Why not turn in a paper I wrote for another class about the same subject?" A good answer is that in some schools it is grounds for academic punishment. Students at Diablo Valley College in Pleasant Hill, California, were amazed to hear about self-plagiarism (personal interviews, anonymous). One student remarked, "What do you mean? I don't have the rights to my own paper?" In response to the notion that self-plagiarism should be punished, another student replied, "It makes some sense, I guess. But are they really going to fail someone for turning in his or her own work?"

Plagiarism--both intentional and unintentional--takes place daily. Fourteen-year-old Hillary Caltagirone, from Arlington High School in LaGrangeville, New York, explained to David Oliver Relin from the New York Times Upfront that "You have to do whatever you have to do to get ahead. I'm going to go to college. I'm going to get a good job. If that

---

Topic sentence, supports 2nd major point

Topic sentence, 3rd major point

Topic sentence, supports 3rd major point

Conclusion

Conclusion

Reminds readers of main point

Makes a final observation

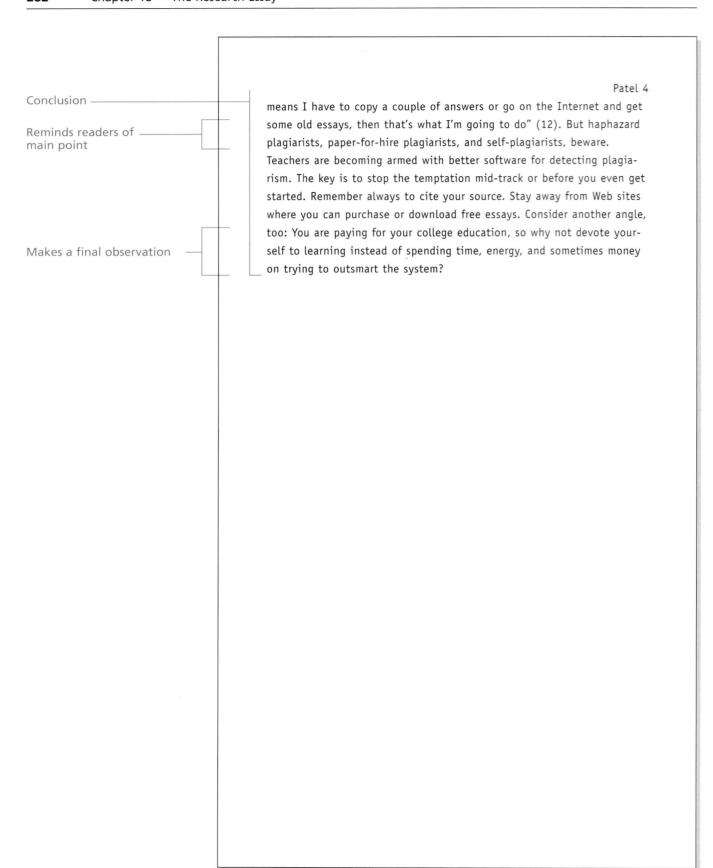

Patel 4

means I have to copy a couple of answers or go on the Internet and get some old essays, then that's what I'm going to do" (12). But haphazard plagiarists, paper-for-hire plagiarists, and self-plagiarists, beware. Teachers are becoming armed with better software for detecting plagiarism. The key is to stop the temptation mid-track or before you even get started. Remember always to cite your source. Stay away from Web sites where you can purchase or download free essays. Consider another angle, too: You are paying for your college education, so why not devote yourself to learning instead of spending time, energy, and sometimes money on trying to outsmart the system?

Patel 5

Works Cited ——————————————————— Heading centered

Carondelet High School student. Personal interview, anonymous.
  25 Apr. 2002.

Chico State University student. Personal interview, anonymous.
  3 Apr. 2002.

Cowen, Trisha. "Your Work, or the Web's?" The Christian Science Monitor
  6 Mar. 2001: 17.

Diablo Valley College students. Personal interviews, anonymous.
  10 Apr. 2002.

Kleiner, Carolyn, Mary Lord, and Lindsay Faber. "The Great Term-Paper
  Buying Caper." U.S. News & World Report 22 Nov. 1999: 63.

"Plagiarize." Merriam-Webster's Collegiate Dictionary. 10th ed. 1999.

Relin, David Oliver. "Truth or Consequences." New York Times Upfront
  1 Jan. 2001: 10-14.

San Diego State University student. Personal interview, anonymous.
  22 Mar. 2002.

Spears, Michael. "What Is Plagiarism?" Plagiarism Q&A. 12 Mar. 2002.
  Central Michigan University. 23 Apr. 2002
  <http://www.ehhs.cmich.edu/~mspears/plagiarism.html>.

Personal interviews

Newspaper article

Personal interviews

Magazine article

Dictionary entry

Newspaper article

Personal interview

Web site

■ **TEACHING TIP** You might point out to students that this essay is an example of classification (see Chapter 12). Ask them to name the categories covered and to list some of the examples that support each category.

## Part Four
# The Four Most Serious Errors

# 19

# The Basic Sentence

*An Overview*

## The Four Most Serious Errors

This book puts special emphasis on the four grammar errors that people most often notice. In your writing, these four errors may make your meaning harder to understand, but even if they don't, they give a bad impression of you.

**THE FOUR MOST SERIOUS ERRORS**

1. Fragments
2. Run-ons
3. Problems with subject-verb agreement
4. Problems with verb form and tense

If you can edit your writing to correct the four most serious errors, it will be clearer, and your grades will improve. By focusing on these errors, this book will help you make a big difference in your writing.

This chapter will review the basic elements of the sentence to help set up the detailed coverage of the four most serious errors in the next four chapters.

## The Basic Sentence

A **sentence** is the basic unit of written communication. A complete sentence in written standard English must have these three elements:

- A **subject**
- A **verb**
- A **complete thought**

> **Ever Thought This?**
>
> "Grammar. I never get it. There's too much to remember."
> —Tony Mancuso, Student
>
> This chapter
> - tells you which four errors are the most important to find and fix
> - gives you practice working with the basic elements of a sentence
> - keeps grammar terms to a minimum
> - simplifies grammar so that you can get it

■ **LEARNING JOURNAL** Your learning journal is a good place to record the errors you make, particularly those you make frequently. Correct the problems and record the edited versions of these sentences too.

To edit your writing, you need a clear understanding of what a sentence *is* and what a sentence *is not.* You can find out if a group of words is a complete sentence by checking to see if it has a subject, a verb, and a complete thought.

## Subjects

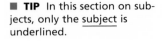

■ **TIP** In this section on subjects, only the subject is underlined.

The **subject** of a sentence is the person, place, or thing that a sentence is about. The subject of a sentence can be a noun (a word that names the person, place, or thing) or a pronoun (a word that replaces the noun, such as *I, you, she,* or *they*). For a complete list of pronouns, see page 376.

To find the subject, ask yourself, **Who or what is the sentence about?**

> **PERSON AS SUBJECT**    Isaac just arrived last night.
>
> [*Whom* is the sentence about? *Isaac*]
>
> **THING AS SUBJECT**    The roller coaster has been shut down.
>
> [*What* is the sentence about? The *roller coaster*]

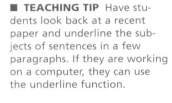

■ **TEACHING TIP** Have students look back at a recent paper and underline the subjects of sentences in a few paragraphs. If they are working on a computer, they can use the underline function.

The subject of the sentence can be either a specific person, place, or thing or a nonspecific person, place, or thing.

> **SPECIFIC PERSON**    Kelli danced in the school musical.
>
> **NONSPECIFIC PERSON**    A dancer has to train carefully.
>
> **SPECIFIC PLACE**    My bedroom is always a mess.
>
> **NONSPECIFIC PLACE**    Public parks are good places to walk your dog.

A **compound subject** consists of two (or more) subjects joined by *and, or,* or *nor.*

> **TWO SUBJECTS**    Kelli and Kate love animals of all kinds.
>
> **SEVERAL SUBJECTS**    The baby, the cats, and the dog play well together.

A **preposition** is a word that connects a noun, pronoun, or verb with some other information about it. A **prepositional phrase** is a word group that begins with a preposition and ends with a noun or pronoun, called the **object of a preposition.** It is important to know that the subject of a sentence is *never* in a prepositional phrase.

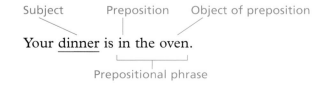

Subject    Preposition    Object of preposition

Your dinner is in the oven.

Prepositional phrase

| PREPOSITION | OBJECT | PREPOSITIONAL PHRASE |
|---|---|---|
| from | the bakery | from the bakery |
| to | the next stoplight | to the next stoplight |
| under | the table | under the table |

### Common Prepositions

| | | | | |
|---|---|---|---|---|
| about | before | except | of | to |
| above | behind | for | off | toward |
| across | below | from | on | under |
| after | beneath | in | out | until |
| against | beside | inside | outside | up |
| along | between | into | over | upon |
| among | by | like | past | with |
| around | down | near | since | within |
| at | during | next to | through | without |

Any time that you see a preposition, you know that it usually begins a prepositional phrase.

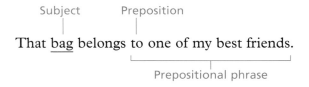

That <u>bag</u> belongs to one of my best friends.

Again, the subject of a sentence is *never* in a prepositional phrase.

<u>One</u> of my best friends won the lottery.

Although you might think the word *friends* is the subject of the sentence, it isn't. *One* is the subject. The word *friends* can't be the subject because it is in the prepositional phrase *of my best friends*. When you are looking for the subject of a sentence, cross out the prepositional phrase.

**PREPOSITIONAL PHRASE CROSSED OUT**

<u>One</u> ~~of the students~~ won the science prize.

■ **ESL** Give students a list of common prepositional phrases that they may not be familiar with (*over the hill, up a creek, beat around the bush,* and so on).

The <u>rules</u> ~~about the dress code~~ are very specific.

The <u>sound</u> ~~of water dripping~~ drives me crazy.

■ **PRACTICE 1  IDENTIFYING SUBJECTS AND PREPOSITIONAL PHRASES**

■ **TIP** For more practices on sentence basics, visit Exercise Central at <**bedfordstmartins .com/realwriting**>.

In each of the following sentences, cross out any ~~prepositional phrases~~ and underline the <u>subject</u> of the sentence.

**EXAMPLE:** The <u>head</u> ~~of the company~~ earned a very high salary.

■ **RESOURCES** *Additional Resources* contains supplemental exercises for this chapter.

1. A <u>company</u> ~~without a chief executive officer~~ conducted a search to find a new leader.

2. The <u>policy</u> ~~of the corporate board~~ was to find an experienced CEO.

3. The <u>people</u> ~~on the short list of candidates~~ had all run other companies.

4. Their <u>work</u> ~~at other businesses~~ had not always made the companies more successful.

5. One <u>man</u> ~~from a bankrupt firm~~ had earned a ten-million-dollar salary.

6. His <u>payments</u> ~~in stock options~~ had been even higher.

7. His <u>appearance</u> ~~before the members of the board~~ did not convince them of his business abilities.

8. One <u>member</u> ~~of the board~~ suggested looking at other kinds of candidates.

9. The <u>workforce</u> ~~within the company~~ included many talented executives.

10. A <u>vice president</u> ~~from the marketing division~~ became the company's new CEO.

## Verbs

■ **TIP** In the examples throughout the remainder of this chapter, the <u>subject</u> is underlined once, and the <u>verb</u> is underlined twice.

Every sentence has a **main verb,** the word or words that tell what the subject does or that link the subject to another word that describes it. Verbs do not always immediately follow the subject: Other words may come between the subject and the verb. There are three kinds of verbs: action verbs, linking verbs, and helping verbs.

## Action Verbs

An **action verb** tells what action the subject performs.

To find the main action verb in a sentence, ask yourself, **What action does the subject perform?**

| | |
|---|---|
| **ACTION VERBS** | The <u>band</u> <u>played</u> all night. |
| | The <u>alarm</u> <u>rings</u> very loudly. |

■ **TEACHING TIP** Have a verb contest. Call out a subject and ask students to write as many action verbs as possible to go with it. Suggest that they work through the alphabet.

## Linking Verbs

A **linking verb** connects (links) the subject to another word or words that describe the subject. Linking verbs show no action. The most common linking verb is *be,* along with all its forms (*am, is, are,* and so on; see the table below). Other linking verbs, such as *seem* and *become,* can usually be replaced by a form of the verb *be,* and the sentence will still make sense.

| | |
|---|---|
| **LINKING VERBS** | The <u>bus</u> <u>is</u> late. |
| | <u>I</u> <u>feel</u> great today. (<u>I</u> <u>am</u> great today.) |
| | My new <u>shoes</u> <u>look</u> shiny. (My new <u>shoes</u> <u>are</u> shiny.) |
| | The <u>milk</u> <u>tastes</u> sour. (The <u>milk</u> <u>is</u> sour.) |

Some words can be used as either action verbs or linking verbs, depending on how the verb is used in a particular sentence.

| | |
|---|---|
| **ACTION VERB** | <u>Justine</u> <u>smelled</u> the flowers. |
| **LINKING VERB** | The <u>flowers</u> <u>smelled</u> wonderful. |

### Common Linking Verbs

| FORMS OF BE | FORMS OF SEEM AND BECOME | FORMS OF SENSE VERBS |
|---|---|---|
| am | seem, seems, seemed | look, looks, looked |
| are | | |
| is | become, becomes, became | appear, appears, appeared |
| was | | |
| were | | smell, smells, smelled |
| | | taste, tastes, tasted |
| | | feel, feels, felt |

### Helping Verbs

A **helping verb** joins the main verb in the sentence to form the **complete verb**. The helping verb is often a form of the verbs *be, have,* or *do.* A sentence may have more than one helping verb along with the main verb.

| Helping Verb | + | Main verb | = | Complete verb |

Sharon <u>was listening</u> to the radio as <u>she</u> <u>was studying</u> for the test.

[The helping verb is *was;* the complete verbs are *was listening* and *was studying.*]

<u>I</u> <u>am saving</u> my money for a car.

<u>Colleen</u> <u>might have borrowed</u> my sweater.

<u>You</u> <u>must pass</u> this course before taking the next one.

<u>You</u> <u>should stop</u> smoking.

---

## Common Helping Verbs

| FORMS OF *BE* | FORMS OF *HAVE* | FORMS OF *DO* | OTHER |
| --- | --- | --- | --- |
| am | have | do | can |
| are | has | does | could |
| been | had | did | may |
| being | | | might |
| is | | | must |
| was | | | should |
| were | | | will |
| | | | would |

---

Before you begin Practice 2, look at these examples to see how action, linking, and helping verbs are different.

**ACTION VERB**      <u>Kara</u> <u>graduated</u> last year.

[The verb *graduated* is an action that Kara performed.]

**LINKING VERB**      <u>Kara</u> <u>is</u> a graduate.

[The verb *is* links Kara to the word that describes her: *graduate.* No action is performed.]

**HELPING VERB**      <u>Kara</u> <u>is graduating</u> next spring.

[The helping verb *is* joins the main verb *graduating* to make the complete verb *is graduating,* which tells what action the subject is taking.]

**PRACTICE 2    IDENTIFYING THE VERB (ACTION, LINKING, OR HELPING VERB + MAIN VERB)**

In the following sentences, underline each <u>subject</u> and double-underline each <u>verb</u>. Then identify each verb as an action verb, a linking verb, or a helping verb + a main verb.

*Helping verb + main verb*
**EXAMPLE:** Bowling <u>was created</u> a long time ago.

*Action verb*
1. The ancient <u>Egyptians</u> <u>invented</u> bowling.

*Linking verb*
2. Dutch <u>settlers</u> <u>were</u> responsible for bowling's introduction to North America.

*Action verb*
3. <u>They</u> <u>bowled</u> outdoors on fields of grass.

*Helping verb + main verb*
4. One <u>area</u> in New York City <u>is called</u> Bowling Green because the <u>Dutch</u>
*Action verb*
<u>bowled</u> there in the 1600s.

*Action verb*
5. The first indoor bowling <u>alley</u> in the United States <u>opened</u> in 1840 in New York.

*Linking verb*
6. Indoor <u>bowling</u> soon <u>became</u> popular across the country.

*Action verb*
7. The largest bowling <u>alley</u> in the United States <u>offers</u> over a hundred lanes.

*Helping verb + main verb*
8. <u>Visitors</u> to Las Vegas <u>can bowl</u> there.

*Helping verb + main verb*
9. Most <u>people</u> <u>would</u> not <u>think</u> of bowling as more popular than basketball.

*Action verb*
10. However, more <u>Americans</u> <u>participate</u> in bowling than in any other sport.

## Complete Thoughts

A **complete thought** is an idea, expressed in a sentence, that makes sense by itself, without other sentences. An incomplete thought leaves readers wondering what's going on.

**INCOMPLETE THOUGHT**    because my alarm didn't go off

**COMPLETE THOUGHT**    <u>I</u> <u>was</u> late because my alarm didn't go off.

**INCOMPLETE THOUGHT**   the people who won the lottery

**COMPLETE THOUGHT**   The <u>people</u> who won the lottery <u>were thrilled</u>.

To determine whether a thought is complete, ask yourself, **Do I get the basic idea, or do I have to ask a question to understand?**

**INCOMPLETE THOUGHT**   in my wallet

[You would have to ask a question to understand, so this is not a complete thought.]

**COMPLETE THOUGHT**   My <u>ticket</u> <u>is</u> in my wallet.

### PRACTICE 3   IDENTIFYING COMPLETE THOUGHTS

Some of the following items contain complete thoughts, and others do not. In the space to the left of each item, write either "C" for complete thought or "I" for incomplete thought. If you write "I," add words to make a sentence. *Answers will vary. Possible answers shown.*

EXAMPLE:   _*I*_   A person I know. *is a private detective*

*I will wait until*
_*I*_   1. ~~Until~~ the store closes at midnight.

_*I*_   2. At the next meeting. *you should say what you think*

_*C*_   3. My keys are missing.

_*I*_   4. The apartment on the third floor. *was for rent*

_*C*_   5. I rented it.

*The Starmode Lounge is where*
_*I*_   6. ~~Where~~ everyone goes on Saturday night.

_*C*_   7. I bought a blue dress.

_*C*_   8. You ought to exercise.

*Mary joined a book club because*
_*I*_   9. ~~Because~~ she likes novels.

_*C*_   10. The baby is awake.

■ **TEAMWORK** Have students read the items in this practice aloud to each other and decide if the items are sentences or incomplete thoughts.

## Chapter Review: The Basic Sentence

1. A **sentence** must have three things: _a subject, a verb, and a complete_ _thought_ .

2. A _subject_ is the person, place, or thing that the sentence is about.

3. A *noun* is _a word that names a person, place, or thing_ .

4. A *prepositional phrase* is _a word group that begins with a preposition and ends with a noun or pronoun_ .

5. What are five common prepositions? _Answers will vary_ .

6. Write an example of a prepositional phrase (not from one of the examples presented earlier): _Answers will vary_ .

7. An action verb tells _what action the subject performs_ .

8. A linking verb _links the subject to a word or a group of words that describe the subject_ .

9. A helping verb _joins the main verb in the sentence to form the complete verb_ .

# 20

# Fragments

*Incomplete Sentences*

## Ever Thought This?

"When my sentence gets too long, I think it probably needs a period, so I put one in, even though I'm not sure it goes there."
— Naomi Roman, Student

This chapter

- explains what fragments are
- shows you how to find them
- gives you practice finding and correcting five common kinds of fragments

■ **LEARNING JOURNAL** Your learning journal is a good place to record fragments you find in your writing. Correct the problems and record the edited versions of these sentences too.

■ **TEACHING TIP** Students should underline the fragments for Practice 1, page 298, and correct them for Practice 9, page 312.

## Understand What Fragments Are

A **sentence** is a group of words that has a subject and a verb and expresses a complete thought, independent of other sentences. A **fragment** is a group of words that looks like a sentence but is missing a subject, a verb, or a complete thought. A fragment is only a piece of a sentence, and it is considered a serious mistake in formal writing.

| | |
|---|---|
| **SENTENCE** | I got home late, so I ate some cold pizza and drank a whole liter of Pepsi. |
| **FRAGMENT** | I got home late, so I ate some cold pizza. *And drank a whole liter of Pepsi.* |

[*And drank a whole liter of Peps*i contains a verb (*drank*) but no subject.]

### In the Real World, Why Is It Important to Correct Fragments?

**SITUATION:** Jeff is applying for a job at a building development corporation. He sends his résumé along with a cover letter to the human resources office. Although he really wants a job with this company, his cover letter hurts his chances. Here is a portion of the letter:

> I have a B. S. from Denver Community College, where I took classes in drafting. Also in computer-assisted design. I studied engineering and engineering graphics, Both of which I enjoyed and did well in. I would like the opportunity to speak with you in person regarding a position at Richmond Homes. In the architecture department. I have good skills and I am a very dedicated, hard worker. I think I could be an asset to the company.

**RESPONSE:** Alan Whitehead, vice president of architecture, responded in the following way to this letter:

> I'm not a stickler for perfect grammar, and our business is building, not writing. But I noticed the errors in the letter right away. The résumé looks decent, but those kinds of mistakes tell me that Jeff is either sloppy or lacking in basic writing skills. I'm not a perfect writer myself, so I always have to spend time proofreading my writing before sending it. I don't need staff who can't write or who don't take the time to do things right; we have lots of applicants for every position.

■ **TIP** For more of Alan Whitehead's thoughts about the importance of good writing, see the profile of him in Chapter 9, page 118.

People outside the English classroom notice major grammar errors, and though they may not assign you a course grade, they do judge you by your communication skills.

## Practice Finding and Correcting Fragments

Fragments are missing a subject, a verb, or a complete thought. How do you find these problems in your own writing? Look for the **five trouble spots** that often signal sentence fragments. When you see these trouble spots, you need to make sure the word group has all of the elements of a sentence.

■ **RESOURCES** *Additional Resources* contains tests and supplemental exercises for this chapter as well as a transparency master for the summary chart at the end of the chapter.

**TROUBLE SPOTS: SENTENCE FRAGMENTS**

- **A word group that starts with a preposition.** Examples of prepositions: *at, in, with*

  **FRAGMENT**   It's hard to find time to study. *With all of my other work.*

- **A word group that starts with a dependent word.** Examples of dependent words: *after, because, that, who*

  **FRAGMENT**   The group is meeting this morning. *After my first class ends.*

- **A word group that starts with an *-ing* verb form.** Examples of *-ing* verb forms: *running, studying, listening*

  **FRAGMENT**   People at my company gossip. *Making everyone nervous.*

- **A word group that starts with *to* and a verb.** Examples of *to* and a verb: *to understand, to hear, to see*

  **FRAGMENT**   I asked my professor for help. *To understand the difficult concept.*

- **A word group that starts with an example or explanation of something mentioned in the previous sentence.** Examples of words that might start a fragment: *for example, for instance, like, such a*s

  **FRAGMENT**   Employees need to know of all exits from the building. *For instance, the nearest fire exit.*

When you find a fragment in your own writing, you can usually correct it in one of two ways.

**BASIC WAYS TO CORRECT A FRAGMENT**

- Add what is missing (a subject, a verb, or both).
- Attach the fragment to the sentence before or after it.

> ### PRACTICE 1   **FINDING FRAGMENTS**

Find and underline the three <u>fragments</u> in Jeff's letter on page 296.

## Fragments That Start with Prepositions

■ **TIP** Remember, the subject of a sentence is *never* in a prepositional phrase (see p. 288).

Whenever a preposition starts what you think is a sentence, check for a subject, a verb, and a complete thought. If the group of words is missing any of these three elements, it is a fragment.

> **FRAGMENT**    I pounded as hard as I could. *Against the door.*
>
> [*Against the door* lacks both a subject and a verb.]

Correct a fragment that starts with a preposition by connecting it to the sentence either before or after it. If you connect such a fragment to the sentence after it, put a comma after the fragment to join it to the next sentence.

---

### FINDING AND FIXING FRAGMENTS:
Fragments That Start with a Preposition

---

#### FIND

I pounded as hard as I could. (Against) the door.

1. **Circle** any (preposition) that starts a word group.
2. **Ask:** Is there a subject in the word group? *No.*   A verb? *No.*
   **Underline** any <u>subject</u>, and **double-underline** any <u>verb</u>.
3. **Ask:** Does the word group express a complete thought? *No.*
4. If the word group is missing a subject or verb or doesn't express a complete thought, it is a fragment. *This is a fragment.*

---

#### FIX

                                                           *a*
I pounded as hard as I could./ Against the door.
                                      ^

5. **Correct the fragment** by joining it to the sentence before or after it.

## Common Prepositions

| | | | | |
|---|---|---|---|---|
| about | before | except | of | to |
| above | behind | for | off | toward |
| across | below | from | on | under |
| after | beneath | in | out | until |
| against | beside | inside | outside | up |
| along | between | into | over | upon |
| among | by | like | past | with |
| around | down | near | since | within |
| at | during | next to | through | without |

■ **PRACTICE 2    CORRECTING FRAGMENTS THAT START WITH PREPOSITIONS**

In the following items, circle any (preposition) that appears at the beginning of a word group. Then correct any fragment by connecting it to the previous or the next sentence. If you need help, look back at the chart on page 298 that shows the correction steps.

**EXAMPLE:** (For) several years when they are young, Children often have imaginary friends.

*Answers may vary. Possible edits shown.*

1. Some parents worry, (About) their children's imaginary companions.

2. Other parents think the imaginary friend is a sign, (Of) the child's creativity.

3. Some parents think imaginary companions are a waste, (Of) time and energy.

4. When children behave badly, they may blame the imaginary friend, (For) their actions.

5. Children should be taught the difference, (Between) lies and imagination.

6. (During) the period of time when a child has an imaginary friend, Parents can learn a lot about the child.

7. A child may not want to admit to being afraid, (Of) the dark.

■ **TIP** For more practice correcting fragments, visit Exercise Central at <bedfordstmartins .com/realwriting>. Also, the Writing Guide Software with this book has tutorials on fragments.

8. Children may use imaginary friends to tell their parents, ⟨About⟩ their fears.

9. Children usually give up their imaginary companions, ⟨After⟩ grade school.

10. ⟨After⟩ its disappearance, Parents who have gotten interested in the imaginary friend may be sorry to see it go.


## Fragments That Start with Dependent Words

A **dependent word** (also called a **subordinate conjunction**) is the first word in a dependent clause.

> **SENTENCE WITH A**
> **DEPENDENT WORD**    We got home early *because* we left early.
>
> [*Because* is a dependent word introducing the dependent clause *because we left early.*]

■ **DISCUSSION** Ask students to jot down what they think the word *dependent* means in the real world and to give an example. After getting some responses, ask how *dependent* in *dependent clause* is similar to *dependent* in the real world.

A dependent clause cannot be a sentence because it doesn't express a complete thought, even though it has a subject and a verb. Whenever a dependent word starts what you think is a sentence, stop to check for a subject, a verb, and a complete thought.

> **FRAGMENT**    *Since I moved.* I have eaten out every day.
>
> [*Since I moved* has a subject (*I*) and a verb (*moved*), but it doesn't express a complete thought.]

■ **COMPUTER** Suggest that students become aware of the dependent words they use most by doing a computer search for them as they edit their own writing. They can then make sure that dependent clauses are attached to sentences.

### *Common Dependent Words*

| | | |
|---|---|---|
| after | if | what(ever) |
| although | since | when(ever) |
| as | so that | where |
| because | that | whether |
| before | though | which |
| even though | unless | while |
| how | until | who/whose |

When a word group starts with *who, whose,* or *which,* it is not a complete sentence unless it is a question.

> **FRAGMENT**    That is the police officer. *Who gave me a ticket last week.*
>
> **QUESTION**    *Who* gave you a ticket last week?

| | |
|---|---|
| **FRAGMENT** | He is the goalie. *Whose team is so bad.* |
| **QUESTION** | *Whose* team are you on? |
| **FRAGMENT** | Sherlene went to the HiHo Club. *Which does not serve alcohol.* |
| **QUESTION** | *Which* club does not serve alcohol? |

Correct a fragment that starts with a dependent word by connecting it to the sentence before or after it. If the dependent clause is joined to the sentence before it, you do not usually need to put a comma in front of it. If the dependent clause is joined to the sentence after it, put a comma after the dependent clause.

---

**FINDING AND FIXING FRAGMENTS:**
Fragments That Start with a Dependent Word

**FIND**

(Because) a job search is important. People should take the time to do it right.

1. **Circle** any (dependent word) that starts either word group.
2. **Ask:** Is there a subject in the word group? *Yes.*   A verb? *Yes.*   **Underline** any subject, and **double-underline** any verb.
3. **Ask:** Does the word group express a complete thought? *No.*
4. If the word group is missing a subject or verb or doesn't express a complete thought, it is a fragment. *This is a fragment.*

**FIX**

Because a job search is important, People should take the time to do it right.

5. **Correct the fragment** by joining it to the sentence before or after it. Add a comma if the dependent word group comes first.

■ **TIP** For more on commas with dependent clauses, see Chapters 27 and 34.

---

■ **PRACTICE 3   CORRECTING FRAGMENTS THAT BEGIN WITH DEPENDENT WORDS**

In the following items, circle any (dependent word) that appears at the beginning of a word group. Then correct any fragment by connecting it to the previous or the next sentence. If you need help, look back at the chart above that shows the correction steps.

**EXAMPLE:** (When) people are asked about their ideal jobs/, ~~The~~ <sup>t</sup>

answers depend on what they want from their work.

*Answers may vary. Possible edits shown.*

1. (Unless) you think about what you really want from your job/, ~~You~~ <sup>y</sup> might make the wrong decision about your future.

2. Some people want a job that pays very well/ (Until) they discover the <sup>u</sup> sacrifices involved.

3. (If) you think a high salary is very important/, ~~You~~ <sup>y</sup> should consider how many hours you are willing to work each week to earn the money.

4. Stress can make a high-paying job unpleasant/ (Since) there is often a <sup>s</sup> lot of pressure on highly paid employees.

5. Some jobs are "dead ends" and don't leave room for advancement/ (Even though) they pay well. <sup>e</sup>

6. Jobs like firefighting, construction work, and logging are difficult to do over a number of years/ (Because) they make intense physical <sup>b</sup> demands.

7. (When) a survey recently ranked the best and worst American jobs/, ~~Those~~ jobs with a possibility of promotion, short work weeks, and low <sup>t</sup> stress rated highest.

8. (Because) jobs in math and computing pay well and cause little stress/, ~~Nine~~ out of ten of the top jobs were in those fields. <sup>n</sup>

9. Taxi driving and working in an oil field ranked in the bottom ten/ (Because) those jobs are stressful, physically difficult, and not very secure. <sup>b</sup>

10. (Whether) you want low stress, job security, or pleasant working conditions/, ~~It's~~ a good idea to prepare for your ideal job. <sup>i</sup>

## Fragments That Start with –*ing* Verb Forms

An **-ing verb form** (also called a **gerund**) is the form of a verb that ends in *-ing: walking, writing, running.* Unless it has a helping verb (*was walking, was writing, was running*), it can't be a complete verb in a sentence. Sometimes an *-ing* verb form is used at the beginning of a complete sentence.

**SENTENCE**     Walking is good exercise.

[The *-ing* verb form *walking* is the subject; *is* is the verb. The sentence expresses a complete thought.]

Sometimes an *-ing* verb form introduces a fragment. When an *-ing* verb form starts what you think is a sentence, stop and check it for a subject, a verb, and a complete thought.

**FRAGMENT**     I was running as fast as I could. *Hoping to get there on time.*

[*Hoping to get there on time* lacks a subject and a verb.]

Correct a fragment that starts with an *-ing* verb form either by adding whatever sentence elements are missing (usually a subject and a helping verb) or by connecting it to the previous or the next sentence. Usually, you will need to put a comma before or after the fragment to join it to the complete sentence.

---

**FINDING AND FIXING FRAGMENTS:**
Fragments That Start with *-ing* Verb Forms

**FIND**

I was running as fast as I could. (Hoping) to <u>get</u> there on time.

1. **Circle** any (*-ing* verb) that starts a word group.
2. **Ask:** Is there a subject in the word group? *No.*   A verb? *Yes.*   **Underline** any <u>subject</u> and **double-underline** any <u>verb</u>.
3. **Ask:** Does the word group express a complete thought? *No.*
4. If the word group is missing a subject or verb or doesn't express a complete thought, it is a fragment. *This is a fragment.*

**FIX**

                                            *h*
I was running as fast as I could/, ̬Hoping to get there on time.

                                    *I was still hoping*
I was running as fast as I could. ~~Hoping~~ to get there on time.

5. **Correct the fragment** by joining it to the sentence before or after it. **Alternative:** Add the missing sentence elements.

■  **PRACTICE 4  CORRECTING FRAGMENTS THAT START WITH *–ING* VERB FORMS**

In the following items, circle any ⟨*-ing* verb⟩ that appears at the beginning of a word group. Then correct any fragment either by adding the missing sentence elements or by connecting it to the previous or the next sentence. If you need help, look back at the chart on page 303 that shows the correction steps.

**EXAMPLE:** People sometimes travel long distances in unusual ways.
                        *They are trying*
⟨Trying⟩ to set new world records.
   ^

*Answers may vary. Possible edits shown.*
                                                                    *w*
1. In 1931, Plennie Wingo set out on an ambitious journey,⟨Walking⟩
   backward around the world.

                                                          *h*
2. ⟨Wearing⟩ sunglasses with rearview mirrors,⟨He set out on his trip early
   one morning.

3. After eight thousand miles, Wingo's journey was interrupted by a
        *h*
   war,⟨Halting⟩ his progress in Pakistan.

4. For two and a half years during the late 1970s, Hans Mullikin was
                                    *He was crawling*
   en route to the White House. ⟨Crawling⟩ from Texas to Washington,
   D.C.

                                                          *t*
5. Mullikin's trip took so long because he lingered,⟨Taking⟩ time out to
   earn money as a logger and a Baptist minister.

                                                          *p*
6. ⟨Taking⟩ unusual transportation to the White House,⟨Protesters have
   often been able to get publicity.

7. Farmers hoping for government help traveled from the Great Plains to
                *They were driving*
   Washington. ⟨Driving⟩ large, slow-moving harvesting machines.

                                        *Reporters covered*
8. The farmers' cause was helped by the media. ⟨Covering⟩ their trip from
   beginning to end.

                                                                *l*
9. Americans may also have heard the story of Alvin Straight,⟨Looking⟩
   for his long-lost brother as he traveled across the Midwest.

10. ⟨Suffering⟩ from increasingly poor eyesight,⟨Straight made his trip on a
    riding lawn mower.

## Fragments That Start with *to* and a Verb

When what you think is a sentence begins with *to* and a verb (called the *infinitive* form of the verb), you need to make sure that it is not a fragment.

| | |
|---|---|
| **FRAGMENT** | Each week the newspaper runs a consumer watch. *To tell readers about potential scams.* |
| **CORRECTED** | Each week the newspaper runs a consumer watch to tell readers about potential scams. |

If a word group begins with *to* and a verb, it must have another verb, or it is not a complete sentence. When you see a word group that begins with *to* and a verb, first check to see if there is another verb. If there is not another verb, it is a fragment.

| | |
|---|---|
| **SENTENCE** | *To run* a complete marathon was my goal. |

[*To run* is the subject; *was* is the verb.]

| | |
|---|---|
| **FRAGMENT** | Cheri got underneath the car. *To change the oil.* |

[There is not another verb in the word group that begins with *to change*.]

To correct a fragment that starts with *to* and a verb, join it to the sentence before or after it, or add the missing sentence elements.

---

**FINDING AND FIXING FRAGMENTS:**
Fragments That Start with *to* and a Verb

↓

**FIND**

Cheri got underneath the car. To change the oil.

1. **Circle** any *to-plus-verb combination* that starts a word group.
2. **Ask:** Is there a subject in the word group? *No.*  A verb? *Yes.* **Underline** any **subject** and **double-underline** any **verb**.
3. **Ask:** Does the word group express a complete thought? *No.*
4. If the word group is missing a subject or verb or doesn't express a complete thought, it is a fragment. *This is a fragment.*

↓

↓

---

**FIX**

*t*
Cheri got underneath the car./To change the oil.
^

*To change the oil,*
Cheri got underneath the car. ~~To change the oil.~~
^

*She needed to*
Cheri got underneath the car. ~~To~~ change the oil.
^

5. **Correct the fragment** by joining it to the sentence before or after it. If you put the *to*-plus-verb word group first, put a comma after it. **Alternative:** Add the missing sentence elements.

---

### PRACTICE 5   CORRECTING FRAGMENTS THAT START WITH *TO* AND A VERB

In the following items, circle any examples of (*to and a verb*) that begin a word group. Then correct any fragment either by adding the missing sentence elements or by connecting it to the previous or next sentence. If you need help, look back at the chart above that shows the correction steps.

*t*
**EXAMPLE:** Computers have made it easy./(To keep) people all around
^
the world connected with one another.
*Answers may vary. Possible edits shown.*

*a*
1. (To send) a message to an old friend or a family member,/A person
^
today often chooses e-mail instead of a letter.

*t*
2. Computer users often receive requests./(To forward) a message to others
^
in their electronic address books.

*That goal is to*
3. Sometimes, such requests are hoaxes that have just one goal.(To ensure)
^
the circulation of thousands of unnecessary e-mail messages.

*t*
4. Elementary school classes have also sent out e-mail messages for recipients./(To pass) on to everyone they know.
^

5. (To send) a message back to the class with the person's location./~~This is~~
another requirement of such e-mail assignments.

*They want to*
6. The classes are taking part in an experiment.(To see) how far and how
^
fast the e-mail message will travel.

7. Teachers who assign this experiment find that it excites the students/
~~t~~
(To get) messages from all over the world.
^

8. But in some schools, thousands of e-mail messages from assignments
like this have clogged computer servers and made it impossible for
~~t~~
teachers/(To get) important messages from the school system or parents.
^

9. Many teachers have learned the hard way/(To make) sure that the origi-
~~t~~
nal message tells recipients when the assignment ends.
^

10. (To start) people sending e-mail messages to classes from around the
*is simple*
globe. It's often much easier than to stop them.
^

## Fragments That Start with Examples or Explanations

As you reread what you have written, pay special attention to groups of
words that are examples or explanations of information you presented in the
previous sentence. They may be fragments.

**FRAGMENT**    I thought of other ways to get out of my locked apartment. *For example, through the window.*

**FRAGMENT**    I don't like climbing out of windows. *Especially from the
third floor.*

[*For example, through the window* and *Especially from the third floor* lack subjects, verbs, and
complete thoughts.]

This last type of fragment is harder to recognize because there is no single
word or kind of word to look for. Here are a few starting words that may signal a fragment, but fragments that are examples or explanations do not always start with these words.

especially          for example          like          such as

When a group of words that you think is a sentence gives an example of information in the previous sentence, stop to check it for a subject, a verb, and
a complete thought.

**FRAGMENT**    I decided to call someone who could help me get out of
my apartment. *Like a locksmith.*

**FRAGMENT**    An answering machine answered my call. *Not the locksmith.*

**FRAGMENT**    I considered getting out of my apartment by using the
fire escape. *The one outside my window.*

[*Like a locksmith, Not the locksmith,* and *The one outside my window* lack verbs and complete thoughts.]

■ **TIP** *Such as* and *like* do
not often begin complete
sentences.

Correct a fragment that starts with an example or explanation by connecting it to the previous or the next sentence. Sometimes you can add whatever sentence elements are missing (a subject or verb or both) instead. When you connect the fragment to a sentence, you may need to change some punctuation. For example, fragments that are examples and fragments that are negatives are often set off by a comma.

### FINDING AND FIXING FRAGMENTS:
Fragments That Are Examples or Explanations

#### FIND

I decided to call someone who could help me get out of my apartment. (Like a locksmith.)

1. **Circle** the word group that is an (example or explanation.)
2. **Ask:** Does the word group have a subject, a verb, and a complete thought? *No.*
3. If the word group is missing a subject or verb or doesn't express a complete thought, it is a fragment. *This is a fragment.*

#### FIX

I decided to call someone who could help me get out of my apartment/, Like a locksmith.

You may need to add some words to correct fragments:

I considered getting out of my apartment by using the fire escape. The one outside my window.
*was strong enough to hold me*

4. **Correct the fragment** by joining it to the sentence before or after it or by adding the missing sentence elements.

■ PRACTICE 6   **CORRECTING FRAGMENTS THAT ARE EXAMPLES OR EXPLANATIONS**

In the following items, circle any word groups that are (examples or explanations). Correct any fragment either by connecting it to the previous or the next sentence or by adding the missing sentence elements. If you need help, look back at the chart above that shows the correction steps.

**EXAMPLE:** The local high school raised money in an unusual way.
*It accepted*
~~Accepting~~ paid advertising from fast-food companies.
∧
*Answers may vary. Possible edits shown.*

1. Public schools in the United States are supposed to survive on money
   *s*
   collected by the government, ~~S~~uch as property taxes.
   ∧

2. A chronic shortage of cash for maintenance and supplies, ~~This~~ is the
   biggest problem many schools face today.

3. In the 1990s, many people believed that businesses held the answer to
   *l*
   the problems of public institutions, ~~L~~ike schools.
   ∧

4. Some schools agreed to permit corporate sponsorship of certain activi-
   *s*
   ties, ~~S~~ports, for example.
   ∧

5. Schools that took money from soft-drink makers were expected to
   *the drinks might be offered*
   allow soft-drink sales in the building. ~~For instance,~~ in the cafeteria and
   in hallway vending machines.

6. Money from fast-food or soft-drink companies may come with other
   *s*
   conditions, ~~S~~uch as a demand that the school sell a certain amount of
   ∧
   the product in order to receive additional funding in the future.

7. Some parents and teachers object that advertisements for fast food and
   *Such ads lead*
   soft drinks contribute to poor student health. ~~Leading~~ young people to
   ∧
   choose less nutritious and more fattening and sugary foods.

8. Other adults feel that schools should train children to think for them-
   *n*
   selves, ~~N~~ot bombard them with advertising.
   ∧

9. Schools that accept advertisements say that they really have little choice
   *They may have*
   in the matter. ~~Having~~ no other way to get enough funding to keep going.
   ∧

10. Many teachers, administrators, and parents consider advertising in
    *it may be*
    school a bad idea. But sometimes necessary.
    ∧

---

■ PRACTICE 7   **CORRECTING VARIOUS TYPES OF FRAGMENTS**

In the following items, circle any word group that is a fragment. Correct
each fragment either by connecting it to the previous or the next sentence
or by adding the missing sentence elements.

**EXAMPLE:** Celebrities' lives seem interesting. (To those of us who are not famous.)

*Answers may vary. Possible edits shown.*

1. (Being a celebrity.) It might not be as much fun as it sounds.

2. (When I was younger,) I desperately wanted to be famous someday.

3. I followed the careers of famous actors and musicians. (Like Julia Roberts and Eddie Vedder.)

4. I wanted to have the things I imagined famous people had. *I looked forward to designer* (Designer clothes, expensive shoes, diamonds, meals in expensive restaurants, a house in Los Angeles, and apartments in New York and Paris.)

5. I was eager. (To be recognized in public places.)

6. Then, I saw Dustin Hoffman once. (On a trip I took to New York City.)

7. He was walking down an avenue in Midtown. (Minding his own business.)

8. (Before I saw the famous actor face to face,) I could see heads turning in the crowd in front of me.

9. Trying not to notice everyone staring at him, Hoffman walked past me. (With a hunted look on his face.)

10. At that moment I lost the urge. (To be noticed wherever I went.)

# Edit Paragraphs and Your Own Writing

Use the Critical Thinking box that follows and the chart, Finding and Fixing Fragments, on page 313 to help you complete the practices in this section and edit your own writing.

| CRITICAL THINKING: EDITING FOR FRAGMENTS |
| --- |

**FOCUS**
Whenever you see one of the five trouble spots in your writing, stop to check for a possible fragment.

**ASK YOURSELF**
• Does it have a subject?
• Does it have a verb?

- Does it express a complete thought in a sentence that is not dependent on other sentences?

**EDIT**

If your answer to any of these questions is "no," you have a fragment that must be corrected.

---

■ **PRACTICE 8    EDITING PARAGRAPHS FOR FRAGMENTS**

Find and correct any fragments in the following paragraphs.
*Answers may vary. Possible edits shown.*

1. (1) Wilma Rudolph was born in 1940 in Tennessee. (2) When she was four, she became ill with scarlet fever and pneumonia. (3) *She was so* So sick that everyone thought she would die. (4) She survived, but one of her legs was damaged. (5) She was told that she would never walk again. (6) Rudolph did manage to walk again despite the doctors' predictions. (7) After years of treatment, braces, and determination, (8) *s*She started running for exercise. (9) In 1960, Rudolph became the second American woman in history to win three gold medals in a single Olympics.

2. (1) Louis Braille was born in France in 1809. (2) In a tragic accident, he punctured one of his eyes when he was three. (3) Infection set in, and he lost sight in both eyes. (4) He attended a special school for the blind where students were taught a system of communication. (5) *It was a* A very cumbersome and difficult system. (6) Becoming fascinated with the idea of inventing a writing system the blind could read, (7) Braille worked for two years on his own idea. (8) *He* To develop*ed* the raised dot system, called Braille, that is used universally.

3. (1) Most people think of Thomas Edison as a famous inventor, (2) ~~The man~~ who invented the light bulb. (3) Most people don't know that Edison was considered learning disabled as a child. (4) An illness had prevented him from entering school until he was eight, and his teachers told his parents that he couldn't learn. (5) His parents took him out of school, (6) *b*Because they did not believe the teachers. (7) He was then homeschooled, (8) *b*By his very determined mother. (9) By the age of ten, Edison was already experimenting with what would become his great inventions.

■ **TEAMWORK** Divide the class into small groups and have each group present a corrected paragraph. Compare the different ways that the groups correct the fragments.

4. (1) Augusta Ada Byron was born in London, England, in 1815. (2) Her famous father, the poet Lord Byron, left her mother/ (3) *i*In 1816 and never returned to England. (4) Ada's mother wanted her daughter to study mathematics/, (5) *n*Not poetry, like her father. (6) Ada was a talented mathematician who soon became interested in an early type of computer. (7) The computer was never built, but Ada designed programs for it/, (8) *e*Earning her recognition in the twentieth century as one of the first computer programmers.

5. (1) Born in Columbus, Ohio, in 1856/, (2) Granville T. Woods, an African American inventor, had to leave school at the age of ten. (3) While working at various jobs, Woods sometimes attended night school/ (4) *b*Because he realized that he needed more education to achieve his goals. (5) He found work on railroads and used his electrical and mechanical skills/ (6) *t*To invent improvements for electric railways. (7) Woods received patents on over sixty of his inventions/, (8) *s*Such as improved air brakes and a telegraph that allowed communication between the train and the station.

■ **PRACTICE 9   EDITING JEFF'S LETTER**

Look back at Jeff's letter on page 296. You may have already underlined the fragments in his letter; if not, do so now. Next, using what you've learned in this chapter, correct each fragment in the letter.

■ **PRACTICE 10   EDITING YOUR OWN WRITING FOR FRAGMENTS**

■ **LEARNING JOURNAL** What kind of fragments do you find most often in your writing? What are some ways to avoid or correct this mistake?

As a final practice, edit fragments in a piece of your own writing—a paper you are working on for this class, a paper you've already finished, a paper for another course, or a recent piece of writing from your work or everyday life. Use the Critical Thinking box on page 310 and the chart on page 313 to help you.

## Chapter Review: Fragments

1. A *sentence* is a group of words that has a ___subject___, a ___verb___, and ___expresses a complete thought___.

2. A ___fragment___ seems to be a complete sentence but is only a piece of one. It lacks a ___subject___, a ___verb___, or a ___complete thought___.

3. What are the five trouble spots that signal possible fragments?

   *A word group that starts with a preposition*

   *A word group that starts with a dependent word*

   *A word group that starts with an -ing verb form*

   *A word group that starts with to and a verb*

   *A word group that starts with an example or explanation*

4. What are the two basic ways to correct fragments?

   *Add what is missing (a subject, a verb, or both).*

   *Attach the fragment to the sentence before or after it.*

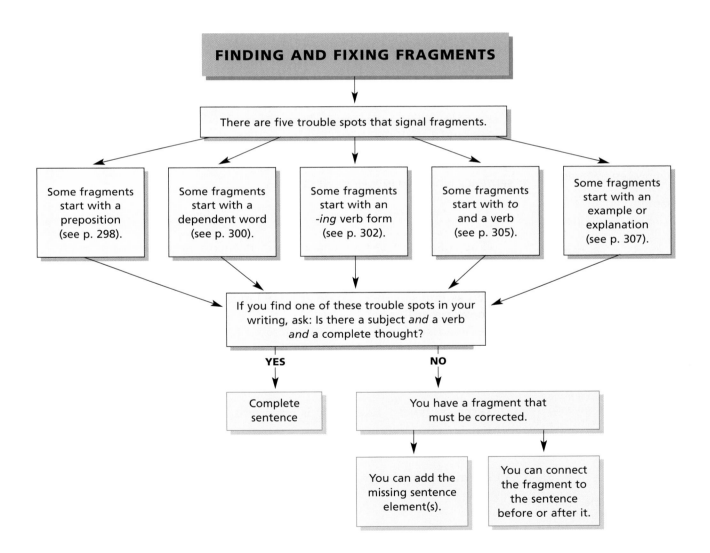

**FINDING AND FIXING FRAGMENTS**

There are five trouble spots that signal fragments.

Some fragments start with a preposition (see p. 298).

Some fragments start with a dependent word (see p. 300).

Some fragments start with an -ing verb form (see p. 302).

Some fragments start with to and a verb (see p. 305).

Some fragments start with an example or explanation (see p. 307).

If you find one of these trouble spots in your writing, ask: Is there a subject *and* a verb *and* a complete thought?

YES → Complete sentence

NO → You have a fragment that must be corrected.

You can add the missing sentence element(s).

You can connect the fragment to the sentence before or after it.

# 21

# Run-Ons

*Two Sentences Joined Incorrectly*

## Ever Thought This?

"I tried putting in commas instead of periods, so I wouldn't have fragments. But now my papers get marked for 'run-ons.'"
    —Jimmy Lester, Student

This chapter

- explains what run-ons are
- shows you how to find them
- gives you practice finding run-ons and shows four ways to correct them

■ **LEARNING JOURNAL** Use your learning journal as a place to record the run-ons you find in your writing. Also write down edited versions of the sentences, with the problems corrected.

■ **TIP** To find and correct run-ons, you need to be able to identify a complete sentence. For a review, see Chapter 19.

## Understand What Run-Ons Are

A sentence is also called an **independent clause**, a group of words with a subject and a verb that expresses a complete thought. Sometimes two independent clauses can be joined to form one larger sentence.

**SENTENCE WITH TWO INDEPENDENT CLAUSES**

Independent clause            Independent clause

The college offers financial aid, and it encourages students to apply.

A **run-on** is two complete sentences that are joined incorrectly and written as one sentence. There are two kinds of run-ons: **fused sentences** and **comma splices**.

A **fused sentence** is two complete sentences joined without any punctuation.

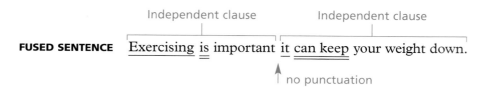

FUSED SENTENCE    Exercising is important it can keep your weight down.

↑ no punctuation

A **comma splice** is two complete sentences joined by only a comma.

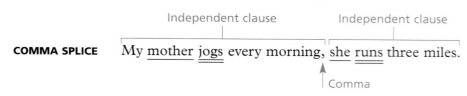

COMMA SPLICE    My mother jogs every morning, she runs three miles.

↑ Comma

**314**

When you join two sentences, you must use the proper punctuation. If you join them with no punctuation or with only a comma, you create a run-on error.

■ **TIP** In the examples throughout this chapter, the <u>subject</u> is underlined once, and the <u>verb</u> is underlined twice.

CORRECTIONS    <u>Exercising</u> <u><u>is</u></u> important; <u>it</u> <u><u>can keep</u></u> your weight down.

My <u>mother</u> <u><u>jogs</u></u> every morning; <u>she</u> <u><u>runs</u></u> three miles.

## In the Real World, Why Is It Important to Correct Run-Ons?

■ **RESOURCES** *Additional Resources* contains tests and supplemental practice exercises for this chapter as well as a transparency master for the summary chart at the end of the chapter.

**SITUATION:** Naomi is applying to a special program for returning students at Mariner College. Here is one of the essay questions on the application, followed by a paragraph from Naomi's response.

**STATEMENT OF PURPOSE:** In two hundred words or less, please describe your intellectual and professional goals and how a Mariner College education will assist you in achieving them.

■ **TEACHING TIP** Students should underline the run-ons for Practice 1, page 316, and correct them for Practice 7, page 327.

For many years I did not take control of my life; I just drifted along without any purpose or goals. I realized one day as I was meeting with my daughter's guidance counselor that I hoped my daughter would not turn out like me. From that moment, I decided I would focus my energy on doing something to help myself and others. I set a goal of becoming a nutritionist. To begin on that path, I took a brush-up course in math at night school, *and* then I took another in chemistry. I passed both courses. *W*ith hard work and persistence I know I can do well in the Mariner College program. I am committed to the professional goal I finally found. *I*t has given new purpose to my whole life.

**RESPONSE:** When Jean Turner, a college admissions director, read Naomi's answer, she noticed the run-ons and made the following comment:

We take these essays very seriously. We want students who are thoughtful, hardworking, and mature. Although Naomi's essay indicates that she has some of these qualities, her writing gives another impression. The errors she makes are numerous and significant; I can't help but wonder if she took the time to really think about this essay. If she is careless on a document that represents her for college admission, will she be careless in other areas as well? It's too bad, because her qualifications are quite good otherwise.

Run-ons, like sentence fragments, are errors that people notice and consider major mistakes.

# Practice Finding and Correcting Run-ons

To find run-ons, focus on each sentence in your writing, one at a time. Until you get used to finding run-ons (or until you don't make the error anymore), this step will take extra time. But if you spend the extra time, your writing will improve.

■ **PRACTICE 1    IDENTIFYING RUN-ONS**

Find and underline the four <u>run-ons</u> in Naomi's writing on page 315.

Once you have found a run-on, there are four ways to correct it.

**FOUR WAYS TO CORRECT A RUN-ON**

- Add a period.
- Add a semicolon.
- Add a comma and a coordinating conjunction.
- Add a dependent word.

## Add a Period

You can correct a run-on by adding a period between independent clauses to make two separate sentences. After adding the period, capitalize the letter that begins the new sentence. Reread your two sentences to make sure they each contain a subject and a verb and express a complete thought.

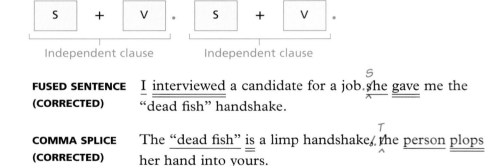

| | Independent clause | | | Independent clause | |
|---|---|---|---|---|---|
| S | + | V | S | + | V |

**FUSED SENTENCE (CORRECTED)**    <u>I</u> <u>interviewed</u> a candidate for a job. ~~s~~he <u>gave</u> me the "dead fish" handshake.

**COMMA SPLICE (CORRECTED)**    The <u>"dead fish"</u> <u>is</u> a limp handshake. ~~,~~ the <u>person</u> <u>plops</u> her hand into yours.

## Add a Semicolon

A second way to correct a run-on is to use a semicolon (;) to join the two sentences. Use a semicolon when the two sentences express closely related ideas. A semicolon can be used only where a period could also be used; the words on each side of the semicolon must be able to stand alone as a complete sentence. Do not capitalize the word that follows a semicolon unless it is the name of a specific person, place, or thing that is usually capitalized — for example, Mary, New York, or Eiffel Tower.

■ **TEACHING TIP** Remind students that a semicolon balances two independent clauses. What is on either side of it must be able to stand alone as a complete sentence.

**FUSED SENTENCE (CORRECTED)**    <u>Slouching</u> <u><u>creates</u></u> a terrible impression <u>it</u> <u><u>makes</u></u> a person seem uninterested, bored, or lacking in self-confidence.

**COMMA SPLICE (CORRECTED)**    <u>It</u> <u><u>is</u></u> important in an interview to hold your head up; <u>it</u> <u><u>is</u></u> just as important to sit up straight.

A semicolon is sometimes used before a transition from one sentence to another, and the transition word is then followed by a comma.

Semicolon   Transition   Comma

<u>I</u> <u><u>stopped</u></u> by the market; however, <u>it</u> <u><u>was closed</u></u>.

Semicolon   Transition   Comma

<u>Sharon</u> <u><u>is</u></u> a neighbor; actually, <u>she</u> <u><u>is</u></u> my friend.

---

**FINDING AND FIXING RUN-ONS:**
Correcting a Run-On by Adding a Period or Semicolon

---

**FIND**

Few <u>people</u> <u><u>know</u></u> the history of many popular holidays <u>Valentine's Day</u> <u><u>is</u></u> one of these holidays.

1. To determine whether there are two independent clauses in a sentence, **underline** the <u>subjects</u> and **double-underline** the <u><u>verbs</u></u>.
2. **Ask:** If there are two independent clauses in the sentence, are they separated by either a period or a semicolon? *No. It is a run-on.*

---

**FIX**

Few people know the history of many popular holidays. Valentine's Day is one of these holidays.

Few people know the history of many popular holidays; Valentine's Day is one of these holidays.

3. **Correct the run-on** by adding a period or a semicolon.

■ **TEACHING TIP** You may want to warn students that if they have written a sentence that is longer than two lines, they should look at it closely to see if it has errors.

■ **TIP** For more practices on run-ons, visit Exercise Central at <bedfordstmartins.com/realwriting>. Also, the Writing Guide Software with this book has tutorials on run-ons.

■ **PRACTICE 2  CORRECTING A RUN-ON BY ADDING A PERIOD OR A SEMICOLON**

For each of the following run-ons, indicate in the space to the left whether it is a fused sentence ("FS") or a comma splice ("CS"). Then correct the run-on by adding a period or a semicolon. Capitalize the letters as necessary to make two sentences. If you need help, look back at the chart on page 317 that shows the correction steps.

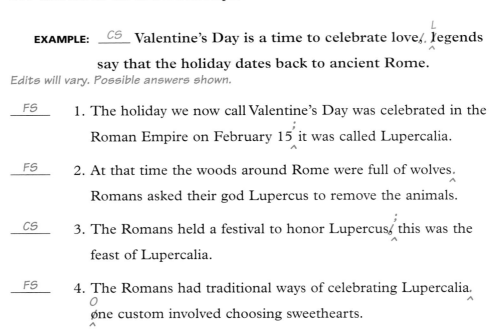

EXAMPLE: __CS__ Valentine's Day is a time to celebrate love, legends
say that the holiday dates back to ancient Rome.

*Edits will vary. Possible answers shown.*

___FS___ 1. The holiday we now call Valentine's Day was celebrated in the Roman Empire on February 15 it was called Lupercalia.

___FS___ 2. At that time the woods around Rome were full of wolves. Romans asked their god Lupercus to remove the animals.

___CS___ 3. The Romans held a festival to honor Lupercus, this was the feast of Lupercalia.

___FS___ 4. The Romans had traditional ways of celebrating Lupercalia. One custom involved choosing sweethearts.

___FS___ 5. The night before the feast, all of the young women wrote their names on pieces of paper. they put the names in a jar.

___CS___ 6. Then, each young man chose a name, this woman would be his sweetheart for the year.

___FS___ 7. The emperor ordered his soldiers not to get married. he was afraid they would want to stay home instead of going to war.

___CS___ 8. A Christian priest named Valentine married several couples secretly, he was arrested.

___CS___ 9. The emperor had Valentine killed on February 14, later the priest was declared a saint.

___CS___ 10. The Romans became Christians and stopped celebrating the feast honoring Lupercus, they began to celebrate St. Valentine's Day on February 14.

## Add a Comma and a Coordinating Conjunction (*and, but, or, nor, so, for, yet*)

You can also correct a run-on by adding a comma and a coordinating conjunction: *and, but, or, nor, so, for,* or *yet*. Think of a coordinating conjunction as a link that joins independent clauses to form one sentence.

If the run-on is a comma splice, it already has a comma, so you need to add only a conjunction. Before adding a conjunction, read the independent clauses aloud to see which word best expresses the relationship between them.

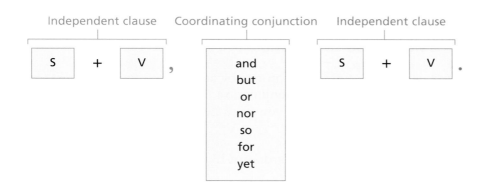

■ **TIP** Notice that the comma does not follow the conjunction. The comma follows the word before the conjunction.

**FUSED SENTENCE**
**(CORRECTED)**
Naomi was qualified for the job, *but* she hurt her chances by mumbling.

**COMMA SPLICE**
**(CORRECTED)**
The candidate smiled, *and* she waved to the crowd.

---

**FINDING AND FIXING RUN-ONS:**
Correcting a Run-On
with a Comma and a Coordinating Conjunction

↓

**FIND**

Foods differ from place to place your favorite treat might disgust someone from another culture.

1. To determine whether there are two independent clauses in a sentence, **underline** the subjects and **double-underline** the verbs.

2. **Ask:** If there are two independent clauses in the sentence, are they separated by either a period or a semicolon? *No. It is a run-on.*

↓

↓

---

**FIX**

Foods differ from place to place, *and* your favorite treat might disgust someone from another culture. ^

3. **Correct the run-on** by adding a comma and a coordinating conjunction between the two independent clauses.

---

> ### PRACTICE 3  CORRECTING A RUN-ON BY ADDING A COMMA AND A COORDINATING CONJUNCTION

Correct each of the following run-ons by adding a comma, if necessary, and an appropriate coordinating conjunction. First underline the <u>subjects</u> and double-underline the <u>verbs</u>. If you need help, look back at the chart above that shows the correction steps.

**EXAMPLE:** Most <u>Americans</u> <u>do</u> not <u>like</u> the idea of eating certain kinds of food, *and* most of us <u>would</u> probably <u>reject</u> horse meat.

*Answers will vary. Possible answers shown.*

1. In most cultures, popular <u>foods</u> <u>depend</u> greatly on availability and tradition, *So* <u>people</u> <u>tend</u> to eat old familiar favorites.

2. <u>Sushi</u> <u>shocked</u> many Americans twenty years ago, *but* today some young <u>people</u> in the United States <u>have grown up</u> eating raw fish.

3. In many societies, certain <u>foods</u> <u>are allowed</u> to ferment, *for* this <u>process</u> <u>adds</u> flavor.

4. <u>Icelanders</u> <u>bury</u> eggs in the ground to rot for months, *and* these fermented <u>eggs</u> <u>are considered</u> a special treat.

5. As an American, <u>you</u> <u>might</u> not <u>like</u> such eggs, *or* the <u>thought</u> of eating them <u>might</u> even <u>revolt</u> you.

6. In general, fermented <u>foods</u> <u>have</u> a strong taste, *so* the <u>flavor</u> <u>is</u> unpleasant to someone unaccustomed to those foods.

7. Many <u>Koreans</u> <u>love</u> to eat kimchee, a spicy fermented cabbage, *but* <u>Americans</u> often <u>find</u> the taste peculiar and the smell overpowering.

8. <u>Herders</u> in Kyrgyzstan <u>drink</u> kumiss, *and* this <u>beverage</u> <u>is made</u> of fermented horse's milk.

9. Americans on a visit to Kyrgyzstan consider themselves brave for

   *but*

   tasting kumiss, ^ local children drink it regularly.

10. We think of familiar foods as normal, ^ favorite American foods might

    *yet*

    horrify people in other parts of the world.

## Add a Dependent Word

A fourth way to correct run-ons is to make one of the complete sentences a dependent clause by adding a dependent word, such as *after, because, before, even though, if, though, unless,* and *when.* (For a more complete list of these words, see the graphic below.) Choose the dependent word (also called a subordinating conjunction) that best expresses the relationship between the two clauses.

You will often use a dependent word when the clause it begins is less important than the other clause or explains the other clause, as in the following sentence.

> When *I get to the train station,* I'll call Josh.

The italicized clause is dependent (subordinate) because it just explains when the most important part of the sentence — calling Josh — will happen. It begins with the dependent word *when.*

Because a dependent clause is not a complete sentence (it has a subject and verb but does not express a complete thought), it can be joined to a sentence without creating a run-on. When the dependent clause is the second clause in a sentence, you usually do not need to put a comma before it unless it is showing contrast.

**TWO SENTENCES**

Halloween was originally a religious holiday. People worshiped the saints.

**DEPENDENT CLAUSE: NO COMMA NEEDED**

Halloween was originally a religious holiday *when people worshiped the saints.*

**DEPENDENT CLAUSE SHOWING CONTRAST: COMMA NEEDED**

Many holidays have religious origins, *though the celebrations have moved away from their religious roots.*

■ **TIP** For more on using commas with dependent clauses, see Chapters 27 and 34.

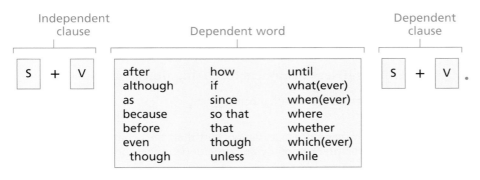

| Independent clause | Dependent word | | | Dependent clause |
|---|---|---|---|---|
| S + V | after | how | until | S + V . |
| | although | if | what(ever) | |
| | as | since | when(ever) | |
| | because | so that | where | |
| | before | that | whether | |
| | even | though | which(ever) | |
| | though | unless | while | |

■ **ESL** Point out that *unless* is as useful as *if,* but it means *if + not.* (I will go *if* I am invited. I will *not* go *unless* I am invited.)

**FUSED SENTENCE (CORRECTED)**    Your final statement should express your interest in the position <u>, although</u> you don't want to sound desperate.

[The dependent clause *although you don't want to sound desperate* shows contrast, so a comma comes before it.]

**COMMA SPLICE (CORRECTED)**    It is important to end an interview on a positive note, *because* that final impression is what the interviewer will remember.

You can also put the dependent clause first. When the dependent clause comes first, be sure to put a comma after it.

Dependent clause        Independent Clause

| Dependent word | S + V , | S + V . |

**FUSED SENTENCE (CORRECTED)**    *When the* The interviewer stands, the candidate should shake hands firmly.

**COMMA SPLICE (CORRECTED)**    *After the* The interview is over, the candidate should stand and smile politely.

---

**FINDING AND FIXING RUN-ONS:**
Correcting a Run-On by Making a Dependent Clause

---

**FIND**

Alzheimer's disease is a heartbreaking illness, it causes steady deterioration of brain capacity.

1. To determine whether there are two independent clauses in a sentence, **underline** the subjects and **double-underline** the verbs.
2. **Ask:** If there are two independent clauses in the sentence, are they separated by a period, a semicolon, or a comma and a coordinating conjunction? *No. It is a run-on.*

---

**FIX**

*because*
Alzheimer's disease is a heartbreaking illness, it causes steady deterioration of brain capacity.

3. If one part of the sentence is less important than the other, or if you want to make it so, **correct the run-on** by adding a dependent word to the less important part.

■ PRACTICE 4    CORRECTING A RUN-ON BY MAKING A
DEPENDENT CLAUSE

Correct each of the following run-ons by adding a dependent word to make
a dependent clause. First underline the <u>subjects</u> and double-underline the
<u>verbs</u>. If you need help, look back at the chart on page 322 that shows the
correction steps.

EXAMPLE: A <u>parent</u> with Alzheimer's <u>can be</u> a difficult patient, *since*
people with the disease often <u>cannot recognize</u> family
members. *Answers will vary. Possible answers shown.*

1. *When a*
   A <u>person</u> <u>is diagnosed</u> with Alzheimer's disease, the whole <u>family</u>
   <u>may feel</u> depressed.

2. *Although the*
   The <u>disease</u> <u>affects</u> people at different rates, the final <u>result</u> <u>is</u> usually a
   serious loss of memory.

3. The <u>progress</u> of Alzheimer's <u>is</u> often gradual *as* the <u>victim</u> <u>begins</u> to forget
   simple things and make little mistakes.

4. *After patients*
   <u>Patients</u> <u>can</u> no longer take care of themselves, the <u>burden</u> <u>falls</u> on
   family members.

5. *Because*
   Alzheimer's <u>patients</u> <u>need</u> the same kind of care that newborns need,
   their <u>children</u> <u>may feel</u> strange caring for their dependent parents.

6. Many <u>children</u> of Alzheimer's patients <u>feel</u> guilty *when* their <u>jobs</u>, <u>homes</u>, and
   <u>families</u> <u>keep</u> them from giving all their attention to their parents.

7. *Since the*
   The <u>expense</u> of caring for Alzheimer's patients <u>can be</u> huge, many
   <u>patients</u> and their <u>families</u> <u>need</u> help.

8. <u>Children</u> of Alzheimer's patients <u>need</u> to take care of their own needs
   *so that*
   <u>they</u> <u>can do</u> the right thing for their parents.

9. <u>Life</u> after Alzheimer's <u>can</u> never <u>be</u> the same, *although* the <u>patient</u> <u>can feel</u>
   happy at times.

10. Support <u>groups</u> <u>can help</u> families cope *when* Alzheimer's <u>strikes</u> a loved one.

## A Word That Can Cause Run-Ons: *Then*

Many run-ons are caused by the word *then*. You can use *then* to join two sentences, but if you add it without the correct punctuation, your sentence will

be a run-on. Often writers use just a comma before *then,* but that makes a comma splice.

**COMMA SPLICE**     I picked up my laundry, then I went home.

Use any of the four methods you have just practiced to correct run-ons caused by *then.* These methods are shown in the following examples.

I picked up my laundry. *T*hen I went home.

I picked up my laundry; then I went home.

*and*
I picked up my laundry, then I went home.

*before*
I picked up my laundry then I went home.

---

## PRACTICE 5   CORRECTING VARIOUS TYPES OF RUN-ONS

In the following items, correct any run-ons. Use each method of correcting run-ons—adding a period, adding a semicolon, adding a comma and a co-ordinating conjunction, or adding a dependent word—at least twice.

**EXAMPLE:** Corporate scandals have damaged many Americans'
*B*
faith in business leaders. both government and businesses are

trying to make companies more honest.
*Answers will vary. Possible answers shown.*

*When the*
1. ~~The~~ collapse of Enron, WorldCom, Tyco, and other companies in 2001 and 2002 brought calls for corporate reform, every government figure from the president on down made speeches about holding companies responsible for their actions.

2. Some reformers wanted businesses to claim stock options as an ex-
*C*
pense. companies had previously seen options, which could be worth millions, as gifts that did not cost the company any money.

3. Congress and the White House did not require companies to declare
*but*
the cost of stock options, a few major American corporations decided to take steps to make their shareholders happier.

4. Coca-Cola was one of the largest corporations to change its account-ing practices; the company announced that it would declare stock options as an expense.

5. Business leaders praised Coca-Cola for this announcement *, and* other
   companies made the same change after Coca-Cola led the way.

6. In late 2002, Coca-Cola made another bold accounting reform *when* it
   announced the end of earnings forecasts.

7. A company's earnings forecast predicts how much money the company
   will make in the next quarter*. A* company looks strong if it meets the
   expectations and weak if it does not.

8. According to some economics experts, earnings forecasts can put
   tremendous pressure on a company*;* executives may even cheat to
   make the company look financially strong.

9. Coca-Cola's financial statements will still provide information about
   how the company does business *; however,* they will not predict how many dollars
   and cents the corporation will earn in the future.

10. *Although many* ~~Many~~ investors feel that Coca-Cola's reforms are a positive step for the
    corporate world, some would place more trust in the stock market if
    the government insisted that all companies do the same thing.

## Edit Paragraphs and Your Own Writing

Use the Critical Thinking box that follows and the chart, Finding and Fixing Run-ons, on page 328 to help you complete the practices in this section
and edit your own writing.

### CRITICAL THINKING: EDITING FOR RUN-ONS

**FOCUS**
Read each sentence aloud, and listen carefully as you read.

**ASK YOURSELF**
- Am I pausing in the middle of the sentence?
- If so, are there two subjects and two verbs?
- If so, are there two complete sentences in this sentence? (If I break
  the sentence into two sentences, does each make sense when I read
  it aloud? Would each make sense if it weren't next to the other one?)
- If there are two complete sentences in this sentence, are they sepa-
  rated by punctuation?
- If the answer is "no," the sentence is a fused sentence.

(continued)

- If there is punctuation between them, is it a comma only, with no coordinating conjunction?
- If the answer is "yes," the sentence is a comma splice.

**EDIT**

If the sentence is a fused sentence or a comma splice, correct it using one of the four methods for correcting run-ons.

■ **TEACHING TIP** Have students read the paragraphs aloud to listen for errors.

### PRACTICE 6   EDITING PARAGRAPHS FOR RUN-ONS

Find and correct the run-ons in the following paragraphs.
*Answers will vary. Possible answers shown.*

1. (1) The Internet once seemed like an exciting new way to make
money. Everyone wanted to earn a living online. (2) The trick was to
find a way to make people pay for something on the Internet. (3) Selling advertising space on Web sites was one popular way to try to earn
money, but most computer users were not especially interested in the ads.
(4) A flashing banner that popped up at the top of a screen rarely made
Internet customers want to find out more; instead, it tended to make
them resentful of the company sponsoring the ad. (5) Spam has become
another way to spread Internet advertising. Spammers flood e-mail
addresses with unsolicited mail selling golf balls, insurance, and so on.
(6) Spam, too, is irritating to computer users; no one wants to spend
time throwing away the electronic equivalent of junk mail. (7) Internet
advertising faces some of the challenges of television advertising because people
want to fast-forward through the advertisements that interrupt their
viewing. (8) Although people still love the Internet, they are more reluctant than ever to invest in online companies or to click through on
ads that pop up online. (9) The willingness of people to surf the Web
daily has not changed. Nevertheless, using the Internet to earn money is
probably even more difficult today than it was in the nineties.

2. (1) The Internet may seem to be unlimited, but there may soon be a
shortage of good domain names. (2) Domain names are those "dot-
com" addresses that Internet users type in when they want to go to a site
on the Web. (3) When people want to create a Web site, they need a
domain name that hasn't been used before. (4) Some people have been

claiming site names that they don't plan to use. ^they hope to sell them
^T^

later. (5) A few people own a large number of domain names, ^the names
^T^

are considered an investment today. (6) Names that a user might type in
when searching for information on a general topic are hard to find now.
(7) The people who own the Web sites at those addresses get more business, ^their domain names are more valuable. (8) Sometimes people who
^so^

own a good domain name sell the name for huge profits, ^companies
^C^

have been willing to pay over a million dollars for a domain name that
they want.

**PRACTICE 7   EDITING NAOMI'S APPLICATION ANSWER**

Look back at Naomi's writing on page 315. You may have already underlined the run-ons; if not, underline them now. Then correct each run-on.

**PRACTICE 8   EDITING YOUR OWN WRITING FOR RUN-ONS**

As a final practice, edit run-ons in a piece of your own writing—a paper you
are working on for this course, a paper you've already finished, a paper for
another course, or a recent piece of writing from your work or everyday life.
Use the Critical Thinking box on page 325 and the chart on page 328 to
help you.

■ **LEARNING JOURNAL** What
kind of run-ons do you find
most often in your writing?
What are some ways to avoid
or correct this mistake?

## Chapter Review: Run-Ons

1. A sentence can also be called an *independent clause*_____.

2. A *run-on sentence*_____ is two complete sentences that are joined incorrectly and written as one sentence.

3. A *fused sentence*_____ is two complete sentences joined without any
   punctuation.

4. A *comma splice*_____ is two complete sentences joined by only a
   comma.

5. What are the four ways to correct run-ons?
   *Add a period.*_____
   *Add a semicolon.*_____

*Add a comma and a coordinating conjunction.* _____

*Add a dependent word.* _____

6. What word in the middle of a sentence may signal a run-on? *then* _____

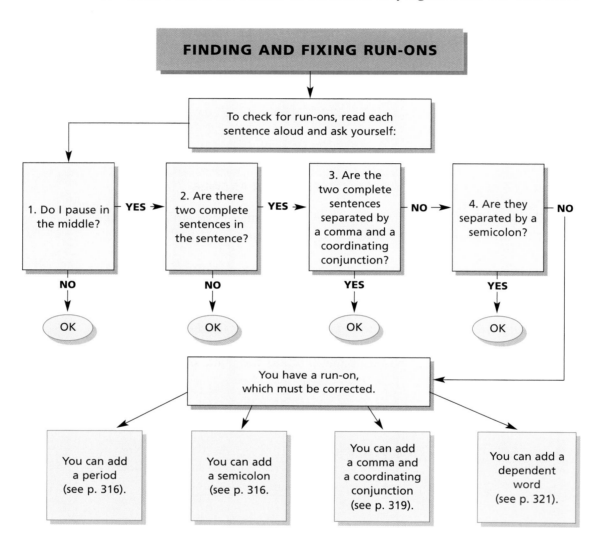

**FINDING AND FIXING RUN-ONS**

To check for run-ons, read each sentence aloud and ask yourself:

1. Do I pause in the middle? — **YES** → 2. Are there two complete sentences in the sentence? — **YES** → 3. Are the two complete sentences separated by a comma and a coordinating conjunction? — **NO** → 4. Are they separated by a semicolon? — **NO**

**NO** → OK    **NO** → OK    **YES** → OK    **YES** → OK

You have a run-on, which must be corrected.

You can add a period (see p. 316).

You can add a semicolon (see p. 316.

You can add a comma and a coordinating conjunction (see p. 319).

You can add a dependent word (see p. 321).

# 22

# Problems with Subject-Verb Agreement

## When Subjects and Verbs Don't Match

## Understand What Subject-Verb Agreement Is

In any sentence, the **subject and the verb must match—or agree—**in number. If the subject is singular (one person, place, or thing), then the verb must also be singular. If the subject is plural (more than one), the verb must also be plural.

**SINGULAR**    The <u>athlete</u> <u>runs</u> around the track.

**PLURAL**    The <u>athletes</u> <u>run</u> around the track.

**Regular verbs** (with forms that follow standard rules) have two forms in the present tense: one that ends in *-s* and one that has no ending. The third-person subjects *he, she, it,* and singular nouns always use the form that ends in *-s.* First-person subjects (*I*), second-person subjects (*you*), and plural subjects use the form with no ending. The chart that follows shows the differences.

|  | SINGULAR | PLURAL |
|---|---|---|
| *First person* | I walk. | We walk. |
| *Second person* | You walk. | You walk. |
| *Third person* | He (she, it) walk<u>s</u>. | They walk. |
|  | Joe walk<u>s</u>. | Joe and Alice walk. |
|  | The student walk<u>s</u>. | The students walk. |

### In the Real World, Why Is It Important to Correct Errors in Subject-Verb Agreement?

**SITUATION:** Regina Toms (name changed) wrote the following brief report about a company employee whom she was sending to the employee assistance program. (These programs help workers with various problems, such as alcoholism or mental illness, that may affect their job performance.)

### Ever Thought This?

"I know sometimes the verb is supposed to end with *-s* and sometimes it isn't, but I always get confused."
—Mayerlin Fana, Student

This chapter

- explains what *agreement* between subjects and verbs is
- explains the simple rules for *regular verbs*
- identifies five trouble spots that can cause confusion
- gives you practice finding and fixing errors in subject-verb agreement

■ **LEARNING JOURNAL** Use your learning journal as a place to record problems with subject-verb agreement that you find in your writing. Also write down edited versions of the sentences, with the problems corrected.

■ **TIP** To find and correct errors in subject-verb agreement, you must be able to identify subjects and verbs. For a review, see Chapter 19.

Mr. XXX, who has been a model employee of the company for five years, _has_ have recently behaved in ways that _are_ is inappropriate. For example, last week he was very rude when a colleague asked him a question. He has been late to work several times and has missed work more often than usual. When I spoke to him about his behavior and asked if he _has_ have problems, he admitted that he had been drinking more than usual. I would like him to speak to someone who understand more about this than I do.

---

**RESPONSE:** When Walter Scanlon received Regina's report, he responded in this way:

I immediately formed an opinion of her based on this short piece of correspondence: that she was either not very well educated or not very considerate of the addressee. Ms. Toms may indeed be intelligent and considerate, but those qualities are not reflected in this report. In this fast-paced world we live in, rapid-fire faxes, e-mails, and brief telephone conversations are likely to be our first mode of contact. Since one never gets a second chance to make a first impression, make the first one count!

---

Problems with subject-verb agreement are serious errors. Most people notice them and consider them major mistakes.

## Practice Finding and Correcting Errors in Subject-Verb Agreement

How can you find problems with subject-verb agreement in your own writing? Learn to look for the five trouble spots that often signal these problems.

### Trouble Spots: Subject-Verb Agreement

**The verb is a form of *be, have,* or *do.***

| | |
|---|---|
| **INCORRECT** | I be in a great mood today. |
| **CORRECT** | I am in a great mood today. |

**Words or phrases come between the subject and the verb.**

| | |
|---|---|
| **INCORRECT** | The dogs *that live in the parking lot* barks all night. |
| **CORRECT** | The dogs that live in the parking lot bark all night. |

**There is a compound subject (more than one subject for one verb).**

| INCORRECT | The student and her friend studies together. |
|---|---|
| CORRECT | The student and her friend study together. |

**The subject is an indefinite pronoun.**

| INCORRECT | Everyone eat in the cafeteria. |
|---|---|
| CORRECT | Everyone eats in the cafeteria. |

**Note:** An indefinite pronoun stands in for a general person, place, or thing (or a general group of people, places, or things). For example, *he, she,* or *you* replaces the names of particular people. However, *all, everyone,* and *every-thing* stand in for general groups and therefore are indefinite pronouns. For a longer list of indefinite pronouns, see page 341.

**The verb comes before the subject.**

| INCORRECT | Where are the bus to Main and Center Streets? |
|---|---|
| CORRECT | Where is the bus to Main and Center Streets? |

**PRACTICE 1   IDENTIFYING PROBLEMS WITH SUBJECT-VERB AGREEMENT**

Find and underline the four problems with subject-verb agreement in Regina Toms's paragraph on page 330.

## The Verb Is a Form of *Be, Have,* or *Do*

The verbs *be, have,* and *do* do not follow the rules for forming singular and plural forms; they are **irregular verbs**.

**FORMS OF THE VERB *BE***

| PRESENT TENSE | SINGULAR | PLURAL |
|---|---|---|
| *First person* | I am | we are |
| *Second person* | you are | you are |
| *Third person* | she, he, it is | they are |
| | the student is | the students are |

| PAST TENSE | | |
|---|---|---|
| *First person* | I was | we were |
| *Second person* | you were | you were |
| *Third person* | she, he, it was | they were |
| | the student was | the students were |

■ **TEACHING TIP** Misuse of the verb *be* is a very common error among some groups of students. If your students often use *be* for all forms and tenses of the verb *be*, you may want to have them flag or paperclip this chart for ease of reference.

**FORMS OF THE VERB *HAVE*, PRESENT TENSE**

| | SINGULAR | PLURAL |
| --- | --- | --- |
| *First person* | I have | we have |
| *Second person* | you have | you have |
| *Third person* | she, he, it has | they have |
| | the student has | the students have |

**FORMS OF THE VERB *DO*, PRESENT TENSE**

| | SINGULAR | PLURAL |
| --- | --- | --- |
| *First person* | I do | we do |
| *Second person* | you do | you do |
| *Third person* | she, he, it does | they do |
| | the student does | the students do |

These verbs cause problems for many writers because they are hard to memorize. They are also difficult because in casual conversation people sometimes use the same form in all cases: *He do the gardening. They do the gardening.* People also sometimes use the word *be* instead of the correct form of *be: She be on vacation.*

In college and at work, you need to use the correct forms of these verbs, making sure that they agree with the subject in number. If you confuse the forms, refer to the charts until you feel confident that your use is correct.

*are*
They ~~is~~ sick today.

*is*
She ~~be~~ at the library every morning.

*does*
Mark ~~do~~ the laundry every Wednesday.

*has*
Without a doubt, Joan ~~have~~ the best taste in shoes.

---

**FINDING AND FIXING PROBLEMS WITH SUBJECT-VERB AGREEMENT:** Making Subjects and Verbs Agree When the Verb Is *Be, Have,* or *Do*

---

**FIND**

<u>I</u> (am / is / are) a believer in naps.

1. **Underline** the <u>subject</u>.
2. **Ask:** Is the subject in the first (*I*), second (*you*), or third person (*he/she*)? *First person.*
3. **Ask:** Is the subject singular or plural? *Singular.*

↓

---

**FIX**

I (am)/ is / are) a believer in naps.

4. **Choose** the verb by matching it to the form of the subject (first person, singular).

---

 **PRACTICE 2    CHOOSING THE CORRECT FORM OF *BE, HAVE,* OR *DO***

In each sentence, underline the subject of the verb *be, have,* or *do,* and circle the (correct form of the verb). If you need help, look back at the chart above that shows the correction steps.

■ **TIP** For more practices on subject-verb agreement, visit Exercise Central at **<bedfordstmartins.com/ realwriting>**. Also, the Writing Guide Software with this book has tutorials on subject-verb agreement.

**EXAMPLE:** Most people (does /do)) not get enough sleep.

1. Sleep (is)/ are) necessary for people to function well.

2. Most people (has /(have)) to get eight hours or more of sleep to be completely alert.

3. Electric lights (was /(were)) once uncommon, so people usually went to bed when the sun went down.

4. Today, darkness ((does)/ do) not make us go to sleep.

5. Almost every home ((has)/ have) electricity, so people stay up long after sundown.

6. Modern Americans (has /(have)) such busy lives that they often sleep less than they should.

7. A working college student ((doesn't)/ don't) often have time to get eight hours of sleep.

8. Job duties (has /(have)) to be done, but schoolwork is equally important.

9. If you study when you (be /(are)) tired, you remember less information.

10. Busy people today try to get by on very little sleep, but it (is)/ are) unhealthy to be sleep-deprived.

■    **PRACTICE 3    USING THE CORRECT FORM OF** *BE, HAVE,* **OR** *DO*

In each sentence, underline the subject of the verb *be, have,* or *do,* and fill in the correct form of the verb indicated in parentheses.

**EXAMPLE:** She _____ *has* _____ (*have*) often looked at the stars on clear, dark nights.

1. Stars _____ *are* _____ (*be*) clustered together in constellations.

2. Every constellation _____ *has* _____ (*have*) a name.

3. I _____ *do* _____ (*do*) not know how they got their names.

4. Most constellations _____ *do* _____ (*do*) not look much like the people or creatures they represent.

5. You _____ *have* _____ (*have*) to use your imagination to see the pictures in the stars.

6. Twelve constellations _____ *are* _____ (*be*) signs of the zodiac.

7. One _____ *is* _____ (*be*) supposed to look like a crab.

8. Other star clusters _____ *have* _____ (*have*) the names of characters from ancient myths.

9. Orion, the hunter, _____ *is* _____ (*be*) the only one I can recognize.

10. He _____ *does* _____ (*do*) not look like a hunter to me.

## Words Come between the Subject and the Verb

In short sentences, you may have no trouble finding the subject and the verb. In longer sentences, words often come between the subject and the verb, so it is more difficult to find them and to make sure they agree. Most often, either a prepositional phrase or a dependent clause comes between the subject and the verb.

■ **COMPUTER** Have students highlight prepositional phrases in their writing and read only the nonhighlighted parts of their sentences.

### *Prepositional Phrase between the Subject and the Verb*

A **prepositional phrase** starts with a preposition and ends with a noun or pronoun: I took my bag *of books* and threw it *across the room.*

The subject of a sentence is never in a prepositional phrase. When you are looking for the subject of a sentence, you can cross out any prepositional phrases. This strategy should make it easier for you to find the real subject and decide whether it agrees with the verb.

■ **TIP** For a list of common prepositions, see page 289.

The leader of the bikers (wear/wears) ten gold nose rings.

The speaker of the U.S. House of Representatives (give/gives) many interviews.

---

**FINDING AND FIXING PROBLEMS WITH SUBJECT-VERB AGREEMENT:** Making Subjects and Verbs Agree When They Are Separated by a Prepositional Phrase

**FIND**

Periods of drought (affects / affect) the water supply in our area.

1. **Underline** the subject.
2. **Cross out** any prepositional phrase the follows the subject.
3. **Ask:** Is the subject singular or plural? *Plural.*

**FIX**

Periods of drought (affects / affect) the water supply in our area.

4. **Choose** the form of the verb that matches the subject.

---

■ PRACTICE 4   **MAKING SUBJECTS AND VERBS AGREE WHEN THEY ARE SEPARATED BY A PREPOSITIONAL PHRASE**

In each of the following sentences, cross out the prepositional phrase between the subject and the verb, and circle the correct form of the verb. Remember, the subject of a sentence is never in a prepositional phrase. If you need help, look back at the chart above that shows the correction steps.

**EXAMPLE:** Rainfall over the past two years (has / have) measured

well below average for this region.

1. People ~~in my neighborhood~~ (likes /(like)) to keep their grass and flowers watered.

2. Water shortages ~~after a hot, dry summer~~ (is /(are)) often severe.

3. A town ~~under drought restrictions~~ ((contains)/ contain) many brown, dead gardens and lawns.

4. The idea ~~of buying rain barrels~~ ((was)/ were) suggested by a member of the town council.

5. Barrels ~~for collecting rain~~ (was /(were)) common fifty years ago.

6. The gutters ~~below the roof of a house~~ (channels /(channel)) water into a downspout.

7. The roof ~~on most average-sized houses~~ ((directs)/ direct) hundreds of gallons of water into the downspout after an inch of rain.

8. A rain barrel ~~under each downspout~~ ((collects)/ collect) water that falls on the roof.

9. A half-inch ~~of rainfall from recent showers~~ ((has)/ have) put enough water in my rain barrel to keep my garden alive in spite of drought restrictions.

10. Gardeners ~~with limited access to water~~ (benefits /(benefit)) from getting a rain barrel.

### Dependent Clause between the Subject and the Verb

A **dependent clause** has a subject and a verb, but it does not express a complete thought. When a dependent clause comes between the subject and the verb, it usually starts with the word *who, whose, whom, that,* or *which.*

The subject of a sentence is never in a dependent clause. When you are looking for the subject of a sentence, you can cross out any dependent clauses. This strategy should make it easier for you to find the real subject and decide whether it agrees with the verb.

The <u>coins</u> ~~that I found last week~~ (<u>seem</u>/seems) very valuable.

The obese <u>person</u> ~~whose stomach was stapled~~ (eat/<u>eats</u>) very little now.

> ### FINDING AND FIXING PROBLEMS WITH SUBJECT-VERB AGREEMENT: Making Subjects and Verbs Agree When They Are Separated by a Dependent Clause

---

#### FIND

The <u>security systems</u> ~~that shopping sites on the Internet provide~~ (is / are) surprisingly effective.

1. **Underline** the <u>subject</u>.
2. **Cross out** any ~~dependent clause~~ that follows the subject. (Look for the words *who, whose, whom, that,* or *which* because they can signal such a clause.)
3. **Ask:** Is the subject singular or plural? *Plural.*

---

#### FIX

The security systems that shopping sites on the Internet provide (is / (are)) surprisingly effective.

4. **Choose** the form of the verb that matches the subject.

---

### PRACTICE 5  MAKING SUBJECTS AND VERBS AGREE WHEN THEY ARE SEPARATED BY A DEPENDENT CLAUSE

In each of the following sentences, cross out any ~~dependent clauses~~. Then correct any problems with subject-verb agreement. If there is no problem, write "OK" next to the sentence. If you need help, look back at the chart above that shows the correction steps.

**EXAMPLE:** My cousins ~~who immigrated to this country from~~
                          *have*
Ecuador ~~has~~ jobs in a fast-food restaurant.
          ^

                                          *is*
1. The restaurant ~~that hired my cousins~~ ~~are~~ not treating them fairly.
                                          ^

                               *have*
2. People ~~who work in the kitchen~~ ~~has~~ to report to work at 7:00 A.M.
                               ^

3. The boss ~~who supervises the morning shift~~ tells the workers not to punch in until 9:00 A.M. *OK*

4. The benefits ~~that full-time workers earn~~ have not been offered to my cousins. *OK*

5. Ramón, ~~whose hand was injured slicing potatoes~~, need<sup>s</sup> to have physical therapy.

6. No one ~~who works with him~~ has helped him file for worker's compensation. *OK*

7. The doctors ~~who cleaned his wound and put in his stitches at the hospital~~ expect<sup>s</sup> him to pay for the medical treatment.

8. The managers ~~who run the restaurant~~ insist<sup>s</sup> that he is not eligible for medical coverage.

9. My cousins, ~~whose English is not yet perfect~~, feel<sup>s</sup> unable to leave their jobs.

10. The restaurant ~~that treats them so badly~~ offers the only opportunity for them to earn a living. *OK*

## The Subject Is a Compound Subject

A **compound subject** consists of two (or more) subjects joined by *and, or,* or *nor.* If two subjects are joined by *and,* they combine to become a plural subject, and the verb must be plural too.

Plural subject

The <u>teacher</u> *and* her <u>aide</u> <u>grade</u> all of the exams.

If two subjects are separated by the word *or* or *nor,* they are not combined. The verb should agree with whichever subject is closer to it.

Singular subject

Either the <u>teacher</u> *or* her <u>aide</u> <u>grades</u> all of the exams.

Plural subject

The <u>teacher</u> *or* her <u>aides</u> <u>grade</u> all of the exams.

Plural subject

Neither the <u>teacher</u> *nor* her <u>aides</u> <u>grade</u> all of the exams.

> ## FINDING AND FIXING PROBLEMS WITH SUBJECT-VERB AGREEMENT: Making Subjects and Verbs Agree in a Sentence with a Compound Subject

### FIND

Watermelon (or) cantaloupe (makes / make) a delicious and thirst-quenching snack.

1. **Underline** the subjects.
2. **Circle** the (word between the subjects.)
3. **Ask:** Does that word join the subjects to make them plural or keep them separate? *Keeps them separate.*
4. **Ask:** Is the subject that is closer to the verb singular or plural? *Singular.*

### FIX

Watermelon or cantaloupe ((makes)/ make) a delicious and thirst-quenching snack.

5. **Choose** the verb form that agrees with the subject that is closer to the verb.

■ **TIP** Whenever you see a compound subject joined by *and,* try replacing it in your mind with *they.*

---

■ **PRACTICE 6   CHOOSING THE CORRECT VERB IN A SENTENCE WITH A COMPOUND SUBJECT**

In each of the following sentences, underline the word (*and* or *or*) that joins the parts of the compound subject. Then circle the (correct form of the verb.) If you need help, look back at the chart above that shows the correction steps.

**EXAMPLE:** My mother <u>and</u> my sister (has /(have)) asked a nutritionist for advice on a healthy diet.

1. A tomato <u>and</u> a watermelon (shares /(share)) more than just red-colored flesh.

2. A cooked tomato <u>or</u> a slice of watermelon ((contains)/ contain) a nutrient called lycopene that seems to protect the human body from some diseases.

3. Fruits and vegetables (is /(are)) an important part of a healthy diet, most experts agree.

4. Nutrition experts and dieticians (believes /(believe)) that eating a variety of colors of fruits and vegetables is best for human health.

5. Collard greens or spinach ((provides)/ provide) vitamins, iron, and protection from blindness to those who eat them.

6. Carrots and yellow squash (protects /(protect)) against cancer and some kinds of skin damage.

7. Too often, a busy college student or worker ((finds)/ find) it hard to eat the recommended five to nine servings of fruits and vegetables a day.

8. A fast-food restaurant or school cafeteria ((is)/ are) unlikely to have many fresh vegetable and fruit selections.

9. A salad or fresh fruit ((costs)/ cost) more than a hamburger in many places where hurried people eat.

10. Nevertheless, a brightly colored vegetable and fruit (adds /(add)) vitamins and healthy fiber to any meal.

## The Subject Is an Indefinite Pronoun

An **indefinite pronoun** does not replace a specific person, place, or thing: It is general. Most indefinite pronouns are either always singular or always plural.

| | |
|---|---|
| **SINGULAR** | Everyone wants the semester to end. |
| **PLURAL** | Many want the semester to end. |
| **SINGULAR** | Either of the meals is good. |

Often an indefinite pronoun is followed by a prepositional phrase or dependent clause. Remember that the verb of a sentence must agree with the subject of the sentence, and the subject of a sentence is *never in a prepositional phrase or dependent clause*. To choose the correct verb, focus on the indefinite pronoun—you can cross out the prepositional phrase or dependent clause.

Everyone in all of the classes (want/wants) the term to end.

Few of the students (is/are) looking forward to exams.

Several who have to take the math exam (is/are) studying together.

## *Indefinite Pronouns*

| ALWAYS SINGULAR | | | ALWAYS PLURAL |
|---|---|---|---|
| another | everybody | no one | any |
| anybody | everyone | nothing | both |
| anyone | everything | one (of) | few |
| anything | much | somebody | many |
| each (of)★ | neither (of)★ | someone | several |
| either (of)★ | nobody | something | |

★When one of these words is the subject, mentally replace it with *one. One* is singular and takes a singular verb. **NOTE:** *Some* is generally plural, although there are exceptions—for example: *Some of the candy is missing.*

## FINDING AND FIXING PROBLEMS WITH SUBJECT-VERB AGREEMENT: Making Subjects and Verbs Agree When the Subject Is an Indefinite Pronoun

### FIND

One  of my best friends (lives / live) in California.

1. **Underline** the subject.
2. **Cross out** any prepositional phrase or dependent clause that follows the subject.
3. **Ask:** Is the subject singular or plural? *Singular.*

### FIX

One of my best friends (lives)/ live) in California.

4. **Choose** the verb form that agrees with the subject.

### PRACTICE 7   CHOOSING THE CORRECT VERB WHEN THE SUBJECT IS AN INDEFINITE PRONOUN

In each of the following sentences, cross out any prepositional phrases or dependent clauses that come between the subject and the verb. Then underline the subject, and circle the correct verb. If you need help, look back at the chart on page 341 that shows the correction steps.

> **EXAMPLE:** One of the strangest human experiences (results/result) from the "small-world" phenomenon.

1. Everyone (remembers/remember) an example of a "small-world" phenomenon.

2. Someone whom you have just met (tells/tell) you a story.

3. During the story, one of you (realizes/realize) that you are connected somehow.

4. One of your friends (lives/live) next door to the person.

5. Someone in your family (knows/know) someone in the person's family.

6. Each of your families (owns/own) a home in the same place.

7. One of your relatives (plans/plan) to marry his cousin.

8. Some (believes/believe) that if you know one hundred people and talk to someone who knows one hundred people, together you are linked to one million people through friends and acquaintances.

9. Someone in this class probably (connects/connect) to you in one way or another.

10. Each of you probably (knows/know) a good "small-world" story of your own.

## The Verb Comes before the Subject

In most sentences, the subject comes before the verb. Two kinds of sentences often reverse the usual subject-verb order: questions and sentences that begin with *here* or *there*. In these two types of sentences, you need to check for errors in subject-verb agreement.

### Questions

In questions, the verb or part of the verb comes before the subject. To find the subject and verb, you can turn the question around as if you were going to answer it.

■ **TEAMWORK** Divide the class down the middle. One side asks questions (students go in turns according to where they are sitting). The other side turns the questions around (anyone can answer by raising his or her hand or calling out the answer). Keep a fairly fast pace.

Where <u>is</u> the <u>bookstore</u>? / The <u>bookstore</u> <u>is</u> . . .

<u>Are</u> <u>you</u> excited? / <u>You</u> <u>are</u> excited.

When <u>is</u> the <u>bus</u> <u>going</u> to leave? / The <u>bus</u> <u>is going</u> to leave . . .

### Sentences That Begin with Here or There

When *here* or *there* begins a sentence, the subject often follows the verb. Turn the sentence around to find the subject and verb.

*Here* <u>is</u> your <u>key</u> to the apartment. / Your <u>key</u> to the apartment <u>is</u> here.

*There* <u>are</u> four <u>keys</u> on the table. / Four <u>keys</u> <u>are</u> on the table.

---

**FINDING AND FIXING PROBLEMS WITH SUBJECT-VERB AGREEMENT:** Making Subjects and Verbs Agree When the Verb Comes before the Subject

---

**FIND**

What classes (is / are) the professor teaching?

1. If the sentence is a question, **turn the question into a statement:** *The professor (is/are) teaching the classes.*

   There (is / are) two good classes in the music department.

2. If the sentence begins with *here* or *there*, **turn it around:** *Two good classes (is /are) in the music department.*

3. **Identify** the subject in each of the two new sentences. *It's "professor" in the first sentence and "classes" in the second.*

4. **Ask:** Is the subject singular or plural? *"Professor" is singular; "classes" is plural.*

---

**FIX**

The professor ((is)/ are) teaching the classes.

Two good classes (is /(are)) in the music department.

5. **Choose** the form of the verb in each sentence that matches the subject.

> ### PRACTICE 8 CORRECTING A SENTENCE WHEN THE VERB COMES BEFORE THE SUBJECT

Correct any problem with subject-verb agreement in the following sentences. If a sentence is already correct, write "OK" next to it. If you need help, look back at the chart on page 343 that shows the correction steps.

                   *does*
**EXAMPLE:** What electives do the school offer?

   *is*
1. What are the best reason to study music?

      *are*
2. There is several good reasons.

3. There is evidence that music helps students with math. *OK*

4. What is your favorite musical instrument? *OK*

     *are*
5. Here is a guitar, a saxophone, and a piano.

      *are*
6. There is very few people with natural musical ability.

         *do*
7. What time of day does you usually practice?

8. There is no particular time. *OK*

         *do*
9. What musician does you admire most?

       *is*
10. Here are some information about the importance of regular practice.

> ### PRACTICE 9 CORRECTING VARIOUS PROBLEMS WITH SUBJECT-VERB AGREEMENT

In the following sentences, identify any verb that does not agree with its subject. Then, correct the sentence using the correct form of the verb.

                  *have*
**EXAMPLE:** CD sales has fallen in the past few years, according to

     industry statistics.

  *Do*
1. Does consumers who download music files really buy fewer recordings?

2. Many people in the music industry believes that downloading hurts sales.

                         *doesn't*
3. Perhaps sometimes a music fan don't bother to buy a recording after

    downloading the latest CD from a popular artist.

                   *s*
4. Of course, nobody like music playing on a computer better than the

    same music playing on a great sound system.

5. In an MP3 file, a song's lyrics and music sounds less clear than on a CD.

6. There *are* ~~is~~ other problems with downloads in addition to sound quality.

7. A user's computer or sometimes the telephone line become *s* occupied during a download, which may take a long time.

8. Nevertheless, everyone still seem *s* to want downloaded music, so companies are turning to tricks instead of lawsuits to stop the practice of sharing music files.

9. For example, the music industry may offer online files supposedly containing an artist's new songs, but a user who downloads the files discover *s* that the songs are incomplete or missing.

10. The recording companies hope that frustration *is* ~~are~~ finally going to make listeners give up trying to download music from the Internet.

## Edit Paragraphs and Your Own Writing

Use the Critical Thinking box that follows and the chart, Finding and Fixing Problems with Subject-Verb Agreement, on page 348 to help you complete the practices in this section and edit your own writing.

### CRITICAL THINKING: EDITING FOR SUBJECT-VERB AGREEMENT

**FOCUS**
Whenever you see one of the five trouble spots in your writing, stop to check for problems with subject-verb agreement.

**ASK YOURSELF**
- Where is the subject in this sentence? Where is the verb?
- When I read them aloud together, do they sound right?
- Do they match in terms of number? (Both singular? Both plural?)

**EDIT**
If your answer to either or both of the last two questions is "no," you have a problem with subject-verb agreement that must be corrected.

**PRACTICE 10    EDITING PARAGRAPHS FOR SUBJECT-VERB AGREEMENT**

Find and correct any problems with subject-verb agreement in the following paragraphs.

1. (1) A study I came across while doing research for my sociology class rate^s U.S. cities by "most things to do." (2) The categories be ~~are~~ sun, sea, snow, nature, sports, and culture. (3) Each of the cities ~~were~~ ^was assigned a total from 0 to 100 points in each category. (4) The points were determined by the number of recreational activities available. (5) Los Angeles and San Diego, which share a warm, coastal climate, have perfect scores. (6) Either of these places ~~are~~ ^is a good place to visit. (7) Miami, New York, and Washington, D.C., are the other cities ranked in the top five.

2. (1) Another study measures the fastest and slowest talkers. (2) Postal workers in different cities talk^s at different speeds when explaining the class of mail. (3) Workers in Columbus, Ohio, speak the fastest. (4) Atlanta and Detroit ~~has~~ ^have the next fastest talkers. (5) There ~~is~~ ^are also fast talkers in Boston and Bakersfield, California. (6) The slowest talkers in the country are in Sacramento, California. (7) Other postal workers who speak very slowly live^s in Los Angeles; Shreveport, Louisiana; and Chattanooga, Tennessee. (8) How do you think your city ranks?

3. (1) The color of chicken eggs come^s from the pigment in the outer layer of the shell. (2) Colors of the shell range from pure white to deep brown. (3) The only determining factor of egg color is the breed of the chicken. (4) Each of the breeds produce^s a slightly different-colored egg. (5) There is a simple way to tell what color egg a hen will produce. (6) Hens with white earlobes lay^s white eggs. (7) Any of the hens with red earlobes produce^s brown eggs.

4. (1) Many writers of fiction invent^s places that are not real. (2) In children's books, there ~~is~~ ^are many familiar lands that no human being has ever visited. (3) You probably remember the Land of Oz, the home of the famous wizard. (4) Oz, which turned out to be a dream Dorothy had, was not real even in the book. (5) ~~Have~~ Has anyone heard of the home of Winnie-the-Pooh? (6) The teddy bear and his friends ~~was~~ ^were supposed to have lived in the Hundred Acre Wood. (7) Authors who invent characters like these make up new worlds for other people to enjoy. (8) What ~~is~~ are your favorite places that don't exist?

5. (1) Teenagers who are sexually active continue to risk infection with the AIDS virus. (2) There *are* is a lot of young people in the United States getting bad information about this dangerous disease. (3) One reason for this problem is that too many adults don't know how to communicate effectively with teenagers. (4) Peer counseling, which is a growing trend in this country, help*s* to solve that problem. (5) Peer counselors, who are trained to discuss AIDS with teenagers, are teenagers themselves. (6) Teenagers who might not listen to warnings from an adult *are* is more likely to pay attention to another teenager. (7) A peer counselor and the teenager being counseled dresses and talk*s* alike. (8) Information that teenagers need to know to stay healthy is easier to accept when it comes from a peer.

---

■ **PRACTICE 11   EDITING REGINA'S LETTER**

Look back at Regina Toms's report on page 330. You may have already underlined the subject-verb agreement errors; if not, do so now. Next, using what you've learned in this chapter, correct each error.

---

■ **PRACTICE 12   EDITING YOUR OWN WRITING FOR SUBJECT-VERB AGREEMENT**

Use your new skill at editing for subject-verb agreement on a piece of your own writing—a paper you are working on for this class, a paper you've already finished, a paper for another course, or a recent piece of writing from your work or everyday life. Use the Critical Thinking guide on page 345 and the chart on page 348 to help you.

■ **LEARNING JOURNAL** What kinds of problems with subject-verb agreement do you find most often in your writing? What are some ways to avoid or correct these mistakes?

---

## Chapter Review: Problems with Subject-Verb Agreement

1. The *subject*_____ and the *verb*_____ in a sentence must agree (match) in terms of number. They must both be *singular*_____, or they must both be plural.

2. *Five*_____ trouble spots can cause errors in subject-verb agreement:
   • When the verb is a form of *be*_____, *have*_____, or *do*_____.
   • When a *prepositional phrase*_____ or a *dependent clause*_____ comes between the subject and the verb.

- When there is a _compound_ subject joined by *and, or,* or *nor.*
- When the subject is an _indefinite_ pronoun.
- When the _verb_ comes _before_ the subject.

---

**FINDING AND FIXING PROBLEMS WITH SUBJECT-VERB AGREEMENT**

Five trouble spots can cause problems with subject-verb agreement.

| Verb is a form of *be, have,* or *do* (see p. 331). | Words come between subject and verb (see p. 334). | Subject is a compound subject (see p. 338). | Subject is an indefinite pronoun (see p. 340). | Verb comes before subject (see p. 342). |

If you find one of these trouble spots in your writing . . .

1. Make sure you find the real subject and the real verb of the sentence.

2. Read them aloud to make sure they sound right together.

3. If you are unsure about the correct form of the verb, check the charts in this book.

4. Correct any problems you find with subject-verb agreement.

# 23

# Verb Problems

## Mistakes in Verb Form and Verb Tense

## Understand What Verb Form and Verb Tense Are

**Verb forms** are the different ways a verb can be spelled and pronounced. For example, here are three different forms of the same verb:

like        likes        liked

To choose the correct form, you need to consider how the verb is used in a sentence: whether it is singular or plural, past or present tense, and so on.

I like my sister's new apartment.

She likes the low rent.

My sister liked her last apartment, but it was too expensive.

**Verb tense** tells *when* the action of a sentence occurs: in the past, in the present, or in the future. Verbs change their form and use helping verbs to indicate different tenses. (Helping verbs—such as *am/is, have, do,* and *will*—are listed on p. 292.)

| | |
|---|---|
| **PRESENT TENSE** | Michael sings quite well. |
| **PAST TENSE** | He sang on the ride home. |
| **FUTURE TENSE** | He will sing for us again soon. |

Using the wrong form of a verb is one of the errors that people notice most.

### Ever Thought This?

"I hear the word 'tense' and I get all tense. I don't understand all the terms."
—Ken Hargreaves, Student

This chapter

- explains what *verb forms* and *verb tenses* are
- explains the present and past tenses of verbs
- gives you a list of irregular verbs
- gives you practice finding and correcting errors in verb form and tense

■ **TIP** In the examples throughout this chapter, the subject is underlined, and the verb is double-underlined.

■ **LEARNING JOURNAL** Use your learning journal as a place to record verb problems that you find in your writing. Also write down edited versions of the sentences, with the problems corrected.

■ **TIP** To find and correct problems with verbs, you need to be able to identify subjects and verbs. For a review, see Chapter 19.

## In the Real World, Why Is It Important to Use Correct Verbs?

**SITUATION:** Martina is a new intern at an accounting firm. She'd like to get a part-time secretarial position there because she knows that she'll learn a lot about accounting, which she's studying in college. Since Martina is trying to make a good impression, she takes on extra work and tells her supervisor about it in a note:

■ **TEACHING TIP** Students should underline the verb errors for Practice 1, below, and correct them for Practice 16 on page 370.

Last night, I file^d Mr. Shackler's letters, and I also make^made copies of those folders you give^gave me. I enjoy this work and hope I can do more of it.

**RESPONSE:** Although Martina's boss was impressed by her responsibility and intelligence, she also noticed that Martina made several grammar errors. When a part-time secretarial position did open up at the firm, Martina was not considered for it because her boss was worried that Martina's poor writing skills would make a bad impression on clients.

## Practice Using Correct Verbs

■ **TIP** For more about making verbs match subjects, see Chapter 22.

English verbs can be very complicated. You can learn some general rules about them, but many verb forms must simply be memorized. The best way to learn the correct forms is to read, write, and speak them as often as possible.

Some people leave off verb endings or use a nonstandard pattern for verb forms in their everyday speech. When these people write, they sometimes spell verbs the same way they would say them. This can lead to mistakes in verb form that are very obvious to most readers. If you use verb forms in your everyday speech that are different from the ones shown in this chapter, be particularly careful to check for standard forms in your writing.

■ **RESOURCES** *Additional Resources* contains tests and supplemental practice exercises for this chapter as well as a transparency master for the summary chart at the end of the chapter.

■ **PRACTICE 1**    **IDENTIFYING PROBLEMS WITH VERB FORM**

Find and underline the three problems with verb form in Martina's note.

### Regular Verbs

Most verbs in English are **regular verbs**—their forms follow standard rules. Practice using the right forms so that you do not leave endings off when you use these verbs in your writing.

#### Two Regular Present-Tense Forms: -s Ending and No Ending

The **present tense** is used for actions that are happening at the same time that they are being written about (the present). It is also used for things that happen all the time. There are two forms for the present tense of regular verbs:

| *-S* ENDING | NO ENDING |
|---|---|
| jumps | jump |
| walks | walk |
| lives | live |

Use the *-s* ending when the subject is *he, she, it,* or the name of one person or thing. Use no ending for all other subjects.

---

### *Regular Verb Forms in the Present Tense*

|  | SINGULAR | PLURAL |
|---|---|---|
| *First person* | I jump. | We jump. |
| *Second person* | You jump. | You jump. |
| *Third person* | She (he, it) jump<u>s</u>. | They jump. |
|  | The child jump<u>s</u>. | The children jump. |

---

■ **DISCUSSION** A common error is using only the present tense in writing. If your students do this, ask why. A common answer is that they know the present form and are less certain about others. Point out that using the present-tense form of a verb where the past tense is correct is as serious an error as using an incorrect past form.

■ **PRACTICE 2   USING THE CORRECT FORM FOR REGULAR VERBS IN THE PRESENT TENSE**

In each of the following sentences, first underline the <u>subject</u>, and then circle the (correct verb form).

■ **TIP** For more practices on verb problems, visit Exercise Central at <**bedfordstmartins .com/realwriting**>. Also, the Writing Guide Software with this book has tutorials on this topic.

**EXAMPLE:** I (tries /(try)) to keep to my budget.

1. My <u>classes</u> (requires /(require)) much of my time these days.

2. In addition to attending school, <u>I</u> (works /(work)) twenty hours a week in the college library.

3. The other <u>employees</u> (agrees /(agree)) that the work atmosphere is pleasant.

4. Sometimes <u>we</u> even (manages /(manage)) to do homework at the library.

5. The <u>job</u> ((pays)/ pay) a fairly low wage, however.

6. My <u>roommate</u> ((helps)/ help) with the rent on the apartment.

7. Because he isn't in school, <u>he</u> often ((wonders)/ wonder) how I get by.

8. <u>I</u> (uses /(use)) my bicycle to get everywhere I need to go.

9. The <u>bicycle</u> ((allows)/ allow) me to stay in shape both physically and financially.

10. I know that I won't be in school forever, so for now, <u>life</u> on a budget
(satisfies)/ satisfy) me.

### One Regular Past-Tense Form: -ed Ending

The **past tense** is used for actions that have already happened. An *-ed* ending is needed on all regular verbs in the past tense.

|              | PRESENT TENSE    | PAST TENSE        |
| ------------ | ---------------- | ----------------- |
| *First person*  | I <u>avoid</u> her. | I <u>avoid</u>**ed** her. |
| *Second person* | You <u>help</u> me. | You <u>help</u>**ed** me. |
| *Third person*  | He <u>walks</u> fast. | He <u>walk</u>**ed** fast. |

■ **TIP** If a verb already ends in *-e*, just add *-d: dance/danced.* If a verb ends in *-y*, usually the *-y* changes to *-i* when *-ed* is added: *spy/spied; try/tried.*

■ **PRACTICE 3    USING THE CORRECT FORM FOR REGULAR VERBS IN THE PAST TENSE**

In each of the following sentences, fill in the correct past-tense form of the verb in parentheses.

**EXAMPLE:** Minutes after the plane <u>landed</u> (*land*), my best
friend <u>arrived</u> (*arrive*) through the gate door.

Several years ago I <u>traveled</u> (*travel*) from Boston to Seattle on Christmas Eve. As we <u>approached</u> (*approach*) the Seattle area, we <u>learned</u> (*learn*) that the airport was fogged in. The captain <u>reported</u> (*report*) that he was considering landing in Portland, 180 miles south. While the airliner <u>circled</u> (*circle*) the area, passengers <u>asked</u> (*ask*) nervous questions about how much fuel <u>remained</u> (*remain*). When I <u>gazed</u> (*gaze*) out the window, I could see the fog down below us. It <u>looked</u> (*look*) thick and white. I <u>worried</u> (*worry*) about visibility. Finally the captain <u>decided</u> (*decide*) to attempt a landing. Some passengers <u>expressed</u> (*express*) concern, but most of us were glad not to be going to Portland. Soon we <u>plunged</u> (*plunge*) deep into the fog and <u>waited</u> (*wait*) for something to happen; suddenly the runway's blue landing lights <u>rushed</u> (*rush*) up to meet us. A moment later the plane <u>touched</u> (*touch*) down, and the entire aircraft <u>seemed</u> (*seem*) to shudder with relief.

### One Regular Past Participle: -ed Ending

The **past participle** is a verb that can be used with helping verbs, such as *have*. For all regular verbs, the past-participle form is the same as the past-tense form: It uses an *-ed* ending. (To learn about when past participles are used, see pp. 361–65.)

| PAST-TENSE FORM | PAST-PARTICIPLE FORM |
|---|---|
| My kids <u>watched</u> cartoons. | They <u>have watched</u> cartoons before. |
| George <u>visited</u> his cousins. | He <u>has visited</u> them every year. |

### PRACTICE 4    USING THE CORRECT FORM FOR THE PAST PARTICIPLES OF REGULAR VERBS

In each of the following sentences, underline the <u>helping verb</u> (a form of *have*), and fill in the correct form of the verb in parentheses.

**EXAMPLE:** Throughout history, parents <u>have</u> _____*worried*_____

(*worry*) when their children were sick.

1. Until the view of antibiotic use changed in the past ten years, modern

    parents <u>had</u> generally _____*expected*_____ (*expect*) a doctor to prescribe

    antibiotics for a child's illness.

2. Medical professionals <u>have</u> _____*realized*_____ (*realize*) in the past few

    years that antibiotics are prescribed too often.

3. A virus that <u>has</u> _____*infected*_____ (*infect*) a child is not cured by

    antibiotics.

4. Only a child who <u>has</u> _____*contracted*_____ (*contract*) a bacterial infection

    needs antibiotics.

5. By the late 1980s, antibiotics <u>had</u> apparently _____*defeated*_____

    (*defeat*) most bacterial infections, but then bacteria began to fight

    back.

6. Doctors <u>have</u> _____*determined*_____ (*determine*) that the overuse of anti-

    biotics can make bacteria stronger.

7. In the past, a parent who <u>had</u> not _____*received*_____ (*receive*) a pre-

    scription for a child's ear infection often felt that the doctor had made

    a mistake.

8. The American Medical Association has ___*tried*___ (*try*) to spread the word that most children's infections go away without antibiotics.

9. Some parents have ___*turned*___ (*turn*) to over-the-counter medications instead of antibiotics, but doctors believe that such treatments are often unnecessary.

10. A physician who has ___*examined*___ (*examine*) a sick child should decide whether the child needs medicine or not.

## Irregular Verbs

**Irregular verbs** do not follow the regular pattern for endings of the different verb forms. Practice using these verbs so that you learn to use the correct forms in your writing.

■ **ESL** It is helpful for students to *hear* the verb forms, particularly for irregular verbs. If you have access to a language lab, you might have them listen to verb tapes. If students can record, have them record examples for each other, using personalized examples.

### Irregular Verb Forms

| PRESENT-TENSE FORM | PAST-TENSE FORM | PAST PARTICIPLE |
|---|---|---|
| am/are/is | was/were | been |
| become | became | become |
| begin | began | begun |
| bite | bit | bitten |
| blow | blew | blown |
| break | broke | broken |
| bring | brought | brought |
| build | built | built |
| buy | bought | bought |
| catch | caught | caught |
| choose | chose | chosen |
| come | came | come |
| cost | cost | cost |
| do | did | done |
| draw | drew | drawn |
| drink | drank | drunk |
| drive | drove | driven |
| eat | ate | eaten |

| PRESENT-TENSE FORM | PAST-TENSE FORM | PAST PARTICIPLE |
|---|---|---|
| fall | fell | fallen |
| feed | fed | fed |
| feel | felt | felt |
| fight | fought | fought |
| find | found | found |
| forget | forgot | forgotten |
| get | got | gotten |
| give | gave | given |
| go | went | gone |
| grow | grew | grown |
| have/has | had | had |
| hide | hid | hidden |
| hit | hit | hit |
| hold | held | held |
| hurt | hurt | hurt |
| keep | kept | kept |
| know | knew | known |
| lay | laid | laid |
| leave | left | left |
| let | let | let |
| lie | lay | lain |
| light | lit | lit |
| lose | lost | lost |
| make | made | made |
| mean | meant | meant |
| meet | met | met |
| pay | paid | paid |
| put | put | put |
| quit | quit | quit |
| read | read | read |
| ride | rode | ridden |
| run | ran | run |
| say | said | said |
| see | saw | seen |

(continued)

■ **TEACHING TIP** Give students a few minutes in class, or ask them as a homework assignment, to review the list of irregular verbs and underline the fifteen verbs they use most frequently.

| PRESENT-TENSE FORM | PAST-TENSE FORM | PAST PARTICIPLE |
|---|---|---|
| sell | sold | sold |
| send | sent | sent |
| show | showed | shown |
| shut | shut | shut |
| sing | sang | sung |
| sink | sank | sunk |
| sit | sat | sat |
| sleep | slept | slept |
| speak | spoke | spoken |
| spend | spent | spent |
| stand | stood | stood |
| steal | stole | stolen |
| stick | stuck | stuck |
| sting | stung | stung |
| swim | swam | swum |
| take | took | taken |
| teach | taught | taught |
| tear | tore | torn |
| tell | told | told |
| think | thought | thought |
| throw | threw | thrown |
| understand | understood | understood |
| wake | woke | woken |
| wear | wore | worn |
| win | won | won |
| write | wrote | written |

## Present-Tense Forms for Two Irregular Verbs

| BE | | HAVE | |
|---|---|---|---|
| I am | we are | I have | we have |
| you are | you are | you have | you have |
| he, she, it is | they are | he, she, it has | they have |
| the editor is | the editors are | | |
| Beth is | Beth and Caryn are | | |

### Irregular Present-Tense Forms

Only a few verbs are irregular in the present tense. However, these verbs are very common, so it is important to learn the correct forms.

**PRACTICE 5** **USING THE CORRECT FORMS FOR *BE* AND *HAVE* IN THE PRESENT TENSE**

In each of the following sentences, fill in the correct form of the verb indicated in parentheses.

**EXAMPLE:** Because of my university's internship program, I

_____*am*_____ (*be*) able to receive academic credit

for my summer job.

1. I _____*have*_____ (*have*) a job lined up with a company that provides

   private security to businesses and residential developments.

2. The company _____*has*_____ (*have*) a good record of keeping its

   clients safe from crime.

3. The company _____*is*_____ (*be*) part of a fast-growing industry.

4. Many people no longer _____*have*_____ (*have*) faith in the ability of

   the police to protect them.

5. People with lots of money _____*are*_____ (*be*) willing to pay for

   their own protection.

6. Concern about crime _____*is*_____ (*be*) especially noticeable in

   so-called gated communities.

7. In these private residential areas, no one _____*has*_____ (*have*) the

   right to enter without authorization.

8. If you _____*are*_____ (*be*) a visitor, you must obtain a special

   pass.

9. Once you _____*have*_____ (*have*) the pass, you show it to the secu-

   rity guard when you reach the gate.

10. In a gated community, the residents _____*are*_____ (*be*) likely to

    appreciate the security.

### Irregular Past-Tense Forms

Irregular verbs do not use the *-ed* ending for the past-tense form. They show the past tense with a change in spelling or in some other way.

| PRESENT-TENSE FORM | PAST-TENSE FORM |
|---|---|
| I begin today. | I began yesterday. |
| You sleep very soundly. | You slept late this morning. |
| I let the dog in today. | I let the dog in yesterday. |

The verb *be* is tricky because it has two different forms for the past tense: *was* and *were*.

### The Verb Be, *Past Tense*

| | SINGULAR | PLURAL |
|---|---|---|
| *First person* | I was | we were |
| *Second person* | you were | you were |
| *Third person* | he, she, it was | they were |
| | the student was | the students were |

There is no simple rule for how to form irregular verbs in the past tense. Until you memorize them, consult the chart on pages 354–56.

PRACTICE 6   **USING THE CORRECT PAST-TENSE FORM OF THE VERB *BE***

In the paragraph that follows, fill in each blank with the correct past-tense form of the verb *be*.

**EXAMPLE:** During college, my sister _____*was*_____ not able to have much of a social life.

(1) My sister _____*was*_____ always afraid of visits to the doctor. (2) Therefore, my parents and I _____*were*_____ very surprised when she announced that she wanted to become a doctor herself. (3) We thought that medicine _____*was*_____ a strange choice for her. (4) "Since you _____*were*_____ a little girl, you have disliked doctors," I reminded her. (5) I _____*was*_____ sure she would change her mind very quickly. (6) She admitted that she _____*was*_____ still afraid, but she hoped that understanding medicine would help her overcome her

fears. (7) Her premedical courses in college _____*were*_____ very difficult, but finally she was accepted into medical school. (8) We _____*were*_____ very proud of her that day, and we knew that she would be a great doctor.

## PRACTICE 7   USING THE CORRECT FORM FOR IRREGULAR VERBS IN THE PAST TENSE

In each of the following sentences, fill in the correct past-tense form of the irregular verb in parentheses. If you do not know the answer, find the word in the chart of irregular verb forms on pages 354–56.

**EXAMPLE:** It _____*took*_____ (*take*) many years for baseball players in the Negro Leagues to get recognized for their abilities.

1. The Negro Leagues _____*began*_____ (*begin*) in 1920, founded by pitcher Andrew "Rube" Foster.

2. Segregation _____*made*_____ (*make*) it impossible for black players to play on the all-white major league teams at that time.

3. The Negro Leagues_____*gave*_____ (*give*) black athletes the opportunity to play professional baseball.

4. Some Negro League players _____*became*_____ (*become*) legendary.

5. People across the country _____*knew*_____ (*know*) the name of Satchel Paige, the pitcher for the Kansas City Monarchs.

6. The Kansas City Monarchs's infielder, Jackie Robinson, _____*laid*_____ (*lay*) the groundwork for all future black baseball players.

7. Robinson _____*left*_____ (*leave*) the Negro Leagues in 1947 to become the first black player to join a major league team, the Brooklyn Dodgers.

8. Other Negro League players _____*hit*_____ (*hit*) home runs and _____*stole*_____ (*steal*) bases but did not become famous.

9. The Negro Leagues _____*shut*_____ (*shut*) down in 1960.

10. Supporters _____*built*_____ (*build*) the Negro Leagues Baseball Museum in Kansas City, Missouri.

**PRACTICE 8   USING THE CORRECT FORM FOR PAST-TENSE IRREGULAR VERBS**

In the following paragraph, replace any incorrect present-tense verb forms with the correct past-tense form of the verb.

(1) In 1900, my great-grandfather *grews* wheat and raised a few cattle on his farm in Wyoming. (2) When my grandmother and her brothers were young, they *go* to the fields every day to help their father. (3) The family *does* not have much money, and they hoped for good weather every year. (4) Droughts and damaging storms often cost them a lot. (5) One year, high winds *blow* down the barn, and hailstorms *break* their windows. (6) Another year, very little rain *falls*, and they almost *lose* the farm. (7) Somehow, they *keep* going in spite of their difficulties. (8) Their life was hard, but the whole family *understands* that the rewards of owning their own land were worthwhile.

*[handwritten annotations above verbs: grew, went, did, blew, broke, fell, lost, kept, understood]*

### Irregular Past Participles

For regular verbs, the **past-participle form** (used with helping verbs such as *have*) is the same as the past-tense form; they both use the *-ed* ending. For irregular verbs, the past-participle form is often different from the past-tense form.

|  | PAST-TENSE FORM | PAST-PARTICIPLE FORM |
|---|---|---|
| **REGULAR VERB** | I walked home. | I have walked home before. |
| **IRREGULAR VERB** | I drove home. | I have driven home before. |

It is difficult to predict how irregular verbs form the past participle. Until you are familiar with them, find them in the chart on pages 354–56.

**PRACTICE 9   USING CORRECT PAST-PARTICIPLE FORMS FOR IRREGULAR VERBS**

In each of the following sentences, fill in the correct helping verb (a form of *have*) and the correct past-participle form of the verb in parentheses. If you do not know the correct form, find the word in the chart on pages 354–56.

**EXAMPLE:** Four of my good friends ____*have lost*____ (*lose*) their jobs since September.

1. Probably you ____*have heard*____ (*hear*) that the United States is facing economic problems.

2. Until recently, I ___had thought___ (*think*) that my job was safe.

3. The recession ___had hurt___ (*hurt*) several of my friends, but I was still employed.

4. In the last two weeks, however, I ___have seen___ (*see*) signs of trouble at my job.

5. My company ___has sold___ (*sell*) some of its divisions to other companies.

6. In addition, it ___has laid___ (*lay*) off some workers in my division.

7. Although my boss ___has told___ (*tell*) me that my position is safe, I still wonder.

8. I worry that I ___have become___ (*become*) too dependent on my job.

9. I ___have begun___ (*begin*) to think about how I can cut back on expenses.

10. This experience ___has made___ (*make*) me think about putting money aside for hard times.

## Using Past Participles

So far in this chapter, you have studied only the form of past participles; now you will study what they are used for.

A **past participle**, by itself, cannot be the main verb of a sentence. But when a past participle is combined with another verb, called a **helping verb**, it can be used to make the present perfect tense and the past perfect tense.

■ **TEACHING TIP** As you introduce this section, remind students that the purpose of this chapter is not to memorize the terms but to use verbs correctly in writing.

### Have/Has + *Past Participle* = *Present Perfect Tense*

Use a present-tense form of the verb *have* plus the past participle to make the **present perfect tense**. The present perfect tense is used for an action begun in the past that either continues into the present or was completed at some unspecified time in the past.

Present tense of
*have* (helping verb)            Past participle

**PRESENT PERFECT TENSE**  My car has stalled several times recently.

[This sentence says the stalling began in the past but may continue into the present.]

**PAST TENSE**  My car stalled.

[This sentence says that the car stalled once and that it's over.]

■  PRACTICE 10    **USING THE PRESENT PERFECT TENSE**

In each of the following sentences, circle the (correct verb tense).

**EXAMPLE:** For many years now, the laws of most states
(allowed/(have allowed)) only doctors to write
prescriptions for patients.

1. In the past few years, a number of states (began/(have begun)) to allow
physician assistants and nurse practitioners to write prescriptions.

2. Before the changes in the laws, physician assistants and nurse practitioners ((saw)/have seen) patients with common illnesses.

3. However, if the patients ((needed)/have needed) a prescription, a doctor
had to write it.

4. Many doctors (said/(have said)) that the changes are a good idea.

5. Physician assistants and nurse practitioners (spent/(have spent)) years in
training by the time they get their licenses.

6. Since the new laws took effect, physician assistants and nurse practitioners (wrote/(have written)) many common prescriptions.

7. Recently, some people (expressed/(have expressed)) concern that physician assistants and nurse practitioners might make mistakes in writing
prescriptions.

8. However, the possibility of a mistake in a prescription (always existed/
(has always existed)).

9. For the past several years, pharmacists (kept/(have kept)) track of
prescription errors.

10. Doctors made all but one of the mistakes they (found/(have found)) so
far.

## Had + *Past Participle* = *Past Perfect Tense*

Use *had* (the past-tense form of *have*) plus the past participle to make the
**past perfect tense**. The past perfect tense is used for an action begun in
the past that was completed before some other past action.

Past tense of      Past participle
*have* (helping verb)

**PAST PERFECT TENSE**    My <u>car</u> <u>had stalled</u> several times before I called the mechanic.

[This sentence says that both the *stalling* and *calling the mechanic* happened in the past, but the stalling happened before the calling.]

**PAST TENSE**      My <u>car</u> <u>stalled</u>.

**PRESENT PERFECT TENSE**      My <u>car</u> <u>has stalled</u> several times recently.

---

  ■   **PRACTICE 11**   **USING THE PAST PERFECT TENSE**

In each of the following sentences, circle the (correct verb tense).

> **EXAMPLE:** By the time firefighters finally arrived, the fire (destroyed/(had destroyed)) most of the building.

1. Tenants who (rushed/(had rushed)) outside when the fire began now watched in shock and disbelief as the firefighters turned their hoses on the blaze.

2. Firefighters were relieved to see that everyone (got/(had gotten)) out of the building safely.

3. Although there were no major injuries, paramedics ((treated)/had treated) two of the tenants for mild smoke inhalation.

4. A cat that never before (ventured/(had ventured)) out of its apartment came racing down the stairs at the first sign of flames.

5. Firefighters also ((rescued)/had rescued) a pet rabbit.

6. As the sun set that evening, authorities (declared/(had declared)) the building a total loss.

7. Once the fire finally (burned/(had burned)) itself out, investigators began sifting through the ashy ruins.

8. The next day investigators reported that someone (left/(had left)) a saucepan filled with water on top of a lighted stove burner.

9. After all the water (boiled /(had boiled)) away, the bottom of the saucepan began to melt.

10. Investigators also ((suggested)/ had suggested) that a roll of paper towels may have been left on top of the stove.

### Be + *Past Participle* = *Passive Voice*

A sentence that is written in the **passive voice** has a subject that performs no action. Instead, the subject is acted upon. To create the passive voice, combine a form of the verb *be* with a past participle.

Form of *be*        Past participle
(helping verb)

**PASSIVE**        The newspaper was thrown onto the porch.

[The subject, *newspaper,* did not throw itself onto the porch. Some unidentified person acted upon the newspaper.]

Most sentences are written in the **active voice**, which means that the subject performs the action.

**ACTIVE**        The delivery person threw the newspaper onto the porch.

[The subject, *delivery person,* performed the action: He or she threw the newspaper.]

Use the passive voice when no one person performed the action, when you don't know who performed the action, or when you want to emphasize the receiver of the action. Do not overuse the passive voice. When you know who performed the action, it is usually preferable to identify the actor.

**ACTIVE**        The bandleader chose Kelly to do a solo.

**PASSIVE**        Kelly was chosen to do a solo.

[If you wanted to emphasize Kelly's being chosen rather than the bandleader's choice, you might decide to use the passive voice.]

---

### FINDING AND FIXING VERB PROBLEMS:
#### Changing from Active to Passive Voice

↓

**FIND**

~~He~~ sent the payment over two weeks ago.

1. **Underline** the subject, and **double-underline** the verb.
2. **Ask:** What word in the sentence is receiving the action? *Payment.*
3. **Cross out** the ~~subject~~.

↓

> **FIX**
>
> *The payment*
> **He** ~~sent the payment~~ over two weeks ago.
>
> 4. Make the word that is receiving the action the subject by moving it to the beginning of the sentence.
>
> *The payment was*
> ~~He~~ sent ~~the payment~~ over two weeks ago.
>
> 5. Add the correct form of the verb *be* in front of the main verb.
>
> *The payment was      by him*
> ~~He~~ sent ~~the payment~~ over two weeks ago.
>
> 6. You can either delete the performer of the action or put this information after the verb and the word *by.*
>
> **NOTE:** If the original sentence uses a form of *have* followed by a past participle, form the passive voice by using a form of *have* + *been* + the past participle:
>
> *The payment     been*
> **He has** ~~sent~~ the payment.

## PRACTICE 12 USING THE PASSIVE VOICE

Rewrite the following sentences in the passive voice. If you need help, look back at the chart above that shows the correction steps.

*My bill was*
**EXAMPLE:** ~~You~~ added ~~my bill~~ incorrectly.

*The Civil War was*
1. ~~Soldiers~~ fought ~~the Civil War~~ from 1861 to 1865.

*The movie     been*
2. ~~Critics~~ had praised ~~the movie~~ highly even before its opening day.

*Paint was*
3. ~~Vandals~~ smeared ~~paint~~ on the statues in the park.

*We were*
4. ~~An anonymous caller~~ told ~~us~~ the good news at 7:00 this morning.

*The winner     been*
5. ~~A voice~~ has announced ~~the winner~~.

## Consistency of Verb Tense

**Consistency of tense** means that all verbs in a sentence that describe actions happening at the same time are in the same tense. If all of the actions happen in the present or happen all the time, use the present for all verbs in the sentence. If all of the actions happened in the past, use the past tense for all verbs.

When you edit your writing, make sure that any time a verb tense changes it is because the action the verb describes happened at a different time. Otherwise, the shift in tenses causes an inconsistency.

**INCONSISTENT**    The <u>movie</u> <u><u>started</u></u> just as <u>we</u> <u><u>take</u></u> our seats.

[The actions both happened at the same time, but *started* is in the past tense, and *take* is in the present tense.]

**CONSISTENT,**    The <u>movie</u> <u><u>starts</u></u> just as <u>we</u> <u><u>take</u></u> our seats.
**PRESENT TENSE**

[The actions and verb tenses are both in the present.]

**CONSISTENT,**    The <u>movie</u> <u><u>started</u></u> just as <u>we</u> <u><u>took</u></u> our seats.
**PAST TENSE**

[The actions *started* and *took* both happened in the past, and both are in the past tense.]

---

## FINDING AND FIXING VERB PROBLEMS:
### Using Consistent Verb Tense

### FIND

A <u>company</u> <u><u>offered</u></u> me a job in customer service, but <u>I</u> <u><u>take</u></u> another job instead.

1. **Underline** the subjects, and **double-underline** the verbs.
2. **Ask:** What tense is the first verb in? *Past.*
3. **Ask:** What tense is the second verb in? *Present.*
4. Unless the actions take place at different times, the tenses must be consistent. Are the tenses consistent? *No.*

### FIX

                                                                                         *took*

A company offered me a job in customer service, but I ~~take~~ another job instead.

5. **Cross out** the ~~incorrect verb form~~ and **replace it with a form that is consistent with the first verb**.

---

PRACTICE 13    **USING CONSISTENT VERB TENSE**

In each of the following items, double-underline the <u>verbs</u> in the sentence, and correct any unnecessary shifts in verb tense. Write the correct form of the verb in the blank space provided. If you need help, look back at the chart on page 366 that shows the correction steps.

> **EXAMPLE:** _____*represent*_____ Many people who <u>work</u> in customer
>
> service <u>represented</u> their company to the public.

1. ___*seem*___ No one <u>keeps</u> statistics on customer satisfaction, but many people <u>seemed</u> to feel unhappy with modern customer service.

2. ___*see*___ People who <u>analyze</u> trends in American culture <u>saw</u> a problem with the customer-service industry.

3. ___*were*___ In the past, companies <u>trained</u> service people, and the workers <u>are</u> proud of their ability to please customers.

4. ___*are*___ Today, most companies <u>don't</u> provide training because they <u>were</u> cutting costs.

5. ___*aren't*___ Also, companies sometimes <u>have</u> to settle for employees who <u>weren't</u> always polite.

6. ___*treat*___ Polite service people <u>are</u> hard to find, and many workers <u>treated</u> customers very rudely.

7. ___*are*___ People who study trends <u>think</u> that good manners <u>were</u> generally considered less important today than in the past.

8. ___*are*___ The new trend toward rudeness <u>goes</u> both ways, since customers <u>were</u> also more likely to be unpleasant to service people.

9. ___*is*___ Rude or indifferent service people <u>can cost</u> businesses money, for it <u>was</u> less expensive to keep an old customer than to find a new one.

10. ___*is*___ Customers <u>are</u> willing to pay higher prices if the service <u>was</u> good.

### PRACTICE 14   CORRECTING VARIOUS VERB PROBLEMS

In the following sentences, find and correct any problems with verb tenses or verb forms.

> **EXAMPLE:** Sheena ~~be~~ *is* tired of the tattoo on her left shoulder.

1. Many of Sheena's friends ~~was~~ *were* getting tattoos ten years ago.

2. Sheena had never consider *ed* a tattoo until several of her friends got them.

3. Sheena was twenty-two when she ~~goes~~ *went* to the tattoo parlor.

4. After looking at many designs, she had chose *n* a purple rose, which she gave to the tattoo artist.

5. Her sister liked the tattoo, but her mother faints *ed*.

6. Tattoos ~~are~~ *were* very popular among young Americans in the 1990s.

7. Today, however, a typical person with a ten-year-old tattoo express *es* some regret about following that 1990s trend.

8. Many people who *have* now reached their thirties want to get rid of their tattoos.

9. Dermatologists have ~~saw~~ *seen* the development of a new trend toward tattoo removal.

10. A few years ago, when a person *had* decided to have a tattoo removed, doctors had to cut out the design.

11. That technique ~~leaved~~ *left* scars.

12. Today, doctors ~~using~~ *use* laser light to break up the ink molecules in the skin.

13. Six months ago, Sheena start *ed* to have treatments to remove her tattoo.

14. The procedure hurt~~ed~~ every time she saw the doctor, but she hoped it would be worth the pain.

15. Purple ink ~~have~~ *has* longer staying power than black, blue, and red, so Sheena's treatments will continue for more than two years.

## Edit Paragraphs and Your Own Writing

Use the Critical Thinking box that follows and the chart, Finding and Fixing Verb Problems, on page 372 to help you complete the practices in this section and edit your own writing.

## CRITICAL THINKING: EDITING FOR VERB TENSE AND FORM

**FOCUS**

Look for the verbs in your sentences.

**ASK YOURSELF**

### About each verb:
- Is this the main verb in the sentence?
- Is this a regular verb? An irregular verb?
- Have I used the tense that will tell when the action happened?
- Have I used the correct form of the verb?

### About the overall sentence:
- Is my sentence about the present? About the past? About something that happened before something else?
- If the verbs in the sentence are not all in the same tense, is it because the actions actually happen at different times?

**EDIT**

Edit to correct any problems with verb form or tense.

---

**PRACTICE 15   EDITING PARAGRAPHS FOR CORRECT VERBS**

Find and correct any problems with verb form or tense in the following paragraphs.

1.  (1) When Teresa saw her friend Jan drop makeup into her bag, she frown. *ed* (2) She *knew* know that Jan was stealing. (3) She also *knew* knowed that Jan would be mad if Teresa said anything. (4) What if someone from security had seen Jan! (5) As they *left* leave the store, Teresa's heart beated *d* hard. (6) When nothing happened, she was relieve. (7) Still, she *felt* feel bad, so she spoke to Jan. (8) Jan *said* say she was sorry and has returned the makeup. *felt* (9) Teresa be feeling much better.

2.  (1) George Crum, a Native American chef, invent *ed* potato chips in 1853. (2) A customer *had* has returned an order of french fries with a note that they were too thick. (3) Crum decide *d* to make superthin fries to get even. (4) The customer loved the thin fries, and since then they *have* become a favorite snack. (5) In the 1920s, Herman Lay *brought* brang the potato chip to grocery stores. (6) The chips sold first in the South, and their popularity quickly spread. (7) Since then, people *have eaten* ate millions of chips.

3.  (1) William Topaz McGonagall *spent* spended most of his life in the city of Dundee, Scotland, before his death in 1902. (2) He *was* be a

flamboyant figure, and he like^d to attract attention of all kinds. (3) He once ~~boughted~~ *bought* the right to play the title part in a performance of Shakespeare's *Macbeth*. (4) In the play, Macbeth is supposed to die in a duel. (5) When McGonagall played the part, however, he ~~was refusing~~ *refused* to die. (6) In the past century, critics ~~had~~ *have* called McGonagall the world's worst poet. (7) He ~~begun~~ *began* to write poetry at the age of forty-seven, and he eventually ~~writed~~ *wrote* more than two hundred poems. (8) He was only ~~pay~~ *paid* for his work once, for a poem he composed for a soap commercial. (9) McGonagall's poems often mention*ed* the river Tay, which flow*s* through Dundee. (10) To celebrate McGonagall, who ~~are~~ *is* a cult hero in Dundee, the citizens ~~has~~ *have* recently carved a verse from one of his terrible poems into the sidewalk along the Tay.

■ **LEARNING JOURNAL** What kind of verb problems do you find most often in your writing? What are some ways to avoid or correct these mistakes?

### PRACTICE 16    EDITING MARTINA'S NOTE

Look back at Martina's note on page 350. You may have already underlined the verb errors; if not, do so now. Next, using what you've learned in this chapter, correct each error.

### PRACTICE 17    EDITING YOUR OWN WRITING FOR VERB TENSE AND FORM

Use your new skill at editing verbs on a piece of your own writing—a paper you are working on for this class, a paper you've already finished, a paper for another course, or a recent piece of writing from your work or everyday life. Use the Critical Thinking guide on page 369 and the chart on page 372 to help you.

## Chapter Review: Verb Problems

1. Verb ____*tense*____ indicates when the action in a sentence happens.

2. What are the two present-tense forms for regular verbs?
   ____*-s ending and no ending*____

3. How do regular verbs in the past tense end? ____*-ed ending*____

4. The past-participle verb form is used with a ____*helping*____ verb.

5. Verbs that do not follow the regular pattern for verb forms are called
   _____*irregular*_____ .

6. An action that is happening right now uses the _____*present*_____
   tense.

7. An action that began and ended in the past uses the _____*past*_____
   tense.

8. An action that started in the past but might continue into the present
   uses the *present perfect tense* .

9. An action that happened in the past before something else that happened in the past uses the *past perfect tense* .

10. You should usually avoid using the _____*passive*_____ voice, which has
    a subject that performs no action but is acted upon.

11. Verb tenses are consistent when actions that happen at the same
    _____*time*_____ are in the same _____*tense*_____ .

## FINDING AND FIXING VERB PROBLEMS

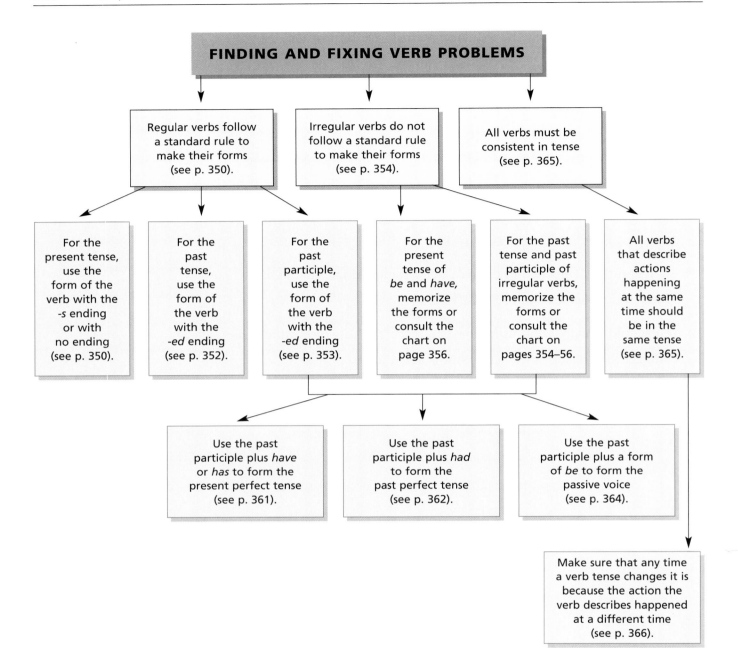

Regular verbs follow a standard rule to make their forms (see p. 350).

Irregular verbs do not follow a standard rule to make their forms (see p. 354).

All verbs must be consistent in tense (see p. 365).

For the present tense, use the form of the verb with the -s ending or with no ending (see p. 350).

For the past tense, use the form of the verb with the -ed ending (see p. 352).

For the past participle, use the form of the verb with the -ed ending (see p. 353).

For the present tense of *be* and *have,* memorize the forms or consult the chart on page 356.

For the past tense and past participle of irregular verbs, memorize the forms or consult the chart on pages 354–56.

All verbs that describe actions happening at the same time should be in the same tense (see p. 365).

Use the past participle plus *have* or *has* to form the present perfect tense (see p. 361).

Use the past participle plus *had* to form the past perfect tense (see p. 362).

Use the past participle plus a form of *be* to form the passive voice (see p. 364).

Make sure that any time a verb tense changes it is because the action the verb describes happened at a different time (see p. 366).

# Part Five
# Other Grammar Concerns

# 24

# Pronouns

## *Using Substitutes for Nouns*

## Understand What Pronouns Are

**Pronouns** replace nouns or other pronouns in a sentence so that you do not have to repeat them.

> *her*
> Sheryl got into ~~Sheryl's~~ car.
>                 ^

> *He*
> I like Mario. ~~Mario~~ is a good dancer.
>               ^

The noun or pronoun that a pronoun refers to is called the **antecedent**, which means "coming before." In most cases, a pronoun refers to a specific noun or pronoun mentioned nearby.

> antecedent noun
>       ⌐─┴─⌐
> I picked up my new glasses. They are cool.
>                          └─┬─┘
>                pronoun replacing antecedent

■ **LEARNING JOURNAL** Use your learning journal as a place to record sentences with pronoun problems that you find in your writing. Also write down edited versions of the sentences, with the problems corrected.

■ **RESOURCES** *Additional Resources* contains tests and supplemental exercises for this chapter as well as a transparency master for the chart at the end.

## Practice Using Pronouns Correctly

### Identify Pronouns

Before you practice finding and correcting common pronoun errors, it will help you to practice identifying pronouns based on the discussion and the chart on page 376.

## Common Pronouns

| PERSONAL PRONOUNS | POSSESSIVE PRONOUNS | INDEFINITE PRONOUNS | |
|---|---|---|---|
| I | my | all | many |
| me | mine | another | much |
| you | your/yours | any | neither |
| she/he | hers/his | anybody | nobody |
| her/him | hers/his | anything | none |
| it | its | both | no one |
| we | our/ours | each | nothing |
| us | our/ours | either | one |
| they | their/theirs | everybody | several |
| them | their/theirs | everyone | somebody |
| | | everything | someone |
| | | few | something |

■ **TIP** For more practice with pronoun usage, visit Exercise Central at <**bedfordstmartins .com/realwriting**>. Also, the Writing Guide software with this book has tutorials on this topic.

▇ **PRACTICE 1    IDENTIFYING PRONOUNS**

In each of the following sentences, circle the (pronoun,) underline the noun it refers to, and draw an arrow from the pronoun to the noun.

> **EXAMPLE:** In 2002, a gold coin made news when it sold for the highest price of any coin in history.

1. When the U.S. mint began to make gold coins in 1850, they had a face value of twenty dollars.

2. The sculptor Augustus Saint-Gaudens redesigned the gold pieces in 1907, so Americans began to call the coins "saints" after him.

3. After President Franklin Roosevelt took the country off the gold standard in 1933, he ordered all 1933 "saints" to be melted down.

4. Two coins were given to the Smithsonian Institution, and they were supposed to be the only surviving 1933 gold twenty-dollar pieces.

5. A coin stolen from the mint somehow ended up with the <u>delegates</u> of the royal family of Egypt; (they) asked for permission to take the coin to Egypt.

■ **ESL** ESL students may have particular trouble with pronouns and benefit from extra practice exercises.

6. Probably by mistake, the <u>Treasury Department</u> granted (its) permission to the request.

7. When Egypt's <u>King Farouk</u>, a coin collector, obtained the world's rarest coin, (he) must have felt quite lucky.

8. When <u>Farouk</u> was deposed, (his) coin collection was sold, and the coin disappeared.

9. <u>Stephen Fenton</u>, a later owner of the coin, had to go to court in the United States to prove that (he) had the right to sell the gold piece.

10. When the "<u>saint</u>" was auctioned in 2002, (it) brought a price of over 6.6 million dollars.

## Check for Pronoun Agreement

A pronoun must agree with (match) the noun or pronoun it refers to in terms of number. **Number** is the amount of something, which is either one (singular) or more than one (plural).

If a pronoun is singular, it must also match the noun or pronoun it refers to in gender (*he, she,* or *it*).

**CONSISTENT**     Magda sold *her* old television set.

[*Her* agrees with *Magda* because both are singular and feminine.]

**CONSISTENT**     The Wilsons sold *their* old television set.

[*Their* agrees with the *Wilsons* because both are plural.]

Watch out for singular, generic nouns. If a noun is singular, the pronoun that refers to it must be singular as well.

**INCONSISTENT**   Any student can tell you what *their* least favorite course
                   is.

[*Student* is singular, but the pronoun *their* is plural.]

**CONSISTENT**     Any student can tell you what *his* or *her* least favorite
                   course is.

[*Student* is singular, and so are the pronouns *his* or *her.*]

To avoid using the phrase *his* or *her,* make the subject plural.

> **CONSISTENT**    Most students can tell you what *their* least favorite course is.

Two types of words often cause errors in pronoun agreement: indefinite pronouns and collective nouns.

### Indefinite Pronouns

An **indefinite pronoun** does not refer to a specific person, place, or thing: It is general. Most indefinite pronouns are either always singular or always plural. Whenever a pronoun refers to an indefinite pronoun, check for agreement.

Someone left ~~their~~ *her* purse in the cafeteria.

The monks got up at dawn. Everybody had ~~their~~ *his* chores for the day.

| *Indefinite Pronouns* | | | |
|---|---|---|---|
| **ALWAYS SINGULAR** | | | **ALWAYS PLURAL** |
| another | everyone | nothing | any |
| anybody/anyone | everything | one (of) | both |
| anything | much | somebody | few |
| each (of) | neither (of) | someone | many |
| either (of) | nobody | something | several |
| everybody | no one | | |

**NOTE:** The indefinite pronoun *some* is generally plural, although there are exceptions—for example: *Some of the candy is missing.*

**TEACHING TIP** Have students focus on the "significant seven" indefinite pronouns: *any, each, either, neither,* and words ending in *-one, -thing,* or *-body.*

**NOTE:** Many people object to use of only the masculine pronoun *he* when referring to a singular indefinite pronoun, such as *everyone.* Although grammatically correct, using the masculine form alone to refer to an indefinite pronoun is considered sexist. Here are two ways to avoid this problem:

1. Use *his or her.*

   Someone posted *his or her* e-mail address to the Web site.

2. Change the sentence so that the pronoun refers to a plural noun or pronoun.

   Some students posted *their* e-mail addresses to the Web site.

**COMPUTER** Students who use *their* as singular can use the find or search functions on their computer to check each use of *their* in their own writing.

■ **PRACTICE 2   USING INDEFINITE PRONOUNS**

Circle the correct pronoun or group of words in parentheses.

(1) Anyone who wants to start (their / his or her) own business had better be prepared to work hard. (2) One may find, for example, that (his or her / their) work is never done. (3) There is always something waiting, with (its / their) own peculiar demands. (4) Nothing gets done on (their / its) own. (5) Anybody who expects to have more freedom now that (he or she no longer works / they no longer work) for a boss may be disappointed. (6) After all, when you work as an employee for a company, there is always someone above you who must make decisions as (they see / he or she sees) fit. (7) When you are your own boss, there is no one else to place (themselves / himself or herself) in the position of final responsibility.

(8) Somebody starting a business may also be surprised by how much tax (they / he or she) must pay. (9) Each employee at a company pays only about half as much toward social security as what (they / he or she) would pay if self-employed. (10) And neither medical nor dental coverage can be obtained as inexpensively as (it / they) can when a person is an employee at a corporation.

## Collective Nouns

A **collective noun** names a group that acts as a single unit.

| *Common Collective Nouns* | | |
|---|---|---|
| audience | company | group |
| class | crowd | jury |
| college | family | society |
| committee | government | team |

■ **TEAMWORK** In small groups, have students expand the list of collective nouns. See which group adds the most, and have all students write the added words next to the box.

Collective nouns are usually singular, so when you use a pronoun to refer to a collective noun, it too must usually be singular.

*its*
The team had ~~their~~ sixth consecutive win of the season.

*its*
The jury returned ~~their~~ verdict.

If the people in a group are acting as individuals, however, the noun is plural and should be used with a plural pronoun.

The class brought *their* papers to read.

---

**FINDING AND FIXING PRONOUN PROBLEMS:**
Using Collective Nouns and Pronouns

↓

**FIND**

The <u>committee</u> changed (its/their) meeting time.

1. **Underline** any <u>collective nouns</u>.
2. **Ask:** Is the collective noun singular (a group acting as a single unit) or plural (people in a group acting as individuals)? *Singular.*

↓

**FIX**

The committee changed (its̲)/their) meeting time.

3. **Choose** the pronoun that agrees with the subject.

---

■  **PRACTICE 3    USING COLLECTIVE NOUNS AND PRONOUNS**

Fill in the correct pronoun in each of the following sentences. If you need help, look back at the chart above that shows the correction steps. Also, you may want to refer to the list of common pronouns on page 376.

   **EXAMPLE:  A large group entered the bowling alley, and**

   _____*they*_____ **drank twenty root beer floats.**

1. The bowling alley is across the street from the baseball stadium, and

   a crowd often makes _____*its*_____ way to the bowling alley after

   the ball game.

2. My team won _____*its*_____ third tournament in the bowling alley

   two weeks ago.

3. The local high school's senior class will have _____*its*_____ gradu-

   ation party there.

4. This is a diverse community, and most of _____*its*_____ members have come to the bowling alley at one time or another.

5. The owner became ill and sold the bowling alley to a corporation last year, and _____*it*_____ recently announced a decision to turn the place into a parking lot.

6. The corporate board publicly announced that _____*it*_____ had commissioned a study and found the bowling alley unprofitable.

7. After the announcement, a large crowd raised _____*their*_____ voices outside the town hall to express fondness for the bowling alley.

8. A committee of concerned local residents put _____*their*_____ heads together to find a solution.

9. An alliance of bowling alley supporters asked _____*their*_____ representatives on the town council to approach the corporate board.

10. The local government has tried _____*its*_____ hardest to mediate between the corporation and the supporters of the bowling alley, but the issue has not yet been resolved.

## Make Pronoun Reference Clear

If the reader isn't sure what noun or pronoun a pronoun refers to, the meaning of a sentence becomes confusing. You should edit any sentence that has an ambiguous, vague, or repetitious pronoun reference.

### Avoid Ambiguous or Vague Pronoun Reference

An **ambiguous pronoun reference** is one in which the pronoun could refer to more than one noun.

**AMBIGUOUS**      Michael told Jim *he* needed a better résumé.

[Did Michael tell Jim that Michael himself needed a better résumé? Or did Michael tell Jim that Jim needed a better résumé?]

**EDITED**      Michael advised Jim to revise his résumé.

**AMBIGUOUS**      I put the glass on the shelf, even though *it* was dirty.

[Was the glass or the shelf dirty?]

**EDITED**      I put the dirty glass on the shelf.

A **vague pronoun reference** is one in which the pronoun does not refer clearly to any particular person, place, or thing.

| | |
|---|---|
| **VAGUE** | When Tom got to the clinic, *they* told him it was closed. |
| | [Who told Tom the clinic was closed?] |
| **EDITED** | When Tom got to the clinic, the nurse told him it was closed. |
| **VAGUE** | Before I finished printing my report, *it* ran out of paper. |
| | [What was out of paper?] |
| **EDITED** | Before I finished printing my report, the printer ran out of paper. |

A **repetitive pronoun reference** is one in which the pronoun repeats a reference to a noun rather than replacing the noun.

The nurse at the clinic he told Tom that it was closed.

The newspaper, it says that the new diet therapy is promising.

■ **ESL** Repetitious pronoun reference is a very common error among ESL students. Read aloud some sentences with this problem (from their own writing, if possible), and ask students to raise their hands when they hear a repetitive pronoun reference.

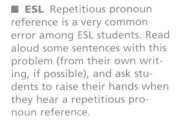

**FINDING AND FIXING PRONOUN PROBLEMS:**
Avoiding Ambiguous or Vague Pronoun References

**FIND**

The <u>cashier</u> said (they) were out of milk.

1. **Underline** the <u>subject</u>.
2. **Circle** the (pronoun).
3. **Ask:** Who or what does the pronoun refer to? *No one. "They" does not refer to "cashier."*

**FIX**

*the store was*
The cashier said ~~they were~~ out of milk.
                         ^

4. **Correct the pronoun reference** by revising the sentence to make the pronoun more specific.

■ **PRACTICE 4    AVOIDING AMBIGUOUS OR VAGUE PRONOUN REFERENCES**

Edit each sentence to eliminate any ambiguous or vague pronoun references. Some sentences may be revised in more than one way. If you need help, look back at the chart on page 382 that shows the correction steps.

*some experts*

**EXAMPLE:** The nutritionist explained that ~~they~~ are no longer certain
^

that eating fat is unhealthy.

*Answers may vary.*

1. I have been trying to get plenty of exercise and to eat a nutritious diet,
*this method*
but ~~it~~ hasn't helped me lose weight.
^

*nutritional experts*
2. I paid attention twenty years ago when ~~they~~ said that too much fat
^

caused weight gain.

*the amount*
3. My diet at the time contained a certain amount of fat, but ~~it~~ did not
^

worry me.

4. Then my mother told my sister that the family needed to cut back on
*my mother*
fat, and ~~she~~ began to stock up on fat-free foods.
^

5. When I read the ingredients on the package of fat-free cookies, how-
*much of the fat had simply been*
ever, I learned that ~~they simply~~ replaced ~~much of the fat~~ with extra
^

sugar.

*someone*
6. I told my mother that ~~they~~ should invent a better diet.
^

*the food*
7. Nevertheless, at each meal I tried to eliminate fat, but ~~it~~ did not taste
^

the same to me.

*my diet*
8. I added more pasta to my diet, but ~~it~~ left me feeling unsatisfied.
^

*nutritionists*
9. Now ~~they~~ claim that eating fat makes a person feel less hungry.
^

10. Some experts say that fat can contribute to weight loss, and I am ready
*eating fat*
to try ~~it~~.
^

**FINDING AND FIXING PRONOUN PROBLEMS:**
Avoiding Repetitious Pronoun References

---

**FIND**

Television <u>advertising</u>  sometimes <u>has</u> a negative influence on young viewers.

1. **Underline** the subject and **double-underline** the verb.
2. **Circle** any  in the sentence.
3. **Ask:** What noun does the pronoun refer to? *Advertising.*
4. **Ask:** Do the noun and the pronoun that refers to it share the same verb? *Yes.* Does the pronoun just repeat the noun rather than replace it? *Yes.* If the answer to one or both questions is yes, the pronoun is repetitious.

---

**FIX**

Television advertising ~~it~~ sometimes has a negative influence on young viewers.

5. **Correct the sentence** by crossing out the ~~repetitious pronoun~~.

---

PRACTICE 5   **AVOIDING REPETITIOUS PRONOUN REFERENCES**

Correct any repetitious pronoun references in the following sentences. If you need help, look back at the chart above that shows the correction steps.

> **EXAMPLE:** Car commercials ~~they~~ want viewers to believe that buy-
> ing a certain brand of car will bring happiness.

1. Young people ~~they~~ sometimes take advertisements too literally.

2.  ~~In a~~ beer advertisement, ~~it~~ might imply that drinking alcohol makes people more attractive and popular.

3. People who see or hear an advertisement ~~they~~ have to think about the message.

4. Parents should help their children understand why advertisements ~~they~~ don't show the real world.

5.  A recent study,/ it said that parents can help kids overcome the influ-
    ence of advertising.

## Use the Right Type of Pronoun

Three important types of pronouns are subject pronouns, object pronouns,
and possessive pronouns. Notice their uses in the following sentences.

Object    Subject

The dog barked at *him,* and *he* laughed.

Possessive

As Josh walked out, *his* phone started ringing.

| *Pronoun Types* | | | |
|---|---|---|---|
| | **SUBJECT** | **OBJECT** | **POSSESSIVE** |
| *First person singular/plural* | I/we | me/us | my, mine/ our, ours |
| *Second person singular/plural* | you/you | you/you | your, yours/ your, yours |
| *Third person singular* | he, she, it | him, her, it | his, her, hers, its |
| *Third person plural* | they who/who | them whom/whom | their, theirs its, whose |

■ **TIP** Never put an apostrophe in a possessive pronoun.

Read the following sentence and replace the underlined noun <u>Andreas</u> with
pronouns. Note that the pronouns are all different.

*his*                    *he*
When Andreas made an A on <u>Andreas's</u> final exam, <u>Andreas</u> was proud
*him*
of himself, and the teacher congratulated <u>Andreas</u>.

### Subject Pronouns

A **subject pronoun** serves as the subject of a verb.

*He* lives next door to a graveyard.

*I* opened the door too quickly.

## Object Pronouns

**Object pronouns** either receive the action of a verb (the object of the verb) or are part of a prepositional phrase (the object of the preposition).

**OBJECT OF THE VERB**    Jay gave *me* his watch.

**OBJECT OF THE PREPOSITION**    Jay gave his watch to *me*.

For a list of prepositions, see page 289.

## Possessive Pronouns

**Possessive pronouns** show ownership.

Dave is *my* uncle.

That book is *yours*, I think.

Three trouble spots make it difficult to know what type of pronoun to use.

**THREE PRONOUN TROUBLE SPOTS**

- Compound subjects and objects
- Comparisons
- Sentences that need *who* or *whom*

## Pronouns Used with Compound Subjects and Objects

**TIP** When you are writing about yourself and someone else, always put yourself after everyone else. *My friends and I went to a club,* not *I and my friends went to a club.*

A **compound subject** has more than one subject joined by a conjunction such as *and* or *or*.

A **compound object** has more than one object joined by a conjunction. (For a list of conjunctions, see p. 416.)

**COMPOUND SUBJECT**    Beth and *I* worked on the project.

**COMPOUND OBJECT**    My boss gave the assignment to Beth and *me*.

To decide what type of pronoun to use in a compound construction, try leaving out the other part of the compound and the conjunction. Then say the sentence aloud to yourself.

**TIP** Many people make the mistake of using *I* in the phrase *between you and (me/I)*. The correct pronoun with *between* is the object *me*. If you get confused, try substituting the word *with* for the word *between*.

~~Joan and~~ (me / I) went to the movies last night.

[Think: *I* went to the movies last night.]

The car was headed right for ~~Tom and~~ (she / her).

[Think: The car was headed right for *her*.]

If a pronoun is part of a compound object in a prepositional phrase, use an object pronoun.

I will keep that information just between you and (I / me).

[*Between you and me* is a prepositional phrase, so an object pronoun, *me*, is required.]

---

**FINDING AND FIXING PRONOUN PROBLEMS:**
Using Pronouns in Compound Constructions

↓

**FIND**

My ~~friend and~~ me talk at least once a week.

1. **Underline** the subject and **double-underline** the verb, and **circle** any (object or objects) (words that receive the action of the verb).

2. **Ask:** Is there a compound subject or object? *Yes — "friend and me" is a compound subject.*

3. **Ask:** Do the nouns in the compound construction share a verb? *Yes, "talk".*

4. **Cross out** one of the subjects so that only the pronoun remains.

5. **Ask:** Does the sentence sound right with just the pronoun as the subject? *No.*

↓

**FIX**

*I*
My friend and ~~me~~ talk at least once a week.
 ^

6. **Correct the sentence** by replacing the incorrect pronoun with the correct one.

---

▇ **PRACTICE 6   EDITING PRONOUNS IN COMPOUND CONSTRUCTIONS**

Edit each sentence using the proper type of pronoun. If a sentence is already correct, write a "C" next to it. If you need help, look back at the chart above that shows the correction steps.

**EXAMPLE:** Don King approached Zaire's President Mobutu, and
*he*
Mobutu and ~~him~~ reached an agreement.
 ^

1. In 1974, George Foreman was the heavyweight boxing champion, and
*he*
~~him~~ and Muhammad Ali agreed to a fight for the title.
 ^

2. President Mobutu of Zaire wanted to make his country famous, so the
*him*
financial backing for the fight came from ~~he~~ and the people of Zaire.
 ^

3. Because American officials considered Mobutu a strong anticommu-
*they and he*
nist, ~~them and him~~ were allies, but Mobutu was a corrupt dictator who
 ^
stole money intended for his impoverished country.

4. According to the agreement with Mobutu, he and Don King guaranteed Foreman and Ali five million dollars each for the championship bout.  *C*

5. Foreman angered the people of Zaire immediately when ~~him~~ *he* and his German shepherd dog were seen getting off the airplane.

6. German shepherds were part of Zaire's unhappy past, when the streets were patrolled by them and the Belgian colonial police; people were afraid of the dogs.  *C*

7. The people loved Muhammad Ali, and pictures of he *him* and his entourage in Zaire showed adoring crowds everywhere.

8. Foreman was younger and stronger, so most boxing fans believed that in a bout between him and Ali, Foreman would win an easy victory.  *C*

9. Ali may have feared losing the fight, but when ~~him~~ *he* and Foreman finally got in the ring, Ali absorbed punch after punch.

10. Foreman became so tired that the end of the fight came for he *him* and Ali in the eighth round; Ali knocked out the champion and regained the world heavyweight title.

### Pronouns Used in Comparisons

Using the right type of pronoun in comparisons is particularly important because using the wrong type can change the meaning of the sentence. Editing comparisons can be tricky because they often imply words that aren't actually included in the sentence.

Bob trusts Donna more than *I*.

[This sentence means Bob trusts Donna more than I trust her. The implied words are *trust her*.]

Bob trusts Donna more than *me*.

[This sentence means Bob trusts Donna more than he trusts me. The implied words are *he trusts*.]

To decide whether to use a subject or object pronoun in a comparison, try adding the implied words and saying the sentence aloud.

The registrar is much more efficient than (us /(we)).

[Think: The registrar is much more efficient than *we are*.]

Susan rides her bicycle more than (he/ him).

[Think: Susan rides her bicycle more than *he does*.]

■ **TIP** Add the additional words to the comparison when you speak and write. Then others will not think you are incorrect.

**FINDING AND FIXING PRONOUN PROBLEMS:**
Using Pronouns in Comparisons

↓

**FIND**

The other band attracts a bigger audience (than) us on Friday nights.

1. **Circle** the (word that indicates a comparison.)
2. **Ask:** What word or words that would come after the comparison word are implied but missing from the sentence? *Do.*
3. **Ask:** If you add the missing word or words, does the pronoun make sense? *No.*

↓

**FIX**

                                                                    *we (do)*
The other band attracts a bigger audience than u̲s on Friday
                                                                        ^
nights.

4. **Correct the sentence** by replacing the incorrect pronoun with the correct one.

▨ PRACTICE 7    **EDITING PRONOUNS IN COMPARISONS**

Edit each sentence using the correct pronoun type. If a sentence is correct, put a "C" next to it. If you need help, look back at the chart above that shows the correction steps.

   **EXAMPLE:** My cousin and I both started bands, but I was more
                                   *she*
               successful than h̶e̶r̶.
                                 ^

1. My cousin is a better guitar player than m̶e̶. *I*
                                            ^

2. I did not want to compete with someone who plays as well as h̶e̶r̶. *she*
                                                                  ^

3. I became a singer instead, but my cousin thought that her band's
   singer was better than I. *C*

4. When she did not ask me to join her band, I started my own with
   friends who had been musicians much longer than ~~her~~. *she*

5. The members of my band and hers knew each other well because we
   played in the same places as they for several months. *C*

6. Soon, we were attracting so many more fans than my cousin's band
   that the biggest local club paid us much more than ~~they~~. *them*

7. A music producer came to see us play, but he wanted a new teen-
   pop sensation in the area more than ~~we~~, so we did not get a record
   contract. *us*

8. The teen singer became much more famous than ~~me~~ or my cousin. *I*

9. My cousin was not as fascinated as ~~me~~ by stardom, and she helped me
   get over my disappointment. *I*

10. In the end, I think she probably handled our rivalry more profession-
    ally than I. *C*

### *Choosing between* Who *and* Whom

*Who* is always a subject; *whom* is always an object. If a pronoun performs an action, use the subject form *who*. If a pronoun does not perform an action, use the object form *whom*.

> **WHO = SUBJECT**    I would like to know *who* delivered this package.
>
> **WHOM = OBJECT**    He told me to *whom* I should report.

**■ TIP** *Whoever* is a subject pronoun; *whomever* is an object pronoun.

In sentences other than questions, when the pronoun (*who* or *whom*) is followed by a verb, use *who*. When the pronoun (*who* or *whom*) is followed by a noun or pronoun, use *whom*.

> The pianist (who/ whom) played was excellent.
> [The pronoun is followed by the verb *played*. Use *who*.]

> The pianist (who /whom) I saw was excellent.
> [The pronoun is followed by another pronoun: *I*. Use *whom*.]

### PRACTICE 8 CHOOSING BETWEEN *WHO* AND *WHOM*

In each sentence, circle the correct word, *who* or *whom*. Remember, if the pronoun is followed by a verb, use *who*. If it is followed by a noun or pronoun, use *whom*.

**EXAMPLE:** Police officers (who/whom) want to solve a crime—
or prevent one—are now relying more than ever on
technology.

1. Face-recognition software, now being introduced, is supposed to
identify possible criminals (who/whom) cameras have photographed
in public places.

2. Use of such software, which can compare security camera images with
mugshots from a criminal database, can help law enforcement officials
determine (who/whom) they want to question about a crime.

3. Police will try to detain any person (who/whom) is identified by the
software as a criminal.

4. There are bound to be innocent people (who/whom) resemble criminals closely enough that the software will single them out.

5. However, police and nervous Americans are hopeful that this method
can help to identify terrorists (who/whom) appear in airports or other
sensitive locations.

## Make Pronouns Consistent in Person

**Person** is the point of view a writer uses—the perspective from which he
or she writes. Pronouns may be in first person (*I, we*), second person (*you*),
or third person (*he, she,* or *it*). (See the chart on p. 385.)

| | |
|---|---|
| **INCONSISTENT PERSON** | *I* wanted to sign up for a computer class, but the person said *you* had to know word processing. |

[The sentence starts in the first person (*I*) but shifts to the second person (*you*).]

| | |
|---|---|
| **CONSISTENT PERSON** | *I* wanted to sign up for a computer class, but the person said *I* had to know word processing. |

[The sentence stays with the first person, *I*.]

| | |
|---|---|
| **INCONSISTENT PERSON** | As soon as *a shopper* walks into the store, *you* can tell it is a weird place. |

[The sentence starts with the third person (*a shopper*) but shifts to the second person (*you*).]

| | |
|---|---|
| **CONSISTENT PERSON** | As soon as *a shopper* walks into the store, *he* or *she* can tell it is a weird place. |
| **CONSISTENT PERSON, PLURAL** | As soon as *shoppers* walk into the store, *they* can tell it is a weird place. |

**FINDING AND FIXING PRONOUN PROBLEMS:**
Making Pronouns Consistent in Person

**FIND**

<u>I</u> had the right answer, but to win the tickets ⟨you⟩ had to be the ninth caller.

1. **Underline** all of the <u>subject nouns and pronouns</u> in the sentence.
2. **Circle** any ⟨pronouns⟩ that refer to another subject noun or pronoun in the sentence.
3. **Ask:** Is the subject noun or pronoun that the circled pronoun refers to in the first (*I, we*), second (*you*), or third person (*he, she,* or *it*)? *First person.*
4. **Ask:** What person is the pronoun in? *Second.*

**FIX**

                                                                    *I*
I had the right answer, but to win the tickets ~~you~~ had to be the
                                                                    ^
ninth caller.

5. **Correct the sentence** by changing the pronoun to be consistent with the noun it refers to.

■ **PRACTICE 9    MAKING PRONOUNS CONSISTENT IN PERSON**

In the following items, correct the shifts in person. There may be more than one way to correct some sentences. If you need help, look back at the chart above that shows the correction steps.

> **EXAMPLE:** Many college students have access to a writing center
>                      *they*
> where ~~you~~ can get tutoring.
>      ^

*Answers may vary.*

                                      *his or her*
1. A writing tutor must know ~~your~~ way around college writing assignments.
                                ^

2. I have gone to the writing center at my school because sometimes ~~you~~
                                            *I*

    need a second pair of eyes to look over a paper.

3. Students signing up for tutoring at the writing center may not be in
     *their*
    ~~your~~ first semester of college.
    ^

4. Even a graduate student may need help with ~~your~~ *his or her* writing at times.

5. The writing-center tutor is very careful not to correct ~~their~~ *his or her* students' papers.

6. My tutor told me that ~~you~~ *I* had to learn to edit a paper.

7. Every student has to learn to catch ~~your~~ *his or her* own mistakes.

8. A student's tutor is not like ~~your~~ *his or her* English professor.

9. No student gets ~~their~~ *his or her* grade on a paper from a writing tutor.

10. Tutors don't judge but simply help students with ~~your~~ *their* papers.


## PRACTICE 10   CORRECTING VARIOUS PRONOUN PROBLEMS

In the following sentences, find and correct any problems with pronoun use. You may be able to revise some sentences in more than one way, and you may need to rewrite some sentences to correct errors.

**EXAMPLE:** *Students with busy schedules have* ~~Everyone with a busy schedule has~~ probably been tempted to take shortcuts on their coursework.

*Answers may vary.*

1. My class received ~~its~~ *their* term paper grades yesterday.

2. My friend Gene and ~~me~~ *I* were shocked to see that he had gotten an F for his paper.

3. I usually get better grades than ~~him~~ *he*, but he doesn't usually fail.

4. Mr. Padilla, the instructor, ~~who~~ *whom* most students consider strict but fair, scheduled an appointment with Gene.

5. When Gene went to the department office, ~~they~~ *the office assistant* told him where to find Mr. Padilla.

6. Mr. Padilla *didn't think that Gene* ~~told Gene that he didn't think he~~ had written the paper.

7. The paper ~~it~~ contained language that was unusual for Gene.

8. The instructor said that ~~you~~ *he* could compare Gene's in-class writing with this paper and see significant differences.

9. Mr. Padilla, who had typed suspicious passages from Gene's paper
   into a search engine, found two online papers containing sentences
   that were also in Gene's paper.

10. Gene ~~told Mr. Padilla~~ *admitted* that he had made a terrible mistake.

11. Gene told my girlfriend and ~~I~~ *me* later that he did not realize that borrow-
    ing sentences from online sources was plagiarism.

12. We looked at the paper, and ~~you~~ *we* could tell that parts of it did not
    sound like Gene's writing.

13. Anyone doing Internet research must be especially careful to docu-
    ment ~~their~~ *the* sources, as Gene now knows.

14. The department decided ~~that they would~~ not *to* suspend Gene from
    school.

15. Mr. Padilla will let Gene take his class again and will help him avoid
    inadvertent plagiarism, and Gene said that no one had ever been more
    relieved than ~~him~~ *he* to hear that news.

## Edit Paragraphs and Your Own Writing

**PRACTICE 11   EDITING PARAGRAPHS FOR PRONOUN USE**

Find and correct any problems with pronoun use in the following paragraphs. You may want to use the chart, Finding and Fixing Pronoun Problems,
on page 397. *Answers may vary. Possible edits shown.*

1. (1) Can a person make ~~their~~ *his or her* own luck? (2) People ~~whom~~ *who* consider themselves lucky may actually be luckier than those who think they
are unlucky. (3) If you and ~~me~~ *I* feel optimistic and in control of the
future, we are more likely to have good luck. (4) Some people try to
increase their chances of having good luck by carrying good-luck
charms. (5) Rabbit feet are common charms, but ~~they~~ *people* say ~~they~~ *the feet* didn't
bring the rabbit any luck! (6) Seventy percent of students ~~they~~ believe
that good-luck charms bring academic success. (7) "Lucky" rituals are

also common among students; for example, ~~you~~ *they* might wear the same shirt for every test. (8) Experts say that people who want good luck should try to meet new people who might bring them a lucky break.

2. (1) ~~On~~ *T*elevision*,* ~~they have~~ *has* broadcast game shows since the 1950s. (2) Early game shows did not offer huge amounts of prize money. (3) They did give ~~you~~ *contestants* the chance to show off ~~your~~ *their* knowledge to a large television audience. (4) Every contestant on early game shows had to try ~~their~~ *his or her* best to answer very difficult questions. (5) The audience was eager to see ~~their~~ *its* favorite contestants win. (6) To make the audience happy, game-show officials provided some contestants with the answers in advance. (7) ~~They~~ *The officials* helped ~~them~~ *the contestants* win. (8) Eventually, a contestant ~~whom~~ *who* had been told to lose got angry. (9) The game show had stopped giving him the answers. (10) Instead, ~~they~~ *the officials* had given ~~them~~ *answers* to another player who was more popular than ~~him~~ *he*. (11) He publicized the cheating, and game shows had a bad reputation for a while.

3. (12) Of course, game shows ~~they~~ never completely went away, as viewers know. (13) A few years ago, ~~they~~ *the shows* became more popular than ever. (14) The prizes on the most popular shows increased to a million dollars or more for a few lucky winners who answered questions correctly. (15) People like you and ~~I~~ *me* could become contestants simply by calling a phone number. (16) Researchers said that the questions contestants had to answer for the newer shows were easier than ~~it was~~ *they were* in the 1950s. (17) Ordinary people liked to watch other ordinary people win. (18) In the 1950s, the shows couldn't find enough ordinary people ~~whom~~ *who* could win the big prizes. (19) That's the reason ~~they~~ *the shows* gave ~~them~~ *contestants* the answers. (20) The questions ~~they~~ *some hosts* asked in the newer shows made it possible for some contestants to win without cheating and without being geniuses. (21) Easier questions were a compromise, but most people could live with it. (22) Now, reality shows are even more popular than game shows, and former hit game shows have been canceled. (23) You and ~~me~~ *I* would rather watch *Joe Millionaire* than answer questions to try to be him!

■ **LEARNING JOURNAL** Do you understand the terms *pronoun agreement* and *pronoun reference*? How would you explain them to someone else?

■ **PRACTICE 12    EDITING YOUR OWN WRITING FOR PRONOUN USE**

As a final practice, edit a piece of your own writing for pronoun use. It can be a paper you are working on for this course, a paper you've already finished, a paper for another course, or a recent piece of writing from your work or everyday life. Use the chart on page 397 to help you. Record in your learning journal any problem sentences you find, along with a corrected version of these sentences.

## Chapter Review: Pronouns

1. Pronouns replace _____*nouns*_____ or other _____*pronouns*_____ in a sentence.

2. A pronoun must agree with (match) the noun or pronoun it replaces in _____*number*_____ and _____*gender*_____.

3. An _____*indefinite pronoun*_____ does not refer to a specific person, place, or thing. What are three examples of this kind of pronoun? *Answers will vary. Possible answers: anybody, something, few*

4. A _____*collective noun*_____ names a group that acts as a single unit. What are two examples? *Answers will vary. Possible answers: crowd, jury*

5. In an _____*ambiguous*_____ pronoun reference, the pronoun could refer to more than one noun.

6. In a _____*vague*_____ pronoun reference, the pronoun does not refer clearly to any particular person, place, or thing.

7. In a _____*repetitious*_____ pronoun reference, the pronoun repeats a reference to a noun rather than replacing it.

8. Subject pronouns serve as the subject of a verb. Write a sentence using a subject pronoun. *Answers will vary. Possible answer: We went to the movies last night.*

9. What are two other types of pronouns? *object pronouns and possessive pronouns*

10. What are three trouble spots in pronoun use?

*compound subjects and objects* _____

*comparisons* _____

*sentences that need who or whom* _____

11. When you must decide whether to use *who* or *whom,* use the following

    technique: Use *who* when the pronoun is followed by a _____*verb*_____.

    Use *whom* when the pronoun is followed by a __*noun or pronoun*__.

12. What are examples of first-, second-, and third-person pronouns?

    First person:  _____*I*_____

    Second person: _____*you*_____

    Third person:  __*he, she, or it*__

13. Pronouns should be _____*consistent*_____ in person.

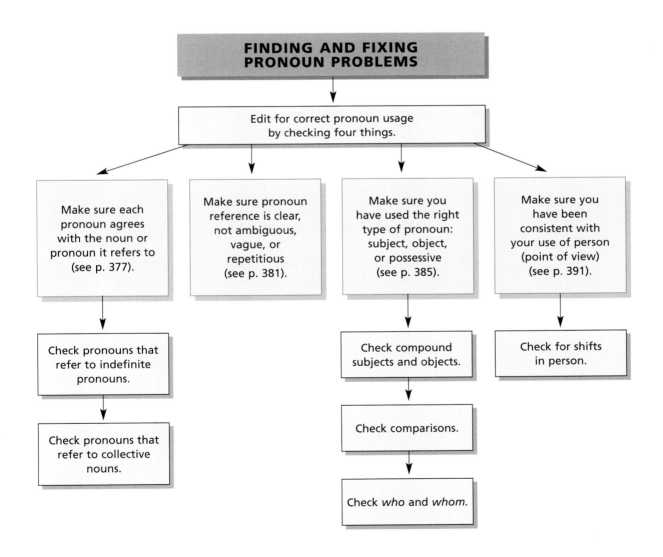

# 25

# Adjectives and Adverbs

*Describing* **Which One?** *or* **How?**

## Understand What Adjectives and Adverbs Are

■ **LEARNING JOURNAL**
Use your learning journal as a place to record sentences with adjective and adverb problems that you find in your writing. Also write down edited versions of the sentences, with the problems corrected.

■ **TIP** To understand this chapter on adjectives and adverbs, you need to know what nouns and verbs are. For a review, see Chapter 19.

Adjectives and adverbs describe or modify (give more information about) other words. They can come before or after the words they modify. You can use more than one adjective or adverb to modify a word.

**Adjectives** describe or modify nouns (words that name people, places, or things) and pronouns (words that replace nouns). They add information about *what kind, which one,* or *how many.*

The *final* exam was today.

It was *long* and *difficult.*

The *three shiny new* coins were on the dresser.

**Adverbs** describe or modify verbs (words that tell what happens in a sentence), adjectives, or other adverbs. They add information about *how, how much, when, where, why,* or *to what extent.* Adverbs often end with *-ly.*

■ **ESL** Refer students to Chapter 30, where the standard order of adjectives is presented.

| | |
|---|---|
| **MODIFYING VERB** | Sharon *enthusiastically* accepted the job. |
| **MODIFYING ADJECTIVE** | The *very* young lawyer handled the case. |
| **MODIFYING ANOTHER ADVERB** | The team played *surprisingly* well. |

## Practice Using Adjectives and Adverbs Correctly

### Choosing between Adjectives and Adverbs

Many adverbs are formed by adding *-ly* to the end of an adjective.

| ADJECTIVE | ADVERB |
|---|---|
| She received a *quick* answer. | Her sister answered *quickly*. |
| The *new* student introduced himself. | The couple is *newly* married. |
| That is an *honest* answer. | Please answer *honestly*. |

■ **DISCUSSION** To get students focused on adjectives and adverbs, throw out a few sentences containing adjectives, with students in the class as the subjects (*Dan is wearing a black leather jacket*). Ask the student in the sentence what the adjectives are.

The similarity between adjectives and adverbs can make it difficult to choose between them. To decide whether to use an adjective or an adverb, find the word it is describing or modifying. If that word is a noun or pronoun, use an adjective. If it is a verb, adjective, or another adverb, use an adverb.

### ■ PRACTICE 1   CHOOSING BETWEEN ADJECTIVES AND ADVERBS

In each sentence, underline the word in the sentence that is being described or modified, and then circle the correct word in parentheses.

■ **TIP** For more practice with adjective and adverb usage, visit Exercise Central at <bedfordstmartins.com/realwriting>. Also, the Writing Guide Software with this book has tutorials on this topic.

> **EXAMPLE:** People are (common /*commonly*) aware that smoking causes health risks.

1. Many smokers are (*stubborn*/ stubbornly) about refusing to quit.

2. Others who are thinking about quitting may decide (sudden /*suddenly*) that the damage from smoking has already been done.

3. In such cases, the (*typical*/ typically) smoker sees no reason to stop.

4. The news about secondhand smoke may have made some smokers stop (quick /*quickly*) to save the health of their families.

5. Now, research shows that pet lovers who smoke can have a (*terrible*/ terribly) effect on their cats.

6. Cats who live with smokers (frequent /*frequently*) develop lymphoma.

7. Veterinarians point out that the cats of smokers may reek (strong /*strongly*) of smoke.

8. Cats like to have their fur (*clean*/ cleanly), and they lick the fur to groom themselves.

■ **RESOURCES** *Additional Resources* contains tests and supplemental practice exercises for this chapter as well as a transparency master for the chart at the end.

9. When they are grooming, cats may ingest a (*significant*/ significantly) dose of tobacco smoke.

10. Perhaps some smokers who feel that it's too late for their own health will (serious /*seriously*) consider quitting for the sake of their pets.

## Using Comparative and Superlative Forms

■ **ESL** Point out that comparative constructions often use the word *than*.

To compare two persons, places, or things, use the **comparative** form of adjectives or adverbs.

> Carol ran *faster* than I did.

> Johan is *more intelligent* than his sister.

To compare three or more persons, places, or things, use the **superlative** form of adjectives or adverbs.

> Carol ran *fastest* of all the women runners.

> Johan is the *most intelligent* of the five children.

■ **TIP** For more on changing a final *-y* to *-i* when adding endings, and on other spelling changes involving endings, see Chapter 33.

Comparatives and superlatives can be formed either by adding an ending to an adjective or adverb or by adding a word. If an adjective or adverb is short (one syllable), add the endings *-er* to form the comparative and *-est* to form the superlative. Also use this pattern for adjectives that end in *-y* (but change the *-y* to *-i* before adding *-er* or *-est*). If an adjective or adverb is longer than one syllable, add the word *more* to make the comparative and the word *most* to make the superlative.

### Comparative and Superlative Forms

| ADJECTIVE OR ADVERB | COMPARATIVE | SUPERLATIVE |
| --- | --- | --- |
| **ADJECTIVES AND ADVERBS OF ONE SYLLABLE** | | |
| tall | taller | tallest |
| fast | faster | fastest |
| **ADJECTIVES ENDING IN -Y** | | |
| happy | happier | happiest |
| silly | sillier | silliest |
| **ADJECTIVES AND ADVERBS OF MORE THAN ONE SYLLABLE** | | |
| graceful | more graceful | most graceful |
| gracefully | more gracefully | most gracefully |
| intelligent | more intelligent | most intelligent |
| intelligently | more intelligently | most intelligently |

Use either an ending (*-er* or *-est*) or an extra word (*more* or *most*) to form a comparative or superlative—not both at once.

> Tiger Woods is the ~~most~~ greatest golfer in the world.

■ **PRACTICE 2   USING COMPARATIVES AND SUPERLATIVES**

In the space provided in each sentence, write the correct form of the adjective or adverb in parentheses. You may need to add *more* or *most* to some adjectives and adverbs.

**EXAMPLE:** My grandfather's reflexes are _____*slower*_____ (*slow*)
than they used to be.

1. One of the _____*scariest*_____ (*scary*) experiences of my life happened in my grandfather's car.

2. He was driving me and my sister to school, and another car stopped in front of us _____*more quickly*_____ (*quick*) than he expected.

3. He made the _____*fastest*_____ (*fast*) stop he could, but he still hit the back of the other car.

4. My sister's seat belt was fastened _____*more loosely*_____ (*loose*) than it should have been, and she ended up in the hospital.

5. I was _____*luckier*_____ (*lucky*) than my sister, and I was not hurt.

6. The accident provided my mother with the _____*most damaging*_____ (*damaging*) evidence she had seen yet that my grandfather was no longer a safe driver.

7. My mother had to make one of the _____*hardest*_____ (*hard*) decisions of her life.

8. She told me later that her conversation with my grandfather was the _____*most serious*_____ (*serious*) talk they had had since she had reached adulthood.

9. My grandfather insisted that he was not a dangerous driver, but he finally admitted that he had been _____*more certain*_____ (*certain*) of his ability to handle a car when he was younger.

10. My mother told my grandfather that she had never been _____*prouder*_____ (*proud*) of him than when he handed her the keys to his car.

### Good, Well, Bad, and Badly

■ **TIP** Irregular means not following a standard rule.

Four common adjectives and adverbs have irregular forms: *good, well, bad,* and *badly.*

| Comparative and Superlative Forms | | |
|---|---|---|
| | **COMPARATIVE** | **SUPERLATIVE** |
| **ADJECTIVE** | | |
| good | better | best |
| bad | worse | worst |
| **ADVERB** | | |
| well | better | best |
| badly | worse | worst |

People often get confused about whether to use *good* or *well.* *Good* is an adjective, so use it to describe a noun or pronoun. *Well* is an adverb, so use it to describe a verb or an adjective.

**ADJECTIVE**   She has a *good* job.

**ADVERB**   He works *well* with his colleagues.

*Well* can also be an adjective to describe someone's health: I am not *well* today.

■ **PRACTICE 3   USING GOOD AND WELL**

Complete each sentence by circling the correct word in parentheses. Underline the word that *good* or *well* modifies.

> **EXAMPLE:** A (good / well) pediatrician spends as much time talking
>
> with parents as he or she does examining patients.

1. The ability to communicate (good / well) is something that many

   parents look for in a pediatrician.

2. With a firstborn child, there is a (good / well) chance that every visit to

   the doctor will cause the parent at least some anxiety.

3. Parents can become particularly worried when their infant doesn't feel

   (good / well) because the child can't say what the problem is.

4. Doctors today are equipped with (good/ well) <u>diagnostic tools</u>, however.

5. An otoscope helps a doctor <u>see</u> (good /well) when he or she looks into a patient's ear, for example.

6. A fever and an inflamed eardrum are (good/ well) <u>indicators</u> of a middle-ear infection.

7. Children who have chronic ear infections may not <u>hear</u> as (good /well) as children who have fewer infections.

8. If the pediatrician presents clear options for treatment, parents can make a (good /well)-<u>informed</u> decision about treating their child's illness.

9. Some parents decide that ear-tube surgery is a (good/ well) <u>solution</u> to the problem of chronic ear infections.

10. Within an hour after ear-tube surgery, most <u>children</u> are (good /well) enough to go home.


■ **PRACTICE 4   USING COMPARATIVE AND SUPERLATIVE FORMS OF *GOOD* AND *BAD***

Complete each sentence by circling the (correct comparative or superlative form) of *good* or *bad* in parentheses.

**EXAMPLE:** Men tend to sleep (better/ best) than women do.

1. One of the (worse /worst) gaps in human knowledge about sleep disorders used to be that little research had been done using female subjects.

2. Until the 1990s, most scientists considered male subjects a (better/ best) choice than female ones for sleep research.

3. Now that (better/ best) research on sleep disorders in women is available, scientists know that women suffer more than men from certain kinds of sleep problems.

4. One of the (worse /worst) problems for new mothers is loss of sleep.

5. Whether because of habit or some biological cause, women are (better/ best) than men at hearing the sound of a child crying in the middle of the night.

6. New sleep research shows that women suffer (worse/ worst) than men do from insomnia, whether they are parents or not.

7. In the past, many women who complained of being tired were diagnosed with depression instead of with sleep disorders; the treatment often failed to help and sometimes made the problems (worse/ worst).

8. So far, the (better/ best) explanation that researchers can offer for women's sleep problems is that sleeplessness may be related to levels of hormones.

9. But hormone therapies, according to some scientists, can create health problems that are (worse/ worst) than the ones they are supposed to solve.

10. No one is certain yet of the (better/ best) solution for insomnia and sleep problems in women, but the increasing availability of information will probably improve the situation.

## Edit Paragraphs and Your Own Writing

■ **PRACTICE 5    EDITING PARAGRAPHS FOR CORRECT ADJECTIVES AND ADVERBS**

■ **TEAMWORK** Copy an article from the newspaper or some other source, and have students find all the adjectives and adverbs, drawing arrows from the modifiers to the words they modify. This can be done in small groups in class or assigned as homework and gone over the next day in class.

Find and correct any problems with adjectives and adverbs in the following paragraphs. You may want to use the chart, Editing for Correct Usage of Adjectives and Adverbs, on page 407 to help you.

1. (1) One of the jobs ~~commonliest~~ *most commonly* held by teenagers is a position in a fast-food restaurant. (2) Managers of fast-food franchises consider hiring teenagers a ~~well~~ *good* idea. (3) Teens will work for ~~more~~ lower pay than many other workers, so the restaurant can keep its prices down. (4) The jobs do not require a lot of skill, so the restaurants do not need to spend money offering training to ~~newly~~ *new* workers. (5) Jobs in fast food are not glamorous, but they are plentiful; a teenager who wants to work in a fast-food restaurant can usually find a job ~~quick~~ *quickly*. (6) But few teenagers, and probably even fewer of their parents, realize that fast-food work has a drawback: It can be *more* dangerous than many other summer jobs. (7) Fast-

food restaurants keep large amounts of cash on hand, and this fact is known ~~good~~ *well* by people who want to commit a robbery. (8) Today, fast-food franchises are robbed more often than convenience stores because criminals have a ~~worser~~ *worse* chance of success in a convenience-store holdup. (9) Many teenagers think that a fast-food job is boring but a ~~harmlessly~~ *harmless* way to spend a summer. (10) Unfortunately, a robbery can make a fast-food job ~~excitinger~~ *more exciting* than any worker wants it to be.

2. (1) One of the ~~importantest~~ *most important* things I've learned since starting college is to avoid waiting until the last minute to begin my work. (2) I used to think that I could successfully write a paper the night before it was due. (3) This technique worked ~~good~~ *well* for me in high school. (4) But when I tried it in my history class during my first year in college, I received a bad grade, much ~~badder~~ *worse* than I had expected. (5) I promised myself that I would do ~~gooder~~ *better* than that in the future. (6) I've also learned to work ~~persistent~~ *persistently* at a task, even when I feel frustrated. (7) If a task is ~~more~~ harder than I expected, I will arrange to ask the professor or a tutor for help. (8) This often turns out to be the ~~faster~~ *fastest* way of all to solve the problem. (9) If no outside help is available, I will usually put the work away for a few hours, or overnight, and resume my efforts when I feel ~~more~~ better about my ability to concentrate.

3. (10) Patience is also a ~~usefully~~ *useful* habit. (11) I tend to do a ~~strong~~ *stronger* job when I work more ~~slow~~ *slowly* than when I work faster. (12) Sometimes I dive into a project too ~~quick~~ *quickly*, before I have a full understanding of what is expected of me. (13) I also get in trouble if I try to tackle something when I'm overtired or not feeling ~~good~~ *well*. (14) Then I have to start over, and I end up ~~needless~~ *needlessly* wasting time. (15) It's a ~~well~~ *good* idea to do my most important work when I'm feeling my ~~bestest~~ *best*.

---

■ **PRACTICE 6    EDITING YOUR OWN WRITING FOR CORRECT ADJECTIVES AND ADVERBS**

■ **LEARNING JOURNAL**
What mistake in using adjectives or adverbs do you make most often in your writing? What are some ways to avoid or correct this mistake?

As a final practice, edit a piece of your own writing for correct use of adjectives and adverbs. It can be a paper you are working on for this course, a paper you've already finished, a paper for another course, or a recent piece of writing from your work or everyday life. Record in your learning journal any problem sentences you find, along with their corrections. You may want to use the chart on page 407 to help you.

## Chapter Review: Adjectives and Adverbs

1.  Adjectives and adverbs describe or _____*modify*_____ (give more infor-
    mation about) other words.

2.  Adjectives modify _____*nouns*_____ and _____*pronouns*_____ .

3.  Adverbs modify _____*verbs*_____, _____*adjectives*_____, or
    _____*other adverbs*_____ .

4.  Many adverbs are formed by adding an _____*-ly*_____ ending to
    an adjective.

5.  The comparative form of an adjective or adverb is used to compare
    how many people, places, or things? _____*two*_____ It is
    formed by adding an _____*-er*_____ ending or the word
    _____*more*_____ .

6.  The superlative form of an adjective or adverb is used to compare
    how many people, places, or things? _____*three or more*_____ It is
    formed by adding an _____*-est*_____ ending or the word
    _____*most*_____ .

7.  What four words have irregular comparative and superlative forms?
    _*good, well, bad, badly*_

8.  *Good* is an (adjective/ adverb) and *well* is an (adjective /adverb).

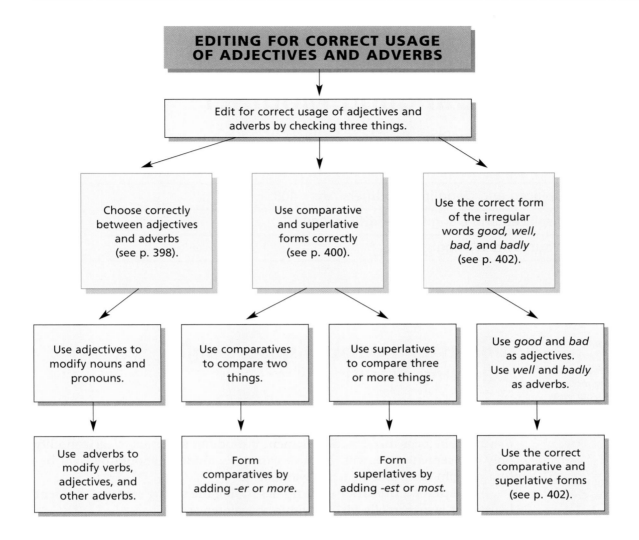

**EDITING FOR CORRECT USAGE OF ADJECTIVES AND ADVERBS**

Edit for correct usage of adjectives and adverbs by checking three things.

Choose correctly between adjectives and adverbs (see p. 398).

Use comparative and superlative forms correctly (see p. 400).

Use the correct form of the irregular words *good, well, bad,* and *badly* (see p. 402).

Use adjectives to modify nouns and pronouns.

Use comparatives to compare two things.

Use superlatives to compare three or more things.

Use *good* and *bad* as adjectives. Use *well* and *badly* as adverbs.

Use adverbs to modify verbs, adjectives, and other adverbs.

Form comparatives by adding *-er* or *more.*

Form superlatives by adding *-est* or *most.*

Use the correct comparative and superlative forms (see p. 402).

# 26

# Misplaced and Dangling Modifiers

*Avoiding Confusing Descriptions*

■ **LEARNING JOURNAL** Use your learning journal as a place to record sentences with misplaced or dangling modifiers that you find in your writing. Also write down edited versions of the sentences, with the problems corrected.

■ **TIP** For a review of basic sentence elements, see Chapter 19.

## Understand What Misplaced and Dangling Modifiers Are

**Modifiers** are words or word groups that describe or give more information about other words in a sentence. To communicate the right message, a modifier must be near the sentence element it modifies and must clearly modify only one sentence element. In most cases, the modifier should be right before or right after that sentence element.

A **misplaced modifier** ends up describing the wrong sentence element because it is incorrectly placed within the sentence.

> **MISPLACED**      Linda saw the White House *flying over Washington, D.C.*
>
> [Was the White House flying over Washington?]
>
> **CLEAR**      *Flying over Washington, D.C.,* Linda saw the White House.

A **dangling modifier** is said to "dangle" because the sentence element it is supposed to modify is implied but not actually in the sentence; with nothing to attach itself to, the modifier is left dangling. A dangling modifier usually appears at the beginning of a sentence and seems to modify the noun or pronoun that immediately follows it.

> **DANGLING**      *Rushing to class,* the books fell out of my bag.
>
> [Were the books rushing to class?]
>
> **CLEAR**      *Rushing to class,* I dropped my books.

Even though readers can often guess what you are trying to say, misplaced and dangling modifiers can create confusion. Be sure to look for and correct misplaced and dangling modifiers in your writing.

# Practice Correcting Misplaced and Dangling Modifiers

## Misplaced Modifiers

To correct a misplaced modifier, place the modifier as close as possible to the sentence element it modifies. The safest choice is often to put the modifier directly before the sentence element it modifies.

*Wearing my bathrobe,*
I went outside to get the paper. wearing my bathrobe.

Three constructions in particular often lead to misplaced modifiers. Be sure to check your writing for these three trouble spots, which are detailed below.

### Trouble Spots: Misplaced Modifiers

1. **Limiting Modifiers, Such as *Only, Almost, Hardly, Nearly,* and *Just*** These words need to be right before — not just close to — the words or phrases they modify.

   *only*
   I only found two old photos in the drawer.

   [I may have found other things in the drawer.]

   *almost*
   Joanne almost ate the whole cake.

   [Joanne actually ate; she didn't "almost" eat.]

   *nearly*
   Thomas nearly spent two hours waiting for the bus.

   [Thomas spent close to two hours waiting; he didn't "nearly spend" them.]

2. **Phrases**

   **PREPOSITIONAL PHRASES**

   *for her father*
   She was shopping for a present all afternoon. for her father.

   [She shopped for her father's present; she wasn't doing her father's shopping.]

   *for the front door*
   Kayla hid the key under the rock. for the front door.

   [The key was for the front door; the rock wasn't for the front door.]

   **PHRASES BEGINNING WITH *-ING* VERB FORMS**

   *Using my credit card,*
   I bought the puppy. using my credit card.

   [The puppy was not using the credit card.]

   *Wearing a glove,*
   Kim caught the ball. wearing a glove.

   [The ball was not wearing the glove; Kim was.]

■ **TEACHING TIP** With an introductory modifier, the noun that follows the comma should be the one that is doing the action or being described. Remind students that possessive nouns and possessive pronouns can't be modified.

■ **RESOURCES** *Additional Resources* contains tests and supplemental practice exercises for this chapter as well as a transparency master for the chart at the end.

■ **TEAMWORK** As homework, have each student write a sentence that is funny because of a misplaced or dangling modifier. Collect the sentences and read some aloud, asking the class for corrections.

### 3. Clauses Beginning with *Who, Whose, That, or Which*

*that was infecting my hard drive*

Joel found the computer virus attached to an e-mail message. ~~that was infecting my hard drive.~~

[What was infecting the hard drive, the virus or the message?]

### ▨ PRACTICE 1   CORRECTING MISPLACED MODIFIERS

■ **TIP** For more practice correcting misplaced and dangling modifiers, visit Exercise Central at <**bedfordstmartins.com/ realwriting**>. Also, the Writing Guide Software with this book has tutorials on this topic.

Find and correct any misplaced modifiers in the following sentences. If a sentence is correct, write a "C" next to it.

**EXAMPLE:** ~~Wearing a baseball cap to cover his bald spot,~~ I often see

*wearing a baseball cap to cover his bald spot*

my next-door neighbor. *Answers may vary. Possible edits shown.*

*who always appear in public with trendy hats on their heads*

1. Celebrities might as well announce their baldness. ~~who always appear in public with trendy hats on their heads.~~

*Only a*

2. ~~A~~ person afraid of going bald ~~only~~ wears a hat all the time.

*A*                                                                           *hiding a bald spot*

3. ~~Hiding a bald spot, a~~ good friend should tell any celebrity to get a haircut and stop pretending.

*who carefully arrange their hair to hide a bald spot*

4. Men are not fooling observers. ~~who carefully arrange their hair to hide a bald spot.~~

5. A few years ago, my mother wanted my father to stop combing his hair over his bald spot.  *C*

6. He thought no one could tell that his hair ~~was getting thin~~, which was

*, was getting thin*

once his pride and joy.

*in photographs*

7. My mother produced proof that his bald spot was obvious to everyone. ~~in photographs.~~

*nearly*

8. After he saw the pictures, my father let my mother ~~nearly~~ cut off all of his hair.

*on his new look*

9. Compliments came from all kinds of people. ~~on his new look.~~

10. Baldness does not have to be embarrassing, but trying to conceal a

*under a hat or a strange hairdo*

bald spot makes people look ridiculous. ~~under a hat or a strange hairdo.~~

## Dangling Modifiers

When an opening modifier does not modify any word in the sentence, it is a **dangling modifier**. Writers often fail to include the word being modified because they think the meaning is clear. To be certain that your sentence says what you intend it to say, be sure to include the word being modified.

*I drove*
Distracted by the bright lights, my car ~~drove~~ off the road.

[The word being modified, *I*, was not included in the original sentence.]

There are two basic ways to correct dangling modifiers. Use the one that makes the most sense. You can add the word being modified right after the opening modifier so that the connection between the two is clear.

*I*                    *on my bike.*
Trying to eat a hot dog, ~~my bike~~ swerved.

Or you can add the word being modified in the opening modifier itself.

*While I was trying*
~~Trying~~ to eat a hot dog, my bike swerved off the path.

**PRACTICE 2    CORRECTING DANGLING MODIFIERS**

Find and correct any dangling modifiers in the following sentences. If a sentence is correct, write a "C" next to it. It may be necessary to add new words or ideas to some sentences.

*Because I had invited*
**EXAMPLE:** ~~Inviting~~ my whole family to dinner, the kitchen was filled

with all kinds of food.  *Answers may vary. Possible edits shown.*

*While I was preparing*
1. ~~Preparing~~ a big family dinner, the oven suddenly stopped working.

2. In a panic, we searched for Carmen, who can solve any problem.  *C*

*With everyone trying*
3. ~~Trying~~ to help, the kitchen was crowded.

*we could see that*
4. Looking into the oven, the turkey was not done.

*we almost cancelled dinner.*
5. Discouraged, ~~the dinner was about to be cancelled.~~

*As I was staring*
6. ~~Staring~~ out the window, a pizza truck went by.

7. Using a credit card, Carmen ordered six pizzas.  *C*

*One*                    *and*
8. ~~With one~~ quick phone call six large pizzas solved our problem.

■ **COMPUTER** Have students highlight introductory phrases in their writing. Then ask them to look at the first word after the phrase to make sure that it is the noun or pronoun the phrase describes.

■ **TEACHING TIP** Students sometimes try to correct a dangling modifier by adding a subordinating conjunction (such as *while*) without sufficiently reworking the sentence itself. Point out that adding *while* alone does not correct the problem with this sentence: *While trying to eat a hot dog . . .*

9. ~~Returning~~ *When I returned* to the crowd in the kitchen, family members still surrounded the oven.

10. Delighted with Carmen's decision, *they cheered* ~~cheers filled the room.~~

# Edit Paragraphs and Your Own Writing

■ PRACTICE 3 **EDITING PARAGRAPHS FOR MISPLACED AND DANGLING MODIFIERS**

Find and correct any misplaced or dangling modifiers in the following paragraphs. You may want to refer to the chart, Editing for Misplaced and Dangling Modifiers, on page 414.

*Answers may vary. Possible edits shown.*

1. (1) Believing they can do nothing to make a difference in the environment, *people often waste* energy. ~~is often wasted.~~ (2) Individuals *who make environmentally good choices* can have an effect *, such as buying a gas-guzzling car or SUV,* ~~who make environmentally good choices.~~ (3) Bad choices can have an effect too, ~~such as buying a gas-guzzling car or SUV.~~ (4) By saving energy, consumers can also save money. (5) Some products *that cost more up front* will save people money for many years. ~~that cost more up front.~~ (6) With solar shingles installed on their roofs, homeowners who paid more for the shingles will have dramatically lower energy bills for the life of the house. (7) Rated for energy efficiency, household appliances can help the environment and the owner's budget. (8) Individuals *who do the right thing for the environment* can make a difference ~~who do the right thing for the environment.~~

2. Dear Mr. Bolton:

(1) I am responding to your advertisement in the *Courier-Ledger* seeking a summer intern for your law practice. (2) A hard worker, *I have strong* ~~my~~ qualifications. ~~are strong.~~ (3) I am currently working on a bachelor's degree in political science and ~~nearly~~ have taken *nearly* fifty credit hours of courses, including classes in jurisprudence, law and public policy, and business law.

(4) Business law is especially of interest to me. (5) Sometimes I *, while sitting in class,* dream of becoming a corporate attorney. ~~while sitting in class.~~ (6) Someday I'd like to work for one of the major firms in New York. (7) ~~Already~~ *I am already*

planning to go on to law school, *and* my grade point average is in the top 10 percent of my class.

(8) I realize that I will not earn much money as an intern. (9) But ~~someday~~ I am confident that *someday* I will be able to find a good-paying job. (10) Thinking of the experience I could gain, *I find* a summer job at your firm ~~is~~ highly appealing.

■ PRACTICE 4   **EDITING YOUR OWN WRITING FOR MISPLACED AND DANGLING MODIFIERS**

As a final practice, edit a piece of your own writing for misplaced and dangling modifiers. It can be a paper you are working on for this course, a paper you've already finished, a paper for another course, or a recent piece of writing from your work or everyday life. Record in your learning journal any problem sentences you find, along with their corrections. You may want to use the chart on page 414.

■ **LEARNING JOURNAL**
Which is more difficult for you, finding misplaced and dangling modifiers or correcting them? What can you do to help yourself find or correct them more easily?

## Chapter Review: Misplaced and Dangling Modifiers

1. _____Modifiers_____ are words or word groups that describe or give more information about other words in a sentence.

2. A _misplaced modifier_ describes the wrong sentence element because it is incorrectly placed within the sentence.

3. When an opening modifier does not modify any word in the sentence, it is a _dangling modifier_ .

4. Edit both misplaced and dangling modifiers by making sure that
   a. the sentence element to be modified is _____*in*_____ the sentence.
   b. it is placed as _____*close*_____ as possible to the modifier.

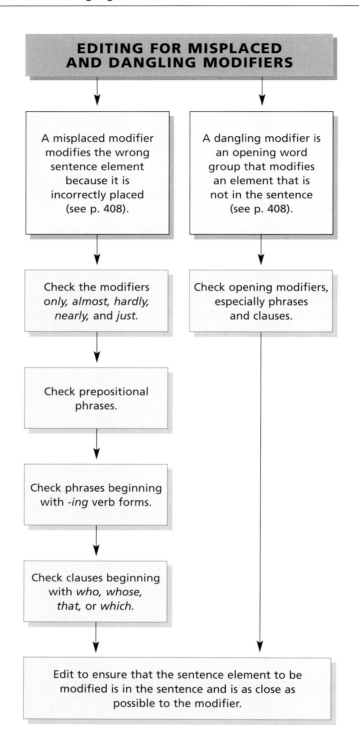

**EDITING FOR MISPLACED AND DANGLING MODIFIERS**

A misplaced modifier modifies the wrong sentence element because it is incorrectly placed (see p. 408).

A dangling modifier is an opening word group that modifies an element that is not in the sentence (see p. 408).

Check the modifiers *only, almost, hardly, nearly,* and *just.*

Check opening modifiers, especially phrases and clauses.

Check prepositional phrases.

Check phrases beginning with *-ing* verb forms.

Check clauses beginning with *who, whose, that,* or *which.*

Edit to ensure that the sentence element to be modified is in the sentence and is as close as possible to the modifier.

# 27

# Coordination and Subordination

## Joining Ideas

## Understand What Coordination and Subordination Are

If all of your sentences are short, they will seem choppy and hard to read. To vary the rhythm and flow of your writing, use coordination or subordination to join sentences that contain related ideas.

**Coordination** can be used to join two sentences when the ideas in them are equally important.

| | |
|---|---|
| **TWO SENTENCES** | The continent of Antarctica is unpopulated. Scientists are studying its habitability. |
| **JOINED THROUGH COORDINATION** | The continent of Antarctica is unpopulated, but scientists are studying its habitability. |

**Subordination** can be used to join two sentences when one idea is less important than the other. Adding a dependent word (such as *although*, *because*, *if*, or *that*) to one sentence shows that it is subordinate to, or less important than, the other.

| | |
|---|---|
| **TWO SENTENCES** | Mount Erebus in Antarctica is a volcano. It erupts periodically. |
| **JOINED THROUGH SUBORDINATION** | *Because* Mount Erebus in Antarctica is a volcano, it erupts periodically. |

[*Because* makes the first part of this sentence subordinate and puts more emphasis on the second part, the idea that Mount Erebus erupts.]

■ **LEARNING JOURNAL** Use your learning journal as a place to record short, choppy sentences that could be joined by coordination or subordination. Also write down edited versions of the sentences, once you have connected them.

■ **TIP** To understand this chapter, you need to be familiar with basic sentence elements. For a review, see Chapter 19.

■ **TIP** The word *subordinate* means "lower in rank" or "secondary." In the workplace, for example, you are subordinate to your boss. In the army, a private is subordinate to an officer.

■ **RESOURCES** *Additional Resources* contains tests and supplemental practice exercises for this chapter as well as a transparency master for the chart at the end.

■ **TIP** For more on the use of commas, see Chapter 34.

■ **TEACHING TIP** Emphasize that conjunctions are not interchangeable (*but* can't fill in for *so,* for example). Write two independent clauses on the board (*Tom was hungry/he had a sandwich*). Ask students which conjunctions would work. Ask how the sentence would have to change to use others.

# Practice Using Coordination and Subordination

## Coordination Using Coordinating Conjunctions

A **conjunction** is a word that joins words, phrases, or clauses. **Coordinating conjunctions** are the words *and, but, for, nor, or, so,* and *yet.* (You can remember them by thinking of FANBOYS—*for, and, nor, but, or, yet, so.*) They join ideas of equal importance. To join two sentences that have ideas of equal importance, put a comma and one of these conjunctions between the sentences. Choose the conjunction that makes the most sense for the meaning of the two sentences.

| Equal idea | , and<br>, but<br>, or<br>, nor<br>, so<br>, for<br>, yet | Equal idea |
|---|---|---|

Antarctica is huge          , and        it is 98 percent ice.
[*And* simply joins two ideas.]

It is beautiful         , but        it is very cold.
[*But* indicates a contrast.]

It is very dry        , for        it receives only as much rain as a desert.
[*For* indicates a reason or cause.]

The vegetation is not lush        , nor        is it leaf bearing.
[*Nor* indicates a negative.]

Perhaps people could live there        , or        it could be used for other purposes.
[*Or* indicates alternatives.]

Much remains to be learned        , so        scientists will continue to study the area.
[*So* indicates a result.]

It is a hard place to work        , yet        it may be a resource for the future.
[*Yet* indicates a possibility.]

■ **PRACTICE 1**   **JOINING IDEAS WITH COORDINATING CONJUNCTIONS**

In each of the following sentences, fill in the blank with an appropriate coordinating conjunction. There may be more than one correct answer for some sentences.

**EXAMPLE:** Companies want workers with diverse skills, _____*but*_____ parents may find that child-rearing experience does not always impress potential employers.

*Answers will vary.*

■ **TIP** For more practice with coordination and subordination, visit Exercise Central at <**bedfordstmartins.com/ realwriting**>. Also, the Writing Guide Software with this book has tutorials on this topic.

1. Parents who quit work to care for children may worry about making enough money, _____*or*_____ they may fear that small children will be hard to deal with all day long.

2. Those problems can cause people to think twice about leaving their jobs, _____*yet*_____ the real problem for many people may come when they want to go back to work.

3. Finding a job can be difficult in any circumstances, _____*so*_____ a job-seeker's résumé needs to be as impressive as possible.

4. Résumé experts say that every gap in employment should be explained, _____*for*_____ prospective employers want to know what a person did during that time.

5. Many parents fear that employers will see that they have spent a few years raising children, _____*and*_____ their résumés will go straight to the bottom of the pile.

6. Employers may not realize that parenting requires all kinds of skills, _____*so*_____ a person returning to work after raising young children must make employers see that the experience was valuable.

7. The wrong description can make child care sound like dull, unimaginative work, _____*but*_____ a good résumé can demonstrate how challenging and diverse the job of raising children can be.

8. Some parents who want to return to careers find ways to fill gaps on their résumés, _____*and*_____ others come up with ways to get around the problem of résumés altogether.

9. Skills that a worker had before leaving a career can be used in a new business, _____*so*_____ a person who starts a business does not have to worry about creating a perfect résumé.

10. Parents who leave careers have new challenges to consider,

_____*but*_____ they should be aware that further challenges will

await them when they decide to return to work.

**PRACTICE 2 COMBINING SENTENCES WITH COORDINATING CONJUNCTIONS**

Combine each pair of sentences into a single sentence by using a comma and a coordinating conjunction. To choose a coordinating conjunction, consider how the ideas in the two sentences are related to each other. In some cases, there may be more than one correct answer.

**EXAMPLE:** E-mail has become common in business communica-
                                         *, so people*
tion. People should mind their e-mail manners.

*Answers may vary. Possible edits shown.*

1. Many professionals use e-mail to keep in touch with clients and
                    *so business people*
contacts. They must be especially careful not to offend anyone with

their e-mail messages.

2. However, anyone who uses e-mail should be cautious. It is dangerously
                                                          *for it*

easy to send messages to unintended recipients.

3. Employees may have time to send personal messages from work. They
                                                                    *but they*

should remember that employers often have the ability to read their

workers' messages.

4. R-rated language and jokes may be deleted automatically by a com-
                    *or they*
pany's server. They may be read by managers and cause problems for

the employee sending or receiving them.

5. No message should be forwarded to everyone in a sender's address
                    *and senders*
book. Senders should ask permission before adding a recipient to a

mass-mailing list.

6. People should check the authenticity of mailings about lost children,
                                                                    *for most of*
dreadful diseases, and terrorist threats before passing them on. Most

such messages are hoaxes.

7. Typographical errors and misspellings in e-mail make the message
                                *yet using*
appear less professional. Using all capital letters—a process known as

*shouting*—is usually considered even worse.

8. Many people find attachments unwelcome. ~~They~~ *and they* are likely to be deleted unread if the recipient does not recognize the e-mail address of the sender.

9. Viruses are a major problem with attachments. ~~No~~ *but no* one wants to receive even a harmless attachment if it takes a long time to download.

10. People who use e-mail for business want to be taken seriously. ~~They~~ *so they* should make their e-mails as professional as possible.

## Coordination Using Semicolons

A **semicolon** is a punctuation mark that can join two sentences through coordination. When you use a semicolon, make sure that the ideas in the two sentences are not only of equal importance but also very closely related.

■ **TEACHING TIP** Remind students that a semicolon balances two independent clauses; what's on either side must be able to stand alone as a complete sentence.

| Equal idea | ; | Equal idea |
|---|---|---|
| Antarctica is a mystery | ; | no one knows too much about it. |
| Its climate is extreme | ; | few people want to endure it. |
| My cousin went there | ; | he loves to explore the unknown. |

A semicolon alone does not tell readers much about the relationship between the two ideas. To give more information about the relationship, use a semicolon followed by a word that indicates the relationship; such words are known as **conjunctive adverbs**. They must be followed by a comma.

■ **TIP** When you connect two sentences with a conjunctive adverb, the statement following the semicolon remains a complete thought. If you use a subordinating word such as *because*, however, the second statement becomes a dependent clause and a semicolon is not needed: *It receives little rain because it is incredibly cold.*

| Equal idea | ; also,<br>; as a result,<br>; besides,<br>; however,<br>; in addition,<br>; in fact,<br>; instead,<br>; still,<br>; then,<br>; therefore,<br>; yet, | Equal idea |
|---|---|---|
| Antarctica is largely unexplored | ; as a result, | it is unpopulated. |
| It receives little rain | ; also, | it is incredibly cold. |
| It is a huge area | ; therefore, | scientists are becoming more interested in it. |

■ PRACTICE 3    **JOINING IDEAS WITH SEMICOLONS**

Join each pair of sentences by using a semicolon alone.

**EXAMPLE:** Tanning booths can cause skin to age/; ~~They~~ may also
                                                    *they*

promote cancer.

1.  Exposure to the sun can cause both short-term and long-term side
                        *using*
    effects/; ~~Using~~ tanning booths has similar risks.

2.  Using a tanning booth does not mean that you will definitely harm
                    *what*
    yourself/; ~~What~~ it does mean is that you are taking a chance.

3.  It's easy to ignore long-term health dangers/; ~~The~~ desire to look good is
                                                *the*
    often of more immediate concern.

4.  Some people wear no clothes in a tanning booth/; ~~This~~ behavior can
                                                    *this*
    damage skin that is normally covered by a bathing suit.

5.  Ultraviolet light can injure the eyes/; ~~Tanning~~-salon patrons should
                                        *tanning*
    always wear protective goggles.

■ PRACTICE 4    **COMBINING SENTENCES WITH SEMICOLONS AND
CONNECTING WORDS (CONJUNCTIVE ADVERBS)**

Combine each pair of sentences by using a semicolon and a connecting
word. Choose a conjunctive adverb that makes sense for the relationship between the two ideas. In some cases, there may be more than one correct
answer. Consult the chart on page 419.

**EXAMPLE:** Seventy percent of mothers now work outside the home/;
                        *as a result, family*
                **Family** life in the United States has changed.

*Answers may vary. Possible edits shown.*
                                                        *then, the*
1. Only 40 percent of mothers worked outside the home in 1970/; ~~The~~

   American workforce changed.
                                                    *however, mothers*
2. Many families today need two incomes to survive/; ~~Mothers~~ often feel

   guilty about spending too little time with their children.

3. A new study shows that children of working parents don't necessarily
                        *in fact, they*
   feel neglected/; ~~They~~ think they get to spend enough time with their

   mothers and fathers.

4. Children whose parents work and children with a parent at home rate
   their parents about equally*/;*~~Children~~ *still, children* with working parents want their
   parents to be less tired.

5. Compared with earlier generations, parents today generally have fewer
   children*/;*~~Fathers~~ *in addition, fathers* today usually are more nurturing.

6. More Americans are working longer hours today*/;*~~They~~ *as a result, they* think their
   children want them to work less.

7. For most children, their parents' jobs are not the problem*/;*~~They~~ *however, they* want
   their time with their parents to be more relaxed.

8. Children think that their fathers should be more available*/;*~~Most~~ *yet, most*
   children think their dads are teaching them important values.

9. Most working parents try not to give up time with their families*/;*~~They~~ *instead, they*
   cut out personal time and hobbies.

10. A parent's relationship with a child is more important than the
    number of hours they spend together*/;*~~Parents~~ *therefore, parents* should try to find out
    what is going on in the lives of their children.

## Subordination Using Subordinating Conjunctions

As noted earlier, a **conjunction** is a word that joins words, phrases, or clauses. **Subordinating conjunctions** join two ideas when one idea is more important than the other or when one idea explains the other. The idea that has the subordinating conjunction in front of it becomes a subordinate clause or dependent clause; because of the subordinating conjunction, it no longer expresses a complete thought and cannot stand by itself as a sentence.

Choose the conjunction that makes the most sense with the two sentences. Here are some of the most common subordinating conjunctions.

| Main idea | | | Subordinate idea |
|---|---|---|---|
| | after | since | |
| | although | so that | |
| | as | unless | |
| | as if | until | |
| | because | when | |
| | before | where | |
| | even though | while | |
| | if | | |

■ **TEACHING TIP** Do the same kind of exercise with subordinating conjunctions as you did with coordinating conjunctions. Write two sentences on the board and have students suggest how the sentences would have to change to accommodate different subordinating conjunctions.

■ **ESL** Point out that unlike the conjunctive adverbs on page 419, these subordinating conjunctions are never used with a semicolon in front of them or a comma after.

| Scientists study the interior of Mount Erebus | because | it might provide clues about global warming. |
| It is difficult to study the interior | since | it is composed of boiling lava. |

When a subordinate idea ends a sentence, it usually does not need to be preceded by a comma unless it is showing a contrast.

You can also put a subordinating conjunction and subordinate idea at the beginning of a new sentence. When the subordinate idea comes first, use a comma to separate it from the rest of the sentence.

| Subordinating conjunction | Subordinate idea | , | Main idea |
|---|---|---|---|
| When | it erupts | , | Mount Erebus hurls lava bombs. |
| Because | it is dangerous | , | scientists are hesitant to go inside. |

---

**EDITING FOR COORDINATION AND SUBORDINATION:**
Joining Ideas through Subordination

↓

**FIND**

**It is hard to sleep in the city. It is always very noisy.**

1. **Ask:** What is the relationship between the two complete sentences? *The second sentence explains the cause of the first.*

2. **Ask:** What subordinating conjunctions express that relationship? *"Because," "as," or "since."*

↓

**EDIT**

*because it*
**It is hard to sleep in the city./ It is always very noisy.**

3. **Join the two sentences** with a subordinating conjunction that makes sense.

---

■ **PRACTICE 5    JOINING IDEAS THROUGH SUBORDINATION**

In the following sentences, fill in the blank with an appropriate subordinating conjunction. In some cases, there may be more than one correct choice.

If you need help, look back at the chart on page 422 that shows the correction steps.

**EXAMPLE:** _____*When*_____ the Treasury Department redesigned the twenty-dollar bill, many people thought that it looked like Monopoly money.

*Answers may vary. Possible answers shown.*

1. The Treasury Department decided to change the design of American paper money _____*because*_____ it was too easy for criminals to make copies of the old bills.

2. _____*Since*_____ security was the only reason for the change, the basic elements of each bill remain the same.

3. The portrait on each denomination shows the same person as the old bills did _____*so that*_____ the new money is somewhat familiar.

4. _____*Although*_____ the person in the portrait is the same, the portraits themselves are different.

5. _____*While*_____ discussing the security measures, Treasury Department officials considered changing the color of the bills.

6. The bills are printed on the same paper as they were before _____*because*_____ the feel of the paper tells most Americans immediately whether or not a bill is real.

7. _____*When*_____ you look closely at one of the new bills, you can see security fibers printed with the bill's denomination.

8. The paper also has a watermark that is invisible _____*unless*_____ you hold the bill up to the light.

9. The new bills do have simpler graphics _____*because*_____ the new security measures take up too much space to fit on the elaborate original design.

10. _____*After*_____ so many years of the old design, the new bills seem strange to many people.

---

> ### EDITING FOR COORDINATION AND SUBORDINATION:
> Joining Contrasting Ideas through Subordination

> **FIND**
>
> Revising your writing on a computer saves time. You can lose your work if you forget to save your document.
>
> 1. **Ask:** Which of the two sentences expresses the more important idea? *The second one.*
> 2. **Ask:** What subordinating conjunction expresses the relationship between the two ideas? *Although.*

> **EDIT**
>
> *although you*
> Revising your writing on a computer saves time./You can lose your work if you forget to save your document.
>
> 3. **Join the two sentences** with the subordinating conjunction that best expresses the relationship between the two ideas.

**PRACTICE 6    COMBINING SENTENCES THROUGH SUBORDINATION**

Combine each pair of sentences into a single sentence by using an appropriate subordinating conjunction either at the beginning of or between the two sentences. Use a conjunction that makes sense with the two sentences. In some cases, there may be more than one correct answer. If you need help, look back at the chart above.

*because composing*
**EXAMPLE:** Most business executives now type their own letters./

~~Composing~~ on computer is faster than writing by hand.

*Answers may vary. Possible edits shown.*

*when computers*
1. Almost all college students used typewriters until the 1980s./ ~~Computers~~

   became more affordable.

*after computers*
2. Typewriters were used less often./ ~~Computers~~ became more widespread.

*although there*
3. Computers offer many advantages./There are also some drawbacks.

*If you*                                                              *a*
4. ~~You~~ have not saved what you have written./A power outage could

   cause you to lose your work.

5. ~~Computers~~ *When computers* became widely used in the 1980s/, ~~Professors~~ *professors* were surprised to hear students say, "The computer ate my paper."

6. ~~You~~ *When you* have written a rough draft of a paper/, ~~You~~ *you* should print it out.

7. Some people like to print out a document to proofread it/ *because they* ~~They~~ fail to catch all their mistakes on the screen.

8. ~~The~~ *While the* quality of computer screens is getting better/, ~~People~~ *people* still complain about eyestrain.

9. ~~Spell-checking~~ *Even though spell-checking* programs prevent many errors/, ~~Only~~ *only* a person is able to recognize sound-alikes such as *their* and *there*.

10. Using a grammar-check program can also cause problems/ *if writers* ~~Writers~~ assume that the computer understands grammar rules and do not check their work themselves.

# Edit Paragraphs and Your Own Writing

### PRACTICE 7   EDITING PARAGRAPHS FOR COORDINATION AND SUBORDINATION

In the following paragraphs, join the underlined sentences by using either coordination or subordination. Do not forget to punctuate correctly. You may want to use the chart, Editing for Coordination and Subordination, on page 427. *Answers may vary. Possible edits shown.*

1. (1) Viewers of network television sometimes complain that the commercial breaks seem to get longer and longer. (2) <u>It is not just their imagination</u>/; (3) <u>~~Most~~ *most* network programs have been shortened by thirty seconds or more.</u> (4) The networks are not making these changes just to be annoying. (5) <u>The networks want more advertising to cover the rising costs of television shows</u>/; (6) <u>*even though the* ~~The~~ networks now demand $100,000 or more for a thirty-second commercial.</u> (7) Understandably, the creators of shows are unhappy with the changes. (8) <u>A half-hour show can now run only twenty-one minutes</u>/, (9) <u>*and an* ~~An~~ hour-long show lasts only about forty-four minutes.</u>

2. (1) *Although*
Herman Melville is now considered one of the greatest American writers/,(2) *his* His books were mostly forgotten at the time of his death in 1891. (3) His novel *Moby-Dick,* perhaps the most admired work in all of American literature, was viewed as nothing more than a curious adventure story that might hold the interest of teenage boys. (4) The book's more complex themes remained invisible/ (5) *until a* A new generation of literary critics rediscovered them in the 1920s.

(6) The Dutch painter Vincent van Gogh was another nineteenth-century artist unappreciated during his lifetime. (7) Buyers were not interested in his work/,(8) *and even* Even van Gogh himself thought much of it "ugly." (9) Sadly, the most inspired period in the artist's life ended with his suicide in July 1890. (10) He had moved to Arles, France, in February 1888/, *where he* (11) He created some of his most famous works, including the disturbingly powerful *Starry Night.*

(12) Great art is often far ahead of its time/, *so it* (13) It is frequently misunderstood. (14) Numerous writers and painters better known in their day than Melville or van Gogh have long since been forgotten. (15) These people gave the public what it wanted/, *but they* (16) They failed to create anything of lasting worth.

■ **LEARNING JOURNAL** How would you explain coordination and subordination to someone who had never heard of them?

■ **PRACTICE 8    EDITING YOUR OWN WRITING FOR COORDINATION AND SUBORDINATION**

As a final practice, edit a piece of your own writing for coordination and subordination. It can be a paper you are working on for this course, a paper you've already finished, a paper for another course, or a recent piece of writing from your work or everyday life. Record in your learning journal any choppy problem sentences you find, along with the edited versions of the sentences. You may want to use the chart on page 427.

# Chapter Review: Coordination and Subordination

1. ___*Coordination*___ and ___*subordination*___ can be used to join sentences with related ideas.

2. _____*Coordination*_____ can be used to join two sentences when the ideas in them are equally important.

3. Subordination can be used to join two sentences when one idea is
   *more important than the other or explains the other* _____.

4. What are two ways of joining sentences through coordination?
   *Use a comma and a coordinating conjunction.*
   *Use a semicolon alone or a semicolon and a conjunctive adverb.*

5. List five common coordinating conjunctions. *Answers will vary.*
   *Possible answers: for, and, nor, but, or*

6. List five common subordinating conjunction. *Answers will vary.*
   *Possible answers: although, because, since, if, unless*

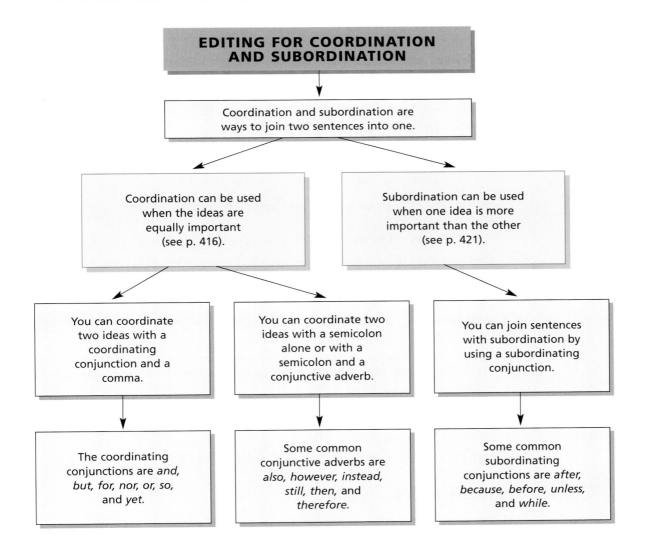

**EDITING FOR COORDINATION AND SUBORDINATION**

Coordination and subordination are ways to join two sentences into one.

Coordination can be used when the ideas are equally important (see p. 416).

Subordination can be used when one idea is more important than the other (see p. 421).

You can coordinate two ideas with a coordinating conjunction and a comma.

You can coordinate two ideas with a semicolon alone or with a semicolon and a conjunctive adverb.

You can join sentences with subordination by using a subordinating conjunction.

The coordinating conjunctions are *and, but, for, nor, or, so,* and *yet.*

Some common conjunctive adverbs are *also, however, instead, still, then,* and *therefore.*

Some common subordinating conjunctions are *after, because, before, unless,* and *while.*

# 28

# Parallelism

## *Balancing Ideas*

■ **LEARNING JOURNAL** Use your learning journal as a place to record sentences with problems in parallelism that you find in your writing. Also record edited versions of these sentences, with the problems corrected.

■ **TIP** To understand this chapter, you need to be familiar with basic sentence elements, such as nouns and verbs. For a review, see Chapter 19.

## Understand What Parallelism Is

**Parallelism** in writing means that similar parts in a sentence have the same structure: Their parts are comparable and balanced. Parallelism makes your writing flow smoothly and helps avoid misunderstandings. To create parallelism, use similar structures to express similar ideas. Put nouns with nouns, verbs with verbs, and phrases with phrases.

| | |
|---|---|
| **NOT PARALLEL** | I enjoy <u>basketball</u> more than <u>playing video games</u>. |

[*Basketball* is a noun, but *playing video games* is a phrase.]

| | |
|---|---|
| **PARALLEL** | I enjoy <u>basketball</u> more than <u>video games</u>. |

| | |
|---|---|
| **NOT PARALLEL** | On our anniversary, we <u>ate</u>, <u>danced</u>, and <u>were singing</u>. |

[Verbs must be in the same tense to be parallel.]

| | |
|---|---|
| **PARALLEL** | On our anniversary, we <u>ate</u>, <u>danced</u>, and <u>sang</u>. |

| | |
|---|---|
| **NOT PARALLEL** | This weekend we can go <u>to the beach</u> or <u>walking in the mountains</u>. |

[*To the beach* and *walking in the mountains* are both phrases, but they have different forms. *To the beach* should be paired with another prepositional phrase: *to the mountains.*]

| | |
|---|---|
| **PARALLEL** | This weekend we can go <u>to the beach</u> or <u>to the mountains</u>. |

## Practice Writing Parallel Sentences

■ **ESL** Refer ESL students to Chapter 30. Many of the parallel constructions depend on using infinitives and idioms correctly.

### Parallelism in Pairs and Lists

When you present two or more items in a series joined by the words *and* or *or,* use a similar form for each item.

**428**

| NOT PARALLEL | The criminal conspiracy involved <u>an accountant</u>, and <u>an assistant from the mayor's office was also part of it.</u> |
| PARALLEL | The criminal conspiracy involved <u>an accountant</u> and <u>an assistant from the mayor's office.</u> |
| NOT PARALLEL | The story was <u>in the newspaper</u>, <u>on the radio</u>, and <u>the television.</u> |
| PARALLEL | The story was <u>in the newspaper</u>, <u>on the radio</u>, and <u>on the television.</u> |

■ **TEACHING TIP** Help students see that the problem with parallelism in this sentence is that the preposition *on* has been left out of the last phrase.

## PRACTICE 1   USING PARALLELISM IN PAIRS AND LISTS

In each sentence, underline the <u>parts of the sentence that should be parallel.</u> Then edit the sentence to make it parallel.

■ **TIP** For more practice with making sentences parallel, visit Exercise Central at <bedfordstmartins.com/ realwriting>. Also, the Writing Guide Software with this book has tutorials on this topic.

> **EXAMPLE:** Coyotes now roam the <u>western mountains</u>, the <u>central</u>
> *suburbs*
> plains, and <u>t̶h̶e̶y̶ ̶a̶r̶e̶ ̶i̶n̶ the suburbs of</u> the East Coast of
> ^
> t̶h̶e̶ ̶U̶n̶i̶t̶e̶d̶ ̶S̶t̶a̶t̶e̶s̶.

■ **RESOURCES** *Additional Resources* contains tests and supplemental practice exercises for this chapter as well as a transparency master for the chart at the end.

*Answers may vary. Possible edits shown.*

1. Wild predators, such as wolves, are vanishing because people <u>hunt</u>
   *take*
   them and <u>a̶r̶e̶ ̶t̶a̶k̶i̶n̶g̶</u> over their land.
   ^

2. Coyotes are <u>surviving</u> and <u>*doing* t̶h̶e̶y̶ ̶d̶o̶</u> well in the modern United States.
   ^

3. The success of the coyote is due to its <u>varied diet</u> and <u>*adaptability* a̶d̶a̶p̶t̶i̶n̶g̶ ̶e̶a̶s̶i̶l̶y̶</u>.
   ^

4. Coyotes are sometimes <u>vegetarians</u>, sometimes <u>scavengers</u>, and some-
   *hunters*
   times <u>t̶h̶e̶y̶ ̶h̶u̶n̶t̶</u>.
   ^

5. Today, they are <u>spreading</u> and <u>*populating* p̶o̶p̶u̶l̶a̶t̶e̶</u> the East Coast for the first
   ^
   time.

6. The coyotes' new range <u>surprises</u> and <u>*worries* i̶s̶ ̶w̶o̶r̶r̶y̶i̶n̶g̶</u> many people.
   ^

7. The animals have chosen an area <u>*more populated and less wild than* t̶h̶a̶t̶ ̶i̶s̶ ̶m̶o̶r̶e̶ ̶p̶o̶p̶u̶l̶a̶t̶e̶d̶ ̶a̶n̶d̶ ̶i̶t̶'̶s̶ ̶n̶o̶t̶</u>
   ^
   <u>a̶s̶ ̶w̶i̶l̶d̶ ̶a̶s̶</u> their traditional home.

8. Coyotes can adapt to <u>rural</u>, o̶r̶ <u>suburban</u>, or <u>*urban life.* e̶v̶e̶n̶ ̶l̶i̶v̶i̶n̶g̶ ̶i̶n̶ ̶a̶ ̶c̶i̶t̶y̶.</u>
   ^

9. One coyote was <u>identified</u>, <u>tracked</u>, and <u>t̶h̶e̶y̶ captured h̶i̶m̶</u> in Central
   Park in New York City.

10. Suburbanites are getting used to the <u>sight</u> of coyotes.<u>*and sound* a̶n̶d̶ ̶h̶e̶a̶r̶i̶n̶g̶</u>
    ^            ^
    t̶h̶e̶m̶.

## Parallelism in Comparisons

In comparisons, the items being compared should have parallel structures. Comparisons often use the words *than* or *as*. When you edit for parallelism, check to make sure that the items on either side of those words (the things being compared) are parallel.

| | |
|---|---|
| **NOT PARALLEL** | Driving downtown is as fast as the bus. |
| **PARALLEL** | Driving downtown is as fast as taking the bus. |
| | |
| **NOT PARALLEL** | To admit a mistake is better than denying it. |
| **PARALLEL** | To admit a mistake is better than to deny it. |
| | Admitting a mistake is better than denying it. |

Sometimes in order to make the parts of a sentence parallel, you may need to add or drop a word or two.

| | |
|---|---|
| **NOT PARALLEL** | A tour package is less expensive than arranging every travel detail yourself. |
| **PARALLEL, WORD ADDED** | *Buying* a tour package is less expensive than arranging every travel detail yourself. |
| | |
| **NOT PARALLEL** | The sale price of the shoes is as low as paying the regular price for two pairs. |
| **PARALLEL, WORDS DROPPED** | The sale price of the shoes is as low as the regular price for two pairs. |

### PRACTICE 2   USING PARALLELISM IN COMPARISONS

In each sentence, underline the parts of the sentence that should be parallel. Then edit the sentence to make it parallel.

EXAMPLE: Leasing a new car may be less expensive than ~~to buy~~ *buying* one.

*Answers may vary. Possible edits shown.*

1. Car dealers often require less money down for leasing a car than for *purchasing* ~~the purchase of~~ one.

2. The monthly payments for a leased car may be as low as ~~paying for a loan~~ *loan payments*.

3. You should check the terms of leasing to make sure they are as favorable as ~~to buy~~ *the terms of buying*.

4. You may find that ~~to lease~~ *leasing* is a safer bet than <u>buying</u>.

5. You will be making less of a financial commitment <u>by leasing</u> a car than ~~to own~~ *by owning* it.

6. <u>Buying</u> a car may be better than ~~a lease on~~ *leasing* one if you plan to keep it for several years.

7. A <u>used car</u> can be more economical than <u>getting a new one</u>.

8. However, ~~maintenance of~~ *maintaining* a new car may be easier than <u>taking care of</u> a used car.

9. A <u>used car</u> may not be as impressive as ~~buying~~ a <u>brand-new vehicle</u>.

10. <u>To get a used car</u> from a reputable source can be a better decision than ~~a~~ *to buy* <u>new vehicle</u> that loses value the moment you drive it home.

## Parallelism with Certain Paired Words

When a sentence uses certain paired words, called **correlative conjunctions**, the items joined by them must be parallel. These words link two equal elements and show the relationship between them. Here are the paired words:

■ **COMPUTER** Students can use the find or search function to locate the first word in correlative conjunctions. They should read the sentences with those constructions carefully to make sure the second word is present and that parallel structure is used.

| | | |
|---|---|---|
| both . . . and | neither . . . nor | rather . . . than |
| either . . . or | not only . . . but also | |

When you use the first part of a pair, be sure you always use the second part as well.

**NOT PARALLEL**     Bruce wants *both* <u>to be rich</u> *and* <u>freedom</u>.

[*Both* is used with *and,* but the items joined by them are not parallel.]

**PARALLEL**     Bruce wants *both* <u>to be rich</u> *and* <u>to be free</u>.

**NOT PARALLEL**     He can *neither* <u>fail the course</u> and <u>quitting his job</u> is also impossible.

**PARALLEL**     He can *neither* <u>fail the course</u> *nor* <u>quit his job</u>.

■ **PRACTICE 3**     **USING PARALLELISM WITH CERTAIN PAIRED WORDS**

In each sentence, circle the (paired words) and underline the <u>parts of the sentence that should be parallel</u>. Then edit the sentence to make it parallel. You may need to change one of the paired elements to make the sentence parallel.

**EXAMPLE:** A cellular telephone can be (either) a lifesaver (or) ~~it can be~~
*an annoyance*
**annoying**.
      ^
*Answers may vary. Possible edits shown.*

1. Fifteen years ago, most people (neither) had cellular telephones (nor)
   *wanted*
   ~~did they want~~ them.
        ^

2. Today, cell phones are (not only) carried by businesspeople and taxi
   drivers (but also) ~~are found~~ in the hands of teenagers.

3. Cell phones are not universally popular: Some commuters would
                                                  *be*
   (rather) ban cell phones on buses and trains (than) ~~being~~ forced to listen
                                                            ^
   to other people's conversations.

                                                      *convenient*
4. No one denies that a cell phone can be (both) useful (and) ~~convenience~~
                                                                   ^
   ~~is a factor~~.

5. A motorist stranded on a deserted road would probably (rather) have a
                                    *be forced*
   cell phone (than) ~~to walk~~ to the nearest gas station.
                         ^

6. When cell phones were first introduced, some people feared that they
   (either) caused brain tumors (or) ~~they~~ were a dangerous source of electro-
   magnetic radiation.

7. Most Americans today (neither) worry about radiation from cell phones
                        *fear*
   (nor) ~~other~~ injuries.
            ^

8. The biggest risk associated with cell phones, many people feel, is (either)
                                                    *that people get*
   that drivers are distracted by them (or) ~~people getting~~ angry at someone
                                                    ^
   talking too loudly in public on a cell phone.

9. While scientists have determined that cell phones probably do not
   cause brain tumors, some experiments on human cells have shown
   that energy from cellular phones may (both) affect people's reflexes (and)
   ~~it might~~ alter the brain's blood vessels.

10. Some scientists think that these experiments show that cell-phone use
                                                          *also mental ones*
    might have (not only) physical effects on human beings (but ~~it also~~) could
                                                                      ^
    ~~influence mental processes~~.

◼ **PRACTICE 4   COMPLETING SENTENCES WITH PAIRED WORDS**

For each sentence, complete the correlative conjunction and add more information. Make sure that the structures on both sides of the correlative conjunction are parallel.

**EXAMPLE:** I am both impressed by your company *and enthusiastic to*

*work for you* .

*Answers will vary. Possible answers shown.*

1. I could bring to this job not only youthful enthusiasm *but also relevant*

*experience* .

2. I am willing to work either in your Chicago *or in your San Francisco*

*office* .

3. My current job neither encourages creativity *nor allows flexibility*

.

4. I would rather work in a difficult job *than work in an unchallenging job*

.

5. In college I learned a lot both from my classes *and from other students*

.

# Edit Paragraphs and Your Own Writing

◼ **PRACTICE 5   EDITING PARAGRAPHS FOR PARALLELISM**

Find and correct any problems with parallelism in the following paragraphs. You may want to refer to the chart, Editing for Parallelism, on page 435.
*Answers will vary. Possible edits shown.*

1. (1) Karaoke started about twenty years ago in Japan, found many fans in that country, and ~~it~~ became a popular form of entertainment around the world. (2) The word *karaoke* combines part of the word *kara*, meaning "empty," with part of the word *okesutura,* ~~which means~~ *meaning* "orchestra." (3) A karaoke recording of a song contains the music without vocals, and karaoke performers sing the lyrics. (4) In Japan, where houses are small, close together, and ~~they are~~ not soundproofed, people travel to special karaoke rooms to sing. (5) Karaoke rooms allow

◼ **TEAMWORK** Have students form small groups. Then have each group write five sentences that are not parallel. Each group should then exchange sentences with another group and correct the other group's sentences.

customers to sing, relax, and ~~they can~~ enjoy being the center of attention for a little while. (6) Many Westerners are surprised to learn that most Japanese are neither reluctant nor ~~do they find it~~ *embarrassed* ~~embarrassing~~ to sing in public. (7) Japanese karaoke singers know that they can entertain either by singing well or *by singing* ~~they can sing~~ badly. (8) To them, *entertaining* ~~to entertain~~ is more important than showing off a beautiful voice.

2. (1) As a young man, Sigmund Freud, the founder of psycho-analysis, was determined to use the methods of science to unlock the secrets of human behavior. (2) But as biographer Peter Gay explains, the effort was slow, time-consuming, and ~~that it was~~ often discouraging. (3) A medical doctor by training, in the 1890s Freud began studying and *documenting* ~~to document~~ causes of hysteria, and he discovered that many of his female patients had been sexually abused by their fathers. (4) Through this discovery, Freud came to understand how traumatic events from childhood that are ignored or *forgotten* ~~one forgets them~~ can cause emotional problems later.

(5) To test his theories, Freud analyzed himself. (6) Studying his own violent and erotic impulses was frightening and *disturbing* ~~disturbed him~~. (7) But it was deeply rewarding as well, not only to Freud as a scientist but also *to* Freud as an individual. (8) His own neurotic symptoms gradu-ally disappeared. (9) Soon he published his most famous book, *The Interpretation of Dreams*. (10) Here he describes how even in sleep the subconscious mind often distorts and *disguises* ~~is disguising~~ forbidden wishes so that they become unrecognizable. (11) A dream takes on meaning only when understood symbolically—"interpreted" through the methods of psychoanalysis.

■ **PRACTICE 6    EDITING YOUR OWN WRITING FOR PARALLELISM**

■ **LEARNING JOURNAL** How would you explain parallelism to someone who had never heard of it? How would you ex-plain how to edit for it?

As a final practice, edit a piece of your own writing for parallelism. It can be a paper you are working on for this course, a paper you've already finished, a paper for another course, or a recent piece of writing from your work or everyday life. Record in your learning journal any problem sentences you find, along with their corrections. You may want to use the chart on page 435.

# Chapter Review: Parallelism

1. Parallelism in writing means that *similar parts in a sentence are comparable and balanced*.

2. In what three situations do problems with parallelism most often occur?
   *with pairs and lists, with comparisons, and with certain paired words*

3. What are three pairs of correlative conjunctions? *Answers will vary.*
   *Possible answers: both/and, neither/nor, rather/than*

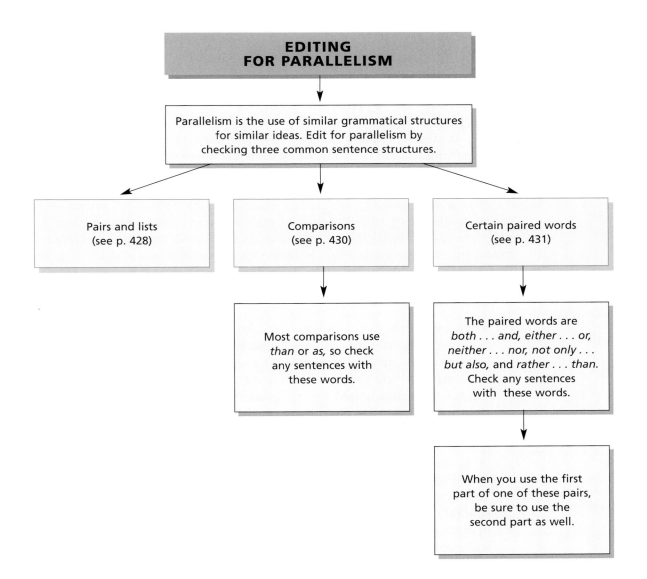

**EDITING FOR PARALLELISM**

Parallelism is the use of similar grammatical structures for similar ideas. Edit for parallelism by checking three common sentence structures.

Pairs and lists
(see p. 428)

Comparisons
(see p. 430)

Certain paired words
(see p. 431)

Most comparisons use *than* or *as,* so check any sentences with these words.

The paired words are *both . . . and, either . . . or, neither . . . nor, not only . . . but also,* and *rather . . . than.* Check any sentences with these words.

When you use the first part of one of these pairs, be sure to use the second part as well.

# 29

# Sentence Variety

*Putting Rhythm in Your Writing*

■ **LEARNING JOURNAL**
Use your learning journal as a place to record an example of a brief passage with short, similar-sounding sentences. Also record an edited version after you have introduced sentence variety.

## Understand What Sentence Variety Is

Having **sentence variety** in your writing means using assorted sentence patterns, lengths, and rhythms. Most of us like variety: We don't want to eat the same dinner every night, or own ten shirts of the same style and color, or listen to the same song ten times in a row.

If your sentences all have the same pattern and are the same length, your readers will quickly tire of them and may not keep reading long enough to understand your point. Many writers use too many short, simple sentences, mistakenly thinking that short is always easier to understand than long. In fact, that is not true, as you can see in these examples.

### WITH SHORT, SIMPLE SENTENCES

Many people do not realize how important their speaking voice is. This is particularly true in a job interview. What you say is important. How you say it is nearly as important. The way you say it is what creates the impression of you that the interviewer forms. Mumbling while slouching is a particularly bad way of speaking. It makes the speaker appear sloppy and lacking in confidence. It also makes it difficult for the interviewer to hear. Talking too fast is another bad speech behavior. The speaker runs his or her ideas together. The interviewer can't follow them or distinguish what's important. A third common bad speech behavior concerns what are called verbal "tics." Verbal tics are things like saying "um" or "like" or "you know" all the time. Practice for an interview. Sit straight. Look the person to whom you're speaking directly in the eye. Speak up. Slow down. One good way to find out how you sound is to leave yourself a voice-mail message. If you sound bad to yourself, you need practice speaking aloud. Don't let poor speech behavior interfere with creating a good impression.

**WITH SENTENCE VARIETY**

Many people do not realize how important their speaking voice is, particularly in a job interview. What you say is important, but how you say it is nearly as important because that is what creates the impression of you that the interviewer forms. Mumbling while slouching is a particularly bad way of speaking. Not only does this make the speaker appear sloppy and lacking in confidence, but it also makes it difficult for the interviewer to hear. Talking too fast is another bad speech behavior. The speaker runs his or her ideas together, and the interviewer can't follow them or distinguish what's important. A third common bad speech behavior concerns what are called verbal "tics," things like saying "um" or "like" or "you know" all the time. When you practice for an interview, sit straight, look the person to whom you're speaking directly in the eye, speak up, and slow down. One good way to find out how you sound is to leave yourself a voice-mail message. If you sound bad to yourself, you need practice speaking aloud. Don't let poor speech behavior interfere with creating a good impression.

Good writing results when you mix long and short sentences and use a variety of patterns. Sentence variety is what gives your writing good rhythm and flow.

■ **COMPUTER** Students can get a visual measure of the length of their sentences by inserting two returns after every period in a paragraph. (They can search for periods to do this.)

## Practice Creating Sentence Variety

To create sentence variety, you need to edit your writing so that it has sentences of different types and lengths. Most writers tend to write short sentences that start with the subject, so this chapter will focus on techniques for starting with something other than the subject and for writing a variety of longer sentences. Two additional techniques for achieving sentence variety—coordination and subordination—are covered in Chapter 27.

Remember that the goal is to use variety to achieve a good rhythm. Do not simply change all your sentences from one pattern to another pattern, or you still won't have variety: You'll have just another set of similar-sounding sentences. Also, when you are changing the patterns of your sentences, check to make sure that your revised sentences are correct.

■ **RESOURCES** *Additional Resources* contains tests and supplemental practice exercises for this chapter as well as a transparency master for the chart at the end.

### Start Some Sentences with Adverbs

**Adverbs** are words that modify or describe verbs, adjectives, or other adverbs; they often end with -*ly*. As long as the meaning is clear, adverbs can be placed at the beginning of a sentence instead of in the middle. Adverbs at the beginning of a sentence are usually followed by a comma. If an adverb indicates time, such as *often* or *always*, a comma may not be needed. However, always use a comma if the reader should pause slightly after reading the adverb.

■ **TIP** For more about adverbs, see Chapter 25.

| ADVERB IN MIDDLE | Stories about haunted houses *frequently* surface at Halloween. |
| ADVERB AT BEGINNING | *Frequently,* stories about haunted houses surface at Halloween. |
| ADVERB IN MIDDLE | These stories *often* focus on ship captains lost at sea. |
| ADVERB AT BEGINNING | *Often* these stories focus on ship captains lost at sea. |

■ **TIP** For more practice with sentence variety, visit Exercise Central at <**bedfordstmartins .com/realwriting**>. Also, the Writing Guide Software with this book has tutorials on this topic.

■ **PRACTICE 1   STARTING SENTENCES WITH AN ADVERB**

Edit each sentence so it begins with an adverb.

**EXAMPLE:** *Unfortunately, rabies* Rabies ~~unfortunately~~ remains a problem in the United States.

1. *Once, rabies* ~~Rabies once~~ was a major threat to domestic pets in this country.

2. *Now, the* ~~The~~ disease is ~~now~~ most deadly to wildlife such as raccoons, skunks, and bats.

3. *Frequently, people* ~~People frequently~~ fail to have their pets vaccinated against rabies.

4. *Mistakenly, they believe* ~~They believe mistakenly~~ that their dogs and cats are no longer in danger.

5. *Worriedly, veterinarians note* ~~Veterinarians note worriedly~~ that wildlife can infect pets and people with rabies.

■ **PRACTICE 2   STARTING SENTENCES WITH AN ADVERB**

In each sentence, fill in the blank with an adverb that makes sense. Add a comma when necessary. There may be several good choices for each item. In the example sentence, other adverbs that would have been good choices are *fortunately, eventually,* and *perhaps,* as well as many others.

**EXAMPLE:** ____*Luckily,*____ a new method of vaccination may help reduce the amount of rabies in some wild animals.

*Answers will vary.*

1. ____*Recently,*____ an oral vaccine that prevents rabies in raccoons and skunks has been developed.

2. _____*Often,*_____ the vaccine can be placed in bait that the animals like to eat.

3. _____*Thankfully,*_____ this method of vaccination has stopped the spread of rabies in coyotes in southern Texas.

4. _____*Additionally,*_____ it has saved humans' and pets' lives, public health officials agree.

5. _____*Unfortunately,*_____ the problem of rabies in bats has not yet been solved.

---

■ **PRACTICE 3** **WRITING SENTENCES THAT START WITH AN ADVERB**

Write three sentences that start with an adverb. Use commas as necessary. Choose among the following adverbs: *often, sadly, amazingly, luckily, lovingly, aggressively, gently, frequently, stupidly.*

1. _*Answers will vary.*_____

2. _____

3. _____

## Join Ideas Using an *-ing* Verb Form

One way to combine sentences is to use an **-ing verb form** (the form of a verb that ends in -*ing*) to make one of the sentences into a phrase.

The *-ing* verb form indicates that the two parts of the sentence are happening at the same time. When you use an *-ing* verb form to combine two sentences, the more important idea (the one you want to emphasize) should be in the main clause, not in the phrase you make by adding the *-ing* verb form.

■ **TEACHING TIP** Explain to students that in their own writing they will need to consider the context when deciding which sentence contains the more important idea.

| | |
|---|---|
| **TWO SENTENCES** | A pecan roll from our bakery is not dietetic. It contains eight hundred calories. |
| **JOINED WITH -*ING* VERB FORM** | *Containing* eight hundred calories, a pecan roll from our bakery is not dietetic. |

To combine sentences this way, add *-ing* to the verb in one of the sentences and delete the subject. You now have a modifier phrase that can be added to the beginning or the end of the other sentence, depending on what makes the most sense.

The fat content is also high. ~~It equals~~ *equaling* the fat in a huge country breakfast.

■ **ESL** Remind students that an *-ing* verb form that modifies the subject cannot be the main verb in the sentence.

If you add a phrase starting with an *-ing* verb form to the beginning of a sentence, put a comma after it. If you add the phrase to the end of a sentence, you will usually need to put a comma before it, as in the preceding example, unless the phrase is essential to the meaning of the sentence.

If you put a phrase starting with an *-ing* verb form at the beginning of a sentence, be sure the word that the phrase modifies follows immediately. Otherwise, you will create a dangling modifier.

■ **TIP** For more on finding and correcting dangling modifiers, see Chapter 26, and for more on joining ideas, see Chapter 27.

| | |
|---|---|
| **TWO SENTENCES** | I ran through the rain. My raincoat got all wet. |
| **DANGLING MODIFIER** | Running through the rain, my raincoat got all wet. |
| **EDITED** | Running through the rain, I got my raincoat all wet. |

## EDITING FOR SENTENCE VARIETY:
### Combining Sentences Using an *-ing* Verb Form

**FIND**

The police officer called for back-up. She hoped she wasn't too late.

1. **Underline** the subject and **double-underline** the verb in each sentence.
2. **Ask:** Are the actions in both sentences happening at the same time? *Yes.*
3. **Ask:** Which sentence expresses the more important idea (the one you want to emphasize)? *The first one.*
4. **Circle** the sentence that *does not* express the more important thought.
5. **Cross out** the subject of that sentence.

**EDIT**

*hoping*
The police officer called for back-up, She hoped she wasn't too late.

6. **Combine the two sentences** by turning the verb for that subject into an *-ing* verb.

■ PRACTICE 4  **JOINING IDEAS USING AN *-ING* VERB FORM**

Combine each pair of sentences into a single sentence by using an *-ing* verb form. Add or delete words as necessary. If you need help, look back at the chart above that shows the correction steps.

**EXAMPLE:** Some people read faces extremely accurately, ~~They~~ *interpreting*
⌃
interpret nonverbal cues that other people miss.

*Answers may vary. Possible edits shown.*

*Testing*
1. ~~A recent study tested~~ children's abilities to interpret facial expressions,
⌃ *a recent*
~~The~~ study made headlines.
⌃

*Participating in the study, physically*
2. ~~Physically~~ abused children ~~participated in the study.~~ ~~They~~ saw photo-
⌃
graphs of faces changing from one expression to another.

3. The children told researchers what emotion was most obvious in each
*choosing*
face, ~~The children chose~~ among fear, anger, sadness, happiness, and
⌃
other emotions.

*serving*
4. Nonabused children also looked at the faces, ~~They served~~ as a control
⌃
group for comparison with the other children.

5. All of the children in the study were equally good at identifying most
*responding*
emotions, ~~They all responded~~ similarly to happiness or fear.
⌃

6. Battered children were especially sensitive to one emotion on the faces,
*identifying*
~~These children identified~~ anger much more quickly than the other
⌃
children could.

*Having*                                                      *the abused children*
7. ~~The abused children have~~ learned to look for anger, ~~They~~ protect
⌃                                                             ⌃
themselves with this early-warning system.

8. Their sensitivity to anger may not help the abused children later in
*perhaps hurting*
life, ~~It perhaps hurts~~ them socially.
⌃

*Tending*                                                 *abused children*
9. ~~The abused children tend~~ to run from anger they observe, ~~They~~ have
⌃                                         ⌃
difficulty connecting with teachers or friends who exhibit anger.

*often hanging*
10. The human brain works hard to acquire useful information, ~~It often~~
⌃
~~hangs~~ onto the information after its usefulness has passed.


> **PRACTICE 5    JOINING IDEAS USING AN -*ING* VERB FORM**

Fill in the blank in each sentence with an appropriate -*ing* verb form. There
are many possible ways to complete each sentence.

**EXAMPLE:** _Approaching_ the plate, Hernandez eyed the pitcher calmly.

_Answers will vary._

1. The pitcher stepped off the mound, _delaying_ his first pitch.

2. _Clutching_ his bat, Hernandez waited.

3. _Striding_ back onto the mound, the pitcher released his devastating fastball.

4. Hernandez swung too late, _missing_ the ball.

5. "Strike," called the umpire, _pointing_ his finger sharply.

■ **PRACTICE 6   JOINING IDEAS USING AN _-ING_ VERB FORM**

Write two sets of sentences and join them using an _-ing_ verb form. To help you complete this practice, look back at the chart on page 440.

**EXAMPLE:**   a. _Carol looked up._

b. _She saw three falling stars in the sky._

**COMBINED:**   _Looking up, Carol saw three falling stars in the sky._

1.  a. _Answers will vary._

b. _____

**COMBINED:** _____

2.  a. _____

b. _____

**COMBINED:** _____

## Join Ideas Using an _-ed_ Verb Form

■ **TIP** For more on helping verbs, see Chapters 19 and 23.

Another way to combine sentences is to use an **_-ed_ verb form** (the form of a verb that ends in _-ed_) to make one of the sentences into a phrase. You can join sentences this way if one of them has a form of _be_ as a helping verb along with the _-ed_ verb form.

**TWO SENTENCES**   Leonardo da Vinci was a man of many talents. He was noted for his painting.

**JOINED WITH _-ED_ VERB FORM**   _Noted_ for his painting, Leonardo da Vinci was a man of many talents.

To combine sentences this way, drop the subject and the helping verb from the sentence that has an *-ed* verb form. You now have a modifier phrase that can be added to the beginning or the end of the other sentence, depending on what makes the most sense.

*Interested*        *Leonardo*

~~Leonardo was interested~~ in many areas~~.~~ ^, ^~~He~~ investigated problems of

geology, botany, mechanics, and hydraulics.

If you add a phrase that begins with an *-ed* verb form to the beginning of a sentence, put a comma after it. If you add the phrase to the end of the sentence, you will usually need to put a comma before it unless the meaning of the sentence would change without the phrase.

If you put a phrase starting with an *-ed* verb form at the beginning of a sentence, be sure the word that the phrase modifies follows immediately. Otherwise, you will create a dangling modifier. Sometimes, as in the preceding example, you will need to change the word that the phrase modifies from a pronoun to a noun.

## EDITING FOR SENTENCE VARIETY:
### Combining Sentences Using an *-ed* Verb Form

### FIND

Champion <u>cyclists</u> <u>can travel</u> at high speeds over long periods.

~~They~~ (are) <u>noted</u> for their endurance.

1. **Underline** the subject, and **double-underline** the verb in each sentence.
2. **Circle** any (form of the verb *be*) that is a helping verb paired with an *-ed* verb form.
3. **Cross out** the ~~helping verb~~ and the ~~subject~~ of that sentence.

### EDIT

*Noted for their endurance, champion*

~~Champion~~ cyclists can travel at high speeds over long periods.
^

~~They are noted for their endurance.~~

*, noted for their endurance,*

Champion cyclists ^ can travel at high speeds. ~~They are noted~~

~~for their endurance.~~

4. **Attach the remaining phrase** to the other sentence either by moving it to the beginning of the sentence and adding a comma *or* by moving it directly after the word it describes.

■ **PRACTICE 7   JOINING IDEAS USING AN -ED VERB FORM**

Combine each pair of sentences into a single sentence by using an -ed verb form. If you need help, look back at the chart on page 443 that shows the correction steps.

> *Forced*
**EXAMPLE:** The oil company was forced to take the local women's
>                  ^
>                                      *the oil*
> objections seriously. The company had to close for ten
>                                    ^
> days during their protest.

*Answers may vary. Possible edits shown.*

*Angered by British colonial rule in 1929, the*
1. The women of southern Nigeria were angered by British colonial rule
   ^
   in 1929. They organized a protest.

*Covered with pipelines and oil wells,*
2. Nigeria is now one of the top ten oil-producing countries. The nation
   ^
   is covered with pipelines and oil wells.

*Pumped*                                                              *the*
3. The oil is pumped by American and other foreign oil companies. The
   ^                                                              ^
   oil often ends up in wealthy western economies.

*Squandered by corrupt rulers in many cases, the*
4. The money from the oil seldom reaches Nigeria's local people. The
   ^
   cash is squandered by corrupt rulers in many cases.

*Polluted*                                          *the Nigerian countryside*
5. The Nigerian countryside is polluted by the oil industry. The land
   ^                                                        ^
   then becomes less profitable for local villagers.

*Insulted*
6. Many Nigerians are insulted by the way the oil industry treats them.
   ^*many Nigerians*
   They want the oil companies to pay attention to their problems.
   ^

*Inspired*
7. Local Nigerian women were inspired by the 1929 women's protests.
   ^ *local Nigerian women*
   They launched a series of protests against the oil industry in the
   ^
   summer of 2002.

8. The women prevented workers from entering or leaving two oil company offices. The offices were located in the port of Warri.

*Concerned*
9. Workers at the oil company were concerned about the women's threat
   ^              *many workers at the oil company*
   to take their clothes off. Many workers told company officials that
                            ^
   such a protest would bring a curse on the company and shame to its
   employees.

10. The company eventually agreed to hire more local people and to invest in local projects, ~~The projects are~~ intended to supply electricity and provide the villagers with a market for fish and poultry.

---

■ **PRACTICE 8   JOINING IDEAS USING AN *-ED* VERB FORM**

Fill in the blank in each sentence with an appropriate *-ed* verb form. There are several possible ways to complete each sentence.

**EXAMPLE:** ____*Trusted*____ by people around the world for centuries, herbs can be powerful medical tools.

*Answers will vary.*

1. Common American plants are made into medicine, such as St. John's wort, ____*used*____ as an antidepressant.

2. ____*Manufactured*____ in laboratories, popular herbs are widely available in capsule form.

3. ____*Regarded*____ as "natural" medicines, herbs are often believed to be harmless.

4. ____*Uninformed*____ about the effects of herbal medicines, some people take them without understanding possible consequences.

5. Some herbs may interact badly with other drugs ____*prescribed*____ by a doctor.

---

■ **PRACTICE 9   JOINING IDEAS USING AN *-ED* VERB FORM**

Write two sets of sentences and join them using an *-ed* verb form. If you need help, look back at the chart on page 443.

**EXAMPLE:**   a. *Chris is taking intermediate accounting.*

b. *It is believed to be the most difficult course in the major.*

**COMBINED:**   *Chris is taking intermediate accounting, believed to be the most difficult course in the major.*

1.  a.  *Answers will vary.*

b.  _____

**COMBINED:** _____

2. a. _____

   b. _____

**COMBINED:** _____

## Join Ideas Using an Appositive

■ **TEACHING TIP** Say aloud a sentence that has as its subject something familiar to students in the class (for example, the president, a celebrity). Ask them to suggest a good appositive.

An **appositive** is a noun phrase that renames a noun. Appositives can be used to combine two sentences into one.

| | |
|---|---|
| **TWO SENTENCES** | Fen-Phen was found to be toxic. It was a very popular diet drug. |
| **JOINED WITH AN APPOSITIVE** | Fen-Phen, a very popular diet drug, was found to be toxic. |

[The phrase *a very popular diet drug* renames the noun *Fen-Phen.*]

To combine two sentences this way, turn the sentence that renames the noun into a noun phrase by dropping the subject and verb. The appositive phrase can appear anywhere in the sentence, but it should be placed before or after the noun it renames. Use a comma or commas to set off the appositive.

             *, a dangerous compound,*
The drug caused a few deaths. ~~It was a dangerous compound.~~

---

### EDITING FOR SENTENCE VARIETY:
### Combining Sentences Using an Appositive

#### FIND

<u>The school</u> <u><u>was completed</u></u> last fall. <u>~~It~~</u> <u><u>~~was named~~</u></u> Florence Sawyer High School.

1. **Underline** the <u>subject</u> and **double-underline** the <u><u>verb</u></u> in each sentence.
2. **Ask:** Does one sentence rename a noun in the other sentence? *Yes. In the second sentence, "It" renames "school."*
3. **Cross out** the ~~subject~~ and ~~verb~~ of that sentence.

#### EDIT

         *, Florence Sawyer High School,*
The school was completed last fall. ~~It was named Florence Sawyer High School.~~

4. **Combine the sentence and the remaining appositive phrase** by placing the appositive phrase directly before or directly after the noun it describes. Be sure to use a comma or commas to set off the appositive phrase.

### PRACTICE 10    JOINING IDEAS USING AN APPOSITIVE

Combine each pair of sentences into a single sentence by using an appositive. Be sure to use a comma or commas to set off the appositive. If you need help, look back at the chart on page 446 that shows the correction steps.

EXAMPLE:    Levi's jeans *, perhaps the most famous work clothes in the world,* have looked the same for well over a century. ~~They are perhaps the most famous work clothes in the world.~~

*Answers may vary. Possible edits shown.*

1. Jacob Davis~~, was~~ a Russian immigrant working in Reno, Nevada~~. He~~ was the inventor of Levi's jeans.

2. Davis came up with an invention *, the riveted seam,* that made work clothes last longer. ~~The invention was the riveted seam.~~

3. Davis bought denim from a wholesaler~~. The wholesaler was~~ Levi Strauss.

4. In 1870, he offered to sell the rights to his invention to Levi Strauss for the price of the patent~~. Patents then cost~~ about seventy dollars.

5. Davis joined the firm in 1873 and supervised the final development of its product~~. The product was~~ the famous Levi's jeans.

6. Davis oversaw a crucial design element~~. The jeans all had~~ orange stitching.

7. ~~The curved stitching on the back pockets was~~ *Another* choice Davis made *, the curved stitching on the back pockets,*~~. It~~ also survives in today's Levi's.

8. *A* ~~The stitching on the pockets has been~~ trademark since 1942 *the stitching on the pockets*~~. It is~~ very recognizable.

9. During World War II, Levi Strauss temporarily stopped adding the pocket stitches because they wasted thread~~. It was~~ a valuable resource.

10. Until the war ended, the pocket design was added with a less valuable material~~. The company used~~ paint.

### PRACTICE 11    JOINING IDEAS USING AN APPOSITIVE

Fill in the blank in each sentence with an appropriate appositive. There are many possible ways to complete each sentence.

**EXAMPLE:** The off-campus housing office, <u>*a small room crowded with*</u> <u>*desperate students*</u>, offered little help.

*Answers will vary.*

1. My sister, <u>*a college freshman*</u>, needed to find an apartment before she started school.

2. As she looked for a place to live, she faced a serious obstacle, <u>*sky-high rents*</u>.

3. Searching for apartments in the area near the campus, <u>*a quiet, tree-lined*</u> <u>*neighborhood*</u>, she found nothing suitable.

4. She applied for housing in a dormitory, <u>*a high-rise on the campus*</u>, but the waiting list already contained sixty-two names.

5. She finally found a place she could afford, <u>*a dark, cramped apartment*</u>, in a neighborhood with a high crime rate.

## Join Ideas Using an Adjective Clause

■ **TIP** For more about adjectives, see Chapter 25.

An **adjective clause** (sometimes called a *relative clause*) is a group of words with a subject and a verb that modifies or describes a noun. An adjective clause often begins with the words *who, which,* or *that,* and it can be used to combine two sentences into one.

| | |
|---|---|
| **TWO SENTENCES** | Lauren has won many basketball awards. She is captain of her college team. |
| **JOINED WITH AN ADJECTIVE CLAUSE** | Lauren, *who is captain of her college team*, has won many basketball awards. |

■ **TEACHING TIP** Explain to students that in their own writing they will need to consider the context when deciding which sentence contains the more important idea.

To join sentences this way, use *who, which,* or *that* to replace the subject of a sentence that describes a noun in another sentence. You now have an adjective clause that you can move so that it follows the noun it describes. The sentence with the more important idea (the one you want to emphasize) should become the main clause. The less important idea should be in the adjective clause.

■ **TIP** Use *who* to refer to a person, *which* to refer to places or things (but not to people), and *that* for people, places, or things. When referring to a person, *who* is preferable to *that.*

Rocío attributes her success to the Puente Project. <sup>*which*</sup> It helped her meet the challenges of the college.

[The more important idea here is that Rocío gives the Puente Project credit for her success. The less important idea is that the Puente Project helped her cope with college.]

**NOTE:** Punctuating adjective clauses can be tricky. If an adjective clause can be taken out of a sentence without completely changing the meaning of the sentence, put commas around the clause.

Lauren, *who is captain of her college team,* has won many basketball awards.

[The phrase *who is captain of her college team* adds information about Lauren, but it is not essential; the sentence *Lauren has won many basketball awards* means almost the same thing as the sentence in the example.]

If an adjective clause is an essential part of the meaning of a sentence, do not put commas around it.

Lauren is an award-winning basketball player who overcame childhood cancer.

[*Who overcame childhood cancer* is an essential part of this sentence. The sentence *Lauren is an award-winning basketball player* is very different in meaning from the whole sentence in the example.]

---

**EDITING FOR SENTENCE VARIETY:**
Combining Sentences Using an Adjective Clause

**FIND**

Carson moved to California last year. <u>He works for a software company.</u>

1. **Decide** which of the sentences expresses the more important idea. *The first sentence does.*

2. **Ask:** Does the sentence that *does not* contain the more important idea modify or describe a noun or pronoun in the other sentence? *Yes, the second sentence modifies Carson.*

3. **Underline** that <u>sentence.</u>

4. **Replace** the subject of the underlined sentence with *who, which,* or *that.* It is now an adjective clause. ***He works for a software company.*** ⟶ ***Who works for a software company.***

**EDIT**

*, who works for a software company,*
Carson moved to California last year. ~~He works for a software company.~~

5. **Combine the sentences and the adjective clause** by placing the adjective clause directly before or after the noun or pronoun it describes. Put commas around the clause if it is not an essential part of the sentence.

◼ **PRACTICE 12    JOINING IDEAS USING AN ADJECTIVE CLAUSE**

Combine each pair of sentences into a single sentence by using an adjective clause beginning with *who, which,* or *that.* If you need help, look back at the chart on page 449 that shows the correction steps.

*, who has been going to college for the past three years,*

**EXAMPLE:** My friend Erin had her first child last June. ~~She has been going to college for the past three years.~~

*Answers will vary. Possible edits shown.*

1. While Erin goes to classes, her baby boy stays at a day-care center.
*which*
~~The day-care center~~ costs Erin about $100 a week.

2. Twice when her son was ill Erin had to miss her geology lab.
*, which*
~~The lab~~ is an important part of her grade for that course.

*, who live about seventy miles away,*
3. Occasionally, Erin's parents come up and watch the baby while Erin is studying. ~~They live about seventy miles away.~~

*that*
4. Sometimes Erin feels discouraged by the extra costs. ~~The costs~~ have resulted from her having a child.

*who have never been mothers themselves*
5. She feels that some of her professors aren't very sympathetic. ~~These are the ones who have never been mothers themselves.~~

*, who wants to be a good mother and a good student,*
6. Erin understands that she must take responsibility for both her child and her education. ~~She wants to be a good mother and a good student.~~

*, which were once straight A's,*
7. Her grades have suffered somewhat since she had her son. ~~They were once straight A's.~~

*, who hopes to go to graduate school someday,*
8. Erin wants to earn honors at her graduation. ~~She hopes to go to graduate school someday.~~

*, who is the person in her life she cares about most,*
9. Her son is more important than an A in geology. ~~He is the person in her life she cares about most.~~

*, who*
10. Erin still expects to have a high grade-point-average. She has simply given up expecting to be perfect.

◼ **PRACTICE 13    JOINING IDEAS USING AN ADJECTIVE CLAUSE**

Fill in the blank in each of the following sentences with an appropriate adjective clause. Add commas, if necessary. There are many possible ways to complete each sentence.

**EXAMPLE:** The firefighters _____ *who responded to the alarm* _____

entered the burning building.

*Answers will vary. Possible edits shown.*

1. A fire ___ *that was probably caused by faulty wiring* ___ began in our house in the middle of the night.

2. The members of my family ___ *who were home at the time of the fire* ___ were all asleep.

3. My father ___ *, who has always been a light sleeper,* ___ was the first to smell smoke.

4. He ran to our bedrooms ___ *, which were on the second floor,* ___ and woke us up with his shouting.

5. The house *, which was the only home I had ever lived in,* was damaged, but everyone in my family reached safety.

# Edit Paragraphs and Your Own Writing

■ **PRACTICE 14   EDITING PARAGRAPHS**

Create sentence variety in the following paragraphs. Join at least two sentences in each of the paragraphs. Try to use several of the techniques covered in this chapter. There are many possible ways to edit each paragraph. You may want to refer to the chart, Editing for Sentence Variety, on page 453.
*Answers will vary. Possible edits shown.*

1. (1) Immunizations *, which* have saved countless lives in this century. (2) ~~Immunizations~~ have recently become controversial. (3) A few children *a very small minority,* have reactions to the vaccines. (4) ~~They are a very small minority.~~ (5) *Worrying* ~~Some parents worry~~ that vaccinations are harmful, *some parents* (6) ~~They~~ are speaking out against routine immunization. (7) But without immunization, more children would have terrible childhood diseases. (8) Immunization is slightly risky but necessary.

2. (1) Movies were made possible by Thomas Edison. (2) ~~He was~~ the inventor of the motion picture camera. (3) One of the first films showed scenes of an oncoming train. *which* (4) ~~The scenes~~ frightened audiences early in the twentieth century. (5) Audiences today are not as easily frightened. (6) They are accustomed to the magic of movies.

(7) One type of magic gets more amazing as technology im-
proves. (8) ~~This magic is called~~ *Called* "special effects~~.~~," (9) ~~Magic~~ *this magic* is not cheap.
(10) Blockbuster movies get more expensive every year because they
have bigger and flashier special effects. (11) Hollywood studios *, which* are
corporations trying to earn a profit~~.~~, (12) ~~They~~ spend millions to make
blockbusters. (13) They do everything they can to make sure that people
see the movies. (14) The studios do not necessarily want new and unusual products.

(15) There is another kind of magic in moviemaking~~.~~ (16) ~~This~~ *that*
~~magic~~ makes us remember why we loved movies in the first place.
(17) A great movie does not necessarily need special effects. (18) It may
be small and personal~~.~~, (19) ~~It may capture~~ *capturing* our imagination or our
heart. (20) The movies we love may show us the invention of a completely new world~~.~~, (21) ~~It can be a world~~ unimagined even by Thomas
Edison.

■ **PRACTICE 15** **EDITING YOUR OWN WRITING FOR SENTENCE VARIETY**

■ **LEARNING JOURNAL** Do
you tend to write short, similar-
sounding sentences? Which
sentence patterns covered in
this chapter do you think you
will use most often when
you are editing for sentence
variety?

As a final practice, edit a piece of your own writing for sentence variety. It
can be a paper you are working on for this course, a paper you've already
finished, a paper for another course, or a recent piece of writing from your
work or everyday life. Record in your learning journal any examples of
short, choppy sentences you find, along with the edited versions of these
sentences. You may want to use the chart on page 453.

## Chapter Review: Sentence Variety

■ **TEAMWORK** After students
have completed the chapter,
small groups can reexamine
the sample paragraph showing
sentence variety (p. 437). Have
students try to identify which
kinds of sentence variety the
author has used.

1. Having sentence variety means <u>using assorted sentence patterns, lengths,</u>
   <u>and rhythms</u>.

2. If you tend to write short, similar-sounding sentences, what five techniques should you try? <u>starting some sentences with adverbs, combining</u>
   <u>sentences using an -ing verb form, combining sentences using an -ed verb form,</u>
   <u>combining sentences using an appositive, and combining sentences using an</u>
   <u>adjective clause</u>

3. An <u>appositive</u> is a noun phrase that renames a noun.

4. An _____*adjective*_____ clause often starts with *who*, _____*which*_____,
   or _____*that*_____. It modifies or describes a noun or pronoun.

5. Use commas around an adjective clause when the information in it is
   (essential / (not essential)) to the meaning of the sentence.

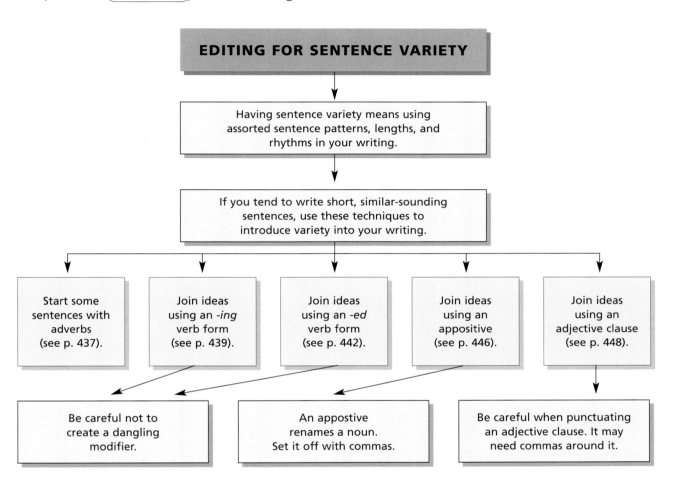

# 30

# ESL Concerns

## Areas of Special Interest to Nonnative Speakers and Speakers of Nonstandard English

■ **TIP** This chapter focuses on problems that many nonnative speakers of English have when they write papers for college, but native speakers may find it useful as well.

■ **LEARNING JOURNAL** Use your learning journal as a place to record sentences with problems that may be related to the fact that you speak English as a second language or that your spoken English differs from the English expected in college writing. Also record edited versions of these sentences, with the problems corrected.

■ **TIP** For more on subjects, nouns, and pronouns see Chapter 19. For more on dependent clauses, see Chapter 20.

If English is not your first language or if you grew up speaking a different version of English than what is expected in college papers, you may need some help with certain aspects of English that may be very different from your own first or your current spoken language. This chapter will focus on those areas.

## Nouns and Articles

### Subjects

The **subject** of a sentence is the person, place, or thing the sentence is about. It is either a noun, a pronoun (a word that substitutes for a noun), or a word or phrase that functions like a noun. Be sure to include a subject in every sentence and every clause, even a dependent clause, which doesn't express a complete thought.

*It is*
~~Is~~ raining here today.
^

*he*
My boss has taught me a great deal, although ~~is~~ difficult to work for.
                                                            ^

### Count and Noncount Nouns

A **noun** is a word that names a person, place, or thing. English nouns fall into two categories, depending on whether they name items that can be counted.

| | |
|---|---|
| **COUNT NOUN** | I bought two new *chairs*. |
| **NONCOUNT NOUN** | I bought some new *furniture*. |

The noun *chair* (plural, *chairs*) is a **count noun** because it names a distinct individual item that can be counted.

The noun *furniture* is a **noncount noun** because it represents a general category or group that cannot be divided easily into distinct, countable items. It would not make sense to say in English, *I bought two new furnitures.* Here are some more examples.

| COUNT | NONCOUNT |
|---|---|
| apple/apples | fruit |
| tree/trees | grass |
| dollar/dollars | money |
| beach/beaches | sand |
| fact/facts | information |

Count nouns can be made plural. Noncount nouns usually cannot be plural; they are usually singular.

■ **TIP** *Singular* means one; *plural* means more than one.

| | |
|---|---|
| **NONCOUNT NOUNS** | I got ~~two~~ *informations* to use in my paper. |
| | The coach looked over the team's *equipments*. |

**NOTE:** Some noncount nouns, such as *fruit, money,* and *sand,* are sometimes treated as count nouns (*the fruits of one's labor*).

## Articles

The words *a, an,* and *the* are called **articles**; they are used with nouns. You can choose *a, an, the,* or no article at all. Use *a* before words that start with a consonant sound; use *an* before words that start with a vowel sound: *a dog, an elevator.* The chart that follows shows how to use articles and when to use no article at all.

### Articles with Count and Noncount Nouns

| COUNT NOUNS | ARTICLE |
|---|---|
| **SINGULAR** | |
| **Identity Known** | *the* |
| | I want to read *the book* on taxes that you recommended. |
| | [The sentence refers to one particular book: the one that was recommended.] |
| | I can't stay in *the sun* very long. |
| | [There is only one sun.] |

■ **RESOURCES** For more advice and recommendations on teaching ESL students, see *Practical Suggestions.* For tests and supplemental practice exercises for this chapter, see *Additional Resources.*

| | |
|---|---|
| **Identity Not Known** | *a* or *an* |
| | I want to read *a book* on taxes. |
| | [It could be any book on taxes.] |

**PLURAL**

| | |
|---|---|
| **Identity Known** | *the* |
| | I enjoyed *the books* we read. |
| | [The sentence refers to a particular group of books: the ones we read.] |
| **Identity Not Known or a General Category** | (no article at all or another kind of word such as *this, these, that, some*) |
| | I usually enjoy *books.* |
| | [The sentence refers to books in general.] |
| | She found *some books.* |
| | [I don't know which books she found.] |

| **NONCOUNT NOUNS** | **ARTICLE** |
|---|---|

**SINGULAR**

| | |
|---|---|
| **Identity Known** | *the* |
| | I put away *the food* we bought. |
| | [The sentence refers to particular food: the food we bought.] |
| **Identity Not Known or a General Category** | (no article at all or another kind of word such as *this, these, that, some*) |
| | There is *food* all over the kitchen. |
| | [The reader doesn't know what food the sentence refers to.] |
| | Give *some food* to the neighbors. |
| | [The sentence refers to food in general.] |

■ **TIP** Never use *a* or *an* with noncount nouns.

---

■ PRACTICE 1   **EDITING NOUNS AND ARTICLES**

Edit the following paragraph, adding and changing articles and nouns as necessary. Also add a subject to any sentence that is missing one.

■ **TIP** For more exercises helpful to nonnative or non-standard speakers of English, visit Exercise Central at <bedfordstmartins.com/realwriting>.

EXAMPLE:
            *The weather*
            Weather was very bad in the December and January last
            ^
            year.

■ **TEACHING TIP** It might help students to know that *a few* is a very common expression in English (*a few days, a few weeks*).

            *It snowed*                      *The days*              *the*
(1) Snowed a lot last winter. (2) Days were short, and sky was usually
    ^                              ^              *the*           ^*a*
covered with clouds. (3) I seldom saw a̸ sun. (4) After the few weeks, I
                                     ^*a*            ^
                                                *a*
began to feel depressed. (5) I went to see doctor about the problem be-
                                           *a* ^                    *The*
cause I had always considered myself the happy person. (6) A doctor
                                      ^                     ^

asked me if I had ever noticed this sadness in *a*[the] winter before. (7) I realized that *a* short, dark days have often made me gloomy. (8) ~~Doctor~~[The doctor] diagnosed me with *a* disease called "seasonal affective disorder." (9) Now, when I feel sad during *a*[the] winter months, I have *a* solution. (10) I turn on *a*[an] electric light that is specially made to imitate *the* light of the sun. (11) ~~May~~[It may] be an unusual thing to do, but *it* makes me feel much better while I wait for *a* spring to come.

## Verbs

**Verbs** tell what action the subject in a sentence performs or link the subject to a word that describes it.

### Using the *-ing* Form or the *to* Form after Certain Verbs

A **gerund** (or *-ing* form of a verb) is a verb form that ends in *-ing* and functions as a noun. An **infinitive** is a verb form that has no ending but is preceded by the word *to*. These verb forms (gerunds and infinitives) cannot function as the main verbs in sentences; the sentences must have another word that functions as the main verb. In the sentences that follow, the gerund and the infinitive are objects — they receive the action of the verbs.

| | |
|---|---|
| **GERUND** | I <u>enjoy</u> *swimming*. |
| **INFINITIVE** | I <u>like</u> *to swim*. |

How do you decide whether to use a gerund or an infinitive as the object of a verb? The decision often depends on the main verb in a sentence. Some verbs can be followed by either a gerund or an infinitive, some can be followed only by a gerund, and some can be followed only by an infinitive. Knowing which to use can be tricky because the correct form is based on common practice, not logic. Practice using the correct structures for the verbs you use most often.

■ **TIP** For verbs plus prepositions, see page 460. For the position of verbs in questions, see page 463. For other problems with verbs, see Chapter 23.

■ **TIP** In the examples in this section, the <u>verbs</u> in the sentences are double-underlined.

---

### *Verbs That Are Followed by Either an Infinitive or a Gerund*

| begin | hate | remember | try |
|---|---|---|---|
| continue | like | start | |
| forget | love | stop | |

These verbs can be followed by either an infinitive or a gerund. Sometimes the meaning is about the same.

He hates *to study* math. = He hates *studying* math.

Sometimes the meaning changes depending on whether you use an infinitive or a gerund.

Mario stopped *to smoke*.

[This sentence means that Mario stopped what he was doing and smoked a cigarette.]

Mario stopped *smoking*.

[This sentence means that Mario no longer smokes.]

| *Verbs That Are Followed by an Infinitive* | | | |
| --- | --- | --- | --- |
| agree | decide | offer | refuse |
| ask | expect | plan | want |
| beg | fail | pretend | |
| choose | hope | promise | |
| claim | need | | |

Teresa agreed *to help*.

Roberto chose *to ignore* my advice.

| *Verbs That Are Followed by a Gerund* | | | |
| --- | --- | --- | --- |
| admit | discuss | keep | risk |
| avoid | enjoy | miss | suggest |
| consider | finish | practice | |
| deny | imagine | quit | |

The man admitted *robbing* the bank.

He avoids *paying* bills.

## Progressive Tense

The **progressive** tense consists of a form of the verb *be* plus the *-ing* form of a verb. It is used to indicate a continuing activity. Use the present progressive tense to indicate that an action is in progress now.

Kim is <u>reading</u> a novel about Asian American immigrants.

*is cleaning*
Greg ~~cleans~~ his basement today.
     ^

Not all verbs can form the progressive tense. Certain verbs that indicate sensing or a state of being are not usually used this way.

---

### *Verbs That Usually Cannot Form the Progressive Tense*

| | | | |
|---|---|---|---|
| appear | have | mean | taste |
| believe | hear | need | understand |
| belong | know | see | want |
| cost | like | seem | weigh |

---

I ~~am~~ belonging to several student associations on campus.

*means*
The author ~~is meaning~~ that unions have damaged our economy.
           ^

---

██  **PRACTICE 2**  **EDITING VERBS**

Edit the following paragraph to make sure that the verbs are used correctly.

*believe*
(1) Many students ~~are believing~~ that the college should provide on-
                  ^
campus day care. (2) These students want ~~improving~~ their ability to get
                                    *to improve*
a good job. (3) They consider ~~to get~~ a better job a worthwhile goal. (4)
              *getting*      ^
They come to college where they try to take courses that will make them
attractive to employers. (5) The courses ~~are~~ costing a lot, but the expense is worth it to these students. (6) Unfortunately, since they con-
                                              *have*
tinue to be responsible for their families, they often ~~are having~~ difficulty
                                                       ^
                                          *is becoming*
arranging for child care. (7) Today, this problem ~~becomes~~ more serious.
                                                  ^
(8) Students stop taking the courses they really need, so they don't
                                          *to help*
achieve their goal. (9) Shouldn't the college agree ~~helping~~ these stu-
                                                    ^
dents? (10) The college would also benefit because more and better
students would want to come to a college that met more of the students'
needs.

■ **TIP** For a complete list of prepositions, see page 289.

# Prepositions

A **preposition** is a word (such as *about, above, between, of*) that connects a noun, pronoun, or verb with some other information about it; some prepositions have two words. Knowing which preposition to use can be difficult because the correct preposition is often determined by idiom or common practice rather than by its actual meaning.

An **idiom** is any combination of words that is always used the same way, even though there is no logical or grammatical explanation for it. The best way to learn idioms is to practice writing and speaking the correct forms.

## Prepositions with Adjectives

Adjectives are often followed by prepositions. Here are some common examples.

| | | |
|---|---|---|
| afraid of | full of | scared of |
| ashamed of | happy about | sorry for |
| aware of | interested in | tired of |
| confused by | proud of | |
| excited about | responsible for | |

            *about*
Marina is excited ~~of~~ getting a good grade in the course.

            *of*
However, she is tired ~~with~~ all this work.

## Prepositions with Verbs

■ **TIP** To improve your ability to write and speak standard English, read magazines and your local newspaper, and listen to television and radio news programs. Also read magazines and newspaper articles aloud; it will help your pronunciation.

Many verbs consist of a verb plus a preposition (or adverb). The meaning of these verbs usually has nothing to do with the literal meaning of the verb plus the preposition, but taken together the verb and the preposition have a particular meaning in English. Often, the meaning of the verb changes completely depending on which preposition is used with it.

You must *take out* the trash.

You must *take in* the exciting sights of New York City.

Here are a few common examples.

| | |
|---|---|
| arrived in | My train *arrived in* New York. |
| call off | They *called off* the wedding. |
| call on | The professor never *calls on* me. |
| count on | You can *count on* me. |
| drop in | Sometimes, friends *drop in*. |
| fill in | Please *fill in* the blanks. |

| fill out | Please *fill out* this application form. |
| fill up | I will *fill up* the gas tank. |
| go over | He wants to *go over* what we learned last week. |
| grow up | All children *grow up*. |
| hand in | You may *hand in* your homework now. |
| look up | I decided to *look up* the word in the dictionary. |
| pick out | Richard *picked out* a dependable car. |
| pick up | Allison *picked up* her cat at the kennel. |
| put off | I often *put off* my work until the last minute. |

■ PRACTICE 3   **EDITING PREPOSITIONS**

Edit the following sentences to make sure that the correct prepositions are used.

EXAMPLE:  I am very interested to political subjects.
*(in)*

1. I was very happy for my first English class in the United States.
*(about)*

2. Ever since I arrived to this country, I have been preparing to continue my education.
*(in)*

3. My English was poor at first, and I was ashamed for my inability to understand what people were saying.
*(of)*

4. I still have to look out a vocabulary word sometimes, but I am definitely improving.
*(up)*

5. My English classes were full with people from all over the world, and I found them very interesting.
*(of)*

6. The teacher was excited for the chance to teach us, and she made us want to learn.
*(about)*

7. The texts she had picked on for us to read were the only thing I did not like.
*(out)*

8. She asked us to go under many pieces about immigrants' experiences in the United States.
*(over)*

9. I was soon tired from reading about immigrants, and I wanted to read and talk about subjects that had nothing to do with immigration.
*(of)*

10. My desire to discuss other topics, such as mathematics, religion, and
politics, has helped me to become aware ~~about~~ <sup>of</sup> many other people in
my class who share my interests.

### PRACTICE 4   EDITING PREPOSITIONS

Edit the following paragraph to make sure that the correct prepositions are
used.

(1) People were once afraid ~~to~~ <sup>of</sup> comets in the sky. (2) They thought
that these giant snowballs were signs of bad luck. (3) There are historical examples of rulers calling ~~down~~ <sup>off</sup> battles and holidays when they saw
comets in the sky. (4) Today, most people are excited ~~for~~ <sup>about</sup> the idea of seeing a comet, as long as there is no danger of its colliding with the earth.
(5) Scientists are interested ~~to~~ <sup>in</sup> learning more about each comet that
passes through our solar system. (6) Since there is no way we can travel
to visit comets, we need to wait until they come to us.

# Negatives and Questions

## Negatives

To form a negative statement, you can usually use one of these words.

| never | nobody | no one | nowhere |
|-------|--------|--------|---------|
| no    | none   | not    |         |

The word *not* is often combined with a verb in a shortened form called
a **contraction**.

They *aren't* finished. = They *are not* finished.

In standard English, there can be only one negative word in each clause.

Caryl will ~~not~~ ask no one for help.

Caryl will not ask ~~no one~~ <sup>anyone</sup> for help.

When you write a negative statement using the word *not*, the *not* must
come after the first helping verb in the sentence. If there is no helping verb,
you must add a form of *do* as well as *not* to make a negative statement.

**■ TIP** A clause is a group of
words with a subject and a
verb. It may or may not be
able to stand on its own as a
sentence.

## Common Helping Verbs

| FORMS OF *BE* | FORMS OF *HAVE* | FORMS OF *DO* | OTHER VERBS |
|---|---|---|---|
| am | have | do | can |
| are | has | does | could |
| been | had | did | may |
| being | | | might |
| is | | | must |
| was | | | should |
| were | | | will |

| | |
|---|---|
| **POSITIVE** | Jane *will go* with us. |
| **NEGATIVE** | Jane *will not go* with us. |
| **POSITIVE** | I *enjoyed* listening to the music. |
| **NEGATIVE** | I *did not enjoy* listening to the music. |

[Notice that the verb *enjoyed* changed to *enjoy* once the helping verb *did* was added.]

## Questions

To turn a statement into a question, move the helping verb in the statement so that it comes before the subject. If the only verb is a form of *be,* it should also be moved before the subject. If there is no helping verb or form of *be* in the statement, you must add a form of *do* and put it before the subject. Be sure to end the question with a question mark.

| | |
|---|---|
| **STATEMENT** | Jim *can drive* tonight. |
| **QUESTION** | *Can* Jim *drive* tonight? |
| **STATEMENT** | He *is* unhappy. |
| **QUESTION** | *Is* he unhappy? |
| **STATEMENT** | You *passed* the test. |
| **QUESTION** | *Did* you *pass* the test? |

[Notice that the verb *passed* changed to *pass* once the helping verb *did* was added.]

■    PRACTICE 5    **WRITING NEGATIVE STATEMENTS AND QUESTIONS**

For each positive statement, write one negative statement and one question.

**EXAMPLE:**

**POSITIVE STATEMENT:** Our professor gives us interesting assignments.

**NEGATIVE:** *Our professor does not give us interesting assignments.*

**QUESTION:** *Does our professor give us interesting assignments?*
*Answers may vary. Possible edits shown.*

1. **POSITIVE STATEMENT:** We were writing about why we want to take this course.

   **NEGATIVE:** *We were not writing about why we want to take this course.*

   **QUESTION:** *Were we writing about why we want to take this course?*

2. **POSITIVE STATEMENT:** We are working on papers about our family histories.

   **NEGATIVE:** *We are not working on papers about our family histories.*

   **QUESTION:** *Are we working on papers about our family histories?*

3. **POSITIVE STATEMENT:** My family has lived in this country for five years.

   **NEGATIVE:** *My family has not lived in this country for five years.*

   **QUESTION:** *Has my family lived in this country for five years?*

4. **POSITIVE STATEMENT:** We enjoy all there is to do and see here.

   **NEGATIVE:** *We do not enjoy all there is to do and see here.*

   **QUESTION:** *Do we enjoy all there is to do and see here?*

5. **POSITIVE STATEMENT:** The weather is difficult to get used to.

   **NEGATIVE:** *The weather is not difficult to get used to.*

   **QUESTION:** *Is the weather difficult to get used to?*

# Adjectives

■ **TIP** For more on adjectives, see Chapter 25.

**Adjectives** modify or describe nouns and pronouns. Many sentences have several adjectives that modify the same word.

The *big old red* truck rolled by.

When you use more than one adjective to modify the same word, you should use the conventional order for adjectives in standard English. The list that follows indicates this order.

1. Judgment/overall opinion: *awful, friendly, intelligent, strange, terrible*
2. Size: *big, huge, tiny, large, short, tall*

3. Shape: *round, square, fat, thin, circular, square*

4. Age: *old, young, new, youthful*

5. Color: *blue, green, yellow, red*

6. Nationality/location: *Greek, Italian, California, southern*

7. Material: *paper, glass, plastic, wooden*

| | |
|---|---|
| **EXAMPLE, ORDER OF ADJECTIVES:** | The (1) *friendly* (2) *large* (3) *fat* (4) *old* (5) *green* (6) *northern* (7) *shell* tortoise was crossing the road. |

■ **TIP** If you can insert *and* between the adjectives and the sentence still makes sense, use commas between the adjectives. If the sentence does not make sense with *and* between the adjectives, do not use commas.

## PRACTICE 6    ORDERING ADJECTIVES

For each item, write a sentence using the noun listed and the adjectives in parentheses. Be sure to put the adjectives in the correct order: judgment or overall opinion, size, shape, age, color, nationality or location, and material.

**EXAMPLE:** desk (wooden, huge, old)

*The huge old wooden desk was covered with papers.*
*Answers may vary. Possible edits shown.*

1. hair (black, long)

*Her long black hair was beautiful.*

2. jacket (leather, new, brown)

*The new brown leather jacket is too expensive.*

3. man (old, scary)

*I ran from the scary old man.*

4. calculator (tiny, new)

*The tiny new calculator is hard to use.*

5. chair (green, ugly, plastic)

*The ugly green plastic chair sat by the pool all winter.*

## PRACTICE 7    CORRECTING VARIOUS ESL PROBLEMS

In the following sentences, find and correct any problems with subjects, count and noncount nouns, articles, gerunds and infinitives, progressive tenses, prepositions, negatives, questions, and adjective order.

**EXAMPLE:** Some people ~~are believing~~ believe that bomb-sniffing dogs make

no mistakes.  *Answers may vary. Possible edits shown.*

1. In the summer of 2002, Florida police officers became interested ~~of~~ *in*
   three Arab American medical students who were traveling to Miami.

2. ~~Woman~~ *A woman* in a restaurant thought she had heard the students talking
   about terrorism.

3. ~~Was~~ *It was* the job of bomb-sniffing dogs to investigate the students' car.

4. The dogs thought the car contained explosives, but an official search
   ~~no turned~~ *did not turn* up anything.

5. Why the dogs ~~were~~ *were* wrong?

6. Most well-trained dogs ~~are wanting~~ *want* to please the people they work
   with, who are called *handlers*.

7. A police dog can tell if its handler feels excitement or ~~a~~ fear.

8. The dog expects ~~finding~~ *to find* something when the handler is excited.

9. When the Florida dogs made their mistake, three young men were
   falsely accused of being ~~the~~ terrorists.

10. ~~Is~~ *Can* anything ~~can~~ be done to help dogs make fewer mistakes?

11. Dog experts have suggested ~~to keep~~ *keeping* police dogs off their leashes when
    the dogs are working.

12. U.S. ~~most~~ *Most* police dogs work on the leash, which can lead to errors.

13. A Dutch ~~new~~ *new* training program has also found that dog handlers
    sometimes unconsciously direct their dogs toward particular suspects.

14. ~~Was~~ *There was* a government scientist identified by bloodhounds as a possible
    suspect in the 2001 anthrax mailings.

15. ~~Never he was~~ *He was never* arrested, and his lawyers say that the handlers wanted
    their dogs to identify him.

16. Dogs may also pretend to pick ~~on~~ *up* a scent in order to get rewards.

17. Like human beings, they ~~are liking~~ *like* the special treats they get when
    someone is pleased with them.

18. Of course, well-trained detective dogs have been responsible *for* ~~of~~ the
    ^
    discovery of some explosives and chemical weapons.

19. However, new researches on preventing training mistakes may make
    dogs and their handlers even more effective against crime.

20. Police departments will continue to count *on* ~~of~~ the expert noses of dogs, but
    ^
    people should not forget that even the best dogs can sometimes be wrong.

# Chapter Review: ESL Concerns

1. A noun is  *a word that names a person, place, or thing*          .

2. A count noun names  *a particular individual item that can be counted*          .

3. A noncount noun names  *a general category that cannot be divided or*          
   *counted individually*          .

4. List the three articles used with nouns  *a, an, the*          .

5. If the identity of a noun is known, what article do you use?  *the*          

6. Use the article  _____ *a* _____  for singular count nouns when their identity is unknown or not specific.

7. Use  _____ *a* _____  before words that start with a consonant sound. Use
   _____ *an* _____  before words that start with a vowel sound.

8. A gerund is  *a verb form that ends in "-ing" and functions as a noun*          .

9. An infinitive is  *a verb form that has no ending but is preceded by "to"*          .

10. The progressive tense of a verb is used when an action is  *a continuing*          
    *activity*          .

11. List five common phrases in which an adjective is followed by a prepo-
    sition.  *Answers will vary. Possible answers: afraid of, aware of, excited about,*          
    *tired of, happy to*          

12. What are five common verb-plus-preposition phrases?  *Answers will vary.*          
    *Possible answers: call off, drop in, go over, hand in, pick out*

13. When you are turning a statement into a question, move the ___*helping*___ ___*verb*___ so that it comes before the ___*subject*___ .

14. In the following sentence, fill in the blanks with adjectives using the conventional order for adjectives. *Answers will vary.*

My _____, _____, _____, _____ uncle is visiting for a month.

# Part Six
# Word Use

# 31

# Word Choice

*Avoiding Language Pitfalls*

## Understand the Importance of Choosing Words Carefully

In conversation, much of your meaning is conveyed by your facial expression, your tone of voice, and your gestures. In writing, you have only the words on the page to make your point, so you must choose them carefully. If you use vague or inappropriate words, your readers may not understand what you have to say. Carefully chosen, precise words tell your readers exactly what you mean.

Two resources will help you find the best words for your meaning: a dictionary and a thesaurus.

### Dictionary

You need a dictionary. You can get a good paperback dictionary for a minimal investment, and a number of good dictionaries are now available free online. Dictionaries are a useful resource for all kinds of useful information about words: spelling, division of words into syllables, pronunciation, parts of speech, other forms of words, definitions, and examples of use. Following is a sample dictionary entry.

| spelling and end-of-line division | pronunciation | parts of speech | other forms |
| --- | --- | --- | --- |

**con • crete** (kon′krēt, kong′-, kon krēt′), *adj., n., v.* **-cret • ed,** — definition
**-cret • ing,** *adj.* **1.** constituting an actual thing or instance; real; — example
perceptible; substantial: *concrete proof.* **2.** pertaining to or concerned with
realities or actual instances rather than abstractions; particular as
opposed to general: *concrete proposals.* **3.** referring to an actual substance

■ **LEARNING JOURNAL** Use your learning journal as a place to record sentences with the types of problems covered in this chapter. Also write down edited versions of these sentences, with the problems corrected.

■ **RESOURCES** *Additional Resources* contains tests and supplemental practice exercises for this chapter.

■ **TIP** Several online dictionaries are available. Just a few of them are <**dictionary.com**>, <**yourdictionary.com**>, and <**m-w.com**> (Merriam-Webster OnLine). Online thesauruses include <**www.thesaurus.com**> and <**www.bartleby.com/ thesauri**>. The Merriam-lWebster site also offers an online thesaurus.

■ **ESL** ESL students may want to use a dictionary written especially for nonnative speakers (such as the *Longman Dictionary of American English*) in addition to a standard English dictionary.

or thing, as opposed to an abstract quality: The words *cat, water,* and *teacher* are concrete, whereas the words *truth, excellence,* and *adulthood* are abstract. . . .

—*Random House Webster's College Dictionary*

### Thesaurus

A thesaurus gives **synonyms** (words that have the same meaning) for the word you look up. Like a dictionary, it comes in inexpensive and even electronic editions. Use a thesaurus when you can't find the right word for what you mean. Be careful, however, to choose a word that has the precise meaning you intend. If you are not sure how a word should be used, look it up in the dictionary.

> **Concrete**, *adj.* 1. Particular, specific, single, certain, special, unique, sole, peculiar, individual, separate, isolated, distinct, exact, precise, direct, strict, minute; definite, plain, evident, obvious; pointed, emphasized; restrictive, limiting, limited, well-defined, clear-cut, fixed, finite; determining, conclusive, decided.
>
> —J. I. Rodale, *The Synonym Finder*

## Practice Avoiding Four Common Word-Choice Problems

Four common problems with word choice may make it hard for you to get your point across. You can eliminate them by using specific words that fit your meaning and make your writing clearer.

### Vague and Abstract Words

Your words need to create a clear picture for your readers. Vague and abstract words are too general. They don't give your readers a clear idea of what you mean. Here are some common vague and abstract words.

■ **COMPUTER** Tell students they can use a computer's search or find function to locate these words in their own writing.

**VAGUE AND ABSTRACT WORDS**

| | | | |
|---|---|---|---|
| a lot | dumb | nice | school |
| awful | good | OK (okay) | small |
| bad | great | old | thing |
| beautiful | happy | person | very |
| big | house | pretty | whatever |
| car | job | sad | young |

When you see one of these words or another general word in your writing, try to replace it with a concrete or more specific word. A **concrete** word names something that can be seen, heard, felt, tasted, or smelled. A **specific** word names a particular individual or quality. Compare these two sentences:

| VAGUE AND ABSTRACT | An old man crossed the street. |

| CONCRETE AND SPECIFIC | An eighty-seven-year-old priest sprinted across Main Street. |

The first version is too general to be interesting. The second version creates a clear, strong image. Some words are so vague that it is best to avoid them altogether.

| VAGUE AND ABSTRACT | It's like, *whatever*. |

[This sentence is neither concrete nor specific.]

■ **TEACHING TIP** Take students to a spot on campus and have them write descriptions of the same scene. Then have them compare what they wrote, noting the use of concrete and specific language as well as of vague and abstract words.

## ■ PRACTICE 1 AVOIDING VAGUE AND ABSTRACT WORDS

In the following sentences, underline any words that are vague or abstract. Then edit each sentence by replacing the vague or abstract words with concrete, specific ones. You may invent any details you like.

■ **TIP** For more practice on choosing words effectively, visit Exercise Central at <bedfordstmartins.com/realwriting>.

EXAMPLE: The ~~zoo~~ in my ~~city is big~~.
      *Bronx Zoo*     *neighborhood sprawls over hundreds of acres.*

*Answers will vary. Possible edits shown.*

1. I visit the ~~local zoo a lot.~~
   *Bronx Zoo at least twice a year.*

2. The animals ~~seem happy there.~~
   *behave as they would in the wild instead of pacing restlessly.*

3. Living in a cage would be ~~awful~~, but the ~~zoo in my city~~ doesn't have cages.
   *painfully boring and uncomfortable*   *Bronx Zoo*

4. The new gorilla habitat is ~~nice.~~
   *like the gorillas' native habitat.*

5. The zoo has ~~some very pretty~~ birds.
   *two different species of*   *with purple and turquoise feathers.*

6. ~~Sometimes~~ the zoo has ~~young~~ animals.
   *Every spring*   *newborn*

7. Watching the bats is ~~great.~~
   *like watching a creepy old movie or a thrilling air show.*

8. The zoo raises money to ~~do good things~~ for wildlife around the world.
   *preserve natural habitats*

9. The ~~zoo has a lot of information available for~~ visitors.
   *zoo's exhibits teach*   *about wildlife conservation.*

10. I would like to ~~have a job~~ at the ~~zoo someday.~~
   *work as a wildlife biologist*   *Bronx Zoo after I finish college.*

## Slang

**Slang** is informal and casual language that is often shared by a particular group—for example, teenagers. Slang should be used only in informal situations. Avoid it when you write, especially for college classes or at work. Use language that is appropriate for your audience and purpose.

■ **TEAMWORK** Students can collaborate to list slang words and then translate them into edited English.

| SLANG | EDITED |
|---|---|
| If I don't get this job, I'll be *bummed*. | If I don't get this job, I will be disappointed. |
| Getting this job would be really *phat*. | Getting this job would be exciting. |

■ **PRACTICE 2 AVOIDING SLANG**

In the following sentences, underline any slang words. Then edit the sentences by replacing the slang with language appropriate for a formal audience and purpose. Imagine that you are writing to a supervisor at work.

> so critical of me
**EXAMPLE:** I want to know why you have been ~~on my case so much~~
> ^
> recently.
> *Answers will vary. Possible edits shown.*

> reprimand me
1. I don't see why it is necessary for you to ~~chew me out~~ so often.
> ^

> improve my performance
2. During my last evaluation you asked me to ~~get my act together~~, and I
> ^
feel that I have done so.

> enthusiastic
3. I was really ~~fired up~~ about the last project I worked on.
> ^

> relaxed
4. I wish that our relationship could be more ~~laid back~~.
> ^

> a wonderful                                remain
5. This is ~~an awesome~~ place to work, and I'd like to ~~hang around~~ here for
> ^                                          ^
at least another year.

> I get along well
6. ~~I'm buddies~~ with all of my coworkers in this department.
> ^

> have a disagreement about
7. Jim Hoffman and I did once ~~get into it over~~ scheduling.
> ^

> we get along fine
8. Working with him was tense for a while, but ~~we're cool~~ now.
> ^

> complaining about me,
9. If anyone has been ~~talking me down~~, I would like to know about it.
> ^

> tell me about it.
10. If you see a problem with my work, please ~~give me the 411~~.
> ^

## Wordy Language

People sometimes use too many words to express their ideas. They may think that using more words will make them sound smart and important. But too many words can get in the way of a writer's point and weaken it.

Wordy language includes phrases that contain too many words, unnecessarily qualify (comment on) a statement, or use slightly different words without adding any new ideas.

| | |
|---|---|
| **WORDY** | I'm not interested *at this point in time*. |
| **EDITED** | I'm not interested now. |

[The phrase *at this point in time* uses five words to express what could be said in one word: *now*.]

| | |
|---|---|
| **WORDY** | *In the opinion of this writer,* I think the directions are clear. |

[The qualifying phrase *in the opinion of this writer* is not necessary and weakens the statement.]

| | |
|---|---|
| **WORDY** | The suspect was *evasive* and *avoided answering the questions*. |
| **EDITED** | The suspect was evasive. |

[The words *evasive* and *avoided answering the questions* repeat the same idea without adding anything new.]

**COMMON WORDY EXPRESSIONS**

| WORDY | EDITED |
|---|---|
| As a result of | Because |
| Due to the fact that | Because |
| In spite of the fact that | Although |
| It is my opinion that | I think |
| In the event that | If |
| The fact of the matter is that | (*Just state the point.*) |
| A great number of | Many |
| At that time | Then |
| In this day and age | Now |
| At this point in time | Now |
| In this paper I will show that . . . | (*Just make the point; don't announce it.*) |
| Utilize | Use |

■ **COMPUTER** Students can use a computer's search or find function to locate these phrases (or others like them) in their writing.

■ **PRACTICE 3    AVOIDING WORDY LANGUAGE**

In the following sentences, underline the wordy or repetitive language. Then edit each sentence to make it more concise. Some sentences may contain more than one wordy phrase.

**EXAMPLE:** Television has had a huge effect on politics ~~as a result of~~ *because* ~~the fact that~~ it brings politicians into people's homes.

*Answers may vary. Possible edits shown.*

1. ~~It is a well-known fact that~~ ~~television~~ *Television* helped Richard Nixon lose the 1960 presidential election.

*Many*
2. ~~A great number of~~ voters disliked Nixon's appearance during televised
debates with John F. Kennedy.

*Although*
3. ~~In spite of the fact that~~ technicians encouraged Nixon to wear makeup
for the debate, he refused.

*looked*
4. He ~~gave the appearance of being~~ sweaty and pale next to tanned, calm
Kennedy.

5. ~~The fact of the matter is that~~ Nixon did not look much better on
television during his presidency from 1968 to 1974.

6. Like Kennedy, President Ronald Reagan ~~was a chief executive who~~
looked good on television.

*because*
7. He had experience standing in front of cameras ~~due to the fact that~~ he
had been an actor.

8. Reagan's ~~cheerful, happy~~ smile made people forget questions they had
about his political experience.

*Some*
9. ~~In this day and age, some~~ people have pointed out that looking good
*most important*
on television is one of the requirements ~~of the most paramount impor-~~
~~tance~~ for future presidents.

10. Anyone who does not resemble a news anchorperson ~~in appearance~~ is
*now.*
not likely to go far in national politics ~~at this point in time.~~

## Clichés

**Clichés** are phrases used so often that people no longer pay attention to
them. To get your point across and to get your readers' attention, replace
clichés with fresh language that precisely expresses your meaning.

| CLICHÉS | EDITED |
| --- | --- |
| I can't *make ends meet.* | I don't have enough money to live on. |
| My uncle *worked his way up the corporate ladder.* | My uncle started as a shipping clerk but ended up as a regional vice president. |
| This roll is *as hard as a rock.* | This roll is so hard I could bounce it. |

**COMMON CLICHÉS**

| | |
|---|---|
| as big as a house | light as a feather |
| the best/worst of times | no way on earth |
| better late than never | 110 percent |
| break the ice | playing with fire |
| crystal clear | spoiled brat/rotten |
| a drop in the bucket | starting from scratch |
| easier said than done | sweating blood/bullets |
| few and far between | too little, too late |
| hell on earth | work like a dog |
| last but not least | |

■ **COMPUTER** Students can use a computer's search or find function to locate these phrases (or others like them) in their writing.

---

■ **PRACTICE 4    AVOIDING CLICHÉS**

In the following sentences, underline the clichés. Then edit each sentence by replacing the clichés with fresh language that precisely expresses your meaning.

                                                     *excruciating*

**EXAMPLE:** Riding a bicycle one hundred miles a day can be ~~hell on~~

                               *work extremely hard.* ^

      ~~earth~~ unless you're willing to ~~give 110 percent.~~

*Answers will vary. Possible edits shown.*

                          *devote every bit of your strength to the challenge*

1. You have to persuade yourself to ~~sweat blood and work like a dog~~ for
   up to ten hours.

   *It is impossible to*

2. ~~There's no way on earth you can~~ do it without extensive training.

                      *the very last mile,*         *an enormously difficult*

3. Staying on your bike until ~~the bitter end~~, of course, is ~~easier said than~~
   *task.*
   ~~done~~.

                   *maintain your determination*

4. It is important to ~~keep the fire in your belly~~ and keep your goal of
                ^ *always present*
   finishing the race ~~crystal clear~~ in your mind.

5. No matter how long it takes you to cross the finish line, remind your-
         *finishing at all is a tremendous achievement.*
   self that ~~it's better late than never~~.

6. Even if you aren't a champion racer, training for a bike race will keep
       *in top physical condition.*
   you ~~fit as a fiddle~~.

         *discipline*                        *continue to*

7. It may take ~~a will of iron~~ to make yourself train, but you should ~~keep~~
   *work hard.*
   ~~your nose to the grindstone~~.

*protect themselves*
8. Bike racers should always ~~play it safe~~ by wearing helmets.
^

*watch carefully*
9. When you train for road racing, ~~keep an eye peeled~~ for cars.
^

*injured* ^ *killed!*
10. You don't want to end up ~~flat on your back~~ in the hospital or ~~six feet~~
^ ^

~~under!~~

# Edit Paragraphs and Your Own Writing

**■  PRACTICE 5   EDITING PARAGRAPHS FOR WORD CHOICE**

Find and edit any examples of vague and abstract language, slang, wordy language, or clichés in the following paragraphs. You may want to refer to the chart, Editing for Word Choice, on page 480.

*Answers will vary. Possible edits shown.*
*ordinary citizens now,*
1. (1) Space travel is not available to ~~the average Joe at this point in~~
^
~~time,~~ but that situation may change. (2) In ~~the year~~ 1997, Congress
*legalized* *Many*
~~declared the legality of~~ private manned space flights. (3) ~~A lot of~~ entre-
^ *speculating* ^
preneurs are ~~betting the farm~~ that space tourism will happen ~~pretty~~
^ *be inexpensive.*
soon. (4) But a vacation on the moon won't ~~come cheap, however.~~
*wealthy* ^
(5) Only people ~~with deep pockets~~ will be able to afford half a million
*dollars* ^ *One*
~~smackers~~ for a cruise around the moon. (6) ~~This one~~ company plans a
^ ^
moon community, and a night at the hotel there will cost $1,500. (7) If
anyone is interested in a more permanent visit to space, an option
*be buried*
already exists. (8) For ~~a cost of~~ $4,800, people who want to ~~spend~~
^
~~eternity~~ in space can have their ashes launched from a rocket.
*devastating*
2. (1) Throughout recorded history, humans have done ~~bad~~ things
^
to the environment. (2) For example, the need for firewood ~~really~~
*destroyed* *Because*
~~screwed up~~ the forests of Europe. (3) ~~Due to the fact that~~ wood has
^ ^
a high carbon-to-hydrogen ratio, the burning of wood is a dirty and
*used*
inefficient source of fuel. (4) Coal was ~~utilized~~ as an alternative, but
*also harmful to the environment.* ^ *When*
~~as we know,~~ coal is ~~not so nice either.~~ (5) ~~At this point in time when~~ oil
^ ^
furnaces began to replace coal furnaces, the air in many cities slowly
became somewhat cleaner.
*Amazingly,*
(6) ~~Another thing that blows my mind is that~~ whales were the main
^
source of fuel for lamps for much of the nineteenth century. (7) Each

year, thousands of sperm whales were caught and killed, until ~~the time came when~~ they were almost extinct. (8) When petroleum oil was discovered in 1859, people thought that their energy problems were over ~~forever after.~~ (9) However, ~~in my opinion I feel that~~ our dependence on oil is a <u>significant</u> ~~big-time~~ problem. (10) During the energy crisis of the 1970s, for example, we really had to <u>restrict our fuel consumption.</u> ~~bite the bullet.~~ (11) It is <u>foolish</u> ~~dumb~~ to continue to use fossil fuels when scientists have shown that these fuels contribute to global warming.

■ PRACTICE 6    EDITING YOUR OWN WRITING FOR WORD CHOICE

As a final practice, edit a piece of your own writing for word choice. It can be a paper you are working on for this course, a paper you've already finished, a paper for another course, or a recent piece of writing from your work or everyday life. Record in your learning journal any problem sentences you find, along with their corrections. You may want to use the chart on page 480.

# Chapter Review: Word Choice

1. What two resources will help you choose the best words for your meaning? <u>a dictionary and a thesaurus</u>

2. What are four common word-choice problems? <u>vague and abstract words, slang, wordy language, and clichés</u>

3. Replace vague and abstract words with <u>concrete</u> and <u>specific</u> words.

4. When is it appropriate to use slang in college writing or in writing at work? <u>never</u>

5. What are three common kinds of wordy language?

   <u>using phrases that contain too many words</u>

   <u>using phrases that unnecessarily qualify/comment on a statement</u>

   <u>repeating yourself in slightly different words without adding anything new</u>

6. <u>Clichés</u> are phrases that are overused. Why should you avoid them in your writing? <u>People no longer pay attention to them.</u>

■ **LEARNING JOURNAL**
Which language pitfall do you get trapped by most often? Why do you think you have this problem? How can you avoid it in your writing?

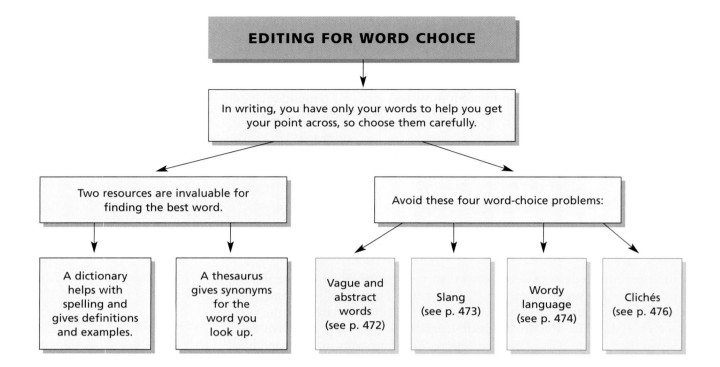

EDITING FOR WORD CHOICE

In writing, you have only your words to help you get your point across, so choose them carefully.

Two resources are invaluable for finding the best word.

A dictionary helps with spelling and gives definitions and examples.

A thesaurus gives synonyms for the word you look up.

Avoid these four word-choice problems:

Vague and abstract words (see p. 472)

Slang (see p. 473)

Wordy language (see p. 474)

Clichés (see p. 476)

# 32

# Commonly Confused Words

*Avoiding Mistakes with Sound-Alikes*

## Understand Why Certain Words Are Commonly Confused

People often confuse certain words in English because they sound alike and may have similar meanings. In speech, words that sound alike are not a problem. In writing, however, words that sound alike may be spelled differently, and readers rely on the spelling to understand what you mean. When you write a word that sounds like the one you want but is spelled differently and has a different meaning, it confuses your readers. Edit your writing carefully to make sure that you have used the correct words.

**STRATEGIES FOR EDITING SOUND-ALIKES**

- **Proofread carefully**, using the techniques discussed on page 494.
- **Use a dictionary** to look up any words you are unsure about.
- **Focus on finding and correcting mistakes** you make with the twenty-seven sets of commonly confused words covered in this chapter.
- **Develop a personal list of words** you confuse often. In your learning journal or on an index card, record the words that you confuse in your writing, and jot down their meanings. Before you turn in any piece of writing, consult your personal list of words to make sure you have used them correctly.

## Practice Using Commonly Confused Words Correctly

Study the different meanings and spellings of these twenty-seven sets of commonly confused words. Complete the sentence after each set of words, filling in each blank with the correct word.

■ **LEARNING JOURNAL** Use your learning journal as a place to start a personal list of words you commonly confuse. When you edit your papers, be sure to check for those words.

■ **RESOURCES** *Additional Resources* contains tests and supplemental exercises for this chapter.

■ **TIP** Some commonly confused words sound similar but not exactly alike, such as *conscience* and *conscious*, *loose* and *lose*, and *of* and *have*. To avoid confusing these words, practice pronouncing them correctly.

## A/An/And

**a:** used before a word that begins with a consonant sound
*A* friend of mine just won the lottery.

**an:** used before a word that begins with a vowel sound
*An* old friend of mine just won the lottery.

**and:** used to join two words
My friend *and* I went out to celebrate.

*A* friend *and* I ate at *an* Italian restaurant.

Other lottery winners were _____*an*_____ algebra teacher _____*and a*_____ bowling team.

## Accept/Except

**accept:** to agree to receive or admit (verb)
I will *accept* the job offer.

**except:** but, other than
All the stores are closed *except* the Quik-Stop.

I *accept* all the job conditions *except* the low pay.

Do not _____*accept*_____ gifts from clients _____*except*_____ those who are also personal friends.

## Advice/Advise

**advice:** opinion (noun)
I would like your *advice* before I make a decision.

**advise:** to give an opinion (verb)
Please *advise* me what to do.

Please *advise* me what to do; you always give me good *advice*.

If you don't like my _____*advice*_____, please _____*advise*_____ me how to proceed.

■ **TIP** For more practice using commonly confused words correctly, visit Exercise Central at <www.bedfordstmartins.com/realwriting>.

## Affect/Effect

**affect:** to make an impact on, to change something (verb)
The whole city was *affected* by the hurricane.

**effect:** a result (noun)
What *effect* will the hurricane have on the local economy?

Although the storm will have many negative *effects*, it will not *affect* the price of food.

The _____*effect*_____ of the disaster will _____*affect*_____ many people.

## Are/Our

> **are:** a form of the verb *be*
> > The workers *are* about to go on strike.
>
> **our:** a pronoun showing ownership
> > The children played on *our* porch.
>
> My relatives *are* staying at *our* house.
>
> _____*Our*_____ new neighbors _____*are*_____ moving in today.

■ **TEACHING TIP** It is helpful to complete these sentences as a class or to assign them as homework and then go over them in class. Have students read the sentences aloud so they can focus on differences in pronunciation.

## By/Buy

> **by:** next to, on or before
> > Meet me *by* the entrance.
> > Make sure the bill is paid *by* the fifteenth of the month.
>
> **buy:** to purchase (verb)
> > I would like to *buy* a new CD player.
>
> When I walk *by* the cottage, I know I'd like to *buy* it.
>
> _____*By*_____ next year, I will be able to _____*buy*_____ a washing machine.

## Conscience/Conscious

> **conscience:** a personal sense of right and wrong (noun)
> > Jake's *conscience* wouldn't allow him to cheat.
>
> **conscious:** awake, aware (adjective)
> > The coma patient is now *conscious*.
> > I am *conscious* that it's getting late.
>
> The judge was *conscious* that the accused had acted according to his *conscience* even though he had broken the law.
>
> The man said he was not _____*conscious*_____ that what he had done was illegal or his _____*conscience*_____ would not have let him do it.

■ **TIP** Remember that one of the words is *con-science;* the other is not.

## Fine/Find

> **fine:** of high quality (adjective); feeling well (adverb); a penalty for breaking a law (noun)
> > This jacket is made of *fine* leather.
> > After a day in bed, Jacob felt *fine*.
> > The *fine* for exceeding the speed limit is fifty dollars.
>
> **find:** to locate, to discover (verb)
> > Did Clara *find* her glasses?
>
> I *find* gardening to be a *fine* pastime.
>
> Were you able to _____*find*_____ a place to store your _____*fine*_____ jewelry?

### Its/It's

**its:** a pronoun showing ownership
The dog chased *its* tail.

**it's:** a contraction of the words *it is*
*It's* about time you got here.

*It's* very hard for a dog to keep *its* teeth clean.

_____It's_____ no surprise that the college raised ____*its*____ tuition.

■ **TIP** If you are not sure whether to use *its* or *it's* in a sentence, try substituting *it is.* If the sentence doesn't make sense with *it is,* use *its.*

### Knew/New/Know/No

**knew:** understood, recognized (past tense of the verb *know*)
I *knew* the answer, but I couldn't think of it.

**new:** unused, recent or just introduced (adjective)
The building has a *new* security code.

**know:** to understand, to have knowledge of (verb)
I *know* how to bake bread.

**no:** used to form a negative
I have *no* idea what the answer is.

I never *knew* how much a *new* car costs.

The ____*new*____ teacher ____*knew*____ many of her students already.

There is ___*no*___ way Tom could ____*know*____ where Celia is hiding.

I ____*know*____ that there is ____*no*____ cake left.

### Loose/Lose

**loose:** baggy, relaxed, not fixed in place (adjective)
In hot weather, people tend to wear *loose* clothing.

**lose:** to misplace, to forfeit possession of (verb)
Every summer I *lose* about three pairs of sunglasses.

If the ring is too *loose* on your finger, you might *lose* it.

I ____*lose*____ my patience with ____*loose*____ rules in schools.

### Mind/Mine

**mind:** to object to (verb), the thinking or feeling part of one's brain (noun)
Toby doesn't *mind* if I borrow his CDs.
Estela has a good *mind*, but often she doesn't use it.

**mine:** belonging to me (pronoun), a source of ore and minerals (noun)
That coat is *mine*.
My uncle worked in a coal *mine* in West Virginia.

That writing problem of *mine* was on my *mind*.

If you don't ____*mind*____, the gloves you just took are ____*mine*____.

### Of/Have

**of:** coming from, caused by, part of a group, made from (preposition)
 The leader *of* the band played bass guitar.

**have:** to possess (verb; also used as a helping verb)
 I *have* one more course to take before I graduate.
 I should *have* started studying earlier.

If I'd known we were out *of* coffee, I would *have* bought some.

Sidney could ____*have*____ been one ____*of*____ the winners.

**NOTE:** Do not use *of* after *would, should, could,* and *might.* Use *have* after those words.

### Passed/Past

**passed:** went by, went ahead (past tense of the verb *pass*)
 We *passed* the hospital on the way to the airport.

**past:** time that has gone by (noun); gone by, over, just beyond (preposition)
 In the *past,* I was able to stay up all night and not be tired.
 The snow fell *past* my window.

This *past* school year, I *passed* all of my exams.

Trish ____*passed*____ me as we ran ____*past*____ the one-mile marker.

### Peace/Piece

**peace:** no disagreement, calm
 Could you quiet down and give me a little *peace*?

**piece:** a part of something larger
 May I have a *piece* of that pie?

The feuding families found *peace* after they sold the *piece* of land.

To keep the ____*peace*____, give your sister a ____*piece*____ of candy.

### Principal/Principle

**principal:** main (adjective), chief, head of a school or leader in an organization (noun)
 Brush fires are the *principal* risk in the hills of California.
 Ms. Edwards is the *principal* of Memorial Elementary School.
 Corinne is a *principal* in the management consulting firm.

**principle:** a standard of beliefs or behaviors (noun)
> Although tempted, she held on to her moral *principles.*

The *principal* questioned the delinquent student's *principles.*

The ___principal___ problem is that you want me to act against my

___principles___ .

### Quiet/Quite/Quit

**quiet:** soft in sound, not noisy (adjective)
> The library was very *quiet.*

**quite:** completely, very (adverb)
> After cleaning all the windows, Alex was *quite* tired.

**quit:** to stop (verb)
> She *quit* her job.

After the band *quit* playing, the hall was *quite quiet.*

■ **COMPUTER** Tell students that although a spell checker won't help them with the spelling of most of these words, they can use the search or find function to find every instance of the words they have trouble with.

If you would ___quit___ shouting and be ___quiet___, you would find

that the scenery is ___quite___ pleasant.

### Right/Write

**right:** correct, in a direction opposite from left (adjective)
> You definitely made the *right* choice.
> When you get to the stoplight, make a *right* turn.

**write:** to put words on paper (verb)
> Will you *write* your phone number for me?

Please *write* the *right* answer in the space provided.

You were ___right___ to ___write___ to the senator.

### Set/Sit

**set:** a collection of something (noun), to place an object somewhere (verb)
> Paul has a complete *set* of Johnny Cash records.
> Please *set* the package on the table.

**sit:** to rest with one's rear end supported by a chair or other surface
> I need to *sit* and rest for a few minutes.

If I *sit* down now, I won't have time to *set* the plants outside.

Before you ___sit___ on that chair, ___set___ the magazines on

the floor.

## Suppose/Supposed

**suppose:** imagine, assume to be true
> I *suppose* you would like something to eat.
> *Suppose* you won a million dollars.

**supposed:** past tense of *suppose,* intended
> Karen *supposed* Thomas was late because of traffic.

I *suppose* you know that Rita was *supposed* to be home by 6:30.

I ___*suppose*___ you want to leave soon because we are ___*supposed*___ to

arrive before the guests.

## Than/Then

**than:** a word used to compare two or more things or persons
> It's colder inside *than* outside.

**then:** at a certain time, next in time
> I got out of the car and *then* realized the keys were still in it.

Clara ran more miles *than* she ever had before, and *then* she collapsed.

Back ___*then*___ I smoked more ___*than*___ three packs a day.

## Their/There/They're

**their:** a pronoun showing ownership
> I borrowed *their* clippers to trim the hedges.

**there:** a word indicating location or existence
> Just put the keys *there* on the desk.
> *There* are too many lawyers.

**they're:** a contraction of the words *they are*
> *They're* about to leave.

*There* is a car in *their* driveway, which indicates that *they're* home.

___*Their*___ beach house is empty except for the one week that

___*they're*___ vacationing ___*there*___ .

> ■ **TIP** If you aren't sure whether to use *their* or *they're,* substitute *they are.* If the sentence doesn't make sense, use *their.*

## Though/Through/Threw

**though:** however, nevertheless, in spite of
> *Though* he's short, he plays great basketball.

**through:** finished with (adjective), from one side to the other (preposition)
> I'm *through* arguing with you.
> The baseball went right *through* the window.

**threw:** hurled, tossed (past tense of the verb *throw*)
> She *threw* the basketball.

Even *though* it was illegal, she *threw* the empty cup *through* the window onto the road.

_____*Though*_____ she didn't really believe it would bring good luck, Jan _____*threw*_____ a penny _____*through*_____ the air into the fountain.

### To/Too/Two

**to:** a word indicating a direction or movement (preposition), part of the infinitive form of a verb
> Please give the message *to* Sharon.
> It is easier *to* ask for forgiveness than *to* get permission.

**too:** also, more than enough, very (adverb)
> I'm tired *too*.
> Dan ate *too* much and felt sick.
> That dream was *too* real.

**two:** the number between one and three
> The lab had only *two* computers.

They went *to* a restaurant and ordered *too* much food for *two* people.

When Marty went _____*to*_____ pay for his meal, the cashier charged him _____*two*_____ dollars _____*too*_____ much.

### Use/Used

**use:** to employ or utilize (verb)
> How do you plan to *use* that blueprint?

**used:** past tense of the verb *use*. *Used to* can indicate a past fact or state, or it can mean "familiar with."
> He *used* his lunch hour to do errands.
> He *used* to go for a walk during his lunch hour.

She *used* to be a chef, so she knows how to *use* all kinds of kitchen gadgets.

She is also *used* to improvising in the kitchen.

Tom _____*used*_____ the prize money to buy a boat; his family hoped he would _____*use*_____ it for his education, but Tom was _____*used*_____ to getting his way.

### Who's/Whose

**who's:** a contraction of the words *who is*
> *Who's* at the door?

**whose:** a pronoun showing ownership
> *Whose* shoes are these?

*Who's* the person *whose* car sank in the river?

The student _____*whose*_____ name is first on the list is the one _____*who's*_____ in charge.

■ **TIP** If you aren't sure whether to use *whose* or *who's*, substitute *who is*. If the sentence doesn't make sense, use *whose*.

### Your/You're

**your:** a pronoun showing ownership
   Did you bring *your* wallet?

**you're:** a contraction of the words *you are*
   *You're* not telling me the whole story.

*You're* going to have *your* third exam tomorrow.

_____*Your*_____ teacher says _____*you're*_____ very good with numbers.

■ **TIP** If you aren't sure whether to use *your* or *you're*, substitute *you are*. If the sentence doesn't make sense, use *your*.

### PRACTICE 1  USING THE RIGHT WORD

In each of the following items, circle the (correct word) in parentheses.

1. I just can't (accept / except) your decision.

2. She (use / used) to live next door.

3. (Their / There / They're) on (their / there / they're) way to the mountains.

4. The baby has more toys (than / then) he knows what to do with.

5. You should always act in accordance with your (principals / principles).

6. After cheating on the test, she had a very guilty (conscience / conscious).

7. His enthusiasm (knows / nos) (know / no) bounds.

8. Are you going to (your / you're) class today?

9. I should (of / have) left (are / our) car at the garage.

10. I need to (buy / by) some food for dinner.

## Edit Paragraphs and Your Own Writing

### PRACTICE 2  EDITING PARAGRAPHS FOR COMMONLY CONFUSED WORDS

Edit the following paragraphs to correct errors in the use of commonly confused words.

1. (1) When ~~your~~ [you're] driving, ~~its~~ [it's] hard to know exactly when your gas tank needs to be filled. (2) ~~Accept~~ [Except] for a few new models, cars' gas gauges don't tell you when you will run out or need to ~~by~~ [buy] gas. (3) The gauge reads *empty* when the gas level has ~~past~~ [passed] below a certain point. (4) However, ~~their~~ [there] is still gas in the car when ~~it's~~ [its] gas gauge first points at E. (5) Most people ~~no~~ [know] this, and they sometimes keep driving when they should ~~of~~ [have] stopped to fill up. (6) ~~Than~~ [Then] they run out of gas and ~~loose~~ [lose] time and perhaps their tempers trying to get ~~too~~ [to] a gas station. (7) The technology in some new cars allows drivers to ~~no~~ [know] more precisely ~~then~~ [than] they once could exactly how much gas is left in ~~there~~ [their] tanks, so they know when ~~their suppose~~ [they're supposed] to fill up.

2. (1) More and more women are purchasing handguns, against the ~~advise~~ [advice] of law enforcement officers. (2) Few of these women are criminals or plan to commit crimes. (3) They ~~no~~ [know] the risks of guns, and they ~~except~~ [accept] those risks. (4) They buy weapons primarily because ~~their~~ [they're] tired of feeling like victims. (5) They don't want to contribute ~~too~~ [to] the violence in ~~are~~ [our] society, but they also realize that women are the victims of violent attacks far ~~to~~ [too] often. (6) Many women ~~loose they're~~ [lose their] lives because they can't fight off ~~there~~ [their] attackers. (7) Some women have made a ~~conscience~~ [conscious] decision to arm themselves for protection. (8) The National Rifle Association (NRA) has even produced a series of advertisements with this aim as ~~it's~~ [its] main message.

(9) But does buying a gun make things worse rather ~~then~~ [than] better? (10) Having a gun in ~~you're~~ [your] house makes it three times more likely that someone will be killed there—and that someone is just as likely to be you or one of your children as ~~a~~ [an] assailant. (11) Most young children can't tell the difference between a real gun and a toy gun when they ~~fine~~ [find] one. (12) Every year, ~~their~~ [there] are tragic examples of children who accidentally shoot and even kill other youngsters while they are playing with guns. (13) A mother ~~who's~~ [whose] children are injured while playing with her gun will never again think that a gun provides ~~piece~~ [peace] of mind. (14) Reducing the violence in ~~are~~ [our] society—not redistributing it—may be a better solution.

■ **PRACTICE 3   EDITING YOUR OWN WRITING FOR COMMONLY CONFUSED WORDS**

As a final practice, edit a piece of your own writing for commonly confused words. It can be a paper you are working on for this course, a paper you've already finished, a paper for another course, or a recent piece of writing from your work or everyday life. Add any misused words you find to your personal list of the words you confuse most often.

■ **TEACHING TIP** Ask students for a few more commonly confused words. Start them off by putting one set on the board and then list others that they suggest.

## Chapter Review: Commonly Confused Words

1.  What are four strategies you can use to avoid confusing words that sound alike or have similar meanings?

    *Proofread carefully.*

    *Use a dictionary to look up any words you are unsure about.*

    *Focus on finding and correcting mistakes you make with the twenty-seven sets of*

    *commonly confused words covered in this chapter.*

    *Develop a personal list of words you confuse often.*

2.  What are the top five commonly confused words on your personal list?

    *Answers will vary.*

# 33

# Spelling

## *Using the Right Letters*

■ **LEARNING JOURNAL** Use your learning journal as a place to start a personal spelling list—a list of words that you misspell repeatedly. When you edit your papers, be sure to check for words on your spelling list.

As part of their editing, successful writers who are also poor spellers **proofread** their writing before submitting it, to find and correct spelling, punctuation, and capitalization errors.

## Understand the Importance of Spelling Correctly

■ **TEACHING TIP** Keep at least two dictionaries in the classroom. Let students know where they are, but also emphasize that they should buy their own.

Some very smart people are very poor spellers. Unfortunately, spelling errors are easy for readers to spot, and they make a bad impression. In fact, spelling errors can be considered the fifth most serious error that writers make.

If you are serious about improving your spelling, you need to have two important tools—a dictionary and a spelling list—and use them.

### Dictionary

A dictionary contains the correct spellings of words, along with information on how the words are pronounced, what they mean, and where they came from. Buy a dictionary; everyone needs one. You might also use one of the many dictionaries that are now available online.

■ **TIP** Online dictionaries can also help you with spelling. Merriam-Webster OnLine, at <m-w.com>, has a feature called the "wild card search" in which you can substitute a "?" for any single character you don't know and an "*" for any string of characters. The search engine then returns a list of possible words for you to choose from.

When proofreading your papers, consult a dictionary whenever you are unsure about the spelling of a word. *Checking a dictionary is the single most important thing you can do to improve your spelling.* For a sample dictionary entry, see page 471.

Buy a current dictionary rather than an old one because current editions have up-to-date definitions and words that are new to the language, such as *dot-commer, eye candy, identity theft,* and *road rage*. If you have trouble finding words in a regular dictionary, get a spelling dictionary, which is designed to help you find a word even if you have no idea how to spell it.

## Spelling List

Most people misspell the same words over and over. Keeping a list of these words will show you what your problem words are and will help you learn to spell them correctly.

Set aside a section of your course notebook or journal for your spelling list. Every time you edit a paper, write down the words that you misspelled. Put the correct spelling first, and then in parentheses put the way you actually wrote it. After you have recorded the spelling errors for three pieces of writing, spend ten minutes analyzing your spelling list. Ask yourself:

- What words have I misspelled more than once?
- What do I get wrong about them? Do I always misspell them the same way?
- What are my personal spelling "demons"? ("Demons" are the five to ten words that you tend to spell wrong over and over.)
- What other mistakes do I tend to make repeatedly (leaving the final -*s* off words, for example)?

Write your demon words (five to ten words), spelled correctly, on an index card, and keep the card somewhere handy so that you can consult it whenever you write.

Every couple of weeks, go back to your spelling list to see if your problem words have changed. Are you misspelling fewer words in each paper? What are your current spelling demons? Using a spelling list will definitely improve your spelling.

■ **RESOURCES** *Additional Resources* contains tests and supplemental exercises for this chapter.

■ **TEACHING TIP** Telling students they will have to turn in their spelling lists reinforces the importance of their making them. If you have time, you can make up individualized spelling quizzes.

# Practice Spelling Correctly

You can improve your spelling in several ways. First learn to find and correct spelling mistakes in your writing. At the same time, work on becoming a better speller so that you make fewer mistakes to begin with.

## Three Steps for Finding and Correcting Mistakes

Every time you write a paper, proofread it for spelling errors by focusing only on spelling. Don't try to correct your grammar, improve your message, and check your spelling at the same time. Remember to check the dictionary whenever you are unsure about the spelling of a word and to add all the spelling mistakes you find to your personal spelling list.

### Step 1. Use a Spell Checker

Most word-processing programs have spell checkers. A spell checker finds and highlights a word that may be misspelled, suggests other spellings, and gives you the opportunity to change the spelling of the word. (Some word-processing programs automatically highlight potentially misspelled words.)

Use a spell checker after you have completed a piece of writing but before you print it out.

Never rely on a spell checker to do your editing for you. A spell checker ignores anything it recognizes as a word, so it will not help you find words that are misused or misspellings that are also words. For example, a spell checker would not highlight any of the problems in these phrases:

| | |
|---|---|
| Just *to* it. | (Correct: Just *do* it.) |
| pain in the *nick* | (Correct: pain in the *neck*) |
| my writing *coarse* | (Correct: my writing *course*) |

### Step 2.  Use Proofreading Techniques

Use some of the following proofreading techniques to focus on the spelling of one word at a time. Different techniques work for different people, so try them all and then decide which ones work best for you.

**PROOFREADING TECHNIQUES**

- Print out your paper before proofreading. (Many writers find it easier to detect errors on paper than on a computer screen.)
- Put a piece of paper under the line that you are reading.
- Cut a "window" in an index card that is about the size of a long word (such as *misunderstanding*), and place it over your writing to focus on one word at a time.
- Proofread your paper backward, one word at a time.
- Print out a version of your paper that looks noticeably different: Make the words larger, make the margins larger, triple-space the lines, or do all of these.
- Read your paper aloud. This strategy will help you if you tend to leave words out.
- Exchange papers with a partner and proofread each other's papers. You should only identify possible misspellings. The writer of the paper should be responsible for checking the spelling and correcting any spelling errors.

### Step 3.  Check Your Personal Spelling List

After you have proofread each word in your paper, look at your personal spelling list and your list of demon words one more time. Have you used any of these words in your paper? If so, go back and check their spelling again. You may be surprised to find that you missed seeing the same old spelling mistakes.

■ **TIP**  For more spelling practice, visit Exercise Central at <bedfordstmartins.com/ realwriting>.

**PRACTICE 1   USING THE THREE STEPS FOR FINDING AND CORRECTING MISTAKES**

Take the last paper you wrote — or one that you are working on now — and use the three steps for finding and correcting spelling mistakes. How many spelling mistakes did you find? Were you surprised? How was the experience different from what you normally do to edit for spelling? How confident are you that your paper now contains no spelling mistakes?

## Four Strategies for Becoming a Better Speller

Learning to find and correct spelling mistakes that you have already made is only half the battle. You also need to become a better speller so that you do not make so many mistakes in the first place. Here are four strategies.

### Strategy 1. Master Ten Troublemakers

The ten words in the following list were identified by writing teachers around the United States as the words most commonly misspelled by students of all ages and backgrounds. Master these and you will be ahead of the crowd. Because there are only ten, you should be able to memorize them.

A phrase related to the spelling of a word often helps people remember the correct spelling. Silly as these memory aids may seem, they can work, so try them or think of your own.

**THE TEN TROUBLEMAKERS**

| TROUBLEMAKERS | COMMON MISSPELLINGS | MEMORY AIDS |
|---|---|---|
| 1. **a lot** | alot | *a lot* is a lot of words |
| 2. **develop** | develope | *lop* off the *e* |
| 3. **receive** | recieve | *i* before *e* except after *c*, or when sounded like *a*, as in *neighbor* or *weigh* |
| 4. **separate** | *seperate* | there's *a rat* in there |
| 5. **until** | *untill* | sounds like *one l* |
| 6. **light** | *lite* | light *is* right |
| 7. **necessary** | necesary, nesesary | a *c* and two *s*'s are *necessary* |
| 8. **argument** | arguement | no *gue* (pronounced *gooey*) arguments! |
| 9. **definite** | definate, defenite | people *definitely* have two *eyes (i's)* |
| 10. **surprise** | surprize | *surprise* is no *prize* |

### Strategy 2. Master Your Personal Spelling Demons

Once you know what your spelling demons are, you can start to conquer them. If your list of spelling demons is long, you may want to start by focusing on the top five or the top three. When you have mastered these, you can go on to the next few. Different techniques work for different people. Try them all, and then stick with the ones that work for you.

**TECHNIQUES FOR MASTERING YOUR SPELLING DEMONS**

- Create memory aids, like those shown for the ten troublemakers.
- Break the word into parts and try to master each part. You can break it into syllables (*Feb ru ar y*) or separate the prefixes and endings (*dis ap point ment*).
- Write the word (correctly) ten times.
- Say the letters of the word out loud. See if there's a rhythm or a rhyme you can memorize.
- Write a paragraph in which you use the word at least three times.
- Say the word out loud, emphasizing each letter and syllable even if that's not the way you normally say it. For example, say *pro bab ly* instead of *prob ly*. Try to pronounce the word this way in your head each time you spell it.
- Ask a partner to give you a spelling test.

### Strategy 3.  Master Commonly Confused Words

Chapter 32 covers twenty-seven sets of words that are commonly confused because they sound similar, such as *write* and *right* or *its* and *it's*. If you can master these commonly confused words, you will avoid many spelling mistakes.

### Strategy 4.  Learn Six Spelling Rules

This section covers spelling situations in which people often think, *What do I do here?* If you can remember the rules, you can correct many of the spelling errors in your writing.

Before the six rules, here is a quick review of vowels and consonants.

Vowels

**Consonants** are all the letters that are not vowels: *b, c, d, f, g, h, j, k, l, m, n, p, q, r, s, t, v, w, x,* and *z*.

**The letter *y*** can be either a vowel or a consonant. It is a vowel when it sounds like the *y* in *fly* or *hungry*. It is a consonant when it sounds like the *y* in *yellow*.

### Should I Use ie or ei?

> **RULE 1:**   *I* before *e*
>
> Except after *c*.
>
> Or when sounded like *a*
>
> As in *neighbor* or *weigh*.

Many people repeat this rhyme to themselves as they decide whether a word is spelled with an *ie* or an *ei*.

pie**ce** (*i* before *e*)

rece**i**ve (except after *c*)

**ei**ght (sounds like *a*)

■ **TEAMWORK** For each rule, have students give three additional examples of words that follow the rule. This can be done in small groups or pairs.

**EXCEPTIONS:** *either, neither, foreign, height, seize, society, their, weird*

■ **PRACTICE 2   USING RULE 1**

In the spaces provided, write more examples of words that follow the rule. Do not use words that have already been covered.

*Answers will vary. Possible answers shown.*

1. *niece* _____

2. *siege* _____

3. *believe* _____

4. *deceive* _____

5. *freight* _____

6. *sieve* _____

### Should I Drop the Final e or Keep It when Adding an Ending to a Word?

**RULE 2:**  **Drop the final** *e* when adding an ending that begins with a vowel.

> hop**e** + ing = hoping

> imagin**e** + ation = imagination

**Keep the final** *e* when adding an ending that begins with a consonant.

> achiev**e** + ment = achievement

> definit**e** + ly = definitely

**EXCEPTIONS:** *argument, awful, simply, truly,* and others

■ **PRACTICE 3   USING RULE 2**

For each item, circle the (first letter) in the ending, and decide whether it is a consonant or a vowel. Then add the ending to the word and write the new word in the space.

1. peace + (f)ul = *peaceful* _____

2. separate + (l)y = *separately* _____

3. believe + (i)ng = *believing* _____

4. schedule + (e)d = *scheduled* _____

5. value + (a)ble = *valuable* _____

6. write + (i)ng = *writing* _____

7. pure + (e)r = *purer* _____

8. create + (i)ve = *creative* _____

9. shame + (f)ul = *shameful* _____

10. converse + (a)tion = *conversation* _____

### *Should I Change the y to i when Adding an Ending?*

**RULE 3:**   When adding an ending to a word that ends in *y*, **change the y to i** when a consonant comes before the *y*.

lone**ly** + est = lonel**i**est

hap**py** + er = happ**i**er

apolo**gy** + ize = apolo**gi**ze

like**ly** + hood = likel**i**hood

**Do not change the y** when a vowel comes before the *y*.

**boy** + **i**sh = boyish

**pay** + **m**ent = payment

surv**ey** + **or** = surveyor

**buy** + **er** = buyer

**EXCEPTIONS:**   1. When adding *-ing* to a word ending in *y*, always keep the *y*, even if a consonant comes before it: stu**dy** + ing = stud**y**ing.

2. Other exceptions include *daily, dryer, said,* and *paid*.

■   **PRACTICE 4    USING RULE 3**

For each item, circle the letter before the *y*, and decide whether it is a vowel or a consonant. Then add the ending to the word, and write the new word in the space provided.

1. pl**a**y + ful = *playful*

2. pl**y** + ers = *pliers*

3. come**d**y + an = *comedian*

4. car**r**y + er = *carrier*

5. de**f**y + ant = *defiant*

6. pl**a**y + ed = *played*

7. bu**r**y + al = *burial*

8. me**r**ry + ment = *merriment*

9. puf**f**y + ness = *puffiness*

10. pr**a**y + ers = *prayers*

### *Should I Double the Final Consonant when Adding an Ending?*

**RULE 4:**   When adding an ending that starts with a vowel to a one-syllable word, follow these rules.

**Double the final consonant** only if the word ends with a consonant-vowel-consonant.

t**rap** + ed = tra**pp**ed

oc**cur** + ence = occu**rr**ence

pre**fer** + ed = prefe**rr**ed

com**mit** + ed = commi**tt**ed

**Do not double the final consonant** if the word ends with some other combination.

| VOWEL-VOWEL-CONSONANT | VOWEL-CONSONANT-CONSONANT |
|---|---|
| clean + est = cleanest | slick + er = slicker |
| poor + er = poorer | teach + er = teacher |
| clear + ed = cleared | last + ed = lasted |

**RULE 5:** When adding an ending that starts with a vowel to a word with two or more syllables, follow these rules.

**Double the final consonant** only if the word ends with a consonant-vowel-consonant and the stress is on the last syllable.

submit + ing = submitting

control + er = controller

admit + ed = admitted

**Do not double the final consonant** in other cases.

problem + atic = problematic

understand + ing = understanding

offer + ed = offered

**PRACTICE 5     USING RULES 4 AND 5**

For each item, circle the (last three letters) in the main word, and decide whether they fit the consonant-vowel-consonant pattern. In words with more than one syllable, underline the stressed syllable. Then add the ending to each word, and write the new word in the space provided.

1. lift + ed = *lifted*

2. happen + ed = *happened*

3. command + er = *commander*

4. omit + ed = *omitted*

5. cheap + er = *cheaper*

6. disgust + ed = *disgusted*

7. spot + ed = *spotted*

8. slip + ery = *slippery*

9. scrap + ed = *scrapped*

10. return + ed = *returned*

### Should I Add -s or -es?

The endings -s and -es are used to make the plural form of most nouns (*two books*) and the *he/she/it* form of most verbs (*he runs*).

**RULE 6:** **Add -s** to most words, including words that end in *o* preceded by a vowel.

| MOST WORDS | WORDS THAT END IN VOWEL PLUS *O* |
|---|---|
| book + **s** = books | vid**eo** + **s** = videos |
| college + **s** = colleges | ster**eo** + **s** = stereos |
| jump + **s** = jumps | rad**io** + **s** = radios |

**Add -es** to words that end in *o* preceded by a consonant and words that end in *s, sh, ch,* or *x.*

| WORDS THAT END IN CONSONANT PLUS *O* | WORDS THAT END IN *S, SH, CH,* OR *X* |
|---|---|
| pota**to** + **es** = potatoes | class + **es** = classes |
| he**ro** + **es** = heroes | push + **es** = pushes |
| **go** + **es** = goes | ben**ch** + **es** = benches |
|  | fax + **es** = faxes |

**EXCEPTIONS:** *pianos, solos,* and others

### PRACTICE 6    USING RULE 6

For each word, circle the (last two letters,) and decide which of the Rule 6 patterns this word fits. Add *-s* or *-es* and write the new word in the space provided.

1. addre(ss) *addresses*

2. bicy(cle) *bicycles*

3. toma(to) *tomatoes*

4. chur(ch) *churches*

5. stret(ch) *stretches*

6. stud(io) *studios*

7. da(sh) *dashes*

8. constru(ct) *constructs*

9. discov(er) *discovers*

10. b(ox) *boxes*

---

## One Hundred Commonly Misspelled Words

Use this list as an easy reference to check your spelling.

| | | | |
|---|---|---|---|
| absence | a lot | appetite | basically |
| achieve | already | argument | beautiful |
| across | analyze | athlete | beginning |
| aisle | answer | awful | believe |

| | | | |
|---|---|---|---|
| business | especially | knowledge | rhythm |
| calendar | exaggerate | license | roommate |
| career | excellent | lightning | schedule |
| category | exercise | loneliness | scissors |
| chief | fascinate | marriage | secretary |
| column | February | meant | separate |
| coming | finally | muscle | sincerely |
| commitment | foreign | necessary | sophomore |
| conscious | friend | ninety | succeed |
| convenient | government | noticeable | successful |
| cruelty | grief | occasion | surprise |
| daughter | guidance | occurrence | truly |
| definite | harass | perform | until |
| describe | height | physically | usually |
| dictionary | humorous | prejudice | vacuum |
| different | illegal | probably | valuable |
| disappoint | immediately | psychology | vegetable |
| dollar | independent | receive | weight |
| eighth | interest | recognize | weird |
| embarrass | jewelry | recommend | writing |
| environment | judgment | restaurant | written |

# Edit Paragraphs and Your Own Writing

### ■ PRACTICE 7   EDITING PARAGRAPHS FOR SPELLING

Find and correct any spelling mistakes in the following paragraphs.

      (1) In today's schools, there is a ~~rageing~~ *raging* argument about whether to ~~seperate~~ *separate* children of different ~~abilitys~~ *abilities* into classes with others of similar ~~achievment~~ *achievement* levels. (2) Some experts claim that children develope and learn best when they are in mixed-ability classes. (3) These same experts state that ~~divideing~~ *dividing* students will ~~prejudise~~ *prejudice* teachers against the slower

students. (4) When students of lesser ability are grouped together, they
don't learn as fast, their self-esteem drops, their ~~absenses~~ *absences* increase, and
they may drop out. (5) ~~Basicaly,~~ *Basically,* the experts claim, students ~~loose~~ *lose* all
motivation to ~~acheive~~ *achieve*.

(6) Other experts present another side of the ~~arguement~~ *argument*. (7) They
say that grouping ~~buy~~ *by* ability allows students ~~too~~ *to* learn at a more natural
rate. (8) Teachers ~~usally~~ *usually* have ~~alot~~ *a lot* more time to spend with students
because they aren't trying to teach students of all abilities. (9) For example, if students with similar writing skills ~~our~~ *are* together in class, the
teacher either can spend a lot of time with grammar if the class needs
it or can skip over it if the students have ~~masterred~~ *mastered* the basic rules.
(10) These experts claim that grouping by ability provides a more effi-
cient learning ~~enviroment,~~ *environment,* gets a good class ~~rythym~~ *rhythm* going, and results in
the ~~happyest,~~ *happiest,* most enthusiastic learners.

(11) Both sides have ~~intresting,~~ *interesting,* persuasive arguments that they
present to local, state, and federal ~~goverment~~ *government* officials. (12) So far, neither side has persuaded the other, and the heated debate continues.

■ **PRACTICE 8    EDITING YOUR OWN WRITING FOR SPELLING**

As a final practice, edit a piece of your own writing for spelling, using the
techniques described in this chapter. It can be a paper you are working on
for this course, a paper you've already finished, a paper for another course,
or a recent piece of writing from work or everyday life. Record in your learning journal any mistakes you find, along with their corrections.

## Chapter Review: Spelling

1. What are two important tools for good spelling? *a dictionary and a*
   *spelling list*

2. What three steps can you use to find and correct spelling mistakes?
   *Use a spell checker.*

   *Use proofreading techniques.*

   *Check your personal spelling list.*

3. What four strategies can you use to become a better speller?

*Master the ten troublemakers.*

*Master your personal spelling demons.*

*Master commonly confused words.*

*Learn the six spelling rules.*

4.  For each of the six spelling rules presented in this chapter, write one word that shows how the rule works.

    Using *ie* or *ei*: *Answers will vary.*

    Dropping or keeping the final *e* when adding an ending to a word:

    Changing or not changing the *y* to *i* when adding an ending:

    Adding an ending that begins with a vowel to a one-syllable word:

    Adding an ending that begins with a vowel to a word with two or more syllables: 

    Adding -*s* or -*es* to form plural words or the *he/she/it* forms of verbs:

5.  What are five of your own spelling demons? *Answers will vary.*

## Part Seven
# Punctuation and Capitalization

# 34

# Commas

,

## Understand What Commas Do

**Commas (,)** are punctuation marks that help readers understand a sentence. Read aloud the following three sentences. How does the use of commas change the meaning?

| | |
|---|---|
| **NO COMMA** | When you call Sarah I'll start cooking. |
| **ONE COMMA** | When you call Sarah, I'll start cooking. |
| **TWO COMMAS** | When you call, Sarah, I'll start cooking. |

When you use a comma in a sentence, it signals a particular meaning to your readers, so it is important that you understand when and how to use it.

## Practice Using Commas Correctly

### Commas between Items in a Series

Use commas to separate the items in a series (three or more items). This includes the last item in the series, which usually has *and* before it.

| item | , | item | , | item | , | and | item |
|---|---|---|---|---|---|---|---|

To get from South Dakota to Texas, we will drive through *Nebraska*, *Kansas*, and *Oklahoma*.

We can *sleep in the car*, *stay in a motel*, or *camp outside*.

As I drive, *Maria will read*, *Harry will look at the scenery*, and *my father will sleep*.

> ■ **LEARNING JOURNAL** Use your learning journal as a place to record sentences with comma problems. Also write down edited versions of these sentences, with the problems corrected.

> ■ **RESOURCES** *Additional Resources* contains supplemental exercises for this chapter.

> ■ **TIP** How does a comma change the way you read a sentence aloud? Most readers pause when they come to a comma.

■ **TEACHING TIP** Write this incorrectly punctuated sentence on the board: *My daughter is a fast aggressive, and competitive soccer player.* Read it aloud (as if it were correctly punctuated), and ask students if they can hear where the missing comma should go.

■ **TIP** For more practice using commas correctly, visit Exercise Central at <bedfordstmartins .com/realwriting>.

**NOTE:** In magazines and newspapers as well as in some business writing, the comma before the final item is sometimes left out. It is always best to include it, however, so that your meaning will be clear.

■ **PRACTICE 1**     **USING COMMAS IN SERIES**

Edit the following sentences by underlining the items in the series and adding commas where they are needed. If a sentence is already correct, put a "C" next to it.

**EXAMPLE:** Sales of our fruit juices have expanded in the Northeast, the South, and the Midwest.

1. Continued expansion depends on our ability to promote novelty beverages such as papaya, mango, and boysenberry juices in grocery stores and restaurants.

2. We also present juice as an alternative to beverages such as soda, beer, and water.

3. In Washington and California, we are doing well against our major competitors.  C

4. In these areas, our increase in market share over the past three years has been 7 percent, 10 percent, and 7 percent.

5. In areas where our juice is new, we'd like increases of 10 percent, 20 percent, or 25 percent.

6. In each section of the country, the regional sales director will develop a plan, his or her assistant will communicate the plan, and local sales-people will implement the plan for that area.

7. We want to target New England states such as Connecticut, Massachusetts, and Maine, where attitudes about fruit juice are similar to those in Seattle, Portland, and other Northwest cities.

8. Our advertising should emphasize our small-scale production methods, our commitment to quality, and our juices' delicious flavor.  C

9. We should set up displays, provide free samples of our juices, and sponsor contests.

10. Careful planning, hard work, and individual initiative will ensure the growth of our company.  *C*

## Commas in Compound Sentences

A **compound sentence** contains two complete sentences joined by one of these words: *and, but, for, nor, or, so, yet.* Use a comma before the joining word to separate the two complete sentences.

■ **TIP** The words *and, but, for, nor, or, so,* and *yet* are called coordinating conjunctions. For more information, see Chapter 27.

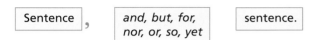

I called my best friend, and she agreed to drive me to work.

I asked my best friend to drive me to work, but she was busy.

I can take the bus to work, or I can call another friend.

**NOTE:** A comma is not needed if the word *and, but, for, nor, or, so,* or *yet* joins two sentence elements that are *not* complete sentences.

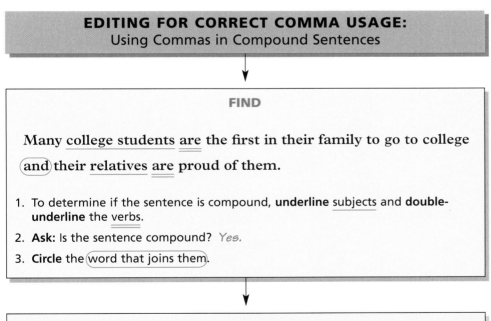

**EDITING FOR CORRECT COMMA USAGE:**
Using Commas in Compound Sentences

**FIND**

Many college students are the first in their family to go to college and their relatives are proud of them.

1. To determine if the sentence is compound, **underline** subjects and **double-underline** the verbs.
2. **Ask:** Is the sentence compound? *Yes.*
3. **Circle** the word that joins them.

**EDIT**

Many college students are the first in their family to go to college, and their relatives are proud of them.

4. **Put a comma** before the word that joins the two sentences.

■    **PRACTICE 2    USING COMMAS IN COMPOUND SENTENCES**

Edit the following compound sentences by adding commas where they are needed. If a sentence is already correct, put a "C" next to it. If you need help, look back at the chart on page 509 that shows the correction steps.

> **EXAMPLE:** Marika wanted to get a college education‸but her
>
> husband didn't like the idea.

1. Marika's hospital volunteer work had convinced her to become a physical therapist, but she needed a college degree to qualify.  *C*

2. Deciding to apply to college was difficult for her‸so she was excited when she was admitted.

3. She had chosen the college carefully‸for it had an excellent program in physical therapy.

4. Marika knew the courses would be difficult‸but she had not expected her husband to oppose her plan.

5. They had been married for twelve years, and he was surprised that she wanted a career.  *C*

6. She tried to tell him about the exciting things she was learning‸but he didn't seem interested.

7. It was hard for her to manage the house and keep up with her classes, but he would not help.  *C*

8. Maybe he was upset that she wanted more education than he had‸or perhaps he was afraid they would grow apart.

9. She didn't want to have to choose between her husband and an education‸and she didn't have to.

10. They talked about their problems‸and now he thinks her career might even help their marriage.

■ **ESL** Because different languages have different intonation patterns, students should not rely on intonation alone to decide where to put commas.

## Commas after Introductory Word Groups

Use a comma after an introductory word or word group. An introductory word group can be a phrase or a clause. The comma lets your readers know when the main part of the sentence is starting.

| Introductory word or word group | , | main part of sentence. |
| --- | --- | --- |

**INTRODUCTORY WORD:** *However,* the president is coming to visit our city.

**INTRODUCTORY PHRASE:** *By the way,* I don't have a babysitter for tomorrow.

**INTRODUCTORY CLAUSE:** *While I waited outside,* Susan went backstage.

### PRACTICE 3    USING COMMAS AFTER INTRODUCTORY WORD GROUPS

In each item, underline any introductory word or word group. Then add commas after introductory word groups where they are needed. If a sentence is already correct, put a "C" next to it.

**EXAMPLE:** According to most medical researchers, the chance of the AIDS virus being spread through athletic contact is very low.

1. As we all know, AIDS is spread mainly through sexual contact and through drug use that involves the sharing of needles.

2. Nonetheless, some people feel that all college athletes should be tested for HIV.

3. Since basketball star Magic Johnson revealed in 1991 that he is HIV-positive, an NBA player must be removed from a game if he is bleeding.

4. Once the wound is properly bandaged, the player is allowed to return to the game.

5. Not surprisingly, many college sports follow similar rules.

6. However, requiring athletes to leave a contest when they are bleeding is quite different from forcing them to be tested for HIV. *C*

7. According to some student athletes, mandatory HIV testing would violate their civil liberties.

8. Using the same argument, many student athletes object to being tested for the use of drugs.  *c*

9. In their view, student athletes should be treated no differently than other students.  *c*

10. In this case, some would say that public health is more important than civil liberties.

## Commas around Appositives and Interrupters

■ **TIP** For more on appositives, see Chapter 29.

An **appositive** comes directly before or after a noun or pronoun and renames it.

Lily, *a senior*, will take her nursing exam this summer.

The prices are outrageous at Chapters, *the campus bookstore*.

■ **TIP** Most of the transitions (time, space, and importance) covered in earlier chapters are interrupters that should be set off with commas.

An **interrupter** is an aside or transition that interrupts the flow of a sentence and does not affect its meaning.

My sister, *incidentally*, has very good reasons for being late.

Her child had a fever, *for example*.

Putting commas around appositives and interrupters tells readers that these elements give extra information but are not essential to the meaning of a sentence. If an appositive or interrupter is in the middle of a sentence, set it off with a pair of commas, one before and one after. If an appositive or interrupter comes at the beginning or end of a sentence, separate it from the rest of the sentence with one comma.

*By the way*, your proposal has been accepted.

Your proposal, *by the way*, has been accepted.

Your proposal has been accepted, *by the way*.

**NOTE:** Sometimes an appositive is essential to the meaning of a sentence. When a sentence would not have the same meaning without the appositive, the appositive should not be set off with commas.

The actor *John Travolta* has never won an Academy Award.

[The sentence *The actor has never won an Academy Award* does not have the same meaning.]

> **EDITING FOR CORRECT COMMA USAGE:**
> Using Commas to Set Off Appositives and Interrupters

---

**FIND**

Tamara my sister-in-law moved in with us last week.

1. **Underline** the subject.
2. **Underline** any appositive (which renames the subject) or interrupter (which interrupts the flow of the sentence).
3. **Ask:** Is the appositive or interrupter essential to the meaning of the sentence? *No.*

---

**EDIT**

Tamara, my sister-in-law, moved in with us last week.

4. If it is not essential, **set it off with commas.**

---

■ **PRACTICE 4   USING COMMAS TO SET OFF APPOSITIVES AND INTERRUPTERS**

Underline any appositives and interrupters in the following sentences. Then use commas to set them off. If you need help, look back at the chart above that shows the correction steps. Some sentences may have more than one appositive or interrupter.

> **EXAMPLE:** Many homeowners, people of all ages and backgrounds, are nervous these days.

1. Gated communities, those fancy neighborhoods with a gate at the entrance, have been part of the American landscape for years.

2. Today, however, they are more popular than ever before.

3. The terrorist attacks of 2001, the hijackings and anthrax scares, have left many people feeling insecure.

4. Gates and guardhouses, visible symbols of protective authority, make anxious Americans feel safer at home.

5. The fear of crime may, in fact, be worse than crime itself in most parts of the United States.

6. Crime in gated communities, mainly vandalism and petty theft, occurs in spite of gates and guards.

7. The criminals behind such acts, neighborhood teenagers, often live inside the gates.

8. Most gated communities, as it happens, do not even have walls around them.

9. The gate, a sign of a safe community, is nothing more than that, a sign.

10. Nervous residents use one mirage, the appearance of security, to help them overcome another, the fear of random violence.

## Commas around Adjective Clauses

An **adjective clause** is a group of words that begins with *who, which,* or *that,* has a subject and verb, and describes a noun right before it in a sentence. Whether or not an adjective clause should be set off from the rest of the sentence by commas depends on its meaning in the sentence.

If an adjective clause can be taken out of a sentence without completely changing the meaning of the sentence, put commas around the clause.

Lily, *who is my cousin,* will take her nursing exam this summer.

Chapters, *which is the campus bookstore,* charges outrageous prices.

I complained to Mr. Kranz, *who is the bookstore manager.*

If an adjective clause is essential to the meaning of a sentence, do not put commas around it. You can tell whether a clause is essential by taking it out and seeing if the meaning of the sentence changes significantly, as it would if you took the clauses out of the following examples.

The only grocery store *that sold good bread* went out of business.

Students *who do internships* often improve their hiring potential.

Salesclerks *who sell liquor to minors* are breaking the law.

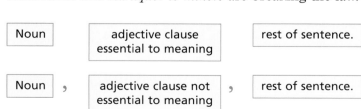

**EDITING FOR CORRECT COMMA USAGE:**
Using Commas to Set Off Adjective Clauses

**FIND**

The woman who is the CEO of eBay is very well-respected.

1. **Underline** any adjective clause (a word group that begins with *who, which,* or *that*).
2. **Read** the sentence without this clause.
3. **Ask:** Does the meaning change significantly without the clause? *Yes.*

**EDIT**

The woman who is the CEO of eBay is very well-respected.

4. If the meaning *does* change, as in this case, **do not put in commas.** (Add commas only if the meaning *does not* change.)

### PRACTICE 5   USING COMMAS TO SET OFF ADJECTIVE CLAUSES

Edit the following sentences by putting commas around adjective clauses where they are needed. Remember that if an adjective clause is essential to the meaning of a sentence, you should not use commas. If a sentence is already correct, put a "C" next to it. If you need help, look back at the chart above that shows the correction steps.

**EXAMPLE:** Elvis Presley, who died in 1977, still has fans around the world.

1. My mother, who has always loved music, was not a big fan of Elvis Presley when she was younger.

2. She considered the teenagers who were Elvis fans out of touch with popular music. *C*

3. The records that she bought as a teenager embarrass her now. *C*

4. I have looked through her collection, which includes hits by Barry Manilow and John Denver.

5. She started to listen to Elvis after a party that friends of hers held on the tenth anniversary of the King's death.  *C*

6. The party, which featured local bands playing Elvis songs, changed her mind about the music.

7. My mother's best friend from high school, who also attended the party, introduced her to a handsome Elvis impersonator.

8. That man, who is still an Elvis impersonator today, is also my father.

9. My father's stage show, which now emphasizes the King's Las Vegas years, is only a little embarrassing to me.

10. The part that I like best about his performances is how impressed my friends are with my dad.  *C*

## Other Uses for Commas

### Commas with Quotation Marks

■ **TIP** For more on quotation marks, see Chapter 36.

**Quotation marks** are used to show that you are repeating exactly what someone said. Use commas to set off the words inside quotation marks from the rest of the sentence.

> "Let me see your license," demanded the police officer.
>
> "Did you realize," she asked, "that you were going eighty miles per hour?"
>
> I exclaimed, "I didn't!"

Notice that a comma never comes directly after a quotation mark.

When quotations are not attributed to a particular person, commas may not be necessary.

> "Pretty is as pretty does" never made sense to me.

### Commas in Addresses

Use commas to separate the elements of an address included in a sentence. However, do not use a comma before a zip code.

> My address is 2512 Windermere Street, Jackson, Mississippi 40720.

If a sentence continues after the address, put a comma after the address.

> I moved here from Detroit, Michigan, when I was eighteen.

## Commas in Dates

Separate the day from the year with a comma. If you give just the month and year, do not separate them with a comma.

My daughter was born on November 8, 1992.

The next conference is in August 2004.

If a sentence continues after the date, put a comma after the date.

On April 21, 2005, the contract will expire.

## Commas with Names

Put commas around the name of someone you are addressing by name.

Don, I want you to come look at this.

Unfortunately, Marie, you need to finish the report by next week.

## Commas with Yes *or* No

Put commas around the word *yes* or *no* in response to a question.

Yes, I believe you are right.

### PRACTICE 6   **USING COMMAS IN OTHER WAYS**

Edit the following sentences by adding commas where they are needed. If a sentence is already correct, put a "C" next to it.

**EXAMPLE:** On December 12, 2001, beachfront property was badly damaged by a fast-moving storm.

1. Some homeowners were still waiting to settle their claims with their insurance companies in January 2003.  *C*

2. Rob McGregor of 31 Hudson Street, Wesleyville, is one of those homeowners.

3. Asked if he was losing patience, McGregor replied, "Yes, I sure am."

4. "I've really had it up to here," McGregor said.  *C*

5. His wife said, "Rob, don't go mouthing off to any reporters."

6. "Betty, I'll say what I want to say," Rob replied.

7. An official of Value-Safe Insurance of Wrightsville, Ohio, said the company will process claims within the next few months.

8. "No, there is no way we can do it any sooner," the official said.

9. Customers unhappy with their service may write to Value-Safe Insurance, P.O. Box 225, Wrightsville, Ohio 62812. *C*

10. The company's home office in Rye, New York, can be reached by a toll-free number.

## Edit Paragraphs and Your Own Writing

### PRACTICE 7   EDITING PARAGRAPHS FOR COMMAS

Edit the following paragraphs by adding commas where they are needed.

1. (1) According to etiquette experts, e-mail users need to practice good manners. (2) Yes, you can answer your e-mail in your bathrobe, but you should still be courteous. (3) Not everyone appreciates receiving jokes, electronic greeting cards, and bogus virus warnings regularly. (4) You should be careful, in particular, to avoid sending dozens of such e-mail messages to someone's office address. (5) E-mail is similar to a telephone call, a quick and informal way to keep in touch. (6) As a rule, you should not e-mail anyone more often than you would call. (7) In addition, you should use the subject header to let the recipient know whether or not the message is important. (8) Proper etiquette is not just for dinner parties, so do your part to improve the manners of the online community.

2. (1) In April 1990, the book *You Just Don't Understand* was published by William Morrow in New York, New York. (2) The subject of the book is the differences in the way men and women use language, including how they listen, how they speak, how they interact, and generally how they communicate. (3) It gives examples of how men and women misunderstand each other, and it describes the causes of and possible so-

lutions to the differences in their language expectations. (4) Deborah Tannen, the author, starts with childhood experiences that shape the way girls and boys use language.

(5) Tannen writes, "Even if they grow up in the same house, girls and boys grow up in different worlds of words. (6) Although they often play together, boys and girls spend most of their time playing in same-sex groups. (7) And although some of their play activities are similar, their favorite games are different, and their ways of using language in their games are also different." (8) Tannen continues, "Boys tend to play outside, for example, in large groups that have a hierarchy. (9) Girls, on the other hand, play in small groups or pairs. (10) Many of their activities (such as playing house) don't have winners or losers."

(11) Later in life, these differences can cause disagreements between men and women. (12) Tannen says, for example, "For everyone, home is a place to be offstage. (13) The comfort of home, however, can have opposite meanings for men and women. (14) For many men, the comfort of the home means freedom from having to talk. (15) They are free to remain silent. (16) For women, on the other hand, home is a place where they feel the greatest need to talk, and they want to talk to those closest to them." (17) Needless to say, conflicts result from these different expectations.

■ **LEARNING JOURNAL** What mistake with commas do you make most often? Why do you think you make this mistake?

## ▐ PRACTICE 8    EDITING YOUR OWN WRITING FOR COMMAS

As a final practice, edit a piece of your own writing for comma usage. It can be a paper you are working on for this course, a paper you've already finished, a paper for another course, or a recent piece of writing from your work or everyday life. In your learning journal, record any examples of sentences with comma problems that you find, along with edited versions of those sentences.

# Chapter Review: Commas

1. A comma (,) is a _punctuation mark_ that helps readers understand your sentence.

2. How do you use commas in these three situations?

   In a series of items, *use a comma to separate three or more items in a series* .

   In a compound sentence, *use a coordinating conjunction and a comma to* *make two sentences into one* .

   When there is an introductory word group, *use a comma after an intro-* *ductory clause or phrase* .

3. An appositive comes before or after a noun or pronoun and *renames* *the noun or pronoun* .

4. An interrupter is an *aside or transition* that interrupts the flow of a sentence.

5. Put commas around an adjective clause when it is *not essential* to the meaning of a sentence.

6. How are commas used with quotation marks? *Use commas to set off the* *words inside quotation marks from the rest of the sentence* .

7. In a date with the month, the day, and the year, a comma goes *between* *the day and the year* .

# 35

# Apostrophes

,

## Understand What Apostrophes Do

An **apostrophe** (') is a punctuation mark that either shows ownership (*Susan's*) or indicates that a letter has been intentionally left out to form a contraction (*I'm, that's, they're*). Although an apostrophe looks like a comma (,), it is not used for the same purpose, and it is written higher on the line than commas are.

apostrophe'   comma,

■ **LEARNING JOURNAL**
Use your learning journal as a place to record sentences with apostrophe problems. Also record edited versions of these sentences, with the problems corrected.

## Practice Using Apostrophes Correctly

### Apostrophes to Show Ownership

- **Add -'s to a singular noun to show ownership even if the noun already ends in -s.**

  *Karen's* apartment is on the South Side.

  They all followed the *college's* rules.

  *James's* roommate is looking for him.

- **If a noun is plural and ends in -s, just add an apostrophe. If it is plural but does not end in -s, add -'s.**

  My *books'* covers are falling off.

  [more than one book]

■ **TIP** *Singular* means one; *plural* means more than one.

■ **RESOURCES** *Additional Resources* contains tests and supplemental exercises for this chapter.

**521**

The *twins'* father was building them a playhouse.

[more than one twin]

The *children's* toys were broken.

The *men's* locker room is being painted.

- **The placement of an apostrophe makes a difference in meaning.**

  My *sister's* six children are at my house for the weekend.

  [one sister who has six children]

  My *sisters'* six children are at my house for the weekend.

  [two or more sisters who together have six children]

- **Do not use an apostrophe to form the plural of a noun.**

  Gina went camping with her *sister's* and their children.

  All of the *highway's* to the airport are under construction.

- **Do not use an apostrophe with a possessive pronoun.** These pronouns already show ownership (possession).

  Is that bag *your's*?

  No, it is *our's*.

| *Possessive Pronouns* | | | |
|---|---|---|---|
| my | his | its | their |
| mine | her | our | theirs |
| your | hers | ours | whose |
| yours | | | |

The single most common error with apostrophes and pronouns is confusing *its* (a possessive pronoun) with *it's* (a contraction meaning "it is"). Whenever you write *it's*, test correctness by replacing it with *it is* and reading the sentence aloud to hear if it makes sense.

■ **PRACTICE 1    USING APOSTROPHES TO SHOW OWNERSHIP**

Edit the following sentences by adding -'s or an apostrophe alone to show ownership and by crossing out any ~~incorrect use~~ of an apostrophe or -'s.

**EXAMPLE:** People must respect other people's need's for personal

space.

1. A person's feelings about personal space depend on his or her's

culture.

2. Personal space is especially important in cultures' that are formal and

reserved.

3. Putting your face too close to another's is considered rude.

4. Fistfights often are preceded by someone's aggressive violation of some-

one else's space.

5. The expression "Get out of my face!" is a warning meant to prevent

the confrontation's violent conclusion.

6. A dog's interaction with a member of it's own species can follow a

similar pattern; dogs are determined to defend what is their's.

7. The hair on dogs' neck's may stand on end.

8. A researcher's recent work examines various species' personal space.

9. For example, seagulls' positions on a log follow a pattern similar to that

of people lined up waiting for a bus.

10. Studies show that an animal's overcrowded environment can lead to

violent behavior.

■ **TIP** For more practice
using apostrophes correctly,
visit Exercise Central at
<bedfordstmartins.com/
realwriting>.

## Apostrophes in Contractions

A **contraction** is formed by joining two words and leaving out one or more
of the letters. When writing a contraction, put an apostrophe where the letter or letters have been left out, not between the two words.

*She's* on her way. = *She is* on her way.

*I'll* see you there. = *I will* see you there.

Be sure to put the apostrophe in the right place.

It *does'n't* really matter.

■ **TIP** Avoid using contractions
in formal papers or reports for
college or work.

## Common Contractions

| | |
|---|---|
| aren't = are not | she'll = she will |
| can't = cannot | she's = she is, she has |
| couldn't = could not | there's = there is |
| didn't = did not | they'd = they would, they had |
| don't = do not | they'll = they will |
| he'd = he would, he had | they're = they are |
| he'll = he will | they've = they have |
| he's = he is, he has | who'd = who would, who had |
| I'd = I would, I had | who'll = who will |
| I'll = I will | who's = who is, who has |
| I'm = I am | won't = will not |
| I've = I have | wouldn't = would not |
| isn't = is not | you'd = you would, you had |
| it's = it is, it has | you'll = you will |
| let's = let us | you're = you are |
| she'd = she would, she had | you've = you have |

■ **ESL** Because contractions are often new to ESL students, you may want to advise them to avoid all contractions in college work that they are submitting for a grade. They should use apostrophes only to show ownership.

### PRACTICE 2   USING APOSTROPHES IN CONTRACTIONS

Read each sentence carefully, looking for any words that have missing letters. Edit these words by adding apostrophes where needed and crossing out ~~incorrectly used apostrophes~~.

> **EXAMPLE:** Although we observe personal space boundaries in our daily lives, they▵re not something we spend much time thinking about.

1. You▵ll notice right away if a stranger leans over and talks to you so his face is practically touching yours.

2. Perhaps you▵d accept this kind of behavior from a family member.

3. There is▵nt one single acceptable boundary we▵d use in all situations.

4. An elevator has its own rules: Don▵t stand right next to a person if there is open space.

5. With coworkers, we're likely to keep a personal space of four to twelve feet.

6. We'll accept a personal space of four feet down to eighteen inches with friends.

7. The last sixteen inches are reserved for people we're most intimate with.

8. When people hug or kiss, they're willing to surrender their personal space to each other.

9. A supervisor who's not aware of the personal space boundaries of his or her employees risks committing a serious transgression.

10. Even if the supervisor doesn't intend anything by the gestures, it's his or her responsibility to act appropriately.

## Apostrophes with Letters, Numbers, and Time

- **Use -'s to make letters and numbers plural.** The apostrophe prevents confusion or misreading.

  In Scrabble games, there are more *e*'s than any other letter.

  In women's shoes, size *8*'s are more common than size *10*'s.

- **Use an apostrophe or -'s in certain expressions in which time nouns are treated as if they possess something.**

  She took four *weeks*' maternity leave after the baby was born.

  *This year's* graduating class is huge.

■ **PRACTICE 3   USING APOSTROPHES WITH LETTERS, NUMBERS, AND TIME**

Edit the following sentences by adding apostrophes where needed and crossing out ~~incorrectly used apostrophes~~.

> **EXAMPLE:** When I returned to work after two weeks' vacation, I had what looked like a decade's worth of work in my box.

1. I sorted letters alphabetically, starting with *A*'s.

2. There were more letters by names starting with *M*'s than any other.

3. When I checked my e-mail, the screen flashed 48's to show that I had forty-eight messages.

4. My voice mail wasn't much better, telling me that in two weeks' time I had received twenty-five messages.

5. I needed another week's time just to return all the phone calls.

# Edit Paragraphs and Your Own Writing

**PRACTICE 4    EDITING PARAGRAPHS FOR APOSTROPHES**

Edit the following paragraphs by adding apostrophes where needed and crossing out ~~incorrectly used apostrophes~~.

1. (1) An astronaut goes through extreme adjustment's in zero gravity. (2) The human body has a hard time keeping it's systems operating normally. (3) The brain can't tell up from down. (4) Immune cell's don't respond the way they should. (5) Heartbeats' can speed up and then slow down for no apparent reason. (6) Sleep is a problem for many astronauts, who may complain that they can't get their "z's." (7) The physical effects of a few week's space travel can imitate what a body experiences after thirty years' aging. (8) Unpleasant as they may be, these effects might help scientist's learn about treating illnesses associated with getting old.

2. (1) People's names often have strange stories attached to them. (2) Oprah Winfrey's first name, for example, is very unusual. (3) It's actually misspelled. (4) It was supposed to be Orpah, a biblical name, but a clerks' error on the birth certificate resulted in Oprah. (5) Somehow, The Orpah Winfrey Show doesn't sound like a popular television program. (6) Oprah, on the other hand, with it's resemblance to *opera*, makes us think of a performer on stage. (7) Winfrey herself is certainly not upset that she didn't end up with her parents' choice of name; her production company's name is Harpo, which is Oprah spelled backward.

(8) While Winfrey is not the only entertainer with an unusual first name, hers' is especially memorable.

(9) As Winfrey's example suggests, names on birth certificates are often mixed up. (10) If a clerk's a's look like o's, for example, Dana becomes Dona and Jarvis becomes Jorvis. (11) But unusual names don't all result from mistakes. (12) You've probably heard of names such as Candy Cane or Spring Raines or Stormy Winters. (13) Some people's names sound like job titles. (14) Think, for example, of a surgeon who's named Carver, or a dentist called Dr. Drill. (15) Early in his career, the baseball pitcher Eric Plunk was known for hitting batters' with his wild pitches. (16) There's no way to explain any of these names except by attributing them to pure chance. (17) Each name has its own meaning and origin; we're all affected by our names, whether we like them or not.

■ PRACTICE 5   **EDITING YOUR OWN WRITING FOR APOSTROPHES**

As a final practice, edit a piece of your own writing for apostrophes. It can be a paper you are working on for this course, a paper you've already finished, a paper for another course, or a recent piece of writing from your work or everyday life. In your learning journal, record any examples of sentences with apostrophe problems that you find, along with edited versions of these sentences.

■ **LEARNING JOURNAL** What type of mistake with apostrophes do you make most often? How can you avoid this mistake or be sure to edit for it?

# Chapter Review: Apostrophes

1.  An apostrophe (') is a punctuation mark that usually either shows ____ownership____ or indicates where a letter or letters have been left out in a ____contraction____ .

2.  To show ownership, add ____'s____ to a singular noun, even if the noun already ends in -s. For a plural noun, add an ____apostrophe____ alone if the noun ends in -s; add ____'s____ if the noun does not end in -s.

3.  Do not use an apostrophe with a ____possessive____ pronoun.

4.  Do not confuse *its* and *it's*. *Its* shows _____ownership_____; *it's* is a
    _____contraction_____ meaning "*it is.*"

5.  A _____contraction_____ is formed by joining two words and leaving out
    one or more of the letters. Use an apostrophe to show where _the letter_
    _or letters have been left out_ .

6.  Use -*'s* to make letters and numbers _____plural_____.

7.  Use an apostrophe or -*'s* in certain expressions in which _time nouns_
    are treated as if they possess something.

# 36

# Quotation Marks

" "

## Understand What Quotation Marks Do

**Quotation marks (" ")** always appear in pairs. Quotation marks have two common uses in college writing: They are used with some quotations, and they are used to set off titles.

A **quotation** is the report of another person's words. There are two types of quotations: **direct quotations** (the exact repetition, word for word, of what someone said or wrote) and **indirect quotations** (a restatement of what someone said or wrote, not word for word). Quotation marks are used only for direct quotations.

> **DIRECT QUOTATION**    He said, "You should get the downtown bus."
>
> **INDIRECT QUOTATION**    He said that I should get the downtown bus.

## Practice Using Quotation Marks Correctly

### Quotation Marks for Direct Quotations

When you write a direct quotation, you need to use quotation marks around the quoted words. These tell readers that the words used are exactly what was said or written.

1. "I don't know what she means," I said to my friend Lina.
2. Lina asked, "Do you think we should ask a question?"
3. "Excuse me, Professor Soames," I ventured, "but could you explain that again?"
4. "Yes," said Professor Soames. "Let me make sure you all understand."

5. After further explanation, Professor Soames asked, "Are there any other questions?"

When you are writing a paper that uses outside sources, use quotation marks to indicate where you quote the exact words of a source.

> We all need to become more conscientious recyclers. A recent editorial in the *Bolton Common* reported, "When recycling volunteers spot-checked bags that were supposed to contain only newspaper, they found a collection of nonrecyclable items such as plastic candy wrappers, aluminum foil, and birthday cards."

When quoting, writers usually use words that identify who is speaking, such as *I said to my friend Lina* in the first example. The identifying words can come after the quoted words (example 1), before them (example 2), or in the middle of them (example 3). Here are some guidelines for capitalization and punctuation.

■ **TEACHING TIP** As you go over the first two rules on capitalization, put a sentence on the board without any quotation marks. Ask students where the quotation marks should go and which letters should be capitalized.

### GUIDELINES FOR CAPITALIZATION AND PUNCTUATION

- Capitalize the first letter in a complete sentence that's being quoted, even if it comes after some identifying words (example 2).
- Do not capitalize the first letter in a quotation if it's not the first word in a complete sentence (*but* in example 3).
- If it is a complete sentence, and it's clear who the speaker is, a quotation can stand on its own (second sentence in example 4).
- Identifying words must be attached to a quotation; they cannot be a sentence on their own.
- Use commas to separate any identifying words from quoted words in the same sentence.
- Always put quotation marks after commas and periods. Put quotation marks after question marks and exclamation points if they are part of the quoted sentence.

■ **TIP** For more on commas with quotation marks, see Chapter 34.

Quotation mark                Quotation mark

Lina asked, "Do you think we should ask a question?"

Comma                 Question mark

- If a question mark or exclamation point is part of your own sentence, put it after the quotation mark.

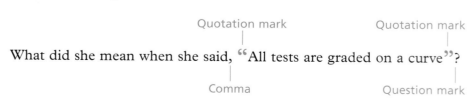

Quotation mark             Quotation mark

What did she mean when she said, "All tests are graded on a curve"?

Comma                Question mark

## Setting Off a Quotation within Another Quotation

Sometimes when you directly quote someone, part of what that person said quotes words that someone else said or wrote. Put single quotation marks (' ') around the quotation within a quotation so that readers understand who said what.

> The student handbook said, "Students must be given the opportunity to make up work missed for legitimate reasons."

> Terry told his instructor, "I'm sorry I missed the exam, but that isn't a reason to fail me for the term. Our student handbook says, 'Students must be given the opportunity to make up work missed for legitimate reasons,' and I have a good reason."

■ **TEACHING TIP** Remind students that they will probably need to use quotation marks when writing narration (Chapter 8) and argument (Chapter 16) and when using direct quotations in the opening or closing paragraphs of any kind of essay. In research essays (Chapter 18), they will also use quotation marks often.

■ **PRACTICE 1  PUNCTUATING DIRECT QUOTATIONS**

Edit the following sentences by adding quotation marks and commas where needed.

**EXAMPLE:** A radio journalist asked a nurse at a critical-care facility, "Do you feel that the medical community needlessly prolongs the life of the terminally ill?"

■ **TIP** For more practice using quotation marks correctly, visit Exercise Central at <bedfordstmartins.com/realwriting>.

1. "If I could quickly answer that question," the nurse replied, "I'd deserve an honorary degree in ethics."

2. She added, "But I see it as the greatest dilemma we face today."

3. "How would you describe that dilemma?" the reporter asked the nurse.

4. The nurse said, "It's a choice of when to use our amazing medical technology and when not to."

5. The reporter asked, "So there are times when you'd favor letting patients die on their own?"

6. "Yes," the nurse replied, "I would."

7. The reporter asked, "Under what circumstances should a patient be allowed to die?"

8. "I can't really answer that question because there are so many variables involved," the nurse replied.

9. "Is this a matter of deciding how to allocate scarce resources?" the reporter asked.

10. "In a sense, it is," the nurse replied. "As a colleague of mine says, 'We shouldn't try to keep everyone alive for as long as possible just because we can.'"

## No Quotation Marks for Indirect Quotations

■ **TEAMWORK** Have students interview one another on a controversial local issue that you have chosen. The interviewer should write up the interview using direct and indirect quotations.

When you report what someone said or wrote but do not use the person's exact words, you are writing an indirect quotation. Do not use quotation marks for indirect quotations. Indirect quotations often begin with the word *that*.

| INDIRECT QUOTATION | DIRECT QUOTATION |
| --- | --- |
| Sam said that there was a fire downtown. | Sam said, "There was a fire downtown." |
| The police told us to move along. | "Move along," directed the police. |
| Tara told me that she is graduating. | Tara said, "I am graduating." |

### PRACTICE 2 PUNCTUATING DIRECT AND INDIRECT QUOTATIONS

Edit the following sentences by adding quotation marks where needed and crossing out ~~quotation marks that are incorrectly used~~. If a sentence is already correct, put a "C" next to it.

**EXAMPLE:** Three days before her apartment was robbed, Jocelyn told a friend, "I have concerns about the safety of this building."

1. "Have you complained to the landlord yet?" her friend asked.

2. "Not yet," Jocelyn replied, "although I know I should."

3. Jocelyn phoned the landlord and asked him to install a more secure lock on the front door. *c*

4. The landlord said that ~~"~~he felt the lock was fine the way it was.~~"~~

5. When Jocelyn phoned the landlord after the burglary, she said, "I know this wouldn't have happened if that lock had been installed."

6. "I'm sorry," the landlord replied, "but there's nothing I can do about it now."

7. Jocelyn asked a tenants' rights group whether she had grounds for a lawsuit. *C*

8. The person she spoke to said that *she probably did.*

9. "If I were you," the person said, "I'd let your landlord know about your plans."

10. When Jocelyn told her landlord of the possible lawsuit, he said that he would reimburse her for the lost items. *C*

## Quotation Marks for Certain Titles

When you refer to a short work such as a magazine or newspaper article, a chapter in a book, a short story, an essay, a song, or a poem, put quotation marks around the title of the work.

| | |
|---|---|
| **NEWSPAPER ARTICLE** | "College Tuition to Rise 25 Percent" |
| **SHORT STORY** | "The Lady or the Tiger?" |
| **ESSAY** | "Snoopers at Work" |

Usually titles of longer works, such as novels, books, magazines, newspapers, movies, television programs, and CDs, are underlined or italicized. The titles of sacred books such as the Bible or the Koran are neither underlined nor surrounded by quotation marks.

| | |
|---|---|
| **BOOK** | The Good Earth or *The Good Earth* |
| **NEWSPAPER** | Washington Post or *Washington Post* |

[Do not underline, italicize, or capitalize the word *the* before the name of a newspaper or magazine, even if it is part of the title: I saw that in the *New York Times*. But do capitalize *The* when it is the first word in titles of books, movies, and other sources.]

If you are writing a paper with many outside sources, your instructor will probably refer you to a particular system of citing sources. Follow that system's guidelines when you use titles in your paper.

**NOTE:** Do not enclose the title of a paragraph or an essay that you have written in quotation marks when it appears at the beginning of your paper. Do not underline it either.

■ **TIP** For more information on citing sources, see Chapter 18.

■ **PRACTICE 3** **USING QUOTATION MARKS FOR TITLES**

Edit the following sentences by adding quotation marks around titles as needed. Underline any book, magazine, or newspaper titles.

> **EXAMPLE:** After the terrorist attacks of September 11, 2001, the 1,200 radio stations belonging to Clear Channel Communications were asked not to play songs with a political message, such as "Imagine" by John Lennon.

1. In 2002, Bruce Springsteen released his first new album in years, containing songs like "Worlds Apart" that dealt with the terrorist attacks on the United States.

2. "The Missing," a review of the Springsteen album in the New Yorker magazine, found Springsteen's new songs unusual because they did not include many specific details about people, as older Springsteen songs like "Born in the U.S.A." had done.

3. No one made that complaint about "John Walker's Blues," a song by Steve Earle based on the story of the young American captured while fighting for the Taliban in Afghanistan.

4. Earle was condemned by some for writing from Walker's point of view; a New York Post headline claimed, "Twisted Ballad Honors Tali-Rat."

5. As a Time magazine article, "Don't Even Tell These Guys About Eminem," pointed out, the controversy was peculiar because it occurred before Earle's song had even been released, and those objecting had apparently neither heard the song nor read its lyrics.

## Edit Paragraphs and Your Own Writing

■ **PRACTICE 4** **EDITING PARAGRAPHS FOR QUOTATION MARKS**

Edit the following paragraphs by adding quotation marks where needed and crossing out any ~~incorrectly used quotation mark~~s. Correct any errors in punctuation.

1. (1) When I first read Edgar Allan Poe's "The Tell-Tale Heart," I thought it was the scariest story ever written. (2) I told all my friends that "they should read it." (3) The narrator is a murderer who knows that readers will "think he is mad." (4) He admits, "True! — nervous — very, very dreadfully nervous I had been and am." (5) However, he insists that he is perfectly sane. (6) As proof, he points out that his sense of hearing is good and says, "I heard all things in the heaven and in the earth." (7) At the end of the story, the narrator confesses to the murder of an old man. (8) His guilt makes him imagine that he is hearing the dead man's heartbeat, so he tells the police that the sound is "the beating of my hideous heart"!

2. (1) When Ruiz first came into my office, he told me that he was a poor student. (2) I asked, "What makes you think that?"

(3) Ruiz answered, "I've always gotten bad grades, and I don't know how to get any better." (4) He shook his head. (5) "I've just about given up."

(6) I told him that "there were some resources on campus he could use and that we could work together to help him."

(7) "What kind of things are you talking about?" asked Ruiz. (8) "What exactly will I learn?"

(9) I said, "There are plenty of programs to help you. (10) You really have no excuse to fail."

(11) "Can you be a little more specific?" he asked.

(12) "Certainly," I said. (13) I told him about the survival skills program. (14) I also pulled out folders on study skills, such as managing time, improving memory, taking notes, and having a positive attitude. (15) "Take a look at these," I said.

(16) Ruiz said, "No, I'm not interested in that. (17) And I don't have time."

(18) I replied, "That's your decision, Ruiz, but remember that education is one of the few things that people are willing to pay for and not get." (19) I paused and then added, "Sounds to me like you're wasting

the money you spent on tuition. (20) Why not try to get what you paid for?"

(21) Ruiz thought for a moment, while he looked out the window, and finally told me that "he'd try."

(22) "Good," I said. (23) "I'm glad to hear it."

■ **PRACTICE 5    EDITING YOUR OWN WRITING FOR QUOTATION MARKS**

As a final practice, edit a piece of your own writing for quotation marks. It can be a paper you are working on for this course, a paper you've already finished, a paper for another course, or a recent piece of writing from your work or everyday life. In your learning journal, record any examples you find of sentences with mistakes in the use of quotation marks. Also write down the edited versions of these sentences.

# Chapter Review: Quotation Marks

1. Quotation marks look like this: _____ " " _____. They always appear in (pairs)/ triples).

2. A quotation is the report of _another person's words_.

3. A direct quotation is the exact _____ *repetition* _____ of what someone (or some outside source) said or wrote. (Use)/ Do not use) quotation marks around direct quotations.

4. An indirect quotation is a _restatement of what someone said or wrote, but_ _not word for word_ . (Use /(Do not use)) quotation marks with indirect quotations.

5. To set off a quotation within a quotation, use _single quotation marks_ .

6. Put quotation marks around the titles of short works such as (give four examples) _Answers will vary. Possible answers: short stories, poems, songs,_ _articles_ .

7. For longer works such as magazines, novels, books, newspapers, and so on, either _____ *italicize* _____ or _____ *underline* _____ the titles.

# 37

# Other Punctuation

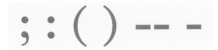

## Understand What Punctuation Does

Punctuation helps readers understand your writing. If you use punctuation incorrectly, you send readers a confusing—or, even worse, a wrong—message. This chapter covers punctuation marks that people sometimes use incorrectly because they aren't quite sure what they are supposed to do.

| | | |
|---|---|---|
| **SEMICOLON** | **;** | Joins two independent clauses into one sentence |
| | | Separates complete items in a list that already has commas within individual items |
| **COLON** | **:** | Introduces a list |
| | | Announces an explanation |
| **PARENTHESES** | **( )** | Set off extra information that is not essential |
| **DASH** | **--** | Sets off words for emphasis |
| | | Indicates a pause |
| **HYPHEN** | **-** | Joins two words that together form a single description |
| | | Shows a word break at the end of a line |

> ■ **LEARNING JOURNAL** Use your learning journal as a place to record sentences in your writing that should have semicolons, colons, parentheses, dashes, and hyphens. Try to find one sample sentence for each of these punctuation marks. Write the sentence both before and after you edit it.

## Practice Using Punctuation Correctly

> ■ **RESOURCES** *Additional Resources* contains tests and supplemental exercises for this chapter.

### Semicolon ;

#### Semicolons to Join Independent Clauses

Use a semicolon to join two very closely related sentences and make them into one sentence.

In an interview, hold your head up and don't slouch; it is important to look alert.

Make good eye contact; looking down is not appropriate in an interview.

### Semicolons in Lists Containing Commas

■ **TEACHING TIP** Caution students not to use semicolons unless they feel certain about how they are used. Since many students use semicolons as a default solution when trying to increase sentence complexity, they end up overusing or misusing them.

When one or more items in a list contain commas, use semicolons to separate the items. Otherwise, it is difficult for readers to tell where one item ends and another begins.

> For dinner, Bob ate an order of onion rings, extra large; a sixteen-ounce steak, medium rare; a baked potato with sour cream, bacon bits, and chives; a green salad; and a huge bowl of ice cream topped with fudge sauce, nuts, whipped cream, and a maraschino cherry.

## Colon   :

### Colons before Lists

Use a colon after an independent clause to introduce a list. An independent clause contains a subject, a verb, and a complete thought. It can stand on its own as a sentence.

> Many companies had booths at the computer fair: Apple, Microsoft, IBM, and Hewlett-Packard, to name just a few.

> The fair featured a vast array of software: financial management applications, games, educational CDs, college-application programs, and so on.

### Colons before Explanations or Examples

Use a colon after an independent clause to let readers know that you are about to provide an explanation or example of what you just wrote.

> The fair was overwhelming: too much hype about too many things.

> I picked up something I've been looking for: a new laptop.

A colon in a sentence *must* follow an independent clause. One of the most common misuses of colons is to use them after a phrase instead of an independent clause. Watch out especially for colons following the phrases *such as* or *for example*.

■ **TIP** See Commas (Chapter 34), Apostrophes (Chapter 35), and Quotation Marks (Chapter 36) for coverage of these punctuation marks. For more information on using semicolons to join sentences, see Chapter 27.

| | |
|---|---|
| **INCORRECT** | Tonya enjoys sports that are sometimes dangerous. Such as: white-water rafting, wilderness skiing, rock climbing, and motorcycle racing. |
| **CORRECT** | Tonya enjoys sports that are sometimes dangerous: white-water rafting, wilderness skiing, rock climbing, and motorcycle racing. |

| INCORRECT | Jeff has many interests. For example: bicycle racing, sculpting, and building musical instruments. |
|---|---|
| CORRECT | Jeff has many interests: bicycle racing, sculpting, and building musical instruments. |

### Colons in Business Correspondence

Use a colon after a greeting (called a *salutation*) in a business letter and after the standard heading lines at the beginning of a memorandum.

Dear Mr. Hernandez:

To: Pat Toney
From: Susan Anker

## Parentheses ( )

Use parentheses to set off information that is not essential to the meaning of a sentence. Parentheses are always used in pairs and should be used sparingly.

My grandfather's most successful invention (and also his first) was the electric blanket.

When he died (at the age of ninety-six) he had more than 150 patents registered.

■ TEACHING TIP Advise students that although an occasional set of parentheses is fine, too many are distracting.

## Dash --

Dashes can be used like parentheses to set off additional information, particularly information that you want to emphasize. Make a dash by writing or typing two hyphens together. Do not put extra spaces around a dash.

The final exam--worth 25 percent of your total grade--will be next Thursday.

There will be no makeup exam--no exceptions--for this course.

A dash can also indicate a pause, much like a comma does.

My uncle went on long fishing trips--without my aunt and cousins.

## Hyphen -

### Hyphens to Join Words That Form a Single Description

Writers often join two or more words that together form a single description of a person, place, or thing. To join the words, use a hyphen.

Being a stockbroker is a high=risk career.

Michelle is the ultimate decision=maker in our department.

Jill was a lovely three=year=old girl.

When writing out numbers from twenty-one to ninety-nine, you should put a hyphen between the numbers.

Seventy=five people participated in the demonstration.

### Hyphens to Divide a Word at the End of a Line

Use a hyphen to divide a word when part of the word must continue on the next line.

Critics accused the tobacco industry of increasing the amounts of nico= tine in cigarettes to encourage addiction and boost sales.

If you are not sure where to break a word, look it up in a dictionary. The word's main entry will show you where you can break the word: dic • tio • nary. If you still aren't confident that you are putting the hyphen in the right place, don't break the word; write it all on the next line.

■ **COMPUTER** Most word-processing programs automatically put a whole word on the next line without hyphenating it ("word wrap"). Most have a hyphenation feature, however, that can be turned on. Be sure to tell students if you prefer one style over the other.

## Edit Paragraphs and Your Own Writing

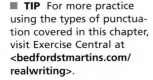  PRACTICE 1  **EDITING PARAGRAPHS FOR OTHER PUNCTUATION MARKS**

■ **TIP** For more practice using the types of punctuation covered in this chapter, visit Exercise Central at <bedfordstmartins.com/realwriting>.

Edit the following paragraphs by adding semicolons, colons, parentheses, dashes, and hyphens where needed. Circle the (punctuation marks) that you add. Keep in mind that in some places more than one type of punctuation may be acceptable. *Answers may vary. Possible edits shown.*

1. (1) We already know that natural light can improve our mood; now it seems that light from the sun has other positive effects. (2) It may be possible for schools to improve student performance with one simple trick: letting the sun shine in. (3) A study of school districts indicates that natural light—even on a cloudy day—can help students learn. (4) The students in the study took standardized tests; those whose schools got more natural light had higher scores. (5) The scores improved by up to twenty-six percent, even when other factors affecting scores were taken into account. (6) In a related study, stores in a retail chain were compared; some had skylights and others did not. (7) The sun-filled stores

had much higher sales—an average of forty percent higher. (8) Natural light in a building apparently has the effect of making people want to have more of any commodity (whether it is education or merchandise) the establishment offers.

2. (1) More than fifty thousand domestic adoptions take place in this country each year; despite minor difficulties, most of them go smoothly. (2) But a few years ago, the case of four-year-old Baby Richard highlighted an important issue: the rights of adoptive parents versus the rights of birth parents. (3) Richard was in a good situation: healthy, happy, loved by the couple who had adopted him at birth. (4) Then Richard's other parents—the biological ones—appeared on the scene. (5) They were prepared to spend years battling the case in court; they desperately wanted their son back.

(6) Toward the end of her pregnancy, the birth mother felt alone, frightened, and confused; angry that her boyfriend had left her two weeks before Richard was born, and unprepared for motherhood. (7) Therefore, a few days after the baby's birth, the baby was put up for adoption; his mother didn't want him. (8) When the boyfriend (the father of the baby) returned later, he was told that the baby had died. (9) Eventually, however, the father discovered that his former girlfriend had lied; his son was still alive. (10) After several years of searching, the biological parents found their long-lost child, who was living happily with his adoptive parents. (11) After years of legal arguments, the Illinois Supreme Court reached its verdict: Baby Richard belonged to the parents whose genes he shared. (12) The adoptive parents—the people who had loved and cared for Baby Richard for his first four years—were bitterly disappointed.

## PRACTICE 2  EDITING YOUR OWN WRITING FOR OTHER PUNCTUATION MARKS

As a final practice, edit a piece of your own writing for semicolons, colons, parentheses, dashes, and hyphens. It can be a paper you are working on for this course, a paper you've already finished, a paper for another course, or a piece of writing from your work or everyday life. You may want to try more

■ **LEARNING JOURNAL** What is one useful piece of information you learned in this chapter?

than one way to use these punctuation marks in your writing. In your learning journal, record any examples of sentences you edited, showing the sentences both before and after you edited them.

## Chapter Review: Other Punctuation

1. Semicolons (;) can be used to *join two independent clauses into one sentence*
   and to *separate complete items in a list where commas are used within the*
   *complete items* .

2. Colons (:) can be used in what three ways?

   *after an independent clause to introduce a list*

   *after an independent clause to provide an explanation or example of what you just*
   *wrote*

   *after a greeting in a business letter or memo heading*

3. A colon in a sentence must always be used after an *independent clause* .

4. Parentheses ( ) set off information that is _____ *not essential* _____ to a
   sentence.

5. *Dashes (--)* _____ also set off information in a sentence, usually
   information that you want to emphasize.

6. Hyphens (-) can be used to join two or more words that together
   *form a single description* and to _____ *break* _____ a word at the
   end of a line.

# 38

# Capitalization
## *Using Capital Letters*

## Understand Three Rules of Capitalization

If you can remember the following rules, you will avoid the most common errors of capitalization.

**THE THREE RULES OF CAPITALIZATION**
Capitalize the first letter

- Of every new sentence
- In names of specific people, places, dates, and things
- Of important words in titles

**■ LEARNING JOURNAL** Use your learning journal as a place to record sentences in your own writing that have errors in capitalization. Try to find one sample sentence for each rule of capitalization. Write the sentence both before and after you edit it.

**■ RESOURCES** *Additional Resources* contains tests and supplemental exercises for this chapter.

## Practice Capitalization

### Capitalization of Sentences

Capitalize the first letter of each new sentence, including the first word of a direct quotation.

The superintendent was surprised.

He asked, "What's going on here?"

**■ PRACTICE 1  CAPITALIZING THE FIRST WORD IN A SENTENCE**

Edit the following paragraph, changing lowercase letters to capital letters as needed.

**■ TEACHING TIP** Remind students that they should not write or type in all capital letters because it will be more difficult for them to recognize and edit their capitalization errors.

543

■ **TIP** For more practice with capitalization, visit Exercise Central at <**bedfordstmartins .com/realwriting**>.

(1) Occasionally a phrase or sentence uttered by a president is so memorable that it becomes part of American history. (2) One example occurred before the start of the Civil War, when Abraham Lincoln stated, "A house divided against itself cannot stand." (3) Almost seventy years later, in the midst of the Great Depression, Franklin Roosevelt declared, "We have nothing to fear but fear itself."

## Capitalization of Names of Specific People, Places, Dates, and Things

The general rule is to capitalize the first letter in names of specific people, places, dates, and things. Do not capitalize a generic name such as *college* as opposed to the specific name: *Carroll State College*. Look at the examples for each group.

### People

■ **TEACHING TIP** Have students come up with their own "specific" and "not specific" examples.

Capitalize the first letter in names of specific people and in titles used with names of specific people.

| SPECIFIC | NOT SPECIFIC |
|---|---|
| Jean Heaton | my neighbor |
| Professor Fitzgerald | your math professor |

| SPECIFIC | NOT SPECIFIC |
|---|---|
| Dr. Cornog | the doctor |
| Aunt Pat, Mother | my aunt, your mother |

The name of a family member is capitalized when the family member is being addressed directly: Happy Birthday, *Mother*. In other instances, do not capitalize: It is my *mother's* birthday.

The word *president* is not capitalized unless it comes directly before a name as part of that person's title: *President* George W. Bush.

### Places

Capitalize the first letter in names of specific buildings, streets, cities, states, regions, and countries.

| SPECIFIC | NOT SPECIFIC |
|---|---|
| Bolton Town Hall | the town hall |
| Arlington Street | our street |
| Dearborn Heights | my hometown |
| Arizona | this state |

| the South | the southern region |
| Spain | that country |

Do not capitalize directions in a sentence.

Drive *south* for five blocks.

## Dates

Capitalize the first letter in the names of days, months, and holidays. Do not capitalize the names of the seasons (winter, spring, summer, fall).

| SPECIFIC | NOT SPECIFIC |
|---|---|
| Wednesday | tomorrow |
| June 15 | summer |
| Thanksgiving | my birthday |

## Organizations, Companies, and Groups

| SPECIFIC | NOT SPECIFIC |
|---|---|
| Taft Community College | my college |
| Microsoft | that software company |
| Alcoholics Anonymous | the self-help group |

## Languages, Nationalities, and Religions

| SPECIFIC | NOT SPECIFIC |
|---|---|
| English, Greek, Spanish | my first language |
| Christianity, Buddhism | your religion |

The names of languages should be capitalized even if you aren't referring to a specific course.

I am taking psychology and *Spanish*.

## Courses

| SPECIFIC | NOT SPECIFIC |
|---|---|
| Composition 101 | writing course |
| Introduction to Psychology | my psychology course |

**■ ESL** Ask ESL students to identify any English capitalization rules that differ from the rules in their first language.

## Commercial Products

| SPECIFIC | NOT SPECIFIC |
|---|---|
| Diet Pepsi | a diet cola |
| Skippy peanut butter | peanut butter |

■ PRACTICE 2 **CAPITALIZING NOUNS**

Edit the following sentences by adding capitalization as needed or removing capitalization where it is inappropriate.

**EXAMPLE:** New <sup>Y</sup>~~y~~ork is one of the best <sup>c</sup>~~C~~ities for a vacation.

1. Unlike most <sup>A</sup>~~a~~merican cities, New York has a great <sup>m</sup>~~M~~ass <sup>t</sup>~~T~~ransportation system, so visitors don't need a car.

2. That's fortunate, for most visitors would not want to drive on the <sup>s</sup>~~S~~treets of Manhattan.

3. You can arrive by <sup>t</sup>~~T~~rain at <sup>P</sup>~~p~~ennsylvania <sup>S</sup>~~s~~tation or <sup>G</sup>~~g~~rand <sup>C</sup>~~c~~entral <sup>S</sup>~~s~~tation.

4. New <sup>Y</sup>~~y~~ork is famous as the home of the Statue of <sup>L</sup>~~l~~iberty.

5. There are many internationally known buildings, such as the <sup>E</sup>~~e~~mpire <sup>S</sup>~~s~~tate <sup>B</sup>~~b~~uilding.

6. If you like <sup>m</sup>~~M~~useums, New York has more than its share: the <sup>M</sup>~~m~~etropolitan <sup>M</sup>~~m~~useum <sup>A</sup>of <sup>A</sup>~~a~~rt, the <sup>A</sup>~~a~~merican <sup>M</sup>~~m~~useum of <sup>N</sup>~~n~~atural <sup>H</sup>~~h~~istory, and the <sup>G</sup>~~g~~uggenheim <sup>M</sup>~~m~~useum, to name just a few.

7. One of the best things about the city is the <sup>r</sup>~~R~~estaurants, which serve food from all over the world.

8. You can dine on <sup>I</sup>~~i~~ndian, <sup>E</sup>~~e~~thiopian, <sup>C</sup>~~c~~uban, or <sup>I</sup>~~i~~talian food within the space of a few blocks.

9. Famous <sup>N</sup>~~n~~ew <sup>Y</sup>~~y~~orkers include <sup>G</sup>~~g~~wyneth Paltrow, Woody <sup>A</sup>~~a~~llen, and <sup>A</sup>~~a~~l <sup>S</sup>~~s~~harpton.

10. The <sup>N</sup>~~n~~ew <sup>Y</sup>~~y~~ork <sup>S</sup>~~s~~tock <sup>E</sup>~~e~~xchange on <sup>W</sup>~~w~~all <sup>S</sup>~~s~~treet is watched around the world.

## Capitalization of Titles

■ **TIP** For more on punctuating titles, see Chapter 36. For a list of common prepositions, see Chapter 19.

When you write the title of a book, movie, television program, magazine, newspaper, article, story, song, paper, poem, and so on, capitalize the first word and all important words. The only words that do not need to be capitalized (unless they are the first word) are *the, a, an,* coordinating conjunctions (*and, but, for, nor, or, so, yet*), and prepositions.

*I Love Lucy* was a long-running television program.

Both *USA Today* and the *New York Times* are popular newspapers.

"Once More to the Lake" is one of Chuck's favorite essays.

### PRACTICE 3   CAPITALIZING TITLES

Edit the following sentences by capitalizing titles as needed.

**EXAMPLE:** Some people believe that the myth of the American West
began with movie westerns like *shane* and *stagecoach*.

1. The American West has been a common topic in popular culture since
   early films like *the big trail.*

2. Western songs, including Gene Autry's version of "back in the saddle
   again" and "the yellow rose of texas," were radio favorites.

3. Television, too, relied on westerns in its early years, making *gunsmoke*
   one of the longest-running shows of all time.

4. Clint Eastwood first became famous in the TV western *rawhide.*

5. John Ford movies, including *the searchers* and *she wore a yellow ribbon,*
   popularized an image of the West.

# Edit Paragraphs and Your Own Writing

### PRACTICE 4   EDITING PARAGRAPHS FOR CAPITALIZATION

Edit the following paragraphs by capitalizing as needed and removing unnecessary capitalization.

(1) The names and accomplishments of some presidents of the
united states are familiar to almost every american. (2) Most people are
familiar with george washington or abraham lincoln, for example.
(3) being president is no guarantee that a person will have lasting fame,
however. (4) How many of us could recall anything about millard
fillmore, the thirteenth president of the united states! (5) The millard
fillmore society celebrates his Birthday every year on january 7. (6) It

also publishes a magazine called *milestones with millard* and sponsors an essay contest. (7) Nevertheless, the facts about fillmore are known mainly to students of History.

(8) Fillmore was the whig party's candidate for vice president in 1848. (9) The candidate for president was zachary taylor, a hero of the mexican war. (10) american voters were divided on the subject of slavery, and the democrats and the free soil party took opposite sides on the issue. (11) Taylor, who remained neutral, was elected, but he died in office, so fillmore became President in 1850. (12) The whig party decided to nominate another mexican war hero, winfield scott, instead of fillmore in 1852, so fillmore was never elected president of the united states. (13) The newspaperman h.l. mencken wrote a column in the new york evening mail in 1917 claiming that fillmore had installed the white house's first bathtub. (14) Mencken had intended the column as a joke, but many people believed it. (15) poor millard fillmore—when he is remembered at all, it is usually to be given credit for something he didn't really do.

■ **PRACTICE 5**  **EDITING YOUR OWN WRITING FOR CAPITALIZATION**

■ **LEARNING JOURNAL** What problem with capitalization do you have most often? How can you edit more effectively for this problem in the future?

As a final practice, edit a piece of your own writing for capitalization. It can be a paper you are working on for this course, a paper you've already finished, a paper for another course, or a recent piece of writing from your work or everyday life. In your learning journal, record any examples of sentences with capitalization problems that you find, along with edited versions of these sentences.

## Chapter Review: Capitalization

1. Capitalize the ____first letter____ of every new sentence.

2. Capitalize the first letter in names of specific ____people____, ____places____, ____dates____, and ____things____.

3. Capitalize the first letter of ____important words____ in titles.

# Part Eight
# Readings for Writers

# 39

# The Basics of Critical Reading

In Chapters 40–48, you will find twenty essays that demonstrate the types of writing you have studied in this book: narration, illustration, description, process analysis, classification, definition, comparison and contrast, cause and effect, and argument. However, these readings provide more than just good models of writing. They also tell fascinating stories, argue passionately about controversial issues, and present a wide range of perspectives.

Some of the essays may even help you work more efficiently, with strategies for successful job interviews and tips on using exercise to improve mental functioning. These essays can also provide you with ideas for your own writing, both in and out of school. Most important, they offer you a chance to practice your reading skills—skills that will help you to become a better writer.

Reading good models will improve your writing by showing you how other writers have handled certain elements—for example, main points and supporting information, organization of ideas, and introductions and conclusions.

The following basics will help you understand and respond to the reading you will do in this course and others. They will also help you get information you need in other areas of your life. For example, you can read expert advice on making money, investing, starting your own business, finding a job, moving, raising a family, protecting yourself from unfair treatment, buying a car at the best price, and so on: The list is endless. When you read carefully, you can find help to get whatever you need.

## ■■ FOUR BASICS OF READING

1.  Preview the essay, article, or chapter.
2.  Find the main idea.
3.  Find the support for the main idea.
4.  Review and respond to what you have read.

**Ever Thought This?**

- I failed the test because I didn't read the directions right.
- I had to redo the application because I put information in the wrong place.
- The insurance agent told me I'm not covered for the damage. I thought I was, but I hadn't read the policy carefully.

■ **TEACHING TIP** Some students may find photos and other visuals to be helpful adjuncts to the readings provided in this part of the book. For visuals that correspond to each rhetorical mode, see Writing Assignment 2 in each chapter of Part Two. See also the photographs provided in the Writing Guide Software.

A piece of advice before getting into the basics: Be an active reader. An active reader takes part in the experience of reading and doesn't passively sit and look at the words. Before beginning to read, prepare to actively engage in reading. Find a place where you can be comfortable and where you won't constantly be distracted or interrupted. You need to be mentally alert and ready to concentrate when you read. Be physically alert too: For most people, reading while lying down or slouching results in sleepiness (and even a tendency to nod off). Instead, try sitting at a table or a desk with a good light source nearby.

# 1. Preview the Reading

Before carefully reading any piece of writing, first skim or preview the whole thing. This applies to any article, chapter, or essay that is assigned to you in college; any report, memo, or e-mail you get at work; or any agreement you are asked to sign in everyday life. Previewing a piece of writing will help you understand it better when you read the whole piece carefully. The following steps of previewing should be done quickly, before you actually read the piece for meaning.

## Read the Title, Headnote, and Introductory Paragraphs Quickly

The title of a chapter or an article will usually give you some idea of what the topic is. In business writing—such as memos and e-mails—the topic is usually stated in the subject line. Writers most often introduce their topic and their main point in the first few paragraphs, so read those and make a note of what you think the main idea might be. Often, an article or chapter will be introduced by a **headnote**, a paragraph (or more) that gives information about the author, the writing itself, or both. The background information in a headnote can help you to understand what an author is trying to say.

## Note Headings, Key Words, and Definitions

Authors of most textbooks and many other pieces of writing use headings to help readers follow their ideas. These headings (such as the heading "Preview the Reading" above) tell you what the subjects of different sections are. As you preview the reading, highlight major headings.

Writers put certain words in **boldface** type because they want them to stand out to readers. Words in boldface are important to the topic, so pay attention to them as you skim a reading. In textbooks, particularly, writers often introduce and define words that are important to the topic and the readers' understanding of it. If, while previewing a document, you see a definition in the text or in the margin, circle or underline it.

## Look for Summaries and Checklists

Many textbooks (such as this one) include features that highlight or summarize main points. Review any summaries, checklists, or chapter reviews to make sure that you understand the main points.

## Read the Conclusion Quickly

Writers normally reinforce their main point in their concluding sentences or paragraphs. Read the conclusion and compare it with the note you made after skimming the introduction.

## Ask a Guiding Question

To help you read more productively, ask yourself a question that you expect the reading will be able to answer. Usually, you can make the title into a question. For example, for the essay by humorist Russell Baker that appears on page 559 ("The Plot against People"), you could ask, "What kind of plot will Baker describe, and who or what will be involved?"

As you read, try to answer your question. A guiding question gives you a purpose when you are reading and helps keep you focused. This book supplies a guiding question for each essay in the Readings section. Be sure to read it before beginning the essay and keep it in mind while you read.

# 2. Find the Main Idea

After previewing the document, begin reading carefully for meaning. Read the first few paragraphs with special care because, as we have noted, writers usually introduce their main idea early. After reading the first few paragraphs, stop and write down what you think the main idea is, in your own words. You can do this in the margin of the piece. If you think the writer has stated the main idea in a single sentence, double-underline that sentence; but remember, putting the main idea into your own words is more useful because it forces you to really understand that idea, instead of just underlining or copying it.

■ **TIP** For more information on the main idea in writing, see Chapter 3.

When you are writing your own paragraphs and essays, you should express your main idea in one sentence. That makes it easier for readers to know what you're trying to show, explain, or prove. It's also a tool for you as a writer: You can easily refer back to your main idea as you develop support to make sure you are sticking to your main point. Similarly, when summarizing the main point of a reading, try to express this point in a single sentence.

■ **PRACTICE 1**   **FINDING THE MAIN IDEA**

The following paragraph has a main idea, but it is not fully expressed in a single sentence. Read the paragraph, and write its main idea in your own words, in a single sentence.

Americans can be divided into three groups: smokers, nonsmokers, and that expanding pack of us who have quit. Those who have never smoked don't know what they're missing, but former smokers, ex-smokers, and reformed smokers can never forget. We are veterans of a personal war, linked by that watershed experience of ceasing to smoke and by the temptation to have just one more cigarette. For almost all of us ex-smokers, smoking continues to play an important part in our lives. And now that it is being restricted in restaurants around the country and many indoor public places, it is vital that everyone understand the different emotional states cessation of smoking can cause. I have observed four of them, and I have classified them as those of the zealot, the evangelist, the elect, and the serene. Each day, each category gains new recruits.

> —Franklin E. Zimring, from "Confessions of a Former Smoker," *Newsweek*, April 20, 1987

Main idea: *Answers will vary; see text below.* _____

Some of you may think that the main idea is the first sentence—that there are three groups of Americans: smokers, nonsmokers, and those who have quit. In this case, however, the first sentence is really a lead-in to the main idea, not the main idea itself. The main idea is that there are four kinds of ex-smoker: the zealot, the evangelist, the elect, and the serene. So what you stated as the main idea should be some variation on that.

### PRACTICE 2   FINDING THE MAIN IDEA

Try finding the main idea in another paragraph taken from the same essay.

I have labeled my final category of former smokers the serene. Serenity is quieter than zealotry and evangelism, and those who qualify are not as self-righteous as the elect. The serene ex-smoker accepts himself and also accepts those around him who continue to smoke. This kind of serenity does not come easily, nor does it seem to be an immediate option for those who have stopped. Rather it is a goal, an end stage in a process of development during which some former smokers progress through one or more of the less-than-positive psychological points on the way. For former smokers, serenity is thus a positive possibility that exists at the end of the rainbow. But all former smokers cannot reach the promised land.

Main idea: *Answers will vary; see text below.* _____

The main idea of this paragraph is that the serene ex-smoker accepts that others smoke, and that the stage of serenity often comes after the ex-smoker has gone through the other, less positive stages (evangelist, zealot, and elect).

The following two paragraphs are similar versions taken from a single piece of writing. Read the first paragraph and write down, in the space provided, what you think the main idea is. Then read the second paragraph. If you think the main idea has changed from the one you wrote down for the first paragraph, write this main idea after the second paragraph.

1.  Of all the components of a good night's sleep, dreams seem to be least within our control. In dreams, a window opens into a world where logic is suspended and dead people speak. A century ago, Freud formulated his revolutionary theory that dreams were the disguised shadows of our unconscious desires and fears; by the late 1970s, neurologists had switched to thinking of them as just "mental noise"—the random byproducts of the neural-repair work that goes on during sleep.
　　　　—Marcia Hill Gossard, from "Taking Control," *Newsweek*, July 15, 2002

Main idea: *Answers will vary.*

2.  Of all the components of a good night's sleep, dreams seem to be least within our control. In dreams, a window opens into a world where logic is suspended and dead people speak. A century ago, Freud formulated his revolutionary theory that dreams were the disguised shadows of our unconscious desires and fears; by the late 1970s, neurologists had switched to thinking of them as just "mental noise"—the random byproducts of the neural-repair work that goes on during sleep. Now, researchers suspect that dreams are part of the mind's emotional thermostat, regulating moods while the brain is "offline." And one leading authority says that these intensely powerful mental events can be not only harnessed but actually brought under conscious control, to help us sleep and feel better.
　　　　—Marcia Hill Gossard, from "Taking Control," *Newsweek*, July 15, 2002

Main idea: *Answers will vary; see text below.*

The point of having you read these two paragraphs was to show that one or two additional sentences, particularly in the introductory paragraph of an essay, can change your perception of what the main idea is.

As you may have discovered, in the second paragraph, the addition of the two last sentences changes the main point. Instead of being about how dreams are out of our control, the paragraph sets up an essay that will discuss how to harness our dreams. This example shows why it's important to give special attention to each sentence in the first couple of paragraphs of an essay and then to actually jot the main idea, in your own words, in the margin. As you read the rest of the piece, you can refer back to the main idea you have written.

## 3. Find the Support for the Main Idea

Support plays different roles in different types of writing:

- When you read the instructions for how to put something together, the support will present the steps of the process, and it is important to understand each step.

■ **TIP** For more information on support in writing, see Chapter 4.

- When you read a memo or e-mail at work, the body of the document will provide reasons for, or details about, the topic described in the subject line.

- When you read a textbook in college, the authors will provide supporting details to explain topics or concepts so that you can understand their significance.

- When you read an essay in an English course, the support helps you understand the main point the author is making.

Often on a test or as a paper assignment, your instructor will ask you to respond to a reading you have been assigned. For example, you may be asked to write about whether you agree or disagree with the author, and why. Only by understanding the support provided in the reading will you be able to judge how successful the author has been in getting you to understand and appreciate his or her main point or position. Whether you agree or disagree with the author's point, you can explain *why* only by referring to the support.

As you read, make some notes to yourself. These will help you understand the selection and also keep you mentally alert. Underline the ideas that you think support the main point. Also note ideas that you agree with (put a check mark in the margin), don't agree with (put an exclamation point in the margin), or don't understand (put a question mark in the margin). Jot down thoughts or reactions you have as you read.

■ **PRACTICE 3** **FINDING MAIN IDEA AND SUPPORT**

The following paragraph is taken from a book that was on the *New York Times* bestseller list. It is also used in college courses. Double-underline the main idea and underline the support.

Any dictatorship takes a psychological toll on its subjects. If you are treated as an untrustworthy person—a potential slacker, drug addict, or thief—you may begin to feel less trustworthy yourself. If you are constantly reminded of your lowly position in the social hierarchy, whether by individual managers or by endless impersonal rules, you begin to accept that unfortunate status. In the biological sciences, there is ample evidence that animals—rats and monkeys, for example—that are forced into a subordinate status within their social systems adapt their brain chemistry accordingly, becoming "depressed" in humanlike ways. Their behavior is anxious and withdrawn; the level of serotonin (the neurotransmitter boosted by some antidepressants) declines in their brains; and they avoid fighting, even in self-defense.

—Barbara Ehrenreich, from *Nickel and Dimed: On Not Getting By in America* (2001)

■  PRACTICE 4   **FINDING MAIN IDEA AND SUPPORT**

The following excerpt is taken from an introduction to business textbook for college. Double-underline the main idea and underline the support.

**NEW SKILLS NEEDED**

The active participation of employees adds new responsibilities and opportunities to jobs at all levels. For starters, employees need new skills. The employee training budgets of U.S. businesses show the kinds of skills companies stress. The most common type of employee training is, and always has been, employee orientation, training that brings new employees up to speed on how the business and its industry work. Nine out of ten large and midsized businesses provide new-employee orientation.

Beyond employee orientation, several new kinds of training are increasingly common. Six out of ten large and midsized businesses now train employees in quality improvement. Three-fourths provide training in leadership skills. More participative approaches to business require managers and supervisors to make the shift from giving orders to coaching teams of employees, and some employee teams are now expected to manage themselves. Seven out of ten large and midsized companies now provide employee training in teamwork because new approaches to business require more cooperation and less personal competition.

Also new is the emphasis on problem-solving skills and creativity — two-thirds of midsized and large companies now train employees in problem solving and well over one-third stress creativity. They recognize that these thinking skills are important for employees at all levels of business.

Finally, more than half of these businesses are now giving employees training in how to deal with change. You are the first generation of

> ■ **TIP** For basic advice on problem solving and teamwork, see Chapter 8 (pages 109–12).

students to receive training in how to cope with and lead change in business.

—K. Blanchard, C. Schewe, R. Nelson, and A. Hiam, from *Exploring the World of Business* (1996) p. 26

## 4. Review and Respond to What You Have Read

After you have read a selection, quickly review the following elements:

- the title
- the main idea (either underlined or written in the margin)
- headings
- support you underlined
- words you highlighted
- definitions
- the conclusion

Reviewing what you have read is much like previewing it, with the addition of rereading the main idea and the support. Previewing helps you read more efficiently, and reviewing helps you retain what you have read. Both steps are important, and well worth the few minutes they take.

After reviewing the selection, take the following steps to make sure you understand it.

First, look at your guiding question and try to answer it.

Second, if you are reading a college textbook, you will probably find study questions at the end of each reading or chapter. Try to answer all of them, even if they aren't assigned.

Third, you should always try to answer the following basic questions about what you've read, even if you don't have study questions:

**BASIC READING QUESTIONS**

What is the author's main point?

What are the supporting points?

Do I understand everything I've just read?

**CRITICAL READING QUESTIONS**

Why is the author making this main point?

How strong are the supporting points?

Does the author use opinions or facts as supporting points?

Do I agree with the opinions?

Do the facts seem sound and relevant?

How has the author tried to convince me of his or her point of view?

Is there another way to look at this topic?

What do I think about the author's message? Why do I think this?

Each essay in this section is accompanied by marginal questions to help you read closely and critically. Try to answer them as you read; they'll help you understand, and respond to, the author's ideas.

Additionally, each essay is followed by several kinds of questions and assignments so that you can practice reviewing and responding to a reading selection.

The best way to be an active reader is to write something about what you have read. If you take notes while you read, you have already started to do this. But now you can try three other kinds of writing.

**SUMMARIZE:** A summary is a short account, in your own words, of the main point and supporting points in a reading. Writing an informal summary helps you understand the author's key points. A summary also reminds you of these key points during class discussion, while preparing for a writing assignment, and when studying for a test.

**RESPOND:** A response is your personal reaction to a reading. We learn new things by connecting them to what we already know. What connections can you make between what you've read and your own life? Have you ever experienced anything similar? How did the reading make you feel? What was your first thought when you finished reading?

**WRITE A PARAGRAPH OR ESSAY:** Try writing your own paragraph or essay on the topic of the reading. Do you agree or disagree with what the author said? Set out your own reasons clearly and persuasively. You also can use the reading as a model: Can you write something similar?

■ **TIP** For more information on summarizing, see Chapter 17. If you keep a reading journal, you can summarize and respond to the readings there.

■ **TEACHING TIP** For more information on reading journals, see *Practical Suggestions.*

## An Active Reader at Work

A sample reading follows. The notes in the margin show how one student, Patrick, read the essay. The notes in black are activities that Patrick did while previewing the reading; the notes in color are comments he made while reading. You might want to use this sample as a model as you work through the readings in the following chapters.

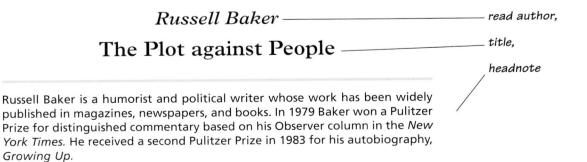

*Russell Baker* —————————— read author,

## The Plot against People ————— title,

headnote

Russell Baker is a humorist and political writer whose work has been widely published in magazines, newspapers, and books. In 1979 Baker won a Pulitzer Prize for distinguished commentary based on his Observer column in the *New York Times.* He received a second Pulitzer Prize in 1983 for his autobiography, *Growing Up.*

*read Guiding
Question*

GUIDING QUESTION
How does Baker classify the three types of inanimate objects, and what
examples does he provide?

*Main point*

Inanimate[1] objects are classified scientifically into three major categories— 1
those that don't work, those that break down, and those that get lost.

The goal of all inanimate objects is to resist man and ultimately to de- 2
feat him, and the three major classifications are based on the method each
object uses to achieve its purpose. As a general rule, any object capable of
breaking down at the moment when it is most needed will do so. The automobile is typical of the category.

*example, something that
breaks down*

With the cunning[2] typical of its breed, the automobile never breaks 3
down while entering a filling station with a large staff of idle mechanics.
It waits until it reaches a downtown intersection in the middle of the
rush hour, or until it is fully loaded with family and luggage on the Ohio
turnpike.

*more examples, things that
break down; what about
computers and printers?*

Thus it creates maximum misery, inconvenience, frustration, and irri- 4
tability among its human cargo, thereby reducing its owner's life span. Washing machines, garbage disposals, lawn mowers, light bulbs, automatic
laundry dryers, water pipes, furnaces, electrical fuses, television tubes, hose
nozzles, tape recorders, slide projectors—all are in league with the automobile to take their turn at breaking down whenever life threatens to flow
smoothly for their human enemies.

*examples of things that
get lost*

Many inanimate objects, of course, find it extremely difficult to break 5
down. Pliers, for example, and gloves and keys are almost totally incapable
of breaking down. Therefore, they have had to evolve a different technique
for resisting man.

*how about socks? and
sunglasses?*

They get lost. Science has still not solved the mystery of how they do it, 6
and no man has ever caught one of them in the act of getting lost. The most
plausible theory is that they have developed a secret method of locomotion[3]
which they are able to conceal the instant a human eye falls upon them.

It is not uncommon for a pair of pliers to climb all the way from the cel- 7
lar to the attic in its single-minded determination to raise its owner's blood
pressure. Keys have been known to burrow three feet under mattresses.
Women's purses, despite their great weight, frequently travel through six or
seven rooms to find hiding space under a couch.

Scientists have been struck by the fact that things that break down 8
virtually never get lost, while things that get lost hardly ever break down. A
furnace, for example, will invariably break down at the depth of the first
winter cold wave, but it will never get lost. A woman's purse, which after all
does have some inherent capacity for breaking down, hardly ever does; it
almost invariably chooses to get lost.

Some persons believe this constitutes[4] evidence that inanimate objects 9
are not entirely hostile to man, and that a negotiated peace is possible. After

*noticed vocabulary*

[1] **inanimate:** not living
[2] **cunning:** shrewd
[3] **locomotion:** movement
[4] **constitutes:** makes up

all, they point out, a furnace could infuriate a man even more thoroughly by getting lost than by breaking down, just as a glove could upset him far more by breaking down than by getting lost.

Not everyone agrees, however, that this indicates a conciliatory[5] attitude among inanimate objects. Many say it merely proves that furnaces, gloves, and pliers are incredibly stupid.   10

The third class of objects—those that don't work—is the most curious of all. These include such objects as barometers, car clocks, cigarette lighters, flashlights, and toy-train locomotives. It is inaccurate, of course, to say that they never work. They work once, usually for the first few hours after being brought home, and then quit. Thereafter, they never work again.   11

*examples of things that don't work*

In fact, it is widely assumed that they are built for the purpose of not working. Some people have reached advanced ages without ever seeing some of these objects—barometers, for example—in working order.   12

*I like his sense of humor*

Science is utterly baffled[6] by the entire category. There are many theories about it. The most interesting holds that the things that don't work have attained the highest state possible for an inanimate object, the state to which things that break down and things that get lost can still only aspire.[7]   13

They have truly defeated man by conditioning him never to expect anything of them, and in return they have given man the only peace he receives from inanimate society. He does not expect his barometer to work, his electric locomotive to run, his cigarette lighter to light, or his flashlight to illuminate, and when they don't, it does not raise his blood pressure.   14

He cannot attain that peace with furnaces and keys, and cars and women's purses as long as he demands that they work for their keep.   15

[5] **conciliatory:** making peace

[6] **baffled:** confused

[7] **aspire:** try for

*noticed vocabulary glosses*

# 40

# Narration

Each essay in this chapter uses narration to get its main point across to the reader. As you read these essays, consider how they achieve the four basics of good narration that are listed below and discussed in Chapter 8 of this book.

## ■■ FOUR BASICS OF GOOD NARRATION

1. It reveals something of importance to the writer (the main point).
2. It includes all of the major events of the story (primary support).
3. It brings the story to life with details about the major events (secondary support).
4. It presents the events in a clear order, usually according to when they happened.

*Elyzabeth Joy Stagg*

## From the Welfare Rolls, a Mother's View

In 1999, Elyzabeth Joy Stagg was a pregnant, jobless single mother, struggling to make ends meet and trying to earn a college degree. Her mixed feelings about her need to rely on welfare led her to write the following essay, which was published in *Newsweek*. After it appeared, Stagg received an outpouring of letters and support. She was delighted to hear that her narration had educated some of her readers about the real lives of welfare mothers.

Today, Stagg continues to educate others as she works with new mothers and their infants. The proud holder of a college degree, a registered nursing license, and a satisfying job in the newborn nursery of a major hospital in Peoria, Illinois, she is glad that she can now afford to buy the things her six-year-old daughter and three-year-old son need—"and some of the things they want." Although relieved that her previous financial hardships are behind her, she still remembers her days as a struggling parent. Her past, she feels, makes her more responsive to the needs of her patients, particularly those who are themselves struggling. She remains grateful for the help she received and says that her experience inspires her to do what she can to help others.

GUIDING QUESTION

What elements of the author's story change your perception of a typical welfare recipient?

I am a single mother of a three-year-old girl, and I'm expecting a son in November. My children have different fathers. I am a welfare mom, a burden to society. I live off your tax dollars.

I first went on welfare when I was pregnant with my daughter, after I lost my job and a house fire took nearly everything I owned. I was living in a hotel paid for by the Red Cross with no possessions, no job, and no boyfriend.

Since then, I've gotten temp jobs that pay enough to let me get off welfare, but when they end, I find myself struggling again. For the last several months I scoured the classifieds[1] and sent out résumés to find a job that would coincide with day care and pregnancy. I ended up serving food part-time at a bar for minimum wage. I tried to supplement that income as best I could, even directing plays and giving swing-dance lessons, but somehow I never seemed to get ahead. Now, due to complications with my pregnancy, I can't work at all and depend totally on welfare.

Being on welfare has taught me a lot. I've learned to go to the grocery store when it's the least busy, so I don't get annoyed looks from the people behind me in line when I pay with coupons and food stamps. I've learned that when I meet with a caseworker periodically, I should get to the welfare office 45 minutes before it opens, or I'll be waiting all day.

The biggest lesson I've learned from being on welfare is that most people assume I don't want to work. When I list my job skills for the caseworkers, they can't seem to understand why I don't have a job. To them, and the rest of society, I am just one of the 7 million people on welfare who survive off less than 1 percent of the federal budget.

But I'm more than just a statistic. I graduated in the top 10 percent of my high-school class. I'm studying nursing at my community college. I've played the flute since I was five. My parents have been married thirty years. I can type more than eighty words a minute. I'm bilingual. I know half a dozen computer programs inside and out. I'm twenty-four years old.

Now that I'm unable to work, I live off the $265 a month I receive from TANF (Temporary Assistance to Needy Families), which doesn't even cover my rent. My utility bills get paid when I receive final disconnect notices and I can take the bills to a community agency for financial assistance. At the end of the month, when my daughter asks for an ice-cream cone I sometimes don't have the extra $2 to buy it for her.

I don't spend my money on anything I don't absolutely need. I borrow videos from the library. I take my daughter to garage sales to look for clothes. I've never bought an alcoholic drink or a cigarette in my life. I don't buy expensive steaks or junk food. I drive a small car that leaks when it rains.

I don't have the kind of relationship I want with either of my kids' fathers. Both men are more than ten years older than I. They've been unable to keep their promises to help me in whatever way I needed. My daughter's father comes in and out of our lives. When he's gone, we miss him. The father of the new baby and I broke up in May because we choose to live different lifestyles. I doubt he will participate in the baby's life when it is born.

I acknowledge that it was my having unprotected sex, and getting pregnant, that caused my situation. I don't regret becoming a mom, but I do

1

2

3

4

5

6

7

8

9

10

**PREDICT:** At this point, what do you predict the author will write about?
*Answers will vary.*

**SUMMARIZE:** What has welfare taught Stagg (paragraphs 4 and 5)?
*Answers will vary, but the biggest lesson is that others assume she doesn't want to work.*

**REFLECT:** Do you share this opinion of those on welfare?
*Answers will vary.*

■ **IDEA JOURNAL** Tell about a time something bad happened to you that was not your fault.

**IDENTIFY:** What is the main point of this paragraph?
*The narrator doesn't spend money on anything she doesn't absolutely need.*

---

[1]**classifieds:** newspaper advertisements that include job listings

> "I feel proud of Miss Stagg. She is doing something for her children, and I know she'll make it."
> —Lidia Figueroa, Student

regret the difficulties I've gone through as a result. My life isn't anything I'd hoped it would be. I find myself constantly having to make choices that force me to compromise what I really want. Do I struggle for a few more years to finish college, or do I work for little money the rest of my life?

My parents tell me I should give the new baby up for adoption. They 11 wonder how I will possibly manage with two kids. I don't wonder. I'll do it because I have to and, more important, because I want to. They're my children, and I wouldn't leave them for anything. It boggles[2] my mind that there are so many parents out there who are not taking responsibility for their kids.

My daughter and my unborn child have forced me to grow up and 12 taught me more about life than any other experience I can possibly think of. They've taught me patience, compromise, love, and that being a mom is a blessing. Although parenthood is often a struggle, I wouldn't trade it for anything.

I'm grateful for the help that welfare has given me in the past. It sub- 13 sidized[3] my day care so I could go back to work and helped me return to school. I will continue to accept public assistance, but only until I can get back on my feet and make it on my own. I want more for my life. I want more for my children.

**IDENTIFY/REFLECT:** What decision does Stagg come to about public assistance in this paragraph? Based on what she writes in this essay, did you expect this decision? *Answers will vary. Stagg decides to continue to accept public assistance.*

■ ■ **SUMMARIZE AND RESPOND**

In your reading journal or elsewhere, summarize the main point of "From the Welfare Rolls, a Mother's View." Then go back and check off support for this main idea. Finally, jot down a brief response to the reading. How did it make you feel? Describe your perception of welfare moms and any experience you or someone you know has had with welfare.

■ **TEACHING TIP** Point out how Stagg uses the narration of her personal experiences to make a point that interests a large audience. Note how she has chosen events and details, such as those in paragraph 3, that help her establish a connection with her readers.

■ ■ **CHECK YOUR COMPREHENSION**

1. An alternate title for this essay could be
    a. "Battling the System."
    b. "Welfare Is Not My First and Final Choice."
    c. "We Have a Responsibility toward Our Children."
    d. "The Importance of Protected Sex."

2. The main idea of this essay is that
    a. people should not be rude to those on welfare.
    b. Stagg is a devoted and responsible parent.
    c. sometimes responsible people need public assistance.
    d. women with children have a right to public assistance.

3. According to the author, how do most people view welfare recipients?
    a. They think welfare recipients don't want to work.

[2] **boggles:** astonishes
[3] **subsidized:** gave money for

b. They have a fairly accurate view of welfare recipients.

c. They think that anyone can reach a point when they will need welfare.

d. They aren't very concerned about welfare recipients.

4. If you are unfamiliar with the following words, use a dictionary to check their meanings: *scoured, coincide* (para. 3); *statistic* (6).

## READ CRITICALLY

1. Stagg provides a number of facts about herself in her first paragraph. What impression of her do these facts create? Why do you think that she creates this impression at the beginning of her essay?

2. How did the facts in the second paragraph change your initial impression of Stagg? What other facts in the essay change that initial impression?

3. What does Stagg mean by the sentence, "But I'm more than just a statistic" (para. 6)? How does the rest of the essay demonstrate that she's "more than just a statistic"?

4. What specific examples of responsible behavior does Stagg provide?

5. What are the key events in Stagg's story? What details does she provide about one of these events?

## WRITE

**WRITE A PARAGRAPH:** Write a paragraph about an experience that changed your impression of someone else or that changed someone else's impression of you.

**WRITE AN ESSAY:** Write a narration essay that demonstrates "I am more than just a/an _____." Choose your own topic, such as "I am more than just a student taking a writing class, an older student, a pretty face, a waiter."

■ **TIP** For a sample narration paragraph, see page 99.

■ **TIP** For a sample narration paragraph, see page 99.

*Walter Scanlon*

# It's Time I Shed My Ex-Convict Status

Walter F. Scanlon (b. 1937) began working with alcohol and drug abusers after he had himself sought out and entered a twelve-step program upon his release from prison. Scanlon had dropped out of high school and then spent more than a decade in hospitals, in jail, and on the streets. Today, he holds a bachelor's degree from Pace University, an M.B.A. from the New York Institute of Technology, and a Ph.D. in psychology from Columbus University. In addition to being a specialist in workplace and family interventions for individuals with drug, alcohol, and other problems, he lectures widely and teaches at Marymount Manhattan College.

Scanlon observes that "there were long periods in my life when most decisions were made for me, not by me. Writing gave me a way to circumvent all that was happening around me and better understand what was happening within me." He is the author of two books, including *Alcoholism and Drug Abuse in the Workplace: Managing Care and Costs Through Employee Assistance Programs* (1991). In the following essay, Scanlon tells the story of the changes in his life over the past thirty years. (For more on Walter Scanlon and an example of his writing at work, see pp. 180–81.)

**GUIDING QUESTION**
Why does Scanlon feel that he should be able to shed his ex-convict status? Is his personal story convincing?

**■ IDEA JOURNAL** Tell about a time when you overcame a difficulty in your life.

**REFLECT:** What is the purpose of the background information in paragraphs 1 and 2? Is it effective?
*Possible answer: The opening*

*engages readers and hooks*

*them into Scanlon's story.*

**IDENTIFY:** Put an X by Scanlon's educational and job accomplishments in this paragraph.

**REFLECT:** Why does Scanlon give the reader these details?
*Possible answer: These*

*examples show how far he*

*has come.*

1    Thirty years ago I decided to drastically turn my life around. With a state-issued olive suit on my back, a high-school equivalency diploma and $40 travel money in my pocket, I became an ex-convict. I had done my time — almost five years in all — and now had the opportunity to redeem myself. I felt almost optimistic. As the huge outer gate of New York state's Clinton Prison slammed behind me, the discharge officer bid me farewell: "Get your act together," he bellowed with a mix of sincerity and humor. "I don't want to see you back here any time soon." A Department of Corrections van sat rumbling at the prison's checkpoint — my ride to the Greyhound bus depot.

2    As we pulled away, the towering walls, razor wire, and iron gates of the prison grew even more awesome, and the looming gun towers more ominous.[1] It was a bright early autumn morning, my thirty-second birthday was days away, and the last ten years of my life had been spent in and out of men's shelters, hospitals, and prisons. I wanted to make it this time.

3    Alcohol and other drugs had been my failing. Realizing I would need help, I sought an organization of other recovering addicts. Within a few days I landed a job in a metal-plating factory and rented a tiny furnished room. *X* On the urging of a new friend who had a similar past, I soon took my first *X* college course. My first grade was a disappointing C, but before long I was *x* scoring A's and B's. I also got better jobs, eventually landing a counseling *X* job in a substance-abuse treatment program. On job applications, I left questions about past arrests and convictions blank. I'd read that this would probably go unnoticed and, if it didn't, it would be better to discuss such matters in person. Time passed and, in a few short years, I completed college. I went on to get my master's degree and, using my graduate thesis as *X* its foundation, I wrote a book on drugs in the workplace. *X*

4    Today I live a full life, enjoying what most people enjoy: movies, books, theater, good food, and good friends. My significant other is a South Asian woman and her diverse circle of friends has enriched my life. My annual income as a substance-abuse specialist is adequate, my standing in the community solid, and my commitment to continued recovery is permanent.

[1] **ominous:** threatening

All of these qualities notwithstanding, I remain, irrevocably,[2] an ex-convict. Although the years have removed all but hazy memories of addiction, hospitalizations, street living, and prison, I secretly carry the baggage of a former offender. As my qualifications for higher-level positions grew, so, too, did the potential for a more detailed scrutiny[3] of my past. Opportunities for better jobs that colleagues took for granted were not so available to me. On virtually every job application, the question continued to haunt me: "Have you ever been convicted of a felony or misdemeanor or denied bond in any state?" Staring blankly at the application, I would often wonder, will this nightmare ever end? For minorities, who have a higher rate of incarceration, the nightmare is even more likely to occur.

To the average person, the ex-convict is an individual of questionable character. And without the experience of meeting a rehabilitated offender, there is little chance that this image will change. It is reinforced by the fact that the only thing usually newsworthy about an ex-convict is bad news — another arrest.

Yet the real news is that many former offenders are, like me, rehabilitated members of society. No one would guess at our pasts. We don't deserve kudos[4] for not committing crimes, but our failings should not supersede[5] decades of personal growth and responsible citizenship. Unfortunately, that's often what happens.

Under employment discrimination laws, hiring decisions cannot be made on the basis of age, sex, or the color of a person's skin. A job applicant does not have to reveal a disability or medical condition, including former drug dependence. Employability is based on the ability to perform the essential function of the job. Yet the former offender, whose past may be directly related to substance abuse, is expected to reveal his transgression.

No one is born an ex-convict; the title is earned and the individual must accept responsibility. Yet wouldn't it be nice if there were an ex-ex-con status? It would feel good not to panic at the sight of a job application and that dreaded question: "Have you ever been convicted of a felony or misdemeanor or denied bond in any state?" This question, without exclusionary criteria ([for example,] within the last ten years), serves no one's interest. To those of us who have paid our debt to society, it's a form of discrimination that undermines our efforts to continue to rebuild our lives.

**5**    IDENTIFY: Underline the sentence that explains why Scanlon was not eligible for higher-level positions.

**6**    ■ TEACHING TIP Point out to students how Scanlon gives plenty of examples in the course of telling his story — for instance, examples of how he turned his life around after prison and of the challenges he faced while doing so.

**7**

**8**    "Scanlon shows that the choices you make in life will never truly disappear."
   —Katilya Labidou, Student

**9**    REFLECT: How might discrimination against ex-convicts hurt their efforts "to continue to rebuild" their lives? *Answers will vary.*

■ **SUMMARIZE AND RESPOND**

In your reading journal or elsewhere, summarize the main point of "It's Time I Shed My Ex-Convict Status." Then go back and check off the support for this main idea. Next, write a brief summary of the essay. Finally, jot down a brief response to the reading. Should ex-convicts, like Scanlon, be able to shed their status?

---

[2] **irrevocably:** permanently

[3] **scrutiny:** inspection

[4] **kudos:** credit, praise

[5] **supersede:** replace

■ **CHECK YOUR COMPREHENSION**

1. An alternate title for this essay could be
    a. "Once an Ex-Convict, Always an Ex-Convict."
    b. "Paying a Debt to Society."
    c. "Rehabilitation Rights."
    d. "Employment Discrimination against Ex-Convicts."

2. The main idea of this essay is that
    a. alcohol and drug use can lead to crime and time in prison.
    b. ex-convicts should not have to reveal their status on job applications.
    c. ex-convicts can be rehabilitated.
    d. ex-convicts make good employees.

3. What does Scanlon mean when he writes that "our failings should not supersede decades of personal growth and responsible citizenship"?
    a. Ex-convicts who have worked hard to enter society should not be held back by their past mistakes.
    b. Ex-convicts need to grow more and prove that they are responsible citizens before they are forgiven for their mistakes.
    c. Mistakes of ex-convicts should always be remembered.
    d. Ex-convicts need to learn from their mistakes.

4. If you are unfamiliar with the following words, use a dictionary to look up their meanings: *drastically, bellowed* (para. 1); *incarceration* (5); *transgression* (8); *misdemeanor, exclusionary, undermines* (9).

■ **READ CRITICALLY**

1. What is Scanlon's tone in this essay?

2. In paragraph 6, according to Scanlon what could be done to begin to change the image of ex-convicts? What reinforces the image most people have of ex-convicts?

3. In paragraph 8, what does Scanlon feel should be the basis of employment? Do you agree with him?

4. In paragraph 9, Scanlon writes that asking a question about conviction "without exclusionary criteria . . . serves no one's interest." Why do you think he added the term "exclusionary criteria" to his statement?

5. What are some of Scanlon's accomplishments after he served his time? Do these help to support his main point? Why or why not?

■  **WRITE**

**WRITE A PARAGRAPH:** Write a paragraph that tells about a time when you did something wrong and made amends for it, but still had it held against you.

■ **TIP** For a sample narration paragraph see page 99.

**WRITE AN ESSAY:** Scanlon uses personal experience in this essay to make a point about discrimination of ex-convicts. To support his thesis, he uses specific and plentiful details. In your essay, write about a time when you felt discriminated against in some way. Like Scanlon, share your personal experience and include details and examples that allow the reader to understand your point of view.

# 41

# Illustration

Each essay in this chapter uses illustration to get its main point across to the reader. As you read these essays, consider how they achieve the four basics of good illustration that are listed below and discussed in Chapter 9 of this book.

## ▪▪ FOUR BASICS OF GOOD NARRATION
1. It makes a point.
2. It gives specific examples that show, explain, or prove the point.
3. It gives details to support these examples.
4. It uses enough examples to get the writer's point across.

*Bill Bryson*

## Snoopers at Work

Bill Bryson (b. 1951) grew up in the United States, moved to England in 1973, married and had four children there, and, after more than two decades, returned to the country of his birth. Recently, he went back to England. After writing a regular newspaper column, he branched out into travel writing—a field he says he entered "entirely by accident." Bryson's travel books include the hilarious bestselling Appalachian Trail memoir, *A Walk in the Woods* (1998); his ode to Australia, *In a Sunburned Country* (2000); a travelogue about a trip to Kenya, *Bill Bryson's African Diary* (2002); and two books about travels in the United States, *The Lost Continent* (1989) and *I'm a Stranger Here Myself* (1999). He has also written two books about the English language.

Bryson's essays in *I'm a Stranger Here Myself,* excerpted here, began as Sunday columns in a British newspaper, *The Mail.* In them, Bryson uses his insight and humor to comment from abroad on aspects of the United States. In the next selection, Bryson illustrates a new American trend that strikes him as particularly disturbing: the invasion of workers' privacy by their employers.

GUIDING QUESTION
As you read this essay consider the number and types of examples the author presents. Are they sufficient and varied enough to convince you that employers and businesses "snoop" on their employees?

Now here is something to bear in mind should you ever find yourself using     1
a changing room in a department store or other retail establishment. It is
perfectly legal — indeed, it is evidently routine — for the store to spy on you
while you are trying on their clothes.

I know this because I have just been reading a book by Ellen Alderman     2
and Caroline Kennedy called *The Right to Privacy,* which is full of alarming
tales of ways that businesses and employers can — and enthusiastically do —
intrude into what would normally be considered private affairs.

The business of changing-cubical spying came to light in 1983 when a     3
customer trying on clothes in a department store in Michigan discovered
that a store employee had climbed a stepladder and was watching him
through a metal vent. (Is this tacky or what?) The customer was sufficiently
outraged that he sued the store for invasion of privacy. He lost. A state court
held that it was reasonable for retailers to defend against shoplifting by engaging in such surveillance.[1]

He shouldn't have been surprised. Nearly everyone is being spied on in     4
some way in America these days. A combination of technological advances,
employer paranoia, and commercial avarice[2] means that many millions of
Americans are having their lives delved into in ways that would have been
impossible, not to say unthinkable, a dozen years ago.

Worse still, there are now scores of information brokers — electronic pri-     5
vate investigators — who make a living going through the Internet digging
out personal information on people for a fee. If you have ever registered to
vote they can get your address and date of birth, since voter registration
forms are a matter of public record in most states. With these two pieces of
information, they can (and for as little as $8 or $10 will) provide almost any
personal information about any person you might wish to know: court
records, medical records, driving records, credit history, hobbies, buying
habits, annual income, phone numbers (including unlisted numbers), you
name it.

Most of this was possible before, but it would take days of inquiries and     6
visits to various government offices. Now it can be done in minutes, in complete anonymity, through the Internet.

Many companies are taking advantage of these technological possi-     7
bilities to make their businesses more ruthlessly productive. In Maryland,
according to *Time* magazine, a bank searched through the medical records
of its borrowers — apparently quite legally — to find out which of them had
life-threatening illnesses and used this information to cancel their loans.
Other companies have focused not on customers but on their own employees — for instance, to check what prescription drugs the employees are taking. One large, well-known company teamed up with a pharmaceutical firm
to comb through the health records of employees to see who might benefit
from a dose of antidepressants. The idea was that the company would get
more serene workers; the drug company would get more customers.

According to the American Management Association two-thirds of com-     8
panies in the United States spy on their employees in some way. Thirty-five

[1] **surveillance:** observation

[2] **avarice:** greed

---

REFLECT: What makes this case different from the others that Bryson presents? Why does he think that the woman will get "a pot of money"?
*Possible answer: This case*

*involves secret surveillance.*

*The video showed the*

*woman changing.*

SUMMARIZE: In your own words, summarize this extended example.
*Answers will vary.*

REFLECT: Consider your own experiences or those of people you know. Do you find this percentage believable?
*Answers will vary.*

"The essay brings up interesting concerns and grabs readers' attention. It shows that the right to privacy is no longer a right."

—Mark Balderas,
Student

percent track phone calls, and 10 percent actually tape phone conversations to review at leisure later. About a quarter of companies surveyed admitted to going through their employees' computer files and reading their e-mail.

Still other companies are secretly watching their employees at work. A secretary at a college in Massachusetts discovered that a hidden video camera was filming her office twenty-four hours a day. Goodness knows what the school authorities were hoping to find. What they got were images of the woman changing out of her work clothes and into a track suit each night in order to jog home from work. She is suing and will probably get a pot of money. But elsewhere courts have upheld companies' rights to spy on their workers. 9

In 1989, when an employee of a large Japanese-owned computer products company discovered that the company was routinely reading employees' e-mail, even though it had assured the employees that it was not, she blew the whistle, and was promptly fired. She sued for unfair dismissal and lost the case. A court upheld the right of companies not only to review employees' private communications but to lie to them about doing it. Whoa. 10

There is a particular paranoia about drugs. I have a friend who got a job with a large manufacturing company in Iowa a year or so ago. Across the street from the company was a tavern that was the company after-hours hangout. One night my friend was having a beer after work with his colleagues when he was approached by a fellow employee who asked if he knew where she could get some marijuana. He said he didn't use the stuff himself, but to get rid of her—for she was very persistent—he gave her the phone number of an acquaintance who sometimes sold it. 11

The next day he was fired. The woman, it turned out, was a company spy employed solely to weed out drug use in the company. He hadn't supplied her with marijuana, you understand, hadn't encouraged her to use marijuana, and had stressed that he didn't use marijuana himself. Nonetheless he was fired for encouraging and abetting[3] the use of an illegal substance. 12

Already, 91 percent of large companies—I find this almost unbelievable—now test some of their workers for drugs. Scores of companies have introduced what are called TAD rules—TAD being short for "tobacco, alcohol, and drugs"—which prohibit employees from using any of these substances at any time, including at home. There are companies, if you can believe it, that forbid their employees to drink or smoke at any time—even one beer, even on a Saturday night—and enforce the rules by making their workers give urine samples. 13

But it gets even more sinister[4] than that. Two leading electronics companies working together have invented something called an "active badge," which tracks the movements of any worker compelled to wear one. The badge sends out an infrared signal every fifteen seconds. This signal is received by a central computer, which is thus able to keep a record of where every employee is and has been, whom they have associated with, how many times they have been to the toilet or water cooler—in short, to log every single action of their working day. If that isn't ominous, I don't know what is. 14

---

[3] **abetting:** assisting
[4] **sinister:** evil

However, there is one development, I am pleased to report, that makes   15
all of this worthwhile. A company in New Jersey has patented a device for
determining whether restaurant employees have washed their hands after
using the lavatory. Now *that* I can go for.

## SUMMARIZE AND RESPOND

In your reading journal or elsewhere, summarize the main point of
"Snoopers at Work." Then go back and check off support for this main idea.
Next, write a brief summary of the essay. Finally, jot down a brief response
to the reading. How did it make you feel? What did you think about the fact
that legally employers and businesses can "snoop" on their employees? What
about the rights of employees?

## CHECK YOUR COMPREHENSION

1. An alternate title for this essay could be
   a. "Legal Monitoring."
   b. "Cameras in the Changing Rooms."
   c. "Spying on the Job."
   d. "Surveillance Tactics."

2. The main idea of this essay is that
   a. drug tests violate personal rights.
   b. employees should take actions against intrusions into their
      personal lives.
   c. computers are making it easy for employees and businesses to
      obtain personal information.
   d. businesses and employers can and do legally intrude into the lives
      of their employees who are on and, in some cases, off the job.

3. According to the author, the practice of "snooping at work" is
   a. minimal enough to be labeled a nuisance.
   b. widespread.
   c. something that occurs only in major corporations.
   d. decreasing because of the threat of lawsuits by employees.

4. If you are unfamiliar with the following words, use a dictionary to
   check their meanings: *anonymity* (para. 6); *ruthlessly* (7); *compelled,
   ominous* (14)

## READ CRITICALLY

1. From where does the author obtain most of his examples? Do you find
   the examples believable?

2. Is the order of the examples effective? Why or why not?

3. Which example of snooping did you find the most offensive? Why?

4. In your opinion, do the TAD (tobacco, alcohol, and drugs) rules go beyond the legal rights of employers? Why or why not?

5. In the last paragraph, the author is apparently pleased with one company's attempt at snooping on its employees. Why? What is the purpose of this example?

### ■ WRITE

■ **TIP** For a sample illustration paragraph, see page 117.

**WRITE A PARAGRAPH:** Write a paragraph that continues the author's idea in this essay. Present additional examples of ways employers or businesses might snoop on their employees, or elaborate on an example presented in the essay. Your examples may be based on personal experiences, observations, or readings.

**WRITE AN ESSAY:** In an essay, expand on the topic of this reading. Consider other types of intrusions as well, such as those committed by the government, schools, or even families. Develop your main point by including specific examples arranged in a logical manner, as Bryson does. Feel free to include the ideas you wrote about in your idea journal or under Summarize and Respond.

*Dianne Hales*

# Why Are We So Angry?

PREDICT: After reading the title, what do you expect this essay to do?
*Answers will vary.*

Dianne Hales specializes in writing about mental health, fitness, and other issues related to the body and mind. She contributes regularly to *Parade* magazine and *Ladies Home Journal,* and she has written several college-level health textbooks. In her critically acclaimed book *Just Like a Woman* (2000), she examined assumptions about the biological differences between women and men; she has also written a comprehensive overview of mental health, *Caring for the Mind* (1996), with her psychiatric husband. Both the American Psychiatric Association and the American Psychological Association have presented Hales with awards for excellence in writing. In addition, she has earned an Exceptional Media Merit Award (EMMA) from the National Women's Political Caucus for health reporting. She lives in Marin County, California.

In the following article, originally in *Parade,* Hales uses vivid examples to illustrate the "rage" phenomenon. She reports on the causes and results of the apparent increase in out-of-control anger—and explains what can be done to relieve the problem.

GUIDING QUESTION
Does the author present specific and plentiful examples to answer the question that she poses in her title?

$S$omething snapped inside Jerry Sola during his evening commute through the Chicago suburbs two years ago. When the driver in front of the fifty-one-year-old salesman suddenly slammed on his brakes, Sola got so incensed[1] that he gunned his engine to cut in front of the man. Still steaming when both cars stopped at a red light, Sola grabbed a golf club from the backseat and got out.

"I was just about to smash his windshield or do him some damage," the brawny, 6-foot-1 former police officer recalls. "Then it hit me: 'What in God's name am I doing? I'm really a nice, helpful guy. What if I killed a man, went to jail and destroyed two families over a crazy, trivial thing?' I got back into my car and drove away."

Like Sola, more and more Americans are feeling pushed to the breaking point. The American Automobile Association's Foundation for Traffic Safety says incidents of violently aggressive driving—which some dub "mad driver disease"—rose 7 percent a year in the 1990s. Airlines are reporting more outbursts of sky rage. And sideline rage has become widespread: A Pennsylvania kids' football game ended in a brawl involving more than one hundred coaches, players, parents, and fans. In a particularly tragic incident that captured national attention, a Massachusetts father—angered over rough play during his son's hockey practice—beat another father to death as their children watched.

No one seems immune to the anger epidemic. Women fly off the handle just as often as men, though they're less likely to get physical. The young and the infamous, such as musicians Sean "Puffy" Combs and Courtney Love—both sentenced to anger-management classes for violent outbursts—may seem more volatile,[2] but even senior citizens have erupted into "line rage" and pushed ahead of others simply because they felt they had "waited long enough" in their lives.

"People no longer hold themselves accountable for their bad behavior," says Doris Wilde Helmering, a therapist and author of *Sense Ability*. "They blame anyone and everything for their anger."

***It's a mad, mad, world.*** Violent outbursts are just as likely to occur in leafy suburbs as in crowded cities, and even idyllic[3] vacation spots are not immune. "Everyone everywhere seems to be hotter under the collar these days," observes Sybil Evans, a conflict-resolution expert in New York City, who singles out three primary culprits: time, technology, and tension. "Americans are working longer hours than anyone else in the world. The cell phones and pagers that were supposed to make our lives easier have put us on call 24/7/365. Since we're always running, we're tense and low on patience. And the less patience we have, the less we monitor what we say to people and how we treat them."

Ironically,[4] the recent boom times may have brought out the worst in some people. "Never have so many with so much been so unhappy," observes Leslie Charles, author of *Why Is Everyone So Cranky?* "There are more of us than ever, all wanting the same space, goods, services, or

1

2

3

4

5

6

7

■ **IDEA JOURNAL** List some examples of publicly displayed anger that you have experienced.

REFLECT: Do you feel that you are one of the many Americans who are pushed to the breaking point? *Answers will vary.*

IDENTIFY: Underline the main point in this paragraph.

"These are all examples that everyone can relate to."
—Katilya Labidou, Student

PREDICT: Pick one of the culprits; how do you think Hales in subsequent paragraphs will show it to be a cause of anger? *Answers will vary*

[1] **incensed:** angered

[2] **volatile:** explosive

[3] **idyllic:** peaceful

[4] **ironically:** opposite to what is or might be expected

IDENTIFY: According to this paragraph, what triggers rage?

*a sense of helplessness*

SUMMARIZE: In your own words, summarize how letting anger out creates problems.

*Answers will vary.*

IDENTIFY: Underline the sentence that presents a solution to releasing anger.

■ **TEACHING TIP** In addition to providing vivid examples, this article traces the causes and effects of what appears to be an increase in angry outbursts. If you are also teaching the cause-and-effect chapters (15 and 47), you might want to point to this essay as an example of how these (and other) writing strategies can be mixed.

attention. Everyone thinks, 'Me first. I don't have time to be polite.' We've lost not only our civility but our tolerance for inconvenience."

The sheer complexity of our lives also has shortened our collective fuse. 8 We rely on computers that crash, drive on roads that gridlock, places calls to machines that put us on endless hold. "It's not any one thing but lots of little things that make people feel like they don't have control of their lives," says Jane Middleton-Moz, a therapist and author. "A sense of helplessness is what triggers rage. It's why people end up kicking ATM machines."

***Getting a grip.*** When his lawn mower wouldn't start, a St. Louis man 9 got so angry that he picked it up by the handle, smashed it against the patio and tore off each of its wheels. Playing golf, he sometimes became so enraged that he threw his clubs 50 feet up the fairway and into the trees and had to get someone to retrieve them. In anger-therapy sessions with Doris Wilde Helmering, he learned that such outbursts accomplish nothing. "Venting" may make you feel better—but only for a moment.

"Catharsis[5] is worse than useless," says Brad Bushman, a psychology 10 professor at Iowa State University whose research has shown that letting anger out makes people more aggressive, not less. "Many people think of anger as the psychological equivalent of the steam in a pressure cooker: It has to be released, or it will explode. That's not true. The people who react by hitting, kicking, screaming, and swearing just feel more angry."

Over time, temper tantrums sabotage physical health as well as psycho- 11 logical equanimity. By churning out stress hormones like adrenaline, chronic anger revs the body into a state of combat readiness, multiplying the risk for stroke and heart attack—even in healthy individuals. In one study by Duke University researchers, young women with "*Jerry Springer Show*-type anger," who tended to slam doors, curse and throw things in a fury, had higher cholesterol levels than those who reacted more calmly.

***How do you tame a toxic temper?*** The first step is to figure out 12 what's really making you angry. Usually the rude sales clerk is the final straw that unleashes bottled-up fury over a more difficult issue, such as a divorce or a domineering boss. Next, monitor yourself for early signs of exhaustion or overload. While stress alone doesn't cause a blow-up, it makes you more vulnerable to overreacting.

When you feel yourself getting angry, control your tongue and your 13 brain. "Like any feeling, anger lasts only about three seconds," says Doris Wilde Helmering. "What keeps it going is your negative thinking." As long as you focus on who or what irritated you—like the oaf who rammed that grocery cart into your heels—you'll stay angry. "Once you come to understand that you're driving your own anger with your thoughts," adds Helmering, "you can stop it."

Since his roadside epiphany, Jerry Sola has conscientiously worked to 14 rein in his rage. "I am a changed person," he says, "especially behind the wheel. I don't listen to the news on the car radio. Instead, I put on nice, soothing music. I force myself to smile at rude drivers. And if I feel myself getting angry, I ask a simple question: 'Why should I let a person I'm never going to see again control my mood and ruin my whole day?'"

[5] **catharsis:** release of emotional tension

### SUMMARIZE AND RESPOND

In your reading journal or elsewhere, summarize the main point of "Why Are We So Angry?" Then go back and check off support for this main idea. Next, write a brief summary of the essay. Finally, jot down a brief response to the reading. Can you identify with the angry people Hales writes about in this essay? Have you ever been one of them?

### CHECK YOUR COMPREHENSION

1. An alternate title for this essay could be
   a. "Anger Management."
   b. "Road Rage."
   c. "Investigating the Anger Epidemic."
   d. "The Breaking Point."

2. The main idea of this essay is that
   a. anger is a widespread occurrence in today's society.
   b. anger is most common in sports.
   c. people should enroll in anger management courses.
   d. road rage must stop.

3. What do experts say about releasing anger?
   a. Releasing anger reduces frustration.
   b. Hitting a pillow is a simple way to release anger.
   c. Releasing anger is not productive.
   d. People in the suburbs are most likely to release anger.

4. If you are unfamiliar with the following words, use a dictionary to check their meanings: *brawl* (para. 3); *immune, epidemic, erupted* (4); *culprits* (6); *gridlock* (8).

### READ CRITICALLY

1. Based on your personal experience and observations, do the examples presented in this essay seem realistic?

2. Throughout the essay, Hales presents information gained from therapists and experts. Does this information strengthen Hales's main point? Would the essay be just as effective without it?

3. What role does technology play in creating anger?

4. Do the steps presented under "How do you tame a toxic temper?" (paras. 12 and 13) seem like a workable solution? Why or why not?

5.  Hales begins her essay with the example of Jerry Sola and ends with it. Why do you suppose she uses this technique?

### WRITE

■ **TIP** For a sample illustration paragraph, see page 117.

**WRITE A PARAGRAPH:** Write a paragraph about a location where you have seen people exhibit their anger. Identify the location, and provide concrete examples of the way people show their anger.

**WRITE AN ESSAY:** Write an essay about a time when either you or someone you knew lost control. What happened? Give concrete examples of the loss of control. What were the consequences? Did you learn anything from the experience about expressing anger? Feel free to include the ideas you wrote about in your reading journal for Summarize and Respond.

# 42

# Description

Each essay in this chapter uses description to get its main point across to the reader. As you read these essays, consider how they achieve the four basics of good description that are listed below and discussed in Chapter 10 of this book.

## ■■ FOUR BASICS OF GOOD DESCRIPTION

1. It creates a main impression—an overall effect, feeling, or image—about the topic.
2. It uses specific details to support the main impression.
3. It supports those examples with details that appeal to the five senses: sight, hearing, smell, taste, and touch.
4. It brings a person, place, or physical object to life for the reader.

## *Andrea Lee*

## Mother

Andrea Lee (b. 1953) began her professional writing career as a journalist, contributing pieces to *New Yorker* magazine while she was an exchange student in Russia and receiving a National Book Award nomination for *Russian Journal* (1981), a nonfiction book about her experience. However, Lee, the daughter of a prominent African American family from Philadelphia, has always loved fiction; she started inventing stories to entertain her relatives at the age of four. "I prefer writing fiction to journalism because to me fiction is far more entertaining and—strange to say—truer to life than journalism," she has said. Her published fiction includes the novel *Sarah Phillips* (1984) and a short-story collection, *Interesting Women* (2002). Lee read pieces from both of these works in 2003 for the Black Writers Reading series at Harvard, the university from which she received her B.A. and M.A. degrees.

*Sarah Phillips,* based on a series of short stories Lee published in the *New Yorker,* tells the story of a young African American girl from a privileged Philadelphia background much like Lee's own. The following excerpt from *Sarah Phillips* presents Sarah's vivid recollections of the sights, smells, and sounds of a summer evening when she was six.

GUIDING QUESTION
As you read Lee's writing, what images are most vivid for you, and what senses do they appeal to?

IDENTIFY: In this paragraph,
identify sensory details related to household smells.
*Possible answers: odors of*

*frying scrapple or codfish,*

*scent of mustard greens,*

*fragrance of clothes*

REFLECT: What do you think
Lee means when she com-
pares the kitchen to the feeling of a workshop?
*Possible answer: The*

*kitchen is cluttered yet rich*

*with possibilities.*

IDENTIFY: Underline the sentence that unites the details
in this paragraph.

In the summer my mother got up just after sunrise, so that when she 1
called Matthew and me for breakfast, the house was filled with sounds and
smells of her industrious mornings. Odors of frying scrapple or codfish
cakes drifted up the back stairs, mingling sometimes with the sharp scent of
mustard greens she was cooking for dinner that night. Up the laundry
chute from the cellar floated whiffs of steamy air and the churning sound of
the washing machine. From the dining room, where she liked to sit ironing
and chatting on the telephone, came the fragrance of hot clean clothes and
the sound of her voice: cheerful, resonant, reverberating a little weirdly
through the high-ceilinged rooms, as if she were sitting happily at the bottom of a well.

Mama was a housekeeper in the grand old style that disdains conve- 2
nience, worships thrift, and condones extravagance only in the form of
massive Sunday dinners, which, like acts of God, leave family members
stunned and reeling. Her kitchen, a long, dark, inconvenient room joined to
a crooked pantry, was entirely unlike the cheerful kitchens I saw on television, where mothers who looked like June Cleaver[1] unwrapped food done
up in cellophane. This kitchen had more the feeling of a workshop, a laboratory in which the imperfect riches of nature were investigated and finally
transformed into something near sublimity.[2] The sink and stove were cluttered with works in progress: hot plum jelly dripping into a bowl through
cheesecloth; chocolate syrup bubbling in a saucepan; string beans and ham
bones hissing in the pressure cooker; cooling rice puddings flavored with al-
mond and vanilla; cooked apples waiting to be forced through a sieve to
make applesauce; in a vat, a brownish aromatic mix for root beer.

Mama took pleasure in the raw materials that became meals. She en- 3
joyed the symmetry, the unalterable rules, and also the freaks and vagaries[3]
that nature brought to her kitchen. She showed me with equal pleasure the
handsome shape of a fish backbone, the little green gallbladder in the middle of a chicken liver; and the double-yolked eggs, the triple cherries, the
peculiar worm in a cob of corn.

On summer evenings, after the dinner dishes had been washed and as 4
the remains of the iced tea stood growing tepid[4] in the pitcher, my mother,
steamy and disheveled,[5] finally would emerge from the kitchen. "Look at
me," she'd murmur, wandering into the living room and patting her hair in
the mirror over the piano. "I look like a Wild Man of Borneo."

She would change into a pair of oxfords[6] and take a walk with me, or 5
with a neighbor. At that time of day, June bugs hurled themselves against
the screens of the house, and my father, covered with mosquito repellent
and smoking cigarette after cigarette, sat reading under the maple tree. In
the diffuse light after sunset, the shadows around the perfectly ordinary

[1] **June Cleaver:** the mother in the TV situation comedy *Leave It to Beaver,* which was originally broadcast from 1957 to 1963

[2] **sublimity:** inspiring awe, impressive

[3] **vagaries:** irregularities

[4] **tepid:** barely warm

[5] **disheveled:** disordered, messed up

[6] **oxfords:** sturdy tied shoes

houses up and down the street made the unambitious details of their de-signs—turrets, round Victorian towers, vague half-timbering—seem for once dramatic. All the backyards of the town seemed to have melted into one darkening common where packs of kids yelled faintly and fought their last battles before bedtime. Cars pulled out of driveways and headed for movie theaters or the shopping centers along the Pike, and the air smelled like honeysuckle and onion grass. When Mama and I walked together, we would wander up and down the long blocks until the streetlights came on.

One evening during the summer that I was six years old, we stopped to visit a neighboring family in which something sad and shocking had hap-pened the previous winter. The father, a district judge named Roland Bar-ber, had driven one gray afternoon to the marshland outside the airport and there had shot himself. His suicide, with hints of further-reaching scan-dal, sent a tremendous shock through the staid[7] circles of my parents' friends, a shock that reached down even into the deep waters that normally insulated me. For a few weeks after the suicide, we held long grisly[8] discus-sions on arcane,[9] even acrobatic ways to do away with oneself.

My mother was carrying a recipe for peach cobbler. It was intended for Mrs. Barber, a bony woman who had fascinated me even before her hus-band's death, because she wore a very thick pair of elasticized stockings. However, after we'd knocked and waited for a while, the front door was fi-nally opened by Phyllis, the Barbers' sixteen-year-old daughter. Mama sometimes referred to Phyllis as "the fair and brainless"; I had seen her plenty of times at the swim club, pretty and somewhat fat-faced, drawing the stares of the men to her plump legs in shorts. That night, though it was only about eight o'clock, she opened the door in a light summer bathrobe and peered out at us without turning on the porch lights. I looked at her with awe. It was the first time I had seen her since I had heard the news about Judge Barber, and the first time I had ever stood right in front of anyone associated with an event that had caused such a convulsion[10] in the adult world. In the light-colored robe, with her wet hair—which normally she wore flipped up at the ends and pulled back with a band, like other high schoolers in the neighborhood—combed back from her forehead, she had a mysterious imposing look that I never would have suspected of her. I immediately ascribed[11] it—as I was ascribing the ordinary shadow of the summer twilight around the doorway—to the extraordinary thing that had happened to her. Her face seemed indefinably swollen, whether with tears or temper, and she kept her top lip tightly clenched as she talked to my mother. She looked beautiful to me, like a dream or an illustration from a book, and as I stared at her, I felt intensely interested and agitated.

In a few minutes, Phyllis went back inside. My mother and I, as we had done many times before, walked quietly up the Barbers' driveway and through the backyard to the swing in the oak tree. Mama stopped to pick a

6

7

8

■ **IDEA JOURNAL** Describe a summer evening.

REFLECT: Paragraphs 6 and 7 take the emphasis off the mother and put it on a neighbor. Offer an explana-tion for this shift. *Possible answer: The shift shows the mother's involve-ment in, and concern for, matters outside the home.*

■ **TEACHING TIP** This excerpt uses vivid sensory details—es-pecially sight, sound, and taste. Have students read the piece, underline images that appeal to the senses, and write in their reading journals the sense each image appeals to. Which para-graph is most vivid? Why?

---

[7] **staid:** proper, orderly

[8] **grisly:** horrible, gruesome

[9] **arcane:** complicated and difficult to imagine

[10] **convulsion:** spasm, fit of agitation and shaking

[11] **ascribed:** to attribute cause to

few tomatoes from the overloaded plants in the Barbers' vegetable garden, and I helped her, though my second tomato was a rotten one that squashed in my fingers.

It was completely dark by then. Lightning bugs flashed their cold green semaphores[12] across the backyards of the neighborhood, and a near-tropical din[13] of rasping, creaking, buzzing night insects had broken out in the trees around us. I walked over and sat down in the oak-tree swing, and Mama, pausing occasionally to slap at mosquitoes, gave me a few good pushes, so that I flew high out of the leaves, toward the night sky.

I couldn't see her, but I felt her hands against my back; that was enough. There are moments when the sympathy between mother and child becomes again almost what it was at the very first. At that instant I could discern[14] in my mother, as clearly as if she had told me of it, the same almost romantic agitation that I felt. While my mother pushed me in the swing, it seemed as if we were conducting, without words, a troubling yet oddly exhilarating dialogue about pain and loss.

In a few minutes I dragged my sneakered feet in a patch of dust to stop the swing. The light of a television had gone on inside the Barber house, and I imagined fat, pretty Phyllis Barber carefully rolling her hair on curlers, alone in front of the screen. I grabbed my mother's hand and said, "It's very sad, isn't it?"

"It certainly is," said Mama.

We took a shortcut home, and by the time we got there, it was time for me to scrub my grimy arms and legs and go to bed. Mama went immediately to the refrigerator and got out an uncooked roast of pork, which she stood contemplating as if it were the clue to something. She smelled of sage and dried mustard when she came upstairs to kiss Matthew and me good-night.

**REFLECT:** This exchange between mother and daughter is the only one that occurs in this story. Why do you think Lee included it?

*Possible answer: The ordinary dialogue is in contrast to the powerful quiet moment that precedes it.*

9

10

11

12

13

## SUMMARIZE AND RESPOND

In your reading journal or elsewhere, summarize the main point of "Mother." Then go back and check off support for the main idea. Finally, jot down a brief response to the reading. What did it make you think or feel? Can you recall a childhood experience of your mother's cooking or of a summer evening?

## CHECK YOUR COMPREHENSION

1. An alternate title for this piece could be
   a. "Good Food in the Kitchen."
   b. "Carefree Summer Strolls."
   c. "A Memorable Summer Evening."
   d. "My Mother's Kitchen."

[12] **semaphores:** visual signal of lights or flags

[13] **din:** high level of noise

[14] **discern:** understand

2. The main idea of this selection is that

    a. it is important for mothers and daughters to have time alone.

    (b.) normal routines are reassuring, particularly when people witness or learn of disturbing experiences.

    c. even people in important and powerful positions can be extremely unhappy.

    d. do unto your neighbor as you would have him or her do unto you (the golden rule).

3. What two things does Lee contrast in great detail?

    a. The impressions of the narrator's home with those of Phyllis Barber's home

    b. The world of children and the world of adults

    c. The atmosphere in the kitchen and the atmosphere outdoors

    (d.) Phyllis Barber's appearance in school with her appearance that evening

4. If you are unfamiliar with the following words, use a dictionary to check their meanings: *churning, resonant, reverberating* (para. 1); *condones* (2); *symmetry* (3); *diffuse* (5); *insulated* (6); *exhilarating* (10).

### READ CRITICALLY

1. Reread paragraphs 1 through 4, underlining the details Lee uses that appeal to the senses, and then review the details you underlined. What general impression do these details create of the atmosphere in the narrator's mother's house? What senses does she appeal to in these paragraphs?

2. Reread paragraphs 6 through 8. What impression do these paragraphs create, and how does that impression compare with the one created in the first four paragraphs? How does the impression created in the first four paragraphs influence the impression in paragraphs 6 through 8?

3. In paragraph 10, Lee writes of the "romantic agitation" that mother and child felt. What do you think she means by calling the experience "a troubling yet oddly exhilarating dialogue about pain and loss"? How can something be both troubling and exhilarating?

4. Why do you think that the mother started cooking as soon as they returned from their walk?

5. The reading concludes with the sentence "She smelled of sage and dried mustard when she came upstairs to kiss Matthew and me good-night." Why is this a good concluding sentence, and what does it indicate?

**WRITE**

■ **TIP** For a sample description paragraph, see page 130.

**WRITE A PARAGRAPH:** Write a paragraph that describes the surrounding atmosphere during a moment you recall vividly. Use physical details that appeal to at least two of the five senses: sight, sound, touch, taste, and smell.

**WRITE AN ESSAY:** Write an essay that uses vivid details to describe an experience that had a strong impact on you. If you wish, use ideas you developed for Summarize and Respond.

## *Chitra Banerjee Divakaruni*
# Common Scents

Chitra Banerjee Divakaruni emigrated from Calcutta, India, to the United States in 1976, when she was nineteen. Working at a series of odd jobs— babysitting, slicing bread, washing laboratory glassware—to pay for her education, she earned a master's degree in English from Wright State University in Dayton, Ohio, and a Ph.D. from the University of California at Berkeley. Divakaruni began postgraduate life as a teacher and turned her focus to creative writing after the death of her grandfather. The loss made her feel that "I was forgetting things, forgetting him, and how things were in India and how people thought" in the land of her birth; writing helped her to remember. She published *The Reason for Nasturtiums,* a collection of poetry, in 1990. Her first book of short stories, *Arranged Marriage,* won the 1996 American Book Award and the PEN Oakland Award. In addition to three books of poetry, three novels, two short-story collections, and a children's book, Divakaruni has written numerous essays and short stories; her works have appeared in more than fifty magazines and in over thirty anthologies.

The essay that follows appeared first in Divakaruni's column in the online magazine *Salon.com.* In it, Divakaruni explores the connection between memory and the sense of smell.

GUIDING QUESTION
How does the author use the sense of smell to describe aspects of her childhood?

"The description of the location is great. I could visualize that same place and even taste the mangoes. My mouth watered wanting a taste of the chicken curry."
—Lidia Figueroa, Student

It's a cool December morning halfway across the world in Gurap, a little    1
village outside Calcutta where we've come to visit my mother. I sit on the veranda and watch my little boys, Anand and Abhay, as they play on the dirt road. They have a new cricket bat and ball, a gift from their grandma, but soon they abandon these to feed mango leaves to the neighbor's goat, which has wandered over. Abhay, who is two, wants to climb onto the goat's back. Anand, who is five and very much the big brother, tells him it's not a good idea, but Abhay doesn't listen.

Behind me the door opens. Even before I hear the flap-flap of her leather    2
chappals,[1] I know who it is. My mother, fresh from her bath, heralded by

[1] **chappals:** Indian footwear, sandals

the scent of the sandalwood soap she has been using ever since I can remember. Its clean, familiar smell pulls me back effortlessly into my childhood.

When I was young, my mother and I had a ritual every evening. She would comb my hair, rub in hibiscus[2] oil and braid it into thick double plaits.[3] It took a long time—there were a lot of knots to work through. But I was rarely impatient. I loved the sleepy fragrance of the oil (the same oil she used, which she sometimes let me rub into her hair). I loved, too, the rhythm of her hands, and the stories (each with its not-so-subtle moral) that she told me as she combed. The tale of Sukhu and Dukhu, the two sisters. The kind one gets the prince, the greedy one is eaten up by a serpent. Or the tale of the little cowherd boy who outwits the evil witch. Size and strength, after all, are no match for intelligence.

What is it about smells that lingers in our subconscious, comforting and giving joy, making real what would otherwise be wooden and wordy? I'm not sure. But I do know this: Every lesson that I remember from my childhood, from my mother, has a smell at its center.

The smell of turmeric,[4] which she made into a paste with milk and rubbed into my skin to take away blemishes, reminds me to take pride in my appearance, to make the best of what nature has given me.

The smell of the rosewater-scented rice pudding she always made for New Year is the smell of hope. It reminds me to never give up. Who knows—something marvelous may be waiting just around the bend.

Even the smell of the iodine she dabbed on my scraped knees and elbows, which I so hated then, is one I now recall with wry gratitude. Its stinging, bitter-brown odor is that of love, love that sometimes hurts while it's doing its job.

Let me not mislead you. I wasn't always so positively inclined toward my mother's lessons—or the smells that accompanied them. When I first moved to the United States, I wanted to change myself, completely. I washed every last drop of hibiscus oil from my hair with Vidal Sassoon shampoo. I traded in my saris for Levi's and tank tops. I danced the night away in discos and returned home in the bleary-eyed morning smelling of vodka and sweat and cigarettes, the perfume of young America.

But when Anand was born, something changed. They say you begin to understand your mother only when you become a mother yourself. Only then do you appreciate all the little things about her that you took for granted. Maybe that's true. Otherwise, that morning in the hospital, looking down at Anand's fuzzy head, why did I ask my husband to make a trip to the Indian store and bring me back a bar of sandalwood soap?

I have my own rituals now, with my boys, my own special smells that are quite different. (I learned early that we can't be our mothers. Most times, it's better to not even try.)

On weekends I make a big chicken curry with turmeric and cloves. Anand helps me cut up the tomatoes into uneven wedges; Abhay finger-

[2] **hibiscus:** a large and colorful tropical flower

[3] **plaits:** braids

[4] **turmeric:** an East Indian plant that, in powdered form, is used as seasoning

■ **IDEA JOURNAL** List some smells that transport you back to your own childhood.

3  **REFLECT:** How do the details in this paragraph help you to understand Divakaruni's childhood and her relationship with her mother? *Possible answer: The details suggest a happy childhood and close relationship between the author and her mother.*

4

**IDENTIFY:** Underline the sentence in paragraph 4 that provides the main or unifying idea for paragraphs 5–7.

5

■ **TEACHING TIP** To suggest how mysterious the effects and associations of smells can be, the author poses several questions about smells (in paras. 4, 9, 14, and 16) that she's not sure how to answer. Students may be unfamiliar with this writing strategy, so you might want to point it out and discuss its possibilities and limitations.

6

7

8  **IDENTIFY:** Put Xs by the details that show the author's attempts to Americanize herself.

9

10 **PREDICT:** What possible rituals might Divakaruni have with her own children? *Answers will vary.*

11

shreds the cilantro[5] with great glee. As the smell of spices fills the house, we sing. Sometimes it's a song from India: *Ay, ay, Chanda mama*—come to me, Uncle Moon. Sometimes it's "Old MacDonald Had a Farm."

When the children are sick, I sprinkle lavender water on a handkerchief    12
and lay it on their foreheads to fend off that other smell, hot and metallic: the smell of fever and fear.

If I have a special event coming up, I open the suitcase my mother gave    13
me at my wedding and let them pick out an outfit for me, maybe a gold-embroidered kurta or a silk shawl. The suitcase smells of rose potpourri.[6] The boys burrow into it and take deep, noisy breaths.

REFLECT: How can a smell provide comfort?
*Possible answer: It may have a pleasant association.*

Am I creating memories for them? Things that will comfort them in the    14
dark, sour moments that must come to us all at some time? Who knows—there is so much out of my own childhood that I've forgotten that I can only hope so.

"Watch out!" says my mother now, but it's too late. The goat, having    15
eaten enough mango leaves, has decided to move on. He gives a great shrug, and Abhay comes tumbling off his back. He lies on the dirt for a moment, his mouth a perfect O of surprise, then runs crying to me. A twinge goes through me even as I hide my smile. A new lesson, this, since motherhood: how you can feel someone else's pain so sharply, like needles, in your own bones.

REFLECT: What does Divakaruni mean by the expression "scent-shop of memories"? Do you think the expression is an effective way for her to get her point across?
*Answers will vary.*

When I pick him up, Abhay buries his face in my neck and stays there a    16
long time, even after the tears have stopped. Is he taking in the smell of my body? Is he going to remember the fragrance of the jabakusum oil that I asked my mother to rub into my hair last night, for old time's sake? I'm not sure. But I do know this—I've just gained something new, something to add to my scent-shop of memories: the dusty, hot smell of his hair, his hands pungent with the odor of freshly-torn mango leaves.

### ■ SUMMARIZE AND RESPOND

In your reading journal or elsewhere, summarize the main point of "Common Scents." Then go back and check off the support for this main idea. Next, write a brief summary of the essay. Finally, jot down a brief response to the reading. Has the smell of something or someone ever brought back memories of something in your past? If so, did you find the association comforting?

### ■ CHECK YOUR COMPREHENSION

1. An alternate title for this essay could be
    a. "A Calcutta Childhood."
    b. "Childhood Memories."
    c. "Creating Rituals."
    (d.) "Scents: A Bridge to the Past."

[5] **cilantro:** coriander leaves used as an herb in cooking
[6] **potpourri:** a mixture of dried flower petals with spices

2. The main idea of this essay is that
   a. scents have the power to evoke memories.
   b. we should all have childhood rituals.
   c. good scents create good memories.
   d. the lessons we learn in childhood never fade.

3. Why does Divakaruni create rituals with her sons?
   a. She wants them to experience different smells in their lives.
   b. She wants them to have structure in their lives as she did when she was a child.
   c. She wants them to learn about their Calcutta culture.
   d. She wants them to be able to associate smell with a comforting childhood ritual.

4. If you are unfamiliar with the following words, use a dictionary to check their meanings: *heralded* (para. 2); *blemishes* (5); *wry* (7); *pungent* (16).

### READ CRITICALLY

1. How would you describe the tone of this essay?

2. Describe how Divakaruni shifts between the present and the past in this essay.

3. What details does Divakaruni include in this essay to make the connection between scent and memories of her childhood?

4. What happened in Divakaruni's life that made her understand her mother?

5. Why did Divakaruni begin rituals with her own children?

### WRITE

**WRITE A PARAGRAPH:** Write a paragraph using a technique similar to the one Divakaruni uses in paragraph 3. That is, think of a particular ritual that you shared with someone, such as a parent. What smells were involved? How were those smells incorporated into the ritual? Think of rituals such as going to the beach, setting up a campsite, and so on.

**WRITE AN ESSAY:** Explore your past and think of a particular smell from childhood that helps you recall a specific memory of an event or person. What memory or memories do you associate with that smell? As Divakaruni does, use descriptive details as you discuss both the smell and the memory it generates. Feel free to include the ideas you wrote about in your idea journal or for Summarize and Respond.

■ **TIP** For a sample description paragraph, see page 130.

# 43

# Process Analysis

Each essay in this chapter uses process analysis to get its main point across to the reader. As you read these essays, consider how they achieve the four basics of good process analysis that are listed below and discussed in Chapter 11 of this book.

## ■■ FOUR BASICS OF GOOD PROCESS ANALYSIS

1. It tells readers what process the writer wants them to know about and makes a point about it.
2. It presents the essential steps in the process, either so readers can do the steps themselves or understand how something works.
3. It explains the steps in detail.
4. It presents the steps in a logical order (usually time order).

*Kirby W. Stanat*

# The Job Interview

Kirby W. Stanat claims to have hired more than eight thousand people in his work as a personnel specialist and recruiter. He spent seven years as the director of Career Planning and Placement at the University of Wisconsin before becoming the university's director of Auxiliary Enterprises. As a placement director, Stanat's function was "teaching students how the hiring process works . . . how the system works and how you can work it."

In "The Job Interview," an excerpt from his book *Job Hunting Secrets and Tactics* (1977), Stanat outlines the process of applying for—and getting—a job. Although the essay focuses on interviews conducted on campus by recruiters from big companies, his advice applies equally well to all job seekers.

"This essay is interesting from beginning to end. It wasn't like the usual article that tells you specifically what to wear and how to act. Stanat makes you see how ridiculous you could look by making some sloppy mistakes in the interview process."
—Nicole Foley, Student

GUIDING QUESTION

What advice does Stanat give about job interviews, and does it sound like good advice?

To succeed in campus job interviews, you have to know where that recruiter is coming from. The simple answer is that he is coming from corporate headquarters.

That may sound obvious, but it is a significant point that too many   2
students do not consider. The recruiter is not a free spirit as he flies from
Berkeley to New Haven, from Chapel Hill to Boulder. He's on an invisible
leash to the office, and if he is worth his salary, he is mentally in corporate
headquarters all the time he's on the road. If you can fix that in your
mind—that when you walk into that bare-walled eight-by-ten cubicle in the
placement center you are walking into a branch office of Sears, Bendix, or
General Motors—you can avoid a lot of little mistakes and maybe some big
ones. If, for example, you assume that because the interview is on campus
the recruiter expects you to look and act like a student, you're in for a shock.
A student is somebody who drinks beer, wears blue jeans, and throws a
Frisbee. No recruiter has jobs for student Frisbee whizzes.

A cool spring day in late March. Sam Davis, a good recruiter who
has been on the college circuit for years, is on my campus talking to
candidates. He comes out to the waiting area to meet the student who
signed up for an 11 o'clock interview. I'm standing in the doorway of my
office, taking in the scene.

Sam calls the candidate: "Sidney Student." There sits Sidney. He's
at a 45-degree angle, his feet are in the aisle, and he's almost lying down.
He's wearing well-polished brown shoes, a tasteful pair of brown pants,
a light brown shirt, and a good-looking tie. Unfortunately, he tops
off this well-coordinated outfit with his Joe's Tavern Class A Softball
Championship jacket, which has a big woven emblem over the heart. If
that isn't bad enough, in his left hand is a cigarette and in his right hand
is a half-eaten apple.

When Sam calls his name, the kid is caught off guard. He ditches the
cigarette in an ashtray, struggles to his feet, and transfers the apple from
the right to the left hand. Apple juice is everywhere, so Sid wipes his
hand on the seat of his pants and shakes hands with Sam. Sam, who by
now is close to having a stroke, gives me that what-the-hell-do-I-have-
here look and has the young man follow him into the interview room.

The situation deteriorates even further—into pure Laurel and
Hardy.[1] The kid is stuck with the half-eaten apple, doesn't know what to
do with it, and obviously is suffering some discomfort. He carries the
apple into the interviewing room with him and places it in the ashtray
on the desk—right on top of Sam's freshly lit cigarette. The interview
lasts five minutes.

I have told that story to scores of students and have asked them, "Did   3
that kid get the job?" Invariably, they answer, "No, he didn't," and, of
course, they're right. The students readily accept the idea that the kid lost
the job in the waiting room. No student has ever asked me, "Did Sam Davis
investigate to find out if the kid had any talent?" or "Did Sam Davis ask
around to see if the kid might be smarter than that?" Of course, Sam did
not.

After Sam gave Sidney the lightning brush-off, I asked Sidney to come   4
into my office. I slammed the door and started to chew him out, because a

REFLECT: Why do you think
Stanat included this example
early on in the essay?
*Possible answer: It pres-*
*ents a vivid example of how*
*an interviewee can make a*
*bad impression.*

---

[1] **Laurel and Hardy:** Actor-comedians who made Hollywood films from 1915 to the 1950s

stunt like that reflects badly on the university and on the placement center and, most important, it certainly doesn't do Sidney any good. I told him, "You handled yourself like some dumb student," and he said, "Well, Mr. Stanat, that's what I am. I am a student." I had to do a lot of talking to convince him that he had blown the interview, that Sam Davis wanted a professional, not a student.

That was an extreme case, but similar things happen, in varying degrees, over and over again in campus placement offices all over the country.

Recruiters want to meet professionals — with professional attitudes, professional objectives, and professional clothes. Behave and dress for the campus interview as if you were going to talk to the president of Ford Motor Company in his office.

Let us move in for a closer look at how the campus recruiter operates.

IDENTIFY: What is the purpose of this short, one-sentence paragraph (para. 7)?
*Possible answer: It provides a transition to a specific example.*

■ TEACHING TIP Have students read the essay and underline the essential steps in the process. Are the author's examples of each step detailed enough? Ask groups to give another detail for each step and then rewrite the process analysis in a simplified how-to format.

SUMMARIZE: How could the interviewer gain a negative impression of you from your résumé?
*Possible answer: The recruiter may gain an impression from the grade point, spelling errors, poor erasures, or missing information.*

Let's say you have a 10 o'clock appointment with the recruiter from XYZ Corporation. The recruiter gets rid of the candidate in front of you at about five minutes to 10, jots down a few notes about what he is going to do with him or her, then picks up your résumé or data sheet. (Students usually fill out standard data sheets provided by the placement center. Sometimes they give the placement center copies of their résumés. These are given to the recruiter before the interview. [Some employment counselors] will strongly advise you, in certain situations, not to submit your résumé before meeting the recruiter. That does not apply when you go through the college placement center. The reason for not submitting your résumé in advance in some other situations is that submitting it could prevent you from getting an interview. But at the placement center, once you sign up for the interview, your interview is guaranteed.)

The importance of your data sheet or résumé comes into play here. Although the recruiter is still in the interview room and you are still in the lobby, your interview is under way. You're on. The recruiter will look over your sheet pretty carefully before he goes out to call you. He develops a mental picture of you. He thinks, "I'm going to enjoy talking with this kid," or "This one's going to be a turkey." The recruiter has already begun to make a screening decision about you.

His first impression of you, from reading your sheet, could come from your grade point. It could come from misspelled words. It could come from poor erasures or from the fact that necessary information is missing. By the time the recruiter has finished reading your sheet, you've already hit the plus or minus column. You might not be very far into either column, but you probably didn't land squarely on the neutral line dividing the two columns. I defy anybody to read ten data sheets or résumés without forming an opinion about all ten candidates.

Let's assume the recruiter got a fairly good impression from your sheet.

Now the recruiter goes out to the lobby to meet you. He almost shuffles along, and his mind is somewhere else. Then he calls your name, and at that instant he visibly clicks into gear. He just went to work. As he calls your name, he looks quickly around the room, waiting for somebody to move. If you are sitting on the middle of your back, with a book open and a cigarette going, and if you have to rebuild yourself to stand up, the interest will run right out of the recruiter's face. You, not the recruiter, made the appointment for 10 o'clock, and the recruiter expects to see a young professional come popping out of that chair like today is a good day and you're anxious to meet him.

At this point, the recruiter does something rude. He doesn't walk across the room to meet you halfway. He waits for you to come to him. Something very important is happening. He wants to see you move. He wants to get an impression about your posture, your stride, and your briskness. If you slouch over to him, sidewinderlike,[2] he is not going to be impressed. He'll figure you would probably slouch your way through workdays. He wants you to come at him with lots of good things going for you. If you watch the recruiter's eyes, you can see the inspection. He glances quickly at shoes, pants, coat, shirt; dress, blouse, hose — the whole works.   13

He'll stick out his hand and say, "Good morning, Bill, my name is Joe Recruiter." Your handshake is extremely important.   14

**Tip:** I would rather have a [person] bring me to my knees with a powerful handshake than give me a weak one. . . .

Next the recruiter will probably say, "Okay, Bill, please follow me," and he'll lead you into his interviewing room.   15

When you get to the room, you may find that the recruiter will open the door and gesture you in — with him blocking part of the doorway. There's enough room for you to get past him, but it's a near thing.   16

As you scrape past, he gives you a closeup inspection. He looks at your hair; if it's greasy, that will bother him. He looks at your collar; if it's dirty, that will bother him. He looks at your shoulders; if they're covered with dandruff, that will bother him. If you're a man, he looks at your chin. If you didn't get a close shave, that will irritate him. If you're a woman, he checks your makeup. If it's too heavy, he won't like it.   17

> **PREDICT:** Pause after the first sentence of this paragraph. How would a student not visually pass inspection?
> *Answers will vary.*

Then he smells you. An amazing number of people smell bad. Occasionally a recruiter meets a student who smells like a canal horse. That student can expect an interview of about four to five minutes (the average interview is twenty-five to thirty minutes). Students who stretch their budgets don't have their clothes dry-cleaned often enough. And every recruiting season a recruiter will run into somebody who stopped at a student union before the interview to wolf down a hamburger with onions and then tried to cover up the smell with breath mints. That doesn't work. The kid ends up smelling like onions and breath mints, and the interview has been severely damaged.   18

Next the recruiter inspects the back side of you. He checks your hair (is it combed in front but not in back?), your heels (are they run down?), your pants (are they baggy?), your slip (is it showing?), your stockings (do they have runs in them?).   19

> ■ **IDEA JOURNAL** How would you present yourself as a "professional" in a job interview?

Then he invites you to sit down.   20

At this point, I submit, *the recruiter's decision on you is 75 to 80 percent made.*   21

> **REFLECT:** Does this high percentage surprise you? Anger you?
> *Answers will vary.*

Think about it. The recruiter has read your résumé. He knows who you are and where you are from. He knows your marital status, your major, and your grade point. And he knows what you've done with your summers. He   22

---

[2] **sidewinderlike:** like a small rattlesnake, in an indirect manner

has inspected you, exchanged greetings with you, and smelled you. There is very little additional hard information that he must gather on you. From now on, it's mostly body chemistry.

Many recruiters have argued strenuously[3] that they don't make such    23
hasty decisions. So I tried an experiment. I told several recruiters that I would hang around in the hall outside the interview room when they took candidates in.

I told them that as soon as they had definitely decided not to recom-    24
mend the candidates they were interviewing, they should snap their fingers loud enough for me to hear. It went like this:

First candidate: thirty-eight seconds after the candidate sat down: Snap!    25
Second candidate: one minute, forty-two seconds: Snap! Third candidate: forty-five seconds: Snap!

One recruiter was particularly adamant.[4] "Hell, no," he said; he didn't    26
rush to judgment on candidates. I asked him to participate in the snapping experiment. He went out in the lobby, picked up his first candidate of the day, and headed for an interview room. As he passed me in the hall, he glared at me. And his fingers went "Snap!"

IDENTIFY: What point in this essay does this example underscore?

*how quickly interviewers*

*form impressions of job*

*candidates*

### ■ SUMMARIZE AND RESPOND

In your reading journal or elsewhere, summarize the main point of "The Job Interview." Then go back and check off support for this main idea. Finally, jot down a brief response to the reading. As a student, is there anything you would like to say to Kirby W. Stanat?

### ■ CHECK YOUR COMPREHENSION

1. An alternate title for this essay could be
   a. "When Students Were Studious."
   b. "Losing the Job."
   c. "Making the Grade: How to Pass a Job Interview."
   d. "No Chemistry Finals Here."

2. The main idea of this essay is that
   a. students should act like students at job interviews.
   b. recruiters are not judgmental.
   c. how you present yourself to the world involves more than what you say.
   d. a good student is not necessarily a good worker.

3. What is the first impression a student makes on the recruiter?
   a. His or her appearance
   b. The information on his or her résumé and how it is presented

[3] **strenuously:** with energy
[4] **adamant:** unyielding

   c.  His or her talent

   d.  Whether he or she is a smoker or a nonsmoker

4.  If you are unfamiliar with the following words, use a dictionary to check their meanings: *emblem, deteriorates* (para. 2).

## ■ READ CRITICALLY

1.  What process is Stanat analyzing? Why is he analyzing it? Use examples from the text to support your answer.

2.  Does Stanat present the steps of the process in chronological order?

3.  In paragraph 24, Stanat says he told the recruiters to "snap their fingers loud enough for me to hear." What is the purpose of the snapping? What function does it serve in his essay?

4.  In paragraph 9 Stanat writes, "Although the recruiter is still in the interview room and you are still in the lobby, your interview is under way." What does he mean by this statement?

5.  Describe the tone the author uses in the essay and how you responded to it.

## ■ WRITE

**WRITE A PARAGRAPH:** List your ideas about what a student should do for a successful job interview. Then write a paragraph that presents your list in chronological order.

**WRITE AN ESSAY:** Write an essay that explains how to balance the various "lives" that today's students have (college, work, family, and so on). You might want to expand on the ideas you expressed in your reading journal for Summarize and Respond. Your essay should be a guide to how to be a student at the beginning of the twenty-first century. Based on your experiences and the challenges you have faced, what advice could you give a younger student?

> ■ **TIP** For a sample process analysis paragraph, see page 145.

## *Malcolm X*

# A Homemade Education

Malcolm X (1925–1965) was one of the best-known African American activists of the 1960s. Born Malcolm Little in Omaha, Nebraska, he first gained fame in the 1950s as a minister for Elijah Muhammad's Nation of Islam. Malcolm X gave fiery speeches in support of black separatism and autonomy, attracting many followers to the organization. At the height of his fame, he was featured in a television special, "The Hate That Hate Produced," and spied on by

■ **TEACHING TIP** In his second paragraph, Malcolm X refers to the problems of writing in slang, but he doesn't go into detail about them. Ask students to comment on what these problems might be. If you want to cover this issue in more detail, see Chapter 31.

the FBI. After learning about the extramarital affairs of his mentor, Elijah Muhammad, Malcolm X broke with the Nation of Islam in 1964. He made a pilgrimage to the Islamic holy city of Mecca in Saudi Arabia that year and met "blond-haired, blue-eyed men I could call my brothers." Upon his return to the United States, his new openness toward working with people of all races did not improve his relationship with those in the Nation of Islam who still resented his leaving the organization and renouncing its leader. On February 21, 1965, he was killed by three gunmen as he spoke at the Audubon Ballroom in New York.

In his speeches and writings, Malcolm X urged his followers to educate themselves. A high-school dropout who had turned to petty crime as a teenager, he realized the importance of a good education after being sentenced to seven years in prison when he was twenty-one. The following selection from *The Autobiography of Malcolm X* (1965) explains the learning process that he put himself through during his years behind bars.

GUIDING QUESTION
What does Malcolm X mean by a "homemade education," and how does he get it?

■ **IDEA JOURNAL** Have you experienced similar frustrations about your ability to communicate with others?

It was because of my letters that I happened to stumble upon starting to acquire some kind of homemade education. 1

I became increasingly frustrated at not being able to express what I wanted to convey in letters that I wrote, especially those to Mr. Elijah Muhammad. In the street, I had been the most articulate[1] hustler out there—I had commanded attention when I said something. But now, trying to write simple English, I not only wasn't articulate, I wasn't even functional. How would I sound writing in slang, the way I would *say* it, something such as "Look, daddy, let me pull your coat about a cat, Elijah Muhammad—" 2

**PREDICT:** Pause after the third paragraph. What role do you think the prison system played in Malcolm X's education?
*Answers will vary.*

Many who today hear me somewhere in person, or on television, or those who read something I've said, will think I went to school far beyond the eighth grade. This impression is due entirely to my prison studies. 3

It had really begun back in Charlestown Prison, when Bimbi first made me feel envy of his stock of knowledge. Bimbi had always taken charge of any conversation he was in, and I had tried to emulate[2] him. But every book I picked up had few sentences which didn't contain anywhere from one to nearly all the words that might as well have been in Chinese. When I just skipped those words, of course, I really ended up with little idea of what the book said. So I had come to Norfolk Prison Colony still going through only book-reading motions. Pretty soon, I would have quit even these motions unless I had received the motivation that I did. 4

**IDENTIFY:** Read paragraphs 5–10 carefully and put an X by the steps Malcolm X took to educate himself.

I saw that the best thing I could do was to get hold of a dictionary—to study to learn some words. I was lucky enough to reason also that I should try to improve my penmanship. It was sad. I couldn't even write in a straight line. It was both ideas together that moved me to request a dictionary along with some tablets and pencils from the Norfolk Prison Colony school. 5

X

---

[1] **articulate:** well-spoken
[2] **emulate:** imitate

*X*   I spent two days just riffling³ uncertainly through the dictionary's pages. I'd never realized so many words existed! I didn't know *which* words I *X* needed to learn. Finally, just to start some kind of action, I began copying.

6

*X*   In my slow, painstaking, ragged handwriting, I copied into my tablet everything printed on that first page, down to the punctuation marks.

7

*X*   I believe it took me a day. Then, aloud, I read back, to myself, everything I'd written on the tablet. Over and over, aloud, to myself, I read my own handwriting.

8

*X*   I woke up the next morning, thinking about those words — immensely proud to realize that not only had I written so much at one time, but I'd written words that I never knew were in the world. Moreover, with a little *X* effort, I also could remember what many of these words meant. I reviewed the words whose meanings I didn't remember. Funny thing, from the dictionary first page right now, that "aardvark" springs to my mind. The dictionary had a picture of it, a long-tailed, long-eared, burrowing African mammal, which lives off termites caught by sticking out its tongue as an anteater does for ants.

9

*X*   I was so fascinated that I went on — I copied the dictionary's next page. And the same experience came when I studied that. With every succeeding *X* page, I also learned of people and places and events from history. Actually the dictionary is like a miniature encyclopedia. Finally the dictionary's A *X* section had filled a whole tablet — and I went on into the B's. That was the way I started copying what eventually became the entire dictionary. It went a lot faster after so much practice helped me to pick up handwriting speed. Between what I wrote in my tablet, and writing letters, during the rest of my time in prison I would guess I wrote a million words.

10

I suppose it was inevitable that my word-base broadened, <u>I could for the first time pick up a book and read and now begin to understand what the book was saying.</u> Anyone who has read a great deal can imagine the new world that opened. Let me tell you something: from then until I left that prison, in every free moment I had, if I was not reading in the library, I was reading on my bunk. You couldn't have gotten me out of books with a wedge. Between Mr. Muhammad's teachings, my correspondence, my visitors — usually Ella and Reginald — and my reading books, months passed without my even thinking about being imprisoned. In fact, up to then, I had never been so truly free in my life.

11

> "I enjoyed knowing that even though Malcolm X was in prison, he still aspired to learn how to read and write. He showed how reading a book opened doors to places he'd never imagined existed before."
> —Lidia Figueroa, Student

11   **IDENTIFY:** Underline the sentence that states the result of all his work.

◼ **SUMMARIZE AND RESPOND**

In your reading journal or elsewhere, summarize the main point of "A Homemade Education." Then go back and check off the support for this main idea. Next, write a brief summary of the essay. Finally, jot down a brief response to the reading. How is it that Malcolm X is able to obtain knowledge? Consider his skill level before and after his self-education process.

---

³**riffling:** leafing through (a book)

■ **CHECK YOUR COMPREHENSION**

1. An alternate title for this essay could be
   a. "An Open Book."
   b. "Freeing the Mind."
   c. "The Dictionary: One Man's Door to Knowledge."
   d. "No More Slang."

2. The main idea of this essay is that
   a. reading makes time go by fast for prisoners.
   b. anyone with desire and commitment can obtain knowledge.
   c. there is a connection between reading and writing.
   d. education is best obtained in steps.

3. To what or whom does Malcolm X attribute his ability to speak, read, and write?
   a. A dictionary
   b. Bimbi
   c. Elijah Muhammad
   d. The prison educational system

4. If you are unfamiliar with the following words, use a dictionary to check their meanings: *hustler* (para. 2); *immensely, burrowing* (9); *inevitable* (11).

■ **READ CRITICALLY**

1. What is Malcolm X's purpose in this essay?

2. In what order did Malcolm X write about the steps he took to increase his word base?

3. Details are important to understanding the steps in a process. In this essay, what details stand out for you?

4. In paragraph 10, what do you think Malcolm X means when he writes that "the dictionary is like a miniature encyclopedia"?

5. What is significant about the last line? What point is Malcolm X making about reading specifically and education in general?

■ **WRITE**

■ **TIP** For a sample process analysis paragraph, see page 145.

**WRITE A PARAGRAPH:** Write a paragraph about how you have improved or might improve your academic performance in an area.

**WRITE AN ESSAY:** Write an essay that traces the steps you took to learn a particular skill or accomplish a particular goal. As Malcolm X does in this essay, be sure to include what you were like before and after you developed your skill or reached your goal.

# 44

# Classification

Each essay in this chapter uses classification to get its main point across to the reader. As you read these essays, consider how they achieve the four basics of good classification that are listed below and discussed in Chapter 12 of this book.

■■
■■ **FOUR BASICS OF GOOD CLASSIFICATION**

1. It makes sense of a group of people or items by organizing them into categories.
2. It uses a single organizing principle.
3. It sorts the group into useful categories.
4. It gives examples of what fits into each category.

*Stephanie Ericsson*

## The Ways We Lie

Stephanie Ericsson was born in 1953 and raised in San Francisco. She has lived in a variety of places, including New York, Los Angeles, London, Mexico, the Spanish island of Ibiza, and Minnesota, where she currently resides. Ericsson's life took a major turn when her husband died suddenly, leaving her two months pregnant. She began a journal to help her cope with the grief and loss and later used her writing to help others with similar struggles. An excerpt from her journal appeared in the *Utne Reader,* and her writings were later published in a book entitled *Companion through the Darkness: Inner Dialogues on Grief* (1993). About her book, Ericsson writes, "It belongs to those who have had the blinders ripped from their eyes, who suddenly see the lies of our lives and the truths of existence for what they are."

In "The Ways We Lie," which also appeared in the *Utne Reader* and is taken from her follow-up work, *Companion into the Dawn: Inner Dialogues on Loving* (1994), Ericsson continues her search for truth by examining and classifying our daily lies.

GUIDING QUESTION

As you read this essay, pay attention to the examples Ericsson provides. What examples of lying can you think of from your own experience?

*to deceive,* then the Catholic Church's conscious covering for Porter created irreparable consequences. The church became a coperpetrator with Porter.

## Stereotypes and Clichés

Stereotype and cliché serve a purpose as a form of shorthand. Our need for vast amounts of information in nanoseconds[9] has made the stereotype vital to modern communication. Unfortunately, it often shuts down original thinking, giving those hungry for truth a candy bar of misinformation instead of a balanced meal. The stereotype explains a situation with just enough truth to seem unquestionable.

All the *isms*—racism, sexism, ageism, et al.—are founded on and fueled by the stereotype and the cliché, which are lies of exaggeration, omission, and ignorance. They are always dangerous. They take a single tree and make it a landscape. They destroy curiosity. They close minds and separate people. The single mother on welfare is assumed to be cheating. Any black male could tell you how much of his identity is obliterated[10] daily by stereotypes. Fat people, ugly people, beautiful people, old people, large-breasted women, short men, the mentally ill, and the homeless all could tell you how much more they are like us than we want to think. I once admitted to a group of people that I had a mouth like a truck driver. Much to my surprise, a man stood up and said, "I'm a truck driver, and I never cuss." Needless to say, I was humbled.

## Out-and-Out Lies

Of all the ways to lie, I like this one the best, probably because I get tired of trying to figure out the real meanings behind things. At least I can trust the bald-faced lie. I once asked my five-year-old nephew, "Who broke the fence?" (I had seen him do it.) He answered, "The murderers." Who could argue?

At least when this sort of lie is told it can be easily confronted. As the person who is lied to, I know where I stand. The bald-faced lie doesn't toy with my perceptions—it argues with them. It doesn't try to refashion reality, it tries to refute[11] it. *Read my lips* . . . No sleight[12] of hand. No guessing. If this were the only form of lying, there would be no such thing as floating anxiety or the adult-children of alcoholics movement.

These are only a few of the ways we lie. Or are lied to. As I said earlier, it's not easy to entirely eliminate lies from our lives. No matter how pious[13] we may try to be, we will still embellish, hedge, and omit to lubricate[14] the daily machinery of living. But there is a world of difference between telling functional lies and living a lie. Martin Buber once said, "The lie is the spirit committing treason against itself." Our acceptance of lies becomes a

14

15

■ **IDEA JOURNAL** Think of another common human behavior. Break it into categories, and give examples for each category.

16 PREDICT: Pause just as you start the "Out-and-Out Lies" section. How do you think Ericsson might define such lies?
*Answers will vary.*

17

18

---

[9] **nanoseconds:** billionths of a second

[10] **obliterated:** wiped out

[11] **refute:** deny

[12] **sleight:** skillful trick

[13] **pious:** religious

[14] **lubricate:** oil

REFLECT: Think back on your answer to the question on page 599 about whether lying ever has any merit. Have your views on this issue changed? Why or why not? *Answers will vary.*

cultural cancer that eventually shrouds[15] and reorders reality until moral garbage becomes as invisible to us as water is to a fish.

How much do we tolerate before we become sick and tired of being sick  19 and tired? When will we stand up and declare our *right* to trust? When do we stop accepting that the real truth is in the fine print? Whose lips do we read this year when we vote for president? When will we stop being so reticent about making judgments? When do we stop turning over our personal power and responsibility to liars?

Maybe if I don't tell the bank the check's in the mail I'll be less tolerant  20 of the lies told to me every day. A country song I once heard said it all for me: "You've got to stand for something or you'll fall for anything."

## ■ SUMMARIZE AND RESPOND

In your reading journal or elsewhere, summarize the main point of "The Ways We Lie." Then go back and check off the support for this main idea. Finally, jot down a brief response to the reading. What did it make you think about or feel? Do you agree with Ericsson's claim that we all tell lies every day? Provide examples from your own experience that support this idea.

## ■ CHECK YOUR COMPREHENSION

1.  An alternate title for this essay could be
    a.  "Lying Never Hurt Anyone."
    b.  "The Check's in the Mail: The Greatest Lie of All."
    c.  "Justification for Lying."
    d.  "Lies in Our Lives."

2.  The main idea of this essay is that
    a.  small lies are OK because everyone lies.
    b.  we should reevaluate the role that lies play in our lives.
    c.  lies told by someone you trust are the worst.
    d.  to trust and be trusted, we must refuse to lie.

3.  What distinction does Ericsson make between telling a functional lie and living a lie?
    a.  Telling a functional lie makes someone feel bad, and living a lie cheats big institutions.
    b.  Telling a functional lie is relatively harmless, but living a lie can have serious consequences.
    c.  Telling a functional lie has no merit, and living a lie is a good idea.
    d.  Telling a functional lie is honest, and living a lie is dishonest.

[15] **shrouds:** covers

4. If you are unfamiliar with the following words, use a dictionary to look up their meanings: *confrontation* (para. 3); *merit* (4); *penance* (6); *irreparable* (13); *cliché, vital* (14); *refashion* (17); *tolerant* (20).

## READ CRITICALLY

1. Describe Ericsson's tone in this essay. For example, what is her tone in paragraph 1 when she tells us that "the baby I'm pregnant with decided to do aerobics on my lungs for two hours"?

2. How does Ericsson organize her essay? How does she classify the ways we tell lies?

3. What images does Ericsson associate with telling lies? Select one that you like, and explain why.

4. What is Ericsson's attitude toward lying? What examples in the essay support your answer?

5. In paragraph 16 Ericsson writes, "At least I can trust the bald-faced lie." What do you think she means by trusting a lie?

## WRITE

**WRITE A PARAGRAPH:** Write a paragraph that describes another category of lies. Be sure to provide examples for your readers.

**WRITE AN ESSAY:** Write an essay that continues Ericsson's classification of the ways we lie. Provide detailed examples from your experiences—or the experiences of people you know—for at least two of the categories she provides. Develop two new categories of your own. Feel free to include the ideas you wrote about in your reading journal for Summarize and Respond.

■ **TIP** For a sample classification paragraph, see page 161.

*Carolyn Foster Segal*

# The Dog Ate My Disk, and Other Tales of Woe

Carolyn Foster Segal (b. 1950) is an associate professor of English at Cedar Crest College in Pennsylvania, where she teaches creative writing, American literature, and film; she also serves as an advisor for the writing minor. In addition to teaching, Segal has published fiction, poetry, and popular and critical essays. She has recently written a series of eleven essays on academic life for the *Chronicle of Higher Education.*

The essay that follows classifies students' excuses for late coursework. Segal notes, "I am not talking about all students or all excuses here. There are certainly legitimate—and sometimes devastating—reasons for missing a deadline; on the other hand, it's quite possible that a few readers might feel guilty." Her essay clearly touched a nerve with other instructors, hundreds of whom sent their own stories of student excuses to Segal after the piece appeared.

**GUIDING QUESTION**
What creative categories of student excuses does Segal present? Are the examples within each category concrete and specific?

■ **IDEA JOURNAL** Can you recall a common excuse that you may have used in school or college in the past or have heard others use?

T aped to the door of my office is a cartoon that features a cat explaining    1
to his feline teacher, "The dog ate my homework." It is intended as a gently humorous reminder to my students that I will not accept excuses for late work, and it, like the lengthy warning on my syllabus, has had absolutely no effect. With a show of energy and creativity that would be admirable if applied to the (missing) assignments in question, my students persist, week after week, semester after semester, year after year, in offering excuses about why their work is not ready. Those reasons fall into several broad categories: the family, the best friend, the evils of dorm life, the evils of technology, and the totally bizarre.

**PREDICT:** Pause here. Predict the type of family excuses Segal will give in this paragraph.
*Answers will vary.*

**The Family.** The death of the grandfather/grandmother is, of course,    2
the grandmother of all excuses. What heartless teacher would dare to question a student's grief or veracity[1]? What heartless student would lie, wishing death on a revered family member, just to avoid a deadline? Creative students may win extra extensions (and days off) with a little careful planning and fuller plot development, as in the sequence of "My grandfather/grandmother is sick"; "Now my grandfather/grandmother is in the hospital"; and finally, "We could all see it coming—my grandfather/grandmother is dead."

Another favorite excuse is the "family emergency," which (always) goes    3
like this: "There was an emergency at home, and I had to help my family." It's a lovely sentiment,[2] one that conjures[3] up images of Louisa May Alcott's *little women* rushing off with baskets of food and copies of *Pilgrim's Progress*, but I do not understand why anyone would turn to my most irresponsible students in times of trouble.

"This is a really witty reading that flows with ease."
—Amy Cork, Student

**The Best Friend.** This heartwarming concern for others extends be-    4
yond the family to friends, as in, "My best friend was up all night and I had to (a) stay up with her in the dorm, (b) drive her to the hospital, or (c) drive to her college because (1) her boyfriend broke up with her, (2) she was throwing up blood [no one catches a cold anymore; everyone throws up blood], or (3) her grandfather/grandmother died."

At one private university where I worked as an adjunct,[4] I heard an    5
interesting spin that incorporated the motifs[5] of both best friend and dead relative: "My best friend's mother killed herself." One has to admire the cleverness here. A mysterious woman in the prime of her life has allegedly

---

[1] **veracity:** truthfulness

[2] **sentiment:** expression of feeling

[3] **conjures:** summons, creates

[4] **adjunct:** additional instructor

[5] **motifs:** patterns

committed suicide, and no professor can prove otherwise! And I admit I was moved, until finally I had to point out to my students that it was amazing how the simple act of my assigning a topic for a paper seemed to drive large numbers of otherwise happy and healthy middle-aged women to their deaths. I was careful to make that point during an off week, during which no deaths were reported.

**The Evils of Dorm Life.** These stories are usually fairly predictable; almost always feature the evil roommate or hallmate, with my student in the role of the innocent victim; and can be summed up as follows: <u>My room-mate, who is a horrible person, likes to party, and I, who am a good person, cannot concentrate on my work when he or she is partying</u>. Variations include stories about the two people next door who were running around and crying loudly last night because (a) one of them had boyfriend/girlfriend problems; (b) one of them was throwing up blood; or (c) someone, some-where, died. A friend of mine in graduate school had a student who claimed that his roommate attacked him with a hammer. That, in fact, was a true story: it came out in court when the bad roommate was tried for killing his grandfather.

**The Evils of Technology.** The computer age has revolutionized the student story, inspiring almost as many excuses as it has Internet businesses. Here are just a few electronically enhanced explanations:

- The computer wouldn't let me save my work.
- The printer wouldn't print.
- The printer wouldn't print this disk.
- The printer wouldn't give me time to proofread.
- The printer made a black line run through all my words, and I know you can't read this, but do you still want it, or wait, here take my disk. File name? I don't know what you mean.
- I swear I attached it.
- It's my roommate's computer, and she usually helps me, but she had to go to the hospital because she was throwing up blood.
- I did write to the newsgroup, but all my messages came back to me.
- I just found out that all my other newsgroup messages came up under a diferent name. I just want you to know that its really me who wrote all those messages, you can tel which ones our mine because I didnt use the spelcheck! But it was yours truley :) Anyway, just in case you missed those messages or dont belief its my writing, I'll repeat what I sad: I thought the last movie we watched in clas was borring.

**The Totally Bizarre.** I call the first story "The Pennsylvania Chain Saw Episode." A commuter student called to explain why she had missed my morning class. She had gotten up early so that she would be wide awake for class. Having a bit of extra time, she walked outside to see her neighbor, who was cutting some wood. She called out to him, and he waved back to her with the saw. Wouldn't you know it, the safety catch wasn't on or was broken, and the blade flew right out of the saw and across his lawn and over her fence and across her yard and severed a tendon in her right hand. So she

6     IDENTIFY: Underline the sentence in which Segal sum-marizes stories about the "evils of dorm life."

7     ■ TEACHING TIP In a class discussion, ask students to list other excuses offered for miss-ing or delayed classwork. Stu-dents may not feel comfortable discussing excuses they them-selves have used, so ask them to list ones they've heard of. Then discuss how these various excuses might be classified.

8     REFLECT: How "bizarre" is the excuse presented in this paragraph? Is it too bizarre to be believable?
*Answers will vary, but the excuse is probably too bizarre to be believable.*

was calling me from the hospital, where she was waiting for surgery. Luckily, she reassured me, she had remembered to bring her paper and a stamped envelope (in a plastic bag, to avoid bloodstains) along with her in the ambulance, and a nurse was mailing everything to me even as we spoke.

That wasn't her first absence. In fact, this student had missed most of the class meetings, and I had already recommended that she withdraw from the course. Now I suggested again that it might be best if she dropped the class. I didn't harp on the absences (what if even some of the story were true?). I did mention that she would need time to recuperate and that making up so much missed work might be difficult. "Oh, no," she said, "I can't drop this course. I had been planning to go on to medical school and become a surgeon, but since I won't be able to operate because of my accident, I'll have to major in English, and this course is more important than ever to me." She did come to the next class, wearing — as evidence of her recent trauma — a bedraggled[6] Ace bandage on her left hand.

You may be thinking that nothing could top that excuse, but in fact I have one more story, provided by the same student, who sent me a letter to explain why her final assignment would be late. While recuperating from her surgery, she had begun corresponding on the Internet with a man who lived in Germany. After a one-week, whirlwind Web romance, they had agreed to meet in Rome, to rendezvous[7] (her phrase) at the papal Easter Mass. Regrettably, the time of her flight made it impossible for her to attend class, but she trusted that I — just this once — would accept late work if the pope wrote a note.

9

10

REFLECT: How do you imagine Segal reacted when she read the note about the pope?
*Answers will vary, but Segal was probably amused.*

## ▉ SUMMARIZE AND RESPOND

In your reading journal or elsewhere, summarize the main point of "The Dog Ate My Disk, and Other Tales of Woe." Then go back and check off support for this main idea. Next, write a brief summary of the essay. Finally, jot down a brief response to the reading. Do any of these excuses sound familiar? Can you add examples of excuses to any of the categories? You might want to look back at ideas you recorded in your idea journal.

## ▉ CHECK YOUR COMPREHENSION

1. An alternate title for this essay could be
   a. "Computer Cop-Outs."
   b. "Homework Hassles."
   c. "How to Lie Effectively."
   d. "Excuses: The Old, the New, and the Creative."

2. The main idea of this essay is that
   a. students have never-ending and often bizarre excuses for not submitting required work.

[6] **bedraggled:** messy, untidy
[7] **rendezvous:** to meet

b.  teachers often downgrade late assignments.

c.  the more bizarre excuse a student gives, the less likely that the teacher can prove the student is lying.

d.  teachers should issue strong warnings and penalties to prevent students from handing in assignments late.

3.  Which excuse can students expand upon to get further deadline extensions?

a.  Best friend

b.  Technology

c.  Dorm life

(d.)  Family

4.  If you are unfamiliar with the following words, use a dictionary to look up their meanings: *bizarre* (para.1); *enhanced* (7); *trauma* (9); *whirlwind* (10).


## ■ READ CRITICALLY

1.  How would you describe the tone of this essay?

2.  Do Segal's categories seem logical and appropriate for the examples she provides?

3.  Which category seems the most developed? The least developed?

4.  What gives Segal authority to write about this subject?

5.  What do you suppose Segal means by the phrase "the grandmother of all excuses" in paragraph 2?


## ■ WRITE

**WRITE A PARAGRAPH:** Think of another category that Segal could have included in this essay. Using that category, create a topic sentence and write a paragraph that provides concrete examples of student excuses.

**WRITE AN ESSAY:** Consider one of your roles in life—as an employee, child, parent, boyfriend, girlfriend, and so on. Then, brainstorm and categorize excuses for not doing something that you are supposed to do as part of that role—for example, coming to work, doing assigned chores, and so on. Next, as Segal does, write an essay where you present and develop each category with examples.

■ **TIP** For a sample classification paragraph, see page 161.

# 45

# Definition

Each essay in this chapter uses definition to get its main point across to the reader. As you read these essays, consider how they achieve the four basics of good definition that are listed below and discussed in Chapter 13 of this book.

## ■■ FOUR BASICS OF GOOD DEFINITION

1. It tells readers what is being defined.
2. It presents a clear and precise basic definition.
3. It uses examples to show what the writer means.
4. It gives details about the examples that readers will understand.

## *Isaac Asimov*

## What Is Intelligence, Anyway?

The son of Russian Jews, Isaac Asimov (1920–1992) emigrated with his family to New York at the age of three. He began writing stories when he was eleven, entered Columbia University at fifteen, and eventually earned a Ph.D. in chemistry. He went on to become one of the greatest and most productive science fiction writers of the twentieth century. He once called writing "my idea of a vacation." Asimov's career spanned more than fifty years and led to numerous awards and honors. In addition to fiction, he wrote histories, scientific essays, children's stories, and pamphlets for the United States Atomic Energy Commission.

In "What Is Intelligence, Anyway?" Asimov combines a sense of humor with an interest in scientific inquiry. His essay asks us to think about our own definitions of intelligence.

GUIDING QUESTION
Does Asimov answer his question, "What is intelligence, anyway?"

"The essay shows that everyone learns differently and at different rates. Intelligence tests aren't always a sure way to find out how intelligent someone is because everyone has strong and weak points."

—Katilya Labidou, Student

What is intelligence, anyway? When I was in the Army, I received a kind of 1 aptitude[1] test that all soldiers took and, against a normal of 100, scored 160. No one at the base had ever seen a figure like that, and for two hours they

[1] **aptitude:** ability, talent

made a big fuss over me. (It didn't mean anything. The next day I was still a buck private with KP[2] as my highest duty.)

All of my life I've been registering scores like that, so that I have the complacent[3] feeling that I'm highly intelligent, and I expect other people think so, too. Actually, though, don't such scores simply mean that I am very good at answering the type of academic questions that are considered worthy of answers by the people who make up the intelligence tests—people with intellectual bents[4] similar to mine?

For instance, I had an auto repairman once, who, on these intelligence tests, could not possibly have scored more than 80, by my estimate. I always took it for granted that I was far more intelligent than he was. Yet, when anything went wrong with my car, I hastened to him with it, watched him anxiously as he explored its vitals,[5] and listened to his pronouncements as though they were divine oracles[6]—and he always fixed my car.

Well, then, suppose my auto repairman devised questions for an intelligence test. Or suppose a carpenter did, or a farmer, or, indeed, almost anyone but an academician.[7] By every one of those tests, I'd prove myself a moron. And I'd *be* a moron, too. In a world where I could not use my academic training and my verbal talents but had to do something intricate or hard, working with my hands, I would do poorly. My intelligence, then, is not absolute but is a function of the society I live in and of the fact that a small subsection of that society has managed to foist[8] itself on the rest as an arbiter[9] of such matters.

Consider my auto repairman, again. He had a habit of telling me jokes whenever he saw me. One time he raised his head from under the automobile hood to say, "Doc, a deaf-and-dumb guy went into a hardware store to ask for some nails. He put two fingers together on the counter and made hammering motions with the other hand. The clerk brought him a hammer. He shook his head and pointed to the two fingers he was hammering. The clerk brought him nails. He picked out the sizes he wanted, and left. Well, doc, the next guy who came in was a blind man. He wanted scissors. How do you suppose he asked for them?"

Indulgently, I lifted my right hand and made scissoring motions with my first two fingers. Whereupon my auto repairman laughed raucously[10] and said, "Why, you dumb jerk, he used his *voice* and asked for them." Then he said, smugly, "I've been trying that on all my customers today." "Did you catch many?" I asked. "Quite a few," he said, "but I knew for sure I'd catch *you*." "Why is that?" I asked. "Because you're so goddamned educated, doc, I *knew* you couldn't be very smart."

And I have an uneasy feeling he had something there.

[2] **KP:** kitchen patrol

[3] **complacent:** pleased with oneself, often without being aware of some defect

[4] **bents:** talents

[5] **vitals:** main parts of something

[6] **oracles:** wise answers

[7] **academician:** college teacher

[8] **foist:** pass off as valuable

[9] **arbiter:** person who decides an issue

[10] **raucously:** in a loud, coarse way

---

2 REFLECT: Do you think that people have judged you, either positively or negatively, by test scores?
*Answers will vary.*

3 SUMMARIZE: Summarize this paragraph in one or two sentences.
*Answers will vary.*

4 ■ TEACHING TIP Ask students to underline the sentence that defines *intelligence* (para. 4) and identify the topic sentence structure (term + *is not* + expected definition). Does Asimov's essay give a clear and precise meaning of the term *intelligence*? (No, he explains that the meaning of *intelligence* is relative.) How does context help define intelligence?

5

6 REFLECT: What do you think the auto repairman meant by his last statement in paragraph 6?
*Possible answer: The repairman is suggesting that education and common sense are two different things.*

7

## ■ SUMMARIZE AND RESPOND

In your reading journal or elsewhere, summarize the main point of "What Is Intelligence, Anyway?" Then go back and check off support for this main idea. Finally, jot down a brief response to the reading. What did it make you think or feel? Give an example of being "smart" that requires more than being educated.

■ **IDEA JOURNAL** Define *intelligence* using one of your strengths (such as the ability to work well with your hands, to figure out how engines work, to diagnose and fix problems, to explain ideas to other people) as the measure of intelligence.

## ■ CHECK YOUR COMPREHENSION

1. An alternate title for this essay could be
   a. "Why I Hate My Auto Repairman."
   b. "More Than One Kind of Intelligence."
   c. "How to Increase Your Score on an Intelligence Test."
   d. "Test Makers: Always Right."

2. The main idea of this essay is that
   a. academicians are not very smart.
   b. people who "get" jokes are more intelligent than people who don't.
   c. all standardized tests should have questions about farming.
   d. there are many different types of intelligence, not just the one measured by standardized tests.

3. What is the author not skilled in?
   a. Understanding jokes
   b. Taking intelligence tests
   c. Working with tools and machines
   d. Verbal talents

4. If you are unfamiliar with the following words, use a dictionary to check their meanings: *private* (para. 1); *estimate, granted, hastened* (3); *devised, intricate* (4).

## ■ READ CRITICALLY

1. In paragraph 2, Asimov writes, "I have the complacent feeling that I'm highly intelligent, and I expect other people think so, too." Do you think he feels the same way by the end of the essay? Why, or why not?

2. What do you think intelligence is? How do you think Asimov would answer this question?

3. How do you think the auto repairman would define *intelligence*?

4. Why do you think Asimov tells readers about the joke? How does the story contribute to the point of his essay?

5. Think of another example that shows how different situations call for different types of intelligence. Where would you put your examples in Asimov's essay?

## ■ WRITE

**WRITE A PARAGRAPH:** Write a paragraph about a time when you used a different type of intelligence than the kind you are tested on in school. For example, you could write about how you fixed a leaky faucet, cheered up a friend who was feeling down, or played a game of tennis.

**WRITE AN ESSAY:** Write an essay that answers the question, "What is intelligence, anyway?" Use examples from your personal experience to help define the concept of intelligence. If you wrote about this topic for Summarize and Respond, you may want to develop your ideas here. Explain why you think Asimov would agree or disagree with your definition.

■ **TIP** For a sample definition paragraph, see page 178.

*Robyn Griggs Lawrence*
# Wabi-Sabi: The Art of Imperfection

Robyn Griggs Lawrence (b. 1964) has been the editor-in-chief of *Natural Home* magazine since 1999. As long as she can remember, she has known that she wanted to write. She graduated from the University of Iowa with a journalism degree in 1986 and then worked as a reporter, copyeditor, and writer, earning publishing credits in the *Chicago Tribune, Cosmopolitan,* and the *Boston Herald.* She has always been concerned about the environment, and having children has only added to that concern; today, she writes and speaks frequently about environmentally conscious living. She lives in Boulder, Colorado.

In the following essay, Lawrence defines the Japanese concept of *wabi-sabi.* She believes that "learning to be still and accept imperfection" makes for a happy home. The topic, she says, fascinated her immediately and seemed a natural outgrowth of her other interests. Her book on wabi-sabi will be published in 2004.

GUIDING QUESTION
Can you understand the philosophy behind and the applications of wabi-sabi?

According to Japanese legend, a young man named Sen no Rikyu sought     1
to learn the elaborate set of customs known as the Way of Tea. He went to tea-master Takeeno Joo, who tested the younger man by asking him to tend the garden. Rikyu cleaned up debris[1] and raked the ground until it was perfect, then scrutinized[2] the immaculate garden. Before presenting his work to

■ **IDEA JOURNAL** What particular things do you like about a space that you feel comfortable in?

---
[1]**debris:** rubbish, refuse
[2]**scrutinized:** studied carefully

IDENTIFY: Underline the sentence that provides a working definition of *wabi-sabi*.

PREDICT: Pause here. What type of examples could Lawrence use to explain what it means to see beauty in "something that may first look decrepit and ugly"?

*Answers will vary.*

"The reading clearly defines *wabi-sabi*. In addition, many examples illustrate the definition."
—Michelle Bassett, Student

the master, he shook a cherry tree, causing a few flowers to spill randomly onto the ground.

To this day, the Japanese revere Rikyu as one who understood to his very core a cultural thread known as *wabi-sabi*. Emerging in the fifteenth century as a reaction to the prevailing aesthetic[3] of lavishness, ornamentation, and rich materials, <u>wabi-sabi is the art of finding beauty in imperfection and profundity[4] in earthiness, of revering authenticity[5] above all</u>. In Japan, the concept is now so deeply ingrained that it's difficult to explain to Westerners; no direct translation exists.

Broadly, wabi-sabi is everything that today's sleek, mass-produced, technology-saturated culture isn't. It's flea markets, not shopping malls; aged wood, not swank[6] floor coverings; one single morning glory, not a dozen red roses. Wabi-sabi understands the tender, raw beauty of a grey December landscape and the aching elegance of an abandoned building or shed. It celebrates cracks and crevices and rot and all the other marks that time and weather and use leaves behind. To discover wabi-sabi is to see the singular beauty in something that may first look decrepit and ugly.

Wabi-sabi reminds us that we are all transient[7] beings on this planet— that our bodies, as well as the material world around us, are in the process of returning to dust. Nature's cycles of growth, decay, and erosion are embodied in frayed edges, rust, liver spots. Through wabi-sabi, we learn to embrace both the glory and the melancholy[8] found in these marks of passing time.

Bringing wabi-sabi into your life doesn't require money, training, or special skills. It takes a mind quiet enough to appreciate muted beauty, courage not to fear bareness, willingness to accept things as they are—without ornamentation. It depends on the ability to slow down, to shift the balance from doing to being, to appreciating rather than perfecting.

You might ignite your appreciation of wabi-sabi with a single item from the back of a closet: a chipped vase, a faded piece of cloth. Look deeply for minute details that give it character; explore it with your hands. You don't have to understand why you're drawn to it, but you do have to accept it as it is.

Rough textures, minimally processed goods, natural materials, and subtle hues are all wabi-sabi. Consider the musty-oily scent that lingers around an ancient wooden bowl, the mystery behind a tarnished goblet. This patina[9] draws us with a power that the shine of the new doesn't possess. Our universal longing for wisdom, for genuineness, for shared history manifests[10] in these things.

---

[3] **aesthetic:** value (artistic)
[4] **profundity:** intellectual or emotional depth
[5] **authenticity:** genuineness
[6] **swank:** fancy
[7] **transient:** short-lived
[8] **melancholy:** sadness
[9] **patina:** finish, glaze
[10] **manifests:** is shown

There's no right or wrong to creating a wabi-sabi home. It can be as simple as using an old bowl as a receptacle for the day's mail, letting the paint on an old chair chip, or encouraging the garden to go to seed. Whatever it is, it can't be bought. Wabi-sabi is a state of mind, a way of being. It's the subtle art of being at peace with yourself and your surroundings. 8

■ **TEACHING TIP** Ask students to think of imperfect things that they treasure, and write their responses on the board. What makes these things special to them? Can students think of a term, like *wabi-sabi*, that captures the nature of these things?

## SUMMARIZE AND RESPOND

In your reading journal or elsewhere, summarize the main point of "Wabi-Sabi: The Art of Imperfection." Then go back and check off support for this main idea. Next, write a brief summary of the essay. Finally, jot down a brief response to the reading. Does Lawrence clearly define this term for you so that you would be able to apply it to your own home and/or lifestyle?

## CHECK YOUR COMPREHENSION

1. An alternate title for this essay could be
   a. "A Japanese Solution."
   b. "Understanding the Power of Understatement."
   c. "Trash to Treasure."
   d. "Un-decorating."

2. The main idea of this essay is that
   a. wabi-sabi can save you money on decorating your home.
   b. wabi-sabi is an art form that Sen no Rikyu originated in Japan.
   c. wabi-sabi involves recycling so it can save the environment.
   d. wabi-sabi is a state of mind that is reflected in a person's home and behavior.

3. Wabi-sabi originated as a reaction against
   a. ornamentation.
   b. authenticity.
   c. processed goods.
   d. transience.

4. If you are unfamiliar with the following words, use a dictionary to look up their meanings: *immaculate, randomly* (para. 1); *revere, lavishness, ornamentation* (2); *crevices* (3); *erosion, embodied, frayed* (4); *muted* (5); *hues, musty, tarnished, goblet* (7); *receptacle, subtle* (8).

## READ CRITICALLY

1. In paragraph 2, Lawrence refers to wabi-sabi with the sentence: "In Japan, the concept is now so deeply ingrained that it's difficult to explain to Westerners; no direct translation exists." Yet her essay is an

attempt to explain the concept. Is she successful? By the end of the essay, do you have a fairly solid understanding of wabi-sabi?

2. Lawrence begins paragraph 5 by stating what wabi-sabi does not require. Based on what you have read in this essay, what does wabi-sabi require?

3. What techniques does Lawrence use in this essay to define the term *wabi-sabi*?

4. Based on suggestions provided in this essay (specifically in paragraphs 6–8), can you think of one way to apply wabi-sabi to your home?

5. As Lawrence points out, wabi-sabi is not just something that we do to our homes; it is something that we do to ourselves. How is wabi-sabi "a state of mind, a way of being" as she writes in the last paragraph?

## ■ WRITE

■ **TIP** For a sample definition paragraph, see page 178.

**WRITE A PARAGRAPH:** Write a paragraph that defines an expression that is common to a particular culture, which is defined as a group of people who share common ideas, customs, and so on. For this assignment, you might consider your work culture, your social culture, or other types of cultures that you are involved in. (Some possible terms include *success*, in a college or work setting, or slang terms like *chilling* or *eye candy*, in an everyday life setting.) As you develop your definition, consider using contrast, as Lawrence does in paragraph 3, and choose well-selected examples.

**WRITE AN ESSAY:** In this essay, Lawrence writes about a cultural concept. In your essay, select another cultural concept and define it in such a way that someone from another culture can understand the term as you do. Again, you can use the broad definition of culture given in Write a Paragraph. For example, the word *macho* has a different meaning in many Hispanic cultures than it commonly does in the United States.

# 46

# Comparison and Contrast

Each essay in this chapter uses comparison and contrast to get its main point across to the reader. As you read these essays, consider how they achieve the four basics of good comparison and contrast that are listed below and discussed in Chapter 14 of this book.

■■ ■ **FOUR BASICS OF GOOD COMPARISON AND CONTRAST**
■ ■

1. It uses subjects that have enough in common to be compared or contrasted in a useful way.
2. It serves a purpose—either to help readers make a decision or to understand the subjects.
3. It presents several important, parallel points of comparison and contrast.
4. It arranges points in a logical organization.

## *Adora Houghton*
## My Indian

Adora Houghton wrote this essay while she was a student at Foothill College in Los Altos Hills, California. In her piece, she compares and contrasts the view of American Indians she learned from books as a child and the reality she later came to understand. The essay was originally published in the anthology *Multitude: Cross-Cultural Readings for Writers* (1993).

GUIDING QUESTION
How does a young girl's image of the Native American change? Does the author's story effectively capture her disappointment and eventual acceptance?

I've always been fascinated by Native Americans—or, as we said when I was growing up, American Indians. Even as far back as first grade, my favorite game was to pretend I was an Indian. I remember how after school I would transform myself into a brave by donning[1] my cloth "buckskin," complete with the headdress I had fashioned out of construction paper and

1

■ **IDEA JOURNAL** Think of a time when your expectations about someone, or a group of people, were inaccurate.

---
[1] **donning:** wearing

IDENTIFY: Put an X by the details Houghton uses to describe her image of Native Americans.

"This is a brilliantly descriptive essay that creates mental images of the contrasting ideas of *Indian*."

—Amy Cork, Student

■ **TEACHING TIP** You might want to point out to students that this essay is also a good example of narration. Ask them why it is an effective narrative, referring to the "four basics" in Chapter 8 if that's helpful.

feathers which I had found in our backyard. In times of war I would use my mother's makeup for war paint! Then, with war paint on and headdress in place, I would hop onto my sawhorse, and off we'd go to imaginary lands of mountains with perilous passes and plains filled with wild buffalo. As I rode my trusty steed,[2] I sometimes dreamed of what it would be like to come face to face with an authentic Indian. But when that dream finally came true, my Indian turned out to be quite different from what I had expected.

I was six years old at that time, or, as I would have described it in 2 the Indian way (according to me), entering my sixth harvest moon. I read everything I could find about Indians—the *Encyclopaedia Britannica* and the book club selections that arrived each month at our house. Actually, since I couldn't read most of those big words, I'd just look at the pretty pictures. They told me all I needed to know. How glamorous the Indians were! How noble! Their long braided hair gleamed in the sun, and their feathers waved *x* gently in the breeze that blew across their weathered faces as they rode their *x* painted ponies through the desert. Some Indians had short spiky hair *x* painted in bright colors. Others wore buckskin clothes with fringes and *x* moccasins on their feet. But what I liked most of all was their jewelry, the carved beads that were sewn onto the edges of their leather coats and the *x* porcupine-quill chokers that adorned their necks. My favorites, of course, *x* were the turquoise and silver combinations that I would study carefully, *x* peering as closely at the picture as possible.

As I grew, so did my fascination. I named myself Wa-bish-kee-pe-nas, 3 which I had found out was Chippewa for One White Pigeon, and to it I added "with blue eyes." I fashioned a backyard camp, making it look as much like the picture in my schoolbook as I could. It consisted of a tepee made from local resources such as branches from our pine trees and my bed linen, and a pole to tie intruders to (which was actually one end of my mother's clothesline). I even had a campfire, just like the ones built when we went camping, only Mother wouldn't let me light it. That year on my birthday, I asked for and received a peace pipe. I attempted to use it one night by stealing one of my dad's cigarettes, emptying the tobacco into it, and trying to smoke it. It didn't work too well, and when Dad found out, he made sure that it would be my last attempt!

One day as I was sitting by my campfire chanting, Dad came out to join 4 me. He told me that a friend of his was in town and asked me if I would like to go meet him the next day. Imagine my excitement when he added that his friend was an Indian!

"An Indian!" I shouted, and my heart beat as hard as a tom-tom. "Of 5 course I'll go!"

All that night I couldn't sleep. I lay in bed, wide awake, thinking that my 6 biggest dream was about to come true. I was going to meet a real, true, live Indian. Perhaps he would take me to his tribe and introduce me to the elders. They would give me a pair of moccasins and my own buckskin coat and call me by my Indian name. Then we would go through a ceremony to make me part of the tribe. I couldn't wait!

Morning finally arrived. I could hardly eat any breakfast. At last Father 7 was ready, and we climbed into the car and took off for our exciting adven-

[2] **steed:** stallion

ture. Pretty soon we stopped in front of a small store. I was a bit perplexed.[3] It seemed like a strange place to meet an Indian. But when I entered I noticed that the store was filled with Indian artifacts.[4] There were medicine wheels and tomahawks, bows and arrows and Kachina dolls. And in the corner, inside a glass case, was the jewelry: bracelets, necklaces, rings, and earrings—all in silver and turquoise, all more exquisite[5] than the pictures I'd seen. I'd never imagined there could be so much Indian jewelry in one place.

As I stood mesmerized[6] by the shiny pieces, a man walked up to my father. I turned to watch the two of them greet each other. The man was slender, dressed in regular street clothes, with short hair framing his thin face. There was something vaguely familiar about his face, with its dark skin and high cheekbones and brown eyes, but before I could quite figure out what it was, he looked at me and smiled.

"Hello!" he said. "You must be Adora. My name's Ed Kee."

"Hello!" I replied. He seemed like a nice guy, but I didn't want to waste any time, so I quickly added, "Are you going to take me to meet Dad's Indian friend?"

The man had an understanding look in his eyes, as if he'd heard that line before.

"I am your Dad's Indian friend."

"You!" My voice went high with shock. "You're an Indian?"

Ed nodded and smiled, and as though he sensed my dismay, he began to tell me about the tribe he came from and some of their myths.[7] They were good stories, but although I tried to listen, I couldn't pay much attention to them because I was so disappointed inside.

<u>He didn't look anything like the Indians I had grown up with and loved, the Indians in my picture-books.</u> He didn't have long braided hair, or even short colored hair. His hair was cut in the latest style, and its color looked almost like my dad's. He didn't wear a buckskin or moccasins or even a shawl. He was attired in blue jeans and a T-shirt that said "Hawaii," and on his feet, of all things, he wore cowboy boots. Worst of all, his name wasn't Running Red Bear or He Who Kills Three Sioux. It was Ed. I had two Eds in my class at school.

In a last effort to salvage[8] the situation, I asked Ed where he lived. I was hoping he'd say it was in a tepee on the top of the hills I could see from my house, or at least in an adobe[9] hut.

But he simply said, "In a house, just like you do."

I was crushed. Everything I envisioned had turned out to be just that, a vision.

Finally, it was time to leave. We said goodbye to Ed, climbed into the car, and drove off. All the way home, I didn't say a word, and my dad knew why.

[3] **perplexed:** confused

[4] **artifact:** objects

[5] **exquisite:** beautiful

[6] **mesmerized:** fascinated

[7] **myths:** traditional stories; can also mean false stories

[8] **salvage:** save

[9] **adobe:** clay

---

8

9
10

11  REFLECT: What does Houghton mean when she writes "as if he'd heard that line before"?
12  *Possible answer: Ed Kee is*
13  *used to hearing that he*
14  *doesn't look "Indian."*

15  IDENTIFY: Underline the topic sentence of this paragraph.

16

17

18  REFLECT: Interpret the line "Everything I envisioned had turned out to be just that, a vision."
19  *Possible answer: she real-*
*izes that she must radically*
*revise her ideas about what*
*it is to be Native American.*

REFLECT: Why does Houghton state that "for a long time I didn't go into the backyard."

*Possible answer: She was*

*disillusioned.*

He tried to explain to me that even though Ed didn't look like my idea of an Indian, it didn't mean he was any less one. It only meant that Indians, like all living beings, change with time and circumstance, and I needed to understand that. He added that what was important was that I should keep my respect for the heritage and the spirit of the Indians, because that would never die. What he said made sense, but I still struggled for days with my disillusionment, and for a long time I didn't go into the backyard.

Then one day, quite some time later, I received a package in the mail. 20 What could it be? I wasn't expecting anything. I opened it with all the excitement of a child on Christmas morning. There was no note and no return address, but inside the box was a beautiful turquoise and silver bracelet. It was simple and elegant and just my size, and I instantly fell in love with it. I started to put it on, and then I noticed an engraving on the back. It read: Ed Kee, Navajo. My Indian! He had kept in mind the disappointment of a little girl and had taken the time to make and send her something special, something that showed he cared, something that was part of who he was.

I ran to my father to show him my bracelet and to tell him that I had 21 finally understood what he had been trying to tell me the day we met my Indian.

### ■ SUMMARIZE AND RESPOND

In your reading journal or elsewhere, summarize the main point of "My Indian." Then go back and check off the support for this main idea. Next, write a brief summary of the essay. Finally, jot down a brief response to the reading. What is Houghton's image of Native Americans before she meets her father's friend? What is it after?

### ■ CHECK YOUR COMPREHENSION

1. An alternate title for this essay could be
   a. "An Unexpected Lesson."
   b. "The Ideal Native American."
   c. "A Turquoise Treasure."
   d. "A Childhood Adventure."

2. The main idea of this essay is that
   a. young children are easily disappointed but quickly recover.
   b. impressions of people that are formed based on how others see them often conflict with reality.
   c. stereotyping people is dangerous.
   d. Native Americans are misunderstood largely because of television and books.

3. The word *myth* in paragraph 14 is generally significant to the entire essay because
   a. Native Americans have many myths in their culture.

b. the young girl Adora had accepted a myth about Native Americans.

c. myths, an essential part of all heritages, should be cherished.

d. myths are an important part of growing up.

4. If you are unfamiliar with the following words, use a dictionary to look up their meanings: *peering* (para. 2); *chanting* (4); *vaguely* (8); *dismay* (14); *heritage, disillusionment* (19).

### ▪ READ CRITICALLY

1. What sentence in the first paragraph could function as the thesis statement for this essay?

2. What details give you a clear picture of what Houghton expected a Native American to look and act like?

3. How does Houghton arrange her details in paragraph 15? What is the effect of this technique?

4. What is meaningful about the turquoise and silver bracelet that she receives from Ed Kee (para. 20)?

5. In paragraph 1, Houghton uses the term "my Indian." She uses the term again at the end of her essay in paragraphs 20 and 21. What is significant about the absence of the term in the rest of the essay and its repetition at the end?

### ▪ WRITE

**WRITE A PARAGRAPH:** Pick a person that you knew at a different point in your life, such as when you were a child, and compare that person with how you see him or her today.

▪ **TIP** For a sample comparison/contrast paragraph, see page 194.

**WRITE AN ESSAY:** In this essay, Houghton learns the lesson that people aren't always as we imagine them to be. In your essay, select a person, place, event, or item that turned out to be different from what you had imagined or expected. As Houghton does, use contrast to point out the differences.

## *Yi-Fu Tuan*
## American Space, Chinese Place

Yi-Fu Tuan (b. 1930), the son of a diplomat, lived in China, Australia, and the Philippines before attending Oxford University, which granted him bachelor's and master's degrees. He moved to the United States in 1951. After earning a Ph.D. in geography from the University of California at Berkeley in 1957, Tuan taught geography and related courses in the United States and Canada for more than forty years. He has won a Guggenheim Fellowship and major awards from the American Geographical Association and the Association of

American Geographers. Tuan's wide-ranging interests have led him to publish books and articles about subjects as diverse as southwestern geography, pets, the relationship between human beings and their surroundings, and the concept of living a good life. He wrote his autobiography, *Who Am I?*, after retiring from his professorship in geography at the University of Wisconsin, Madison, in 1998.

Tuan advises young people to "take full advantage of world culture to expand [their] imagination and sense of aliveness," noting that "no single culture can remotely satisfy an individual's potential for experiencing." In "American Space, Chinese Place," Tuan compares and contrasts two of the cultures he knows best and discusses differences in American and Chinese expectations about interior space and the idea of home.

GUIDING QUESTION
What are the fundamental cultural differences between the American and the Chinese concept of home?

■ **TEACHING TIP** If you have students from other countries in your class, you might ask them to discuss or write about "American space" compared with "space" in their native country.

"I like how the writer made such an uncommon comparison between the culture and history of American and Chinese ideas of home."
— Michelle Bostick, Student

IDENTIFY: Underline the topic sentence of this paragraph.

Americans have a sense of space, not of place. Go to an American home in   1
exurbia,[1] and almost the first thing you do is drift toward the picture window. How curious that the first compliment you pay your host inside his house is to say how lovely it is outside the house! He is pleased that you should admire his vistas.[2] The distant horizon is not merely a line separating earth and sky, it is a symbol of the future. The American is not rooted in his place, however lovely: his eyes are drawn by the expanding space to a point on the horizon, which is his future.

By contrast, consider the traditional Chinese home. Blank walls enclose   2
it. Step behind the spirit wall and you are in a courtyard with perhaps a miniature garden around the corner. Once inside the private compound you are wrapped in an ambiance[3] of calm beauty, an ordered world of buildings, pavement, rock, and decorative vegetation. But you have no distant view: nowhere does space open out before you. Raw nature in such a home is experienced only as weather, and the only open space is the sky above. The Chinese is rooted in his place. When he has to leave, it is not for the promised land on the terrestrial horizon, but for another world altogether along the vertical, religious axis of his imagination.

The Chinese tie to place is deeply felt. Wanderlust[4] is an alien sentiment.   3
The Taoist classic *Tao Te Ching* captures the ideal of rootedness in place with these words: "Though there may be another country in the neighborhood so close that they are within sight of each other and the crowing of cocks and barking of dogs in one place can be heard in the other, yet there is no traffic between them; and throughout their lives the two peoples have nothing to do with each other." In theory if not in practice, farmers have ranked high in Chinese society. The reason is not only that they are engaged in the "root"

[1] **exurbia:** a residential area beyond the suburbs

[2] **vista:** views

[3] **ambiance:** atmosphere

[4] **wanderlust:** desire to travel

industry of producing food but that, unlike pecuniary[5] merchants, they are tied to the land and do not abandon their country when it is in danger.

Nostalgia is a recurrent theme in Chinese poetry. An American reader    4 of translated Chinese poems may well be taken aback—even put off—by the frequency, as well as the sentimentality,[6] of the lament for home. To understand the strength of this sentiment, we need to know that the Chinese desire for stability and rootedness in place is prompted by the constant threat of war, exile, and the natural disasters of flood and drought. Forcible removal makes the Chinese keenly aware of their loss. <u>By contrast, Americans move, for the most part, voluntarily. Their nostalgia for home town is really longing for childhood to which they cannot return: in the meantime the future beckons and the future is "out there," in open space.</u> When we criticize American rootlessness we tend to forget that it is a result of ideals we admire, namely, social mobility and optimism about the future. When we admire Chinese rootedness, we forget that the word "place" means both location in space and position in society: to be tied to place is also to be bound to one's station in life, with little hope of betterment. Space symbolizes hope; place, achievement and stability.

**IDEA JOURNAL** Do you think that Americans are less sentimental about their homes than the Chinese are?

IDENTIFY: Underline the sentences in paragraph 4 that contrast Americans with Chinese in terms of attitudes about space.

## SUMMARIZE AND RESPOND

In your reading journal or elsewhere, summarize the main point of "American Space, Chinese Place." Then go back and check off support for this main idea. Next, write a brief summary of the essay. Finally, jot down a brief response to the reading. Do you agree with Tuan's conclusion about the American concept of home? What evidence can you offer to support your opinion?

## CHECK YOUR COMPREHENSION

1.  An alternate title for this essay could be
    a. "The American vs. the Chinese Concept of Home."
    b. "Ties That Bind Us."
    c. "Differences between Americans and Chinese."
    d. "Home Is Where the Heart Is."

2.  The main idea of this essay is that
    a.  American and Chinese homes are different in many ways.
    b.  some cultures are more nostalgic than others.
    c.  the American philosophy of rootlessness and the Chinese philosophy of rootedness reflect where and how each group lives their lives.
    d.  a home should reflect the owner's personality, regardless of culture.

[5]**pecuniary:** financial

[6]**sentimentality:** characterized by excessive feeling or emotion

3. In this essay, Tuan links "space" to
   a. social mobility and optimism.
   b. optimism and stability.
   c. achievement and stability.
   d. rootedness and optimism.

4. If you are unfamiliar with the following words, use a dictionary to look up their meanings: *terrestrial* (para. 2); *alien* (3); *nostalgia, recurrent, lament, drought, optimism* (4).

### ■ READ CRITICALLY

1. What is Tuan's purpose in this essay?

2. What elements of the American home lead Tuan to conclude that Americans are not rooted? Are these elements sufficient to justify his conclusion?

3. In paragraph 2, do the details presented about the Chinese home create a clear picture that contrasts with the details of the American home in paragraph 1? Why or why not?

4. How does the *Tao Te Ching* quote presented in paragraph 3 explain the Chinese "rootedness in place"?

5. In the last paragraph, what pattern of organization does Tuan use to arrange his details? Is it effective?

### ■ WRITE

■ **TIP** For a sample comparison/ contrast paragraph, see page 194.

**WRITE A PARAGRAPH:** Write a paragraph that compares a room in your home with that same room in someone else's home. How are they alike? How are they different? What reasons can you provide for those similarities and differences — culture, economic level, family size, age?

**WRITE AN ESSAY:** Write an essay in which you explore the differences between how two cultures approach marriage, education, raising children, celebrating a major holiday, and so on. As Tuan does, use contrasting details to point out the differences. Also, as he does, provide a rationale for those differences to help frame your details. If you don't know enough about a different culture to write about this topic, consider an experience with any tradition or event (for example, a holiday at a friend's house, a wedding outside of your family) that was different from what you were accustomed to.

# 47

# Cause and Effect

Each essay in this chapter uses cause and effect to get its main point across to the reader. As you read these essays, consider how they achieve the four basics of good cause and effect that are listed below and discussed in Chapter 15 of this book.

## ■■ FOUR BASICS OF GOOD CAUSE AND EFFECT
## ■■■

1. It makes clear, early on, whether you are writing about causes, effects, or both.
2. It discusses real causes, not just something that happened before another event.
3. It discusses real effects, not just something that happened before another event.
4. It gives clear and detailed examples of causes and/or effects.

*Pat Wingert*

## Uniforms Rule

Pat Wingert earned a B.S. in journalism from the University of Illinois, Champaign-Urbana, and learned her craft working for the Pulitzer Prize–winning columnist Mike Royko at the *Sun-Times.* She became a reporter at the paper herself and later worked for the *Chicago Tribune.* After nine years at the two Chicago newspapers, she left her native city for the Washington bureau of *Newsweek* in 1986 and has worked there ever since. Wingert has cowritten many cover stories over the years on issues related to children, families, and education. She also worked on two important recent stories based in Washington, the sniper attacks of 2002 and the terrorist attack on the Pentagon. Her reporting has won numerous awards, including a National Press Club Award for her *Newsweek* cover story "Kids Who Can't Learn" (November 1997) and several Educational Press Association awards. Wingert lives in Washington, D.C., with her husband and children.

In "Uniforms Rule," originally from *Newsweek* (October 1999), Wingert examines how and why uniforms and other dress codes affect public-school safety and student behavior.

> "Before reading this, I thought uniforms were a bad idea, but the writer's reasons for them made me see another side."
>
> —Chris Fernandez, Student

GUIDING QUESTION
Why would wearing a uniform influence students' behavior?

Kiara Newsome's spotless navy jumper and demure white blouse won't   1
win raves on the runways. But to school reformers, the six-year-old is a real
trendsetter. This fall, Kiara and her classmates at P.S. 15 on Manhattan's
Lower East Side joined hundreds of thousands of students in the nation's
largest school system and donned[1] uniforms for the first time.

SUMMARIZE: Summarize the
reasons in paragraphs 2 and
3 in favor of school uniforms.
*Answers will vary.*

    Kiara likes her new duds " 'cause they're pretty." Her mother, Alelia, is   2
happy because "it's much easier to find the clothes in the morning." Educators in New York and around the country believe uniforms could also
solve some of the toughest problems facing schools today. In the aftermath
of the Littleton, Colo., shootings, many see dress codes as a cheap and
simple way to make schools safer. This fall, Los Angeles, Chicago, Miami,
Boston, Houston, Cleveland, and Washington, D.C., all have a majority of
their students in uniforms. "It's spreading to the suburbs now," says Vince
Ferrandino, president of the National Association of Elementary School
Principals. "It's become a national phenomenon."[2]

    Proponents say clothing rules eliminate the baggy gang-inspired look that   3
makes it easy for students to smuggle in weapons, drugs, and other banned
items. Dress codes also make it easier to spot intruders. "Last week this boy
walked into our cafeteria in jeans, and we knew right away he wasn't one of
ours," says Ramond Rivera, an elementary-school principal in El Paso, Texas,
whose students wear uniforms. "We immediately escorted him out."

■ TEACHING TIP Have stu-
dents circle the effects of the
trend toward requiring schoolchildren to wear uniforms.
Then ask them to double-
underline the causes of the
trend. Have them list at least
two additional causes or effects
that Wingert has not men-
tioned and then prepare a
response to Wingert's essay in
which they either support the
trend or oppose it.

    Researchers say there's very little hard evidence that uniforms improve   4
students' behavior or academic success. They do, however, affect student attitudes. One of the best studies compared two middle schools in Charleston
County, S.C., one with a uniform policy, the other without. A survey of
more than 300 sixth to eighth graders revealed that uniformed students gave
their schools higher scores. "Although school uniforms do not represent a
panacea[3] for all society's problems," says the lead researcher, Richard K.
Murray, a principal in Dorchester, S.C., "research now shows that school
uniforms do significantly affect student perceptions of school climate."

    Keith King of the University of Cincinnati recently published a review   5
of research on the effectiveness of dress codes. He says that overall, students
in uniforms "felt more like a team." That's important, King says, because
"the No. 1 protective factor against school violence is having a student feel
connected to his school and that he fits in."

IDENTIFY: Underline the sentences that identify a positive effect of uniforms in
middle schools and high
schools.

    Uniforms are getting the most attention at middle and high schools,   6
where security and school unity are big issues, along with the extremes of
current teen fashion: spaghetti-strap tanks, face painting, body piercing.
"You'd be amazed at the amount of time administrators have been spending
on what kids are wearing to school," says Susan Galletti, a middle-school
specialist at the National Association of Secondary School Principals
[NASSP]. "With uniforms, all that is eliminated, and they can spend more
time on teaching and learning."

    While some schools stick to traditional plaids and navy blue, others   7
allow polo shirts, chinos, and even capri pants. Still, teens in the throes[4] of
adolescent rebellion often object and in a few cases, they've even sued for

[1]**donned:** put on

[2]**phenomenon:** occurrence or circumstance

[3]**panacea:** remedy for all problems or diseases, cure-all

[4]**throes:** painful struggle

the freedom to choose their own clothes. "The older kids get, the more aware they are of their rights," says Stephen Yurek, general counsel of the NASSP. "If you try to restrict what they can say or wear, you'll start hearing that their rights are being violated." <u>Yurek says the courts have made it clear that students don't have the same rights inside school as they do outside; clothing requirements are not considered a violation of their freedom of expression if there's a valid educational reason for imposing them.</u> To avoid legal hassles, though, most schools will provide uniforms to poor students who can't afford to buy them, and many allow parents to opt out if they have religious objections.

IDENTIFY: Underline the sentence that presents the courts' decision about uniforms in schools.

Educators say the best way to get kids to accept uniforms is to start in the early grades. Noelle Ebright, sixteen, a student at Wilson High School in Long Beach, Calif., has been wearing a uniform for eight years. "I've slowly adapted to it," she says. This year, she says, "all I have to do is grab some khaki bottoms and a white shirt with a collar and I'm out of the house." Still, she admits, "if I had my personal preference, of course I would prefer not to wear one. Any kid would."

8    **■ IDEA JOURNAL** If you have never worn a uniform, how would you feel if you were required to wear one? If you have worn a uniform, did you like doing so?

Some adults sympathize. Norman Isaacs, principal of Millikan Middle School in Sherman Oaks, Calif., has resisted uniforms. He believes clothing gives teachers insights into what's happening with individual students. "Our counselors and teachers monitor the way kids are dressed," he says. "If we see a big change in the way a student dresses, that sends up a signal and tells us we need to address that person."

9

Other critics say they fear the spread of uniforms will smother student creativity. But experienced educators have learned that kids often dream up truly inspired loopholes.[5] El Paso's Rivera remembers the girl who came to school wearing contact lenses that gave her the appearance of having yellow cat eyes. It wasn't a strict violation; no one had thought to include contacts in the dress code. Still, he says, "We had to put a stop to that. . . . It was a distraction to every kid in her class." And a real eye-opener for the principal.

10   REFLECT: Wingert offers an example of a creative loophole. Based on your experience, what other loopholes might students create? *Answers will vary.*

### ■ SUMMARIZE AND RESPOND

In your reading journal or elsewhere, summarize the main point of "Uniforms Rule." Then go back and check off support for this main idea. Finally, jot down a brief response to the reading. What did it make you think or feel? Do you have an opinion on the subject? Do you think wearing uniforms could result in better student behavior?

### ■ CHECK YOUR COMPREHENSION

1.  An alternate title for this essay could be
    a.  "School Uniforms Kill Student Creativity."
    b.  "Dress Codes and Public Schools."
    c.  "School Uniforms and Student Behavior."
    d.  "School Uniforms and Freedom of Expression."

[5] **loopholes:** ways to get around a rule

2. The main idea of this essay is that
   a. teenagers do not care what they wear to school.
   b.) school uniforms have a positive effect on student attitudes.
   c. schools that require uniforms are stricter than schools that do not.
   d. wearing a school uniform cuts down on the time required to get ready for school in the morning.

3. According to research, what is one effect of wearing school uniforms?
   a.) Uniforms make students feel as if they are part of a team and fit in.
   b. Uniforms make students feel like they are in grade school.
   c. Students will always find loopholes in the dress code.
   d. Uniforms will cause an increase in body piercing.

4. If you are not familiar with the following words, use a dictionary to check their meanings: *demure, trendsetter* (para. 1); *proponents* (3); *valid, hassles* (7).

■ **READ CRITICALLY**

1. According to Wingert, what are the effects of wearing school uniforms? What has caused schools to adopt school uniform policies?

2. Why don't the courts consider requiring school uniforms a violation of students' freedom of expression? Do you agree or disagree with this view?

3. How can wearing school uniforms improve school safety?

4. Can you tell from the essay what Wingert's attitude toward school uniforms is? How would you describe the tone of the essay?

5. As a parent, how would you react if your child were required to wear a uniform to school? How would you react if you were required to wear a uniform to class? Is your response different, and if so, why?

■ **WRITE**

■ **TIP** For a sample cause/effect paragraph, see page 212.

**WRITE A PARAGRAPH:** Write a paragraph about what causes students at a particular grade level to feel alienated from their schools or classmates.

**WRITE AN ESSAY:** Write an essay that explores the possible effects of a high school dropping its uniform policy and allowing students to wear whatever they choose. If you addressed this issue in Summarize and Respond, feel free to use those ideas.

*Daryn Eller*

# Move Your Body, Free Your Mind

Daryn Eller, a native Californian, graduated from the University of California, Berkeley, and then spent fifteen years living and working in New York, where she gained the experience and connections that enable her to work as a free-lance writer today. Eller began writing professionally when she was promoted from an assistant at *Mademoiselle* magazine to a copywriter responsible for covering topics like fashion, beauty, and health. "The health was what stuck," she says. She later took a position writing about food and nutrition for *Self* magazine before turning to freelance writing—mainly about nutrition and fitness—in 1990. She lives in Venice, California.

The essay that follows is a favorite of Eller's because it came from her personal conviction that exercise could inspire creativity. After finding that scientific research backed up her gut feeling, she got an assignment to write the piece, which first appeared in *Health* magazine (May 2002). Eller notes, "I continue to use the technique to get my brain working. When I don't have the time to fit in exercise, I take a shower—that seems to work too!" (A side-bar that accompanied this essay appears on page 152. It describes a process.)

GUIDING QUESTION
What are the mental effects of exercise?

This is a true story: I was sitting at my desk, facing the challenge of how to begin a piece about the power of exercise to enhance creative thinking. Naturally, I wanted this beginning to engage you, but nothing all that engaging was coming to mind. Zilch, in fact. So I did what I often do: I went to the pool and swam for an hour. Now here I am, back at my desk typing away, my writer's block well behind me. 1

Exercise can do that for you. "It helps me get a fresh perspective on things," says Katlin Kirker, a forty-five-year-old painter who takes work-break walks on the beach near her home in Venice, California, whenever she feels the need to clear her mind. One writer I know generates so many ideas when running that he tucks a pad of paper and pen into his pocket before leaving the house. 2

It's all too easy to shrug off exercise, especially when you've got a lot of work to do. Why spend the time sweating when you could be pushing some of that paper off your desk? But research suggests that exercise can get the creative juices flowing and may even make you more productive. And it doesn't just apply to "creative types" like writers, musicians, and artists; anyone who needs to solve problems and generate ideas can get a mental boost from a good workout. 3

The best measure so far of the exercise-creativity connection is a 1997 study at Middlesex University in Middlesex, England, involving men and women ages nineteen to fifty-nine. On the first day of the study, the researchers had the group do aerobic[1] exercise for twenty-five minutes and 4

**■ IDEA JOURNAL** Has exercise, or any other technique, ever helped you "free your mind"?

REFLECT: Can you identify with the desire to "shrug off" exercise when you are busy?
*Answers will vary.*

PREDICT: Read most of paragraph 4 but pause when you reach the sentence beginning "As you probably guessed . . ." What do you predict the study proved?
*Answers will vary.*

[1] **aerobic:** exercise that conditions the heart and lungs

then asked them to think of as many uses for empty cardboard boxes and tin cans as they could. On the second day, the group watched an "emotionally neutral" video on rock formations and were given the same creativity test. As you probably guessed, after working out, the volunteers came up with more solutions to the box/tin can dilemma than they did after watching the video.

What is it about exercise that can make people more inventive thinkers? Robert Thayer, Ph.D., a professor of psychology at California State University–Long Beach and author of *Calm Energy: How People Regulated Mood With Food and Exercise,* believes it may have to do with the ability of physical activity to alter some factors that inhibit creativity. One is a lack of energy. "When you exercise, you experience a host of physiological changes, such as an increase in metabolism,[2] more cardiac activity, and the release of neurotransmitters[3] that affect alertness," Thayer says. "These all add to a state of general bodily arousal, and that increases energy."

Another factor could be mood, says Eric Maisel, Ph.D., a California psychotherapist and author of *Write Mind: 299 Things Writers Should Never Say to Themselves (and What They Should Say Instead)*. "What often stops people from creating is that they're depressed, so it's perfectly logical that if exercise reduces your experience of depression, you're more likely to create," he says. "Same with anxiety. Creative blocks can be a form of performance anxiety, so anything that reduces anxiety can help."

Another theory of Maisel's — and the one I relate to the most — is that exercise produces a state Zen Buddhists call the "empty mind." When the mind empties, preoccupations slip away and that nagging little voice inside your head that says "Maybe I'm just not smart enough to figure this out" or "I used to be a good writer but not anymore" shuts up. During those moments of silence, creative thoughts have a chance to develop. "If we're always worried about something or concerned about our to-do list, there is no way for ideas to enter our brain," Maisel says. "But with the emptying of the mind, worries fade away, and when that happens, ideas come."

While you can't exactly prescribe a workout to build creativity like you would to build biceps, the twenty-five minutes of aerobic exercise employed in the Middlesex study is a good place to start. (By the way, in the study, volunteers did instructor-led aerobic exercise, but the researchers speculate that running and walking may be equally, and possibly even more beneficial.) And a longer, harder session may make you even more creative, depending on the reason for your imaginative angst.[4] For instance, if stress is hindering[5] your thought process, an hour of vigorous aerobic exercise could spark a breakthrough. "Heavy exercise, like working out hard at the gym for an hour, has been shown to significantly decrease tension," Thayer says. "But it can also make you very tired afterward, and you may not get a resurgence[6] of energy for a while." Sometimes, though, less is better: If you

---

[2] **metabolism:** the process of converting food into energy

[3] **neurotransmitters:** chemicals that transmit nerve impulses from one nerve cell to another

[4] **angst:** worry

[5] **hindering:** interfering with

[6] **resurgence:** reappearance

REFLECT: Based on your personal experience, does this explanation seem logical to you?
*Answers will vary.*

SUMMARIZE: In your own words, summarize the effects of exercising heavily.
*Answers will vary.*

"I sometimes get writer's block when I sit down to write a paper. This essay gives good advice: When you use your body, your mind is more clear."
—Michelle Bassett, Student

need more energy, Thayer's studies have shown that a fast-paced walk as brief as ten minutes can help. "We've found that short, brisk walks can raise energy for up to two hours afterward," he reports.

You may have to experiment a little to find out what works for you. For me, a moderate workout is best—that is, one long enough to help me get an "empty mind," but not so hard that it tires me out. Once I get to that quiet state, so many ideas start percolating[7] in my head that when I get home I often go straight to my desk to capitalize[8] on the momentum. Need proof that it works? I finished this article, didn't I?

9

■ **TEACHING TIP** Ask students if they would consider trying exercise as a way of "freeing their minds" for school work and other work. You might also remind them that the prewriting techniques described in Chapter 2 can help them with writing tasks specifically.

### ▊ SUMMARIZE AND RESPOND

In your reading journal or elsewhere, summarize the main point of "Move Your Body, Free Your Mind." Then go back and check off support for this main idea. Next, write a brief summary of the essay. Finally, jot down a brief response to the reading. Do the examples, details, and research presented illustrate the psychological benefits of exercise? Does your personal experience verify those benefits?

### ▊ CHECK YOUR COMPREHENSION

1. An alternate title for this essay could be
   a. "Move It or Lose It."
   b. "Add Exercise to Your Life."
   c. "Jump-Start Your Mind by Exercising."
   d. "The Benefits of Exercise."

2. The main idea of this essay is that
   a. weightlifting decreases tension and makes people tired.
   b. certain types of exercises can make people creative and productive.
   c. certain types of exercise are more beneficial than others.
   d. certain exercise programs should be monitored by professionals.

3. According to research,
   a. exercise alters factors that inhibit creativity.
   b. exercise most frequently helps writers, musicians, and artists to generate ideas.
   c. because exercise decreases bodily arousal, it increases mental ability.
   d. exercise is addictive.

4. If you are unfamiliar with the following words, use a dictionary to look up their meanings: *generates* (para. 2); *alter, inhibit, physiological* (5); *preoccupation* (7); *speculate, vigorous* (8).

[7] **percolating:** bubbling

[8] **capitalize (on):** make the most of

## READ CRITICALLY

1. Notice that Eller uses the "I" point of view in the first paragraph. Is this approach effective? Why or why not?

2. What are some of the factors (see paras. 5–7) that inhibit creativity?

3. Does Eller create logical links between causes (exercise) and effects (mental changes)? Based on the information presented, how does physical activity create changes in the mind?

4. To experience the mental rewards of physical activity, what type of exercise session is recommended? Not recommended?

5. What technique does the author use in the last two lines? Is it effective?

## WRITE

■ **TIP** For a sample cause/effect paragraph, see page 212.

**WRITE A PARAGRAPH:** Write a paragraph about how you have used exercise or some other activity to achieve a particular state of mind. What did you do? What were the specific effects of those actions?

**WRITE AN ESSAY:** At the end of her essay, Eller notes the effects that a moderate workout has on her mental state. In your essay, discuss the effects of your involvement in a particular sport, exercise program, or other activity. These effects might be mental, social, or physical. If you wish, include any ideas you developed for Summarize and Respond.

# 48

# Argument

The essays in this chapter use argument to get their main point across. We have provided a pro and con essay for each of two topics—strategies for dealing with drug offenders and approaches for teaching English to non-native speakers. This will allow you to compare and contrast the argumentative strategies used. As you read the essays in each pair, decide which essay you find stronger and why.

Each pairing deals with an issue that was put before voters. In the weeks and months leading up to an election, newspapers, magazines, Web sites, and other media outlets publish pieces like these so that voters are informed. After the election, writers may consider the consequences of a particular outcome.

In some cases, articles aimed at informing voters attempt to present all sides of an issue; in other cases, writers argue for one side of an issue. The essays in this chapter are of this second type. Note, however, that even these types of essays must account for the opposition's arguments.

As you read these essays, consider how they achieve the four basics of good argument that are listed below and discussed in Chapter 16 of this book.

■ **TIP** For more information on writing argument, see Chapter 16. To become a more informed voter, consider visiting the following Web sites: **Project Vote Smart** (<**www.vote-smart.org**>), which provides information about thousands of candidates and elected officials, as well as voter registration forms and other voter assistance; **DemocracyNet** (<**www.dnet.org**>), which also offers information on candidates and issues; and the **League of Women Voters** (<**www.lwv.org**>). This last site includes a voter information page at <**www.lwv.org/voter/index.html**>.

## ■ FOUR BASICS OF GOOD ARGUMENT

1. It takes a strong and definite position on an issue or advises a particular action.
2. It gives good reasons and supporting evidence to defend the position of recommended action.
3. It considers opposing views.
4. It has enthusiasm and energy from start to finish.

■ **TEACHING TIP** The essay assignments following the readings in this chapter ask students to write their own editorials. If you or your students choose these assignments, you might want to ask students to study other editorials first. Ask them to find one that interests them in a local newspaper and to consider how well the writer supports his or her argument. They should bring the editorials to class and be prepared to discuss their reactions.

## Pairing 1: Treatment, Not Jail, for Drug Offenders: Yes or No?

### *Nell Bernstein*

# The Drug War's Littlest Victims

Nell Bernstein (b. 1965) has written frequently about the U.S. foster care system and about the effects of incarceration on American families. Bernstein has won media fellowships from the University of Maryland School of Journalism, the Open Society Institute, and the Soros Foundation. She was awarded a 2000 Media Award from Prevention for a Safer Society for her story in the online magazine *Salon.com*, "When the Jailhouse is Far from Home." Bernstein, who earned a bachelor's degree in comparative literature from Yale University, is the author of *A Rage to Do Better: Listening to Young People from the Foster Care System* (2000). She lives in Berkeley, California.

Note that both this essay and the one that follows refer to Proposition 36, which was passed in California in November 2000. This measure requires probation with treatment for all "nonviolent drug offenders" until their third conviction. In this essay, which first appeared on *Salon.com*, Bernstein argues that treatment instead of prison for drug abusers could help not only the addicts but the innocent victims of their addiction.

GUIDING QUESTION
Who are the "littlest victims" Bernstein refers to in the title? Why are they victims?

"I like the introduction, which is straightforward and to the point. I like the facts that the author provided."

—Mark Balderas, Student

The last time Tracy Carter, a longtime drug user, was sent to the county jail, she ran into her mother. Neither woman was surprised. Carter's parents are both longtime heroin addicts. Her sister is a heroin addict. Carter says she herself was born a heroin addict. So were most of her seven children.

Carter (not her real name), thirty-eight, has been in and out of jail throughout her long career as an addict, mostly for violating her probation. She has come out each time—homeless, jobless, and full of good intentions—and started using again within a matter of weeks or months. This grim routine has left her children trapped in a grueling[1] cycle themselves: bouncing from one home to another; vacillating[2] between faith and despair as their mother makes and breaks promise after promise; and, as they grow up without her, drifting into depression, delinquency, and addictions of their own.

In November 2000, California voters decided it was time for Tracy Carter, and drug users like her, to try something different. With 61 percent of the vote, they passed Proposition 36, a measure that sends most non-

■ **IDEA JOURNAL** Do you agree or disagree that drug offenders should be treated instead of imprisoned?

[1] **grueling:** exhausting
[2] **vacillating:** wavering, shifting

violent drug offenders into treatment rather than to jail. Two years later, similar initiatives are on the ballot in Ohio and the District of Columbia; several more states have implemented[3] or are working on legislative fixes to tough drug laws; and more than 70 percent of Americans are telling pollsters[4] they'd like to see the government ease up on addicts.

X This new climate may be based in pragmatism[5] as much as in compas-
X sion. The number of drug offenders in state and federal prisons has in-
X creased more than tenfold over the past decade, from forty thousand to
X nearly five hundred thousand. Incarcerating them costs five billion dollars
X a year. With a faltering economy draining government coffers[6]—and the war on terrorism competing for dollars formerly reserved for the war on drugs—the price tag for being the world's largest jailer is starting to look a little steep.

A national shift from incarceration to treatment has the potential to save much more than dollars. More than 8 million of America's 75 million children have a parent or parents addicted to drugs or alcohol. Parental drug addiction fuels the foster-care system; it feeds the juvenile justice system. It affects welfare caseloads, school performance, and child health. And parental addiction is self-perpetuating: Up to 70 percent of the children of addicts become addicted to drugs themselves.

Might drug treatment slow the staggering growth in the nation's foster-care system, which has more than doubled in the past fifteen years, to over half a million children? Child-welfare workers think so. In a 1997 survey by the Child Welfare League, child-welfare workers estimated that 67 percent of the parents they dealt with needed treatment, but only 31 percent got it. According to researchers at the National Center on Addiction and Substance Abuse at Columbia University (CASA), parental substance abuse is implicated[7] in seven of ten cases of child abuse and neglect, and is responsible for ten billion dollars of the fourteen billion dollars spent nationally each year on child welfare costs. Nationwide, according to the Office of National Drug Control Policy, five million Americans need drug treatment but only two million receive it.

Might treatment stem the tide of juvenile incarceration, which has left 125,000 adolescents behind bars at last count—many of whom have experienced parental drug addiction and incarceration? Might it aid those hardest cases that stymie[8] welfare reformers—the families that lose their benefits to time limits before they manage to find another means of support, many of whom are thought to have drug problems?

If these are questions we are only just beginning to ask, the children of drug-addicted parents are well ahead of us.

In 1999, in researching a report on foster care, I interviewed and surveyed in writing more than 150 current and former foster youth in California and New York. When I asked the question, "What might have kept your

---

4   IDENTIFY: Put an X by the evidence that presents concrete supporting evidence.

5   SUMMARIZE: Summarize the effects of parental drug addiction.
*Answers will vary.*

6   ■ **TEACHING TIP** If you plan to have students read the essay that follows this one, you might point out that the authors of that piece also use information from CASA—but for a very different purpose. Have them contrast these purposes.

7

8

9

---

[3] **implemented:** put into practice

[4] **pollsters:** people who conduct polls

[5] **pragmatism:** practicality

[6] **coffers:** funds

[7] **implicated:** involved

[8] **stymie:** frustrate

REFLECT: Why does Bernstein include quotes from children?

*Possible answer: The testimony from children is powerful since the essay focuses on these "littlest victims."*

REFLECT: Reread the last sentence of this paragraph. Do you find the statistic to be powerful? Believable? *Answers will vary.*

family together?" one answer came up over and over: help with a parent's drug problem.

"My father was into drugs instead of me," one teenager wrote. "That's why I'm in the system." 10

"If there wasn't drugs," wrote another, "I probably would not know what a system is." 11

Our response to these children has to date lacked imagination: We incarcerate addicted parents and place their children in foster care, or leave them to fend for themselves. CASA researchers spent three years scrutinizing[9] state budgets in an effort to figure out the dollar cost of this approach. In 1998, they determined, the states spent $81.3 billion dealing with drug abuse and its consequences, but of each dollar spent, only four cents went to prevention and treatment. This imbalance, they found, had a particularly powerful impact on the young: The states spent $5.3 billion addressing cases of child abuse and neglect, 79 percent of which could be traced to parental drug or alcohol abuse. 12

But as the nation tentatively[10] embarks on a new way of doing things, early indications are promising. In California, the Department of Corrections has reported a 20 percent drop in the number of drug offenders in its custody since Proposition 36 was implemented, and a 10 percent drop in women inmates overall. As the measure is fully implemented, the state Legislative Analyst's Office estimates, it will save between $100 and $150 million each year in prison costs. 13

When parents do get treatment, the federal Center for Substance Abuse Treatment has found, kids come home and taxpayers save even more money. In a Florida pilot program, for example, 180 women treated in a single residential program regained custody of 580 children who had previously been in the care of the state. 14

Charles (not his real name), eighteen, grew up in Northern California under the old drug enforcement regime.[11] He spent his childhood and adolescence in a series of foster homes and juvenile halls while his crack-addicted mother cycled in and out of jail and prison. When Charles was sixteen, his mother put herself in rehab. Today, she works at a church and has her own two-bedroom apartment. She hasn't used drugs in two years. 15

"It feels good," says Charles. "That little piece that's lost—it's filled the gap there. At first I used to think my mom would be dead, but now I know she's going to see my kids. She'll see me graduate from high school, go on to college. I used to pray at night for a new mommy and daddy. Now I'm getting my mama back." 16

Does large-scale treatment work as an approach to drug addiction? We don't know, because we've never tried it. But as the casualties of our decades-long war on drugs continue to fill not only our nation's prisons but its foster homes, group homes, and juvenile halls, there's plenty of evidence that the alternative has failed the children it was meant to serve. 17

[9] **scrutinizing:** carefully studying

[10] **tentatively:** cautiously

[11] **regime:** administration or structure

Despite years of disappointment and betrayal, children of addicts will   18
likely tell you they are willing to give their parents another chance. Three
decades into a failed war on drugs, voters may finally be ready to do the
same.

## ■ SUMMARIZE AND RESPOND

In your reading journal or elsewhere, summarize the main point of "The
Drug War's Littlest Victims." Then go back and check off the support for this
main idea. Next, write a brief summary of the essay. Finally, jot down a brief
response to the reading. Do drug offenders belong in treatment centers
rather than jail? Why or why not?

## ■ CHECK YOUR COMPREHENSION

1.  An alternate title for this essay could be
    a.  "Drug-Addicted Parents."
    b.  "Welfare Woes."
    c.  "Treatment Programs Break the Addiction Cycle."
    d.  "Foster-Care Problems."

2.  The main idea of this essay is that
    a.  incarcerating addicted parents protects their children.
    b.  the foster-care system needs to be restructured.
    c.  more treatment centers are needed in this country.
    d.  putting nonviolent drug offenders in treatment centers has positive
        effects.

3.  According to this essay, which of the following is *not* a negative effect
    associated with parental drug addiction?
    a.  Parental drug addiction fuels the foster-care system.
    b.  Parental drug addiction is self-perpetuating.
    c.  Parental drug addiction is lessened through treatment programs.
    d.  Parental drug addiction feeds the juvenile justice system.

4.  If you are unfamiliar with the following words, use a dictionary to look
    up their meanings: *grim, delinquency* (para. 2); *initiatives, legislative* (3);
    *compassion, steep* (4); *perpetuating* (5); *staggering* (6); *stem* (7); *embarks*
    (13); *pilot* (14).

## ■ READ CRITICALLY

1.  In what ways does Bernstein appeal to readers' emotions in her
    argument?

2. What evidence does Bernstein present to develop her "pragmatism" point (para. 4)?

3. How does Bernstein use the effects of incarceration to fuel her argument for treatment programs? Does she establish a logical cause/effect relationship that is supported with specific evidence?

4. Why does Bernstein conclude that "early indications are promising" (para. 13)? Based on the evidence presented, do you agree?

5. In paragraph 17, what is Bernstein's response to the question she poses about large-scale treatment? Does her admission help or hinder her argument?

### ■ WRITE

■ **TIP** For a sample argument paragraph, see page 227.

**WRITE A PARAGRAPH:** Write a paragraph about one issue Bernstein presents in this essay—for example, the view that the approach she advocates could save money in tough economic times. You might elaborate on, clarify, or offer refuting evidence.

**WRITE AN ESSAY:** Imagine that your state is facing a similar ballot question—one that will decriminalize illegal drugs and provide treatment for drug addicts as opposed to imprisoning them. Like Bernstein, write an editorial, an essay to be published in your local newspaper. In your essay, expand on the points that she makes or take the opposite position and argue against a measure like Proposition 36. You may use personal experience, information from this essay, or information from another reading to support your position. If you wish, include any ideas you developed for Summarize and Respond.

### *Jim Gogek and Ed Gogek*
## Seeing Criminal Addicts through Middle-Class Eyes

Jim Gogek earned a bachelor's degree in English from the University of Iowa and a master's degree in journalism from New York University. After starting as a copy boy for the Associated Press in 1980, he worked for AP bureaus in Colorado and North Carolina and for newspapers in Florida and California. He is now an editorial writer for the *San Diego Union-Tribune* and a Robert Wood Johnson Fellow in Developing Leadership in Reducing Substance Abuse. Ed Gogek graduated from the University of Illinois College of Medicine and completed his training at the University of Western Ontario. He is a psychiatrist specializing in addiction. Jim and Ed Gogek are brothers who have cowritten several articles about the problems of chemical dependency.

This editorial was first printed in the *San Diego Union-Tribune* in August 2000, just three months before Proposition 36 was passed. This measure requires probation with treatment for all "nonviolent drug offenders" until their third conviction. Arguing against Proposition 36, Jim Gogek and Ed Gogek assert that strict drug laws can force changes in the behavior of addicts who would otherwise never accept treatment.

GUIDING QUESTION
What do the authors mean by "middle-class eyes"? How might that view of the issue shape someone's opinion?

Some baby boomers[1] remember smoking dope and going to rock concerts back in college. Or they might have done a little cocaine once in awhile on a Saturday night, then went out drinking and had a wild time. 1

Was it really that bad? Some may still have a bag hidden in their closet, and smoke a joint on weekends. They still hold a job, have a family. . . . Is it a federal crime? It never seemed to hurt anybody. 2

When they read that nearly one-third of prison inmates are incarcerated for drug crimes, they're incensed.[2] Those poor people should be set free, they say, and given some drug treatment. Why fill our prisons with people whose only crime is doing drugs? 3

Such thinking embraces a faulty and dangerous assumption, one that lies beneath the rationale[3] for decriminalizing illegal drugs, including the effort on the California ballot this fall called Proposition 36. Proponents[4] don't see the downside of decriminalization because they look at their own middle-class lives and their own experience with drugs, and assume people in prison are just like them. 4

They think the person in prison for drugs is someone, maybe much like themselves, who was just walking down the street one day with a bag in his pocket, got arrested and ended up in prison. That's simply not reality. Casual drug use bears almost no resemblance to criminal drug addiction. 5

First of all, criminal addicts are severely addicted, not occasional users. 6

Ernest Jarman, a prison psychologist, is assistant director for substance abuse programs for the California Department of Corrections. He works with the people in prison on drug charges, the ones drug decriminalization proponents believe should be set free. 7

"I've done research for the department for almost ten years, and I don't come in contact with the casual drug user or the weekend drug user," Jarman said. "From my corrections experience, I don't know what that is. . . . We deal in severity here." 8

Claude Meitzenheimer, who runs a treatment program at the Cocoran state prison, says the inmates he treats are society's heaviest drug abusers, round-the-clock junkies and tweakers[5] whose drug use is so all-consuming it makes holding a job, being a parent, or living a normal life utterly impossible. 9

**■ IDEA JOURNAL** If you are (or know) a baby boomer, do the authors' perceptions about baby boomers' attitudes toward drugs ring true or false to you? What are your own attitudes?

IDENTIFY: What is the "dangerous assumption"?
*Possible answer: that criminal addicts are like casual drug users*

IDENTIFY: Underline the sentence that functions as the main point of the essay.

REFLECT: Why do the Gogeks include information from Jarman and Meitzenheimer in this section?
*Possible answer: These "front-line" experts lend credibility to the argument.*

[1] **baby boomers:** Americans born between 1946 and 1964
[2] **incensed:** angered, annoyed
[3] **rationale:** reasoning
[4] **proponents:** supporters
[5] **tweakers:** a slang term for crack or methamphetamine (speed) users

■ **TEACHING TIP** In paragraph 10, the authors criticize the comparison of criminal addicts to casual users and then go on to contrast these groups. Ask students to summarize the contrast they describe. Do students agree with the authors' position here?

"It was interesting to read this article after the Nell Bernstein one. I can almost hear the authors debating the issues."
—Lena Genrick, Student

SUMMARIZE: Summarize the information in this paragraph to provide a brief definition of "undersocialized."
*Possible answer: lacking the*
*basic skills needed to*
*function in society*

Comparing the criminal addict to the casual user is like comparing the hardcore homeless alcoholic passed out on the sidewalk to someone who has a glass of wine with dinner. The middle-class casual drug experience might be smoking a joint before a Bruce Springsteen concert, then going back to work on Monday. The criminal addict drug experience is snorting crystal meth[6] every day for three weeks, smoking pot and drinking a gallon of cheap wine each day to take the edge off, and in the meantime robbing a gas station, driving while extremely intoxicated, and beating up his girlfriend. Eventually, the criminal addict gets arrested for one of these crimes, and drugs are found on him. When he goes before the judge, he often cops a plea down to the drug charge.      10

And that highlights another fact legalization proponents miss. Criminal addicts lead criminal lives. These are not people who just commit drug crimes; they also commit the majority of nondrug crimes.      11

While approximately one-third of state prison inmates are in for drug crimes, research shows that about 80 percent of all inmates have substance abuse problems. Addiction causes most crime, and that's all crime, not just drug crime. For example, most murders are committed under the influence of drugs or alcohol. The inmates locked up for violent crimes or property crimes are no different from those in for drug crimes. They're the same people with the same problems, they just happened to get caught for different things. Many convicts in for drug crimes were arrested for other crimes but then pleaded down to the drug crime.      12

"These are people with big histories of criminal behavior," Meitzenheimer said.      13

Middle-class drug dabblers[7] can't even imagine the world that criminal addicts inhabit. Most criminal addicts didn't grow up in anything resembling a normal home.      14

Jarman: "Many people think that people in prison were raised in a middle-class environment, perhaps like we were. That is not the norm when you go to prison. You find prison is a generational phenomenon[8] in some families. It's not uncommon to find several family members in prison. It's not uncommon to find a father and son team or a mother and daughter team in prison, even on the same prison yard."      15

The criminal addict's life is so addled[9] by addiction, both his own addiction and that of his family, that he never learned anything but a criminal lifestyle.      16

Jarman: "We might call somebody like that undersocialized: They never reached a level of adult functionality where they could survive on their own and where they could be productive. You have to teach these people basic living skills. You don't rehabilitate[10] them, you habilitate[11] them.      17

"Again, we're not talking about middle-class populations. We could be talking about a child who grew up in a crack house, who grew up with par-      18

---

[6] **crystal meth:** methamphetamine (speed)

[7] **dabblers:** people who do something casually, not seriously

[8] **phenomenon:** occurrence

[9] **addled:** confused, shaken up

[10] **rehabilitate:** restore, reform

[11] **habilitate:** to train people to function effectively in society

ents who were criminals, selling drugs, and it simply became very normal behavior for him."

A study by the National Center on Addiction and Substance Abuse at Columbia University bears this out. Forty-two percent of drug users behind bars have family members who have also been in prison. Nearly 70 percent had friends who were also criminals. How many suburban baby boomers can say the same?

The solution to the large numbers of drug addicts in prison is not to let these people go back to their addictions and criminal lives. Criminal addicts need extensive, long-term treatment to become happy, productive, and law-abiding. But they rarely seek treatment by themselves, and don't want it when it's offered.

Almost everyone knows that denial is a symptom of addiction; prisons are full of addicts who deny they have a problem. If we set them free first and then offer treatment, most will refuse it. But by keeping our drug laws strict, providing enough drug treatment in prison and for parolees[12] and probationers,[13] we can coerce[14] criminal addicts into finally getting the help they need.

19

20 REFLECT: This paragraph begins by stating what the solution is *not*. Based on what you have read, provide what the Gogeks might consider a solution.

21 *Possible answer: Treat criminal addicts during imprisonment.*

## ▀ SUMMARIZE AND RESPOND

In your reading journal or elsewhere, summarize the main point of "Seeing Criminal Addicts through Middle-Class Eyes." Then go back and check off support for this main idea. Next, write a brief summary of the essay. Finally, jot down a brief response to the reading. Do you agree with the Gogeks' position on this issue? Why or why not? Do they argue their point logically and provide sufficient and appropriate evidence?

## ▀ CHECK YOUR COMPREHENSION

1. An alternate title for this essay could be
   a. "Misunderstanding Drug Addiction."
   b. "Substance Abuse Programs Do Their Jobs."
   c. "Middle-Class Values."
   d. "Drugs and Alcohol Don't Mix."

2. The main idea of this essay is that
   a. drug programs in today's prisons are effective in helping offenders overcome drug addition.
   b. the middle-class view is based on a solid understanding of criminal drug addiction.
   c. the number of incarcerated drug addicts in prisons can be effectively reduced through treatment centers.

---

[12]**parolees:** those on parole (conditional release) from prison

[13]**probationers:** those whose criminal sentences have been suspended on the promise of good behavior

[14]**coerce:** force

d. those from the middle class who have taken drugs on a casual basis can not understand the dangers associated with criminal drug addiction.

3. According to the Gogeks, what is the relationship between addictive drug use and crime?
    a. Putting people in prison because they are drug addicts will introduce them to a life of crime.
    b. Addictive drug use leads only to crimes that involve drugs.
    c. Inmates in prison for violent crimes are different from those in prison for drug addiction.
    d. Drug addiction causes most crime.

4. If you are unfamiliar with the following words, use a dictionary to look up their meanings: *embraces, assumption, decriminalizing* (para. 4); *severity* (8); *utterly* (9); *intoxicated* (10); *suburban* (19); *extensive* (20).

### READ CRITICALLY

1. What evidence do the Gogeks include to defend the point that "criminal addicts are severely addicted, not occasional users"?

2. Why might middle-class people see those in prison for drugs as being "much like themselves"? Do you think the authors provide enough support for this notion?

3. One way the Gogeks consider opposing arguments is through the question "Why fill our prisons with people whose only crime is doing drugs?" How would they answer this question?

4. How do the Gogeks use the concept of denial to support their argument?

5. Overall, did the Gogeks' argument convince you? Why or why not?

### WRITE

**TIP** For a sample argument paragraph, see page 227.

**WRITE A PARAGRAPH:** Write a paragraph about one issue presented in this essay—for example, the view that middle-class people do not understand the problems associated with criminal drug offenders. You might elaborate on, clarify, or refute arguments made by the Gogeks.

**WRITE AN ESSAY:** Imagine that your state is facing a similar ballot question—one that will decriminalize illegal drugs. Like the Gogeks, write an editorial, an essay to be published in your local newspaper. In your essay, expand on the points that the Gogeks make or take the opposite position and argue in favor of such a measure. You may use personal experience, information from this essay, or information from another reading to support your position. If you wish, include any ideas you developed for Summarize and Respond.

If you have already argued for or against decriminalization in response to the Bernstein piece, here's a possible alternative: Compare and contrast Bernstein's and the Gogeks' argumentation strategies in terms of how well the writers make and support their main points, consider opposing views, and engage you as a reader. (You may think of other points to compare.) Overall, which essay do you think is more effective?

## Pairing 2: English Immersion: Yes or No?

*Lincoln J. Tamayo*

# A "Yes" Vote Will Benefit Kids

Lincoln J. Tamayo emigrated to the United States from Cuba with his parents and grandmother when he was a boy. Tamayo, who learned English as a second language, became a strong supporter of a 2002 Massachusetts referendum (Question 2) to place non-English-speaking public-school students in immersion programs instead of in traditional bilingual education. (With English immersion, all teaching materials and instruction are in English; in bilingual education, students who are not proficient in English are taught in both their native language and English.) As the principal of Chelsea High School in Chelsea, Massachusetts, Tamayo says that he saw "far too many cases of children going through a second and a third year without hearing a word of good English in the classroom." He left his post at the school to serve as the chairman of English for the Children of Massachusetts, a group in favor of the referendum.

"A 'Yes' Vote Will Benefit Kids" is an editorial that appeared in the *Boston Globe* (October 2002) together with an opposing editorial by Tim Duncan (Duncan's piece appears on p. 645). In his editorial Tamayo argues that the referendum would benefit immigrant students. The referendum, known as Question 2, passed with strong public support in November 2002.

GUIDING QUESTION
Is Tamayo's evidence in favor of Question 2 compelling?

My parents and I emigrated[1] here from Cuba. Though we are proud of our   1
heritage and our first language, we have always understood that success in this country is inextricably[2] tied to a command of English. The faster that command is achieved, the better.

■ **IDEA JOURNAL** Do you agree that success in the United States is tied closely to a command of English? What do your own experiences suggest?

As a high school principal in Chelsea (where almost 70 percent of the   2
students speak a language other than English at home) I witnessed the disastrous consequences of a failed policy of transitional bilingual[3] education that has ill-served generations of immigrant students in Massachusetts.

[1] **emigrated:** left a country

[2] **inextricably:** closely

[3] **bilingual:** involving two languages

■ **TEACHING TIP** If you plan to have students read both this editorial and the one by Tim Duncan that follows it, ask them to envision a debate between the two writers. Based on the way the writers make their points, who do students think would win the debate and why? Prompt them to notice such features as tone, authority, and evidence.

**SUMMARIZE:** Briefly, and in your own words, summarize Tamayo's position.

*Answers will vary.*

This is why I left Chelsea in order to lead the ballot question campaign     3
to change our bilingual education laws.

The bilingual education law passed in August by the Legislature will en-     4
sure that almost nothing changes or improves the education of Spanish-
speaking children, who are most likely to be enrolled in bilingual education
programs. Too many of these students will remain trapped in Spanish-
language classrooms for years while learning English very slowly, if at all.

Because of transitional bilingual education, too many Spanish-speaking     5
students are segregated[4] from their English-speaking schoolmates, and this
has contributed significantly to the abysmal[5] educational results for Hispanic students in Massachusetts: the lowest MCAS[6] scores and the highest
dropout rates among all major racial/ethnic groups.

It is time to bring sense into the education of our immigrant and non-     6
English-speaking children. The faster and the more intensely we teach them
English, under the guidance of trained and caring teachers, the sooner these
students will be able to benefit from the educational opportunities that lead
to skilled jobs, higher education, and full participation in our society.

We acquire the ability to communicate by instinct. Thus the learning of     7
a second language is accomplished most easily and effectively in our early
years, when the instinct to communicate is most readily manifested.[7] When
I entered kindergarten in Florida I could not speak English, but with just
two months of good English-language education I began to communicate
well. Tens of thousands of young Cuban immigrants like me learned English
in American classrooms in similar fashion. It is absurd to think that Spanish-
speaking children entering kindergarten or first grade in Massachusetts
need to wait three or four years to participate in regular classes with their
native English-speaking classmates, as claimed by bilingual education "experts."

**REFLECT:** Why does Tamayo put the word "experts" in quotation marks?

*Possible answer: to suggest doubt about their expertise*

Indeed, these "experts" would prefer we ignore the fact that in Califor-     8
nia, where a similar ballot question passed in 1998, statewide test scores indicate that students immersed in English are three times more likely to be
successful on English-language tests than those still attending holdout bilingual education programs, where subjects are taught in the native language.

Three outrageous misrepresentations commonly made by our oppo-     9
nents must be dismissed.

1. Opponents of the ballot question say it prohibits a child's native lan-     10
guage from being used at all in English immersion classrooms, and that
teachers will be sued if they speak a word of any other language in the classroom. That is pure demagoguery.[8]

**SUMMARIZE:** After reading paragraphs 10–12, summarize Tamayo's views on how Question 2 will affect teachers.

*Answers will vary.*

Nothing in Question 2 prohibits a child's native language from being     11
used in a classroom to clarify a new lesson or to place a lesson in appropriate context when necessary. Question 2 also allows waivers[9] for native-
language academic instruction for older students who might have serious
difficulty in quickly acquiring strong English skills.

[4] **segregated:** separated

[5] **abysmal:** terrible

[6] **MCAS:** a test that Massachusetts high-school students must pass in order to receive a diploma; it stands for Massachusetts Comprehensive Assessment System

[7] **manifested:** apparent

[8] **demagoguery:** appeals to people's emotions or prejudices

[9] **waivers:** permission (in this case)

Question 2 does allow for suits against teachers and administrators who 12 *willfully and repeatedly* violate the law by providing (in the absence of waivers) all or almost all instruction and teaching materials in their students' native languages.

2. The new bilingual education "reform" bill that legislators say will 13 give school districts local choice of educational programs is in reality a shallow cover for protecting the supremacy of the same old native-language classes defended by the bilingual education bureaucracy. Are we to believe that the large urban school districts in Massachusetts, dominated by this bureaucracy, will voluntarily choose the most promising and effective programs that focus on the early teaching of English?

3. Question 2 is not anti-immigrant or racist. As an immigrant, I know 14 firsthand that there is nothing more pro-immigrant than to provide a child with the very foundation of success here — a command of English as quickly as possible.

Politicians have had years to make reforms in our bilingual education 15 laws, but they have repeatedly failed to do so. It is time for voters to do the right thing by voting yes on Question 2.

> "This essay made me aware of a problem in our educational system I would never have thought of because English is my first language."
> —Michelle Bostick, Student

**IDENTIFY:** Underline the topic sentence of this paragraph.

## SUMMARIZE AND RESPOND

In your reading journal or elsewhere, summarize the main point of "A 'Yes' Vote Will Benefit Kids." Then go back and check off support for this main idea. Next, write a brief summary of the essay. Finally, jot down a brief response to the reading. Do you agree with Tamayo's position? What past experiences or readings can you offer as support for your position?

## CHECK YOUR COMPREHENSION

1.  An alternate title for this essay could be
    a.  "Learn to Succeed."
    b.  "Segregating Schools."
    c.  "Bilingual Education Is the Path to Academic Achievement."
    d.  "A Sensible Solution: English Language Immersion."

2.  The main idea of this essay is that
    a.  transitional bilingual education has been proven to work.
    b.  Hispanic students have the highest dropout rates among all major racial/ethnic groups.
    c.  the sooner and more intense English language instruction is, the quicker students will benefit academically.
    d.  three years is an appropriate period for students to be in bilingual classrooms before moving to English-speaking classrooms.

3.  What does Tamayo predict will happen if the current bilingual education system does not change?

a. Many Spanish-speaking students will remain trapped in Spanish language classrooms.

b. Non-English-speaking students will continue to benefit from instruction in their own language.

c. The dropout rate for Hispanic students will decrease.

d. The conflict among politicians, teachers, and voters will disappear so that all can focus on making improvements within the current system.

4. If you are unfamiliar with the following words, use a dictionary to look up their meanings: *heritage* (para.1); *disastrous, transitional, ill-served* (2); *immersed* (8); *shallow, supremacy, bureaucracy* (13).

### READ CRITICALLY

1. What gives Tamayo authority to write about this topic?

2. Create a slogan that Tamayo might use as part of his campaign to get voters to vote "Yes" on Question 2.

3. How does Tamayo use the effects of transitional bilingual educational classes to argue his position?

4. What is the function of paragraph 9?

5. How does Tamayo address the opposing arguments? Are his approach and use of evidence effective?

### WRITE

**TIP** For a sample argument paragraph, see page 227.

**WRITE A PARAGRAPH:** Write a paragraph that elaborates on or argues against one point Tamayo has made in his essay—for example, that we acquire the ability to communicate by instinct. You might draw on your personal experience or another reading.

**WRITE AN ESSAY:** Imagine that your state is facing a similar ballot question—one that will require English immersion for all students for whom English is not their native language. Like Tamayo, write an editorial, an essay to be published in your local newspaper. In your essay, expand on the points that Tamayo makes or take the opposite position and argue against such a ballot question. You may use personal experience, information from Tamayo's essay, or information from another reading to support your position. If you wish, include any ideas you developed for Summarize and Respond.

*Tim Duncan*

# To Avoid a Failed System, Vote "No"

Tim Duncan recently served as the chairman of the Committee for Fairness to Children and Teachers. The Massachusetts group formed in opposition to Question 2, a 2002 state referendum requiring public schools to place non-English-speaking students in English immersion classes rather than in traditional bilingual education programs. (For a definition of these programs, see p. 641.) Urging voters to reject a ballot initiative that he said would force schools to adopt a uniform statewide program instead of allowing each school district to choose the course best for its own students, Duncan said, "We trust our own communities [ . . . ] to make these decisions for us."

In the following article, which was paired with the preceding piece by Lincoln J. Tamayo, Duncan argues that the referendum would not serve the interests of Massachusetts children. The referendum was approved by a wide margin in November 2002.

GUIDING QUESTION
What evidence does Duncan present in his argument against Question 2?

1   As if guiding our kids through their school years wasn't daunting[1] enough for parents, on November 5 our children's futures will be on the ballot. Question 2 will decide whether the school my son and his friends attend can continue to teach them—as they have successfully been doing—using the methods that their teachers and we, as parents, have chosen.

■ **IDEA JOURNAL** In what ways can education help children get "the best possible start in life"?

2   All parents understand the value of kids getting the best possible start in life. The education our children get today will help them fulfill their dreams in the future. With that in mind, I'll be voting "no" on Question 2. Here's why:

3   Question 2 would undo valuable education reforms passed by the Legislature only a few months ago with broad bipartisan[2] support. Those reforms will improve the way children learn English; allow greater local control; maintain parental choice; and provide strict accountability for every school district in Massachusetts. Instead, Massachusetts would be left with a "sink-or-swim" scheme imported from California that fails kids, threatens teachers, and costs taxpayers millions.

IDENTIFY: Underline the sentence in paragraph 3 that summarizes Duncan's argument against Question 2.

4   The flaws in the system that Question 2 would impose are numerous, but perhaps the most serious is that it has been a proven failure in California.

5   According to the California Department of Education, fewer than 20 percent of the children in the system have graduated into mainstream classes in each of the four years since a similar ballot question was passed there.

■ **TEACHING TIP** You might point out how Duncan addresses the opposing point of view. For example, in paragraph 6, he mentions what the proponents of Question 2 claim about a similar measure in California and then counters that claim. In paragraph 11, he quotes an opponent about Question 2's potential effects on teachers and then in the next paragraph addresses the opponent's view.

6   Rather than staying in segregated classes for one year, as proponents claim, over one million children in California have been left behind, and are forced to stay in bilingual[3] classes far longer than kids do in Massachusetts.

---

[1] **daunting:** difficult

[2] **bipartisan:** supported by both Democrats and Republicans

[3] **bilingual:** involving two languages

For example, close to 80 percent of English-learning children in Boston are able to do ordinary class work in English within three years or less.

REFLECT: Is Duncan's "financial" argument convincing? Why or why not?
*Answers will vary.*

We simply can't afford to import a failed system to Massachusetts. Nor can we afford the $125 million price tag that Question 2 carries. A task force of educators and professors from MIT, Boston College, and Salem State has studied the "immersion" system that would be introduced if the ballot measure passed. Based on official figures from California and Massachusetts, they estimate that taxpayers would be left with a $125 million tab for the new system.

The Massachusetts Taxpayers Foundation agrees that there would be additional costs to the state. At a time when the deteriorating[4] economy is forcing our state to cut programs for families, seniors, and children, as well as aid to towns and cities, we simply can't afford this costly experiment.

Children and taxpayers will not be the only groups adversely[5] affected by the passage of Question 2. Hidden away in the fine print of the law is a provision that would allow teachers to be sued if they teach a struggling child in their native language. Let me cite the section of the proposed law to make this point clear.

SUMMARIZE: In your own words, explain the law.
*Answers will vary.*

The law itself says, "The parent or legal guardian of any school child shall have legal standing to sue for enforcement of the provisions of this chapter, and if successful shall be awarded reasonable attorney's fees, costs, and compensatory[6] damages."

Ron Unz, the California businessman who is bankrolling[7] Question 2, is quoted in the media as saying "[Teachers] would have to pay out of their own pocket. And I think there's a perfectly reasonable possibility some of them might be driven into personal bankruptcy."

> "Duncan's argument was so effective with its facts and examples that I was heated up and ready to vote no."
>
> —Amy Cork, Student

Despite what Unz thinks, we in Massachusetts have greater respect for our teachers, and understand the incredibly difficult job they do. We've no doubt that most of the people in our state would rather they were allowed to focus on teaching children English, not fighting off lawsuits.

Labels and barbs[8] have been tossed around during the campaign. The initiative has been branded "anti-immigrant" and Unz's racist comments about the secretary of education (who disagrees with the question's proponents) have not helped keep the campaign focused on the harsh realities of Question 2.

Indeed, similar initiatives passed in California and Arizona because of the deep pockets of Unz and his ability to keep the debate away from the true facts surrounding Question 2's immersion system.

REFLECT: Why do you think Duncan mentions Ted Kennedy and President Bush?
*Possible answer: This shows that both liberals and conservatives oppose the initiative.*

But the coalition arrayed[9] against Question 2 in Massachusetts is broad, and in the cold light of day, we understand the immense damage the initiative would inflict. Teachers and parents, labor and business, religious and political leaders alike—from Ted Kennedy to President Bush—oppose this

[4] **deteriorating:** weakening

[5] **adversely:** negatively

[6] **compensatory:** suitable to a loss or pain suffered

[7] **bankrolling:** funding

[8] **barbs:** insults

[9] **arrayed:** arranged

initiative. Why would people from such diverse groups agree that passing Question 2 would be a disaster for Massachusetts?

Quite simply because it fails kids, threatens teachers, and hits taxpayers    16 in the pocket. Vote for our kids, teachers, and our economy. Vote no on Question 2.

### SUMMARIZE AND RESPOND

In your reading journal or elsewhere, summarize the main point of "To Avoid a Failed System, Vote 'No.'" Then go back and check off support for this main idea. Next, write a brief summary of the essay. Finally, jot down a brief response to the reading. Do you agree or disagree with Duncan's position on Question 2? Why?

### CHECK YOUR COMPREHENSION

1. An alternate title for this essay could be
   a. "Question 2 Provides No Answers."
   b. "The Coalition's Challenge."
   c. "A Taxing System."
   d. "English First."

2. The main idea of this essay is that
   a. passing Question 2 will help all students pass.
   b. passing Question 2 will help bilingual students to be quickly and successfully immersed into the school system.
   c. passing Question 2 will have negative effects.
   d. passing Question 2 requires a united effort by teachers and taxpayers.

3. Perhaps the most serious flaw of Question 2, according to Duncan, is that
   a. it is anti-immigrant.
   b. it is anti-teacher.
   c. it does not have bipartisan support.
   d. a similar measure has been a failure in California.

4. If you are unfamiliar with the following words, use a dictionary to look up their meanings: *mainstream* (para. 5); *proponents* (6); *immersion* (7); *provision* (10); *incredibly* (12); *coalition* (15).

### READ CRITICALLY

1. What do you think Duncan is trying to achieve in the first two paragraphs?

2.  Why and how does Duncan use what happened in California as support for his main point? Is his approach effective?

3.  In paragraph 7, what does Duncan mean when he writes that "We simply can't afford to import a failed system to Massachusetts"?

4.  How does Duncan use Question 2's possible effects on teachers as an argument against the measure?

5.  Duncan presents three reasons to support his position. Based on your reading, does he offer solid evidence for each? Explain.

### ■ WRITE

■ **TIP** For a sample argument paragraph, see page 227.

**WRITE A PARAGRAPH:** Write a paragraph that argues for or against one of the points Duncan presents in this essay—for example, that teachers should not have to suffer from consequences of a measure like Question 2.

**WRITE AN ESSAY:** Imagine that your state is facing a similar ballot question—one that will require English immersion for all students for whom English is not their native language. Like Duncan, write an editorial, an essay to be published in your local newspaper. In your essay, expand on the points that Duncan makes or take the opposite position and argue in favor of such a measure. You may use personal experience, information from Duncan's essay, or information from another reading to support your position. If you wish, include any ideas you developed for Summarize and Respond.

If you have already argued for or against English immersion in response to the Tamayo reading, here's a possible alternative: Compare and contrast Tamayo's and Duncan's argumentation strategies in terms of how well the writers make and support their points, consider opposing views, and engage you as a reader. (You may think of other points to compare.) Overall, which editorial do you think is more effective?

# Useful Appendices

## Appendix A

### *The Basics of Writing an Essay*

**NOTE TO TEACHERS:** This appendix is an abbreviated version of the essay sections in Part One (Chapters 1–7) of this book. For ease of learning and instruction, Part One combines coverage of paragraphs and essays wherever the process is the same or where students can benefit from seeing how a paragraph and an essay compare (for example, Chapter 2 shows how the same topic is narrowed for a paragraph and for an essay). However, we realize that some users prefer to have students read about the essay as a separate form after students have learned to write paragraphs. Therefore, this appendix covers just the basics of essay writing.

The process of writing an essay is the same as the process of writing a paragraph:

---

#### Generate Ideas and State Your Main Point

**Consider:** What is my purpose in writing? Given this purpose, what interests me? Who will read this? What do they need to know?

- Narrow and explore your topic (Chapter 2).
- Express your main point (in essays, this is your thesis statement; see Chapter 3).
- Support your main point (Chapter 4).

---

#### Plan

**Consider:** How can I organize my ideas effectively for my readers?

- Arrange your ideas and make an outline (Chapter 5).

---

#### Draft

**Consider:** How can I show my readers what I mean?

- Write a draft, including an introduction that will interest your readers, a strong conclusion, and a title (Chapter 6).

---

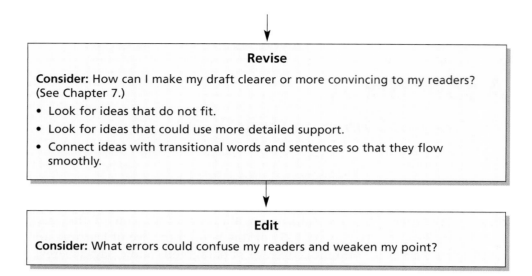

**Revise**

**Consider:** How can I make my draft clearer or more convincing to my readers? (See Chapter 7.)

- Look for ideas that do not fit.
- Look for ideas that could use more detailed support.
- Connect ideas with transitional words and sentences so that they flow smoothly.

**Edit**

**Consider:** What errors could confuse my readers and weaken my point?

The following diagram shows how the parts of an essay correspond to the parts of a paragraph.

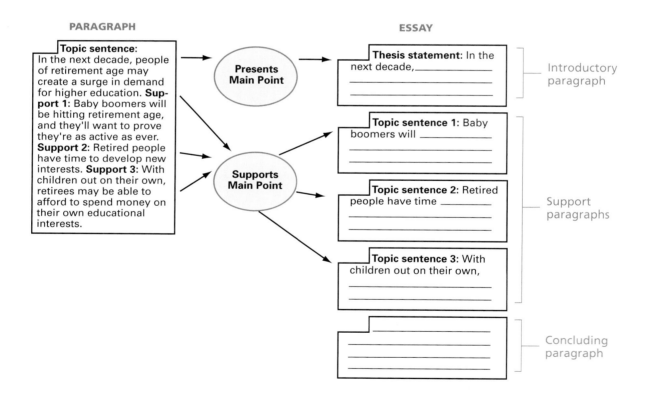

**PARAGRAPH**

**Topic sentence:** In the next decade, people of retirement age may create a surge in demand for higher education. **Support 1:** Baby boomers will be hitting retirement age, and they'll want to prove they're as active as ever. **Support 2:** Retired people have time to develop new interests. **Support 3:** With children out on their own, retirees may be able to afford to spend money on their own educational interests.

**Presents Main Point**

**Supports Main Point**

**ESSAY**

**Thesis statement:** In the next decade,_____ _____ _____

Introductory paragraph

**Topic sentence 1:** Baby boomers will _____ _____ _____

**Topic sentence 2:** Retired people have time _____ _____ _____

**Topic sentence 3:** With children out on their own, _____ _____

Support paragraphs

_____ _____ _____ _____

Concluding paragraph

The rest of this appendix focuses on the essay, presenting more details on the steps described in the flowchart above.

# Narrow and Explore Your Topic

## Narrow Your Topic

Because you have already written paragraphs, you know what the process is: dividing your general topic into smaller parts that you might write about. When you are writing an essay, your topic can be a little broader than for a paragraph, because essays are longer than paragraphs and allow you to develop more ideas. But be careful: Most of the extra length in an essay should come from developing ideas in more depth (giving more examples and details, and explaining what you mean), not from covering a broader topic.

Read these examples of how a general topic was narrowed to a more specific topic for an essay, and an even more specific topic for a paragraph.

| ASSIGNED GENERAL TOPIC | NARROWED ESSAY TOPIC | NARROWED PARAGRAPH TOPIC |
|---|---|---|
| Drug abuse ⟶ | How alcoholism affects family life ⟶ | How alcoholism affects a family's budget |
| Public service opportunities ⟶ | Volunteering at a homeless shelter ⟶ | My first impression of the homeless shelter |
| A personal goal ⟶ | Getting healthy ⟶ | Eating the right foods |
| A great vacation ⟶ | A family camping trip ⟶ | What I learned on our family camping trip |

## Explore Your Topic

Use prewriting techniques to come up with ideas at any time during your writing: to find a topic, to get ideas for what you want to say about it, and to support your ideas. Ask yourself: What interests me about this topic? What do I know? What do I want to say?

Then use one or more of the idea-generating techniques listed below to find the answers. (For examples of these techniques, see pp. 23–29 of Chapter 2.)

**SIX PREWRITING TECHNIQUES**

1. Freewriting
2. Listing/brainstorming
3. Questioning
4. Discussing
5. Clustering/mapping
6. Keeping a journal

---

### CRITICAL THINKING: NARROWING AND EXPLORING YOUR TOPIC

**FOCUS**

Read the general topic you have chosen or been assigned.

**ASK YOURSELF**

- How can I divide this topic?
- Which of these parts would be a good narrowed topic?
- What do I already know about this topic?
- What do I want to write about?

**WRITE**

- Narrow to find a good topic and then use prewriting techniques to explore your ideas about the topic.

## Write a Thesis Statement

Every good piece of writing has a **main idea**—what the writer wants to get across to the readers about the topic, or the writer's position on the topic. If you have narrowed and explored your topic, you may already have a sense of your main idea. Clearly and definitely conveying your main idea to your readers is fundamental to your success as a writer. If your readers don't know from the start what your main idea is, they will not read the rest of what you have written with any clear thought in mind. (For more on developing and writing thesis statements, see Chapter 3, p. 31).

A **thesis statement** in an essay expresses the writer's main idea; it includes both the topic and the main point the writer wants to make about that topic. In many essays, the thesis statement is either the first or the last sentence of the first paragraph.

**EXAMPLE:**

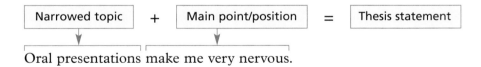

Oral presentations make me very nervous.

**BASICS OF A GOOD THESIS STATEMENT**

- It fits the size of the assignment.
- It contains a single main point or position about the narrowed topic.
- It is specific.
- It is something you can show, explain, or prove.
- It is a forceful statement written with confidence.

| ASSIGNED GENERAL TOPIC | NARROWED ESSAY TOPIC |
|---|---|
| Drug abuse ⟶ | How alcoholism affects family life |

**POSSIBLE THESIS STATEMENT:**

Alcoholism can destroy family life.

[The essay might go on to present several ways in which alcoholism negatively affects the family.]

## CRITICAL THINKING: WRITING A THESIS STATEMENT

**FOCUS**
- Read your narrowed topic.
- Decide what is important to you, personally, about the topic.

**ASK YOURSELF**
- What do I want to show, explain, or prove about the topic?
- How can I state my topic and my main point forcefully and confidently?
- Will the main point I'm considering fit the assignment?
- Can I get behind the main point I'm considering and support it for my readers?

**WRITE**
- Write a forceful, confident thesis statement that includes your topic and your main point about that topic.

# Support Your Thesis

**Support** is the collection of examples, facts, or evidence that show, explain, or prove your main point. **Primary support** consists of the major ideas that back up your main point, and **secondary support** explains (or provides details to back up) your primary support.

**BASICS OF GOOD SUPPORT**

- **It relates to your main point.** The purpose of support is to show, explain, or prove your main point, so use support that is directly related to your main point.
- **It thinks of your readers.** Create support that will show readers what you mean.
- **It is detailed and specific.** Give readers enough detail, particularly through examples, so that they can see what you mean.

In an essay, the primary support for the thesis statement is usually the topic sentence for each of the body (or support) paragraphs. The body of each support paragraph provides secondary support for the thesis because it backs up the primary support.

Detailed, specific support is essential. You could craft the best thesis statement in the world, but if you do not provide adequate, convincing support, your readers will not understand the main point you want to get across. Do not hesitate to try out ideas that may be good support for your thesis: You can always get rid of any that you decide are weak or not related to your point. (For more on supporting a thesis, see Chapter 4, p. 46).

---

**CRITICAL THINKING: SUPPORTING YOUR POINT**

**FOCUS**
- Read your thesis statement.

**ASK YOURSELF**
- What do my readers need to know?
- What facts, details, or observations will help me show, explain, or prove my main point to readers?

**WRITE**
- Use a prewriting technique to generate possible support.
- Select the best primary support from your prewriting.
- Add supporting details.

---

## Make a Plan

From writing paragraphs, you already know that once you have the support you want to use, you need to organize that support so that it has the most impact on the reader. Common methods of organizing ideas are by **time** (chronological), **space**, or **importance**. (For more on these ordering strategies, see Chapter 5, p. 56.)

When you have decided how to order your primary support points, make a more detailed plan for your essay. A good, visual way to plan a draft is to arrange your ideas in an outline. An **outline** for an essay lists the thesis statement, the primary support points for the thesis statement, and secondary supporting details for each of the support points. It provides a map of your ideas that you can follow as you write.

The primary support points for your thesis statement will become topic sentences for paragraphs that will make up the body of the essay. These paragraphs will consist of details that support the topic sentence. To remind yourself of the differences between paragraph and essay structure, see the diagram on page 650 of this appendix.

The outline below is for a typical five-paragraph essay: The introductory paragraph contains the thesis statement; three body paragraphs support the thesis statement; the fifth paragraph is the conclusion. However, essays may include more or fewer than five paragraphs, depending on the topic.

**Thesis statement** (part of introductory paragraph 1)
  A. **Topic sentence for support point 1** (paragraph 2)
    1. **Supporting details for support point 1**
    2.
    3.

**B. Topic sentence for support point 2** (paragraph 3)

    1. **Supporting details for support point 2**

    2.

    3.

**C. Topic sentence for support point 3** (paragraph 4)

    1. **Supporting details for support point 3**

    2.

    3.

**Concluding paragraph** (paragraph 5)

### CRITICAL THINKING: MAKING A PLAN

**FOCUS**

Reread your thesis statement. Also, reread your prewriting or any other ideas you have jotted down about your topic.

**ASK YOURSELF**

- What would be the best way to organize my support points? Time order? Space order? Order of importance?
- What point should come first? What next? What after that?
- Will this organization help me get my point across to my readers?

**WRITE**

Write a plan (an outline) that shows how you want to arrange your points.

## Draft Your Essay

Drafting an essay is very much like drafting a paragraph, but because an essay is longer, three elements become even more important to help your readers understand and follow your point:

- a strong introductory paragraph (sometimes two) that includes your thesis statement and often a preview of what you are going to say in your essay
- a strong conclusion that reminds your readers of your main point and makes an observation based on what you have written
- transitions (both transitional words and transitional sentences) that move your readers smoothly from one idea to the next

**BASICS OF A GOOD DRAFT ESSAY**

- It has an introductory paragraph that draws in readers and includes a thesis statement.
- Its primary support points are topic sentences of paragraphs that each support the thesis statement.

- Its primary support points and secondary supporting details, facts, or examples are arranged in a logical order.
- It has a concluding paragraph that reminds readers of the main point and makes an observation.
- It follows standard essay form and uses complete sentences.

## Write an Introduction

The introduction to your essay should capture your readers' interest and present the main point. Think of your introductory paragraph as a marketing challenge. Ask yourself: How can I sell my essay to readers? You need to market your main point.

The thesis statement is usually either the first or the last sentence in an introductory paragraph.

### BASICS OF A GOOD INTRODUCTION

- It should catch readers' attention.
- It should present the thesis statement.
- It should give readers a clear idea of what the essay will cover.

Here are some common strategies for writing introductions that spark readers' interest. For examples of each of these kinds of introductions, see Chapter 6, pages 71–72.

### Open with a Quote.

A good short quote definitely gets people interested. It must lead naturally into your main point, however, and not be there just for effect. If you start with a quote, make sure that you tell the reader who the speaker is.

### Give an Example or Tell a Story.

People like stories, so opening an essay with a brief, relevant story or example often draws them in.

### Start with a Surprising Fact or Idea.

Surprises capture people's interest. The more unexpected and surprising a fact or idea is, the more likely people are to take notice of it.

### Offer a Strong Opinion or Position.

The stronger the opinion, the more likely it is that people will pay attention. Don't write wimpy introductions! Make your point and shout it!

### Ask a Question.

Starting your essay with a question can encourage readers to continue on to find the answer. But remember: Your question must be one they will care about, and you need to make sure to answer the question through your support.

## Write a Conclusion

The conclusion of your essay is the final chance to make your main point. Because an essay is longer than a paragraph, its conclusion is more than just a final sentence: It is a paragraph that helps the reader recall the main and support points and makes a good final case for the writer's thesis.

**BASICS OF A GOOD ESSAY CONCLUSION**

- It should refer back to the main point.
- It should sum up what has been covered in the essay.
- It should make a further observation or point.

One of the best ways to end an essay is to refer directly to something in the introduction. If you asked a question, re-ask it and answer it. If you started a story, finish it. If you used a quote, use another one—maybe a quote by the same person or maybe one by another person on the same topic. For examples of how the conclusion can refer directly to the introduction, see pages 73–74 of Chapter 6.

## Title Your Essay

Even if your title is the *last* part of the essay you write, it is the *first* thing readers read. Use your title to get your readers' attention and to tell them, in a brief way, what your paper is about. Use vivid, strong, specific words.

**BASICS OF A GOOD ESSAY TITLE**

- It makes people want to read the essay.
- It does not merely repeat the thesis statement.
- It may hint at the main point but does not state it outright.

### CRITICAL THINKING: DRAFTING YOUR ESSAY

**FOCUS**
Review your outline, including your thesis statement and support.

**ASK YOURSELF**
- Does my thesis statement say what I want it to, or do I need to revise it?
- Do my primary support points relate to my thesis statement?

(continued)

- Do I provide supporting details that show, explain, or prove my primary support?
- How should I turn my primary support points into topic sentences for their own paragraphs?
- Is there an introductory technique that might work especially well for my paper's topic and focus?
- What should I say in my concluding paragraph? How can I remind my readers of my main point without just repeating the thesis statement?
- Can I use my introductory technique in my conclusion?
- What observation do I want to make to my readers in my conclusion?
- In my title, how can I get readers' attention and highlight my main point?

**WRITE**

Write a draft essay, including a title.

## Revise Your Essay

**Revising** is changing the ideas in your essay to make your writing clearer, stronger, and more convincing. In other words, it involves looking at the "big picture" and making sure it's the picture you want your readers to "see." When revising, you might add, cut, or change whole sentences or groups of sentences. The process of revising an essay is similar to the process of revising a paragraph: You look at the writing to make sure it has unity, adequate support, and coherence. (For more examples of, and practice with, essay revision, see Chapter 7, pp. 80–81.)

**REVISION STRATEGIES**

- Search for ideas that do not fit.
- Search for ideas that are not as specific or complete as they could be.
- Search for ways to connect ideas so that they flow smoothly from one to the next.
- Search for ways to improve your overall paper.

**FIVE REVISION TIPS**

1. Give yourself a break from your draft (a few hours or a day).
2. Read your draft aloud and listen to your words.
3. Imagine yourself as your reader.
4. Get feedback from a friend, classmate, or colleague (see pp. 81–82 of Chapter 7).
5. Get help from a tutor at your college writing center or lab.

## Revise for Unity

**Unity** in writing means that all the points you make are related to your main point; they are *unified* in support of your main point. As you draft your essay, you may detour from your main point without being aware of it, so check for detours when you revise.

## Revise for Detail and Support

When you revise a paper, look carefully at the support points and supporting details you have developed, and imagine yourself as your reader: Do you have enough information to understand the main point? Are you convinced of the main point?

## Revise for Coherence

Even if you have expressed all of your points and arranged them in a logical order, your writing may still seem choppy, and your ideas may be hard to follow. If so, you need to improve the coherence of your paper.

**Coherence** in writing means that all your points and details connect to form a whole. Individual ideas should be assembled in an order that makes sense and so well connected that they leave readers with a clear overall impression.

Coherence in writing helps readers see how one point leads to another— a piece of writing that lacks coherence can sound like a string of unrelated statements. A good way to make sure that your writing is coherent is to use transitions.

**Transitions** are words, phrases, and sentences that connect your ideas. Use transitions when moving from one main support point to another. Also use them wherever you want to improve the flow of your writing.

---

### CRITICAL THINKING: REVISING YOUR DRAFT ESSAY

**FOCUS**
- After a break, reread your draft with concentration and a fresh perspective.
- If your essay has been reviewed by an instructor or your peers, look over those comments now.

**ASK YOURSELF**
- Did I say what I wanted to say?
- Have I tried to catch readers' attention in my introduction?
- Does the introduction include my thesis statement?
- Do all of the topic sentences support my thesis statement?
- Does everything in each paragraph relate to the topic sentence for that paragraph?
- Do I have enough support for each topic sentence? Can I add any details, examples, or facts?

(continued)

- Does one idea move smoothly to the next?
- Would transitions help?
- Is my support organized in a logical, effective way (for example, by time, space, or order of importance)?
- Does my conclusion remind my readers of my main point? Have I made an observation based on what I've written that ends the essay on a strong note?
- How can I address any concerns or suggestions from my instructor or peers?

**WRITE**

Revise your draft essay, making at least four changes.

**NOTE:** After revising your essay, you should edit it to make sure there are no errors in grammar, spelling, or punctuation. Parts Four through Seven of this book cover editing in detail.

# Appendix B

*How to Make an Oral Presentation*

## Five Surefire Strategies

In college, at work—sometimes even in your everyday life—you will need to make oral presentations. Most people rate public speaking as one of life's most stressful experiences. A number of practical strategies, however, can help you cope with the anxiety that may be caused by this task. Knowing how to prepare for an oral presentation will help you feel confident and in control of the situation.

You have probably witnessed an embarrassing oral presentation, a situation in which the speaker fell apart and the audience felt as uncomfortable as the speaker. The following is an example of such an occurrence.

**SITUATION:** Jean is in the middle of reviewing her presentation notes when she hears herself being introduced. Startled, she gathers her materials into a messy stack of notes and papers, apologizes for not being ready, and walks quickly to the front of the room.

Obviously flustered, she tries to reorganize her notes, shuffling papers, frowning, and sighing loudly. She begins reading her presentation with her head down, speaking quickly and softly. Several people call out, "I can't hear you" or "Speak up."

Jean clears her throat and starts from the beginning. She's so rattled that her voice quivers and then breaks. She looks up, red in the face, and says, "Sorry. I'm really nervous."

She continues but moves too quickly from one point to the next because she doesn't want to bore people. She forgets to introduce or summarize any of her points, so the audience finds it difficult to follow her speech. People start to tune out.

Aware that she's not doing very well, Jean nervously fiddles with her hair while speaking. She reads quickly and with no emphasis, thinking that the sooner she gets through this, the sooner she can sit down. The words that looked so good when she wrote them sound stupid and awkward when she says them aloud.

As Jean turns to the second page, she realizes that her papers are out of order. There is an awkward silence as she searches desperately for the right page. She finally finds it and begins again. Soon she comes to a word that she can't read, and she has to stop again to figure it out. Still fiddling with her hair, she now looks as if she's about to pull it out.

Jean skips the word and continues. Her only goal now is to finish. But she's run out of time because of her fumbling and because her presentation was too long to begin with. The warning signal goes off, indicating that one minute remains.

This is the last straw for Jean. She looks up, bright red and nearly in tears, and says, "I guess I've run out of time. I only got through one of my points. I don't have time for what I really wanted to say." She grabs her papers and returns to her seat.

Jean sits in total misery, sure that everyone is looking at her. She can't listen to anyone else's presentation. All she can do is stare at the floor and wait impatiently for the moment she can escape from the room.

**ANALYSIS:** Jean's presentation was not successful because of some common pitfalls she could easily have avoided. She wasn't adequately prepared, she was obviously very nervous, she hadn't structured her presentation to make her points clear to her audience, she hadn't practiced reading her presentation aloud, and she fled at the end. If she had practiced five simple strategies for making an oral presentation, her experience would have been much less painful, and her presentation would have been much better.

## Strategy 1.  Be Prepared

Jean's first mistake was not being well prepared. She wasn't psychologically ready to speak, and she hadn't organized the materials for her presentation properly. Because she was busy reviewing her notes at the last minute, she was caught off guard. Her papers got messed up, she was startled, and she was off to a bad start.

### *Organize Your Notes.*

Before you go into the room where you are giving your presentation, make sure all of your notes are in order. Number all pages or note cards so you can quickly reorganize them if they get mixed up, and carry all of your materials in a folder.

If you want to review your key points while waiting to make your presentation, try to run through them in your head. Leave the folder closed. If you need to refresh your memory on a particular point, open the folder and carefully go through your notes until you find the answer.

### *Use Your Energy.*

Be aware of when your turn is coming, and focus on being calm. Tell yourself that you're prepared and you know what you're doing. Breathe deeply. Don't worry if your heart is beating hard and fast; that's normal. Nervous energy before a performance of any sort is natural and can make you a more engaging speaker. You just need to learn to channel that energy and make it work for you. Use that adrenaline to fuel your enthusiasm for your topic.

### Build Yourself Up.

Keep breathing normally. However silly it may seem, remind yourself of your strengths and repeat them in your head as your turn to speak approaches: "I know what I'm talking about." "I look good today." "I have a good voice." Remember that your audience isn't waiting for you to fail. Most people understand the stress of oral presentations and are sympathetic. Your audience wants you to do well.

### Carry Yourself Like Royalty.

When it's your turn, take a deep breath, calmly pick up your folder, and walk to the front of the room. Walk slowly, stand straight, and focus on projecting a confident image. Remember that you're in control.

## Strategy 2.  Act with Confidence

Jean's second mistake was not acting with confidence and authority. She was visibly upset as she tried to get her notes in order, and when she did start, she spoke too softly to be heard. When her voice broke, she apologized to the audience and announced her nervousness. Practicing several techniques would have made her appear confident and in control.

### Take Your Time.

After you've walked to the front of the room, take a few moments to calmly arrange your notes and papers before you begin. Relax. The timing of your presentation won't start until you begin speaking, so make sure your materials are where you need them before beginning. Remember that even professional speakers need a few moments to lay out their notes and compose themselves.

### Take Command and Greet Your Audience.

When you're ready to begin, stand up straight and look up and out at the audience. Remember that you are in command of the room. Pause for a few seconds to let people know you're about to begin, and wait for them to give you their attention. When you have their attention, take a deep breath and begin.

Smile and greet the audience, surveying the room as you do so. Your greeting should be simple, like "Good morning and thank you all for coming." If some people in the audience don't know you, be sure to introduce yourself. Don't forget to smile: It will relax you as well as your audience.

### Slow Down and Speak Up.

Make sure that you speak slowly, clearly, and loudly. If you're nervous, you will tend to speak too quickly, so try to slow down your speech a bit. Try to project your voice so that the people in the last row can hear you. It may feel as if you're shouting, but you won't be. Don't be embarrassed to ask if everyone can hear you. Experienced speakers often break the ice by encouraging an audience to tell them if they need to speak up.

## Strategy 3. Structure Your Presentation

Jean's third mistake was not giving her presentation a clear structure, which would have made it easy for her audience to follow her key points. Your presentation should include lots of verbal cues that let people know when you're making a point, what it is, and when you're moving to another point. The structure of an oral presentation must be much more obvious than the structure of a written paper so that people can understand as they are listening.

### Limit Your Topic.

Choose a manageable topic for the time allotted, and limit the number of points you plan to make. Listening is hard work, and most people can absorb only a few key points from a speech. In any presentation, try to limit yourself to three key points, and be sure to support each of them with concrete examples. When you give more complex presentations, you may need to use visual aids—such as transparencies or slides—that will allow you to illustrate and reinforce your points.

### State Your Thesis and Preview Your Key Points.

Let your audience know what your topic is and the main point you are going to make about it. State your thesis (your main point) slowly so that people understand the purpose of your presentation. Tell them: "My topic today is _____," and "I will be arguing [or showing, or explaining] _____."

Tell your audience about the structure of your presentation by giving them a preview of your key points. You might say: "There are three major points I'd like to make about _____. First I'll present _____. Second I'll discuss _____. And my third point will be _____. This presentation should take approximately ten minutes, and there will be time for questions at the end."

### Use Transitions to Move from Point to Point.

Use transitions to let your audience know when you're finished with one point and are about to make another. In your preview, you told the audience what your key points would be. As you speak, you should give clear verbal cues when introducing and summarizing each point. Here is one way to do so.

- "My first point is _____."
- Give examples/explanation.

- Repeat or summarize the first point (to remind the audience of what it is and to let them know you're about to move to another point).
- "My second point is _____."
- Give examples/explanation.
- Repeat or summarize the second point.
- "My third and final point is _____."
- Give examples/explanation.
- Repeat or summarize the third point.

### Conclude by Reviewing Your Key Points.

Let people know when you're coming to the end of your presentation by using a verbal cue such as *in conclusion, to summarize,* or *to review.* Then review your key points. Conclude with a simple, strong sentence that restates the overall purpose of your presentation—the main point you want to make.

## Strategy 4. Practice Your Presentation

Like many people, Jean made the mistake of not adequately practicing her presentation. The right kind of practice would have helped her avoid the following problems: fidgeting with her hair, writing a presentation that sounded awkward when presented orally, losing her place in the middle of her talk, puzzling over her notes, and running out of time.

Even professional speakers practice their speeches. You should allow plenty of time to practice giving your oral presentation.

### Practice Aloud.

Phrases and sentences that sound good in writing often sound awkward when spoken. Read your presentation aloud—several times—to make sure that it sounds right. You'll feel silly, but do it anyway. Stop and make changes when a sentence sounds awkward. Be aware of any distracting habits you may have, such as interrupting your speech with expressions like "uh" or "you know."

Practicing aloud will also help you remember your key points. Practice your speech again and again until you feel comfortable with it. Be sure to practice aloud a final time on the day of your presentation.

### Practice in Front of a Mirror.

You need to see what you look like as you give your presentation, so try practicing in front of a mirror. This may make you feel even sillier than just saying the speech aloud, but it will also make you feel much more confident when you actually give the presentation.

- Stand straight and look up at the mirror frequently. Pretend you are looking out at an audience.

- Be aware of any distracting habits you have while speaking, such as fidgeting with your hair, as Jean did. Some people shift their weight from one leg to another, or sway back and forth, or stand with their legs far apart in a military stance.

- Practice keeping your hands still, except when you want to gesture or point to something for emphasis. You can hold your notes at your side or in front of you, or you can place them on a table or podium.

- Practice keeping your feet slightly apart and your weight evenly distributed. Don't shift from side to side or rock.

- If you know you will be seated when giving your presentation, you should sit in a chair while practicing. Don't jiggle your feet or swing your legs. Keep your feet flat on the floor.

### Practice Working with Your Material.

Figure out in advance how you will handle your notes, papers, and material such as PowerPoint slides. After you've said your presentation aloud a couple of times to get the wording right, decide whether you will work with the whole presentation written out, an outline, or notecards. Some people prefer to work with just an outline and PowerPoint slides.

**THE WHOLE PRESENTATION:** If you think you need the whole presentation — written out word for word — to read from, that's fine, but you still have to practice. You have to be comfortable enough with the written version to be able to deliver it naturally, not as if you're reading, and to look up at your audience without fear of losing your place. If your eyes are glued to the page, you'll lose your audience's attention.

In addition to practicing, you should format your presentation so it will be easy for you to find your place.

- Highlight your key points in color or by underlining so you'll be able to find your place quickly if you get lost.

- Double-space your presentation so you won't have trouble reading it.

- Use a large type size. If you must handwrite your presentation, make sure that you can read your handwriting.

- Write the numbers of your key points in the margin (next to the paragraphs where you introduce those points), write *conc.* next to your conclusion, and so on.

- Make sure your pages are clearly numbered so they can easily be put in order if you mix them up.

- If you are using PowerPoint slides, make sure you know when and in what order to show them. Print out a copy of your slides.

**OUTLINE:** Instead of writing out your entire presentation, word for word, you may want to write your key points in outline form. An outline should include all of the major points you want to make, with examples or explanations. It should also include the points to be made in the introduction and conclusion.

**NOTECARDS:** Some people prefer to work from 3" × 5" notecards rather than pieces of paper. They prepare a separate notecard for each major point, listing the point and an example. If you use notecards, be sure to number them in the top right corner so that you can easily reassemble them if they get out of order.

**MEDIA:** If you are working with media of any kind, including PowerPoint, don't panic if the technology momentarily lets you down or you skip over a slide and need to go back to find the right one. These kinds of glitches happen to everyone. The key is to stay calm and correct the situation; then carry on with confidence.

See if one of your classmates is willing and able to run your PowerPoint slide show, taking cues from you about when to switch slides. That will give you one less thing to worry about.

### Time Yourself.

As you practice aloud, time yourself. You need to be sure that you can finish your presentation within the time limit you've been given.

If you find that you don't have enough time to make your major points, don't just speak more quickly. Go back and revise your presentation. Keep the points simple and the examples clear. If necessary, cut back on the number of points you are making, keeping only the strongest ones.

Be sure to time yourself at least twice after you have your presentation in final form.

## Strategy 5. Create a Good Final Impression

Jean's last mistake was that when she ran short on time, she panicked and ended on a bad note. Practicing aloud and timing yourself will help you avoid this problem, but if you do run short on time, don't panic.

Usually speakers are given a warning signal of some sort to let them know that they need to finish. If you get a warning signal before you've said all you wanted to, remember that it's a warning. You have a little time left to conclude your presentation.

You may have enough time to finish your speech as planned, but if you know you can't cover all of it in the time remaining, you will need to condense it. Reduce the details about your points, and move to a very brief conclusion. You may need to move to your final point and give it without an example. Then say, "Again, here are the major points," repeat them briefly, and conclude.

When the time is over, look up, smile at your audience, thank them for their attention, and ask if they have any questions. Give the audience time to respond. It may take them a while to start asking questions. Wait calmly, and look around the room. If there are no questions, thank the audience again and return to your seat.

# Appendix C

*How to Write a Résumé and a Cover Letter*

A **résumé** presents your experience and skills in brief written form. When you apply for a job, you should have an up-to-date résumé that you can send to a prospective employer or carry with you to an interview. Because the quality of your résumé will often determine whether you are called for an interview, it is worth your time to put together a good one.

It's a good idea to visit your college's career services office, which usually provides handouts and other materials that will help you to create a good résumé. You can also find résumé advice on the Web; however, make sure the sponsor of the site is reputable (such as a college or university). The Internet is also an excellent source of information about how to prepare for an interview, how to dress, and other important considerations.

Another caution: Avoid the temptation to use a résumé-preparation service. You are the only one who knows what you have done and why it is important; you are therefore the only one who can best represent yourself in a résumé. However, counselors at your college's career services office may provide coaching and advice on resume preparation, and it's worthwhile to seek their help if you're having trouble.

A **cover letter** is the letter you write to a prospective employer when you are interested in applying for a position. Usually, you will send a cover letter along with your résumé.

## How to Write a Good Résumé

The following descriptive guide was written by Jill Lee, formerly coordinator of career services at the University of Toledo Community and Technical College. She was featured in a Profile of Success in the first edition of this book.

The appearance of your résumé is very important. Use a good-quality paper, and print copies of your résumé on a laser printer. Spelling and grammar are also important. A spelling error or an obvious grammar error may eliminate you as a job candidate, so proofread your résumé carefully. Emphasize your positive qualities in your résumé, highlighting your skills and accomplishments. Within each section, list the most recent information first and then work back in time. For example, under "Experience" or "Employment" you should list your current or most recent position first, then the one before that, and so on.

A competitive résumé must be concise and well organized. Prospective employers spend an average of six to eight seconds deciding whether to give a résumé serious consideration, so you should be brief and highlight your skills and experience. Try to keep your résumé to one page. Think about what skills and experience you have that would make your résumé stand out to someone who is receiving hundreds of them.

A résumé should include the following categories of information. (See the sample résumé on p. 672.)

## 1. Identifying Information

At the top of the page, put your identifying information: your full name, address, telephone number (including your area code), and e-mail address if you have one. Include your work number if it's all right for someone to contact you there. It's important to include a number where a caller can leave a message. Each piece of information should be on its own line and centered.

## 2. Career Objective

If you have a specific career objective, you can list it under this category. It should be a clearly defined, short-term goal.

**OBJECTIVE:** To obtain a position as an engineering technician

**OBJECTIVE:** To obtain an accounting position

Make sure that your objective matches the career opportunities available at the company you are sending your résumé to.

## 3. Education

Under "Education," be sure to correctly identify your degree(s). Include the date you received each degree, or your "anticipated" or "expected" graduation date. Under most circumstances, you should not include your high school. Note: Associate degrees do not have an -s at the end of the word *associate*.

B.A. in Communication, May 2004 (anticipated)

Associate of Applied Business/Science degree in Medical Technology, May 2000

Under the appropriate degree(s), include the complete name of each school you attended, along with the city and state where it is located.

The University of Toledo Community and Technical College, Toledo, Ohio

List any relevant additional information, such as grade point average (GPA) if it was 3.0 or higher, dean's list, honorary society, or other academic honors or awards.

## 4. Work Experience

List both paid employment and volunteer work or internships, focusing on the experience that is most relevant to your career objective. If you like, you can create both an "Employment" category listing paid positions and a separate "Related Experience" section listing unpaid positions such as computer-lab tutor, campus guide, or senior mentor.

Each entry in the experience section should include the following information:

Title of position

Company name and location (city, state)

Dates of employment/experience

Summarize the positions you've held, and highlight your accomplishments. Include all of the concrete skills and abilities you have developed, particularly those skills relevant to your current career goals. Remember that a résumé is not the place for undue modesty about your achievements. You need to emphasize your skills to prospective employers. Tell an employer what you can do for the company or organization. Imagine a reader who is asking the question, "Why should I hire you?" and provide reasons. Use action verbs to describe your achievements.

*Developed* a proposal for marketing career services

*Assisted* with legal research

*Analyzed* reports and data and *compiled* results

## 5. Skills and Other Experience

List any special abilities and skills in this category, such as computer, budgeting, or math skills; language skills; telephone abilities; and equipment skills. Don't skimp on this section. Brainstorm to make a list of everything you can do. Then pare down your list to the skills that may be relevant to an employer.

If you have participated in sports or community service or were a member of a group that accomplished something noteworthy (such as raising money for a cause, helping to save an historic building, or developing a guide for newcomers), list that experience. These activities may show your teamwork, problem-solving, and leadership skills, among other things.

## 6. References

References are people who will vouch for you. They should be people who have worked closely with you, such as former employers or instructors, who you think will say positive things about you. Be sure to check with the people you plan to list to make sure it's OK to use them as references.

On your résumé, you may list the names, positions, companies, and telephone numbers of your references, or you may simply write "References available upon request." If you state that references are available, make sure you have people and contact numbers lined up.

## 7. Other Possible Headings

You may have qualifications or abilities that you want to include on your résumé but that don't fit neatly into any of the categories. Don't omit them; consider adding categories to fit your qualifications, such as "Special Training" or "Certifications." You want your résumé to include any information that will strengthen your appeal as a potential employee.

**SAMPLE RÉSUMÉ**

**Taylor E. Willey**
**2005 Garden Park Drive**
**Toledo, OH 43612**
**(419) 555-0622**
twilley@hotmail.net

| | |
|---|---|
| CAREER OBJECTIVE | To obtain a position as a legal secretary |
| EDUCATION | Associate degree in Legal Secretarial Technology, June 2003 |
| | The University of Toledo Community and Technical College, Toledo, Ohio |
| | GPA: 3.5 |
| | • Dean's list |
| | • Golden Key National Honor Society |
| WORK EXPERIENCE | **March 2001–present:** |
| | Legal secretary |
| | Johnson's Legal Services |
| | Perrysburg, Ohio |
| | • Combined and entered expert testimony into database |
| | • Drafted distribution and settlement letters |
| | • Entered and updated claims in LawTrac |
| | • Filled out and filed probate forms |
| | • Attended administrative hearings |
| | • Helped organize information for spreadsheets |
| | **January 1997–March 2001:** |
| | Secretary |
| | The University of Toledo, Toledo, Ohio |
| | • Developed an office procedures manual |
| | • Typed documents |
| | • Organized the office |
| | • Provided courteous personal service |
| SKILLS | • Proficient in WordPerfect, Excel, Windows, Lotus Notes, Microsoft Word, PageMaker, QuarkXpress |
| | • Excellent written and oral communication skills |
| | • Excellent editing and proofreading skills |
| | • Certified legal secretary |
| OTHER EXPERIENCE/ SPECIAL SKILLS | • Organized 10 km walk to raise money for a family whose house had burned down. Raised $35,000. |
| | • Sunday school teacher, Grace Methodist Church, Toledo, Ohio |
| | • Volunteer, Green Street Soup Kitchen. Work ten hours per week serving hot meals to needy. |
| REFERENCES | Available upon request |

When you write your own résumé, use the following checklist to make sure it's complete and effective.

## CHECKLIST: HOW TO WRITE A RÉSUMÉ

| STEPS | HOW TO DO THE STEPS (IF APPLICABLE) |
|---|---|
| **1.** Include identifying information. | ❑ Put your name, address, telephone number, and e-mail address centered at the top of the page. |
| **2.** State your career objective; keep it brief and as specific as possible. | |
| **3.** Complete the "Education" category. | ❑ List degrees received, the date you received each degree, and the institution for each. |
| **4.** Complete the "Work Experience" category. | ❑ Start with your most recent position.<br>❑ List the title of each position, the company name and location, and the dates of employment.<br>❑ For each position, particularly the most recent one, list your achievements and/or responsibilities. Start with an action verb (*Designed* a brochure using QuarkXpress). |
| **5.** Complete the "Other Experience/Special Skills" category. | ❑ List any skills you have that are relevant to the position you are seeking (computer, language, office machines, and so on). Include experiences that demonstrate leadership, teamwork, initiative, and so on. |
| **6.** Provide a list of references, or state "References available upon request." | ❑ Check with the people you are listing to make sure that they are willing to give you a reference and that you have their most current contact information. |
| **7.** Revise your draft résumé. | ❑ Add any experiences or skills that you overlooked.<br>❑ Make sure that all information is complete and accurate. |
| **8.** Edit your résumé. | ❑ Carefully read your résumé, checking for and correcting errors in grammar, spelling, and punctuation. |
| **9.** Format and print your résumé. | ❑ Leave enough space between items so that the résumé looks easy to read and attractive.<br>❑ Use bold to highlight key information.<br>❑ Use a high-quality printer and paper, or go to a copy shop to print your résumé. It is important that it look clean, crisp, and professional. |

# How to Write a Good Cover Letter

Although your résumé provides detailed information about your experience and skills, your cover letter is the first item a prospective employer sees, so it is a very important piece of writing.

**A GOOD COVER LETTER**

- considers your audience (the prospective employer), what information that person would value, and the appropriate tone with which to address that person
- keeps your purpose (to become a candidate for employment) in mind
- follows a standard business-letter format
- briefly but specifically summarizes what position(s) you are interested in, what your qualifications are, and why you should be considered for a position
- provides contact information
- is free of grammar, punctuation, and spelling errors

The cover letter on page 675 uses a correct business format, and its parts are labeled to show you how the letter should be set up and what it should include. Note that the writer tells the prospective employer exactly how to reach her.

**SAMPLE COVER LETTER**

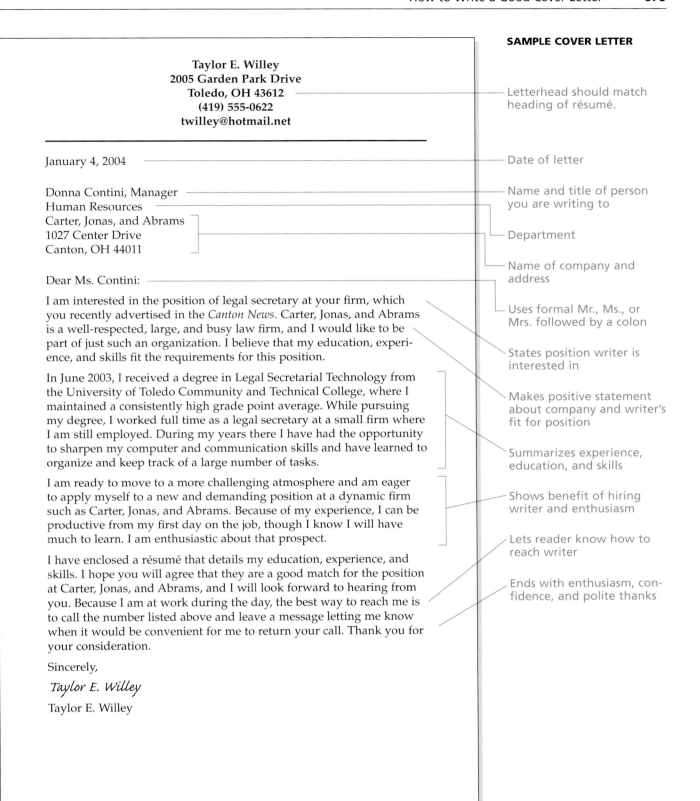

**Taylor E. Willey**
**2005 Garden Park Drive**
**Toledo, OH 43612**
**(419) 555-0622**
**twilley@hotmail.net**

January 4, 2004

Donna Contini, Manager
Human Resources
Carter, Jonas, and Abrams
1027 Center Drive
Canton, OH 44011

Dear Ms. Contini:

I am interested in the position of legal secretary at your firm, which you recently advertised in the *Canton News*. Carter, Jonas, and Abrams is a well-respected, large, and busy law firm, and I would like to be part of just such an organization. I believe that my education, experience, and skills fit the requirements for this position.

In June 2003, I received a degree in Legal Secretarial Technology from the University of Toledo Community and Technical College, where I maintained a consistently high grade point average. While pursuing my degree, I worked full time as a legal secretary at a small firm where I am still employed. During my years there I have had the opportunity to sharpen my computer and communication skills and have learned to organize and keep track of a large number of tasks.

I am ready to move to a more challenging atmosphere and am eager to apply myself to a new and demanding position at a dynamic firm such as Carter, Jonas, and Abrams. Because of my experience, I can be productive from my first day on the job, though I know I will have much to learn. I am enthusiastic about that prospect.

I have enclosed a résumé that details my education, experience, and skills. I hope you will agree that they are a good match for the position at Carter, Jonas, and Abrams, and I will look forward to hearing from you. Because I am at work during the day, the best way to reach me is to call the number listed above and leave a message letting me know when it would be convenient for me to return your call. Thank you for your consideration.

Sincerely,

*Taylor E. Willey*

Taylor E. Willey

---

*Annotations (right margin):*

— Letterhead should match heading of résumé.

— Date of letter

— Name and title of person you are writing to

— Department

— Name of company and address

— Uses formal Mr., Ms., or Mrs. followed by a colon

— States position writer is interested in

— Makes positive statement about company and writer's fit for position

— Summarizes experience, education, and skills

— Shows benefit of hiring writer and enthusiasm

— Lets reader know how to reach writer

— Ends with enthusiasm, confidence, and polite thanks

When you write your own cover letter, use the following checklist to make sure it's complete and effective.

## CHECKLIST: HOW TO WRITE A COVER LETTER

| STEPS | HOW TO DO THE STEPS (IF APPLICABLE) |
|---|---|
| **1.** Include your identifying information. | ❑ Put your name, address, telephone number, and e-mail address in a letterhead that is centered at the top of the page. |
| **2.** Write the date and address of your letter. | ❑ Write the date and skip two or three spaces.<br>❑ Write the name, title, and address of the person you are writing to. Skip two more spaces. |
| **3.** Write your salutation. | ❑ Write Dear Mr./Ms./Mrs./Dr. and the person's last name. Put a colon (:) after the name. Skip two spaces. |
| **4.** Write the body of your letter. | ❑ In the first paragraph, state the position you are interested in.<br>❑ In the second paragraph, briefly but specifically state your qualifications, skills, and strengths.<br>❑ In your final paragraph(s), restate your interest in the position, your enthusiasm, and your confidence in your ability to succeed in the position; indicate how the prospective employer can contact you; and thank him or her for considering you. Skip two spaces. |
| **5.** Write your closing. | ❑ Write *Sincerely* followed by a comma (,). Skip four spaces.<br>❑ Type your name.<br>❑ Sign your name, neatly, above your typed name. |
| **6.** Revise your letter. | ❑ Reread what you have written, and add anything that would strengthen your appeal to the prospective employer. |
| **7.** Edit your letter. | ❑ Carefully edit your letter, making sure that it has no errors in spelling, grammar, or punctuation. |
| **8.** Format and print your letter. | ❑ Make sure that the letter follows the standard format for a letter of application and includes all of the elements.<br>❑ Use a high-quality printer and paper, or go to a copy shop to print your letter. It is important that it look clean, crisp, and professional.<br>❑ Make a copy of your letter for your files. |

# Appendix D

*Computer Basics*

If you are using a computer for this writing course, you should understand how to do the basic functions listed below. If any of them are unfamiliar to you, review the appropriate section in this appendix.

If you still need help, don't fret: Your instructor, your computer lab director, or other students will help you.

**COMPUTER BASICS**

You should know how to

- start a paper
- save your work and manage your files
- revise and edit your work
- format and print your work
- search the Web

Note that many different word-processing programs are available, but if you know the basics of one, you will be able to use others fairly easily. Most of the examples and advice in this appendix are specific to Microsoft Word (Word), a widely used word-processing program.

It helps to be familiar with the basic "menu" of functions for your word-processing software. In Word, this menu runs across the top of the screen and includes such functions as *File, Edit, View, Insert, Format, Tools,* and *Help.*

■ **RESOURCES** If you want to teach the principles of e-mail in your classes, refer to *Additional Resources* for materials on this topic. Additionally, *Practical Suggestions* contains updated advice on using technology in your classroom, including how to use computers to simplify your evaluation of your students' work while providing more detailed feedback. This manual also contains lists of useful Web sites in key areas, such as plagiarism prevention and ESL instruction.

## Starting a Paper

To start a paper in Word, follow the steps below. If you have trouble, or if you use another word-processing program, consult your instructor or lab director.

1. Click on *File* in the main menu.
2. Scroll down to select *New.*
3. You will get a blank page that is ready to use, or a "blank document" icon. If you get this icon . . .
4. Click on the icon, or on the "OK" button, to get a blank page.

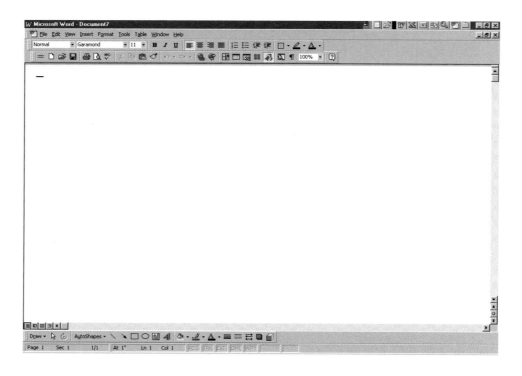

The cursor should then appear at the top of the blank page. You can begin typing your paper.

**NOTE:** For various functions described in this appendix, Word offers shortcut icons—for example, a picture of a blank sheet of paper for starting a document and a picture of a printer for printing. So you could just click on the blank-paper icon to start a new document, instead of following the steps described above.

You can add icons to the toolbar at the top of your screen by selecting *View* from the menu, then *Toolbars,* then *Customize.* The "Commands" option under *Customize* lists icons (and functions) that you can drag to the toolbar.

## Saving Your Work and Managing Your Files

### Saving Your Work

**■ TIP** You can set your computer to automatically save your work at regular intervals. Check with your instructor or computer lab director for details.

To avoid losing what you've written in the event of power outages or other problems, you should save your work regularly while you write—say every fifteen minutes. In Microsoft Word, choose *Save* or *Save As* from the *File* menu, or just click on the icon that looks like a computer disk. If you have started a new document, the computer will ask you to name the file before you save it for the first time.

Developing an easy-to-remember file-naming system is a good first step in managing your writing projects. For example, "Favorite place draft 3-28-04" is better than "English 100 draft." In Microsoft Word, selecting

*Save As* from the *File* menu allows you to create new versions of previous drafts (for example, "Favorite place final version 4-10-04") so that you won't overwrite anything. The old draft will be preserved, and you'll have a new document with your latest changes.

When you finish a computer session, save your work

- on the hard drive of your computer and, if one is available, on the file server for your school/class;

- on a disk, as a backup. (Use a single disk to keep all of the work for a class.)

## Managing Files

It helps to create a folder system to store and organize your files, as illustrated in the graphic below. Computer-based folder systems work much the way paper-based ones do. Whenever you start a new project that will involve a series of documents, you create a new folder and name it for the project. Then you store all of the documents for the project in that folder. Whenever you start a new project, you begin a new folder.

With such a system, you can find the documents you need more easily, and you won't lose track of different versions that your instructor may ask you to keep. Follow these steps to create a folder system for your writing course:

**ELECTRONIC FILE
MANAGEMENT**

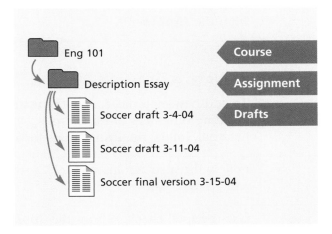

1. Create a folder with the name of your course by selecting *New* and then *Folder* from the *File* menu. (On a Macintosh computer, select *New Folder.*)

2. Within your course folder, create a new folder for each assignment. Save all writing for the assignment in this folder.

3. Whenever you work on a draft, use the *Save As* feature under *File* in your word-processing program to save a new version of your document with a new name.

# Revising and Editing Your Work

While revising, you focus on the "big picture" aspects of your writing: You may change ideas—adding, cutting, and moving whole sentences or paragraphs. Editing, however, involves finding and correcting problems with grammar, style, usage, and punctuation. While editing, you usually add, cut, or change words and phrases.

Clearly, the computer cannot do the thinking for you when you are revising and editing. But it can make these processes easier.

## REVISING AND EDITING ON A COMPUTER

### REVISING

| TASK | HOW TO DO IT |
|---|---|
| Adding sentences or paragraphs | Move your cursor to where you want to add the material, click once, and begin typing. |
| Cutting sentences or paragraphs | Highlight the material you want to cut: Click your mouse button at the start of the material and hold it down while you drag the mouse, until all the material is highlighted. Release the button. Then hit **Delete** on the keyboard. |
| Moving sentences or paragraphs | Highlight the material as described previously. Then select **Cut** from the **Edit** menu. Move your cursor to where you want to place the material and click once. Then select **Paste** from the **Edit** menu. |

### EDITING

| TASK | HOW TO DO IT |
|---|---|
| Adding or changing words or phrases | To add new material, follow the instructions under "Adding sentences or paragraphs," above. To delete old material, follow the instructions below. |
| Cutting words or phrases | Follow the instructions under "Cutting sentences or paragraphs," above. |
| Checking spelling | Use the spell checker; from the **Tools** menu, select **Spelling and Grammar**. |

NOTE: Be sure to use a spell checker before submitting your work for a grade, but remember: Never rely on a spell checker to do your editing for you. A spell checker ignores anything it recognizes as a word, so it will not help you find words that are misused or misspellings that are also words. (For more information on spell checkers and spelling in general, see Chapter 33.)

Some word processors provide grammar checkers, but these tools are often more confusing than helpful, and they can even lead to additional mistakes in your writing. Avoid using these tools unless you instructor approves and gives you specific guidance.

## Formatting and Printing Your Work

Before you print your work, make sure that you have formatted your paper according to any guidelines provided by your instructor.

Practically all instructors require papers to be double-spaced. To double-space your work, make sure that the document containing your work is open. Then highlight all the text and click on the icon that looks like double-spaced lines. (Alternatively, you can select **Paragraph** from the **Format** menu. You will get a pop-up box. Select the "Indents and Spacing" tab in the pop-up box and then select "double" under "Line Spacing." Select "OK.")

Your instructor may have other formatting requirements; for example, you may be asked to add headers or page numbers to your paper. For specific advice on other types of formatting, check with your instructor or computer lab director.

To print your work, click on the icon that looks like a printer, or select **Print** from the **File** menu.

## Searching the Web

Your instructor may ask you to write a paper using outside sources. In addition to the library, the Web is a good source of information; however, because anyone can post anything to the Internet, you need to choose Web sources carefully. Advice on choosing and evaluating Web sources is provided in Chapter 18.

In this section, we focus on using search engines to locate information on the Web. (For a list of search engines, see p. 266.) Because these tools are designed for the express purpose of helping you find information, they are typically quite easy to use. The examples in this section are based on one popular search tool: Google, at <www.google.com>. You can apply the advice for this search engine to most others that you use.

Google, like most other search engines, offers a variety of resources in addition to text-search functions. For example, you can find online discussion forums grouped by topic, directories to Web sites organized by topic, and a searchable database of news sources.

The central feature of any search engine is the search box. To do a basic search, type a keyword (or keywords) of interest into the box and then submit them. Let's say you are interested in getting information on job sharing for a paper you are doing on how job sharing works, and what its advantages and disadvantages are. You enter the words into Google and get these results:

The search engine returned more than two million results or "hits"—much more than you can even scan. Also, some of the hits (for example, the one on the National Association of Diaper Services) just aren't relevant.

Fortunately, Google, like most other search engines, has an "Advanced Search" feature. With advanced searching, you can refine your search in these ways:

- You can ask the search engine to search for more than one word at a time, and ask it to show you only sites that have all of the words. Or you can ask it to show you only sites that have either one word or another.

- You can ask the search engine to search for sites that DO have one word (or set of words) but that DON'T have other word(s).

- You can ask the search engine to look for an exact phrase, such as "job sharing."

Here's what Google's "Advanced Search" form looks like:

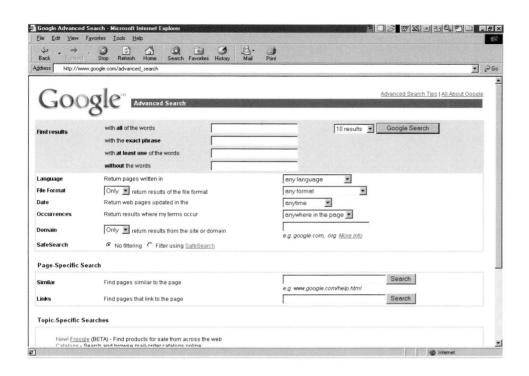

Let's do an advanced search on the job sharing topic using the **exact phrase** "job sharing" but **without** the words "service" and "services"—to eliminate diaper service organizations and the like.

The number of hits is much more manageable—18,000+—and the overall list is more targeted to the topic.

But you can zoom in even more. To get specific sites discussing the advantages and disadvantages of job sharing, repeat the previous search, but type *advantages* and *disadvantages* into the "with **at least one** of the words" search field in "Advanced Search."

You get 500+ very targeted entries.

A final word: All search engines offer functions like "help" or "search tips." If you are using a search engine for the first time, spend some time with these resources; they'll suggest more search options and assist you when you get stuck.

# Answers to Odd-Numbered Editing Exercises

## Chapter 19

**Practice 19-1, page 290**
*Answers:* **1.** Subject: company; prepositional phrase: without a chief executive officer **3.** Subject: people; prepositional phrase: on the short list of candidates **5.** Subject: man; prepositional phrase: from a bankrupt firm **7.** Subject: appearance; prepositional phrase: before the members of the board **9.** Subject: workforce; prepositional phrase: within the company

**Practice 19-2, page 293**
*Answers:* **1.** Subject: Egyptians; verb: invented (action verb) **3.** Subject: they; verb: bowled (action verb) **5.** Subject: alley; verb: opened (action verb) **7.** Subject: alley; verb: offers (action verb) **9.** Subject: people; verb: would think (helping verb + main verb)

**Practice 19-3, page 294**
*Answers and possible edits:* **1.** I (incomplete thought); I will wait until the store closes at midnight. **3.** Correct **5.** Correct **7.** Correct **9.** I (incomplete thought); Mary joined a book club because she likes novels.

## Chapter 20

**Practice 20-2, page 299**
*Answers and possible edits:* **1.** Preposition: about. Some parents worry about their children's imaginary companions. **3.** Preposition: of. Some parents think imaginary companions are a waste of time. **5.** Preposition: between. Children should be taught the difference between lies and imagination. **7.** Preposition: of. A child might not want to admit to being afraid of the dark. **9.** Preposition: after. Children usually give up their imaginary companions after grade school.

**Practice 20-3, page 301**
*Answers and possible edits:* **1.** Dependent word: unless. Unless you think about what you really want from a job, you might make the wrong decision about your future. **3.** Dependent word: if. If you think a high salary is very important, you should consider how many hours you are willing to work each week to earn the money. **5.** Dependent words: even though. Some jobs are "dead ends" and don't leave room for advancement even though they pay well. **7.** Dependent word: when. When a survey recently ranked the best and worst American jobs, those jobs with a possibility of promotion, short work weeks, and low stress rated highest. **9.** Dependent word: because. Taxi driving and working in an oil field ranked in the bottom ten because those jobs are stressful, physically difficult, and not very secure.

**Practice 20-4, page 304**
*Answers and possible edits:* **1.** -*ing* verb: walking. In 1931, Plennie Wingo set out on an ambitious journey, walking backward around the world. **3.** -*ing* verb: halting. After eight thousand miles, Wingo's journey was interrupted by a war, halting his progress in Pakistan. **5.** -*ing* verb: taking. Mullikin's trip took so long because he lingered, taking time out to earn money as a logger and a Baptist minister. **7.** -*ing* verb: driving. Farmers hoping for government help traveled from the Great Plains to Washington. They were driving large, slow-moving harvesting machines. **9.** -*ing* verb: looking. Americans may also have heard the story of Alvin Straight, looking for his long-lost brother as he traveled across the Midwest.

**Practice 20-5, page 306**
*Answers and possible edits:* **1.** *to* + verb: to send. To send a message to an old friend or a family member, a person today often chooses e-mail instead of a letter. **3.** *to* + verb: to ensure. Sometimes, such requests are hoaxes that have just one goal. That goal is to ensure the circulation of thousands of unnecessary e-mail messages. **5.** *to* + verb: to send. To send a message back to the class with the person's location is another requirement of such e-mail assignments. **7.** *to* + verb: to get. Teachers who assign this experiment find that it excites the students to get messages from all over the world. **9.** *to* + verb: to make. Many teachers have learned the hard way to make sure that the original message tells recipients when the assignment ends.

**Practice 20-6, page 308**
*Answers and possible edits:* **1.** Example or explanation: Such as property taxes. Public schools in the United States are supposed to survive on money collected by the government, such as property taxes. **3.** Example or explanation: Like schools. In the 1990s, many people believed that businesses held the answer to the problems of public institutions, like schools. **5.** Example or explanation: For instance, in the cafeteria and in hallway vending machines. Schools that took money from soft-drink makers were expected to allow soft-drink sales in the building. For instance, the drinks might be offered in the cafeteria and in hallway vending machines. **7.** Example or explanation: Leading young people to choose less nutritious and more fattening and sugary foods. Some parents and teachers object that advertisements for fast food and soft drinks contribute to poor student health. Such ads lead young people to choose less nutritious and more fattening and sugary foods. **9.** Example or explanation: Having no other way to get enough funding to keep going. Schools that accept advertisements say that they really have little choice in the matter. They may have no other way to get enough funding to keep going.

**Practice 20-7, page 309**
*Answers and possible edits:* **1.** Fragment: Being a celebrity. Being a celebrity might not be as much fun as it sounds. **3.** Fragment: Like Julia Roberts and Eddie Vedder. I followed the careers of famous actors and musicians like Julia Roberts and Eddie Vedder. **5.** Fragment: To be recognized in public places. I was eager to be recognized in public places. **7.** Fragment: Minding his own business. He was walking down an avenue in Midtown, minding his own business. **9.** Fragment: With a hunted look on his face. Trying not to notice everyone staring at him, Hoffman walked past me with a hunted look on his face.

**Practice 20-8, page 311**

*Possible edits:*  **1.** (1) Correct (3) She was so sick that everyone thought she would die. (5) Correct (7) After years of treatment, braces, and determination, she started running for exercise. (9) Correct  **2.** (1) Correct (3) Correct (5) It was a very cumbersome and difficult system. (7) Correct; combined with (6): Becoming fascinated with the idea of inventing a writing system the blind could read, Braille worked for two years on his own idea.  **3.** (1) Most people think of Thomas Edison as a famous inventor who invented the light-bulb. (3) Correct (5) His parents took him out of school because they did not believe the teachers. (7) He was then homeschooled by his very determined mother. (9) Correct  **4.** (1) Correct (3) Her famous father, the poet Lord Byron, left her mother in 1816 and never returned to England. (5) Ada's mother wanted her daughter to study mathematics, not poetry, like her father. (7) The computer was never built, but Ada designed programs for it, earning her recognition in the twentieth century as one of the first computer programmers.  **5.** (1) Born in Columbus, Ohio, in 1856, Granville T. Woods, an African American inventor, had to leave school at the age of ten. (3) While working at various jobs, Woods sometimes attended night school because he realized that he needed more education to achieve his goals. (5) He found work on railroads and used his electrical and mechanical skills to invent improvements for electric railways. (7) Woods received patents on over sixty of his inventions, such as improved air brakes and a telegraph that allowed communication between the train and station.

# Chapter 21

**Practice 21-2, page 318**

*Answers and possible edits:*  **1.** FS (fused sentence); The holiday we now call Valentine's Day was celebrated in the Roman Empire on February 15; it was called Lupercalia.  **3.** CS (comma splice); The Romans held a festival to honor Lupercus; this was the feast of Lupercalia.  **5.** FS (fused sentence); The night before the feast, all of the young women wrote their names on pieces of paper. They put the names in a jar.  **7.** FS (fused sentence); The emperor ordered his soldiers not to get married. He was afraid they would want to stay home instead of going to war.  **9.** CS (comma splice); The emperor had Valentine killed on February 14. Later the priest was declared a saint.

**Practice 21-3, page 320**

*Possible edits:*  **1.** In most cultures, popular foods depend greatly on availability and tradition, so people tend to eat old familiar favorites.  **3.** In many societies, certain foods are allowed to ferment, for this process adds flavor.  **5.** As an American, you might not like such eggs, or the thought of eating them might even revolt you.  **7.** Many Koreans love to eat kimchee, a spicy fermented cabbage, but Americans often find the taste peculiar and the smell overpowering.  **9.** Americans on a visit to Kyrgyzstan consider themselves brave for tasting kumiss, but local children drink it regularly.

**Practice 21-4, page 323**

*Possible edits:*  **1.** When a person is diagnosed with Alzheimer's disease, the whole family may feel depressed.  **3.** The progress of Alzheimer's is often gradual as the victim begins to forget simple things and make little mistakes.  **5.** Because Alzheimer's patients need the same kind of care that newborns need, their children may feel strange caring for their dependent parents.  **7.** Since the expense of caring for Alzheimer's patients can be huge, many patients and their families need help.  **9.** Life after Alzheimer's can never be the same, although the patient can still feel happy at times.

**Practice 21-5, page 324**

*Possible edits:*  **1.** When the collapse of Enron, WorldCom, Tyco, and other companies in 2001 and 2002 brought calls for corporate reform, every government figure from the president on down made speeches about holding companies responsible for their actions.  **3.** Congress and the White House did not require companies to declare the cost of stock options, but a few major American corporations decided to take steps to make their shareholders happier.  **5.** Business leaders praised Coca-Cola for this announcement, and other companies made the same change after Coca-Cola led the way.  **7.** A company's earnings forecast predicts how much money the company will make in the next quarter. A company looks strong if it meets the expectations and weak if it does not.  **9.** Coca-Cola's financial statements will still provide information about how the company does business; however, they will not predict how many dollars and cents the corporation will earn in the future.

**Practice 21-6, page 326**

*Possible edits:*  **1.** (1) The Internet once seemed like an exciting new way to make money. Everyone wanted to earn a living online. (3) Selling advertising space on Web sites was one popular way to try to earn money, but most computer users were not especially interested in the ads. (5) Spam has become another way to spread Internet advertising. Spammers flood e-mail addresses with unsolicited mail selling golf balls, insurance, and so on. (7) Internet advertising faces some of the challenges of television advertising because people want to fast-forward through the advertisements that interrupt their viewing. (9) The willingness of people to surf the Web daily has not changed. Nevertheless, using the Internet to earn money is probably even more difficult today than it was in the nineties.  **2.** (1) The Internet may seem to be unlimited, but there may soon be a shortage of good domain names. (3) Correct (5) A few people own a large number of domain names. The names are considered an investment today. (7) The people who own the Web sites at those addresses get more business, so their domain names are more valuable.

# Chapter 22

**Practice 22-2, page 333**

*Answers:*  **1.** Subject: sleep; verb: is  **3.** Subject: lights; verb: were  **5.** Subject: home; verb: has  **7.** Subject: student; verb: doesn't  **9.** Subject: you; verb: are

**Practice 22-3, page 334**

*Answers:*  **1.** Subject: stars; verb: are  **3.** Subject: I; verb: do  **5.** Subject: you; verb: have  **7.** Subject: one; verb: is  **9.** Subject: Orion; verb: is

**Practice 22-4, page 335**

*Answers:*  **1.** Prepositional phrase: in my neighborhood; verb: like  **3.** Prepositional phrase: under drought restrictions; verb: contains  **5.** Prepositional phrase: for collecting rain; verb: were  **7.** Prepositional phrase: on most average-sized houses; verb: directs  **9.** Prepositional phrase: of rainfall from recent showers; verb: has

**Practice 22-5, page 337**

*Answers and possible edits:*  **1.** Dependent clause: that hired my cousins. The restaurant that hired my cousins is not treating them fairly.  **3.** Dependent clause: who supervises the morning shift. Correct  **5.** Dependent clause: whose hand was injured slicing potatoes. Ramón, whose hand was injured slicing potatoes, needs to have physical therapy.  **7.** Dependent clause: who cleaned his wound and put in his stitches at the hospital. The doctors who cleaned his wound and put in his stitches at the hospital expect him to pay for the medical treatment. **9.** Dependent clause: whose English is not yet perfect. My cousins, whose English is not yet perfect, feel unable to leave their jobs.

### Practice 22-6, page 339

*Answers:* **1.** Subject joined by: and; verb: share **3.** Subject joined by: and; verb: are **5.** Subject joined by: or; verb: provides **7.** Subject joined by: or; verb: finds **9.** Subject joined by: or; verb: costs

### Practice 22-7, page 341

*Answers:* **1.** Subject: everyone; verb: remembers; prepositional phrase: none **3.** Subject: one; verb: realizes; prepositional phrase: of you **5.** Subject: someone; verb: knows; prepositional phrase: in your family **7.** Subject: one; verb: plans; prepositional phrase: of your relatives **9.** Subject: someone; verb: connects; prepositional phrase: in this class

### Practice 22-8, page 344

*Edits:* **1.** What is the best reason to study music? **3.** Correct **5.** Here are a guitar, a saxophone, and a piano. **7.** What time of day do you usually practice? **9.** What musician do you admire most?

### Practice 22-9, page 344

*Edits:* **1.** Do consumers who download music files really buy fewer recordings? **3.** Perhaps sometimes a music fan doesn't bother to buy a recording after downloading the latest CD from a popular artist. **5.** In an MP3 file, a song's lyrics and music sound less clear than on a CD. **7.** A user's computer or sometimes the telephone line becomes occupied during a download, which may take a long time. **9.** For example, the music industry may offer online files supposedly containing an artist's new songs, but a user who downloads the files discovers that the songs are incomplete or missing.

### Practice 22-10, page 345

*Answers:* **1.** (1) A study I came across while doing research for my sociology class rates U.S. cities by "most things to do." (3) Each of the cities was assigned a total from 0 to 100 points in each category. (5) Correct (7) Correct **2.** (1) Correct (3) Correct (5) There are also fast talkers in Boston and Bakersfield, California. (7) Other postal workers who speak very slowly live in Los Angeles; Shreveport, Louisiana; and Chattanooga, Tennessee. **3.** (1) The color of chicken eggs comes from the pigment in the outer layer of the shell. (3) Correct (5) Correct (7) Any of the hens with red earlobes produce brown eggs. **4.** (1) Many writers of fiction invent places that are not real. (3) Correct (5) Has anyone heard of the home of Winnie-the-Pooh? (7) Correct **5.** (1) Correct (3) Correct (5) Correct (7) A peer counselor and the teenager being counseled dress and talk alike.

# Chapter 23

### Practice 23-2, page 351

*Answers:* **1.** Subject: classes; verb: require **3.** Subject: employees; verb: agree **5.** Subject: job; verb: pays **7.** Subject: he; verb: wonders **9.** Subject: bicycle; verb: allows

### Practice 23-3, page 352

Several years ago I traveled from Boston to Seattle on Christmas Eve. As we approached the Seattle area, we learned that the airport was fogged in. The captain reported that he was considering landing in Portland, 180 miles south. While the airliner circled the area, passengers asked nervous questions about how much fuel remained. When I gazed out the window, I could see the fog down below us. It looked thick and white. I worried about visibility. Finally the captain decided to attempt a landing. Some passengers expressed concern, but most of us were glad not to be going to Portland. Soon we plunged deep into the fog and waited for something to happen; suddenly the runway's blue landing lights rushed up to meet us. A moment later the plane touched down, and the entire aircraft seemed to shudder with relief.

### Practice 23-4, page 353

*Answers:* **1.** Helping verb: had; verb: expected **3.** Helping verb: has; verb: infected **5.** Helping verb: had; verb: defeated **7.** Helping verb: had; verb: received **9.** Helping verb: have; verb: turned

### Practice 23-5, page 357

*Answers:* **1.** have **3.** is **5.** are **7.** has **9.** have

### Practice 23-6, page 358

*Answers:* **1.** was **3.** was **5.** was **7.** were

### Practice 23-7, page 359

*Answers:* **1.** began **3.** gave **5.** knew **7.** left **9.** shut

### Practice 23-8, page 360

*Edits:* **1.** In 1900, my great-grandfather grew wheat and raised a few cattle on his farm in Wyoming. **3.** The family did not have much money, and they hoped for good weather every year. **5.** One year, high winds blew down the barn, and hailstorms broke their windows. **7.** Somehow, they kept going in spite of their difficulties.

### Practice 23-9, page 360

*Answers:* **1.** have heard **3.** had hurt **5.** has sold **7.** has told **9.** have begun

### Practice 23-10, page 362

*Answers:* **1.** have begun **3.** needed **5.** have spent **7.** have expressed **9.** have kept

### Practice 23-11, page 363

*Answers:* **1.** had rushed **3.** treated **5.** rescued **7.** had burned **9.** had boiled

### Practice 23-12, page 365

*Possible edits:* **1.** The Civil War was fought from 1861 to 1865. **3.** Paint was smeared on the statues in the park. **5.** The winner has been announced.

### Practice 23-13, page 366

*Answers:* **1.** Verbs: keeps, seemed; correct verb: seem **3.** Verbs: trained, are; correct verb: were **5.** Verbs: have, weren't; correct verb: aren't **7.** Verbs: think, were; correct verb: are **9.** Verbs: can cost, was; correct verb: is

### Practice 23-14, page 367

*Edits:* **1.** Many of Sheena's friends were getting tattoos ten years ago. **3.** Sheena was twenty-two when she went to the tattoo parlor. **5.** Her sister liked the tattoo, but her mother fainted. **7.** Today, however, a typical person with a ten-year-old tattoo expresses some regret about following that 1990s trend. **9.** Dermatologists have seen the development of a new trend toward tattoo removal. **11.** That technique left scars. **13.** Six months ago, Sheena started to have treatments to remove her tattoo. **15.** Purple ink has longer staying power than black, blue, and red, so Sheena's treatments will continue for more than two years.

### Practice 23-15, page 369

*Edits:* **1.** (1) When Teresa saw her friend Jan drop makeup into her bag, she frowned. (3) She also knew that Jan would be mad if Teresa said anything. (5) As they left the store, Teresa's heart beat hard. (7) Still, she felt bad, so she spoke to Jan. (9) Teresa felt much better. **2.** (1) George Crum, a Native American chef, invented potato chips in 1853. (3) Crum decided to make superthin fries to get even. (5) In the 1920s, Herman Lay brought the potato chip to grocery stores. (7) Since then, people have eaten millions of chips. **3.** (1) William Topaz McGonagall spent most of his life in the city of Dundee,

Scotland, before his death in 1902. (3) He once bought the right to play the title part in a performance of Shakespeare's *Macbeth*. (5) When McGonagall played the part, however, he refused to die. (7) He began to write poetry at the age of forty-seven, and he eventually wrote more than two hundred poems. (9) McGonagall's poems often mentioned the river Tay, which flows through Dundee.

# Chapter 24

### Practice 24-1, page 376

*Answers:*  **1.** Pronoun: they; noun: coins  **3.** Pronoun: he; noun: President Franklin Roosevelt  **5.** Pronoun: they; noun: delegates  **7.** Pronoun: he; noun: King Farouk  **9.** Pronoun: he; noun: Stephen Fenton

### Practice 24-2, page 379

*Answers:*  **1.** his or her  **3.** its  **5.** he or she no longer works  **7.** himself or herself  **9.** he or she

### Practice 24-3, page 380

*Answers:*  **1.** its  **3.** its  **5.** it  **7.** their  **9.** their

### Practice 24-4, page 383

*Possible edits:*  **1.** I have been trying to get plenty of exercise and to eat a nutritious diet, but this method hasn't helped me lose weight.  **3.** My diet at the time contained a certain amount of fat, but the amount did not worry me.  **5.** When I read the ingredients on the package of fat-free cookies, however, I learned that much of the fat had simply been replaced with extra sugar.  **7.** Nevertheless, at each meal I tried to eliminate fat, but the food did not taste the same to me.  **9.** Now nutritionists claim that eating fat makes a person feel less hungry.

### Practice 24-5, page 384

*Edits:*  **1.** Young people sometimes take advertisements too literally.  **3.** People who see or hear an advertisement have to think about the message.  **5.** A recent study said that parents can help kids overcome the influence of advertising.

### Practice 24-6, page 387

*Edits:*  **1.** In 1974, George Foreman was the heavyweight boxing champion, and he and Muhammad Ali agreed to a fight for the title.  **3.** Because American officials considered Mobutu a strong anti-communist, they and he were allies, but Mobutu was a corrupt dictator who stole money intended for his impoverished country.  **5.** Foreman angered the people of Zaire immediately when he and his German shepherd dog were seen getting off the airplane.  **7.** The people loved Muhammad Ali, and pictures of him and his entourage in Zaire showed adoring crowds everywhere.  **9.** Ali may have feared losing the fight, but when he and Foreman finally got in the ring, Ali absorbed punch after punch.

### Practice 24-7, page 389

*Edits:*  **1.** My cousin is a better guitar player than I.  **3.** Correct  **5.** Correct  **7.** A music producer came to see us play, but he wanted a new teen-pop sensation in the area more than us, so we did not get a record contract.  **9.** My cousin was not as fascinated as I by stardom, and she helped me get over my disappointment.

### Practice 24-8, page 390

*Answers:*  **1.** whom  **3.** who  **5.** who

### Practice 24-9, page 392

*Possible edits:*  **1.** A writing tutor must know his or her way around college writing assignments.  **3.** Students signing up for tutoring at the writing center may not be in their first semester of college.  **5.** The writing-center tutor is very careful not to correct his or her students' papers.  **7.** Every student has to learn to catch his or her own mistakes.  **9.** No student gets his or her grade on a paper from a writing tutor.

### Practice 24-10, page 393

*Possible edits:*  **1.** My class received their term paper grades yesterday.  **3.** I usually get better grades than he, but he doesn't usually fail.  **5.** When Gene went to the department office, the office assistant told him where to find Mr. Padilla.  **7.** The paper contained language that was unusual for Gene.  **9.** Mr. Padilla, who had typed suspicious passages from Gene's paper into a search engine, found two online papers containing sentences that were also in Gene's paper.  **11.** Gene told my girlfriend and me later that he did not realize that borrowing sentences from online sources was plagiarism.  **13.** Anyone doing Internet research must be especially careful to document the sources, as Gene now knows.  **15.** Mr. Padilla will let Gene take his class again and will help him avoid inadvertent plagiarism, and Gene said that no one had ever been more relieved than he to hear that news.

### Practice 24-11, page 394

*Possible edits:*  **1.** (1) Can a person make his or her own luck? (3) If you and I feel optimistic and in control of the future, we are more likely to have good luck. (5) Rabbit's feet are common charms, but people say the feet didn't bring the rabbit any luck! (7) "Lucky" rituals are also common among students; for example, they might wear the same shirt for every test.  **2.** (1) Television has broadcast game shows since the 1950s. (3) They did give contestants the chance to show off their knowledge to a large television audience. (5) The audience was eager to see its favorite contestants win. (7) The officials helped the contestants win. (9) Correct (11) Correct (13) A few years ago, the shows became more popular than ever. (15) People like you and me could become contestants simply by calling a phone number. (17) Correct (19) That's the reason the shows gave contestants the answers. (21) Correct (23) You and I would rather watch *Joe Millionaire* than answer questions to try to be him!

# Chapter 25

### Practice 25-1, page 399

*Answers:*  **1.** *Stubborn* modifies *smokers*.  **3.** *Typical* modifies *smoker*.  **5.** *Terrible* modifies *effect*.  **7.** *Strongly* modifies *reek*.  **9.** *Significant* modifies *dose*.

### Practice 25-2, page 401

*Answers:*  **1.** scariest  **3.** fastest  **5.** luckier  **7.** hardest  **9.** more certain

### Practice 25-3, page 402

*Answers:*  **1.** *Well* modifies *communicate*.  **3.** *Well* modifies *feel*.  **5.** *Well* modifies *see*.  **7.** *Well* modifies *hear*.  **9.** *Good* modifies *solution*.

### Practice 25-4, page 403

*Answers:*  **1.** worst  **3.** better  **5.** better  **7.** worse  **9.** worse

### Practice 25-5, page 404

*Edits:*  **1.** (1) One of the jobs most commonly held by teenagers is a position in a fast-food restaurant. (3) Teens will work for lower pay than many other workers, so the restaurant can keep its prices down. (5) Jobs in fast food are not glamorous, but they are plentiful; a teenager who wants to work in a fast-food restaurant can usually find a job quickly. (7) Fast-food restaurants keep large amounts of cash on hand, and this fact is known well by people who want to commit a robbery. (9) Many teenagers think that a fast-food job is boring but a harmless way to spend a summer.  **2.** (1) One of the most important things I've learned since starting college is to avoid waiting until the last minute to begin my work. (3) This technique worked well for me in high school. (5) I promised myself that I would do better than that in the future. (7) If a task is harder than I expected, I will arrange to ask the professor or tutor for help. (9) If no outside help is available, I will usually put the work away for a few hours, or overnight, and resume my efforts when I feel better about my ability to concentrate. (11) I tend to do a stronger job when I work more slowly than when I work faster. (13) I also get in trouble if I try to tackle something when I'm overtired or not feeling well. (15) It's a good idea to do my most important work when I'm feeling my best.

# Chapter 26

### Practice 26-1, page 410
*Possible edits:* **1.** Celebrities who always appear in public with trendy hats on their heads might as well announce their baldness. **3.** A good friend should tell any celebrity hiding a bald spot to get a haircut and stop pretending. **5.** A few years ago, my mother wanted my father to stop combing his hair over his bald spot. **7.** My mother produced proof in photographs that his bald spot was obvious to everyone. **9.** Compliments on his new look came from all kinds of people.

### Practice 26-2, page 411
*Possible edits:* **1.** While I was preparing a big family dinner, the oven suddenly stopped working. **3.** With everyone trying to help, the kitchen was crowded. **5.** Discouraged, we almost cancelled dinner. **7.** Correct **9.** When I returned to the crowd in the kitchen, family members still surrounded the oven.

### Practice 26-3, page 412
*Possible edits:* **1.** (1) Believing they can do nothing to make a difference in the environment, people often waste energy. (3) Bad choices, such as buying a gas-guzzling car or SUV, can have an effect too. (5) Some products that cost more up front will save people money for many years. (7) Correct **2.** (1) Correct (3) I am currently working on a bachelor's degree in political science and have taken nearly fifty credit hours of courses, including classes in jurisprudence, law and public policy, and business law. (5) Sometimes, while sitting in class, I dream of becoming a corporate attorney. (7) I am already planning to go on to law school, and my grade point average is in the top 10 percent of my class. (9) But I am confident that someday I will be able to find a good-paying job.

# Chapter 27

### Practice 27-1, page 416
*Possible answers:* **1.** or **3.** so **5.** and **7.** but **9.** so

### Practice 27-2, page 418
*Possible edits:* **1.** Many professionals use e-mail to keep in touch with clients and contacts, so businesspeople must be especially careful not to offend anyone with their e-mail messages. **3.** Employees may have time to send personal messages from work, but they should remember that employers often have the ability to read their workers' messages. **5.** No message should be forwarded to everyone in a sender's address book, and senders should ask permission before adding a recipient to a mass-mailing list. **7.** Typographical errors and misspellings in e-mail make the message appear less professional; yet using all capital letters — a process known as *shouting* — is usually considered even worse. **9.** Viruses are a major problem with attachments, but no one wants to receive even a harmless attachment if it takes a long time to download.

### Practice 27-3, page 420
*Answers:* **1.** Exposure to the sun can cause both short-term and long-term side effects; using tanning booths has similar risks. **3.** It's easy to ignore long-term health dangers; the desire to look good is often of more immediate concern. **5.** Ultraviolet light can injure the eyes; tanning-salon patrons should always wear protective goggles.

### Practice 27-4, page 420
*Possible edits:* **1.** Only 40 percent of mothers worked outside the home in 1970; then, the American workforce changed. **3.** A new study shows that children of working parents don't necessarily feel neglected; in fact, they think they get to spend enough time with their mothers and fathers. **5.** Compared with earlier generations, parents today generally have fewer children; in addition, fathers today usually are more nurturing. **7.** For most children, their parents' jobs are not the problem; however, they want their time with their parents to be more relaxed. **9.** Most working parents try not to give up time with their families; instead, they cut out personal time and hobbies.

### Practice 27-5, page 422
*Possible answers:* **1.** because **3.** so that **5.** while **7.** when **9.** because

### Practice 27-6, page 424
*Possible edits:* **1.** Almost all college students used typewriters until the 1980s when computers became more affordable. **3.** Computers offer many advantages, although there are also some drawbacks. **5.** When computers became widely used in the 1980s, professors were surprised to hear students say, "The computer ate my paper." **7.** Some people like to print out a document to proofread it because they fail to catch all their mistakes on the screen. **9.** Even though spell-checking programs prevent many errors, only a person is able to recognize sound-alikes such as *their* and *there*.

### Practice 27-7, page 425
*Possible edits:* **1.** (1) No change (3) It is not just their imagination; most network programs have been shortened by thirty seconds or more. (5) The networks want more advertising to cover the rising costs of television shows even though the networks now demand $100,000 or more for a thirty-second commercial. (7) No change (9) A half-hour show can now run only twenty-one minutes, and an hour-long show lasts only about forty-four minutes. **2.** (1) Although Herman Melville is now considered one of the greatest American writers, his books were mostly forgotten at the time of his death in 1891. (3) No change (5) The book's more complex themes remained invisible until a new generation of literary critics rediscovered them in the 1920s. (7) Buyers were not interested in his work, and even van Gogh himself thought much of it "ugly." (9) No change (11) He had moved to Arles, France, in February 1888, where he created some of his most famous works, including the disturbingly powerful *Starry Night*. (13) Great art is often far ahead of its time, so it is frequently misunderstood. (15) These people gave the public what it wanted, but they failed to create anything of lasting worth.

# Chapter 28

### Practice 28-1, page 429
*Answers and possible edits:* **1.** Parts that should be parallel: hunt/are taking over. Wild predators, such as wolves, are vanishing because people hunt them and take over their land. **3.** Parts that should be parallel: varied diet/adapting easily. The success of the coyote is due to its varied diet and adaptability. **5.** Parts that should be parallel: spreading/populate. Today, they are spreading and populating the East Coast for the first time. **7.** Parts that should be parallel: more

populated/it's not as wild as. The animals have chosen an area more populated and less wild than their traditional home.  **9.** Parts that should be parallel: identified/tracked/they captured him. One coyote was identified, tracked, and captured in Central Park in New York City.

### Practice 28-2, page 430

*Answers and possible edits:*  **1.** Parts that should be parallel: for leasing/for the purchase of one. Car dealers often require less money down for leasing a car than for purchasing one.  **3.** Parts that should be parallel: the terms of leasing/to buy. You should check the terms of leasing to make sure they are as favorable as the terms of buying.  **5.** Parts that should be parallel: by leasing/to own. You will be making less of a financial commitment by leasing a car than by owning it.  **7.** Parts that should be parallel: used car/getting a new one. A used car can be more economical than a new one.  **9.** Parts that should be parallel: a used car/buying a brand-new vehicle. A used car may not be as impressive as a brand-new vehicle.

### Practice 28-3, page 431

*Answers and possible edits:*  **1.** Paired words: neither/nor. Parts that should be parallel: had cellular telephones/did they want them. Fifteen years ago, most people neither had cellular telephones nor wanted them.  **3.** Paired words: rather/than. Parts that should be parallel: ban cell phones on buses and trains/being forced to listen to other people's conversations. Cell phones are not universally popular: Some commuters would rather ban cell phones on buses and trains than be forced to listen to other people's conversations.  **5.** Paired words: rather/than. Parts that should be parallel: have a cell phone/be forced to walk to the nearest gas station. A motorist stranded on a deserted road would probably rather have a cell phone than be forced to walk to the nearest gas station.  **7.** Paired words: neither/nor. Parts that should be parallel: worry about radiation from cell phones/other injuries. Most Americans today neither worry about radiation from cell phones nor fear other injuries.  **9.** Paired words: both/and. Parts that should be parallel: affect people's reflexes/it might alter the brain's blood vessels. While scientists have determined that cell phones probably do not cause brain tumors, some experiments on human cells have shown that energy from cellular phones may both affect people's reflexes and alter the brain's blood vessels.

### Practice 28-4, page 433

*Possible edits:*  **1.** I could bring to this job not only youthful enthusiasm but also relevant experience.  **3.** My current job neither encourages creativity nor allows flexibility.  **5.** In college I learned a lot both from my classes and from other students.

### Practice 28-5, page 433

*Possible edits:*  **1.** (1) Karaoke started about twenty years ago in Japan, found many fans in that country, and became a popular form of entertainment around the world. (3) Correct (5) Karaoke rooms allow customers to sing, relax, and enjoy being the center of attention for a little while. (7) Japanese karaoke singers know that they can entertain either by singing well or by singing badly.  **2.** (1) Correct (3) A medical doctor by training, in the 1890s Freud began studying and documenting causes of hysteria, and he discovered that many of his female patients had been sexually abused by their fathers. (5) Correct (7) But it was deeply rewarding as well, not only to Freud as a scientist but also to Freud as an individual. (9) Correct (11) Correct

## Chapter 29

### Practice 29-1, page 438

*Edits:*  **1.** Once, rabies was a major threat to domestic pets in this country.  **3.** Frequently, people fail to have their pets vaccinated against rabies.  **5.** Worriedly, veterinarians note that wildlife can infect pets and people with rabies.

### Practice 29-2, page 438

*Possible answers:*  **1.** Recently  **3.** Thankfully  **5.** Unfortunately

### Practice 29-4, page 440

*Possible edits:*  **1.** Testing children's abilities to interpret facial expressions, a recent study made headlines.  **3.** The children told researchers what emotion was most obvious in each face, choosing among fear, anger, sadness, happiness, and other emotions.  **5.** All of the children in the study were equally good at identifying most emotions, responding similarly to happiness or fear.  **7.** Having learned to look for anger, the abused children protect themselves with this early-warning system.  **9.** Tending to run from anger they observe, abused children have difficulty connecting with teachers or friends who exhibit anger.

### Practice 29-5, page 441

*Possible answers:*  **1.** delaying  **3.** Striding  **5.** pointing

### Practice 29-7, page 444

*Possible edits:*  **1.** Angered by British colonial rule in 1929, the women of southern Nigeria organized a protest.  **3.** Pumped by American and other foreign oil companies, the oil often ends up in wealthy western economies.  **5.** Polluted by the oil industry, the Nigerian countryside then becomes less profitable for local villagers.  **7.** Inspired by the 1929 women's protests, local Nigerian women launched a series of protests against the oil industry in the summer of 2002.  **9.** Concerned about the women's threat to take their clothes off, many workers at the oil company told company officials that such a protest would bring a curse on the company and shame to its employees.

### Practice 29-8, page 445

*Possible answers:*  **1.** used  **3.** Regarded  **5.** prescribed

### Practice 29-10, page 447

*Possible edits:*  **1.** Jacob Davis, a Russian immigrant working in Reno, Nevada, was the inventor of Levi's jeans.  **3.** Davis bought denim from a wholesaler, Levi Strauss.  **5.** Davis joined the firm in 1873 and supervised the final development of its product, the famous Levi's jeans.  **7.** Another choice Davis made, the curved stitching on the back pockets, also survives in today's Levi's.  **9.** During World War II, Levi Strauss temporarily stopped adding the pocket stitches because they wasted thread, a valuable resource.

### Practice 29-11, page 447

*Possible answers:*  **1.** a college freshman  **3.** a quiet, tree-lined neighborhood  **5.** a dark, cramped apartment

### Practice 29-12, page 450

*Possible edits:*  **1.** While Erin goes to classes, her baby boy stays at a day-care center, which costs Erin about $100 a week.  **3.** Occasionally, Erin's parents, who live about seventy miles away, come up and watch the baby while Erin is studying.  **5.** She feels that some of her professors who have never been mothers themselves aren't very sympathetic.  **7.** Her grades, which were once straight A's, have suffered somewhat since she had her son.  **9.** Her son, who is the person in her life she cares about most, is more important than an A in geology.

### Practice 29-13, page 450

*Possible answers:*  **1.** that was probably caused by faulty wiring  **3.** who has always been a light sleeper  **5.** which was the only home I had ever lived in

### Practice 29-14, page 451

*Possible edits:*  **1.** (1) Immunizations, which have saved countless lives in this century, have recently become controversial. (3) A few children, a very small minority, have reactions to the vaccines. (5) Worrying that vaccinations are harmful, some parents are speaking out against routine immunization. (7) Correct  **2.** (1) Movies were made possible by Thomas Edison, the inventor of the motion picture camera. (3) One of the first films showed scenes of an oncoming train, which frightened audiences early in the twentieth century. (5) Correct (7) Correct (9) Called "special effects," this magic is not cheap. (11) Hollywood studios, which are corporations trying to earn a profit, spend millions to make blockbusters. (13) Correct (15) There is another kind of magic in moviemaking that makes us remember why we loved movies in the first place. (17) Correct (19) It may be small and personal, capturing our imagination or our hearts. (21) The movies we love may show us the invention of a completely new world, unimagined even by Thomas Edison.

# Chapter 30

## Practice 30-1, page 456
*Possible edits:* **1.** It snowed a lot last winter. **3.** I seldom saw the sun. **5.** I went to see a doctor about the problem because I had always considered myself a happy person. **7.** I realized that short, dark days have often made me gloomy. **9.** Now, when I feel sad during the winter months, I have a solution. **11.** It may be an unusual thing to do, but it makes me feel much better while I wait for spring to come.

## Practice 30-2, page 459
*Answers:* **1.** Many students believe that the college should provide on-campus day care. **3.** They consider getting a better job a worthwhile goal. **5.** The courses cost a lot, but the expense is worth it to these students. **7.** Today, this problem is becoming more serious. **9.** Shouldn't the college agree to help these students?

## Practice 30-3, page 461
*Edits:* **1.** I was very happy about my first English class in the United States. **3.** My English was poor at first, and I was ashamed of my inability to understand what people were saying. **5.** My English classes were full of people from all over the world, and I found them very interesting. **7.** The texts she had picked out for us to read were the only thing I did not like. **9.** I was soon tired of reading about immigrants, and I wanted to read and talk about subjects that had nothing to do with immigration.

## Practice 30-4, page 462
*Answers:* **1.** People were once afraid of comets in the sky. **3.** There are historical examples of rulers calling off battles and holidays when they saw comets in the sky. **5.** Scientists are interested in learning more about each comet that passes through our solar system.

## Practice 30-5, page 463
*Possible answers:* **1.** Negative: We were not writing about why we want to take this course. Question: Were we writing about why we want to take this course? **3.** Negative: My family has not lived in this country for five years. Question: Has my family lived in this country for five years? **5.** Negative: The weather is not difficult to get used to. Question: Is the weather difficult to get used to?

## Practice 30-6, page 465
*Possible answers:* **1.** Her long black hair was beautiful. **3.** I ran from the scary old man. **5.** The ugly green plastic chair sat by the pool all winter.

## Practice 30-7, page 465
*Possible edits:* **1.** In the summer of 2002, Florida police officers became interested in three Arab American medical students who were traveling to Miami. **3.** It was the job of bomb-sniffing dogs to investigate the students' car. **5.** Why were the dogs wrong? **7.** A police dog can tell if its handler feels excitement or fear. **9.** When the Florida dogs made their mistake, three young men were falsely

accused of being terrorists. **11.** Dog experts have suggested keeping police dogs off their leashes when the dogs are working. **13.** A new Dutch training program has also found that dog handlers sometimes unconsciously direct their dogs toward particular suspects. **15.** He was never arrested, and his lawyers say that the handlers wanted their dogs to identify him. **17.** Like human beings, they like the special treats they get when someone is pleased with them. **19.** However, new research on preventing training mistakes may make dogs and their handlers even more effective against crime.

# Chapter 31

## Practice 31-1, page 473
*Answers and possible edits:* **1.** Vague or abstract words: local zoo a lot. I visit the Bronx Zoo at least twice a year. **3.** Vague or abstract words: awful; the zoo in my city. Living in a cage would be painfully boring and uncomfortable, but the Bronx Zoo doesn't have cages. **5.** Vague or abstract words: some; very pretty. The zoo has two different species of birds with purple and turquoise feathers. **7.** Vague or abstract words: great. Watching the bats is like watching a creepy old movie or a thrilling air show. **9.** Vague or abstract words: a lot; information. The zoo's exhibits teach visitors about wildlife conservation.

## Practice 31-2, page 474
*Answers and possible edits:* **1.** Slang: chew me out. I don't see why it is necessary for you to reprimand me so often. **3.** Slang: fired up. I was really enthusiastic about the last project I worked on. **5.** Slang: an awesome; hang around. This is a wonderful place to work, and I'd like to remain here for at least another year. **7.** Slang: get into it over. Jim Hoffman and I did once have a disagreement about scheduling. **9.** Slang: talking me down. If anyone has been complaining about me, I would like to know about it.

## Practice 31-3, page 475
*Answers and possible edits:* **1.** Wordy/repetitive language: It is a well-known fact that. Television helped Richard Nixon lose the 1960 presidential election. **3.** Wordy/repetitive language: In spite of the fact that. Although technicians encouraged Nixon to wear makeup for the debate, he refused. **5.** Wordy/repetitive language: The fact of the matter is that. Nixon did not look much better on television during his presidency from 1968 to 1974. **7.** Wordy/repetitive language: due to the fact that. He had experience standing in front of cameras because he had been an actor. **9.** Wordy/repetitive language: In this day and age/of the most paramount importance. Some people have pointed out that looking good on television is one of the most important requirements for future presidents.

## Practice 31-4, page 477
*Answers and possible edits:* **1.** Clichés: sweat blood; work like a dog. You have to persuade yourself to devote every bit of your strength to the challenge for up to ten hours. **3.** Clichés: the bitter end; easier said than done. Staying on your bike until the very last mile, of course, is an enormously difficult task. **5.** Cliché: better late than never. No matter how long it takes you to cross the finish line, remind yourself that finishing at all is a tremendous achievement. **7.** Clichés: a will of iron; keep your nose to the grindstone. It may take discipline to make yourself train, but you should continue to work hard. **9.** Cliché: keep an eye peeled. When you train for road racing, watch carefully for cars.

## Practice 31-5, page 478
*Possible edits:* **1.** (1) Space travel is not available to ordinary citizens now, but the situation may change. (3) Many entrepreneurs are speculating that space tourism will happen soon. (5) Only wealthy people

will be able to afford half a million dollars for a cruise around the moon. (7) Correct **2.** (1) Throughout recorded history, humans have done devastating things to the environment. (3) Because wood has a high carbon-to-hydrogen ratio, the burning of wood is a dirty and inefficient source of fuel. (5) When oil furnaces began to replace coal furnaces, the air in many cities slowly became somewhat cleaner. (7) Each year, thousands of sperm whales were caught and killed, until they were almost extinct. (9) However, our dependence on oil is a significant problem. (11) It is foolish to continue to use fossil fuels when scientists have shown that these fuels contribute to global warming.

## Chapter 32

**Practice 32-1, page 489**
*Answers:* **1.** accept **3.** They're; their **5.** principles **7.** knows; no **9.** have; our

**Practice 32-2, page 489**
*Possible edits:* **1.** (1) When you're driving, it's hard to know exactly when your gas tank needs to be filled. (3) The gauge reads *empty* when the gas level has passed below a certain point. (5) Most people know this, and they sometimes keep driving when they should have stopped to fill up. (7) The technology in some new cars allows drivers to know more precisely than they once could exactly how much gas is left in their tanks so they know when they're supposed to fill up. **2.** (1) More and more women are purchasing handguns, against the advice of law enforcement officers. (3) They know the risks of guns, and they accept those risks. (5) They don't want to contribute to the violence in our society, but they also realize that women are the victims of violent attacks far too often. (7) Some women have made a conscious decision to arm themselves for protection. (9) But does buying a gun make things worse rather than better for these women? (11) Most young children can't tell the difference between a real gun and a toy gun when they find one. (13) A mother whose children are injured while "playing" with her gun will never again think that a gun provides peace of mind.

## Chapter 33

**Practice 33-2, page 497**
*Possible answers:* **1.** niece **3.** believe **5.** freight

**Practice 33-3, page 497**
*Answers:* **1.** peaceful **3.** believing **5.** valuable **7.** purer **9.** shameful

**Practice 33-4, page 498**
*Answers:* **1.** playful **3.** comedian **5.** defiant **7.** burial **9.** puffiness

**Practice 33-5, page 499**
*Answers:* **1.** lifted **3.** commander **5.** cheaper **7.** spotted **9.** scrapped

**Practice 33-6, page 500**
*Answers:* **1.** addresses **3.** tomatoes **5.** stretches **7.** dashes **9.** discovers

**Practice 33-7, page 501**
*Answers:* (1) In today's schools, there is a raging argument about whether to separate children of different abilities into classes with others of similar achievement levels. (3) These same experts state that

dividing students will prejudice teachers against the slower students. (5) Basically, the experts claim, students lose all motivation to achieve. (7) They say that grouping by ability allows students to learn at a more natural rate. (9) For example, if students with similar writing skills are together in class, the teacher either can spend a lot of time with grammar if the class needs it or can skip over it if the students have mastered the basic rules. (11) Both sides have interesting, persuasive arguments that they present to local, state, and federal government officials.

## Chapter 34

**Practice 34-1, page 508**
*Answers:* **1.** Continued expansion depends on our ability to promote novelty beverages such as papaya, mango, and boysenberry juices in grocery stores and restaurants. **3.** Correct **5.** In areas where our juice is new, we'd like increases of 10 percent, 20 percent, or 25 percent. **7.** We want to target New England states such as Connecticut, Massachusetts, and Maine, where attitudes about fruit juice are similar to those in Seattle, Portland, and other Northwest cities. **9.** We should set up displays, provide free samples of our juice, and sponsor contests.

**Practice 34-2, page 510**
*Answers:* **1.** Correct **3.** She had chosen the college carefully, for it had an excellent program in physical therapy. **5.** Correct **7.** Correct **9.** She didn't want to have to choose between her husband and an education, and she didn't have to.

**Practice 34-3, page 511**
*Answers:* **1.** As we all know, AIDS is spread mainly through sexual contact and through drug use that involves the sharing of needles. **3.** Since basketball star Magic Johnson revealed in 1991 that he is HIV-positive, an NBA player must be removed from a game if he is bleeding. **5.** Not surprisingly, many college sports follow similar rules. **7.** According to some student athletes, mandatory HIV testing would violate their civil liberties. **9.** Correct

**Practice 34-4, page 513**
*Edits:* **1.** Gated communities, those fancy neighborhoods with a gate at the entrance, have been part of the American landscape for years. **3.** The terrorist attacks of 2001, the hijackings and anthrax scares, have left many people feeling insecure. **5.** The fear of crime may, in fact, be worse than crime itself in most parts of the United States. **7.** The criminals behind such acts, neighborhood teenagers, often live inside the gates. **9.** The gate, a sign of a safe community, is nothing more than that, a sign.

**Practice 34-5, page 515**
*Edits:* **1.** My mother, who has always loved music, was not a big fan of Elvis Presley when she was younger. **3.** Correct **5.** Correct **7.** My mother's best friend from high school, who also attended the party, introduced her to a handsome Elvis impersonator. **9.** My father's stage show, which now emphasizes the King's Las Vegas years, is only a little embarrassing to me.

**Practice 34-6, page 517**
*Answers:* **1.** Correct **3.** Asked if he was losing patience, McGregor replied, "Yes, I sure am." **5.** His wife said, "Rob, don't go mouthing off to any reporters." **7.** An official of Value-Safe Insurance of Wrightsville, Ohio, said the company will process claims within the next few months. **9.** Correct

**Practice 34-7, page 518**
*Answers:* **1.** (1) According to etiquette experts, e-mail users need to practice good manners. (3) Not everyone appreciates receiving

jokes, electronic greeting cards, and bogus virus warnings regularly. (5) E-mail is similar to a telephone call, a quick and informal way to keep in touch. (7) In addition, you should use the subject header to let the recipient know whether or not the message is important. **2.** (1) In April 1990, the book *You Just Don't Understand* was published by William Morrow in New York, New York. (3) It gives examples of how men and women misunderstand each other, and it describes the causes of and possible solutions to the differences in their language expectations. (5) Tannen writes, "Even if they grow up in the same house, girls and boys grow up in different worlds of words. (7) And although some of their play activities are similar, their favorite games are different, and their ways of using language in their games are also different." (9) Girls, on the other hand, play in small groups or pairs. (11) Later in life, these differences can cause disagreements between men and women. (13) The comfort of home, however, can have opposite meanings for men and women. (15) Correct (17) Needless to say, conflicts result from these different expectations.

# Chapter 35

### Practice 35-1, page 522
*Answers:* **1.** A person's feelings about personal space depend on his or her culture. **3.** Putting your face too close to another's is considered rude. **5.** The expression "Get out of my face!" is a warning meant to prevent the confrontation's violent conclusion. **7.** The hair on dogs' necks may stand on end. **9.** For example, seagulls' positions on a log follow a pattern similar to that of people lined up waiting for a bus.

### Practice 35-2, page 524
*Answers:* **1.** You'll notice right away if a stranger leans over and talks to you so his face is practically touching yours. **3.** There isn't one single acceptable boundary we'd use in all situations. **5.** With coworkers, we're likely to keep a personal space of four to twelve feet. **7.** The last sixteen inches are reserved for people we're most intimate with. **9.** A supervisor who's not aware of the personal space boundaries of his or her employees risks committing a serious transgression.

### Practice 35-3, page 525
*Answers:* **1.** I sorted letters alphabetically, starting with A's. **3.** When I checked my e-mail, the screen flashed 48's to show that I had forty-eight messages. **5.** I needed another week's time just to return all the phone calls.

### Practice 35-4, page 526
*Answers:* **1.** (1) An astronaut goes through extreme adjustments in zero gravity. (3) The brain can't tell up from down. (5) Heartbeats can speed up and then slow down for no apparent reason. (7) The physical effects of a few weeks' space travel can imitate what a body experiences after thirty years' aging. **2.** (1) People's names often have strange stories attached to them. (3) It's actually misspelled. (5) Somehow, *The Orpah Winfrey Show* doesn't sound like a popular television program. (7) Winfrey herself is certainly not upset that she didn't end up with her parents' choice of name; her production company's name is Harpo, which is Oprah spelled backward. (9) As Winfrey's example suggests, names on birth certificates are often mixed up. (11) But unusual names don't all result from mistakes. (13) Some people's names sound like job titles. (15) Early in his career, the baseball pitcher Eric Plunk was known for hitting batters with his wild pitches. (17) Each name has its own meaning and origin; we're all affected by our names, whether we like them or not.

# Chapter 36

### Practice 36-1, page 531
*Answers:* **1.** "If I could quickly answer that question," the nurse replied, "I'd deserve an honorary degree in ethics." **3.** "How would you describe that dilemma?" the reporter asked the nurse. **5.** The reporter asked, "So there are times when you'd favor letting patients die on their own?" **7.** The reporter asked, "Under what circumstances should a patient be allowed to die?" **9.** "Is this a matter of deciding how to allocate scarce resources?" the reporter asked.

### Practice 36-2, page 532
*Answers:* **1.** "Have you complained to the landlord yet?" her friend asked. **3.** Correct **5.** When Jocelyn phoned the landlord after the burglary, she said, "I know this wouldn't have happened if that lock had been installed." **7.** Correct **9.** "If I were you," the person said, "I'd let your landlord know about your plans."

### Practice 36-3, page 534
*Edits:* **1.** In 2002, Bruce Springsteen released his first new album in years, containing songs like "Worlds Apart" that dealt with the terrorist attacks on the United States. **3.** No one made that complaint about "John Walker's Blues," a song by Steve Earle based on the story of the young American captured while fighting for the Taliban in Afghanistan. **5.** As a *Time* magazine article, "Don't Even Tell These Guys About Eminem," pointed out, the controversy was peculiar because it occurred before Earle's song had even been released, and those objecting had apparently neither heard the song nor read its lyrics.

### Practice 36-4, page 534
*Answers:* **1.** (1) When I first read Edgar Allan Poe's "The Tell-Tale Heart," I thought it was the scariest story ever written. (3) The narrator is a murderer who knows that readers will think he's mad. (5) Correct (7) Correct **2.** (1) Correct (3) Ruiz answered, "I've always gotten bad grades, and I don't know how to get any better." (5) "I've just about given up." (7) Correct (9) I said, "There are plenty of programs to help you. (11) "Can you be a little more specific?" he asked. (13) Correct (15) "Take a look at these," I said. (17) And I don't have time." (19) I paused and then added, "Sounds to me like you're wasting the money you spent on tuition. (21) Ruiz thought for a moment, while he looked out the window, and finally told me that he'd try. (23) "I'm glad to hear it."

# Chapter 37

### Practice 37-1, page 540
*Possible edits:* **1.** (1) We already know that natural light can improve our mood; now it seems that light from the sun has other positive effects. (3) A study of school districts indicates that natural light—even on a cloudy day—can help students learn. (5) The scores improved by up to twenty-six percent, even when other factors affecting scores were taken into account. (7) The sun-filled stores had much higher sales—an average of forty percent higher. **2.** (1) More than fifty thousand domestic adoptions take place in this country each year; despite minor difficulties, most of them go smoothly. (3) Richard was in a good situation: healthy, happy, loved by the couple who had adopted him at birth. (5) They were prepared to spend years battling the case in court; they desperately wanted their son back. (7) Therefore, a few days after the baby's birth, the baby was put up for adoption—his mother didn't want him. (9) Eventually, however, the father discovered that his former girlfriend had lied; his son

was still alive. (11) After years of legal arguments, the Illinois Supreme Court reached its verdict: Baby Richard belonged to the parents whose genes he shared.

## Chapter 38

**Practice 38-1, page 543**
*Answers:*   **1.** Correct   **3.** Almost seventy years later, in the midst of the Great Depression, Franklin Roosevelt declared, "We have nothing to fear but fear itself."

**Practice 38-2, page 546**
*Answers:*   **1.** Unlike most American cities, New York has a great mass transportation system, so visitors don't need a car.   **3.** You can arrive by train at Pennsylvania Station or Grand Central Station. **5.** There are many internationally known buildings, such as the Empire State Building.   **7.** One of the best things about the city is the restaurants, which serve food from all over the world.   **9.** Famous New Yorkers include Gwyneth Paltrow, Woody Allen, and Al Sharpton.

**Practice 38-3, page 547**
*Answers:*   **1.** The American West has been a common topic in popular culture since early films like *The Big Trail.*   **3.** Television, too, relied on westerns in its early years, making *Gunsmoke* one of the longest-running shows of all time.   **5.** John Ford movies, including *The Searchers* and *She Wore a Yellow Ribbon,* popularized an image of the West.

**Practice 38-4, page 547**
*Answers:*   **1.** The names and accomplishments of some presidents of the United States are familiar to almost every American.   **3.** Being president is no guarantee that a person will have lasting fame, however.   **5.** The Millard Fillmore Society celebrates his birthday every year on January 7.   **7.** Nevertheless, the facts about Fillmore are known mainly to students of history.   **9.** The candidate for president was Zachary Taylor, a hero of the Mexican War.   **11.** Taylor, who remained neutral, was elected, but he died in office, so Fillmore became president in 1850.   **13.** The newspaperman H. L. Mencken wrote a column in the *New York Evening Mail* in 1917 claiming that Fillmore had installed the White House's first bathtub.   **15.** Poor Millard Fillmore, when he is remembered at all, it is usually to be given credit for something he didn't really do.

# Index

## Acknowledgments, Continued

Microsoft Word screen and Internet Explorer toolbars courtesy of Microsoft Corporation.

Walter Scanlon. "It's Time I Shed My Ex-Convict Status." From *Newsweek*, February 21, 2000. Copyright © 2000 Newsweek, Inc. All rights reserved. Reprinted by permission.

Carolyn Foster Segal. "The Dog Ate My Disk, and Other Tales of Woe." From the *Chronicle of Higher Education*, August 11, 2000. Copyright © 2000. Reprinted by permission of the author.

Elyzabeth Joy Stagg. "From the Welfare Rolls, a Mother's View." From *Newsweek*, August 23, 1999, p. 10. Copyright © 1999 Newsweek, Inc. All rights reserved. Reprinted by permission.

Kirby W. Stanat with Patrick Reardon. "The Job Interview." From *Job Hunting Secrets and Tactics*. Copyright © 1977 by Kirby Stanat with Patrick Reardon. Reprinted by permission of the author.

Lincoln J. Tamayo. "A 'Yes' Vote Will Benefit Kids." From the *Boston Globe*, October 28, 2002. Copyright 2002 by Globe Newspaper Company (MA). Reproduced with permission of Globe Newspaper Company (MA) in the format Textbook via Copyright Clearance Center.

Wallace Terry. "When His Sound Was Silenced." First published in *Parade*, December 25, 1994. Copyright © 1994 by Wallace Terry. Reprinted by permission of *Parade* and Scovil Chichak Galen Literary Agency on behalf of the author.

Yi-Fu Tuan. "American Space, Chinese Place." Copyright © 1974 by *Harper's Magazine*. All rights reserved. Reproduced by special permission.

"Types of Plagiarism." Screen shot from the University of Michigan Library. Copyright © 2002 by the Regents of the University of Michigan.

Pat Wingert. "Uniforms Rule." From *Newsweek*, October 4, 1999. Copyright © 1999 by Newsweek, Inc. All rights reserved. Reprinted by permission.

Malcolm X. "A Homemade Education." From *The Autobiography of Malcolm X* by Malcolm X and Alex Haley. Copyright © 1964 by Alex Haley and Malcolm X. Copyright © 1965 by Alex Haley and Betty Shabazz. Used by permission of Random House, Inc.

Franklin E. Zimring. "Confessions of a Former Smoker." Originally published in *Newsweek*, April 20, 1987. Copyright © 1987. Reprinted by permission of the author.

## Photo/Art Credits

Page 1: Robert Ullmann/Design Conceptions
Page 97: David Young-Wolff/PhotoEdit
Page 113: Michael Newman/PhotoEdit
Page 127: Copyright 1996, USA TODAY. Reprinted with permission from *USA Today* and from the United States Olympic Committee.
Page 141: Alexandra Boulat/Cosmos/AURORA
Page 157: © Randy Glasbergen
Page 174: Paul Ekman
Page 190: American Indian College Fund
Page 208: Erika Stone (left panel) /John Launois/Stockphoto.com
Page 223: Mike Thompson, Detroit Free Press
Page 242: Joel Gordon
Page 247: Joel Gordon
Page 285: Jeff Greenberg/eStock
Page 373: Charles Gupton/Corbis
Page 469: Joel Gordon
Page 505: Joel Gordon
Page 549: David Wells/The Image Works

## *Real Writing—Real Rewards!*

**Students:** Take the *Real Writing* Challenge: Become a published paid author. If your instructor sends us a paragraph or an essay that you have written while using *Real Writing,* and we publish it in a forthcoming edition of either this book or *Real Essays,* we will pay you $50 and reward your instructor with an honorarium of $50.

Essays must be approved by and sent by your professor to:
*Real Writing* Paper Submissions
Bedford/St. Martin's
75 Arlington Street, 8th Floor
Boston, MA 02116

**Instructors:** Please submit essays to the above address using the Student Paper Submission form that appears at the back of *Practical Suggestions for Teaching REAL WRITING.* If you do not use *Practical Suggestions* and need a copy of the form, please e-mail a request to developmental@bedfordstmartins.com.

# Correction Symbols

This chart lists typical symbols that instructors use to point out writing problems. The explanation of each symbol includes a step you can take to revise or edit your writing. Included also are suggested chapters to check for more help and information. If your instructor uses different symbols for some errors, write them in the left-hand column for future reference.

| YOUR INSTRUCTOR'S SYMBOL | STANDARD SYMBOL | HOW TO REVISE OR EDIT (NUMBERS IN BOLDFACE ARE CHAPTERS WHERE YOU CAN FIND HELP) |
| --- | --- | --- |
| | adj | Use correct adjective form **25** |
| | adv | Use correct adverb form **25** |
| | agr | Correct subject-verb agreement or pronoun agreement **22; 24** |
| | awk | Awkward expression: edit for clarity **7** |
| | cap | Use capital letter correctly **38** |
| | case | Use correct pronoun case **24** |
| | cliché | Replace overused phrase with fresh words **31** |
| | coh | Revise paragraph or essay for coherence **7** |
| | combine | Combine sentences **29** |
| | con t | Correct the inconsistent verb tense **23** |
| | coord | Use coordination correctly **27** |
| | cs | Comma splice: join the two sentences correctly **21** |
| | d or dic | Diction: edit word choice **31** |
| | dev | Develop your paragraph or essay more completely **4; 6** |
| | dm | Revise to avoid a dangling modifier **26** |
| | frag | Attach the fragment to a sentence or make it a sentence **20** |
| | fs | Fused sentence: join the two sentences correctly **21** |
| | intro | Add or strengthen your introduction **6** |
| | ital | Use italics **36** |
| | lc | Use lowercase **38** |
| | mm | Revise to avoid a misplaced modifier **26** |
| | pl | Use the correct plural form of the verb **23** |
| | ref | Make pronoun reference clear **24** |
| | ro | Run-on sentence; join the two sentences correctly **21** |
| | sp | Correct the spelling error **32; 33** |
| | sub | Use subordination correctly **27** |
| | sup | Support your point with details, examples, or facts **4** |
| | tense | Correct the problem with verb tense **23** |
| | trans | Add a transition **7** |
| | ts | Add or strengthen your topic sentence or thesis statement **3** |
| | u | Revise paragraph or essay for unity **7** |
| | w | Delete unnecessary words **31** |
| | ? | Make your meaning clearer **7** |
| | , | Use comma correctly **34** |
| | ; : ( ) - -- | Use semicolon/colon/parentheses/hyphen/dash correctly **37** |
| | " " | Use quotation marks correctly **36** |

# Useful Lists, Checklists, and Charts

## PREWRITING, DRAFTING, AND REVISING

## BASIC FEATURES OF GOOD WRITING

## PROFILES OF SUCCESS

## CHECKLISTS FOR WRITING PARAGRAPHS AND ESSAYS